On Gangs

SCOTT H. DECKER, DAVID C. PYROOZ,
AND JAMES A. DENSLEY

On Gangs

TEMPLE UNIVERSITY PRESS
Philadelphia • *Rome* • *Tokyo*

TEMPLE UNIVERSITY PRESS
Philadelphia, Pennsylvania 19122
tupress.temple.edu

Library of Congress Cataloging-in-Publication Data

Names: Decker, Scott H., author. | Pyrooz, David, author. | Densley, James
A. (James Andrew), 1982– author.
Title: On gangs / Scott H. Decker, David C. Pyrooz, and James A. Densley.
Description: Philadelphia : Temple University Press, 2022. | Includes
bibliographical references and index. | Summary: "This book introduces
readers to the study of gangs, including key concepts and findings,
competing theoretical approaches, emerging and persistent issues and
questions, and strategies for addressing gangs"— Provided by publisher.
Identifiers: LCCN 2021015326 (print) | LCCN 2021015327 (ebook) | ISBN
9781439920633 (cloth) | ISBN 9781439920640 (paperback) | ISBN
9781439920657 (pdf)
Subjects: LCSH: Gangs.
Classification: LCC HV6437 .D43 2022 (print) | LCC HV6437 (ebook) | DDC
364.106/6—dc23
LC record available at https://lccn.loc.gov/2021015326
LC ebook record available at https://lccn.loc.gov/2021015327

Printed in the United States of America

9 8 7 6 5 4 3 2 1

Dedicated to the legacies of Malcolm Klein and Cheryl Maxson

Contents

Acknowledgments

There has been dramatic growth in gang research over the past three decades. *On Gangs* is a synthesis and reinterpretation of much of this work. As such, we wish to acknowledge those individuals who have contributed to this research, noting a few of the more salient contributors for each of us. Clearly, there are the classic contributors to this body of research, such as Jacobs, Klein, Miller, Moore, Short, and Spergel. There are also more contemporary contributors, such as Esbensen, Harding, Howell, Huff, (Chuck) Katz, Maxson, Melde, (Jody) Miller, Papachristos, and others. And there is a rapidly emerging new generation of young gang researchers, who bring more diversity in backgrounds and perspectives to the field. We acknowledge researchers in each of these categories whose contributions provided a foundation for this work.

Collectively, we also wish to thank our editor Ryan Mulligan and the team at Temple University Press for taking a chance on a book like this, even after the manuscript came in at nearly twice the number of contracted words. Thanks also to the reviewers for feedback that helped shape the direction of the book and significantly improved the final product.

I, Scott Decker, wish to acknowledge a number of individuals who shaped my approach to the study of gangs. This begins with my colleague Richard Wright, whose own ethnographic work is foundational to criminology. In a different way, Street Daddy (Dietrich Smith) provided safe access and understanding to the streets of St. Louis. While not a gang researcher, Charles F. Wellford is still looking over my shoulder, asking about the broader implications of my work. Winnie Reed, formerly of the National Institute of Justice, fought for funding for gang research and convened panels and publication outlets in the 1990s. Her colleague at NIJ, Lois Mock, lobbied for funding for firearms research, which often overlapped with gangs. Phelan Wyrick (currently at NIJ) has been a staunch ally of those who would bring order and science to the study of gangs at multiple Department of Justice agencies through his career. There is a special place for David Curry that recognizes his many contributions and unselfish support for the work of others. Dave, I miss you, buddy. Among professional acknowledgments, perhaps the most consequential is the next generation of gang scholars, led by my coauthors David Pyrooz and James Densley. If this is the future of gang scholarship, it is in good hands. Finally, thanks to my family, especially JoAnn, who frequently asks what part of the word *retirement* includes writing more books. That is a difficult question.

I, David Pyrooz, thank my colleagues, collaborators, and family who hold me to the highest personal and professional standards. That starts with Scott Decker and James Densley, longtime collaborators and friends who serve as role models inside and outside the academy. I am very grateful to my colleagues at CU Boulder (Jason Boardman, Pam Buckley, Del Elliott, Myron Gutmann, Karl Hill, Dave Huizinga, Stef Mollborn, Ryan Masters, Hillary Potter, Mike Radelet, Rick Rogers, and Kyle Thomas) and beyond (Martin Bouchard, Sandra Bucerius, Dena Carson, Finn Esbensen, Gary LaFree, John Leverso, Cheryl Maxson, Jean McGloin, Chris Melde, Rick Moule, Andy Papachristos, Travis Pratt, Caterina Roman, Gary Sweeten, Terry Thornberry, and Scott Wolfe) who continue to push me to think harder and smarter on key issues in criminological and gang research. And thanks to everyone at GRID, who keep me on my toes by ensuring my work has applicability beyond the ivory tower. The students (Kendra Clark, Chantal Fahmy, Meghan Mitchell, Jose Sanchez, Jenn Tostlebe, and Elizabeth Weltman) with whom I have collaborated have influenced my thinking more than they can imagine. Thank you. Among the few silver linings of the COVID-19 pandemic is that I was able to dedicate the needed effort and time to writing this book. To Cyrus and Addy, who, like children across the world, had their school year snatched away from them yet remained unbelievably resilient, your distractions arrived at just the right times when writing this book; your curiosity and enthusiasm know no bounds. And to Natty, who knows that my "thank you" takes on meanings both small and large. Books like this are better because of you.

I, James Densley, would especially like to thank the mentors who first taught me to look at "gangs" differently: Heather Hamill, Federico Varese, and Diego Gambetta. I also owe a huge debt of gratitude to past coauthors and collaborators, who in ways large and small contributed to my understanding of gangs—namely, Ross Deuchar, Thomas Grund, Simon Harding, Susan Hilal, Jordan Hyatt, Keir Irwin-Rogers, Andrew Johnson, David Jones, Tim Lauger, John Leverso, Michelle Lyttle Storrod, Robert McLean, Jillian Peterson, Craig Pinkney, Mo Rahman, Grace Robinson, Caterina Roman, Rick Moule, Robby Roks, Alex Stevens, Marta Urbanik, Elke Van Hellemont, and Andrew Whittaker. To other colleagues who pushed my thinking on gangs through the years, such as Brad Bushman, Marcus Felson, and the Eurogang and Illicit Networks crews, thank you. To the hundreds of gang-involved young people who have shared with me their lived experience of gangs on both sides of the Atlantic, I'm forever grateful. Huge thanks also to the practitioners, particularly Allen Davis, the first "gang cop" who took me under his wing. Like many young gang scholars, I've looked up to Scott Decker since I first read *Life in the Gang* nearly two decades ago. They say, "Never meet your heroes," but from day one, Scott has been a generous (at times hilarious) guide to *Life in the Academy*. Working together for the first time surpassed even the highest of expectations—a privilege and a pleasure. David Pyrooz was equally the perfect coauthor. "What would David do?" has long been my mantra for navigating this field—even more so now. I'm grateful to Jack Daniels for introducing us all those years ago and for the friendship and vibrant exchange of ideas since. Cheers to it all. Finally, special thanks to my family. Emily, our gang was the best decision I ever made. Alex and Andrew, one day, when you're old enough to read it, I hope this book makes you proud, or at the very least not bored.

On Gangs

Introduction

"Mike-Mike" is a twenty-year-old member of the Thundercats, a St. Louis gang that formed in a public housing project. The Thundercats are known in the community as a particularly violent gang. Mike-Mike joined his gang at age fourteen and is widely regarded as the group's leader. He has been heavily involved in drug sales and other crimes, particularly crimes that involve guns, and has been arrested ten times. In interviews with us, he admits that he is frightened by the reckless violence of younger gang members in the community. Because of his two children, both under the age of five, he is trying to withdraw from gang activity. But he finds that it is hard to do because the younger members of his gang look to him for advice.

At age thirteen, another interviewee, Tim, was picked up by police a few miles from his home near Chicago for attempting to steal an automobile. The next year, Tim became involved in a conflict with youths from a nearby middle school. Within two months, he was taken into custody twice for fighting. Two weeks later, he was apprehended for robbery, and the police recorded that the victim of the robbery was a known member of Chicago's Vice Lords gang. That summer Tim was ticketed, along with a number of youths, under Chicago's anti-ganging ordinance. All of the youths, including Tim, were identified in police records as Black Gangster Disciples. The following spring, Tim, then age fifteen, was charged as an offender in a gang-related aggravated assault. Tim was charged again the following year, twice with criminal damage to property and once with unlawful use of a weapon. Finally, Tim moved into the adult criminal justice system.

Why did Mike-Mike and Tim commit these crimes? Is gang membership to blame?

What is life in the gang like? How does it work?

What is the likelihood that Mike-Mike will leave his gang or that Tim will avoid one in prison? Do criminal justice interventions help, or only make things worse?

This book, *On Gangs*, was written to help answer these questions and more. We believe that the study of gangs is important for a variety of reasons. First, it is important for understanding the lives of children and young people, the age cohort most susceptible to gang membership. The nature of gangs reflects a lot about a society, particularly its values, institutions, and methods of achieving goals. Families, schools, neighborhood groups, the political economy, and even the media all influence the growth of gangs and decisions by individuals to join (or resist joining) them.

Second, gangs are, at their core, social groups, and social groups are an integral part of people's lives. Religious congregations, nongovernment organizations, political groups, athletic clubs, and neighborhood collectives draw people together to bring meaning and purpose to their lives from birth to death. Groups are important to understand for anyone who maintains an interest in social life. Understanding the associations, impacts, and nature of gangs is central to the scientific enterprise.

Third, gangs impact lives. People get hurt in gangs and because of them. Fatal and nonfatal injuries reduce life efficacy and expectancy. This extends to the families and friends of victims. Gang members participate extensively in crime and delinquency. People live in fear in their own houses and alter their way of life because they worry about gang violence and intimidation in their own communities.

Fourth, as M. Klein and Maxson (2006) pointed out fifteen years ago, there is a mandate to respond to gangs. Gang members are among the most difficult groups to deal with on the street as well as in jails and prisons, and they pose a considerable risk for practitioners and the public. Civic and political leaders are inevitably presented with the challenge of directing precious human and financial resources to countering gang activity. The criminal justice system has been modified as a result of gangs. New organizational units and strategies have been created in police departments, prosecutor's offices, and correctional facilities to respond to them.

Finally, responding to gangs has (collateral) consequences. There is often little sympathy for gang members when they are victims of crime or recipients of punishment. But we cannot forget that gang members are sons and daughters, brothers and sisters, mothers and fathers, neighbors, friends, and colleagues. How we respond to gangs matters. State and federal policy and practice have generated the need for research and evaluation, and the long road to evidence-based programming has meant that service agencies have had to modify their programs to address the acute needs and risks of their gang clientele or avoid them altogether.

The study of gangs enjoys a long history in the social sciences. In the early 1900s, gangs began attracting the attention of anthropologists, psychologists, and sociologists who were interested in child welfare, community, culture, and social policy. Since then, gang research has undergone many twists and turns, and it truly exploded in volume over the last three decades. In 2015, Pyrooz and Mitchell reviewed the production of knowledge and intellectual history of gang research. They identified over five thousand published works on gangs, including books, refereed articles, and reports. Based on a survey of gang researchers, they identified five major periods:

1. The classic era, when gangs were viewed as "playgroups" (1900 to 1940s)
2. The golden era, when gangs were *the* study of delinquency (1950s)
3. The social problems era, when the view of gangs shifted to a problem to be addressed by the criminal justice system (1960s to current)
4. The empirical turn toward rich ethnographies and longitudinal research design, which yielded major intellectual gains (1990s to current)
5. The international turn with the advent of the Eurogang program of research and the growing significance of gangs outside of the United States, including Africa, Asia, Australia, Canada, Europe, and Latin America (2000s to current)

These eras reflect the framing of gang issues, changes in research design and methodology, funding priorities of the federal government, and sociopolitical influences.

Like many areas in the social sciences, gang research is increasingly specialized, almost its own subfield, like corrections or policing. The late Jim Short, groundbreaking gang scholar and past president of both the American Sociological Association and the American Society of Criminology, argued against this specialization. He viewed gangs from a generalist perspective, contending that they revealed a great deal about human behavior (Short 1996; Short and Hughes 2006, 2015). He argued that the group processes found within gangs had applicability to many groups (criminal or otherwise) and social contexts, and he encouraged gang researchers to focus their efforts outward. But an abundance of myths about gangs and gang members (Howell 2007), thorny theoretical debates about causal inference (namely, whether gangs *caused* the delinquency of gang members; Thornberry et al. 1993), and questions about how to best respond to gangs if they were truly "qualitatively different" from other groups (M. Klein and Maxson 2006, 195) required energies to be directed inward. That led gang research to mature in a way that has been somewhat independent from mainstream criminology in general and even from criminological research in the related areas of co-offending and peer influence.

Specialization typically brings about institutions to support subject areas, but that has not been the case with gang research. There are no mainstream academic journals, divisions in international societies, research centers, or funding bodies devoted to the science of gangs. In many ways, as we expound in this book, the organization of gang research is much like the groups studied: organization is diffuse rather than centralized, roles are functional rather than fixed, meetings are informal rather than coordinated, and bursts of growth are unpredictable rather than deliberate. Some view this as an advantage, allowing researchers to be flexible to emerging trends and exploratory in aim and scope. Others see this as a downside, stunting knowledge by allowing unresolved issues to fester and grow. Regardless, the absence of a central body responsible for organizing knowledge raises the stakes for books like this. Nearly one hundred years and thousands of scholarly works after Thrasher's (1927) *The Gang*, widely regarded as the seminal work on the subject, our aim with this book is to take stock of gang research, capturing mainstream and critical views, in a way that is integrative and authoritative in coverage.

A common theme that runs throughout this book is the tension between continuity and change. It is possible to find many elements of gangs, gang members, and gang crime present today that were present over a century ago. Yet many of the characteristics of gangs, gang members, and gang crime have evolved or emerged over time and represent a new focus of understanding our social world. Certainly, changing gender roles have altered the responsibilities and relationships of men and women in gangs, as have the dramatic changes in technology. We pay attention throughout this book to the old and the new when it comes to the topic of gangs.

This book weaves contemporary research and policy findings around classic and emerging theories of gangs as well as the state of the evidence on the causes, contexts, and consequences of gangs. The book provides students and scholars with links between the gang literature and traditional criminological, criminal justice, sociological, and public health approaches to understanding and responding to crime and criminal justice. We include the perspectives of gang members throughout the book by using quotes from gang members themselves. Over the past thirty years, we have conducted more than a thousand interviews of gang members in Aurora (Colorado), Boston, Chicago, Cleveland, Denver, Fresno, Glasgow (Scotland), Inglewood (California), London (England), Los Angeles, Minneapolis, Oslo, Phoenix, St. Louis, St. Paul, San Diego, Seattle, and Washington, DC, as well as incarcerated gang members in California, Illinois, Missouri, Oregon, and Texas. We believe that the words of these individuals are important in illustrating key points made, especially in the first six chapters.

Our goal in writing this book was to provide a foundation from which readers can learn more about gangs, gang members, and their many activities. We believe that this is important for understanding the social organization and group processes of gangs and that it can also help broaden the understanding of what has become a significant policy issue in the United States and around the world: how do we deal with gangs and gang members? With hundreds of thousands of gang members in the United States and many more overseas, their activities are important to understand if we hope to build effective ways of responding to gangs and crime.

The Origins of *On Gangs*

On Gangs has its roots in the book *Confronting Gangs: Crime and Community* (Curry, Decker, and Pyrooz 2014). The first edition of *Confronting Gangs*, written by G. David Curry and the first author of this book, Scott H. Decker, was published in 1997 by Roxbury Press. That book grew out of a project funded by the National Institute of Justice (NIJ), the research arm of the U.S. Department of Justice (DOJ). Jeremy Travis, NIJ director at the time, commissioned Curry and Decker to write three papers—gangs and crime, drugs and gangs, and responses to gangs—for an NIJ-sponsored conference held in 1995 at the remote (former) Denver Airport. The conference brought Curry and Decker together with Malcolm Klein, Walter Miller, and Irving Spergel, some of the founders of American gang research, and in a wide-open session, Miller accused Klein of setting gang research back twenty years. Suffice it to say, it was a memorable occasion. For one reason or another, NIJ decided not to publish the three papers, so instead Curry and Decker reworked them into a book manuscript, which became *Confronting Gangs*. In retrospect, the first edition of *Confronting Gangs* either looks pretty sparse or accurately reflects the limited scope of gang research at the time, underpinned by police data from a very small number of jurisdictions. This was just before the explosion of more critical and cultural qualitative research and longitudinal survey work done on gangs during what Pyrooz and Mitchell (2015) call the "empirical turn" in gang scholarship.

The second edition of *Confronting Gangs* was published in 2003, also by Roxbury Press. Several new chapters (including "Female Gang Involvement" and "Gangs and Social Institutions") were added that tried to capture the volume and quality of new scholarship. The second edition mostly updated the literature but did not offer much in the way of new perspectives on gangs because it was written for the undergraduate textbook market.

The third edition of *Confronting Gangs* was published in 2013 and added chapters on gangs in international contexts as well as a chapter on gangs in the life course. Another important change to the third edition was that Roxbury Press had been sold to Oxford University Press (OUP). That moved the book into a somewhat different market, straddling the divide between textbook and monograph. As a consequence, a considerable amount of new material was added, as well as a new coauthor, David C. Pyrooz, who was Scott Decker's graduate student at Arizona State University and took a position at Sam Houston State University at the early stages of the book's development.

Dave Curry died in 2015 after a prolonged period of heart problems. This changed the future trajectory of *Confronting Gangs* and was the genesis of this new book. *On Gangs* adds a new voice and another emerging force in our understanding of gangs, James A. Densley, whom Scott first met in 2010 during a visit to the University of Oxford, where James was finishing his Ph.D. (or DPhil as they call it there). Ironic that we add an "Oxford scholar" at the same time the decision was made to move from OUP to a new home, Temple University Press. Scott and David's collaborations are numerous and well known, and David and James have coauthored several articles and op-eds on gangs since they first met at a Eurogang workshop at the University of Kent in 2013. However, this is the first time all three of us have worked together—triad closure, as the social network scholars call it. After three years of preparation, which included hundreds of emails, a few pre-COVID-19 happy hours, and more than a dozen Zoom meetings, *On Gangs* became a reality.

While *On Gangs* can trace its origins to *Confronting Gangs*, it is a very different book. It was our desire to use some of the key themes from *Confronting Gangs* for interpretative lenses but to more fully capture the growth and diversity in the literature. The result is the fourteen-chapter book that follows. We included a strong exposition of the theoretical framework for gangs and communities, the onset and termination of gang membership, and offending and victimization in gangs, as well as new chapters on race/ethnicity and immigration, policing gangs and gang members, gangs in prison, and legislating gangs. Also incorporated were more critical and cultural perspectives on gangs to complement mainstream criminological ideas and empirical research findings. The old "Girls, Women and Gangs" chapter from *Confronting Gangs* became a chapter focused on gender and gender identity that discusses masculinity, femininity, and sexuality as they pertain to gangs. The old "Institutions" chapter now includes deep engagement with gang representations in media and social media. The old "International" chapter is now truly global. The book concludes with a chapter that discusses what works in responding to gangs that integrates standards of best practice in research and compares what goes on in gang research to those standards. We believe that the book has much greater breadth and depth in its coverage of topics.

Since *Confronting Gangs* was published, we have lost a number of notable gang scholars: Jim Short, Dave Curry, Ron Huff, Joan Moore, and Irving Spergel. Our work stands on their shoulders and is better for their many contributions and their friendship.

The Structure of *On Gangs*

This book presents a large volume of research about gangs, gang members, and gang responses and is divided into three parts. Part I includes the core issues in understanding gangs such as definitions and measurement, organization, joining and leaving, victimization and offending, and the community context of gangs. Part II examines emerging and critical issues including gender, race/ethnicity, gangs and social institutions, and gangs in a global context, integrating materials from research about gangs in North America, Central America, South America, Europe, Asia, Africa, and Oceania. Part III is focused on the responses to gangs: policing, legislating, and imprisoning. The book concludes with a chapter that examines programmatic and strategic responses to gangs framed in the context of quality research designs. The research is presented critically—that is, with an eye toward areas where consensus exists regarding findings and where findings are based on robust data and research design. We use the results of research, some of which we completed, to better describe the gang problem and appropriate responses to that problem.

Part I: Core Issues

The first six chapters examine what we call "core issues" about gangs. Core issues are those that have long captured the attention of researchers—definitions and measurement of gangs and gang members, gang organization, joining gangs, leaving gangs, crime and violence, risk factors for gang membership, offending, victimization, and the community context of gangs. Each of the six chapters in this section presents state-of-the-art reviews of the research, reflecting tremendous advances in theory and evidence and new ways of thinking about long-standing problems. Levels of explanation cut across people, groups, and communities. Community context has long been a topic of inquiry among criminologists and sociologists as they attempt to understand the forces that create social problems and craft responses to those problems. However, we also integrate a life-course perspective on gang membership to capture the passage from adolescence to adulthood, which has important implications for understanding gangs and gang membership.

Part II: Emerging and Critical Issues

It seems strange to think of gender and race/ethnicity as "emerging issues" in the study of gangs, especially when even the earliest studies of gangs identified women in gangs and focused on the impact of migration and immigration on the composition of gangs. However, emerging issues are those that have not been subject to a great deal of attention from the research community or have operated at the fringe of gang research. Our aim with these chapters is to capture current issues and critical and cultural criminological perspectives that have emerged with societal changes, from the growing diversity of gangs and gang researchers to the growth of social media, and move this scholarship to the forefront of the minds of scholars, prompting new directions in theory and research. The field of criminology has long dominated the study of gangs. While this has proved advantageous for the production of knowledge, the downside is that the central focus of research has been on crime and violence. This section, therefore, aims to push the boundaries of gang research through the consideration of gangs in the context of key socializing institutions—family, school, labor market, polity, media and technology, religion, and the gang itself.

Part III: Responding to Gangs

In the final section, we detail the response of the criminal justice system to gangs. We begin by examining how the police respond to gangs and how they interact with gang members, because law enforcement is the primary entry point for cases into the criminal justice system. This review is timely given that the last decade has featured one of the most robust debates in U.S. history about what the future of policing in general, and policing gangs and gang violence specifically, ought to look like. Here we engage with critical perspectives, including the growing intolerance of suppression-led responses, along with changes in government surveillance of gangs. Next, we extend the study of gangs into what has been called the "final frontier" for gang research: prison. Our view of prison gangs is equally timely in the context of mass incarceration and the dramatic growth of the U.S. prison population over the past three decades. As an extension of U.S. policing policy and priorities, mass incarceration has had a disproportionate impact on people and communities of color, groups that are also disproportionately labeled by the criminal justice system as "gangs."

Finally, few areas in gang research attract as much controversy as responding to gangs, partly because politics often outpace science. Much has changed since Klein and Maxson notably concluded in 2006 that most responses to gangs appear promising because they have not been subject to rigorous evaluation. This section thus offers a review of gang-related legislation, from sentencing enhancements to civil gang injunctions, and other measures. It also concentrates on scientific advances along with political shifts in the response to gangs in communities. Here we aim to accurately portray growth in the science and the successes and failures of gang prevention and intervention practices and programs.

I

Core Issues

Defining Gangs, Gang Members, and Gang Crime

"We've got a couple right here." Not long after that phrase was uttered, Michael Reinoehl emerged from a parking garage and shot and killed Aaron Danielson. On August 29, 2020, Danielson, who was armed with a loaded handgun, was part of a large group "invading" rival territory, part of an ongoing series of clashes that dated back to 2017. Multiple fights broke out that Saturday evening, resulting in injuries and arrests, culminating with the death of Danielson. Although there had been violence between these groups in the past, this was the first homicide. Just about one month later, Reinoehl was shot and killed by law enforcement officers.

Now let's fill in some missing facts. The site of the scene? Downtown Portland, Oregon, where social unrest unfolded for nearly one hundred continuous days after George Floyd, a Black man, was killed by Minneapolis police in May 2020. The affiliations of the involved parties? Patriot Prayer (Danielson), a far-right, pro-Trump group, and Antifa (Reinoehl), a left-wing, anti-fascist group. Both groups were at odds with each other and with America's elected representatives over the state of the nation. The context of the clash? A pro-Trump caravan of vehicles in conflict with Black Lives Matter protestors. The violence caught the attention of President Donald Trump, who tweeted the next day, "Rest in Peace Jay!"

The first paragraph describes intergroup conflicts between gangs that can be found in just about any city of the United States. Even a brief scan of the fifty-one thousand articles in the National Gang Center's gang-related newsfeed (https://www.nationalgangcenter.gov/gang-related-news) reveals clashes not unlike those that occurred in Portland. Yet the second paragraph complicates matters. The word *gang* is not normally used to describe groups like Patriot Prayer and Antifa. The "gang members" were White. Their violence was political. The context was protest movements.

We begin this book by asking three simple questions:

- What is a gang?
- Who is a gang member?
- What is a gang crime?

The pages that follow demonstrate that the answers to these questions are not simple at all. In fact, there is widespread disagreement about the answers to all three of them. And this disagreement is not just an academic matter. For example, some police departments require a gang motive to classify an act as a gang-related crime, while others just require the involvement of a gang member to classify an act as a gang-related crime (see Maxson and Klein 1996). One can imagine that this could result in either over- or undercounting of gang activity, which, in turn, can have serious consequences for those labeled (or not) as having been involved in it. So, definitions have consequences for how we count gangs, who is officially recorded as a gang member, and what we do to respond to gangs and gang members. For these reasons, we begin this book with a series of discussions about how gangs, gang members, and gang crimes are defined and the size and scope of the gang problem in the United States.

Defining a Gang

The first academic use of the word *gang* as it pertains to the group activities of children was in educator Henry D. Sheldon's (1898) "The Institutional Activities of American Children." Puffer (1912) later offered the first working definition of a gang as a primary social group, and Bogardus's (1926) seminal work on social distance gets an honorable mention for recognizing the "predatory gangs" of Los Angeles, although this work is revered more for being the earliest recorded study of the focus group interview. And then of course there is Thrasher's (1927, 37) oft-cited definition of gangs as "interstitial" groups, a product of the "in-between" areas where formal institutions failed to take hold and flourish in ways that made sense to youth (particularly in transitional segments of a city) and a "manifestation of the period of adjustment between childhood and maturity."

Suffice it to say that people have been talking about gangs for over one hundred years, which is why most people are surprised to learn that there is no agreed-upon definition of a gang among researchers or practitioners. The situation was so muddled that in the 1990s, the U.S. Department of Justice tried to bring some clarity to the definition of a gang. It held a series of meetings between law enforcement, researchers, policymakers, community activists, and others involved in understanding and responding to gangs. They were asked, "What is a gang?" but failed to provide a definitive answer to the question.

The crux of the problem lies in disagreement over the role of involvement in crime as a defining feature of gang membership. Those who study the gang and emphasize its group nature (i.e., characteristics such as cohesiveness, leadership, persistence, and specialization) tend to leave involvement in crime out of the definition. Thrasher (1927), for example, was careful not to include law-violating behavior in his statement on the gang, arguing instead that gangs only facilitate crime. Scholars in this tradition, such as Short, Fagan, Huff, and Curry, argued that criminal inclination is more a function or outcome of gang involvement rather than the raison d'être of the group. They argued that including crime in the definition of the word gang was especially unhelpful for explaining the link between gangs and crime. "Tautology with a capital T" is how Curry (2015, 11) described it—it is redundant to say that gang members commit crime because they are gang members and they are gang members because they commit crime.

Klein (1971, 13) saw things differently. He argued that for a group to be called a gang they had to "have been involved in a sufficient number of delinquent incidents to call forth a consistent negative response from neighborhood residents and/or law enforcement agencies." Otherwise, how are gangs any different from benign peer groups? Likewise, Miller (1975) defined gangs as being mainly the province of law enforcement and others who respond to crime and disorder. Today, the influential Eurogang Program of Research (Esbensen and Maxson 2018; Weerman et al. 2009) is most closely associated with the claim that crime is a central and distinguishing activity of gangs. By focusing on gang members (individuals) rather than gangs (groups) as the unit of analysis in the study of crime, researchers have navigated issues of tautology by studying people who are at liberty to self-nominate (or not) their gang status. Researchers have found that that not all gang members are criminals and not all criminals are gang members. Gang members also vary in the amount and type of crime they commit (see Chapter 6).

These findings are important because it means that there is variation in the criminal activity of gang members to be explained. This logic equally extends to the group level since there is considerable heterogeneity in behavior across gangs, regardless of whether criminal activity is a defining feature of them (Pyrooz and Densley 2018). Still, there are critical and cultural criminologists who in some respects deny that gangs even exist—at least gangs as we know them. They see gangs as social movements of resistance to hegemonic structural forces (Brotherton 2008) and argue that "the criminologists' gang" is essentially the social creation of state control agents and empiricists like us (J. Katz and Jackson-Jacobs 2004).

Hallsworth (2013) and Brotherton (2015), for example, posit that mainstream criminologists impose the gang label with criminal involvement to fit a social and political agenda of managing disorder and protecting the (White) propertied classes. During a more naturalistic study of gangs, they expect gang members to reject criminal involvement as a defining feature of gang life—except, as we demonstrate below, they don't. J. Katz and Jackson-Jacobs (2004) go so far as to claim that gang members are "ghosts" that can be made to appear or disappear simply by changing a definition. This type of criticism is typically directed at criminal justice agents and agencies, especially law enforcement.

In the United States, definitions of gangs used by law enforcement typically are specified in a state's penal code. In California, for example, the penal code criminalizes gang membership. Section 186.22 of the penal code defines a gang as

> any ongoing organization, association, or group of three or more persons, whether formal or informal, having as one of its primary activities the commission of one or more of the [enumerated] criminal acts . . . having a common name or common identifying sign or symbol, and whose members individually or collectively engage in or have engaged in a pattern of criminal gang activity. (California Penal Code § 186.22 (f))

These approaches provide a basis for enforcing laws but often are not as helpful in understanding the problem of gangs and gang members in a broader sense. By this we mean that narrow, legalistic definitions rely on overly specified characteristics that are difficult to measure (see Chapters 11 and 13) and designed solely for law enforcement purposes (e.g., suppression and intelligence-gathering) versus prevention and intervention efforts. Many groups may be interested in prevention and want to focus on younger gang members or those on the verge of affiliating with gangs. Schools and community groups have a legitimate reason to understand gang membership and its role in their domains. Yet a legalistic definition is of little help in crafting family support programs, after-school prevention programs, or education, employment, or training interventions, because it focuses on criminal wrongdoing and ignores risk and protective factors. While the primary purpose of a definition is to determine whether an individual or a group fits within a category (i.e., gang member or gang), such definitions also have implications for the response to gangs. For these reasons, broader definitions that focus less on legalistic aspects have been developed.

There are several alternatives to legalistic definitions of gangs. Such definitions can include those that focus on individual attributes, behavior, and associations. Typically, several key elements are included in the definition of a gang that must be present for a group to be identified as a gang, and we highlight six of them.

First, everyone agrees on at least one thing—any useful definition of a gang must include a group. Some definitions of a gang specify the number of members. And since most delinquent acts or crimes committed by juveniles are done in groups (Zimring and Laqueur 2015), distinguishing between groups and gangs is important. Failure to do so could falsely identify individuals as gang members.

A second element in defining gangs concerns the use of symbols. Most gangs have symbols of membership, helping identify and communicate the collective identity of the gang. These symbols can take a variety of forms. It is important to understand that such symbols may change quickly. While clothes, hand signs, and certain ways of wearing clothes were at one time the most popular indicators of gang membership in this country, that has changed dramatically in the past ten years, in part because these symbols and styles have been commodified and now are a part of global youth culture (Ilan 2015). The rise of computer-mediated communication (including Facebook, Twitter, TikTok, and YouTube) and its widespread use among young people has also fueled the dissemination and growth of new symbols. Symbols may reflect important historic events, persons, or activities, such as deaths or shootings (Frey et al. 2020).

Communication is a third element of gangs and how symbols are transmitted. Most gangs have developed a series of verbal and nonverbal communications. A variety of words have been developed by gangs, typically out of informal trial and error rather than as the result of a purposeful effort to develop such symbols. For example, *Crip* becomes *Crab* if you want to insult a Crip gang member, or the color (Blood) red becomes an affront to the gang when used to cross out Crip blue graffiti. Nonverbal forms of communication include graffiti and hand signs, even emojis on social media. Graffiti is a symbolic form of communication used by gangs (and other groups). Spergel (1995, 87) observed twenty-five years ago that the role of graffiti varies across gangs, communities, and ethnic groups. Traditionally, gang graffiti has been viewed as a method of claiming territory. While there is variation among gangs in their use of graffiti and its meaning, graffiti has spread via media and social media and can be found in many countries around the world.

Gang graffiti can also fuel gang confrontations (Decker 1996, 230). Graffiti can be challenged by writing profanity over it or simply marking it out. The letter K for "kill" can be used to pepper rival graffiti with references to killing members of enemy gangs. The use of K beyond gang contexts is testimony to the growing role that gangs play in popular culture, fueled in part by the widespread availability of social media (Patton et al. 2019). "RIP" added to an opposing gang's graffiti provides an obvious message—rest in peace (Decker 1996, 132). When the graphic nature of graffiti collides with the nearly unlimited graphic possibilities of the internet, it can create a multiplier of new forms of graffiti and new threats. As Patton and colleagues (2019) have pointed out, Twitter represents a near-perfect platform for communicating threats and even identifying targets for assault and shooting. While historically graffiti has been primarily symbolic in nature, social media has facilitated more instrumental ends, by identifying times and locations for violent events.

A fourth defining feature of gangs is that they must be durable. Durability is an outcome, something worthy of study in its own right (Densley 2013; Ouellet, Bouchard, and Charette 2019). Many groups of young people form over a specific issue, only to be disbanded and never seen again. It is common for adolescent friendship groups to form and split apart quickly; gangs do not behave this way. Some have likened the gang to a trolley, in that some individuals hop on or off, but the trolley keeps rolling. This feature of gangs varies considerably, as some Chicago gangs have been in existence since the 1960s, and other gangs in Los Angeles have been around for eighty years. Most gangs in America are considerably newer than that, and many of these new gangs have already come and gone after several years by either merging with other gangs or simply disbanding (Aspholm 2020). Again, the internet has facilitated the creation of new groups that have adopted many of the characteristics of gangs, an issue we return to in Chapters 3 and 10. But the bottom line is that groups that come together for one or two days or one or two events are not durable. Groups that last at least a few months, and despite the turnover of their individual members, are.

Many definitions of gangs include street orientation as a crucial element. This most typically takes the form of gang turf or territory. There is some controversy about this feature because groups that may be considered gangs, such as Antifa and alternative right (alt-right) groups, fluctuate in their street orientation (Pyrooz and Densley 2018; Reid and Valasik 2020). As Densley (2013, 5) observed, street orientation really is a "variable attribute that depends upon the business of the gang," such as street-level drug dealing. Owing to the role of social media in gangs (see Lauger and Densley 2018), moreover, some scholars argue that the term *public-orientation* (Reid and Valasik 2020, 20) better captures the intersection of the street and the internet, or what Lane (2018) calls the "digital street." Still, most contemporary gangs do claim some territory as their own, because that is where the gang began or where most of its members live, and there often is some "set space" within their domain "where gang members come together as a gang" (Tita, Cohen, and Engberg 2005, 280).

The final element in defining a gang is involvement in crime. It is possible to imagine a large number of groups that meet the first five criteria of the definition of a gang yet do not engage in crime. Such groups may include skateboarding crews or basketball teams. However, the first five criteria alone do not make an academic department, the Biology Club, or an athletic team a gang. Rather, what distinguishes a gang from other affinity groups is its involvement in crime, especially violent crime. We recognize that crime is a social construct that varies across time and place and captures a diversity of conduct from public nuisance and status offenses to homicide and serious violence, but we still contend that a good definition of a gang must include involvement in serious crime as a feature of gang activities, if only to separate the gang from other peer groups. Research and practice are clear that gangs are heavily involved in crime and recognize that involvement as a key feature of gang membership, a point we examine in detail in Chapter 6.

A group of researchers, policymakers, and practitioners has been working to study gangs in the United States and Europe since the late 1990s (see Chapter 9). They needed a definition so that they could be sure that what was studied and measured as a gang was consistent across different countries. This was important because what people think of and call a gang in the United States doesn't necessarily resonate in other settings. For example, a gang in the United Kingdom can refer simply to a group of friends. As Ralphs and Smithson (2015, 521) observed, the Dutch *jeugdbendes*, French *bandes*, Norwegian and Swedish *gjengs*, and Danish *bandes* are not functionally equivalent. Based on several years of hard work, however, the group arrived at a "consensus" definition of street gangs, which reads,

> A street gang (or a troublesome youth group corresponding to a street gang elsewhere) is any durable, street-oriented youth group whose own identity includes involvement in illegal activity. (Weerman et al. 2009, 20)

The Eurogang definition includes many of the elements identified above but makes an important distinction between gang definers and gang descriptors: "Gang definers are those elements that are absolutely essential to characterize the group as a gang, while descriptors refer to those elements that help to describe the particular elements of the group"—things like group names, colors, symbols, and tattoos (19). The Eurogang definition has been put to work in over thirty countries, and after more than twenty years of use, Esbensen and Maxson (2021) recently concluded that it remains a reliable and valid definition. The fact that a sixth volume of Eurogang research was published while we were finishing writing this book (Melde and Weerman 2020) is testimony to the influence and staying power of this definitional approach to gangs.

Still, even those who originally worked to develop the Eurogang definition have questioned its utility, largely on the grounds that it is too inclusive (Aldridge, Medina-Ariz, and Ralphs 2012; Smithson, Monchuk, and Armitage 2012). Others critique the definition as again being tautological and not independent of the elements of the definition (Smithson, Ralphs, and Williams 2013). Some have argued that the Eurogang definition does not work well in non-Euro-American contexts, such as Latin America, owing to different structural and cultural traditions (Rodríguez et al. 2017). They also find that street orientation is more typical of American gangs than those found in Europe (Aldridge, Medina-Ariz, and Ralphs 2012). And there are empirical issues with the definition, such as in the ISRD country-by-country comparison where 27 percent of Irish youth identified as gang members, which was nearly double the second-highest percentage which was recorded in France (Haymoz, Maxson, and Killias 2014).

The benefits of using a common definition consistently have been made clear by M. Klein (2012), who argued that "good enough" was never good enough in conducting scientific research, particularly where such research can become the basis for policy. Our own view of defining a gang is that a definition must identify the key components of a concept in a way that can be measured so that objective decisions can be made about whether a *case* is a member of a *category* or not. Take left-wing gangs such as Antifa or right-wing gangs such as the Proud Boys as examples (Pyrooz and Densley 2018; Reid and Valasik 2020). Here, the "brand" has persistence while individual membership is fluid, and some elements of the definition (e.g., turf and permanence) take on greater importance than others. A key element in each of these groups, one generally lacking from many groups with a street focus such as gangs, is a political orientation. This observation underscores the value of a broad definition, one that allows for differing emphasis on some elements over others. In many ways it serves to broaden the study of groups involved in criminal behavior, reminiscent of the classic schematic developed by Thrasher (1927, 70), which we present in Chapter 3. Either way, we must focus squarely on what the group does, and while that may sound simple, hopefully this discussion shows that in practice it is not.

The Eurogang definition is a consensus—not unanimous—definition of gangs. It is sufficiently general to capture the essence of groups described in this book. However, our approach to defining gangs and gang members also draws heavily from our collective experiences interviewing and interacting with gang members nationally and internationally. We have learned a good deal about how gang membership is defined by those individuals whose lives are most affected by gang membership. Here we present the views of some of those individuals to illustrate the two dimensions that most gang members use to describe a gang: (1) criminal involvement and (2) aspects of culture, collective identity, and camaraderie that border on descriptions of the gang as a family.

Most gang members defined their gang in terms of criminal involvement. There is a considerable amount of bravado in their descriptions of gang life, as evident in the responses of these St. Louis gang members. Typically, they described the gang as a family or a loosely based organization of friends who knew they could count on each other. Note in particular how these quotes reflect the activities and beliefs most likely to be valued by adolescents:

> If you want to be a real gang member, you got to bust out windows, steal, sell dope, hang out. The next one you got to do if you in the gang, you got to sell coke or rock, anything. They think it [gang membership] is fun, they can rule everything, take over schools, take over neighborhoods, and they think they own all that.

> You can get to fight whoever you want and shoot whoever you want. To me it's kind of fun; then again, it's kind of not, because you have to go to jail for that shit. I'm tired of that. But other than that, being down for who you want to be with, it's kind of fun.

> It feels kind of good [to be a gang member] 'cause, you know, on one hand you got two families. You got your family, and then they [gang members] all look at you like family. I can do this now, but then on the other hand if I get into some trouble on the streets, it might cause a friend getting killed, it might cause me getting killed, but we all stick together like family.

> To my knowledge, it's a group of fellas. Not just fellas but ones that can depend on each other that's all down for the same thing.

Members of the Chicago gangs we interviewed reported a very different picture of gang membership. Our interviews in Chicago took place with two different groups, the Gangster Disciples and the Latin Kings—gangs that are more organized and have older membership. GDs (as they refer to themselves) typically described the gang as an organization. Indeed, many gang members bristled at the characterization of their group as a gang, believing that such a term unfairly characterized them in negative terms:

> They are a consolidated group of people that are working toward one goal, to better the political, social, and economical development. I don't look at it as no gang because a gang, I always look at it as a wild, radical group of people, but we never acted like that.

Just like a business. The way they operate businesses is the same way we do it in ours. We have different people doing different things. It's not all running around shooting guns and sticking people up and selling drugs and stuff.

But many members of the Gangster Disciples did use criminal involvement to define their group:

Well, in my words, a gang ain't nothing but people come together to do crime and make money and be a family to each other.

I would personally consider it [a gang] a mob of individuals led by a chief or a king that's predominately a criminal activity, though there may be ones that are trying to do something productive and do something for the community and things, but those are few and far in between. Especially they be involved in illegal activity also.

Latin Kings reported many similar definitions of their gang. But they differed from the Gangster Disciples in two important respects. First, Kings emphasized the cultural aspects of their gang, stressing the familial nature of the group. Perhaps as a consequence, Latin Kings were far less politicized than their Black counterparts in Chicago.

It's a second family. They are like your brothers. They will help you out when you need help. Whenever you mess up, they will take care of you too. To me it's like a family; some people want to get out of it, they don't want to be a part of it no more.

It's a group of brothers that agree to go by a set of rules or guidelines. We don't just do gang-type tactics, just go beat people up. We have rules.

Other Latin Kings included involvement in crime as a major factor in their definition of a gang:

We have colors, we have our hand signs, our handshakes, and we represent against our enemies.

When you are gangbanging, you are serious, but there is a lot of people that are not serious when they join because they think it is cool, and maybe sometimes most of the time when kids are young they join for that reason, to be cool, and they end up doing time for the Latin Kings or going to jail or getting shot and having to rely on them.

San Diego gangs were less organized than those we interviewed in Chicago and St. Louis. However, Latino gangs did maintain a stronger orientation to family and group than did their Black counterparts. We interviewed members of the Syndo Mob, a Black gang in San Diego who emphasized criminal involvement in their definition of gangs.

> To me, a gang is you don't give a fuck, and you are just right there with your homeboys, you know, partying. All you do is party and sell drugs. If you hit it off wrong with somebody else from another neighborhood, you just do what you got to do.

> I call it homies; I don't really call it a gang because I wear a green rag or something like that, because that's the way I've been living. Yeah, of course they rob and kill and steal and do all that kind of stuff too, but that's only not necessarily everybody from Lincoln go out and kill.

A few members of this gang did identify affiliational characteristics of gangs:

> When I was getting in trouble, to me, it felt like they were always there for me when I was little. Things got different when I got older.

> What is a gang? A gang, to me, is a group of people that represent something like the area, the neighborhood, the community where they live, and that, to me, would be a gang of people, from a certain neighborhood.

Calle Trienta, also known as the Red Steps, was a Chicano gang in San Diego. Membership and gang definition issues among these individuals reflected a cultural orientation to ethnicity and family. In this manner, they were like their Latino counterparts in Chicago, the Latin Kings:

> Just my homeboys, the people that I hang around with, grew up with, family just like almost, friends. Most of them is family.

> It's just like a neighborhood, some place you belong to. To some people a gang means everything. The gangbangers and the regular gang members, they stay down for the neighborhood or someone who is just down for the neighborhood when they want to be.

Fewer members of this gang identified criminal involvement as the benchmark of gang membership, and many of them included elements of the family in those descriptions:

> They are like a family. [But] my experience with a gang is trouble. They are not a company that works or anything. They sell drugs. Everybody know they are that way. That's why society is scared of them.

The first thing that comes to my mind is fighting with sticks and chains and stuff like that. I always wanted to be somebody that everybody thought was tough.

In sum, most gang members define their gang along one of two basic lines: (1) involvement in crime or (2) the affiliational and cultural aspects of gang membership that make the group like a family in the eyes of many members. While other lenses can be used to distinguish between groups that meet the criteria listed above, we choose not to impose such a filter in defining gangs. For example, we recognize other groups for whom crime and family are key organizing principles, such as organized crime groups, mafias, terrorist groups, and outlaw motorcycle gangs. We do not exclude them from our discussion because we believe they are unimportant or do not engage in crime and cause a good deal of harm. Indeed, we believe just the opposite to be true. But the traditional form of these groups does not conform to the definition of a gang, which we discuss at length in Chapter 3.

Defining a Gang Member

We now move to defining a gang member. Fortunately, this is more straightforward than defining a gang. But as Huff (1996a) has noted, overidentification of gang members has many deleterious consequences; therefore, care must be exercised in the development, application, and use of any and all gang labels.

There are multiple ways to determine whether an individual is a member of a gang. Most criminal justice agencies that identify gang members (police, probation and parole, and jails and prisons) employ a strategy that uses multiple measures of gang membership. This may include such things as self-admission, tattoos, and having known associates who are gang members. In institutional settings, things such as clothing, property, mail, phone calls, graffiti, and informants are commonly used to identify gang members. There is substantial overlap in what is used by law enforcement and in institutional settings to document gang membership (Barrows and Huff 2009). Prison systems typically employ a summative measure, designating as confirmed gang members those who meet three or more of the criteria and as suspected gang members those meet more than one and fewer than three.

Police departments across the country keep detailed records of the names of gang members, and these can be a valuable source of information about the identities of gang offenders. However, there are shortcomings to using police files for research because such information can be dated, be based on misinformation, or fail to reflect changes in gang affiliation by individuals. When an individual has made the decision and taken the steps to leave a gang but is still in a police gang database, the police may continue to treat that individual as an active gang member. This has implications for police gang sweeps, sentencing enhancements (i.e., more time in prison), and access to social services (for a discussion, see Chapters 11 and 12).

But police and other official records are not the only way to identify gang members. Asking gang members and neighborhood residents, especially youths or teachers, to identify gang-involved people can provide another way to determine who is in a gang. Gang members often bear the symbols of their gang affiliation, such as tattoos and clothing. Certainly, the presence of gang tattoos is an indicator of gang involvement—it is a signal of gang membership that is costly for the bearer because wearing it comes with many consequences, such as not being able to get a job (Densley 2012b). The company an individual keeps can also be a key to establishing whether he or she is involved in a gang.

Symbols and behaviors can be used to distinguish gang members from nonmembers, but the most powerful measure of gang membership is self-nomination. By this we mean that simply asking individuals whether they belong to a gang—"claiming" in gang talk—is the best means of identifying who is a gang member. Many studies using diverse methodologies provide support for this contention. Survey research (Esbensen and Huizinga 1993; Esbensen, Winfree, et al. 2001; Matsuda, Esbensen, and Carson 2012), interviews (Decker and Van Winkle 1994; Decker et al. 2014; Mitchell et al. 2018), and official data sources such as police records (Maxson and Klein 1996) all support this view (Melde 2016). In the fields of sociology and criminology, such convergence across methods is rare indeed. Interestingly, comparisons of police gang records to self-reported gang membership in one city showed high levels of concordance with police gang data (C. Katz et al. 2012), something also found by Decker and Pyrooz (2010b) in their review of police reports of the number of gangs and gang members in a city. This indicates that police data have concurrent validity with other measures of gang data, something not to overlook in estimates of the prevalence of gang membership.

Perhaps the most stringent test of self-reported gang membership occurs in assessing the validity of reports of gang membership in prison. Correctional systems keep extensive records of gang members for classification and treatment purposes, but they depend on criminal justice records that follow these individuals from the street and then from prison to prison. In their study of Texas prison gang members, Pyrooz, Decker, and Owens (2020) compared prison records and self-reported gang membership. They found an 82 percent convergence rate, wherein the self-reports of over eight out of ten prisoners were consistent with what the prison records showed. Prisoner reports of the name of their gang were also reliable (86 percent convergence).

While but a single study, these results are certainly promising for the continued use of self-reported gang membership.

Defining a Gang Crime

As Sánchez-Jankowski (2003) observed, there is a difference between gang
member activity, in which individuals in gangs behave as independent agents,
and gang-motivated activity, in which individuals in gangs act as agents of
the organization. This is perhaps most noticeable in the case of homicide (see
Valasik and Reid 2021): you may have gang-related or gang member homicides,
wherein at least one gang member is a party to the event as either offender or
victim (see Maxson and Klein 1996), and gang-motivated homicides, which are
a subsample of the former and result directly from "gang behavior or relationships" and/or some group incentive such as reputation or revenge (Rosenfeld,
Bray, and Egley 1999, 500). We discuss this in detail in Chapter 6. Suffice it to
say that any event where the participants involved were not associated with a
gang and any event where the outcome is unrelated to any known gang activity
is not a gang crime.

Counting Gangs, Gang Members, and Gang Crimes

Given the challenges of defining gangs and gang members, it should come
as no surprise to learn that counting the number of gangs, gang members,
and gang crimes is difficult. To be honest, we have estimates of the number
of each of these things, not the "true" numbers. Over time, the methods used
to estimate the counts for each category have improved, and many observers
believe that the current data provide reasonable estimates of how many gang
members, gangs, and gang crimes there are in the United States.

Many people assume that there is a large database maintained by the FBI
or some other federal authority where all the available information on gang
members and gang-related crime is updated regularly. This has never been
the case. Only over the last three decades has the federal government become
interested in developing such databases on gangs, gang members, or gang-
related crimes. The commitment to understanding the dimensions and size
of the gang problem can be seen in the efforts of the National Gang Center
(NGC), sponsored by the Office of Juvenile Justice and Delinquency Prevention (OJJDP), part of the U.S. Department of Justice (DOJ). However, most of
what we know about the gang problem from 1975 to 1995 is the product of a
series of one-off surveys conducted by different researchers over the last
forty-five years. Here we briefly review their methods and findings.

The first National Youth Gang Survey was led by Walter Miller in 1974–
1975 (W. Miller 1975). Miller was a Harvard anthropologist who had conducted research on gangs and delinquency in Boston and other cities. Miller

selected twelve large U.S. cities to examine the scope of the national gang problem. Each interview began with the question, "In your judgment, is there a 'gang problem' in this city?" Six of the twelve cities met his threshold. His estimates of the number of gangs in those cities ranged from 760 to 2,700 and the number of gang members from 28,500 to 81,500. He did note that there was some evidence of female gang members and that not all gang activity was concentrated in inner-city areas. These observations would prove important to later surveys and put law enforcement on notice that there was a problem with gangs.

Miller's (1982) next survey covered the period of 1974–1982 and included interviews with 173 agencies in 26 intensive study sites. Just over a third of the cities (nine) reported gang problems. Miller concluded that half of the 36 urban areas with populations over one million had a gang problem at some point in the 1970s. In 1982, Miller projected a national estimate of 97,940 gang members in gangs located in 286 cities. The largest concentration of gangs was in California (more than 30 percent of all U.S. gangs). The growth of gang cities in California and the spread to many other states were important findings from this work.

When Spergel and Curry (1993) conducted the National Youth Gang Suppression and Intervention Program in 1988, it represented the first nationally representative survey of gangs. Of the ninety-eight cities or localities screened, 76 percent had organized gangs or gang activities. They identified "chronic gang problem cities" that had a long history of serious gang problems and "emerging gang problem cities," which were smaller cities that had recognized and begun to deal with a usually less serious but often acute gang problem since 1980. For the thirty-five jurisdictions in their study where estimates were available, the researchers reported 1,439 gangs and 120,636 gang members.

The next important step in conducting national surveys of law enforcement to establish an inventory of the number of gang cities, gangs, and gang members was the National Assessment of Law Enforcement Anti-gang Information Resources (Curry et al. 1992). In 1991, the task of arriving at national estimates of the magnitude of the gang problem was undertaken by Curry, Ball, and Fox (1994). In addition to estimating the distribution and scope of the national-level gang crime problem, this study was designed to assess the quality of gang information resources available to local law enforcement. Each police department in the study was asked if their agency identified gangs as engaging in criminal activity within their jurisdiction. The most significant finding from this study was that 91 percent of the largest city police departments reported the presence of gangs. This finding underscored that gangs were no longer a California problem and that they could be found in cities with a wide range of population sizes. These data were used to provide national estimates of the number of gangs (4,881), gang members (249,324), and gang incidents (46,359).

The systematic survey conducted by Curry et al. (1992; see also Curry, Ball, and Decker 1996) provided a scientific basis for defining variables and categories, developing a scientific sampling frame, and reporting data that could reliably be compared across cities and across years. Curry and colleagues further looked at smaller municipalities, as small as those with twenty-five thousand residents. For the first time, reports from small and medium-sized cities and towns revealed a gang problem.

The work done by Miller, Spergel, and Curry was not part of a larger, well-funded ongoing commitment to document gang members, gangs, and gang crime. That changed with the passage of the Crime Bill in 1994 (Decker and Pyrooz, forthcoming), which identified "Criminal Street Gangs" as one of the separate "Titles" to be addressed in the bill. While specific funding for a survey was not included in the legislation that ultimately passed, the emphasis on learning about and responding to gangs was a result of the Crime Bill.

In 1994, the Office of Juvenile Justice and Delinquency Prevention established the National Youth Gang Center (NYGC), which is now the National Gang Center (NGC). In 1995, the NYGC conducted its first national survey, a nonsystematic survey of 4,120 localities that was the largest survey of law enforcement conducted to that point about gangs (John Moore 1997). A total of 1,492 municipal police departments reported gang problems in their jurisdictions, which included 23,388 youth gangs and 664,906 gang members. The numbers produced by the 1995 NYGC were larger than those of any prior one-year survey. The next year the NYGC implemented a design that would result in a more statistically correct estimate of the nation's gang problems. The efforts of this group represent the first wide-scale scientific effort to measure the scope of the nation's gang problem.

Beginning in 1996, the NGC conducted the National Youth Gang Survey (NYGS). The NYGS collects data from a nationally representative sample of city and county law enforcement agencies. In addition to tabulating the national scope of gang problems in terms of numbers of gangs and gang members, the NYGS included additional items that can be of use to policymakers, such as demographics on gangs and gang members, levels of gang involvement in crime, gang migration, and police gang units. The NYGS statistics are the most consistent and systematic of national surveys of law enforcement regarding gang problems.

Unfortunately, the survey was discontinued in 2013 (Asher 2017). That represented a loss of valuable information for law enforcement, criminal justice, and social service professionals and researchers. In 2020, the National Institute of Justice released a call for proposals to reinitiate the NYGS. Meagan Cahill at Rand Corporation was awarded the funding, and we expect national estimates of gang activity to be released in the upcoming years.

History and Trends in Gangs and Gang Behaviors

Are gangs new? Did gangs emerge in the 1980s and 1990s as a new form of youth culture? Were the gangs that existed before the 1980s different from those after 1980s? Are there things we can learn about the response to gangs in earlier times?

Gangs are *not* new, and in fact they are found increasingly all over the world, spread largely through the diffusion of culture and people. We discuss the global nature of gang membership in more detail in Chapter 9. But it is well documented that there are gangs in North, Central, and South America, Europe, Africa, Asia, and Oceania. The best evidence indicates that youth gangs, at least as we would define them now, have existed in the United States since at least the 1870s and have seen four distinct periods of growth and peaks since that time.

M. Klein (1995) has observed that cycles of gang activity vary by history as well as type of gang, geography, and ethnicity. As cities experienced immigration and industrial development in the latter part of the nineteenth century, most saw an increase in organized adolescent groups heavily involved in crime that can be identified as gangs, something we discuss more in Chapter 8. New York, Philadelphia, Boston, Chicago, St. Louis, and Pittsburgh all experienced the emergence of gangs in the late 1800s. These gangs, described primarily by journalists, social welfare groups, and reformers (such as Jacob Riis, Herbert Asbury, and Jane Addams), were disorganized aggregations of recent immigrants. In most cases, Italian and Irish immigrants were overrepresented in the ranks of gang members. These gangs engaged primarily in petty forms of property crime and directing violence against one another and members of rival gangs. It is significant for our current understanding of gangs to note that these gangs were made up of individuals from the bottom of the economic scale in their respective cities, not unlike the nature of gang membership today.

Interestingly, the gangs of the late nineteenth century died out without large-scale interventions by criminal justice or social service agencies. Indeed, these institutions were poorly developed and not well funded. However, two decades later, around the 1920s, the next generation of gangs emerged in American cities. It is important to distinguish between the youth gangs of the 1920s and their more organized adult counterparts, such as the Mafia. The youth gangs of the 1920s had far more in common with their earlier predecessors than they did with members of organized crime syndicates. Most of the youth gang members of the 1920s were in disorganized groups, composed of recent immigrants, typically the children of first-generation immigrants (Thrasher 1927). These gangs had symbols of membership and were more actively involved in crime, including serious crime, than were their counterparts of a generation earlier. Indeed, the literature about these gangs is replete with references to protecting their neighborhood or turf, nonfatal violence, and general property crime. These gangs also faded from the scene, apparently without substantial involvement on the part of the criminal justice system or social service agencies.

The next incarnation of gangs occurred during the 1960s. In many ways, these gangs represented a distinct break with the gangs of the 1890s and the 1920s. For the first time, significant numbers of racial minorities were involved in gang activities (see Chapter 8). However, the economic and demographic parallels between gang involvement in the 1960s and earlier gangs suggests the importance of the underlying causes of gang membership. Black and Latino people were heavily represented in the gangs of the 1960s, and like their earlier counterparts, these individuals generally were located at the bottom of the social and economic ladders of American society. In addition, residential segregation played a role in isolating these individuals from opportunities for success (W. Wilson 1987).

There were other important differences between many of the gangs in the 1960s and their predecessors of the 1920s and the 1890s. First, these new gangs were more extensively involved in criminal activity, especially violence. The availability of guns and automobiles gave these gangs more firepower and the mobility to interact with and fight gangs across a city. Their widespread involvement in crime, in turn, led to increased convictions and prison time, laying the groundwork for mass incarceration. As a consequence, the prison became an important site for the growth and perpetuation of gangs. This illustrates the principle of iatrogenesis, when a cure or intervention works against its intended purpose.

The contemporary period began in the 1980s. We trace the proliferation of gangs in the following section. However, we should note that what differentiates the contemporary period is the rise of the criminal justice system in responding to gangs. Mass incarceration began in this era and helped fuel the growth of street gangs. This occurred through the churning of gang members from the community to the prison and the prison back to the community. This movement of individuals between the street and the prison was fueled by the importation of street gang norms and members as well as the exportation of prison gang norms and behavior to the street (see Chapter 12). During this time, gangs became more violent and more institutionalized on the street and in prison, and they spread from urban settings into suburban and rural areas.

There is tremendous variability among communities in the emergence and persistence of gang activity. Below we offer a descriptive account of gang emergence, persistence, and change across place and time.

In his classic book *The American Street Gang*, Malcolm Klein (1995) traced the proliferation of gangs across United States. He did this using data gathered from two surveys of police gang experts, people who were well positioned to document gangs. There is an irony to this because throughout his career, Klein has been critical of police data on gangs, yet he used them a lot in his own research because they were the only data available. The first survey was based on a nonrandom sample that focused on large and hand-selected cities—in other words, national inferences could not be made. The second survey, with improved methodology, included large cities and a random sample of smaller cities and towns. What Klein observed was "astounding" (18), with a "horrendous" (31) number of cities reporting gang activity. He produced four maps (92–95), capturing gang cities by 1960, 1970, 1980, and 1992, that combined to offer a remarkable visualization of the proliferation of gangs across the country.

Fifty-four cities reported the existence of gangs by 1960. These were cities traditionally thought to have gangs, such as Boston, Chicago, Los Angeles, Philadelphia, and New York City. Klein's data pinned the existence of gangs to cities in only ten states, with California accounting for over half of the cities. By 1970, the number of gang cities jumped to 94. Cities in states such as Connecticut, Florida, Ohio, North Carolina, and Washington were added to the map, but growth remained concentrated in California's Bay Area and Los Angeles megapolis. Another major increase occurred by 1980, as 172 cities reported gang activity, with gangs now found in cities in half of the fifty states.

Whereas Klein's mapping of gang cities in 1960, 1970, and 1980 revealed a hodgepodge of dots, the 1992 map was like no other. The number of cities reporting gangs ballooned to 766. Put simply, gangs went national and could be documented in fifteen times the number of cities with gangs in 1960.

The National Youth Gang Survey employed a methodology not unlike Klein's. Although the idea for such a survey had been long in the making (W. Miller 1975, 1982; Needle and Stapleton 1983; Spergel and Curry 1993), it was formally launched in 1996 and administered annually through 2012. The survey asked knowledgeable law enforcement representatives to report whether their jurisdiction had a gang problem and the year when the current iteration of the gang problem emerged. Table 1.1 contains results on gang emergence partitioned by the four major census regions—distinguishing California in the West and Florida/Texas in the South—in cities with populations exceeding one hundred thousand residents (with notable omissions, such as New York City).

The NYGS findings largely confirm the earlier work of Klein and extend it to the most recent national survey. The largest growth in gang emergence occurred in the late 1980s and early 1990s, right around the time of Klein's survey. Indeed, this could be considered the period when gangs exploded across the country. Midsize cities in California and cities throughout the Midwest and South witnessed the emergence of gangs. Gang proliferation from 1995 forward occurred outside of the West, primarily in the South, especially in midsize cities.

TABLE 1.1 LAW ENFORCEMENT REPORTS ON THE EMERGENCE OF CURRENT GANG PROBLEMS IN LARGE U.S. CITIES BY CENSUS REGION AND PERIOD (N = 223)

Census region	Period of current gang problem emergence			
	1940–1982 (N = 44)	1983–1989 (N = 66)	1990–1994 (N = 68)	1995–2009 (N = 45)
West (N = 88) (without CA: N = 37) (only CA: N = 49)	Albuquerque; Tempe Anaheim; Berkeley; Chula Vista; Corona; Escondido; Fontana; Fresno; Glendale; Hayward; Huntington Beach; Inglewood; Los Angeles; Long Beach; Modesto; Oceanside; Ontario; Oxnard; Pasadena; Pomona; Rancho Cucamonga; Salinas; San Diego; San Francisco; San Jose; Santa Ana; Santa Clara; Stockton; Torrance; Vallejo; West Covina	Anchorage; Denver; Henderson; Honolulu; Lakewood; Mesa; North Las Vegas; Peoria; Phoenix; Portland; Salem; Salt Lake City; Seattle; Spokane; Scottsdale; Tacoma Burbank; El Monte; Fullerton; Garden Grove; Oakland; Sunnyvale; Riverside; Sacramento; San Bernardino; Ventura	Arvada; Bellevue; Boise; Chandler; Colorado Springs; Eugene; Fort Collins; Gilbert; Glendale; Greeley; Las Vegas; Orem; Pueblo; Reno; Tucson; Vancouver; West Valley City; Westminster Concord; Costa Mesa; Daly City; Downey; Fremont; Richmond; Santa Rosa; Simi Valley	Aurora Bakersfield
Midwest (N = 39)	Chicago; Detroit; South Bend	Akron; Aurora; Columbus; Des Moines; Fort Wayne; Green Bay; Joliet; Kansas City (MO); Lansing; Madison; Minneapolis; Omaha; St. Louis; St. Paul; Toledo; Wichita	Cedar Rapids; Cleveland; Dayton; Evansville; Flint; Indianapolis; Lincoln; Milwaukee; Peoria; Rockford; Springfield	Cincinnati; Grand Rapids; Kansas City (KS); Independence; Naperville; Overland Park; Sioux Falls; Topeka

South (N = 73)	Birmingham; Fayetteville (NC); New Orleans; Savannah	Atlanta; Baton Rouge; Columbus; Knoxville; Mobile; Oklahoma City; Shreveport; Tulsa; Washington, DC	Little Rock; Newport News; Alexandria; Norfolk; Chattanooga	Athens; Baltimore; Charlotte; Chesapeake; Columbia; Durham; Greensboro; Hampton; Huntsville; Lafayette; Lexington; Louisville; Memphis; Montgomery; Nashville; Raleigh; Richmond; Virginia Beach; Winston-Salem
(without FL/TX: N = 37)				
(only FL/TX: N = 36)		Abilene; Amarillo; Coral Springs; Forth Worth; Miami; Pasadena; Plano; St. Petersburg; Waco; Wichita Falls	Arlington; Austin; Beaumont; Carrollton; Corpus Christi; Dallas; El Paso; Garland; Grand Prairie; Hialeah; Houston; Laredo; Lubbock; Irving; San Antonio; Tallahassee	Amherst; Brownsville; Cape Coral; Fort Lauderdale; Hollywood; Jacksonville; Mesquite; Orlando; Pembroke Pines
East (N = 23)	Buffalo; Erie; Philadelphia	Boston; Cambridge; Stamford; Waterbury; Worcester	Hartford; Lowell; Newark; Rochester; Pittsburgh; Providence; Springfield; Syracuse	Allentown; Bridgeport; Manchester; Paterson; Jersey City; Tampa; Yonkers

Source: National Youth Gang Survey.

Figure 1.1 indicates the percentage of law enforcement jurisdictions reporting gang problems from 1996 to 2012. We are less interested in the trends (which were stable) than in the sheer percentages, partly because the NYGS shifted its methodology in 2001 (making comparisons over time less valid) but also because there is much stability in recent years. Overall, about 30 percent of nonfederal law enforcement agencies indicate that there are gang problems in their jurisdiction. According to the National Gang Center (https://www.nationalgangcenter.gov/Survey-Analysis/Prevalence-of-Gang-Problems), who administered the survey, that translates to around 3,100 jurisdictions—a number four times greater than Klein's observations from 1992. It is clear that much has changed since Klein's early observations, and not for the better.

There is a strong population gradient to gang problems in cities: the bigger the city, the more likely it is to have gangs. Figure 1.1 breaks out the trends for large cities (>50,000 residents), suburban county agencies, small cities (2,500 to 50,000 residents), and rural county agencies. Only a small share of cities with over 50,000 residents do not report having a gang problem (14 percent), while about half of suburban counties report one. Even a fair

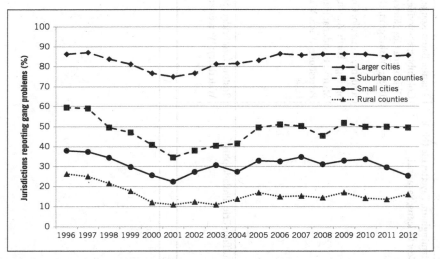

Figure 1.1 Percentage of U.S. jurisdictions reporting gang problems by law enforcement agency type and year

Note: Data are from the National Youth Gang Survey. Sample sizes differ between time periods. From 1996 to 2001, the sample included all police departments serving populations exceeding 25,000 (*N* = 1,216), all suburban county agencies (*N* = 661), a random sample of police departments serving populations between 2,500 and 25,000 (*N* = 398), and a random sample of rural county agencies (*N* = 743). From 2002 to 2012, the sample included all police departments serving populations exceeding 50,000 (*N* = 624), all suburban county agencies (*N* = 739), a random sample of police departments serving populations between 2,500 and 50,000 (*N* = 543), and a random sample of rural county agencies (*N* = 492). Agency type is defined by the 2002–2012 data collection period.

proportion of smaller cities (25 percent) and, surprisingly, rural counties (16 percent) report gang problems in their jurisdictions. These findings at once demonstrate the high prevalence of gangs in U.S. communities and the existence of variation of gangs across locales.

Figure 1.2 displays the trends in the number of gang members and gangs in the United States from 1995 to 2012. On the one hand, the number of gang members reflects individual youths who are either potential offenders or victims in gang-related violence. With observed national increases in violence by juveniles over the first half of the 1990s, increases in gang members may suggest the role of gangs in such increases in violent offenses and the associated costs for young lives. On the other hand, these numbers also reflect the criminalization of large numbers of poor, predominantly minority youths (see Chapter 8). That number has increased to nearly three-quarters of a million gang members in the United States, a number that has remained relatively constant over the past several years.

While most of the surveys have reported the number of gangs in the United States, we feel that this statistic requires caution to interpret. The changing estimates from national surveys of the number of gangs are shown in the gray line in Figure 1.2. The contrast between chronic (longtime) gang cities and emerging cities with a more recent problem made sense in the 1990s, as gangs were new to most jurisdictions. However, gangs have now been around for at least twenty years, and it makes more sense to talk about cities with gangs by reference to their population size and proximity to a major city.

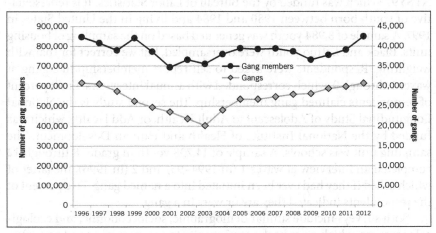

Figure 1.2 Number of gang members and gangs in the United States from 1995 to 2012

Note: The trend for the number of gang members is a solid black line and is depicted on the left y-axis. The trend for the number of gangs is a solid gray line and is depicted on the right y-axis.

Correlates of Gang Involvement

Who joins gangs, and what does the typical gang member look like? These are the questions we explore in this section of the book. But we caution you, even as we try to answer these questions, that there are no simple answers and that the answers are changing because gangs are dynamic social groups in American society. Perilous a task as it is, in this section we examine some of the main sociodemographic correlates of gang membership—gender, race, immigration, cognitive ability, socioeconomic status, and region.

A number of well-developed studies have examined these correlates, but they have limitations. The earliest studies, for example, are based on extensive surveys of youth (Esbensen and Huizinga 1993; Thornberry et al. 1993). While the demographic information derived from these studies is informative, readers could rightly question the generalizability of the experiences of youth in Denver, Colorado, and Rochester, New York, to youth in other areas of the country. A similar concern may be raised about any estimates drawn from the Gang Resistance Education and Training (G.R.E.A.T.) sample of children attending schools in Albuquerque, New Mexico; Chicago, Illinois; Dallas-Fort Worth, Texas; Greeley, Colorado; Nashville, Tennessee; Philadelphia, Pennsylvania; and Portland, Oregon (Esbensen et al. 2010). Relatedly, reports produced by the National Gang Center are derived from surveys of law enforcement. The trade-off of representativeness is that the police may have a different view of gangs that is colored by organizational priorities.

For these reasons, we draw on data from two representative studies of young people. The first is the National Longitudinal Survey of Youth 1997, or NLSY97, which was funded by the Bureau of Labor Statistics. It is representative of youth born between 1980 and 1984 and living in the United States in 1997. A sample of 8,984 youth was generated based on the sampling of housing units. Black and Latino youth were oversampled, but we correct for that with weighting. Respondents were asked to self-report membership in a gang at waves 1 through 9, which corresponded with annual interviews. Eight percent of respondents claimed gang membership. The second study is the National Longitudinal Study of Adolescent to Adult Health, or Add Health, which was funded by the National Institute of Health and Human Development. The sampling unit was schools. A sample of 14,738 youth in grades 8 through 12 completed an interview at waves 1 (in 1994–95) and 2 (in 1996), the latter of which asked if they had ever been initiated into a named gang. Five percent of the respondents indicated they are or were in a gang.

Both surveys include similar demographic, socioeconomic, and ecological measures, which gives us the opportunity to compare gang and non-gang youth across a range of correlates that do not change a lot with time. While these data are representative and contain large subsamples of self-reported gang members, they also have trade-offs based on age, cohort, and period.

In terms of age and cohort, these studies are limited to youth born in the late 1970s and early 1980s. The measurement of gang membership also means we learn nothing about those who join a gang later in life as adults. In terms of period, these are youth who came of age in the "get tough" era of juvenile delinquency and the proliferation of gangs across the United States. Of course, both surveys are now considered dated, having been collected around the turn of the century, but they are nationally representative, and they are the best we have available. Table 1.2 presents these findings.

Demographics

It is popularly believed that the gang is a male domain. Females are rarely central to news and entertainment media, as well as police coverage, of gangs. While we will explore the sources of this gender discrepancy in more detail in Chapter 7, the national figures on gender and gangs indicate that the majority of gang members are indeed male—both datasets tell a remarkably similar story. Over two-thirds of individuals who report being in a gang between early adolescence and emerging adulthood are male. Of course, nearly 50 percent of the population is female, which makes females a distinct, although nontrivial, minority in the gang.

One of the more contentious issues in addressing gangs concerns the race and ethnic identity of gang members. Both the NLSY97 and Add Health reveal consistent patterns of racial/ethnic disparities: White youth are under-represented in gangs, while Black and Latino youth are overrepresented. We should be clear that the under/overrepresentation is not proportional to pop-ular imagery of gangs, whether it is from the police or media. And as we cover in Chapter 8, law enforcement records indicate that White youth con-stitute a small minority—typically around 5–10 percent—of gang members, at least in large U.S. cities. Since the NLSY97 and Add Health data are repre-sentative, they likely document gang members in rural portions of the Unit-ed States who typically escape popular representation.

It is pretty rare for federal elected officials in the United States to call out a single gang, but President Trump made MS-13 a centerpiece of his efforts to clamp down on immigration from Latin America (Dudley 2020). The idea that immigrant youth constitute the bulk, much less a sizeable minority, of gang members does not comport with the data from two national studies. The NLSY97 shows that first-generation immigrants are actually underrep-resented in gangs. In contrast, the Add Health data suggest that such youth are overrepresented in gangs, although the difference was not statistically significant. The main story from both datasets is that native youth—those who trace their lineages to three or more generations—constitute the vast majority of gang members in the United States, or 86 percent in the respec-tive studies. There was a time when gangs were closely linked to immigration

TABLE 1.2 COMPARING GANG AND NON-GANG YOUTH IN TWO REPRESENTATIVE SAMPLES

N (%)	National Longitudinal Survey of Youth, 1997 (N = 8,984)			National Longitudinal Study of Adolescent to Adult Health (N = 14,662)		
	Gang 722 (8.0%)	Non-gang 8,261 (92.0%)		Gang 704 (4.8%)	Non-gang 13,958 (95.2%)	
	Percent or Mean (SD)	Percent or Mean (SD)		Percent or Mean (SD)	Percent or Mean (SD)	
Gender						
Male	70.8%	49.6%	*	69.8%	49.2%	
Race/ethnicity						
White	50.9%	68.0%	*	45.6%	68.2%	*
Black	24.7%	14.6%	*	20.6%	15.1%	*
Hispanic	19.2%	12.1%	*	26.4%	11.6%	*
Asian	2.5%	2.4%		4.0%	3.6%	
American Indian	1.1%	0.8%		2.1%	0.7%	*
Other	1.7%	2.1%		1.4%	0.8%	
Immigration						
First generation	3.1%	4.8%	*	6.8%	5.1%	
Second generation	10.2%	10.0%		6.8%	4.9%	
Third-plus generation	86.2%	84.6%		86.4%	90.0%	
Non-English household	18.1%	13.0%	*	10.1%	7.3%	
Cognitive ability						
ASVAB percentile (SD)	33.7 (26.4)	51.8 (28.7)	*			
Peabody percentile (SD)	38.9 (32.2)	56.0 (33.9)	*			
Picture vocabulary percentile				38.6 (26.3)	49.3 (28.1)	*
Socioeconomic status						
Household poverty	30.4%	16.0%	*	28.6%	18.3%	*
Household size	4.5 (1.6)	4.5 (1.4)		4.7 (1.9)	4.5 (1.6)	
Single-parent household	41.1%	26.4%	*	33.1%	23.2%	*
Parent education, years	11.9 (2.6)	13.0 (2.6)	*	12.3 (2.4)	13.2 (2.4)	*
Ecological (county)						
Poverty rate	13.9 (7.1)	13.0 (6.5)	*	11.4 (6.1)	10.9 (6.2)	
High school diploma rate	74.0 (9.0)	75.4 (8.8)	*	74.6 (9.4)	75.1 (9.1)	
Black population rate	14.4 (1.9)	11.9 (13.8)	*	15.1 (14.1)	13.3 (13.8)	
Hispanic population rate	9.0 (13.8)	8.1 (12.3)		9.6 (14.6)	6.0 (10.0)	*
Unemployment rate	6.6 (2.3)	6.5 (2.1)		7.2 (2.5)	6.8 (2.4)	
Lives in central city	32.6%	25.5%	*	41.9%	32.7%	*
Lives in suburban city	46.0%	54.0%	*	32.9%	38.8%	*

Note: All results are weighted to achieve representativeness. * $p < .05$ (significant difference between gang and non-gang youth).

(e.g., Thrasher 1927), but that observation does not apply to the contemporary period.

Finally, like race/ethnicity and immigration status, cognitive ability is a controversial subject, not least because measures of cognitive ability are thought to be culturally biased. But it is important to consider given that cognitive ability is associated with educational and economic outcomes. Both datasets show a clear pattern of association between cognitive ability and gang membership. In the NLSY97, there was over a half-standard-deviation difference between gang and non-gang members in their average percentile scores on the Armed Services Vocational Aptitude Battery and the Peabody Individual Achievement Test Math Assessment. In the Add Health data, there was under a half-standard-deviation difference between gang and non-gang members in their average percentile scores on the Peabody Picture Vocabulary Test.

Social Ecology and Socioeconomic Status

Both data sources contain information about the counties in which youth live, based on the 1990 decennial census. As readers will see in the next chapter, the county is not the ideal unit for comparison. Indeed, much of the action takes place in neighborhoods within cities. Still, counties are political units where important policy decisions are made.

In terms of macrolevel structural characteristics of counties, the findings are inconsistent across the data sources. In the NLSY97, gang members are more likely to reside in counties with slightly higher levels of poverty, a greater share of Black residents, and a slightly lower proportion of high school diploma earners. The Add Health data reveal that gang members reside in counties with a larger share of Latino residents. There were no differences in unemployment rates.

Gang members are more likely to reside in the central city or urban core of metropolitan statistical areas. For example, Minneapolis and St. Paul are the central cities of the Minneapolis-St. Paul metropolitan statistical area, while the remaining cities nested within the counties are considered suburban. It is a rather crude comparison but one that reveals that gang members are concentrated in the urban areas, which is evident in both datasets. This does not mean that gang members are not found in the suburbs or even rural areas, which is clearly evident in Table 1.2.

This observation seems a logical consequence of the historical characteristics of gangs, but there is evidence that gang membership is more complicated than socioeconomic status alone. The emergence of gangs in suburbs and rural areas presents a challenge to the view that gang members are drawn exclusively from the poorest members of society. Clearly, the concentrations of poverty and isolation that characterize the experiences of many minority group members in large American cities provide fertile recruiting grounds for gangs. However, poverty is not destiny, as most poor youth do not join gangs, and a large number of middle- and upper-class youth become gang members.

Relatedly, the next correlate of gang membership we consider is the socioeconomic status of gang members. Both datasets indicate that a greater proportion of gang members live in poverty than non-gang members. In the NLSY97, gang members were about 90 percent more likely to live in poverty, while in the Add Health gang members were about 60 percent more likely. While the majority of gang members do not come from households living under the poverty line, these differences are indeed stark. Similar differences emerge for youth raised in single-parent households and for years of parent education; both trend in the direction indicating that youth who join gangs are drawn from households of lower socioeconomic status. The parents of gang members completed about twelve years of schooling, equivalent to a high school diploma, while the parents of non-gang members completed about thirteen years of schooling, or about one year of higher education. These are issues we revisit in the next chapter when considering the neighborhood context of gangs.

Conclusion

This chapter has reviewed many important aspects of the challenge of understanding gangs, including definitions; prevalence and frequency of gang problems, gangs, and gang membership; and the correlates of gang involvement. It is important to keep in mind one of the central premises of this book: a key to understanding gangs is knowing who their members are and what they are like. Our work here documents the fact that gangs have existed in America for over one hundred years, though contemporary gangs are larger and more violent than their predecessors. In addition, the late 1980s saw tremendous growth in the number of gangs and gang members. There is a strong population gradient across cities in the nature of their gang problems. History, geography, and population characteristics play a role in the identification of gangs and gang members. But despite the growth of gangs, gang members remain a small fraction of their communities. It is also important to note that gangs can be found in every American state, as well as many countries across the globe. The current gang era has lasted longer than any other period of gang growth in the United States.

2

Structure, Culture, and Gangs in Communities

I n every direction beyond the University of Southern California (USC) is the gangland that has made Los Angeles (in)famous. Just east of the 226-acre (~1-square-kilometer) campus, on the other side of the twelve-lane 110 freeway, is a neighborhood carved up with multiple different Black and Latino gang sets. This includes a 4,800 acre "safety zone" created as part of a civil gang injunction targeting a collection of Gangster Crip sets. Adjacent to the north and west parts of campus is territory claimed by the Harpys, a Sureno gang, also subject to a civil gang injunction. On the south side of campus, the neighborhoods to the south and west of the Los Angeles Memorial Coliseum (featured in the 1984 Summer Olympic Games and the homefield of USC football) are home to various Blood, Crip, and Latino gang sets. This includes the Rolling 40s Neighborhood Crips and Black P. Stones Bloods, notable because purported affiliates were involved in a 2012 melee at a Halloween party hosted in the heart of the campus that left four people with gunshot wounds, squashing the perception that the campus is an oasis immune to violence.

About ten miles away from USC (as the crow flies) is another world-class institution of higher education, the University of California, Los Angeles. Many see the biggest distinction between the universities as UCLA being a public university situated at the base of the Santa Monica mountains, while USC is a private university located just two miles from downtown Los Angeles. But another difference is that, unlike much of the flatlands in Los Angeles south of the San Fernando Valley, there is no gang territory abutting the UCLA campus. Just beyond the campus borders are two communities that are worlds apart, this raises an important question: what gave rise to concentrated gang activity in South Central but not the Westside of Los Angeles? Explaining the concentration and spread of gang activity across places is important for understanding the growth and contraction of community life.

The purpose of this chapter is to describe and explain the existence of gangs in communities, and as such, we aim to accomplish several goals:

- How is gang activity distributed within communities?
- How does gang activity change within communities across time?
- What theories account for the emergence and persistence of gangs in communities?
- What roles do culture and structure play in gang emergence and persistence?
- What does the leading macrolevel empirical research reveal about the variation of gang activity in communities?

We are mindful of the call by Short (Hughes and Broidy 2020; Short 1998) to be more attentive to levels of explanation—micro, meso, and macro. This chapter is about places, not people. We obviously recognize that people inhabit places and groups require people. Our focus is on the powerful economic, political, and social forces found in streets, blocks, neighborhoods, districts, cities, states, and regions that give rise to gangs and their associated activities.

The Unequal Distribution of Gang Activity: A Tale of Two Communities

Just three years after the release of NWA's 1988 triple-platinum album, *Straight Outta Compton*, Ice Cube's *Death Certificate* hit the airwaves, which included the track "My Summer Vacation" (https://www.youtube.com/watch?v=mtTHRgFp _qc). Ice Cube shares the journey of "four gangbangers" from Los Angeles migrating to St. Louis, Missouri, to sell drugs, boarding a flight from LAX, stepping off the plane, renting a car, driving into town, and violently supplanting local crack dealers because they "can't fade South Central."

Like many other cities across the country, St. Louis experienced the growth of gangs in the late 1980s. The senior author was a faculty member at the University of Missouri–St. Louis at the time, and shortly after the release of Ice Cube's album, he was interviewing gang members in St. Louis for his book *Life in the Gang* (Decker and Van Winkle 1996). It was clear in the early 1990s that gang problems were not distributed equally across the city of 350,000 residents (in 2000; it is now below 300,000 residents). It was equally clear that Ice Cube's lyrics captured the St. Louis gang scene, underscoring the role of popular culture in the spread and structure of gang activity. Indeed, the gangs of St. Louis adopted the symbology of Los Angeles gangs, including the Blood and Crip namesakes.

Figure 2.1 illustrates variation in the number and growth of gangs across St. Louis neighborhoods, which in this instance were defined as census tracts. The data on gangs were from the St. Louis Metropolitan Police Department intelligence files containing geographic gang faction territories. We should note that the border running along the east of the city is the Mississippi River. Over a dozen suburban municipalities share a border with the city's west side. St. Louis has long been described as a tale of two cities, where downtown, midtown, and central west end combine to form a dividing line cutting the city in half, separating the relatively more advantaged south side (primarily composed of White residents) from the disadvantaged north side (composed almost exclusively of Black residents).

That dividing line also matters for gang activity. Few neighborhoods on the north side of the city were immune to gangs; the neighborhoods that had no gangs (colored white on the map) were largely industrial or riverfront neighborhoods punctuated by railroads or cemeteries. In contrast, most neighborhoods on the south side of the city were recorded by law enforcement

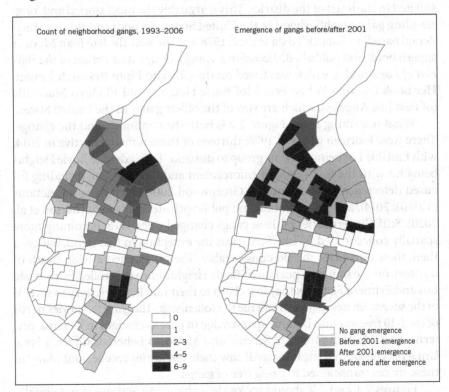

Figure 2.1 Emergence and count of gangs in St. Louis neighborhoods, 1993 to 2006

as having no gangs at all. Some changes occurred between 1993 and 2006. About twenty of the northern St. Louis neighborhoods witnessed the regeneration of gangs. In contrast, gang emergence was more sporadic across time on the south side. The only persistent growth was highly clustered in four contiguous neighborhoods of about twenty thousand residents with various Crip as well as Gangster Disciple and other gang sets. Just like the comparison of the neighborhoods surrounding the USC and UCLA campuses, there is tremendous variation in gang activity within cities. Gangs come and gangs go, but they remain concentrated in specific neighborhoods over time as they proliferate or contract in size.

We return to Los Angeles to illustrate an additional point: there is gang emergence, expansion, contraction, and desistance over time even within neighborhoods. We highlight the work of Valasik (2014), who in his doctoral dissertation plotted the territories of thirty-one gangs in the Hollenbeck policing district of Los Angeles at two snapshots in time, 1978 and 2014 (see Figure 2.2). The date and the place disguise two important facts. First, outside of Los Angeles, "Hollenbeck" may not ring a bell to many, but most readers with some familiarity of (especially Latino) gangs will know Boyle Heights, situated in the heart of the district. This is arguably the most storied and long-standing gang neighborhood in the United States. Second, and this is coincidental based on Valasik's data source, 1978 was the year the late Joan Moore's superb book was published, *Homeboys: Gangs, Drugs, and Prison in the Barrios of Los Angeles*, which was based on the Chicano Pinto Research Project. Her book featured White Fence (of Boyle Heights) and El Hoyo Maravilla (of East Los Angeles), which are two of the oldest gangs in the United States.

What is striking about Figure 2.2 is both the continuity and the change. There were fourteen gangs in 1978; thirteen of them remained active in 2014, with Eastside Los being the only group to disband. This is despite Boyle Heights being hit with the full weight of enforcement and intervention, including focused deterrence (Tita, Riley, and Greenwood 2003), civil gang injunctions (Valasik 2014), and gentrification and public/private investment (Barton et al. 2020). Still, the territories of these gangs changed since 1978, becoming more spatially concentrated. White Fence was the exception to this trend, but even then, their territories shifted considerably. They subsumed a wide swath of territory on the southern portion of Boyle Heights once controlled by Eastside Los and Primera Flats, yet they lost claim to their northern territory to several of the seventeen new gangs to emerge in Hollenbeck. The gang territories north of the I-10 freeway also became sparser, due in part to changes in land use patterns. Eastside 18th Street, El Sereno, and Metro 13 (where California State University, Los Angeles, is located) saw their territories recede, and many of these spaces transitioned to being free of gangs.

Figures 2.1 and 2.2 should make clear that gang activity is not equally distributed across places or across time—it rises and falls in communities

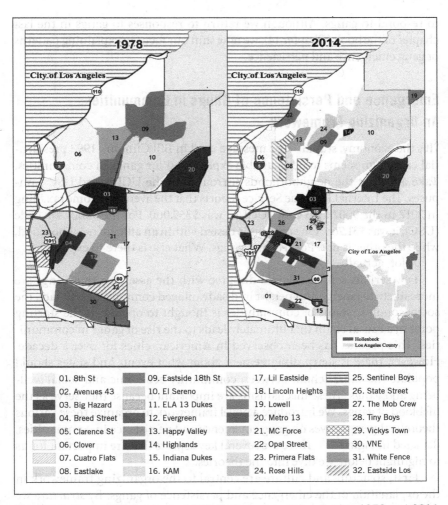

Figure 2.2 Gang territories in the LAPD Hollenbeck policing district, 1978 and 2014
Credit: Reproduced with permission from Matthew Valasik (personal correspondence, July 31, 2020).

and it expands and moves across communities. These observations are not unique to Los Angeles or St. Louis. We chose those cities because of our familiarity with the data and analysis. Anyone with expert knowledge of gang activity in a city—whether it is the police or street outreach or researchers—could attest to these spatial and temporal patterns elsewhere.

But the most important question in our view is *why*. Thus far, the observations we have made about the distribution of gang activity between and within cities shifted from national (Chapter 1) to city to community lenses. Each of these lenses serves important purposes, whether it is for developing theories and conducting research on gangs or crafting policies or developing programs to respond to gangs. Although we return to responses to gangs in the last chapter of the book (Chapter 14), we now shift our focus to explaining patterns of gang emergence and persistence.

Emergence and Persistence of Gangs in Communities: An Organizing Framework

"It's the economy, stupid." The message used in Bill Clinton's 1992 presidential campaign seems to be a suitable explanation for gangs in communities. Take a look at the neighborhoods surrounding the UCLA and USC campuses. The Internal Revenue Service reports that the average income tax filing in 2017 in the 90024 zip code (UCLA) was $359,000. For the 90007 zip code (USC), it was $31,764. One campus is nested within an affluent neighborhood, while the other is not. Poverty and gangs. What else is there to explain?

A lot, actually.

Few serious scholars would disagree with the assertion that gangs are more likely to emerge and persist in disadvantaged communities. In fact, the socioeconomic status of communities is thought to operate as the starting point in a causal chain that ultimately leads to the rise of gangs in communities. This process has been observed in American cities for over a decade. However, there is sharp disagreement about what events and states should populate the causal chain between community economic and social well-being and gangs. These mechanisms are important because they serve as the lifeblood of gangs. We introduce a novel framework to organize these various theoretical perspectives on gang emergence and persistence in communities, depicted in Figure 2.3. There are several key aspects that are important for us to highlight before we dive into the theories.

First, structure and culture are central to the organizing framework in the explanation of the emergence and persistence of gangs. By *structure* we mean the economic, physical, political, and social forces that arrange networks, positions, resources, and roles in core institutions that exist in communities (W. Wilson 2009). Structure puts things into place, and examples abound. Imagine being a young Black child subject to school desegregation policies of the 1980s. How do parents exercise social control when their child is bused hours away to schools far outside the neighborhood? Imagine living in a community where many fathers are imprisoned. Who serves as male role models to young boys? Imagine growing up in one of the twenty-eight high-rises in the since-demolished Robert Taylor Homes housing projects notorious for violence in Chicago. How do children navigate violent environments? Many universities assign students at random to dormitories, rooms, and roommates. Living in a studious versus a rowdy hall could be the difference between a successful and an unsuccessful semester. Poverty,

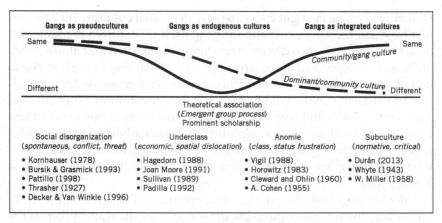

Figure 2.3 Theoretical perspectives on structure, culture, and gangs

income inequality, joblessness, racial composition, residential turnover, population density, and single-parent households—that is structure, or what Sampson and Bean (2006) termed the "hard facts of life."

Culture, in contrast, is more fluid, although "sticky." That is to say, although culture is dynamic, it has persistence, even in the face of change. Sampson and Bean (2006) highlighted a paradigmatic shift from a traditional cultural perspective, as "norms" and "values," to a "culture in action" perspective. In the simplest terms, culture as it is traditionally understood is viewed as internalized to the person, an authentic expression of self, the rational pursuit of mainstream goals, shared values to achieve collective goals, and clear and stable worldviews. The action-oriented approach to culture draws on Swidler's (1986) use of the "toolkit," which focuses on how someone manages rather than sees the world. Culture in this view is (1) intersubjective—definitions, accounts, and interpretations are among us, not embedded within us; (2) performative—the presentation of self varies depending on audiences and venues for evaluation; (3) affective-cognitive—there is high- and low-quality decision-making differentiated by mainstream definitions of means and ends; (4) relational—people construct social hierarchies that contain symbolic boundaries of rank, status, and worthiness; and (5) world-making—the social fields people envision and inhabit consist of players, rules, and rewards that continually evolve. While this notion of culture in action unfortunately remains at the periphery of criminology, it offers advantages to understanding gangs in communities (Harding 2014; Lauger and Horning 2020).

A second aspect of our framework is that we present three overarching perspectives that differentially embrace structure, culture, and their interrelationship. On the far-left end of the continuum, gangs are pseudocultures. Mainstream, community, and gang culture are all indistinguishable from each other. On the far-right end, gangs are integrated cultures. The community in which the gang exists and the gang itself are cut from the same cultural cloth, both of which diverge from dominant culture. The culture stands on its own, independent of the structural factors that may have given rise to it. Both extremes adopt social constructionist views of gangs. As M. Gottfredson and Hirschi (1990, 206) bluntly put it, the attention to gangs "derives more from politics and romance than from the results of research." Others contend that youth collectives in communities are pathologized and labeled as gangs by people in positions of authority—the police, school, or researcher—when in fact they are nothing of the sort (Brotherton 2015; Hallsworth and Young 2008).

Moving away from the extremes are perspectives that embrace the structurally adaptive origins of gangs but differ on the mechanisms. Whereas the left side emphasizes community control, the right side emphasizes youth adaptation. The center views gangs as endogenous cultures. They are half in and half out of community culture, which is half in and half out of dominant culture. Take away the structure, and you take away the gang (and other seemingly distinguishable cultural elements). This is one of the reasons scholars critique most gang responses as Band-Aids to bullet wounds, since they ignore structural roots of gang formation—a macrolevel focus on economic and social forces (e.g., poverty and racism). We acknowledge Sampson and Bean's (2006) point about culture as world-making, thus giving culture a structural component. We must also recognize the early state of understanding the relationship between gangs, structure, and culture; thus, we find this organization to be a useful heuristic.

Finally, we situate leading theories within this overarching perspective on structure and culture. We have written about structural control and adaptation in the past (Curry, Decker, and Pyrooz 2014; Decker, Melde, and Pyrooz 2013), but here we elaborate in greater detail on these theories, especially in relation to their emergent group process and the arguments made in the most prominent applications to gang emergence and persistence. We must be mindful that this is not merely some futile theoretical debate. Different perspectives offer much different prescriptions for policies and practices enacted in communities.

Social Disorganization Theory

Kornhauser's (1978) *Social Sources of Delinquency* was a tour de force in criminological theory. Nearly four decades later, Cullen and Wilcox (2015, 2) declared that no work "before or since . . . matches the sheer brilliance of the theoretical education [she] provided." Kornhauser organized criminological theory into control, strain, and cultural deviance, drawing lines in the sand for the respective theoretical camps. Her influence remains strong today, evidenced not only in the edited volume devoted to her legacy (Cullen et al. 2015) and nearly three thousand citations to her monograph, but also in how we organize theoretical perspectives on communities and gangs in Figure 2.3, including her views on gangs on the far left side of the continuum—gangs as pseudocultures.

Kornhauser's stance was abundantly clear: theories need not privilege gangs, criminal groups, or peers as (sub)cultural influences on behavior. Any "cultural deviance" explanation for bad behavior is little more than a convenient post hoc rationalization; it is an account for falling into disgrace. She stated bluntly that "so abused have been the concepts of culture and subculture in explanation of delinquency that if these terms were struck from the lexicon of criminologists, the study of delinquency would benefit from their absence" (1978, 253). Rather, there is consensus in values that permeate across all communities, as residents neither want crime and disorder nor accept it. Even gangs buy into this consensus, as they too want order and safety in their communities (Sampson 2002, 101), and there are several prominent instances of such arguments in the literature (Leovy 2015; Pattillo 1999; Skarbek 2014; Venkatesh 1997), hence the equivalency of dominant, community, and gang culture in Figure 2.3.

What differs across communities is structure, not culture. Kornhauser (1978) identified one variant of Shaw and McKay's (1942) social disorganization theory as consistent with a control perspective, her preferred theoretical paradigm. Instead of proposing why social problems exist in communities, a control perspective asks, "Why not?" The answer is that communities differ in their ability to regulate themselves. Social disorganization thus refers to community inability to realize common values and maintain effective social controls. Shaw and McKay identified three structural sources of social disorganization. While economic and social disadvantages were the starting point, the next step in the causal process included residential turnover and racial and ethnic heterogeneity, both reflecting and producing change. Disadvantaged areas of cities tended to have poorer housing stock, served as first destinations for immigrant groups, and were quickly abandoned for more desirable locations when the opportunity arose. Thus, these structural factors constrained the breadth and depth of social ties among residents in communities to produce social disorganization. Residents who do not share a common language, desires, or preferences have difficulty realizing common values, while those who intend to reside only temporarily in a neighborhood do not invest in relationships or institutions. And there are limited resources to leverage toward addressing social problems, even if they are to be collectively identified.

There is nothing special about gangs in Kornhauser's (1978) interpretation of social disorganization theory—gangs are a distraction from more important matters in promoting orderly and safe communities. She acknowledged that gangs are a form of "collective behavior" but one that is "spontaneous and unplanned in origin" (52). They exist only because communities are incapable of stamping out the conflicts that foment the transition of the playgroups of yesterday to the gangs of tomorrow, a point we return to shortly. Still, such groups are "not organized to commit delinquent acts," and any appearance of a causal influence on crime or other social problems is a consequence of neighborhood social cohesion and informal social control, or what Sampson, Raudenbush, and Earls (1997) termed *collective efficacy*, not the culture of the group. Kornhauser's view was that the moral codes of the gang were "not characterized by value reversal. Gang boys flout or ignore societal values whose legitimacy and moral validity they tacitly accept" (56). She does not fault the gangs but instead views them as bringing a semblance of order in places where adults and institutions have failed to support youth.

Observations of gangs and corner groups in Boston's North End (Whyte 1943) and Chicago's Near West Side (Suttles 1968) raised serious problems for social disorganization theory: gang problems did not emerge only in communities where there were weak personal ties among residents. Many disadvantaged inner-city communities had very stable patterns of residency, strong personal ties, *and* persistent gang problems (Reiss 1986). This issue had already begun to trouble Shaw and McKay, who joined others by making modifications to social disorganization theory by speaking about "differential social organization," which included advocating for cultural heterogeneity in socially disorganized communities, thus undercutting the notion of a universal cultural system. A good example of this comes from Elijah Anderson's (1999) ethnography of street life in Philadelphia and his distinction between "decent" families committed to middle-class values and "street" families, whose norms are opposed to those of mainstream society. The idea that some community members embraced deviant values raised the ire of Kornhauser, however, because it fell outside the realm of a pure control theory, thus lacking logical consistency and parsimony.

Bursik and Grasmick (1993, 130) recognized that the stability/gangs issue was a "stumbling block" for the social disorganization perspective because a core structural factor (instability) and a core mechanism (social ties) were not performing as planned. However, they were unconvinced that the critique had merit. Part of the reason was due to the evolution of urban life, especially for racial/ethnic groups that represented modern gangs. Mobility patterns changed. Systematic housing discrimination (e.g., redlining) and landlord practices constricted movement, racial/ethnic minorities preferred residence with other racial/ethnic minorities, and resource deprivation contributed to remaining stuck in place. In other words, powerful macrolevel forces were restricting mobility. But Bursik and Grasmick were concerned less with structural factors than with social processes. Indeed, their proposal of a systemic model of control came to constitute a major theoretical advance, one that remained consistent with the control perspective. They held that there was not one but multiple interconnected levels of control in communities, which they categorized into private, parochial, and public.

Personal social control is based on the interpersonal ties between individual community residents that we discussed above. These ties have come to serve as links between people that allow them access to opportunities, role models, and other networks that can expand their opportunities. The latter two levels of control were neglected in the earlier version of social disorganization theory. The parochial level of social control consists of ties between community residents and secondary institutions such as schools and businesses. Ties such as those created by employment opportunities for residents, or the role of school activities in engaging young people in productive activities, are examples of parochial social control. The public level of social control addresses the control of community residents over public resources. Using political power to exert influence on government and the economy is an example of the public level of social control. The public level of social control encompasses such important resources as access to and control over law enforcement and the justice system, as well as securing block grants to build parks or tax incentives for business investment. While personal social control in a community can be high, low levels of parochial and public social control can result in social isolation. By introducing additional levels of community control, Bursik and Grasmick helped make social disorganization theory and its applicability to gang problems a more complete explanation.

Pattillo's (1998) observations in Chicago also represented an advance in social disorganization theory. The gang-active neighborhood she studied on the south side of Chicago was middle-class, socially organized, and racially homogenous (Black), not lower-class, disorganized, and heterogeneous—yet another blow to social disorganization theory. Like Bursik and Grasmick (1993), she illustrated that this neighborhood was not an island. There are broader economic and social forces experienced in communities, particularly the influences of popular media images of gangs and physical and social proximity to gangs. Moving further rightward in Figure 2.3, gangs are culturally distinguishable but tacitly embraced in the community. The reason? Dense ties in the neighborhood, as illustrated in this example:

> One woman at the beat meeting complained of young men "gangbanging" (i.e., congregating) on her corner and of one man in particular who she thought was in charge. But, she said, "I didn't wanna give this young man's name [to the police] because his mama is such a sweet lady." (Pattillo 1998, 763)

Gangs were a double-edged sword. The young men who affiliated with them, including a notorious Chicago gang leader, were the children, nephews, and neighbors of community members. While Pattillo viewed gangs as contributing to lower crime and disorder as well as social organization, high levels of integration also meant that the "criminal minority" were also "given a degree of latitude to operate in the neighborhood" (1998, 770).

Thrasher's (1927) book *The Gang: A Study of 1,313 Gangs in Chicago* represented the foundation of gang research. Thrasher, a product of the Chicago school of sociology, held that "gangland is a phenomenon of human ecology" (23). Consistent with social disorganization theory, gangs were found in the "interstices" of the city, areas characterized by "deteriorating neighborhoods, shifting populations, and the mobility and disorganization of the slum" (22). Whereas other social disorganization statements described the mechanisms permitting social problems in general terms, Thrasher's commentary was very specific with regard to emergent group processes. All playgroups of young people, which form spontaneously based on familiarity and interactions (e.g., families, neighborhoods, and schools), have the potential to become gangs— they are "gangs in embryo" (26). The transition from playgroup to gang occurs not with internal forces leading to organization but with the external forces of collective engagement in conflict. A more definite group-consciousness emerges after it "begins to excite disapproval and opposition" (30), of which the source can be from different neighborhoods, hostile parents or neighbors, storekeepers, or the police. These conflicts are most likely to occur in the interstices of the city, as Thrasher stated:

> The failure of the normally directing and controlling customs and institutions to function efficiently in the boy's experience is indicated by disintegration of family life, inefficiency of schools, formalism and externality of religion, corruption and indifference of politics, low wages and monotony in occupational activities, unemployment, and lack of opportunity for recreation. (37–38)

No punches were pulled in this statement, which is precisely why Thrasher's perspective on gangs, with his focus on conflict-integrating group process, falls on the left side of Figure 2.3. Kornhauser (1978) offered scant praise for most theory and research, but Thrasher was an exception, as he was afforded the esteemed status of a "pure control theorist" (51).

The gangs of 1920s Chicago are much different from contemporary gangs, especially with regard to violence. Whereas the youth gangs of Chicago used rocks, sticks, slingshots, and knives to fight it out, the gang conflicts of today are exceptionally violent and lethal, due in no small part to easier access to and use of firearms. Thrasher's (1927) conflict-based argument needed a facelift for a new era of gangs, and Decker and Van Winkle's (1996) threat perspective offered just that. Their argument is more structural than classic or contemporary versions of social disorganization theory, but Decker and Van Winkle did identify the labor market, residential segregation, disinvestment in social institutions, and disenfranchisement as "forces creat[ing] a neighborhood context within which threats are not effectively controlled, either by formal or informal social control processes" (21). Whereas Thrasher cited conflict, including from conventional sources, Decker and Van Winkle viewed threats, whether real or perceived, from groups internal or external to the neighborhood as the source of intra-gang integration, creating cohesion and solidarity and establishing physical and relational boundaries. This helps explain why non-gang groups, such as breakdancing crews in Milwaukee (Hagedorn 1988) and graffiti/tagging crews in Los Angeles (Bloch 2019; Valasik 2014), can transform into gangs.

Many have also identified threats to neighborhoods or racial threats as sources of group mobilization (e.g., Short and Strodtbeck 1965; Suttles 1968). Adamson's (2000) historical account of Black and White gang formation pointed to interracial conflicts from Chicago to Philadelphia. In the early to mid-1900s, White gangs played a pivotal role in neighborhood defense against the "encroachment" of Black people into traditionally White spaces. Since "urban governments and police forces were weak, ineffective, and often corrupt" (278), White gangs had the tacit approval of adults. That changed with White flight to the suburbs depleting the population of young White boys, leading Black gangs to employ the same predatory tactics as their counterparts. Others have documented these patterns in Los Angeles, where the once-White neighborhoods of South Central transitioned to almost exclusively Black in a few decades, but not without gang conflicts, where car clubs served as the predecessor to Crips and Bloods (Alonso 2004; Davis 1990). Whereas the White gangs disappeared, absorbed into the labor market and political structures owing to personal and parochial networks, the Black gangs remained owing to the cultural separation, economic marginalization, and political powerlessness found in Black communities (Adamson 2000; see also G. Brown, Vigil, and Taylor 2012).

In sum, the way gang dynamics play out at the local level is highly dependent on broader economic and social forces, which set in motion a chain of mechanisms that alter the ability of communities to structure youth activities and control social problems. It is apparent that those forces are strongly influenced by race and ethnicity, which proves consequential for the social organization of communities. Gangs should not form in communities that are integrated into the political economy of cities, since such communities can harness and steer resources to blunt the issues they collectively identify as posing problems, such as violence, property damage, and intimidation.

Underclass Theory

In 1987, William Julius Wilson, a renowned sociologist, wrote one of the most important statements on public policy in the United States, *The Truly Disadvantaged*. Wilson charted the shift in the structure of the labor market from a manufacturing-oriented to a service-oriented economy, known as deindustrialization, which had devastating consequences for urban America. Since the 1970s, there was growth in communities with high levels of concentrated disadvantage—high-poverty (>40 percent), single-parent households, and reliance on government assistance—dislocated from the broader city environs, creating what Wilson termed an "underclass." He assigned responsibility to a labor market that became highly segmented with the shedding of solid union and goods-producing jobs. There was a primary labor market consisting of service-oriented, well-paying, and stable jobs that required advanced education and skills, while the secondary labor market consisted of jobs that required little education or skills, paid poorly, lacked benefits, and were unstable. The burdens of these shifts fell disproportionately on the Black population, already in a precarious social position as a result of decades of discrimination and marginalization. The middle class hollowed out in cities, including Black neighborhoods; those who were able to flee migrated to the ever-expansive suburbs. Those who remained experienced spatial and skills mismatches, as they did not qualify for the good jobs in the city and were too far from good jobs for which they were qualified that existed in the suburbs.

The idea of an underclass perspective had been percolating among gang researchers, most notably with Joan Moore's (1985) observations in East Los Angeles. But W. Wilson (1987) provided the theoretical and empirical scaffolding to apply the underclass perspective to gangs, and few theories have been adopted as swiftly. In just five years, gang researchers made several book-length statements pinning the resurgence of gangs in urban America to deindustrialization—Hagedorn's (1988) *People and Folks*, Sullivan's (1989) *Getting Paid*, Joan Moore's (1991) *Going Down to the Barrio*, and Padilla's (1992) *The Gang as an American Enterprise*, all of which are listed as the most impactful books on gangs (Pyrooz and Mitchell 2015, 37, 51). Moore made the following statement, capturing the sentiment of the times:

> Like many other social scientists, I am impressed by the critical changes in the barrios and ghettos over more than forty years—nearly two generations. Of course there is still poverty and there is still a miasmic air of discrimination, less sharp than in the 1940s, perhaps, but definitely a factor in life choices and opportunities. But there appears to be something new—what some have rather controversially called an "underclass"—a kind of *lumpenproletariat*, a stratum of men and women who simply cycle around with little if any chance to

climb out of the realities of their decayed and defeated neighbor-hoods. (1991, 5–6)

What made Moore's statement compelling was that her observations were made in East, not South Central, Los Angeles, in neighborhoods composed of Latinos, not Black people. Moore was also able to compare distinct genera-tions of the El Hoyo Maravilla and White Fence gangs before and during periods of deindustrialization. And the fact that these observations occurred in economically booming Los Angeles, not struggling Rust Belt cities, was even more compelling, especially when coupled with concordant findings in Milwaukee (Hagedorn 1988), Brooklyn (Sullivan 1989), and Chicago (Padilla 1992).

Bursik and Grasmick (1993) sought to fold the underclass perspective into their systemic model. They recognized that it "might appear that the underclass hypothesis represents an important competing alternative to the systemic social disorganization model" (145). Indeed, the underclass per-spective theorized explicitly about the stable neighborhoods with concen-trated disadvantages, thus challenging social disorganization theory even with Bursik and Grasmick's updating. And the underclass perspective was contemporary, developed to account for a post-1960s view of urban life and race (Venkatesh 1997). Bursik and Grasmick creatively used the same strat-egy to deal with the underclass perspective as they did the empirical obser-vation of stable neighborhoods: public control. They stated,

> We do not believe this body of [underclass] research contradicts the assumptions of a systemic model in any way. Rather, it is simply a difference in emphasis: the traditional social disorganization research has emphasized the private level of systemic control, the "underclass" work has focused on public level. A fully systemic model, with a con-sideration of private, parochial, and public orders of control, can ac-count for the processes described by each set of theories in a logically consistent manner. (146)

Whereas underclass perspectives viewed dislocations as a consequence of deindustrialization, Bursik and Grasmick held that they are a consequence of insufficient institutional linkages, such as political brokers, public invest-ment, and effective policing. If such linkages were to exist, a systemic model grounded in a control-theory perspective could account for the resurgence of gangs in the era of deindustrialization.

We view Bursik and Grasmick's (1993) efforts as compelling but not en-tirely convincing, and for one good reason: they discounted the milieu of contemporary gangs. Scholars making underclass arguments were in the field studying gangs that were much different from the pioneering work of

Thrasher (1927) and to a large extent M. Klein (1971) and Short and Strodt-beck (1965). These gangs were not the playgroups of the past; they were in-volved in serious violence. These gangs did not acculturate to become the union members like in the past; they were criminalized and punished by the full weight of the criminal justice system. And these gangs did not fade away in late adolescence like in the past; people prolonged their membership well into emerging adulthood. The underclass perspective was describing a much different gangland from what Bursik and Grasmick thought could be absorbed into the systemic model. Gangs were (quasi) institutionalizing. Communities would regenerate gangs—second-, third-, or even fourth-generation gangs were increasingly common. Any conception of gangs as an institutional fea-ture of a community stands in sharp contrast to control theories generally and the systemic model specifically. It is hard to argue for a universal value system with the institutionalization of gangs and their associated networks of vio-lence (Papachristos 2009; Kirk and Papachristos 2011).

Figure 2.3 situates the underclass perspective within the "endogenous cultures" area of the continuum. Moore and Hagedorn demonstrated em-pirically that "Chicanos and other minorities were largely excluded" from economic expansion in Los Angeles (Joan Moore 1991, 14) and that the decay of Milwaukee resulted in the industrial ladder being "suddenly snatched away" (Hagedorn 1988, 43). Youth did not stand by idly; they adapted to dein-dustrialization. The youth gangs that Sullivan (1989) observed in Brooklyn were highly skeptical of the relevance of education to their future. But drop-ping out of school meant that they lacked the credentials for an increasingly segmented labor market. These youth were doubly disadvantaged because they also lacked the "soft skills" that appeal for retail sector employment. Thus, maturational reform brought about by employment and marriage never arrived, and instead, as Moore observed,

> in many communities—like Los Angeles, El Paso, and Chicago—gangs that were established decades earlier had become quasi-institutional-ized. . . . They provided outlets for sociability, for courtship, and other normal adolescent activities. . . . As the institutions ordering the role transitions to young adulthood—work and family—become less salient in changing circumstances, these adolescent quasi-insti-tutions begin to be the focus of the lives of young adults. (6–7)

Institutions are supposed to be functional. Moore, Hagedorn, and others viewed gangs as occupying the lacuna of families, schools, and the labor mar-ket. This may sound concordant with Thrasher's (1927) classic line that the gang "fills a gap and affords an escape," but the macro-socioeconomic land-scape for these youth was much different. Gangs were positioned to address the economic shortfall imposed on their members. Padilla (1992) saw gangs as the quintessential enterprise of the informal economy—their rosters were composed of young men who were powerful and motivated players in their communities. It is no surprise, then, that reports emerged of gangs dominating underground markets, such as Venkatesh's (1997) observations in Chicago housing projects.

The underclass perspective on gangs stands apart from social disorganization theory in other ways. While both agree that gangs would subside with improvements in the socioeconomics of communities, there is greater cultural heterogeneity in underclass communities (again, E. Anderson's [1999] "decent" and "street" families), both in community culture deviating from mainstream culture and in gang integration. Joan Moore (1991) saw that the earlier El Hoyo Maravilla and White Fence cliques were better integrated into the community than the recent cliques. While the majority of neighbors viewed the recent cliques either neutrally or positively, the earlier cliques were viewed much more positively. Parents viewed the recent cliques more negatively, with two-thirds disapproval compared to one-third of parents for the earlier cliques. And Moore made it clear that gang culture was distinct from the community, as a gang encouraged "its members to openly subvert and defy the norms and ideals of the schools" (79).

We do not aim to paint a rosy picture of gangs as saviors of youth in underclass communities. Joan Moore's (1991, 44) take was that outsiders tended to impose labels on gangs, where the police call them "criminal" and radicals call them "revolutionary," when in fact "neither captures the essence of the gang." The underclass perspective offers a way to understand gang emergence and continuity in a period that diverged sharply from prior generations. But gangs, even if they were institutionalizing, still diverged from dominant and community culture. As we shift toward the right side of the continuum, we start to observe greater convergence in community and gang culture and divergence in community and dominant culture.

Anomie Theory

"Given the diversity of the United States, only a fool might . . . deny the existence of subcultures in our society." Those words were written by none other than Bursik and Grasmick (1993, 139). In contradicting the foundational assumptions of control theory, even Shaw and McKay (1942) argued for cultural heterogeneity in communities. While they acknowledged that the "dominant tradition in every community is conventional," with this statement they opened up room for culture. And they indeed invoked a cultural explanation for the stability of crime rates in communities, identifying gangs as the source of age-graded transmission of norms and values to the next generation of youth.

Like the underclass perspective, the forces underlying subcultures exist only as a result of the structural factors sustaining them. Unlike the underclass perspective, which viewed gangs as forming due to poor credentials and social dislocations, the anomie/strain perspective viewed gang youth as inventing an alternative cultural system in light of structural constraints. Although we assigned Padilla (1992) to the underclass perspective owing to intellectual proximity to Wilson and contentions about the economic milieu of the gang, he offered a telling statement capturing the sentiment of anomie/strain theory:

> [Young people] have lost faith in the capacity of the society to work on their behalf. Because of this perception of society, many of these young people have organized and created countercultural structures that they believe are capable of delivering the kinds of emotional support and material goods the larger society promises but does not make available to youngsters like themselves. (1–2)

Enter the youth gang, a form of resistance to a social structure that effusively identifies the "ends" but unevenly distributes the "means." The deck is stacked. Gangs form not to reshuffle the deck; they seek a whole new deck of cards altogether. They are, in Merton's (1938) classic, "rebels."

Vigil's (1988) *Barrio Gangs* is typically not associated with anomie/strain theory, and he in fact invoked underclass language in describing barrio life (24–27). However, over a series of works (1988, 2002, 2020), he developed "multiple marginality" as a core concept. He found that the young Latinos involved in the Southern California gangs he studied in the late 1970s were marginalized from aspects of mainstream culture and institutional life—they lived in communities isolated from dominant culture; they lived in families incapable of offering viable alternatives to the street. Marginality brought about adaptation in the form of street socialization, which he described as a "subsociety." Gangs were the collective solution to the problems their members shared in family stress, school failure, and disinterest from institutions. Vigil's (2002, 8) multiple marginality framework posited macrohistorical (e.g., structural racism, repression, and institutional breakdown) and macrostructural (e.g., immigration and poverty) forces triggering ecological, social, and psychological dynamics leading to street socialization. Gangs established their own rules while also perpetuating their own structures, both of which deviated from the dominant and community culture.

Horowitz's (1983) *Honor and the American Dream* offers a powerful account of neighborhoods, culture, and gangs. The gang she studied, the Lions, was composed of Mexican American teenagers who lived in a neighborhood that "rank[ed] very close to the bottom on a socioeconomic hierarchy" in Chicago (31). The neighborhood context described by Horowitz was reminiscent of the systemic model—a poor public school system, weak and predatory banking, high poverty, immigrant concentrations, and dense ties among residents. Horowitz, though, identified a two-dimensional view of culture, a coexistence of a local culture that valued honor, self-respect, and character (to a violent fault in some cases), and a dominant culture—namely, education and employment of the American dream. She traced the cultural products of gangs in a manner that pre-dated early statements on culture in action:

> Cultural symbols acquire meaning when people talk about something, when they agree or disagree about the definition of a situation. People not only use meanings to make sense out of situations but change or reinforce prior meanings in interaction. Consequently, culture is neither static nor necessarily the most stable component of social action, but constantly evolves. (20)

And evolve it did in this community, where the intertwined influences of the expressive honor code conflicted with the influences of the instrumental American dream, a tension felt even by the group of young males involved in gangs. Horowitz had little patience for Kornhauser's take on culture, which she felt was an almost religious standard that was too autonomous, monolithic, internalized, and ends-oriented. Bursik (2015, 122) even admitted a "crisis in faith" upon reading Horowitz. Cultural heterogeneity is the norm, not the exception, especially in disadvantaged communities.

The "golden age" of gang theory is most closely associated with Cloward and Ohlin (1960), A. Cohen (1955), and W. Miller (1958). We set aside a discussion of Miller for the next section because his argument is less about endogenous cultures than about integrated, causal cultures. Both Cloward and Ohlin and Cohen were heavily influenced by the Durkheimian intellectual lineage of anomie, or the (im)balance between "means" and "goals," as well as the Mertonian application to explain deviance. Cloward and Ohlin stated:

> It is our view that pressures toward the formation of delinquent subcultures originate in marked discrepancies between culturally induced aspirations among lower-class youth and the possibilities of achieving them by legitimate means. (78)

Societal goals are rather clear, especially with regard to economic success. The routes to achieve such goals are fuzzier, however. Legitimate routes are highly dependent on community structure; whereas some communities are socially organized to support these routes, others are not. Innovation is brought about by internalizing the goals but lacking the traditional means. Shared frustrations with blocked opportunities, rather than individual frustrations, lead to collective solutions, one of which is the neighborhood gang, or "specialized modes of adaptation to this problem of adjustment" (107).

The core contribution of Cloward and Ohlin (1960) is that innovations are dependent on the distribution of illegitimate—not legitimate—opportunities in the neighborhood. This is closely associated with the differential social organization (or differential association) arguments made by Shaw and McKay (1942) and Sutherland (1947). Criminal subcultures, which are economically oriented, are found in communities with integration between gangs and organized crime and conventional groups. Conflict subcultures, which are violence oriented, are found in communities without such integration. Others have also posited that community type will determine gang type, such as Spergel's (1964) classic work, *Racketville, Slumtown, Haulburg* (see also Spergel 1984).

A. Cohen's (1955) *Delinquent Boys: The Culture of the Gang* is perhaps the best representation of the anomie perspective. Whereas Cloward and Ohlin focused more on the origins of delinquency, Cohen was concerned with the origins of the gang (Hagedorn 1988, 113). And whereas Cloward and Ohlin focused mostly on a narrower version of status attainment (economic), Cohen was concerned with status generally (Bursik and Grasmick 1993, 136). Cohen focused on community institutions as the location for conferring status—especially schools, but also businesses, sports, and community centers. The problem Cohen identified was that these locations were staffed by middle-class individuals who fostered middle-class values. Lower-class youth, Cohen posited, were held to a standard to which they were destined to fail. Teachers saw them as lacking ambition and discipline to succeed educationally. Despite educational achievement serving as a traditional means to achieve culturally defined success, there is a lack of reinforcements in lower-class families and homes owing to alternative pressing needs or value systems. But myriad exposure to the "middle-class measuring rod" leads to status frustrations that produce a "reaction formation." Middle-class norms and values are reversed to construct an alternative cultural system consisting of status criteria that youth could realistically achieve—features that Cohen classically defined as negativistic, versatile, hedonistic, and autonomous, all of which ran counter to middle-class values. The gang was thus a solution to the problems of adjustment that have long concerned anomie theory. Either striving for reforms that flatten differences across lower- and middle-class cultures or lessening the cultural conflict that exists in institutions would serve to disrupt gang formation.

Subcultural Theory

The right side of the structure/culture continuum in Figure 2.3 is represented by subcultural theory. In this view, gangs and community cultures are one and the same, fully rather than partially overlapping, and both are distinct from dominant culture. It is possible that culture in such communities is endogenous to structure, but community and gang culture ultimately takes on a life of its own, unmoored to structural forces. Gangs are normative manifestations of community culture, which is what distinguishes this perspective from the anomie theories discussed above that also emphasize subculture (albeit as adaptations). In a pure subcultural perspective, the entire notion of "gangs" is highly classed and raced since the imposition of the gang label is based on appraisals that are external to the community—media, police, politicians, and researchers. Perhaps the earliest example of this dynamic is found in Whyte's (1943) landmark book, *Street Corner Society*, where he studied the social structure of corner groups and gangs in an Italian slum in the North End of Boston. To outsiders, the community of poor immigrants had all the trappings of social disorganization; to insiders, however, the community was socially organized, and the gangs were a "focal point for the organization" (258). Kornhauser (1978) reserved her most stinging critiques for these types of "cultural deviance" perspectives, contending that they were far too deterministic and ignorant of basic and common human wants and needs.

W. Miller (1958) theorized that a far different set of values permeated lower-class culture, values that naturally lead to increased levels of delinquency and gang involvement. In offering what Bursik and Grasmick (1993, 134) called the "purest cultural perspective," Miller identified a set of "focal concerns" that were defining, widespread, and persistent features of the lower-class communities he studied. The focal concerns included fate, or appealing to luck rather than agentic control over the future; autonomy, or a rebellious individualistic disposition; trouble, or violating the law or conventional norms as a means to achieve social status; toughness, or physical prowess and hypermasculine tendencies; excitement, or publicly engaging in precocious and risky activities; and smartness, or "street" rather than "book" smarts in "getting by" on others. Gang youth did not develop these focal concerns as a result of conflict, collective efficacy, or blocked opportunities; they were acculturated living in their own neighborhoods. Whereas these focal concerns were normative in their community, they deviated from dominant culture, and groups formed as a consequence of shared activities and interests and geographic proximity.

Miller's (1958) focal concerns perspective was criticized by Kornhauser (1978) for proposing a distinctive lower-class culture and by others such as Hagedorn (1988), who identified focal concerns as a politically conservative and outdated "culture of poverty" argument. It is noteworthy that extensive data collection led to Miller's theorizing as part of the Boston Special Youth Program, including three years of field observations, contact cards, official records, and census data. This makes Miller's theory more along the lines of Joan Moore (1991) and Thrasher (1927) than Cloward and Ohlin (1960) and Kornhauser (1978), the latter of whom appraised existing scholarship. Moule (2015), who summarized Miller's legacy of scholarship, contended that his 1958 article captured only a snippet of the broader perspective.

Enter *City Gangs*. This was slated to be Walter Miller's (2011) magnum opus from his Boston data collection efforts, but the book was still unpublished when he passed away in 2004. There is a reason for this, as Decker (2011, 15) wrote in the book's foreword:

> Walter had prepared a manuscript, *City Gangs*, which was submitted to John Wiley and Sons, publishers, and scheduled for publication. This book was to be his account of the gangs and individuals in the seven corner groups that had been studied as part of the Boston Special Youth Program. But the original manuscript was extremely long; it ran more than 600 pages and the publisher wanted substantial cuts in the length of the manuscript. Walter responded to this by adding several more chapters to the book, increasing its length to over 900 pages. The book was never published. Until now.

Few books on gangs and communities capture in such rich detail the structure and culture of communities as *City Gangs* (freely available at https://ccj .asu.edu/gangresearch). It is truly remarkable. Miller documented the housing stock; the demographic, economic, and social makeup of Roxbury; the social organization of the "slum"; and of course the gangs. Miller no doubt doubled down on his cultural argument, stating,

> Virtually none of the available data furnished support for an image of the community as disordered, unstable, or unintegrated; on the contrary, the bulk of evidence pointed to a way of life that was organized and cohesive. (103)

And,

> Characteristic attributes of city gangs—including their propensity to violate laws—are in fundamental respects a product of the urban lower class subculture. On this assumption an explanation of city gangs and gang delinquency requires, as one essential constituent, an explanation for an urban lower class. (105)

Miller did not see gangs as deviant; they were a normative feature of the community. The members of gangs did not possess social or intellectual handicaps. Young boys, and many girls (which he documented), were members of gangs and adhered to the cultural standards reflective of the community in which they lived. The problem was not the community; the problem, in true anthropologist form, was the gaze set on the community by outsiders looking in. Had *City Gangs* been published in a timely fashion, Moule (2015, 471) argued, Miller's contributions would have been "even more widely recognized and appreciated" and likely subject to empirical testing rather than simply caricatured in debates over structure and culture.

The external gaze is not just classed but also racial, according to critical race theorists such as Durán (2013). He does not deny the existence of gangs—after all, he discloses that he was a gang member—but contends that the application of the gang label and responses to gangs are heavily racialized. Peering into Latino communities, White-dominant society interprets the core ideals and patterns of behaviors of young people as gang-like. White youth do not receive such labels because elites, or people in positions of power, are from the same communities and share the same culture; thus, their behavior is viewed as deviant rather than gang. Collectives of White youth involved in crime often receive the "extremist" label, while Black and Latino youth receive the gang label (Reid and Valasik 2020). Durán sees such typecasting as ironic, especially for Latinos, given that the Southwest (his study sites are in Colorado, Texas, and Utah) is made up of colonial settlements. Like Vigil (2002), Durán takes the long view on gangs, as he sees macrohistorical factors of systemic oppression, marginalization, unequal environments, and social exclusion as core sources of activities that White-dominant society labels as gang activity (see Chapter 8). These factors are coupled with color-blind racist policies and practices—which target strong substitutes for race—such gang policing, civil gang injunctions, sentencing enhancements, and gang databases, leading to a backlash among young Latinos (Durán 2018).

The subcultural perspective, in the end, sees the gang and the community as one and the same. The problem is not with the culture of the community; the problem is with the culture of people who impose evaluations on the community. This can be based on class, race, ethnicity, or other markers that are associated with cultural relativism.

Empirical Research on Gangs in Communities

About eight years ago, we reviewed the state of the macrolevel evidence on gangs in communities (Curry, Decker, and Pyrooz 2014; Decker, Melde, and Pyrooz 2013). We now update that review to 2020. Tables 2.1 and 2.2 contain

TABLE 2.1 KEY EMPIRICAL STUDIES EXAMINING GANG PRESENCE IN COMMUNITIES

Authors (year)	Study design		Measures and findings		
	Unit of analysis and sample features	Temporal features	Outcome (DV)	Structural variables	Mechanisms
Jackson (1991)	U.S. cities Population > 100,000 (randomly selected) (N = 51)	1981 (DV) 1970, 1980 (IVs) cross-sectional	Gang presence	+ (youth population) − (retail/wholesale employment change) ns (manufacturing employment change; poverty; unemployment; pop. size; pop. density; Black pop.; Hispanic pop.; Native in-state pop.; Black/White inequality; HH activity; crime rate; temperature)	N/A
Tita, Cohen, and Engberg (2005)	Census block groups Pittsburgh (blocks >25% Black) (N = 165)	1991–1995 (DV) 1990 (IVs) cross-sectional	Gang set space	+ (population density; underclass index; vacant housing units) − (rental housing units; median rent) ns (age composition; boarded housing; Black pop. growth; Black pop; residential stability; per capita income; poverty; unemployment; block size)	N/A
Pyrooz, Fox, and Decker (2010)	U.S. cities Population > 200,000 (N = 100)	2002–2006 (DV) 2000 (IVs) cross-sectional	Gang members	+ (SE disadvantage; racial/ethnic heterogeneity) ns (population density; youth population)	N/A
Katz and Schnebly (2011)	Census tracts Mesa, AZ (N = 93)	2001 (DV) 1990, 2000 (IVs) cross-sectional	Gang member residences	+ (economic disadvantage; social disadvantage; residential stability) ns (pop. density; vacant housing; violent crime)	N/A
Costanza and Helms (2012)	U.S. cities Population > 100,000 (N = 154)	1992 (DV) 1990 (IVs) cross-sectional	Gangs	+ (divorce rate; violent crime) ns (SE disadvantage; pop. size; unemployment; family income)	N/A
Watkins (2017)	U.S. cities Population > 150,000 (N = 133)	2002, 2004–2006 (DV) 2000 (IVs) cross-sectional	Gang members (adults only)	ns (SE disadvantage; racial/ethnic heterogeneity; residential stability; youth pop; pop. density; violent crime; year of gang emergence)	ns (not in labor force; full-time work, wages; retail, service, manufacturing employment)

Note: Cross-sectional and longitudinal refer to between-unit and within-unit differences, respectively (studied contemporaneously or prospectively).

Abbreviations: DV, dependent variable; IV, independent variable; +, positively associated; ns, unrelated/null; HH, household; pop., population; SE, socioeconomic; N/A, not applicable.

TABLE 2.2 KEY EMPIRICAL STUDIES EXAMINING GANG VIOLENCE IN COMMUNITIES

| Authors (year) | Study design | | | Measures and findings | | |
	Unit of analysis and sample features	Temporal features	Outcome (DV)	Structural variables	Mechanisms
Curry and Spergel (1988)	Community areas Chicago (N = 75)	1978–1985 (DV) 1980 (IVs) cross-sectional	Gang-motivated homicide	+ (economic disadvantage; Hispanic) ns (Black)	N/A
Rosenfeld et al. (1999)	Census block groups St. Louis (N = 588)	1985–1995 (DV) 1990 (IVs) cross-sectional	Gang-motivated homicide	+ (SE disadvantage; Black; pop. size) ns (residential stability)	+ (spatial lag)
Kubrin and Wadsworth (2003)	Census tracts St. Louis (N = 110)	1985–1995 (DV) 1990 (IVs) cross-sectional	Gang-motivated homicide (Black perpetrators only)	+ (SE disadvantage; residential stability) ns (young Black males; pop. size)	ns (spatial lag)
Papachristos and Kirk (2006)	Neighborhood clusters Chicago (N = 343)	1995 (DV) 1990, 1994–1995 (IVs) cross-sectional	Gang-motivated homicide	+ (SE disadvantage; immigrant concentration) ns (residential stability)	– (collective efficacy)
Pyrooz (2012b)	U.S. cities Population > 200,000 (N = 88)	2002–2006 (DV) 2000 (IVs) cross-sectional	Gang-related homicide	+ (SE disadvantage) ns (residential stability; pop. heterogeneity; youth pop.; pop. density)	N/A
Tita and Radil (2011)	Census block groups Los Angeles (Hollenbeck district) (N = 120)	2000–2002 (DV) 2000 (IVs) cross-sectional	Gang-related violence	+ (extreme poverty; high poverty; block size; Hispanic pop.) ns (HH income; female-headed HH; rental units; adults without high school diploma; residential stability; vacant housing; youth pop.)	+ (network lag) ns (spatial lag)

(Continued)

TABLE 2.2 KEY EMPIRICAL STUDIES EXAMINING GANG VIOLENCE IN COMMUNITIES (*Continued*)

| Authors (year) | Study design | | | Measures and findings | | |
	Unit of analysis and sample features	Temporal features	Outcome (DV)	Structural variables	Mechanisms
Chris Smith (2014)	Neighborhood clusters Chicago (N = 342)	1994–2005 (DV) 1990, 1994–2002 (IVs) longitudinal	Gang-motivated homicide	+ (public housing demolition; SE disadvantage) − (coffee shops)	N/A
Valasik et al. (2017)	Census tracts Los Angeles (Hollenbeck district) (50 tracts × 4 decennial)	1978–2012 (DV) 1980, 1990, 2000, 2010 (IVs) cross-sectional and longitudinal	Gang-related homicide	+ (longitudinal: SE disadvantage) ns (longitudinal: SE disadvantage; cross-sectional and longitudinal: residential stability; youth pop;; pop. heterogeneity)	+ (spatial lag)
Valasik (2018)	500-foot grid cells Los Angeles (Hollenbeck district) (N = 7,192)	2009, 2009–2011 (DVs) 2009, 2010s (IVs) cross-sectional	Gang-related assault and homicide	+ (metro rail stops) ns (business, transportation, housing, school, and recreation locations)	+ (police stop locations; gang residences; gang set space) ns (spatial lag)

Note: Cross-sectional and longitudinal refer to between-unit and within-unit differences, respectively (studied contemporaneously or prospectively).

Abbreviations: DV, dependent variable; IV, independent variable; +, positively associated; −, negatively associated; ns, unrelated/null; HH, household; pop., population; SE, socioeconomic; N/A, not applicable.

a summary of findings from empirical research on gangs in communities. The volume of research led us to report this summary in separate tables for gang presence and violence, as Askey (2017) shrewdly observed that there is not always congruence between the residences of gangs, gang territory and set space, and gang violence. We focus only on studies with a geographic unit of analysis, such as neighborhoods or communities. We include only studies with a higher standard of evidence—that is, multivariate studies controlling for multiple influences. Explanatory variables are differentiated by whether they tap the structure that fixes things into place or mechanisms that bring about gang activity in communities, consistent with what we described in Figure 2.3.

Dissatisfying as it may be, our main conclusion is that the evidence base is far too sparse to afford any explanatory primacy for gang presence to social disorganization, underclass, anomie, or subculture theories. Very few of the fifteen studies actually test mechanisms tied to one or more theories, instead opting for readily available data from the U.S. Census Bureau. Many of the (violence) studies included a spatial lag that allows the violence in one neighborhood to influence the violence in another neighborhood. While this spatial lag allows a theoretical interpretation consistent with social influence, through either mimicking of actions or cross-border interactions, Tita and Radil (2011) pointed out that this does not differentiate among the bundle of possible social influences. We highlight one study in each table that perhaps best captures the important mechanism facilitative of gang activity.

Watkins (2017) examined the role of the labor market in promoting adult involvement in gangs. The focus on adults is important because the work of W. Wilson (1987) and gang theorists (Hagedorn 1988; Joan Moore 1991) explicitly identified problematic adaptations made in response to deindustrialization among this population. Watkins determined whether the availability, nature, and quality of work—the economic mechanisms that would lead to gangs—was associated with higher rates of adult gang involvement. He used data from the National Youth Gang Survey, which asked law enforcement agencies to report or estimate the number or proportion of gang members in their city who were eighteen years or older. Overall, Watkins found that the evidence in support of the underclass perspective was trending in the right direction, but it did not exceed the bar for significance in scientific research. This does not mean that the underclass perspective is wrong, as there are multiple additional ways to test the theory as well as a general need for more research on the topic.

All of the theoretical discussion above was focused on the presence of gangs in communities, not gang violence. What gives rise to gangs and what gives rise to gang violence may be different. Still, there is enough geographic overlap in these outcomes that we can glean value for theories of gangs in communities. Papachristos and Kirk's (2006) study in Chicago stood apart from all other studies because it formally tested a mediating mechanism (i.e., collective efficacy) and relied on survey data from a large sample of Chicago residents nested within neighborhoods to measure this mechanism. Papachristos and Kirk found that socioeconomic disadvantage, population heterogeneity, and residential stability were related to collective efficacy, consistent with Sampson, Raudenbush, and Earls's (1997) model, which in turn could explain differences in the number of gang homicides across communities. Score one for Kornhauser (1978) and social disorganization theory. Yet too few studies exist to reach any firm conclusions, and improvements in data and measurement are needed before real advances can be made in this literature.

Conclusion

This chapter established that there are differences in gang activity within and between places. It also established that gang activity ebbs and flows across time. A new organizing framework was offered to understand prevailing theoretical perspectives on gangs in communities. This provides a solid foundation from which to organize perspectives on gangs, especially in terms of establishing the cultural meaning attached to the gang vis-à-vis the normative orientations of communities, and identifies mechanisms requiring empirical testing. The updated review of empirical studies on gangs in communities suggests that progress is slow in this area, despite the enormous theoretical implications for urban theories and practical implications for community intervention. Some new studies have added great value to our understanding of these issues, yet the testing of mechanisms is too rare to bring much clarity to the literature. Our next chapter continues to focus on gangs but shifts attention from their patterns of emergence to their forms and functions.

3

Gang Structure and Organization

Humans (and many other mammals for that matter) work in groups to accomplish objectives more efficiently and effectively than in isolation. Put simply, groups can be more effective in producing desirable outcomes, and often, groups provide a more efficient means of accomplishing tasks. This aspect of group behavior is focused on the instrumental, goal-oriented aspects of executing actions. But group activities also contribute to other important functions, such as solidarity, consensus, and permanence. These symbolic functions of groups are no less important than the instrumental aspects, often providing motivation and a sense of belonging and creating synergies. For both these reasons, groups are not mere collections of individuals; they add something to those individuals. Or, as Aristotle said, "The whole is greater than the sum of its parts."

Groups exhibit considerable variety. They vary by size, complexity, specialization, geographical reach, and the ability to accomplish and coordinate complex tasks. The variety of groups is affected by their degree of isolation from other groups. They can be integrated or separate from mainstream values and groups and the individual characteristics (age, gender, education, etc.) of their members. We treat organization as a characteristic of groups. Perhaps the most important thing about groups is that they are diverse. The kind of diversity we are talking about here is multidimensional. By that we mean groups differ in their structural and symbolic components and across time. Think of a corporation like Apple or General Motors that serves consumers. It has a business model, symbols, a supply chain, and a training model (among other things) that are catalogued in manuals, regulations, and procedures. Yet owing to differences in markets, there is variation in the implementation of these formal guidelines. Groups must also be adaptive to change. Imagine a corporation "sitting out" the technology revolution or a traditional dine-in restaurant not offering takeout during the COVID-19 pandemic. Survival requires adaptability. Groups also vary across time, owing to the movement of human capital in and out and up and down in an organization as well as to changes in the external environment within which the group exists. To ignore either form of variation—within and across groups, at one time and across time—is to miss important characteristics about such groups. After all, even the most rigidly structured, rule-bound organization has a dynamic quality.

We argue that as groups composed of individuals in dynamic social settings, gangs too reflect these processes. In our view, too much of the research on gangs (and as a consequence much of the policy) is based on a view of such groups as static and fails to acknowledge the diversity in gangs and their change over time. Such a circumstance is not limited to the study of gangs. Indeed, a static view of organized crime or terrorist groups hinders understanding and responding to such groups. The ever-changing nature of communication technology alone represents a powerful change in how gangs do their business. When the senior member of the authorship team started his work with gangs, pagers were the mode of communication, and they would be called from pay phones. Needless to say, pagers and pay phones are now the stuff of old-time movies.

At the same time, gangs aren't just any group. Most delinquency is committed in groups, but if the gang were just a collection of individuals whose behavior in the group was the same as when they were on their own, we wouldn't be very interested in them. M. Klein and Maxson (2006, 195) observed that gangs are "qualitatively different" from other groups. This means that when individuals are with their gang, their behavior takes on a different character. These differences may include motivation, encouragement, and pressure to engage in crime, as well as role models that facilitate involvement in crime. This difference is what we typically call *group process*, a topic examined in greater detail in Chapter 6.

This chapter asks the following questions:

- How are gangs organized?
- What are features and characteristics of gang organization—leaders, rules, roles, and meetings?
- How are the structural relationships within gangs related to involvement in crime and routine social activities?
- What do gangs do? In this context, we are specifically interested in depicting the activities of gangs on a continuum from specialization to generalist activities.

In answering these questions, we compare gangs to a number of other groups that are also involved in crime, including organized crime groups and radical and extremist groups. We argue that governance and ideology are important points of distinction when examining gangs and other groups involved in crime.

The Organizational Structure of Gangs

It is appropriate to begin our discussion with an important question: What is gang organization? There is not a settled answer to this, but the approach taken by Pyrooz et al. (2012) provides a good starting point. They argue that

> gang organization is the degree to which the group effectively and efficiently coordinates and carries out activities. There are various dimensions of organization, one of which is group structure. (88)

It is instructive to note that this definition was the product of a cross-national study of gangs, and as a consequence it should apply to a wide variety of gangs. If groups are organized structurally, they should be able to accomplish some of their goals effectively and efficiently. Whether we are referring to Starbucks rolling out a new coffee product or the Gangster Disciples helping finance the election of a local politician (see Chapter 10), we find a definition that measures task completion to be a useful starting point in understanding gang organization. But there is variation in how gangs accomplish tasks as well as in organizational structures. Below, we contrast two ideal types of how gangs are organized.

One view of gang organization is that gangs are hierarchical or vertically organized. Such gangs have a formal structure that enforces rules and acts in ways that resemble a business. An alternative view argues that many gangs are horizontal and that organizational ties are based on informal relationships. As is generally the case with gangs, there is considerable diversity between these two extremes, but they serve as "ideal types" in the Weberian sense (i.e., they do not necessarily reflect reality because objectively nothing can, but they can help clarify one's observations). The first type depicts gangs as well organized, or instrumental-rational groups, and the second suggests that they are disorganized, informal-diffuse groups that are loosely confederated. These views emerged from debates about whether gangs controlled street drug markets in the 1990s. Based on research in Milwaukee (Hagedorn 1994) and St. Louis (Decker and Van Winkle 1996), the aim was to determine whether gang members who sold drugs were organized distributors or freelance dealers. The evidence supported the latter view.

From the instrumental-rational perspective, gangs have a vertical structure that allows them to enforce discipline in the gangs and have well-known values shared by the group. Other features of highly organized gangs include age-graded levels of membership, well-defined leadership roles, regular meetings, control of the profits from drug sales, written codes of conduct, expansion into legitimate business operations, and influence on the political process (Decker, Katz, and Webb 2008). These are the characteristics that we would expect to find among organized groups, whether formal or informal. Voluntary organizations and profit-generating businesses function in this manner, with identifiable goals and measurable outcomes. But is there evidence to support this perspective among gangs?

A number of studies find evidence consistent with the instrumental-rational perspective. These studies include Mieczkowski's (1986) work in in Detroit, Padilla's (1992) research in Chicago, Sánchez-Jankowski's (1991) study in Boston, New York, and Chicago, and Skolnick's (1990) investigation of prisoners in California. A fitting example of this kind of gang can be found in research conducted in a Chicago public housing complex by Sudhir Venkatesh. Venkatesh (1997) described the "Black Kings" as a gang with the power to influence community affairs. The gang persuaded the neighborhood "Council" (nominated leaders of buildings) against petitioning for greater police patrol in favor of the gang acting as security. In turn, this strengthened the gang's hierarchically structured drug distribution ring. This example supports the claim that gangs have become "corporatized" and were transitioning—at least in Chicago—from socially oriented to economically oriented associations. That said, these observations are dated. The transition to the status of "supergangs" was followed by the division or fragmentation of these gangs into smaller groups that were focused more on generating profit than on loyalty to the gang or each other. Today, Chicago's supergangs have broken down further into horizonal "cliques" (Aspholm 2020).

In general, it is our view that gangs, especially street gangs, tend not to be very well organized and that the vertical features of gang organization get more attention than they deserve. In fact, Felson (2006) described "Big Gang Theory," which depicts gangs as well-organized criminal organizations, as a myth. Felson is joined by Howell (2007; Howell and Griffiths 2015), a former official in the Office of Juvenile Justice and Delinquency Prevention who now works with the National Gang Center, in viewing this as a myth about gangs. Felson and Howell contend that gangs adopt the characteristics (e.g., symbols, views, behaviors, and language) of feared groups to ward off competitors and natural predators (i.e., other gangs) in their environment. But in reality, most gangs lack the strategic intelligence and resources to become highly organized, not least because they are composed largely of children and young people.

Our view is found in the informal-diffuse perspective on gang organization (Decker and Curry 2000; Decker and Pyrooz 2013), which describes gangs as diffuse and poorly regulated groups of individuals who pursue group goals but remain committed to individual self-interest. This can be seen, for example, in the use of profits from drug sales and other crimes largely for their own ends. In informal-diffuse gangs, leadership emerges in response to particular situations and circumstances, levels of membership are transient, meetings are rare, and codes of conduct have a very general locus, such as "secrecy" and "loyalty." Most importantly, gang members use the profits from crime not for the gang but for their own purposes, including partying, girls, and their own entertainment. From this perspective, while gang members may be heavily involved in crime, that criminality is versatile and does not reflect loyalty to the gang.

This perspective is supported by studies conducted by a number of researchers including Decker and Curry (2000, 2002a), Decker, Katz, and Webb (2008), and Decker and Van Winkle 1994, 1996), all in St. Louis; Fagan (1989) in three cities; Fleisher (1995, 1998) in Kansas City; Hagedorn (1994, 1998a) in Milwaukee; Huff (1996b) in Columbus, Ohio; McGloin (2005) in Newark; Lauger (2012) in Indianapolis; and Harding (2020) and McLean and Densley (2020) in the United Kingdom. Durán's (2018) work is particularly important in this regard, as it relies on data from two cities (El Paso, Texas, and Las Cruces, New Mexico) and thus provides a comparative framework. Importantly, he places gang membership in a broader cultural and institutional perspective, one that documents gang membership as far from a master status.

Similarly, Tapia (2019), working on the "El Paso-Juarez borderland," documents the transitional nature of gangs, which generally lack the internal structure to effectively regulate the lives of their members. Gundur (2019) combines observations and interviews in the Paso del Norte area, paying particular attention to issues of immigration and the role of ex-prisoners on the street. His work is important in that it too provides insights into multiple study sites and reinforces those who argue that the informal-diffuse perspective more accurately reflects the reality of gang structure in these cities. These examinations of gang organization have largely been conducted on the streets, but recent work by Pyrooz and Decker (2019) finds that prison gangs have lost their grip over members and prisons in recent years. This suggests that the informal-diffuse perspective provides a more salient picture of gang organization in the current context.

In their research on the two most organized gangs in Chicago and San Diego, Decker, Bynum, and Weisel (1998) found that the Gangster Disciples of Chicago were the only gang that could be described as instrumental-rational. However, interviews with members of the GDs still revealed a general lack of organization in drug dealing and financial matters—for example,

I never seen the money that I made go into the organization.

Please, not me. If I'm gonna stand up here and sit up here then use mine [profit] for their benefit, I don't think so. I ain't no sucker.

So, even in one of the most organized gangs in (at the time) one of the most organized gang cities, gang members used the money they made selling drugs for their own purposes, not those of the gang. This illustrates the extent to which gangs control or, as the case may be, fail to control the behavior of their members.

The research that does support the instrumental-rational perspective typically comes from large cities with chronic gang problems, such as Chicago, Detroit, and Los Angeles. We might expect that gangs in cities with emerging gang problems could evolve into economically driven or corporatized groups. After all, as one of us (Densley 2014b) documented among gangs in London, they take on these characteristics due to financial motives or protective necessity (see also Pitts 2008; A. Whittaker et al. 2020). There is both theory and research to support the notion that gangs evolve and transition over time (Ayling 2011; Densley 2013; Gottschalk 2017; McLean 2018; Roks and Densley 2020; Thrasher 1927). The conclusion that gangs are dynamic and change in response to internal and external social factors is an important one to keep in mind in future examinations of gang structure. One example is the interest in "Hybrid Gangs" (Starbuck, Howell, and Lindquist 2001). These are largely seen to be transitional groups that display considerable diversity in membership race/ethnicity, residential location, activities, and even group loyalties. Such groups date to Thrasher (1927) and generally are short-lived transitional groups. But they reflect the dynamic nature of gangs, frequently challenging stereotypes about membership and activities. Criminologists are at the early stages of understanding the impact of advanced communication technology such as smart phones and social media on group organization (Moule, Pyrooz, and Decker 2014; Storrod and Densley 2017; A. Whittaker, Densley, and Moser 2020), a topic we examine in more depth in Chapter 10.

Among the most important developments in the study of groups involved in crime is the work of Swedish criminologist Jerzy Sarnecki (2001). His treatise *Delinquent Networks* demonstrated the powerful analytic capabilities of network analysis, a tool largely ignored by criminologists until recently. Any organization can be thought of as a network-based social system. Network analysis captures social interaction and the interdependence of actors in the social world. In their review chapter on "Social Network Analysis and Gangs," Sierra-Arévalo and Papachristos (2015b) noted the impressive growth of this method of data analysis and its implications for understanding gangs, gang members, and the relationships within gangs and between gangs and other groups. Building on the first sociograms developed by M. Klein in 1971, "mapping gangs" (Kennedy, Braga, and Piehl 1997) can shed light on the underlying structure of the group (e.g., Grund and Densley 2012, 2015) and on its group processes in relation to other groups; thus, it can help pinpoint where best to intervene to reduce crime and violence (Sierra-Arévalo and Papachristos 2017). McGloin's (2005) network analysis of the street gangs in Newark, New Jersey, for example, identified gang members who functioned as "cut-points" in the network—removing them would fragment the gang entirely. And as Papachristos (2009) memorably showed with Chicago network data, having a unique position in the social structure of a gang could get you killed.

As Sierra-Arévalo and Papachristos (2015b) noted, the focus on network ties and their strength has considerable relevance for understanding gangs. The work of Descormiers and Morselli (2011) is an excellent example of the complications of studying one group or individuals in one group. The diversity in relationships (such as symmetry and asymmetry) and the continuum between conflict and cooperation are not always straightforward. These complications are made clear by the work of Vargas (2014) and Ouellet, Bouchard, and Charette (2019) in their respective examinations of the role of gang leaders. The latter focus on cohesion and embeddedness, two critical features of gang organization that are key to the survival of a gang. Despite this, these features work differently in large and small groups, with large groups persisting by having closed structures and small groups surviving with more open structures. It is clear that network analysis is a tool well suited for the study of gangs and their internal and external relationships.

The most important conclusion from this discussion is that gangs vary. This variation has been observed from Thrasher (1927) to M. Klein and Maxson (2006) to contemporary work, including that of the authors of this text. It is useful to conclude that gang organization varies along a continuum with informal-diffuse at one end and instrumental-rational at the other, much like Thrasher's figure. However, when a gang becomes well organized, it may well have the ability to engage in self-governance and demonstrate persistence. It is important to understand the organizational differences across gangs. As a sociological concept, such an understanding sheds light on the nature of human organization and collective behavior. As a criminal justice problem, such an understanding sheds light on criminal behavior.

We find that Thrasher's "natural history of the gang" (Figure 3.1) continues to be an important statement about the structure and "sentiment" of groups involved in crime. By *structure*, we mean the relationships and stratification within groups. For example, some groups are highly formal with well-defined roles and responsibilities. In such groups, relationships are specified by some formal known process and persist beyond the "first generation" of members. In other groups, relationships among individuals are

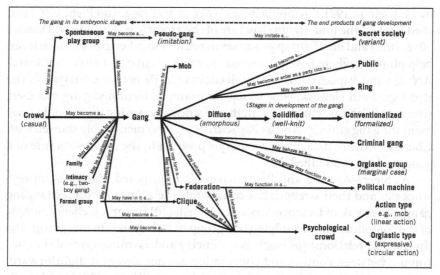

Figure 3.1 Reproducing Frederic Thrasher's natural history of the gang

not specified, certainly not by formal rules or written systems. These groups often do not persist beyond the first generation of members, and the groups are in a regular state of change, evolving as new members join and former members leave. We also believe that it is important to understand the "sentiment" or values and commitments to each other that are held by group members. By *sentiment*, we mean the value consensus among members as well as the strength of bonds among members. In some groups, the sentiment that binds members together is less formal, not specified by formal processes.

Figure 3.1 remains important for a variety of reasons. First, it places gangs in the context of other groups. We believe that an understanding of gangs is best arrived at when they are viewed in such a context. This perspective better allows us to see what gangs have in common with other groups and what is unique to the gang. This is important because if gangs are different from other groups in important ways (as we believe to be the case), then our understanding of them and the development of strategies to mitigate their deleterious effects cannot be built on old models.

A second reason this figure is important is that it is dynamic—that is to say, it allows for a view of gangs in transition. Follow the meridian of the figure from a (casual) crowd that "may become a" gang and, in the process of doing so, move through three different stages of development: diffuse, solidified, and conventionalized. In the course of that development, gangs may become noncriminal groups (secret societies, public groups, political machines, etc.) or criminal gangs. This perspective on groups avoids the all-too-common view of groups as immutable and unchanging.

A third compelling feature of this figure is that it provides a basis for merging a variety of perspectives in understanding gangs. From Weberian bureaucratic order to Durkheimian cultural values, and inclusive of contemporary analyses of group behavior (Perrow 2000; Schelling 1985) that more completely depict the nature of gang structure and values, this figure engages a more comprehensive view of what a gang is and how it is evolving. The consideration of crowds and their fundamental tradition as action or orgiastic based also allows for the inclusion of theories of social movements and mass behavior. We argue later in this chapter that while other groups that engage in crime (such as drug smugglers, human traffickers, mafias, political extremists, and terrorists) share many features with gangs, they are distinct. The understanding of their distinctive features contributes to the understanding of gangs for policy and practice.

The Features and Characteristics of Gangs

While the preceding section dealt with the manifestations of the polar extremes of organizational structure, this section considers the specific features and characteristics of gangs. Los Angeles–based gang researchers M. Klein (1995) and Klein and Maxson (2006) developed a five-category typology of gangs. This typology does not directly address our continuum from instrumental-rational to informal-diffuse, but it suggests a useful way to identify different kinds of gangs based on their structural characteristics. Based on interviews with a sample of gang experts (including the police), they identified the following attributes of gangs: size in members, age range of members, duration of existence, presence of subgroupings, territoriality, and crime versatility. Their analysis of these characteristics resulted in five gang typologies (Table 3.1), including traditional, neotraditional, compressed, collective, and specialty gangs.

TABLE 3.1 THE KLEIN-MAXSON (2006) TYPOLOGY OF GANGS						
Type	Group size (members)	Age range (years)	Longevity (years)	Subgroups	Territory claimed	Offending patterns
Traditional	Large (>100)	Wide (20–30)	Long (>20)	Yes	Yes	Versatile
Neotraditional	Medium (>50)	No pattern	Short (<10)	Yes	Yes	Versatile
Compressed	Small (<50)	Narrow (<10)	Short (<10)	No	No	Versatile
Collective	Medium (>50)	Medium (>10)	Medium (10–15)	No	No	Versatile
Specialty	Small (<50)	Narrow (<10)	Short (<10)	No	Yes	Specialized

Klein and Maxson found that traditional gangs had the highest rate of involvement in crime. Once size was considered, however, they found that specialty gangs had the highest rates of arrests per member. In other words, traditional gangs attracted the most attention from police by virtue of the number of gang members, while specialty gang members had more attention from the police per capita.

Gangs can influence individuals through the way that they are organized. For example, do the members of informal-diffuse gangs have higher rates of offending than the members of instrumental-rational gangs? In theory, informal-diffuse gangs should engage in broader offending and victimization profiles since they are an aggregation of criminally inclined individuals, while more organized gangs are able to control and limit the excesses of gang member behavior that may attract attention from authorities. Alternatively, Decker, Katz, and Webb (2008) argued that organization makes gangs more efficient in accomplishing collective goals and completing discrete tasks. From this perspective, increases in organization exert pressure on gang members to pursue the collective goals of the group, which could range from attending meetings to executing drive-by shootings or even refraining from the use of some forms of violence.

Six studies have directly investigated whether the gang's organizational structure influences the criminal behavior and victimization of gang members. The first two studies, Bjerregaard (2002) and Esbensen, Winfree, et al. (2001), used an indirect approach to examine this relationship. Part of their goal was to determine how the attitudinal and behavioral portrait of gang members changed when comparing loosely to vertically organized gangs. Bjerregaard did this using a sample of over sixteen hundred (mostly) Black and Latino inner-city high school students in California, Illinois, Louisiana, and New Jersey, asking youth if their gang was "just a bunch of guys" or an "organized gang." Esbensen and colleagues' sample consisted of nearly six thousand middle school students in eleven urban, rural, and suburban cities (Las Cruces, New Mexico; Omaha, Nebraska; Phoenix, Arizona; Philadelphia, Pennsylvania; Kansas City, Missouri; Milwaukee, Wisconsin; Orlando, Florida; Will County, Illinois; Providence, Rhode Island; Pocatello, Idaho; and Torrance, California). They compared youths in gangs, delinquent gangs, and organized delinquent gangs. Both sets of researchers found that as the definition of a gang was restricted to more organized groups, the seriousness of gang member attitudes and delinquency increased. These findings suggest that membership in more organized gangs corresponds with greater involvement in serious delinquency, even though those gangs were not highly organized. Several additional studies examine the impact of organizational structure on groups involved in crime, such as youth gangs in the California Youth Authority (D. Scott and Maxson 2016), prisoners in Texas (Mitchell et al. 2017), outlaw motorcycle clubs (Piano

2017), and mafias (Catino 2014). This mixed bag of studies generally supports the position that criminal involvement and victimization are related to group organization and cohesion, but unfortunately it is largely the case that there is a single study for each group, something we find hardly definitive.

A more direct test of the relationship between gang organization, delinquency, and victimization was carried out by Sheley et al. (1995). They interviewed 373 incarcerated youth in California, Illinois, Louisiana, and New Jersey and found that members of structured gangs—gangs with more than fifty members that held meetings, had leadership, and claimed turf—engaged in more drug sales, robberies, and gun carrying than those in unstructured gangs. The effect of gang structure on gun carrying was especially strong.

Decker et al. (2008) surveyed recently arrested juveniles in Arizona prisons. Using an index of gang organization (see the next section), they found that gang members from more organized gangs were more likely to be the victims of violent crime. They also found that members of more organized gangs engaged in violent offending and drug selling at higher rates than members of less organized gangs. This led them to conclude that "the more organized the gang, even at low levels of organization, the more likely it is that members will be involved in violent offenses, drug sales, and violent victimizations" (169).

Bouchard and Spindler (2010) examined whether group organization influenced drug dealing and violent and property offenses among 523 self-reported delinquent youth in the Canadian province of Quebec. Youth were identified as gang members, delinquent group members, or non–group members. Gang members and delinquent group members were compared to determine whether the organizational structure of the group was associated with increased delinquent activities. Group organization was associated with increases in drug dealing and violent offending, but not property offending.

Finally, Pyrooz and colleagues (2012) carried out a cross-national test of this relationship using Esbensen, Winfree, et al.'s (2001) eleven-city sample, Decker et al.'s (2008) Arizona arrestee sample, and a sample of youth from Trinidad and Tobago. Unlike previous research, this study found only "mixed support for the relationship between gang organizational structure and offending and victimization" (99). When aspects of the gang organization index were studied individually, their relationships were inconsistently related to offending and victimization across the separate research sites. This finding underscores the importance of more work in this area, as understanding how gang organization influences individual behavior remains an important and yet unresolved topic.

We now transition to examining the presence of specific features or characteristics of gangs. Here we review the presence of specific features of gang organizational structures, including leaders, rules, roles, meetings, and how money is handled within the gang. These organizational features are important because they have the potential to show how gangs organize themselves both in the commission of crime and in everyday life in the gang.

Gang Leaders

Most gangs have leaders with dominant or "charismatic" (in a Weberian sense) personalities. This conclusion should not come as a surprise, as few organizations can survive without some form of leadership. In most cases, gang leaders function less like corporate executives and more like captains of sports teams. Often, they assume their position because of their longevity with the group, their symbolic value to the group, and the support of most members rather than because they possess a unique or highly practiced set of skills (Densley 2013). Some may assert themselves (Short and Strodtbeck 1963), but gang leadership often is fluid and can change from one activity to another. Leaders also change as individual members of the gang age, move out of gangs, go to prison, or become interested in other pursuits. We find little specialization among gang members. There are some activities where one individual takes the lead (e.g., getting guns, relationships with other gangs, and selling drugs) and others play a secondary role. But today's leader in wholesaling drugs could be tomorrow's follower in exacting revenge from a rival.

One of the key features about gang structures and roles is that they are dynamic. The study of groups, particularly groups with large numbers of adolescent members, must always be mindful of the ever-changing nature of membership, relationships, and activities. This is also true for the role of leaders within gangs. Two important studies, one in Chicago (Vargas 2014) and another in Montreal (Ouellet, Bouchard, and Charette 2019), make this point clear. Vargas examined the effect of the arrest of the leader of a gang on its activities, persistence, and structure. He found that the effect of a gang leader's arrest varied by gang type, with weaker gangs going underground and other, more structured gangs persisting in the face of what he determined to be a frequent event. The latter gangs were larger and of longer provenance, enabling them to better "weather the storm" created by disruptions in gang leadership.

Not surprisingly, leadership roles are better defined in more traditional gangs that have been around the longest in cities where gangs have operated the longest. Thus, in Chicago and Los Angeles, we find gang leaders who are older, more specialized in their activities, and more powerful. In emerging gang cities, leadership roles have a far more informal character. In these gangs, the leader can change more quickly over time or from one activity to another. Since gang membership entails heavy involvement in criminal activity, it is not surprising to find that leaders change regularly as members go to prison. In the most organized Chicago gangs, such as the Gangster Disciples, going to prison often enhances the status of an individual in the gang, and many leadership activities take place from the state or federal prison system (Chapter 12).

Chicago gang members we spoke with told us the following things about gang leaders:

Leaders give orders.

Leaders take on full responsibility as to guiding an organization, keeping within the guidelines of the organization that Larry Hoover [the imprisoned leader of the Gangster Disciples in Chicago] set out for us to abide by.

The leader makes the rules, and everybody got to do what he say.

The picture of leadership found in San Diego and St. Louis gangs was quite different from Chicago. Indeed, most of the gang members we talked with in St. Louis and San Diego could not identify leadership roles:

Everybody calls their own shots. Nobody has the juice.

We all together. We had a leader, but since he's a dead homie, we ain't got another one.

Gang Rules

Most organizations need rules to survive. Rules create expectations among members of an organization and help pattern behavior. They set boundaries, and in doing so they can be used to identify individuals who violate the rules. The authors of this book have interviewed well over a thousand gang members, and when asked, most said that their gang had rules and could list several. However, those rules tend to be general and rarely come with punishments. A relatively small number of gangs have actual written sets of rules or constitutions (Brotherton and Barrios 2004). Most gangs have a set of rules that are understood among members. These rules typically include prohibitions against snitching on other gang members to the police, cheating other gang members out of their deserved profits from illegal activity, and pretending to be a member of another gang by wearing the "wrong" colors or other symbols. A hallmark of formal rules is a description of the punishments and a process by which punishments are to be determined. Gang rules, by and large, lack this structure and instead are just informally "understood."

Most gangs have informal systems of punishments. The punishment an individual receives can depend on the individual's status in the gang as much as what the individual did. Thus, brothers or sisters of longtime members may get a break that another member would not. This lack of procedural regularity in the rules should hardly come as a surprise. After all, the average gang member is a teenager. We would not expect to find elaborate, formal systems of rules, punishments, and procedures developed by young people, whose lives generally are not characterized by the desire for order and regularity that is the case for adults.

When rules are broken, even those with a loose, informal structure, some gang members suggested that the penalties could be severe:

> You might get shot; you might get beat. Your mom might get hurt, anything, anybody that's close to you. You know what I'm sayin', just to send you a message like not to do that no more.

San Diego gang members echoed these sentiments. One member offered that the only rule was:

> not to backstab your partner. That's the main one.

Another reported:

> Don't ever snitch on your own homeboys.

Gang members in chronic gang cities such as Chicago or Los Angeles, however, related quite a different story. Rules among gang members in these cities were more formal, had penalties, and under some circumstances had a formal procedure for adjudicating rule violations. An important characteristic of these rules is that they are written. A number of gang members from the Gangster Disciples and Latin Kings talked of gang constitutions:

> They got two sets of law, 1 through 16 and 1 through 22. Each and every member has to study and learn the laws, because the only way you can be in violation based on the gang's philosophy is to violate one of those laws.

> They are written down until you learn them. You got a certain amount of time to learn them.

Gang Roles

We have described gangs as having either a formal or informal structure. There is substantial variation in these structures, as our review has underscored. There is one organizational characteristic, however, on which the two types of gangs converge: the presence of specialized roles within the gang. While there are gradations in "rank" within gangs, they are hardly formal.

Almost all gang members were able to identify different roles in their gang. In the least-organized gangs, this distinction may only be between core and fringe members, with the former participating more fully in decisions and activities. But few gangs are quite so informal in their identification of roles. In most gangs there are at least three levels of roles: (1) leaders, (2) experienced gang members, and (3) regular members. Only a few members of a gang occupy leadership roles. These roles typically include individuals who have been in the gang the longest or have achieved some distinctive status owing to their criminal activity or specialized knowledge. More experienced gang members assume some specialized role within the gang, such as procuring drugs or weapons or stealing cars. These individuals are likely to have been members of the gang for several years and have earned their rank as a consequence of special skills or achievements (e.g., Harding 2014). Sometimes this rank is represented in the street nicknames of gang members, such as in London, where "elder," more senior gang members will hand down their alias to their "younger" protégés (Densley 2012a). For example, Caesar's "younger" protégé might be called "Little Caesar," signaling criminal mentorship or, in cases where age differences are wide, child criminal exploitation (Harding 2020). The majority of gang members, however, are generalists, offering little to the gang beyond their involvement in hanging out, selling drugs, and being involved in violence.

The lack of diversity reflected in gang roles was summed up by a St. Louis gang member: "Everybody just basically did the same kind of thing. If you was a leader, then you was the one tellin' 'em, 'Do this, do that.'"

In St. Louis, gang members spoke of some level of equality among members:

It's all one thing. It's just the older guys and then the youngsters.

They [all gang members] are equal, they are all hard-core, they are all treated equal.

Gang Meetings

Most organizations hold regular meetings. The available evidence indicates that, in some form or another, most gangs do get together. However, these get-togethers rarely look like the meetings of a large corporation or government agency. It is difficult to imagine all 250 members of the Rolling Sixties Crips in St. Louis or the Calle Trienta in San Diego gathering in a park or at a mall to have a meeting. Imagine if the 18th Street gang in Los Angeles attempted to convene a meeting of hundreds of members. Such public gatherings would likely draw law enforcement attention. Meetings, when they do occur, are much more likely to involve a small group of key decision-makers who then funnel the word on to other members. Subgroups of friends or individuals who live close to each other may gather to discuss gang issues. Chicago gang members told Decker, Bynum, and Weisel (1998) about hundreds of gang members gathering to do calisthenics as a group in the neighborhood park. As one St. Louis gang member told Decker and Van Winkle (1996) when they asked about gang meetings, "We just chill on the corner and talk to each other." Typical activities at such "meetings" included smoking weed, drinking, listening to music, and doing handshakes. These are hardly the stuff of well-organized groups.

Gang Money

In *All the President's Men*, Bob Woodward and Carl Bernstein's (2014) account of the 1972 Watergate scandal, "follow the money" became shorthand for the methods they used to unravel the high crimes and misdemeanors of the Nixon administration. We believe that understanding gang organization and roles is enhanced by following that same dictum. As the detective trying to stop the gang in the HBO series *The Wire* memorably said, "You follow drugs, you get drug addicts and drug dealers. But you start to follow the money, and you don't know where the fuck it's gonna take you." A key feature of organized crime is the reinvestment of profits to advance the interests of the group. This organizational structure represents the corporate model and can be contrasted with a model of individual entrepreneurship. Street gangs are quite different from this. With few exceptions, gangs function as entrepreneurial organizations, where individuals sell drugs or commit crimes for their own benefit.

Comparing Gangs to Other Criminal Groups

Thrasher's (1927) study of gangs placed gangs in the broader context of other groups, particularly groups involved in crime. We reconstruct the figure he used to depict the place of the gang relative to other groups, as well as the transition of gangs from informal playgroups to formal groups involved in organized crime (Figure 3.1).

Thrasher compared gangs to playgroups, mobs, organized crime groups, and other groups, some involved in crime and some not. We reiterate our key contention about gang organization: gangs are often conflated with both non-crime groups on the one hand and more organized crime groups on the other hand. It is our contention that a group of criminals should not be confused with a more organized crime group, such as a gang. One way to avoid this is to place gangs in the broader context of other crime groups such as transnational organized crime, drug smuggling, ideology-based hate groups, human trafficking, and terrorist groups. The structure, processes, beliefs, and activities of these groups provide a useful way to distinguish among them.

TABLE 3.2 ORGANIZATION STRUCTURES OF GANGS AND OTHER CRIME GROUPS		
Corporate groups	*Cells*	*Episodic groups*
Differentiated structure	Purposive	Localized
National presence	Small	Cafeteria offending
Older members	Focused	Young members
Long life of the group	Specialists	Not purposive
Prison involvement	Isolate	Hanging out
Profit motives dominate	Cross-national	Unsupervised teenage groups

We believe that the comparison of groups using Table 3.2 below provides a comparative framework for understanding groups involved in crime. We argue that the level of organization declines as we move from left to right in the table. Groups may "skip" a stage or rapidly become more structured to address tasks that they face, such as opportunities to respond violently to rivals or to steal ATMs. But many of the groups never move out of the column they start in. There is also movement of individuals from column to column as they age, encounter opportunities, or gain new associates or skills.

The corporate group is vertically structured, with a strong instrumental-rational orientation. It has a national or international presence, has older members, and has been around longer. Groups such as the Hells Angels and highly structured prison gangs such as Le Eme or the Aryan Brotherhood (see Chapter 12 for a discussion of prison gangs) fit into this classification quite well. This structure is more effective in achieving large-scale goals, in part because of the size of such groups. Two additional characteristics set these groups apart: (1) their ability to handle money and (2) their ability to regulate the conduct of members in an efficient and patterned manner.

Cells are quite different from corporate groups. As self-contained units with highly specialized roles, members, and missions, they can be differentiated from corporate groups quite easily. But such groups are also characterized by high levels of secrecy and difficulty accessing the groups from the outside. Very few gangs fall into this category, but this is an effective structure for targeted engagements such as acts of terrorism or "ram-raiding" and intense controlled robberies of ATMs or high-value targets such as jewelry stores. Many terrorists such as those involved in the 9/11 attacks on the United States use this form of organization. These groups also include small drug smuggling rings. Such groups depend on the discretion of members to "keep their mouths shut" about their activities, something that most street offenders seem incapable of doing. Any links between terrorists and drug smugglers in such an organizational structure are highly purposive and focused specifically on the achievement of goals. Cells are also often short-lived; they execute their tasks and dissolve.

The final category is episodic groups. These embody the characteristics of the informal-diffuse organizations and include most groups and individuals involved in crime. Given the organizational characteristics of most street gangs, many come to represent episodic groups because their existence is rarely long-term (with notable exceptions) and members age out or are sent to prison, where they find opportunities for engaging with more organized crime groups (see Chapter 12).

There is not much evidence to link gangs to other organized crime groups, despite public and media attention to the contrary. The late Carlo Morselli (2009) made an insightful observation about why this misperception occurs: media and law enforcement conflate high levels of violence with high levels of organization. However, there is much to learn by comparing gangs to other criminal groups, particularly those with persistence and some degree of organizational structure. The organizational features of a gang are important to its ability not only to achieve goals but also to survive. As Ouellet, Bouchard, and Charette (2019) demonstrated, gangs persist regardless of threats to the gang if two conditions are met: cohesion and embeddedness. If gangs have strong internal cohesion and members are strongly embedded within the group, the gang can survive external threats and (in some cases) re-form as a new group.

We engage in such a comparison below focusing on four groups involved in crime: (1) terrorist and hate groups, (2) (transnational) organized crime groups, and (3) drug smugglers. Like most social organizations, gangs are in transition, changing in response to internal and external pressures. It may well be that as Thrasher (1927) suggests in Figure 3.1, gangs are either evolving into more organized groups or merging with such groups to expand the realm of their activities.

We believe that there are four key areas in which gangs can be compared to and distinguished from other groups involved in crime:

1. Differences in goals, with symbolic goals more important to gangs and economic ends more important to more organized groups.
2. Differences in organizational structures, which are less well defined in gangs, reflecting the ages of gang members as well as differences in the levels of cooperation, commitment, and leadership.
3. Differences in activity, such as the extent to which a group attempts to regulate and control the production and distribution of a given commodity or service unlawfully. Profit-making activities are sporadic and opportunistic in gangs, unlike the activities of organized crime groups, terrorists, and drug smugglers, where the pressure to turn a profit results in more highly structured organizations.
4. Differences in the importance of turf or territory.

Gangs and Terrorist and Hate Groups

Gangs and terrorist groups appear to have a lot in common, particularly the importance of violence to achieving goals. Unfortunately, most of the comparisons of gangs and terrorist groups have been synthetic—that is, there is very little data to compare the two groups in a meaningful way (e.g., Densley 2014a). Decker and Pyrooz (2015) have argued that the study of terrorist groups could learn a good deal from gang research, though stopping short of the argument that there is considerable overlap between the two. Curry (2011) conducted a synthetic comparison of gangs, terrorist groups, and organized crime groups. He found a number of similarities between gangs and terrorist groups: members of both groups are mostly male, violence is a common theme, both groups exhibit certain levels of solidarity and elements of collective behavior, and both groups use violence as a form of "self-help," often to even a score. But Curry concluded that these were only similarities on the surface of the groups and that there were many differences. The primary differences include the profit motive in gangs that is largely absent from terrorist groups, the international connections held by terrorist groups, the generalist "cafeteria-style offending" patterns of gang members (M. Klein 1971, 125), and a commitment to a political ideology among members of terrorist groups, which is generally lacking among gang members.

Many argue that the similarities between gangs and terrorists are largely due to the fact that terrorist groups are not as highly structured as is publicly believed (Sageman 2008; Decker and Pyrooz 2015). Varese (2011) noted the same thing regarding organized crime, which functions in ways consistent with networking theory. S. Zhang (1997) has studied criminal organizations such as human trafficking groups for some time. He summarizes the relationship between criminal organizations and terrorist groups as follows:

> The nexus between organized crime and terrorism is at best a tenuous one. This is mainly because criminal organizations and terrorist groups are diametrically different social entities. In fact, criminal organizations, whether they are loosely connected groups of human smugglers or well-organized drug cartels, cannot be more dissimilar to terrorists along two dimensions—ideological and operational. (134)

Curry (2011) described two notable occasions when gang and terrorist activities did intersect. The first coordinated effort between the two groups is the well-documented attempt by Libya to enlist members of the Chicago street gang El Rukn in acts of terror, including bombing buildings and taking down an airliner (Possley and Crawford 1986). The plot was unsuccessful, as El Rukn gang members contacted the Libyans from a telephone in a federal prison (where all phone calls are monitored, as the sign above the phone clearly indicates). The second incident involved Jose Padilla, a Latin King gang member who traveled to the Middle East and was charged in a federal conspiracy to use a radioactive bomb. He was easily taken into custody and convicted. These cases demonstrate why gangs are not good co-conspirators in organized crime—their activities draw a lot of attention from the police, and members of these groups are not effective at clandestine operations. Because discipline is a key element of successful organized crime activity, gangs have rarely been included in more organized crime activities because of the inability to effectively control the behavior of their members.

Another group that causes us to think about the intersection of gangs and terrorism is Mara Salvatrucha or MS-13. In July 2020, President Donald Trump and Attorney General William Barr announced with aplomb that in an attempt to "disrupt, dismantle and destroy" MS-13, Joint Task Force Vulcan would take down the leadership of the organization (Department of Justice, Office of Public Affairs 2020). The plan was to target MS-13 leaders and successfully arrest and prosecute them. Known as "the whole of government approach," it combined federal resources across U.S. attorney jurisdiction, federal law enforcement, and cooperation from Central American "host countries" such as Guatemala, El Salvador, Mexico, and Honduras. Thirteen individuals were indicted in four federal jurisdictions and charged under the Continuing Criminal Enterprise (CCE) and Racketeer Influenced and Corrupt Organizations (RICO) statutes (for a discussion of gang legislation, see Chapter 13). MS-13 is thought to be closely aligned to the Mexican Mafia prison gang. There are an estimated ten thousand MS-13 members in the United States, or less than 1 percent of the estimated 1.4 million gang members across the country. It is difficult to imagine that an operation that does not touch gang members in any South American or Caribbean nations and brings charges against only thirteen individuals will make a dent in a gang of over ten thousand members in the U.S. and many more overseas. Treating MS-13 as a terrorist group only confers a certain status on the gang that increases its standing and reputation in prison, on the street, and multinationally.

Recent collaborations between researchers who study gangs and those who study extremist groups offer empirical insights into the potential overlap between the two groups. Pyrooz et al. (2018) asked whether gang members and extremists were "cut from the same cloth" or whether individual differences between the two existed. They examined the potential overlap between members of the two groups on group involvement, demographic, socioeconomic status, religion, and family measures. Tellingly, only 6 percent of the extremists reported gang ties, and those extremists with gang ties more closely resembled non-gang extremists than they did the gang members. Further support for this view of the divergence between gang members and extremists was found in other work by this team (M. Becker et al. 2020). Becker et al. examined pathways into extremism and gang membership, and while some overlap did exist (largely around age and age-graded activities), there was little similarity in how the two groups were joined.

We are often asked whether White supremacist, Neo-Nazi, and other hate groups are gangs. These groups share some features with gangs: group structure, mostly male, engaging in expressive violence, and often episodic. But as Pyrooz et al. (2018) found in their empirical comparison of gang members in extremists based on Profiles of Individual Radicalization in the United States (PIRUS) data, motives, structure, and group characteristics differ considerably between gangs and such groups. Hate groups are distinguished by their strong ideological beliefs, have allegiance (at least symbolically) with international groups, and are focused on producing political outcomes. Membership in such groups is based on isolation from other groups (Corb and Grozelle 2014), typically racial and ethnic minorities, and fear of such groups is a central component that motivates individuals to join them (Minkenberg 1998).

The key differentiator between radical and extremist groups and street gangs is that the former tends to have a "discernable political, ideological, or religious motivation" for their actions (Department of Homeland Security 2016). This is a point of distinction between terrorist groups and crime syndicates (an ideological, political, or religious ideology). Financial profits are secondary to political ends for terrorist groups, while for criminal syndicates profits are the primary goal. Dishman (2001) and others have argued that there is a wide gulf between terrorists and transnational criminal organizations, with the latter preferring to keep a low profile and remain more clandestine. Motivations and expressive goals form the basis for terrorist groups (including narco-terrorists in Columbia), leading organized crime groups to distance themselves from them out of concern for the public nature of terrorists airing their political grievances. Thus, while there are similarities in the structure and characteristics of individual members, links between gangs and such groups are few and far between.

However, some gangs do have political or ideological aspects (e.g., Brotherton and Barrios 2004), and even the most hardened extremists are neither learned scholars nor subject matter experts in politics, ideology, or religion. Their understanding of the causes said to motivate their actions is often very shallow, contradictory, and even convenient. This is why Reid and Valasik (2020) argued that White power and supremist groups really are "gangs," much like Pyrooz and Densley (2018) argued that Antifa met gang criteria. However, Reid and Valasik (2020, 20) somewhat contradict their own argument by adding the prefix *alt-right* to the word *gang*, defined as "a durable, public-oriented group (both digitally and physically) whose adoption of signs and symbols of the White power movement and involvement in illegal activity is part of its group identity." Readers will notice that this definition is essentially a reworking of the consensus Eurogang effort (see Chapter 1) centered on the political and ideological features of one group that rejects mainstream conservatism and advocates for White supremacy, mostly on the internet. The problem here is that signs and symbols have long been considered descriptors, not definers, of gangs (M. Klein and Maxson 2006). While the alt-right presently are *en vogue*, we are not convinced they are so special that they need a bespoke gang definition.

Gangs and Organized Crime Groups

As von Lampe (2015) argued, many people wrongly assume that organized crime is a matter of structure (hence, *organized*) or being engaged in illicit enterprise (i.e., a profit orientation). The problem is, many groups, including gangs, can be very structured and entrepreneurial; the two do not make organized crime. Instead, as Varese (2010, 45) argued, "an organized crime group attempts to regulate and control the production and distribution of a given commodity or service unlawfully." The operative words here are *regulate* and *control*. Any group can sell drugs. Not any group can be the sole suppliers of drugs in a given domain. Only when groups tip into extralegal governance do they become organized crime. Governance is in fact the very definition of organized crime. The emphasis here is very clearly on what the gang does, not just how it is structured—although it is true that in order to govern effectively and efficiently, structure often matters.

We discuss governance is more detail below. Here we want to stress that in a global world, with increased access to information technology, transnational organized crime groups have been shown to govern without a hierarchical organizational structure and to create disorder without a physical presence. This is in further contrast to what organized crime and other transnational groups such as human traffickers are traditionally thought to be. These changes led Varese (2011) to describe the new organized crime as a series of loosely connected nodes (individuals, organizations, firms, and information sharing tools) that depend on expertise to function rather than hierarchy and force. Such groups have been referred to as a "leaderless nexus" (Dishman 2005) reflecting a transformation in transnational organized crime.

The organizational structure of crime groups has been decentralized in the technological age, when information, not structure or labor, is the key to successful international crime. In this view, crime has evolved from demanding large numbers of more or less well-controlled individuals to a situation where a small number of equals can execute criminal acts successfully. Many organized crime groups function in this way. It is important to remind readers that traditional organized crime groups remain active, especially at the international level. When these groups attempt to control the supply of protection—that is, "protection against extortion; protection against theft and police harassment; protection in relation to credit obtained informally and the recovery of loans; and the settlement of a variety of social disputes . . . protection for thieves, prostitutes, loan sharks and drug dealers"—they are known as "mafias" (Varese 2018, 48–49). The Sicilian Cosa Nostra (Gambetta 1996), Chinese Mafia (P. Wang 2017), Hong Kong Triads (Chu 2000), Russian Mafia (Varese 2001), and Japanese Yakuza (P. Hill 2006) are all examples.

We also include outlaw motorcycle gangs such as the Hells Angels, Bandidos, and Pagans in the category of organized crime (for a review, see Lampe and Blokland 2020). Motorcycle gangs tend to have older members (at least old enough to ride a motorcycle) and focus on a narrower range of (profit-driven) criminal offenses than gangs (J. Quinn 2001; J. Quinn and Koch 2003). Racketeering, prostitution, and narcotics trafficking are key activities for such groups. In a study of street gangs, drug distribution networks, and organized crime, Morselli (2009) found that each of these criminal networks were decentralized and had flat structures with an adaptable set of relations. This structure enabled the group to function more effectively and avoid detection. These loosely confederated networks are the antithesis of vertically structured hierarchical crime groups that characterize the instrumental-rational organizations. Such a structure is facilitated by computer-mediated communication and represents another step in the evolution of dynamic groups involved in crime; indeed, Roks and Densley (2020) documented how one Dutch street gang evolved into an outlaw motorcycle gang as its members aged out of street life but still desired some form of (criminal) group identity.

Research on another form of transnational organized crime—namely, human trafficking and smuggling (Aronowitz 2001; S. Zhang 2007, 2008; Turner and Kelly 2009)—describes these groups as small networks of individuals that function largely without a hierarchy or system of internal discipline. S. Zhang's (2008) exhaustive ethnographic work on human trafficking found "flat" organizations, with little role differentiation in roles and few recognized leaders. The structure of such groups was "amorphous," where even "snakeheads" who formerly exerted strong control over group members now lacked effective control. These human trafficking networks have operated based on "trust," despite the large profits and international scope involved in the enterprise. Zhang offered this description of such groups:

> These smuggling organizations are made up of loosely affiliated individuals with diverse backgrounds, and the relationships among core members are mostly horizontal, with no clear structure of leadership. (131)

This sounds remarkably similar to the way that American street gangs have been described by M. Klein and Maxson (2006), Howell and Griffiths (2015), Curry, Decker, and Pyrooz (2014), and others.

So, are gangs organized crime? Only in rare cases and under certain conditions do gangs evolve to that level. Recent ethnographic studies from London, England, and Glasgow, Scotland, for example, show how global drug markets and new technologies have integrated gangs and organized crime groups (Densley 2013; McLean 2018; McLean, Densley, and Deuchar 2018; McLean et al. 2019; A. Whittaker et al. 2020). The drug-selling gang described by Levitt and Venkatesh (2000), moreover, controlled access to the drug market in the area they ran and was involved in wars with a competing gang to increase its market share. In his comprehensive review of organized crime definitions, Varese (2010, 47) argues, "It would not be enough to describe this gang as just a network or an illicit enterprise . . . it also bore greater ambitions, namely, that of being the only seller of drugs. . . . [It] aspire[d] to govern." In other words, Venkatesh's gang was more than a gang—it was an organized crime group. But it was also the exception, not the rule.

Gangs and Drug Smugglers

Large-scale international drug smuggling is another example of organizations that respond to changes in their environment. Clearly, these enterprises generate large sums of money. This has led many, particularly in law enforcement (Decker and Chapman 2008), to conclude that such enterprises are highly organized and thus fall into the instrumental-rational category in our framework for understanding gangs and other organizations involved in crime. However, just as the high levels of violence are mistakenly assumed to reflect high levels of gang organization, drug smuggling lacks the formal, corporate organizational structure ascribed to it. Williams (1998) has studied international drug smuggling and other forms of smuggling for years. He argued that international drug smuggling was horizontally organized, with small groups of individuals who knew each other and were responsible for most of the steps in the smuggling operation. Similarly, Zaitch (2002) studied cocaine smuggling from Columbia to the Netherlands. He found a strong role for ethnicity and kinship relations in a business that depended more on informal trust and established relationships than on formal agreements. Decker and Chapman (2008) interviewed thirty-four high-level drug smugglers in U.S. federal prisons. The average smuggler had been caught with over seven hundred pounds of cocaine. These researchers identified discrete cells of smugglers that were largely based on kinship or affective relationships. Morselli's (2001) work painted a similar picture of the organization of drug smugglers. He described the organizational structure of these groups as flatter, more informal, and less hierarchical than has often been the case.

The members of groups involved in large-scale drug smuggling tend to be older than gang members and have a more sophisticated involvement in crime. By this we mean that their discipline, both as individuals and as groups, is better developed than that of gangs and gang members. Their crimes are more complicated, often involving international transport of goods (drugs) and the transfer of large sums of money. As such, drug smugglers have more formal characteristics to their organizations than do street gang members (Benson and Decker 2010). That said, such organizations display both instrumental and informal characteristics in common with gangs, including a desire to maximize profit, informal communication and relationships within the group, and an emphasis on secrecy.

Gangs and Governance

Political scientists have turned their attention to assessing the governance functions in diverse groups that are not in government or the public sector. This emphasis on "extralegal" and "non-state" governance has focused specifically on prison gangs but is applicable to street gangs as well. The goal has been to examine groups such as voluntary associations, informal groups, and, in some cases, gangs. This perspective seeks to find patterned characteristics of organizations that create obligations among individuals that resemble the more formal governance found in political and administrative structures of governments. From this perspective, to be effective, organizations must control the behavior of individuals and groups through a system of cooperation, functional role division, planning, and specialization. The key to organizational effectiveness is the provision and regulation of desirable commodities. For gangs, these may be drugs, guns, and money or more basic needs such as protection. This approach is built on the work of Schelling (1985), who distinguished between "crime that is organized" and "organized crime." The former describes most crime committed by gangs (more or less), while the latter is more consistent with highly organized and disciplined functional crime groups.

Lessing (2017; Lessing and Willis 2019) and Skarbek (2011, 2014, 2020) have examined the role of prison gangs, often with ties to street gangs, in "governing" in prison. Prison gangs are hypothesized as effective organizations owing to their ability to govern (see Chapter 12 for evidence to the contrary). This view of governance depends heavily on the provision and regulation of desirable commodities. Campana and Varese (2018) recently advanced an alternative view of extralegal governance based on three (indirect) measures: (1) the ability of a group to generate fear in a community, (2) its ability to coerce legal businesses, and (3) its ability to influence official figures. Their view extends beyond the prison and includes a measurement strategy and empirical data. It emphasizes the role of violence (or the threat of violence) as a key factor in producing successful governance.

Conclusion

This chapter presented a framework for the broad understanding of gangs as groups. We found that the degree of organization and goal orientation are two important characteristics that distinguish groups involved in crime. While gangs do have many organizational features in common with other groups involved in crime, they are distinguished by their emphasis on symbolic features of life in the gang. The role of expressive violence and informal patterns of solidarity among gang members is in large part what distinguishes them from groups motivated more by their instrumental pursuits. While gangs combine an interest in symbolic and instrumental pursuits, the commitment to symbolic ends is much stronger than among drug smugglers or human traffickers, for example. It is important to note that gangs exhibit more diversity than most other groups involved in crime. This diversity is evident in the individual characteristics of gang members, their human and social capital, and their external environments. Gangs are also dynamic, changing and evolving over time and space. As Ouellet, Bouchard, and Charette (2019) concluded, cohesion and embeddedness are two moderating characteristics that condition the transitions gangs and gang members make.

4

Joining the Gang

The study of criminal behavior over the life course has grown dramatically since the 1990s. Such an approach is by no means new, as classic life-history studies of criminals resembled the spirit of life-course criminology (N. Anderson 1923; Shaw 1930). What is new is the ability to document patterns of criminal behavior because of survey information collected systematically over time and the availability of official criminal history information. As a result of this, researchers have been able to track when individuals start committing crime, the rate at which they commit crimes, and when they desist from their involvement in crime (Sampson and Laub 1993; Piquero, Farrington, and Blumstein 2003). What we have just described are the key questions about criminal careers: onset, continuity, and desistance. People maintain different patterns of involvement in criminal behavior in their lives, and understanding differences across people is very important to researchers, practitioners, and policymakers concerned about crime.

The parameters of criminal careers naturally extend to the study of gang membership because people join the gang, participate in the gang, and then eventually leave the gang (Pyrooz, Sweeten, and Piquero 2013). Gang membership has its own life course, and in this chapter, we focus on the start of it—joining the gang. We ask the following questions:

- Who is in the gang, and who is out?
- Why do some people end up in gangs and others do not?
- Why do youth join gangs?
- How do youth join gangs?

These questions collectively address the motives, methods, and processes for joining gangs, some of the factors associated with prolonged gang careers, and the heterogeneity or variability among gang members and their involvement. But we start by detailing the key life-course concepts of gang membership.

A Life-Course Perspective on Gang Membership

Figure 4.1 presents a foundation for understanding the key concepts of gang membership in the life course, as adapted from gang (Decker and Lauritsen 2002; Thornberry et al. 2003; Pyrooz 2014b; Pyrooz, Sweeten, and Piquero 2013) and life-course (Elder 1994; Piquero, Farrington, and Blumstein 2003; Sampson and Laub 1993) studies. Before turning to these concepts, it is important that we provide a brief description of the figure, as it organizes our thinking about gang membership in the life course. Age runs along the x-axis of the figure, and readers can think of it as the life course of an individual. We concentrate on early adolescence to emerging adulthood because we know that gangs are overwhelmingly a youth-oriented phenomenon and many people "age out" of gang life. The probability of gang membership follows along the y-axis, and readers can think of it as the likelihood that someone is in a gang. Low values indicate a smaller chance of gang involvement (e.g., around age ten), whereas high values indicate clearly recognizable involvement in gangs (e.g., around age fifteen). The figure is hypothetical, of course, but grounded in research. Gang membership, like criminal offending, is strongly age-graded, and participation generally occurs after age ten years (Pyrooz 2014b). Data from a nationally representative survey of youth showed that the rate of gang membership rapidly increased during the preteen years, with most youth joining gangs between ages twelve and fifteen years (Pyrooz and Sweeten 2015).

The two key transitions for understanding gang membership are onset and termination, which refer to the first and last reported instances of identification as a gang member. These parameters dictate several important features of gang membership, including the motives and methods for joining and leaving gangs. The vertical lines that represent onset and termination seen in Figure 4.1 indicate the period in which the probability of gang membership surpasses or declines below the 50 percent threshold. This means that identification and deidentification as a gang member marks a point when the probability of gang membership is closer to 1 (yes) or 0 (no).

In relation to life-course criminology and criminal career parameters, the onset and termination of gang membership takes on added significance. Elder (1994), the eminent University of North Carolina sociologist, referred to the life course as comprising transitions, trajectories, and turning points. The onset and termination parameters act as transitions in the life course,

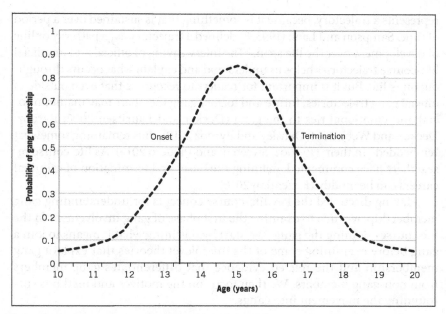

Figure 4.1 Gang membership in the life course

marking the movement into or out of the state of gang membership. Transitions are important events dotted throughout the life course that bring meaning to lives; events such as graduating high school, moving away to college, getting married, or having a baby are examples. These events foreshadow changes in lives, some larger than others. For some individuals, joining and leaving a gang may not be significant events because gang membership is normalized or expected. For other individuals, transitions into or out of gangs may constitute significant life events. Life events known as *turning points* are key to understanding the larger life course, as such events redirect the life course in significant ways (Laub, Sampson, and Sweeten 2006). The onset of gang membership is considered a turning point because it is associated with dramatic changes in the behaviors and attitudes of people who join a gang (Melde and Esbensen 2011; Thornberry et al. 2003).

Between onset and termination is duration, which answers the question: How long do individuals remain in gangs? The typical gang member stays active in gangs for only about two years, according to data from a nationally representative survey of youth (Pyrooz 2014b), but the term *active* doesn't really capture the extent of duration because there are periods of gang membership before and after active status when one's connection to the gang or level of gang involvement is nonzero, either ramping up or tailing off. In relation to Elder's life-course concepts, the duration of gang membership thus better represents a trajectory, because it is something that is sustained over a period of time. Sampson and Laub (1993, 8) defined a trajectory as "a pathway or line of development over the life span." The interweaving of official and unofficial life-course trajectories helps us understand and explain what occurs throughout one's life. But it is important for readers to recognize that even outside of official gang trajectories, future and former gang members may maintain social and emotional ties to the gang (Decker and Lauritsen 2002; Pyrooz, Decker, and Webb 2014; Densley and Pyrooz 2019), thus remaining somewhat "embedded" in them (Pyrooz, Sweeten, and Piquero 2013). As life-course researchers have commented, defining the onset and termination of criminal careers can be muddy (Kazemian 2016).

Having discussed the key life-course concepts for understanding gang membership, we turn to examine the first phase of gang involvement in the life course—joining the gang. We start by outlining what it means to join a gang before examining some of the microlevel theories that explain gang membership and the related evidence that differentiates gang members from non-gang members. We then focus on the motives and methods surrounding the movement into gangs.

Gang Embeddedness

Pyrooz and Sweeten (2015) estimate that about four hundred thousand adolescents join gangs each year in the United States. Perhaps the simplest way to determine who is in a gang and who is out would be to ask a bona fide member of that gang, the assumption being that on the streets, one's reputation as a gang member should be "common knowledge" to one's peers (Chwe 2001). Indeed, "gang membership" really only exists as a concept if other gang members share knowledge of it, know that they share it, and know that others know they share it (Densley 2013). Still, gang membership is never a simple in/out dichotomy, because not all gang members are equally involved in the gang. From "elders" to "youngers" (Densley 2012a) and leaders to "foot soldiers" (Levitt and Venkatesh 2000), people are differentially embedded in the gang.

Some refer to the individuals who are the most loosely tied to the gang as "wannabes." We do not like to use this term when referring to gang members or young people who may imitate gang behavior or styles but are not fully initiated members. In the late 1980s, a number of cities (such as Cleveland, Columbus, and St. Louis) denied that they had real gang problems and real gang members by dismissing the obvious signs of such activities as simply the product of wannabes. These efforts were counterproductive because they let gang members gain a foothold in their communities and, as a consequence, it was more difficult to minimize the influence of gangs and respond to the problems they created. As a young gang member being held for a crime in the St. Louis juvenile detention center told us,

> There ain't no such thing as a wannabe. He can shoot, he can kill you just like a real gang member.

Based on M. Klein's (1971) study of Los Angeles gang members, many researchers have distinguished gang members according to core and fringe status. Core gang members were individuals involved in the gang for more than a year, were actively involved in the commission of crimes with other gang members, and tended to be older (at least age sixteen) and more involved in gang activities. Fringe gang members, on the other hand, had less involvement in the activities of the gang, especially drive-by shootings, initiations, and meetings, should they occur.

Of course, core and fringe also fail to capture the gradations of gang membership. Pyrooz, Sweeten, and Piquero (2013) contended that additional levels of gang membership exist. After all, if, as Thornberry and colleagues (2003, 6) recognized, "not all gang members are created equal," then a core/fringe categorization only expands gang membership from one (gang member) to two (core or fringe gang member) categories. Based on their study of over two hundred gang members in Philadelphia and Phoenix, Pyrooz, Sweeten, and Piquero (2013) outlined five components that distinguish gang members, as follows:

1. Contact with the gang, which taps the everyday patterns of social interaction (in this case, time spent in gang settings)
2. Position in the gang, including leader, top person but not a leader, and member, which accounts for rank or influence and the structural location of gang members in the gang
3. Importance of the gang, a cognitive indicator of the value they assign to their affiliation with the gang
4. Friends outside the gang, which taps components of peer influence and the spread of information from intimate others
5. Participation in gang assaults, an indicator that captures individual involvement in serious, group-based activities

Together, these five items capture what Pyrooz and colleagues called *gang embeddedness*, which refers to "individual immersion within an enduring deviant network" (3). This latent, continuous construct accounts for a wide range of gang members, from gang associates to regular gang members to gang leaders to OGs (original gangsters). Similarly, it accounts for a wide range of ideas that are often used to distinguish gang members, including rank, status, criminal behavior, involvement, and identity. Lauger (2020) argued that identity is especially important because gang members embrace many roles in life beyond gang membership, but their prioritization of membership (and their outward performance of the role) is shaped by the collective identity of the gang itself, the breadth and depth of the gang member's relationships with other gang members, and conceptions of "gang" found beyond the group, such as in movies and music (see Chapter 10). Importantly, gang embeddedness recognizes that there are older members who have logged a considerable number of years as members of their gangs (perhaps as many as five or six years), are in a position to obtain rank, and, as a consequence, are afforded special status and perform unique duties. Yet, OGs do not necessarily "put in work" like they used to and are thus less embedded in the gang than younger, more active gang members. In appealing to M. Klein's (2011, 1038) call that "you can take the member out of the gang, but sometimes you cannot take the gang out of the member," gang embeddedness appreciates different forms of identity and adherence to gangs.

There is a dynamic component to gang embeddedness because it fluctuates over time. Prospective gang members ramp up their level of embeddedness before joining the gang or getting initiated into the gang, and it reaches its peak after greater immersion in the gang via participation and involvement in gang activities. At the same time, non-gang youth can have levels of gang embeddedness by virtue of neighborhood or family connections, but it will likely remain much lower than that of full-fledged gang members. Finally, former gang members' levels of embeddedness should decline as they continue to move away from the gang, as their contact, positioning, and identification with the gang decline, a topic we return to in Chapter 5.

Why Do Some People End Up in Gangs When Others Do Not?

Data from a nationally representative survey of youth in the United States put the prevalence of youth gang membership at about 2 percent (Pyrooz and Sweeten 2015). For every youth who enters a gang, there are about fifty who do not. Are youth who join a gang different from youth who don't join a gang? In this section, we focus on theoretical perspectives that explain gang membership and the extent to which they are supported by empirical evidence.

Before delving into the list of theories, some ground rules are in order. First, there is no such thing as a one-person gang. Gangs are groups, as we learned in Chapters 1 and 3. Second, owing to a combination of historical, socioeconomic, and political factors, gangs are distributed nonrandomly across communities, as we learned in Chapter 2. In areas where gangs are present, there are of course more opportunities for gang involvement, and as Cloward and Ohlin (1960) argued, structure dictates opportunity. If the social structure does not produce gangs, it is unlikely that a youth will be involved in a gang—"no gang, no gang member" (Densley 2015, 236). From numerous studies we have been involved in and the hundreds of interviews we have conducted with gang members, it is rare that one individual cleanly starts a gang from scratch absent any prior gang ties. Not all theories recognize this assumption equally, but it is important that readers are made aware of this.

We begin by detailing several general theories of crime that have been applied to gang membership. As several scholars (Drake and Melde 2014; M. Klein and Maxson 2006; Pyrooz and Densley 2016; Sánchez-Jankowski 1991) observed, none of the "big three" criminological theories discussed here (control, strain, and social learning) are "gang" theories per se. However, the specific connection of each general theory to gang membership is made explicit, as we identity the precise mechanisms that increase the likelihood that someone ends up in a gang. We also discuss two additional classes of theories that were designed specifically for gang membership (gang membership trait theory and gang membership integrated theory), plus another theory, signaling, that is used in fields such as economics and biology to understand communication patterns and has in recent years been applied to gang membership. Similar to how we covered macrolevel theories in Chapter 2, we then provide readers with evidence supporting or refuting these microlevel perspectives.

Criminal Propensity Theory

Some people are more likely to engage in crime than others—that is, they have a greater propensity for criminal behavior. Propensity theories assume that this likelihood does not change substantially over the life course because the physical, temperamental, and psychological traits responsible for one's proneness to crime do not change. Self-control theory, for example, contends that people with self-control deficits are impulsive and self-centered, seek immediate gratification, and engage in risk-taking and crime-analogous behaviors (M. Gottfredson and Hirschi 1990). The perspective is tied to gang membership because propensity theorists argue that criminally prone individuals naturally "flock together" to form gangs (Glueck and Glueck 1950). There is nothing special about gangs from a criminal propensity standpoint, for they are nothing more than loose collections of crime-prone individuals. Gang membership is one of many risky behaviors analogous to crime that people with shared deficits in self-control, neuropsychological functioning, or some other stable trait "select" into, assuming the opportunity is available.

Social Bond Theory

Propensity theory emphasizes how seemingly static controls internal to the individual, such as impulse control, affect gang membership. Social bond theory focuses on dynamic controls external to the individual, such as ties to family, school, and other aspects of society, that diminish one's propensity for deviant behavior (Hirschi 1969). Like propensity theory, therefore, social bond theory is a social control perspective, just with a different emphasis. As advanced by Hirschi (1969) in the book *Causes of Delinquency*, social bonds are based on attachments we have to family, friends, teachers, and coworkers; commitments we make to educational or career goals, as measured by investments in time and energy; our involvement in prosocial activities that bind us to others and leave limited time for engagement in antisocial behavior; and finally, our belief in the values and norms of mainstream society. These four aspects of social control are thought to prevent problem behaviors, such as gang membership. Unlike propensities, social bonds shift over the life course (Sampson and Laub 1993). Adolescents with weakened social bonds might navigate into gangs in their early teenage years, but as people age, deeper attachments to others and a greater stake in conformity decrease the likelihood of throwing it all away to join a gang. Because social bond theory shares a theoretical lineage with control theory, gangs in this perspective are simply collections of individuals who are weakly bonded to conventional society. Thus, as social integration increases, the likelihood of someone being a gang member should decrease. It is for this reason that many gang prevention programs are focused on increasing social bonds or mainstream ties.

General Strain Theory

When experiencing strains, people are pressured by anger or emotions for internal correction (Agnew 1992). A failure to achieve positively valued goals (e.g., as a result of discrimination), any loss of positive stimuli (e.g., the death of a loved one), or the presentation of negative stimuli (e.g., physical or emotional abuse) all constitute sources of strain. There are several adaptations to strains, including cognitive, behavioral, and emotional coping strategies. People cope with strain differently, however, which means that getting involved in gangs or crime will depend on constraints such as external coping resources (e.g., family and peer support), internal coping resources (e.g., self-efficacy and problem-solving skills), prior coping experiences (e.g., drinking or going for a run), attribution (i.e., who is to blame), and access to illegitimate means (e.g., weapons). The likelihood of gang membership is elevated when individuals experience strains and lack conventional coping mechanisms. From this point of view, gangs are a mechanism to correct the pressures and rejections experienced in other life domains, such as family, school, and prosocial peer groups. If there were any theoretical perspective consistent with the "fictive kinship" of the gang (Stack 1975)—that is, the idea that gangs act as surrogate families—general strain theory would be it. That said, Agnew (2017) has argued that general strain theory explanations of gang membership work best in conjunction with social control and, as we discuss next, social learning theories.

Social Learning Theory

People are influenced to engage in criminal and deviant behavior based on small-group interactions and communication. This perspective refers to social influences, such as peer pressure. Within this context, there is an evolving learning process that involves the transmission of defining behaviors as right or wrong through imitation, modeling, conditioning, and reinforcement (Akers 2009). Put simply, the people with whom adolescents associate—family, mentors, and especially peers—will influence them in significant ways. This can occur through mechanisms such as fear, ridicule, and loyalty that produce compliance, and status enhancement (e.g., acceptance and reward systems) in adolescent peer networks (Warr 2002). People will be influenced according to the frequency, intensity, duration, and priority of their relationships with others, who in turn help create and mold definitions of behaviors (Akers 2009). The likelihood that someone ends up in a gang is influenced by gang-favorable definitions they are exposed to. Social learning theory explanations of gang membership focus on the reinforcement of gang membership among the friends and acquaintances (think peer pressure). Thus, having family members in gangs, peers in gangs, and neighborhood gang influences will likely lead to positive evaluations of gang membership, increasing the likelihood that youth join gangs.

Gang Membership Trait Theory

Based on qualitative gang research, where researchers have observed and carried out in-depth interviews with gang members, several studies have proposed common characteristics among gang members. Yablonsky (1962), for example, argued that there are specific traits associated with gang membership. He held that gang members could be distinguished from non-gang youth by sociopathic or psychopathic personalities, a rather provocative contention. Similarly, Sánchez-Jankowski (1991) argued that there were personality differences between gang and non-gang members, something he called defiant individualism. In areas characterized by structural disadvantages, he argued that the characteristics of gang members included intense competitiveness, a sense of mistrust, self-reliance, emotional detachment, defiance, and survivalism—traits that can be tested for using existing social-psychological scales for constructs such as social dominance orientation and trust propensity (Densley, Cai, and Hilal 2014). These perspectives share many similarities with criminal propensity and social control theories of gang membership, whereby people with these characteristics end up together in groups that are referred to as gangs.

Gang Membership Integrated Theories

Three groups of researchers have proposed integrated theories of gang membership. Thornberry (1987) proposed an interactional theory of adolescent delinquency, which he and his colleagues (2003) extended to explain gang membership. There are several fundamental components of interactional theory as it is applied to gang membership. First, the theory starts with structural disadvantage and argues that it increases the likelihood of gang membership. But, second, structural disadvantage does not operate directly on gang membership. Instead, it sets off several of the mechanisms described in the microlevel theories of gang membership. These mechanisms include weakened social bonds, precocious behaviors (e.g., early dating), and antisocial belief systems. Third, these mechanisms not only independently lead to life stressors and delinquency but also combine to increase the likelihood of entering a gang. Importantly, this theory is tied to specific age-related behaviors and thus has a developmental foundation that is linked to behaviors appropriate for a certain age.

Howell and Egley (2005) proposed an extension of Thornberry and colleagues' (2003) interactional theory as it applies to gang membership. Like interactional theory, Howell and Egley's proposal is developmental, but their main objective was to explain gang membership at younger ages. They held that there was a "stepping stone" pattern to gang membership that encompassed four stages: (1) a preschool stage, beginning with conduct problems at age three to four, (2) a school entry stage, where aggressive and disruptive behavior during early school years is coupled with elementary school failure, (3) a later childhood stage, where delinquency, prosocial peer rejection, and antisocial peer associations take place, and (4) an adolescence stage, where risk factors accumulate and interact across a range of life domains and lead to gang membership. Unlike many other theories of gang membership, Howell and Egley contend that, without positive intervention at later stages, the origins of gang membership are in play as early as preschool.

Wood and Alleyne (2010) conducted research in England and also proposed an integrated theory of gang membership that they termed *unified theory*. Similar to Thornberry et al. (2003), they emphasized that previous theories "pay scant attention to the social psychological processes involved in joining a gang" (Wood and Alleyne 2010, 106). They began by arguing that there are environmental and social factors as well as individual characteristics that shape adolescent social perceptions, including gangs. These perceptions, in turn, lead to selection into peer groups. Similar to social learning theory, peer groups reinforce and help mold worldviews, attitudes, and behaviors. If peer groups lead to greater social controls, the likelihood of gang membership declines. However, if peer groups provide opportunities for criminal learning, then psychological factors such as moral disengagement and antisocial cognitive schemas (what E. Anderson [1999] calls "street codes") may provide the psychological infrastructure that facilitates adolescent gang membership. Wood and Alleyne's theory shares many similarities with other theories of gang membership but makes explicit that social-psychological processes are the only direct or immediate factor leading to gang membership.

Signaling Theory

Signaling theory asks us to think differently about selection into gangs by emphasizing the process by which youth actively sell themselves into gang membership. Signaling, the idea that one party credibly conveys some information about itself to another party, was initially developed by the economist Michael Spence, who won a Nobel Prize for his efforts. Spence (1974) argued that education credentials translated to higher earnings in the job market not because education improved ability but because the credential was a credible signal of intangible traits such as perseverance. This logic was first applied to understanding how criminal groups recruit by sociologist Gambetta (2009), but it was one of us (Densley) who applied it to gangs. Contrary to propensity theory, a penchant for and proficiency in crime and violence was not a stable trait, Densley (2012b, 2013, 2015) argued, but rather a dynamic quality that could set one prospective gang member apart from another. Gangs separate the wheat (those with the quality) from the chaff (those without) by attending to reliable signals of that quality, purposefully sent to them by gang prospects. Signaling theory thus advances the idea that selection into gangs is a reciprocal process and that gangs rationally weigh the attractiveness of potential gang members based on certain criteria for entry. Prospective gang members signal their potential value to the gang by engaging in violent and criminal acts that are beyond the capacity of the non-gang member. Furthermore, a latent dimension of signaling underlies many crime-analogous behaviors such as truancy or fighting, for they are deliberate actions that draw the attention of the gang (Pyrooz and Densley 2016).

Risk Factors and Empirical Support for Microlevel Theories

Theories of gang membership each specify several variables that should differentiate someone who joins a gang from someone who avoids a gang (Curry, Decker, and Pyrooz 2014). Here we focus only on measures of the four general theories, because integrated and signaling theories tap similar variables, and they have undergone far greater empirical testing.

Criminal propensity theory emphasizes static or time-stable characteristics of people that change only incrementally and without rank-order shifts across people. These characteristics include low self-control; impulsivity; risk-seeking; self-centeredness or lack of empathy; neuropsychological deficits; psychopathic tendencies, including hyperactivity, fearlessness, or antisociality; conduct disorders; and delinquency or violence involvement. Such characteristics are expected to elevate individual involvement in crime and delinquency. In turn, prosocial peer groups will shun such youth, which increases the likelihood that they will end up in the company of a delinquent peer group, such as a gang.

Social bond theory emphasizes indicators of attachment, commitment, involvement, and beliefs in conventional institutions. Characteristics of social bonds include parental attachment; family support; parental monitoring; unstructured socializing; school commitment and performance; attachment to teachers; and involvement in community, school, or religious activities. The absence of such relationships reflects weakened bonds to society, which allow youth to deviate from conventional standards of behaviors. As these bonds weaken, the likelihood of joining a gang increases.

General strain theory emphasizes stress or strains that one is experiencing or has experienced in the past. Characteristics that could lead to gang joining include low self-esteem or self-concept, social isolation, adverse life events, broken home, negative school environment, limited or blocked opportunities, victimization, residential instability, family substance use, family poverty, and neighborhood social disorganization. The emotions or anger resulting from strains create pressure for internal correction that forces individuals to seek devices for coping. Depending on the type of strain and access to conventional coping resources, gang membership could be one avenue to deal with strains.

Social learning theory emphasizes indicators of antisocial interactions and communications that occur in significant social fields, such as peers, family, and neighborhoods. Influences that could result in gang-favorable definitions include familial gang involvement; associations with delinquent peers, gang-involved peers, or prosocial peers; commitment to peers; neighborhood gangs; positive and negative behavioral reinforcements; legal cynicism; low guilt or low morality; and neutralization of deviant behavior. Such relationships are expected to influence individual perceptions of gangs. If gangs are not defined negatively, then gang membership could result as gang behaviors are reinforced, modeled, or supported by gang associations.

These variables, which we have organized into theories, are better known as *risk factors* for gang affiliation. Maxson's (2011) review of the literature found consistent support for only a handful of them: (1) experiencing a critical or negative life event such as an injury or parental divorce, (2) nondelinquent problem behaviors such as risk-taking or impulsivity, (3) having prodelinquent attitudes, (4) low levels of supervision by parents, and (5) associating with delinquent peers. Hennigan et al. (2014) refined this list by breaking down the latter category into having delinquent peers and a commitment to street-oriented peers. At the same time, there were no unique predictors of gang membership relative to other problematic behaviors such as violent offending (Esbensen et al. 2010).

The risk factor concept is appealing to practitioners and policymakers because if gang members can be identified before they join a gang based on certain characteristics, then this is where limited resources should be directed. However, direct comparisons of individual risk factor items are difficult because individual studies use different research instruments to measure risk factors differently. A recent test of M. Gottfredson and Hirschi's (1990) idea that selection on self-control renders the gang moot, for example, used G.R.E.A.T. II survey data to show that self-control was one (but not the only) source of selection into gangs, levels of self-control worsened during active periods of gang membership, and gang membership maintained a direct association with delinquency (Pyrooz et al. 2021).

Raby and Jones (2016) conducted a systematic review of 102 studies from thirteen countries (76 percent from the United States) to identify predictive risk factors for gang affiliation. They organized their findings according to Howell and Egley's (2005) six categories of risk—the individual, peer group, family, school, and community developmental domains, plus cumulative risk. Consistent with other reviews (e.g., Howell and Griffiths 2015; Higginson et al. 2018 M. Klein and Maxson 2006; Krohn and Thornberry 2008), Raby and Jones (2016) found that youth who experienced risk in any of these domains had greater odds of joining a gang.

Raby and Jones examined not just the quantity of the evidence but its quality. Prospective studies that measured someone's risk for gang membership when they were not already in the gang, using longitudinal samples and cohort designs, were preferred to cross-sectional studies that tested gang membership at one point in time, often retrospectively. In cross-sectional studies, cause is indistinguishable from effect. If someone is already in a gang, they will likely have definitions favorable to gang membership, have siblings or cousins in a gang, have delinquent reinforcements, and, of course, associate with their fellow gang members—all facts that will artificially inflate support for social learning variables. Only prospective studies were truly predictive, but because no studies of gang membership included random allocation to gangs (for obvious ethical and pragmatic reasons), any causal claims are elusive. Many studies also failed to adequately control for confounding factors such as levels of gang presence in the community, which, as discussed in Chapter 2, obviously is important.

TABLE 4.1 EVIDENCE ON THEORIES OF GANG MEMBERSHIP BASED ON RABY AND JONES'S (2016) SYSTEMATIC REVIEW

Risk factor	Criminal propensity	Social bond	General strain	Social learning
Lack of interpersonal skills	✓			
Low self-esteem			✓	
Genetic factors	✓			
Low parental supervision		✓		
Familial gang involvement				✓
Poverty			✓	
Time with antisocial peers				✓
School failure / low academics		✓		
Antisocial or low-socioeconomic-status environment			✓	
Total	2	2	3	2

When focused only on quality studies using longitudinal data, Raby and Jones found that low self-esteem and a lack of interpersonal skills on the individual level were most predictive of gang joining. In the family domain, there was some modest evidence of a genetic route into gangs (e.g., the low-activity form of the MAOA or "warrior" gene has been linked to increased levels of aggression and violence [Beaver et al. 2010]), but low parental supervision, familial gang involvement, and poverty were predictive variables. Spending time with antisocial peers was another predictive risk indicator. School failure and low academic performance were others. And being raised in urban, antisocial, or socioeconomically deprived environments was predictive of gang affiliation at the community level. Based on these findings, therefore, we can say that there is some support for each of the big four theories, as presented in Table 4.1.

The fact that all theories receive at least some support has led some researchers, especially integrated theorists, to emphasize cumulative risk across known risk factors for gang membership (Eitle, Gunkel, and Van Gundy 2004; K. Hill et al. 1999; Thornberry et al. 2003; Esbensen et al. 2010). Raby and Jones (2016) found that cumulative risk was itself an independent, predictive risk variable, albeit mediated by preteen stress exposure, poverty, and ethnicity. Cumulative risk is an important way of thinking about gang affiliation. For example, Thornberry and colleagues (2003), using information gathered from youth in Rochester, New York, found that male youth with fewer than ten risk factors had a 1 percent chance of gang membership, whereas young men with over twenty-one risk factors had a 44 percent chance of gang membership. However, the "problem of prediction" (Drake and Melde 2014) is such that that even cumulative risk cannot differentiate future gang members from youth who avoid gangs better than the flip of a coin (M. Klein and

Maxson 2006). Even among youths experiencing risk across a wide range of factors, the majority of the "riskiest" adolescents do not end up in gangs.

Decker, Melde, and Pyrooz (2013) suggested a number of areas for future research into risk factors for gang membership. For instance, there is a need to identify the intensity at which certain factors in an adolescent's life become risky. Is there an appropriate cut point for being considered at risk on individual risk factors or as a result of accumulated risk? Are some factors risky only in combination with other factors? What risk factors are most important for prediction? Is the effect of accumulated risk factors impacted by the order in which these factors are accumulated across the life course? The influence of risk factors changes in the course of child and adolescent development (Howell, Lipsey, and Wilson 2014). For instance, exposure to delinquent peers in early adolescence may be risky only if youth have already experienced other individual risk factors. These are open questions for future research.

Why Do Youth Join Gangs?

Risk factors speak to variance (i.e., difference and correlation), but joining the gang is really a process (Maxwell 2012). Motivations for joining a gang are different from methods or mechanisms of doing so and different still from the risk factors associated with gang membership (Densley 2015). Motivations for gang joining are more subjective, containing qualitative features relating to the justifications or reasoning for joining a gang. Given what we know about the nature of gangs, it is important to gain a better understanding of why youth would join a group that puts them at greater risk for personal victimization and nearly doubles their chances of getting arrested for bad behaviors (based on nationally representative data; see Densley and Pyrooz 2020) and going to prison (see Chapters 6, 11, and 12). Below, we review what researchers have found about the motivations for gang joining based not only on personal observations but also on interviews with gang members.

No single path exists that can capture the reasons or the processes by which individuals come to join a gang. Responses to the question—why did you join a gang?—typically include (1) family or peer influences; (2) protection; (3) money or material influences; (4) belonging, excitement, or status; and (5) some other reason. Of course, there is considerable overlap across these components, and they cannot be separated from the political economy in which they are formed (Densley and Stevens 2015), but a key issue to understand in this context is whether individuals are pulled or pushed into gang membership (Decker and Van Winkle 1996; Densley 2015). Young people who are pulled into membership join their gang because of the attractions it offers them—the promise or expectation of friendship, opportunities to make money, or the ability to provide something for the neighborhood. Being pushed into the gang conveys a very different motivation. Individuals who see themselves as pushed into gang membership join their gang out of fear for physical consequences if they do not do so, or because they see themselves as powerless to resist the temptations of gang life.

There is considerable evidence about the distinction between pushes and pulls, a distinction that is important because it can help guide responses to gang problems. Most available evidence supports the view that individuals are pulled toward their gangs because of what they see as the positive features of gang involvement. Most gang members report that they joined their gangs to maintain affiliations with their friends or because a number of their friends were members. Let's face it; teenagers have a powerful urge to be around their friends, and adolescence is a time of life when the need to affiliate with one's peers and reject or minimize the importance of relationships with one's parents is greatest. So, the role of friendship in gang joining should come as no great surprise.

But friends aren't the only strong influence on motivating youth to join gangs. Family and neighborhood play an equal (if not greater) role, to the extent that in some contexts, youth may join gangs almost by osmosis or "street socialization" (Vigil 1988; Johanne Miller 2020). Among some families and in some neighborhoods, for example, gangs represent a source of cultural pride and identification. Joan Moore (1978, 1991), Vigil and Long (1990), Padilla (1992), and others document the important role these gangs play in their communities by providing support for the neighborhood and broader cultural values. Likewise, Kissner and Pyrooz (2009) detailed the importance of having siblings, cousins, uncles and aunts, parents, and even grandparents in gangs. While these family members do not necessarily provide encouragement to enter gangs (although some do), they may not discourage gang involvement, either because they see nothing wrong with it or because they were involved in gangs in their youth. This creates "intergenerational continuity" in gang participation (Augustyn, Ward, and Krohn 2017). For the above reasons, when interviewing 252 gang members in Rochester, New York, Thornberry et al. (2003) found that family or friends was the primary reason for gang joining given by the majority of gang members.

Other gang members point to the promise of making money, typically through drug sales but often through other crimes such as robbery or burglary (Padilla 1992; Sánchez-Jankowski 1991; Skolnick 1990). Gang members routinely describe the opportunity to make money that membership in a gang offers them. And that opportunity is not one that requires long hours, hard work, and slow progression through the ranks. Selling drugs, whether by gang members or by others, produces quick profits and is consistent with the desire for immediate gratification that characterizes many adolescents' view of the relationship between work and money (Decker and Van Winkle 1996; Levitt and Venkatesh 2000). While Levitt and Venkatesh (2000) reported that foot soldiers are poorly compensated for their efforts, the appearance of the opportunity for serious profits kept them motivated. Money provides other secondary attractions to gang membership, particularly as money allows its members to satisfy consumer needs (spending money on food, movies, and clothes) and to impress members of the opposite sex.

It was Thrasher (1927) who characterized the motivation to associate with gangs as the "quest for a new experience." Global media presentations and local community myths make gang life seem very compelling (Van Hellemont and Densley 2019). The gang image is "seductive" to some (J. Katz 1988), particularly as an example of resistance identity (Hagedorn 2008). Gang membership is exciting, adventurous, fun, and risky. When in the company of fellow gang members, youths steal from stores, vandalize buildings, get into fights, drink alcohol and smoke cigarettes, and run away from police. Gang membership affords a level of respect, power, and sense of belonging not normally provided to youth, especially racialized youth from marginalized settings (see Chapter 8). Thus, joining a gang provides not only immediate status (Harding 2014) but also an infusion of social capital via access to a network of fellow gang members with resources. Gang hangouts are often the central point for neighborhood get-togethers, where there is access to drugs, alcohol, and girls. Prospective gang members recognize the status enhancements tied to joining a gang. For some, this is enough to tip the scale in favor of gang joining.

There is a darker side to gangs and urban life that compels some young people to join their gang. A substantial fraction of young people turns to gangs seeking protection from rival gangs or just from the violence that lurks in many urban neighborhoods, or as a means of delivering "street justice" when formal justice is lacking (B. Jacobs and Wright 2006; Leovy 2015). By virtue of living in certain neighborhoods or attending certain schools with active gang members, there is sometimes an expectation that most young men are affiliated with a gang. Many young men in Padilla's (1992) and Decker and Van Winkle's (1996) studies reported that they eventually joined a gang because they got tired of being accused of being a member of one gang or another. Living in a neighborhood dominated by one gang would certainly lead outsiders to presume gang membership over time.

But there is another reason, one more troubling, that compels many young people to join their gang—fear of the consequences of not being a member. Quite simply, a number of individuals are targeted for membership because of where they live, who they are, or the perception that they can be forced into gang membership. Evidence exists that gangs strategically recruit new members (e.g., Sánchez-Jankowski 1991), at times in ways close to "intimidation and coercion," resulting in pragmatic but ultimately "reluctant gangsters" (Pitts 2008). This is especially likely in neighborhoods where gangs dominate the local scene and is the likely reason that Decker and Van Winkle (1996) found that "protection" was the most common motivation for gang joining among gang members in St. Louis.

Recent findings from the United Kingdom highlight the complexity of gang joining (Harding 2020; McLean, Robinson, and Densley 2020; Robinson, McLean, and Densley 2019). Some youth were forced into "county lines" drug gangs in order to work off their own drug debts. For them, gang membership was nothing more than a form of indentured servitude that was truly exploitative. Other youth, by contrast, joined the same gangs of their own volition. Owing to boredom, poverty, and a sense of hopelessness about their legitimate job prospects, they said they had no choice but to join the gang and sell drugs, and they enjoyed far greater autonomy and satisfaction in gang life than their indebted counterparts.

It is instructive to see once again the views of gang members. One gang member in London, England, argued that racialized and marginalized youth suffer from such a lack of effective criminal justice that they join gangs in an effort to protect and police themselves:

> Out here you're not living under police protection. No matter how many times the police said they'll protect you, they're not going to protect you. So we find our own protection. We protect our own . . . 'cus the police ain't doing shit for us, we police ourselves. We equip ourselves with tools to protect ourselves, you understand? We're a phone call away. Where the police? Police just tell you to go file a report. (Densley 2013, 23)

In London, joining the gang for protection was often stressed:

> It's inevitable. You wouldn't be in a gang if there wasn't other gangs coming to trouble you in the first place. (Densley 2013, 118)

But family ties also were important, because they not only facilitated entry into the gang but also dictated a gang member's trajectory within it:

> If you're family, you're part and parcel of it. You've already proved yourself because you're part of that bloodline. Do you know what I mean? Like, if you came through me, you're automatically known, "Oh well, that's [name's] cousin," do you know what I mean? Or, "That's his cousin," or that you're someone's cousin, you're someone's

brother. And that in itself makes a difference. That in itself puts you steps ahead of someone who might have been around three or four years longer than the next guy. (Densley 2013, 115)

Reflecting their higher levels of organization (recall our discussion in Chapter 3), members of the Gangster Disciples in the chronic gang city of Chicago who were being held in Joliet Prison in Illinois stated their views:

> I got cut across the face by opposition, Vice Lords, and although my family kept me away from that life, believe me, when this happened, they assessed the surrounding circumstances and automatically got in it.

> I didn't even know at the time that I was in a gang. I was recognized because of my big brother and father were members.

And other imprisoned GDs saw joining the gang as part of the normal turn of events in their neighborhoods:

> I wouldn't say I joined it, I wasn't forced, I joined it because it was the right thing to do at that appropriate time. I didn't see that by joining them it would be prosperous in any form or fashion; it was just something to do at the time, back then.

> The gang was a neighborhood thing—young, ignorant. It's not like people joined gangs for specific purposes; it's not like that.

Another inmate offered a similar opinion:

> Mainly, growing up, my friends was into it [the Gangster Disciples], and I was around it, so I fell into it.

Gang members in San Diego, at the time an emerging gang city, echoed the same reasons offered by Chicago gang members for joining their gang. Despite the differences in cities, the reasons were very similar. One offered that they joined out of "curiosity." For others, the neighborhood had a lot to do with getting in the gang:

> I didn't really join. It was just where I stay, where I grew up at; that's where it was. Like, you walk to the store or something or walk to school, and they were all from the gang.

> I think really I just wanted to get in it.

Actually, what it is, it's just that you grow up with people and you hang together and you kind of watch each other's back. Someone come to your neighborhood, and as long as it's one on one you let it go, but if they bring another then you check 'em.

Gang members from St. Louis provided similar responses to questions about why they joined their gang. Most offered explanations that focused on informal reasons or long-standing friendships:

I ain't going to say it's going to be my life, but it was just something that came up to me where I was staying. I was just with the fellas, and it just happened that I became one of them.

When I moved over here [to St. Louis], I started hanging with them. We herded together and stuff. I just started hanging with them.

To be in a gang, you have friends. It's kinda good to be with some friends instead of going out 'cause if you ain't got no friends, it's really hard to get along out there.

Other gang members in St. Louis pointed to money as their motivation in joining the gang. However, even these gang members recognized the importance of the informal aspects of gang membership:

Money. Money and just being around a whole bunch of guys that like to do stuff that you like to do.

Help me make money. Help me protect myself. Really everything.

In Phoenix, a forty-two-year-old former gang member said that he and his friends joined their gang when they were bored:

Didn't have anything to do. So we started GTAs [Grand Theft Auto]. You know, anything to do something, 'cause we didn't have Parks and Rec and things of that nature when I was growing up, you know.

The fact that gang members cite money, status, protection, family, and friendship as primary motives for gang membership suggests a very real choice calculus (Decker and Van Winkle 1996; Descormiers and Corrado 2016; D. Peterson, Taylor, and Esbensen 2004; Sánchez-Jankowski 1991; Thornberry et al. 2003). Youth can be pushed into gangs by particular circumstances or pulled into them by certain "selective incentives" (see Densley 2015, 244). Beyond the risks of joining gangs, in other words, there are enticements for joining gangs that motivate prospective gang members to rationally weigh the attractiveness of doing so. In their study of female gang membership in Los Angeles and Glasgow, Scotland, Deuchar et al. (2020) found that for some youth, joining gangs was a way out of past experiences, such as child abuse and neglect; for others, gang affiliation was a way in because past experiences had normalized gang membership; and for others still, joining the gang was viewed as a way up to social mobility.

How Do Youth Join Gangs?

Regardless of the motivation for joining a gang, becoming a member typically takes place over time, and the individual gradually adopts a gang identity. Once again, joining a gang is a process, not an event. But once the decision has been made (or in some cases, coerced), the next important step in the gang process is initiation. In relation to Figure 4.1, this occurs at the time of onset. Most documented gangs in the United States have some form of initiation, although it is worth noting that many groups do, from college fraternities to organized crime syndicates. At most English soccer clubs, there is a tradition that new players get up on a chair at dinner and sing a song in front of their new teammates. At the sharper end of life, Sicilian Mafia recruit "men of honor" with symbolic rituals, including the taking of oaths and blood drawing (Gambetta 1996, 146–147). Gonzo journalist Hunter S. Thompson (1996, 45) once documented the Hells Angels motorcycle gang initiating new members with "a bucket of dung and urine . . . poured on the newcomer's head in a solemn baptismal."

Within and between street gangs, there is variation in how initiation rituals occur, yet most are rather crude with few formal aspects to them. Many involve some form of violence, typically by current members of the gang directed against the initiate. Descormiers and Corrado (2016) document three general types of gang initiation. The first is "the crime commission," in which someone is asked to "work" for the gang and commit one or more nonviolent crimes (namely, theft or drug sales) in order to join (1347). The second type of initiation is the "ego violent event" (1348) whereby inductees endure a severe beating from a number of current members for a predetermined number of minutes. The most common example reported is that of being "jumped in" or "beaten in" (Sánchez-Jankowski 1991). Observers of the gang scene in Los Angeles, San Diego, St. Louis, Chicago, and Milwaukee (among other cities) report that this is the preferred method in most gang initiations.

A "beat in" combines expressive and instrumental functions for the gang because it is symbolic of group matriculation and it formally tests how tough a new recruit is. In this scenario, the individual being initiated either stands in the middle of a circle and must fight his or her way out, or must run between two lines of gang members (also known as the "gauntlet"), who pummel him or her with their fists, feet, and occasionally other objects such as bricks, rocks, and sticks. Bolden (2020, 21–25), a former gang member turned scholar, chronicled the beating he underwent at school for his initiation into the Rigsby Court Gangster Bloods, a gang in San Antonio. Such tests of courage and strength are often quite brutal—Bolden broke his wrist while evading teachers breaking up the fight—but end with hugs for the new member and the offering of a few words of unity for the gang. The fact that violence is a part of the very first experience within the gang is quite important. It sends a message to the new gang member that violence is important to the gang, is expected of all members, and constantly lurks beneath the surface of gang life (Decker and Van Winkle 1996).

The third type of initiation is "expressive violence toward others" (Descormiers and Corrado 2016, 1349), such as when a gang member embarks "on a mission" to commit an armed robbery, a drive-by shooting, an assault, a rape, or even a murder at the gang's behest (e.g., Decker 1996, 255). This "baptism" by fire is designed to "weed out the weak and uncommitted" (Vigil 1996, 151). When carried out jointly with other gang members, violent actions incentivize loyalty in the form of *kompromat* or "hostage-information" because everyone is bound together in the illegal deed (Gambetta 2009, 61).

The initiation of female gang members merits comment at this time, though we address female gang membership in Chapter 7. Most observers of the female gang scene report that females tend to be initiated in the same way that males are, through beating in, often by both males and females. A number of highly publicized reports also document rapes of prospective female gang members. In a gendered variation on the ego violent event, women are "sexed in" (Jody Miller 2001; K. Quinn et al. 2019). However, one might argue that sexual assault is not really a form of fair initiation because it positions women as inherently subordinate to men, differentially embedded in the gang. Otherwise, joining patterns that occur for males and females appear to be similar, except perhaps in cases where women are integrated into gangs (with or without their consent) via "bad boy" boyfriends who are gang members (Deuchar et al. 2020).

The picture of life in a gang that has emerged to this point has emphasized the diversity of initiation experiences. The views of gang members are important in this regard. Again, we present the views of active gang members on the issue of initiation. First, we examine the views of members of the Gangster Disciples from Chicago. They may be the most organized gang in the United States, yet they report initiation rituals similar to if not less organized than those in other cities:

> For the initiation, I had to prove my loyalty, prove how much I wanted to become a part of it and basically what I believed in.

> To become a part of it, you just have to become sincere.

Other GDs said that they had to endure physical violence as part of their initiation:

> Just get beat up.

And some members reported that they had to engage in crime:

> Steal and hold drugs.
>
> I proved myself through doing crimes.
>
> Back then you had to prove your loyalty. So there was a guy that had turned State [evidence] on a member in the neighborhood, and we took care of him.

London gang members likewise had to demonstrate proficiency in crime and violence to gain entry into the gang, at times literally staging performances to catch the eye of senior gang members; but even then, it took time to earn the trust of the gang, which was achieved only through repeat interaction:

> It might be something as simple as, you know, we bring a whole lot of girls, we're sort of having a barbecue. You know, all the guys in the gang are there . . . You see what they're like in that environment and that's how you work people out . . . After a few drinks, can I leave the room and trust this boy with my girl? Can I trust this boy with the money on the table? When it comes to girls and money, that's when you see people's true colors. (Densley 2013, 128)

In the emerging gang cities of San Diego and St. Louis, gang initiation focused much more on violence. In almost all cases, potential gang members were "beaten in" as their initiation. In many cases, this was described as being "jumped in." The first three responses were from Chicano gang members in San Diego:

> Some people get their ass kicked into the dirt.
>
> I had to prove to them that I'm down. Prove to them, get in fights.
>
> Actually, they beat the crap out of me.

Their initiation experiences mirrored those of St. Louis gang members from Black gangs:

> I had to have fifteen dudes jump me.

Kill a couple of people, shoot them. Lay somebody on the ground and stomp them.

I had to get into a fight; I had to lie there and be hit, take the pain.

Youth join gangs in other ways. Gang members can be "tagged in" via gang tattoos or other forms of branding (Decker and Van Winkle 1996), which function as a "credible commitment" to the gang because any highly visible or provocative ink "burns bridges" with non-gang life, binding someone to the group (Campana and Varese 2013; Densley 2015). People also are "blessed-in" (i.e., given free access) to the gang by virtue of having older friends and relatives who were already in the gang (Joan Moore 1991). While this is not technically a form of initiation, it emphasizes the importance of existing network ties and "criminal social capital" (Descormiers and Corrado 2016, 1350) or having someone else "vouch" for you in the joining process (Densley 2012b, 313). These all are examples of "costly induction" that force prospective gang members to pay their dues to the gang up front and, in so doing, establish a common basis of trust with their gang colleagues (Densley 2015, 247).

Gangs' reliance on formal initiations may be overstated (Best and Hutchinson 1996), but the concept does get at the idea that gangs are active in the selection process, a key tenet of the signaling theory introduced earlier (Pyrooz and Densley 2016). Think of joining a gang like a dance—sometimes a step forward, sometimes a step back. Either the prospective gang member takes the initiative and the gang follows, or the gang takes the lead and the prospect falls in line. Either way, the prospect must signal, through words and deeds, their intent to join the gang, and the gang must signal, through actions of its own, the want or need for new members. Thus, joining the gang is perhaps best conceived as a negotiated process.

How someone enters the gang also likely dictates their trajectory within the gang, including offending patterns (Pyrooz and Densley 2016). Leary's (1990) work on inclusion and exclusion argues that when people are actively sought out by groups, they tend to experience maximum inclusion, whereas when groups ostracize people, they experience maximum exclusion. Gang embeddedness is a continuum that captures the individual's relationship to the gang. In Figure 4.2, we apply Leary's acceptance–rejection continuum to capture the gang's relationship to the individual, or how the gang feels about the new recruit in their ranks.

Gangs need to know who they can trust to perform the gang member role (and not bring with them unwanted police attention). A gang prospect may well desire the social and personal benefits that gang membership affords (e.g., money or protection), but if the prospect's intentions or initial "quality" threaten the gang's stability or identity, then the gang may decline them entry (Densley 2015) or sideline them to the extent that they only ever experience

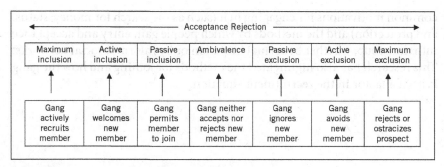

Figure 4.2 Inclusion and exclusion in gangs

exclusion or ambivalence from the gang, never inclusion. This, in turn, could dictate an individual's access to formal information and decision-making channels, or informal social gatherings, where information exchange and decisions otherwise take place. It likely also predicts the duration of gang membership. A signaling perspective on gang joining assumes that gangs need their members to produce, not simply consume; thus, they are better served selecting new members based on reliable indicators of their production value. As Densley's (2012a, 2013) research with gangs in London showed, this puts pressure on the gang prospect to signal to the gang the qualities it is looking for, such as loyalty and bravery, and to do so in a way that is costly or hard to fake, thus satisfying the gang's need for proof of intent.

Conclusion

This chapter discussed the onset stage of gang membership in the context of the life course and what it means to join a gang in terms of levels of gang involvement or embeddedness, a way of capturing gradations of membership based on rank or identity. Not all gang members are created equal, which in part explains the individual pathways people take to enter the gang. Major theories of crime, plus integrated and signaling theories, each offer insights into these risks of gang affiliation. The best evidence suggests that low self-esteem, a lack of interpersonal skills, low parental supervision, familial gang involvement, poverty, time spent with antisocial peers, school failure and low academic performance, and being raised in urban, socioeconomically deprived environments are all predictive risk indicators of gang affiliation. Based on these findings, we can say that there is some support for each of the major theories of gang membership, but the risk factor paradigm is still limited in its scope to predict who joins gangs and why, owing in part to the limitations of using variance to get at process. After all, joining the gang is a process, and qualitative research has provided important insights into the common motivations for engaging in it (such as the search for money, status, and protection) and the methods by which people gain entry and acceptance into the group, whether by formal initiation or by informal social networks. This research has also highlighted the methods for joining and how the gang is itself a factor in the recruitment equation.

5

Continuity and Change in Gang Membership

There is nothing "once and for all" in any decision to change.
Each day brings a new embarking. It's always a recalibration
and a reassessing of attitude and the old tired ways of
proceeding, which are hard to shake for any of us.

—FATHER GREG BOYLE, *TATTOOS ON THE HEART*

P opular stereotypes tend to assume that gang membership is binary—
you're in or you're out—and that once you're in, you're in for life. The
popular musical *West Side Story*, for example, presents warring gangs
the Sharks and the Jets, with a Jets leader articulating the notion that gang
membership and loyalty is permanent, "from your first cigarette to your last
dyin' day. . . . When you're a Jet, you stay a Jet" (Wise and Robbins 1961).
However, in this chapter, we see that not only is membership not binding
until death but also it is normal for it to run its course and for members to
exit. Moreover, those exits may take a variety of forms and motivations as
different individuals weigh the changing costs, benefits, and meanings of
membership according to diverse and changing sets of values across populations and throughout the life course.

One of the reliable facts of human behavior is the relationship between
the past and the present, and crime is no exception. Nagin and Paternoster
(2000) introduced the terms *population heterogeneity* and *state dependence*
to categorize sharply diverging perspectives on continuity in offending—the
factors that prolong criminal careers. Population heterogeneity perspectives
emphasize stable individual differences in factors such as impulsivity, risk-
seeking, and cognitive ability as the explanation for the sturdy correlation
between past and present offending. In contrast, state dependence perspectives emphasize cumulative disadvantages in life experiences such as adverse
childhood experiences, criminal justice system involvement, and gang membership leading to continuity.

Another fact about offending is that nearly everyone desists. Perspectives on desistance differentially emphasize structure and agency in bringing about conformity (Paternoster et al. 2015). On one end, Laub and Sampson's (2003) theory of age-graded informal social controls views entering into structured roles—such as marriage, military, and employment—as the necessary and sufficient conditions for desistance. On the other end, Paternoster and Bushway's (2009) rational choice theory emphasizes that identity shifts—the "feared self" and the "possible self"—facilitate changing views of the benefits and costs of crime. And studies reveal that explanations for desistance are different from those of onset, or what Uggen and Piliavin (1998) termed *asymmetrical causation*.

As we discussed in Chapter 4, there is value in applying theories and methods from the criminal career paradigm and developmental and life-course criminology to gang membership. Whereas the previous chapter focused on the onset of gang membership, this chapter focuses on persistence and disengagement, addressing the following questions:

- What is continuity and change in gang membership, and how do we measure it?
- How long do people remain in gangs?
- What keeps people in gangs?
- Why do people leave gangs?
- How do people leave gangs?

In the last decade, there has been an explosion of research on these questions. Indeed, in an earlier book (Curry, Decker, and Pyrooz 2014) we combined onset, continuity, and change into a single chapter. But research on this topic has increased not only in volume, enough to warrant multiple reviews of the literature (D. Carson and Vecchio 2015; Tonks and Stephenson 2019), but also in theoretical and methodological sophistication.

Defining Persistence and Disengagement

Many people have a stake in determining who is an active gang member and who is a former gang member. The groups that are perhaps most concerned with this distinction are those in the criminal justice system. The police are interested in establishing the motives for crime and violence and gathering intelligence on gangs and gang members (Chapter 11). Prosecutors and judges must make decisions with respect to bail, admission of evidence, and sentencing enhancements (Chapter 13). Correctional officials are required to find adequate housing for incarcerated people and assign them to rehabilitative programs (Chapter 12). Many others are also concerned with this distinction, such as the gang and rival gangs. The gang needs to determine who is willing to fight or retaliate, while rival gangs may put less stock in targeting someone who left the gang. Yet as D. Carson and Vecchio (2015, 259) noted, there are "difficulties in discerning when an ex-gang member, in fact, becomes an ex-gang member."

Part of the reason distinguishing current and former gang members is not clear cut is that leaving a gang is a process. As the quote from Father Boyle above suggests, this process is neither smooth nor linear. Many readers may relate by considering personal experiences with romantic dissolution, religious apostasy, employment retirement, or recovery from substance abuse. Rarely do these transitions occur quickly or without emotional or social challenges. The unwinding of beliefs and relationships is typically protracted with pushes and pulls to and from competing roles. And as the quote from *West Side Story* suggests, it is commonly believed that gang membership never ceases and that the entire notion of disengagement therefore lacks value altogether.

In Chapter 4 we presented a hypothetical trajectory of gang membership (Figure 4.1). *Persistence* in gang membership refers to the duration for which someone identifies as a gang member. Whereas self-identification as a gang member marks entry into the gang, deidentification signifies exit. These are the points where someone is more likely to be a current than a non-gang member (entry) or be a former than a current gang member (exit). Such thresholds are latent rather than observed, and we assume that self-nomination adequately taps the shifts between gang status. Still, self-identification and deidentification impose a rigid categorization of gang status that is mostly blind to the nuances involved in the process of leaving the gang.

Disengagement refers to the process of shifting from peak to trivial levels of embeddedness in gangs, which is represented in the negative slope in Figure 4.1. We prefer to focus on embeddedness rather than identity. Embeddedness, which includes elements of behaviors, beliefs, and experiences, better taps immersion in gang dynamics than identity alone. We also prefer to describe this process as "disengagement" rather than "desistance," a correction to our earliest writing on the topic (Densley 2013; Pyrooz and Decker 2011). "Desistance" is too closely associated with criminal offending and the ceasing of activities, while "disengagement" better captures the release or separation from something to which one was connected. This also acknowledges that people can be disengaging from gang membership yet still remain active in the gang, which is consistent with conceiving of gang membership as a trajectory and disengagement as a redirection.

This brings us to update a typology introduced a decade ago. In Table 5.1, we present a typology that classifies people based on gang embeddedness and identification. Our previous representation focused on criminal offending and

TABLE 5.1 GANG MEMBERSHIP AND GANG EMBEDDEDNESS TYPOLOGY			
		Gang membership self-identification	
		Current	Former
Level of gang embeddedness	Nontrivial	A. Gang member	B. Residual ties
	Trivial	C. Disembedded	D. True desistance

gang identification (Decker and Lauritsen 2002; Pyrooz and Decker 2011). We see offending motivated by gang-related group processes as distinguishable from offending unrelated to gangs. While both are important, the latter is tangential to the key questions in discerning gang status. Cell A refers to people who claim they are gang members and have meaningful levels of embeddedness in gangs—they are, simply put, gang members. Like Cell A, there is little ambiguity in Cell D. True disengagement indicates that neither identity nor embeddedness is consistent with the gang lifestyle. In both of these instances, embeddedness and identity are congruent.

Cells B and C, however, are what Bolden (2013) described as ambivalent gang statuses. Cell B accounts for those who no longer claim an active affiliation but still engage in gang activities. We refer to those who meet these criteria as *residual ties*, acknowledging that emotional and social connections to the gangs unwind over time. This is the flip side of the "wannabe" or "peripheral" gang member. Cell C is perhaps the most controversial category. Disembedded gang members claim affiliation in name only, as they are not embedded in the gang, yet the gang is a fixture of their identity—akin to original gangsters, veteranos, or what Brenneman (2011, 139) termed *pandillero calmado*, a "settled-down gang member." The resulting classifications from this typology are not exercises in futility—moving from Cells A to D should correspond with rank-order decreases in the risk of crime and violence perpetration and victimization, while connections to conventional and prosocial institutions should increase.

Continuity in Gang Membership

West Side Story images of gangs have been long displaced by films, television series, and documentaries such as *Straight Outta Compton*, *Narcos*, and *Bastards of the Party*. In the early 1990s, two cult classics—*American Me* and *Blood In, Blood Out*—traced the lives of young, gang-involved Angelinos in their transition from the street to prison. Both films portrayed gang membership as a lifelong commitment. Yet there was no scientific evidence to support or refute such assertions at the time the films were released. Gang researchers did not know the answers mostly because they did not ask the questions. That has since changed. The criminal career paradigm offered the terminology to consider gang careers. The proliferation of longitudinal research designs and the self-nomination method offered the data and tools to study gang careers. Developmental and life-course criminology offered the theoretical foundation to understand the contouring of gang membership. And with that, we can consider how long people remain in gangs and what is associated with prolonged involvement in gangs.

Duration of Gang Membership

Table 5.2 provides a summary of findings from nine prospective studies of the duration of self-reported gang membership. We focus only on prospective studies because they interview the same individuals over multiple points in time. Prospective studies look forward by capturing gang careers as they unfold. Retrospective studies, in contrast, look backward by asking individuals to report when they joined and left the gang. Both approaches are valuable, but we privilege prospective studies because they tend to be more representative and less susceptible to memory recall biases. These studies tracked gang membership for as few as three years (Weerman, Lovegrove, and Thornberry 2015) to as many as ten years (Leverso and Matsueda 2019). The initial year of data collection occurred as early as 1988 (Thornberry et al. 2003) to as recent as 2006 (Melde and Esbensen 2014). Combined, these studies tracked twenty-four hundred gang members in twenty different cities and one U.S.-representative sample.

The overwhelming conclusion from this summary of studies is that gang careers are rather brief. Either the majority or near-majority of people who were gang-involved claimed this affiliation for one year. This finding is consistent across study period, sample type, and study site or region. The fact that gang membership is fleeting in the life course indicates that gangs exert relatively little control over their members and their decisions to leave the gang. As discussed in Chapter 4, it is necessary for gangs to maintain an active recruitment strategy in order to replenish their ranks. Only a minority of gang members claimed an affiliation for three or more years—as low as 8 percent (Melde, Diem, and Drake 2012) to as high as 28 percent (Pyrooz 2014b) in U.S. studies. The implication is that most gang members cycle out of the gang without intervention, which could be taken to mean that intervention is moot or at least that resources in gang programming should be channeled to persistent gang members.

The results from Table 5.2 belie what we think are two important facts about the duration of gang membership. First, focusing only on cohorts of people who enter gangs discounts the importance of age. It is true that these studies are mostly of young people, but they ignore differences in the age-graded patterning of gang membership. Figure 5.1 illustrates the importance of age by reporting six trajectories of gang membership based on data representative of five birth cohorts—1980 to 1984—in the United States from

TABLE 5.2 PROSPECTIVE STUDIES ON THE DURATION OF GANG MEMBERSHIP

Authors (year)	Study years, site	Sample type	N	1 year	2 years	3 years	4+ years
Thornberry et al. (2003)	1988–1992, Rochester, NY	High-risk, youth	207	55%	28%	12%	5%
K. Hill, Lui, and Hawkins (2001)	1988–1993, Seattle, WA	High-risk, youth	124	69%	17%	11%	3%
Leverso and Matsueda (2019)	1989–1998, Denver, CO	High-risk, youth	226	57%	22%	12%	10%
Rachel Gordon et al. (2004)	1991–2002, Pittsburgh, PA	High-risk, youth	165	48%	25%	27%	—
Melde, Diem, and Drake (2012)	1995–1999, 6 U.S. cities	School, youth	140	58%	34%	6%	2%
Pyrooz (2014b)	1997–2005, United States	Population, Y/A	726	49%	23%	11%	17%
Pyrooz, Sweeten, and Piquero (2013)	2000–2010, Philadelphia and Phoenix 2002–2004,	Delinquent, Y/A	226	62%	13%	8%	16%
Weerman, Lovegrove, and Thornberry (2015)	The Hague, Netherlands	School, youth	73	78%	21%	1%	—
Melde and Esbensen (2014)	2006–2011, 7 U.S. cities	School, youth	512	63%	20%	9%	8%

Note: Studies are ordered chronologically. Year refers to article publication rather than data collection. Y/A indicates studies that include youth (age < 18) and adults (age ≥ 18). Dashes indicate no information about gang membership for that duration. N indicates the number of self-reported gang members. Some studies combined years or did not report information for the duration period.

the National Longitudinal Survey of Youth 1997 (NLSY97) (Pyrooz 2014b). Three of the trajectories are adolescence-oriented, as people join and leave gangs in their preteen, middle teenage, or late teenage years; their mean duration in the gang is one to two years. The modal trajectory, adolescence-limited, joined the gang in the early teenage years, reached peak probability of gang membership (over 60 percent) around age fourteen, and then left the gang in the late teenage years. The three remaining trajectories diverge from common understandings of gang membership in the life course. The adult-onset trajectory is distinguished not by duration but by gang onset in adult years and is the third-most-common pattern followed. The early and late persistent trajectories both reported prolonged membership in gangs—five

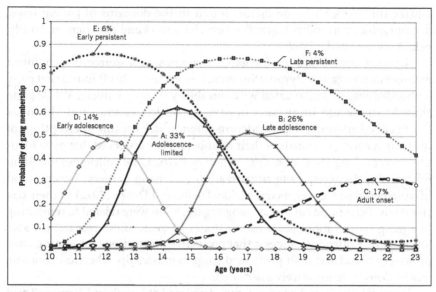

Figure 5.1 Age-graded trajectories of gang membership in the life course, NLSY97
Credit: Data are from the National Longitudinal Survey of Youth 1997 (Pyrooz 2014b).

and seven years, respectively—differentiated by the age at which they joined the gang. These are also the rarest of the six patterns of gang membership.

Second, some individuals remain in gangs for many years and in some instances for decades. Indeed, the oldest current gang member we interviewed in the LoneStar Project (a longitudinal study of trajectories, associations, and reentry among prison inmates in Texas) was fifty-seven years old and told us he had joined the Rolling 60s Crips at age thirteen (Pyrooz and Decker 2019). We should neither sensationalize their gang careers nor treat them as outliers. While these descriptive findings illustrate the duration and age-graded nature of gang membership in the life course, they do not tell us who stays in gangs for the longest periods. This leads us to focus on studies examining the sources of continuity in gang membership.

Sources of Continuity in Gang Membership

What prolongs membership in gangs? Questions of persistence differ from those of disengagement. Several panel studies have examined the correlates of prolonged gang trajectories, including research conducted in Denver (Leverso and Matsueda 2019); Las Cruces Lincoln, Omaha, Philadelphia, Phoenix, and Portland (Melde, Diem, and Drake 2012); Philadelphia and Phoenix (Pyrooz, Sweeten, and Piquero 2013); Seattle (K. Hill, Lui, and Hawkins 2001); and the U.S.-representative NLSY97 (Hashimi, Apel, and Wakefield 2021). We summarize this work based on factors found in the domains of gang/groups, demographics and individual differences, behaviors and experiences, family, neighborhood, and school.

There is much support for gang dynamics as a source of prolonged membership in gangs. Pyrooz, Sweeten, and Piquero (2013) found that gang embeddedness was associated with durability in gang careers. While gang embeddedness taps immersion in gang dynamics, Leverso and Matsueda (2019) called attention to gang identification, which captures perceptions of the gang meeting the needs of their members. They observed that gang identification prolonged membership. Whereas Pyrooz and colleagues found no relationship between gang organization and gang careers, Leverso and Matsueda did in Denver, as did Melde, Diem, and Drake (2012) in their six-city study. Perceptions of higher gang organization were related to remaining in a gang two or more years rather than one year. These researchers also found some evidence to suggest that protective motivations for joining were positively associated with prolonged gang membership, whereas economic motivations were negatively associated.

Race, ethnicity, and gender, topics discussed at length in Chapters 7 and 8, were associated with continuity in gang membership, although the results are noisy. Melde, Diem, and Drake (2012) was the only study to find no demographic differences in prolonged gang membership, whereas Hashimi, Apel, and Wakefield (2021), Leverso and Matsueda (2019), and Pyrooz, Sweeten, and Piquero (2013) did find such differences. There is a fair amount of support to suggest that Latinos remain in gangs for longer periods than White youth and limited support for differences between Black and White youth. Gender also matters, as gang careers are lengthier for males than for females.

There is evidence of behavioral and individual differences in gang careers. Delinquency and victimization are inconsistently related to continuity in gang membership across these studies, with positive, null, and negative effects, preventing us from reaching any firm conclusions. Arrest was related to duration of gang membership (Hashimi, Apel, and Wakefield 2021), which comports with our prior work on imprisonment and gang membership (Pyrooz, Gartner, and Smith 2017). Low self-control (e.g., impulse control, empathy, and temperance) and externalizing behaviors (e.g., aggression, oppositionality, and hyperactivity) were associated with longer gang careers (K. Hill, Lui, and Hawkins 2001; Pyrooz, Sweeten, and Piquero 2013).

School, religion, family, and neighborhood were mostly unrelated to the duration of gang careers, with two important exceptions found in the work of Hashimi, Apel, and Wakefield (2021). Based on their use of the NLSY97, they found that youth who lived in gang-active neighborhoods remained in gangs for lengthier periods, as did youth who moved to new residences with greater frequency. Whether the underlying conditions of the neighborhood or the interactive pressures of the gang were responsible for this was unclear. That said, it is striking that these studies do not identify marriage, cohabitation, parenthood, educational achievement, school connection, family structure, socioeconomic status, or siblings as sources of continuity in gang membership.

Altogether, these findings tell us that many different factors are associated with prolonged membership in a gang. That said, the strongest evidence points to individual- and group-level factors as the sources of continuity in gang membership—namely, the ties that bind people to groups and the organizational features of the gang itself. Demographics, behaviors, and other individual differences also matter, but the evidence is too premature to reach firm conclusions, especially given how few studies exist on the topic. Now that we have taken stock of what is known about continuity, we shift our focus to change, or the transition out of the gang.

Disengagement from Gangs

For decades, so much attention was aimed at understanding joining gangs and differences between gang and non-gang members (Chapter 4) that researchers neglected to probe issues related to leaving gangs. Early accounts of leaving were largely descriptive, offering statements about the next developmental stage to which gang members transitioned. Thrasher (1927, 242), for example, saw romantic relationships and marriage as knifing-off ties to the gang, stating, "The gang which once supplanted the home, now succumbs to it; for the institutional gap in the social framework has been filled." Sánchez-Jankowski (1991) offered a passing mention of five possible post-gang transitions, most of which were maladaptive: criminal persistence, association with organized crime, incarceration, premature mortality, or, potentially, legitimate employment.

Horowitz (1983, 179–184) and Vigil (1988, 106–109) provided the first sustained discussions of leaving gangs. Horowitz, based on her research with the Lions gang in Chicago, reported that peripheral members fluidly came and went without becoming ensnared in gang life. For core members, though, she appealed to employment, marriage, and military enlistment, akin to the age-graded informal social controls highlighted by Laub and Sampson (2003). Vigil (1988), in contrast, saw maturational reform undergirding the motivations for leaving the gang, with people drifting away from the gang once they start "wising-up" to lasting consequences of their actions (107), akin to Paternoster and Bushway's (2009) identity theory of desistance.

The earliest standalone discussions of leaving the gang were provided by Fong and Vogel (1995), who discussed the motivations for "defecting" from Texas prison gangs, and Decker and Lauritsen (2002), who outlined the motivations for leaving and the tension between persistence and disengagement among street gang members in St. Louis. In applying a developmental and life-course framework to gang membership, Pyrooz and Decker (2011) identified gang disengagement as a process and outlined the need to uncover the motives and methods for leaving gangs. Since then, the literature on this topic has exploded, and we have documented over forty contributions to this area of research, nearly all of which were published in the last decade. And so, now that we have provided some background, we turn to a conceptual framework capable of accounting for disengagement from gangs.

Conceptual Framework

Figure 5.2 outlines the process of disengagement from gangs—transitioning from peak to nominal levels of embeddedness. Motivations and methods are the core processes involved in this transition. In their absence, continuity in gang membership is the likely pathway. Decker and colleagues (2014), drawing on Ebaugh's (1988) theory of role exit, offered a stage-based model of disengagement. Their model focused primarily on subconscious and conscious transformations in identity and self-concept that gang members experience. The initial stage is the generation of first doubts about staying in the role of gang member. At this stage, there is no commitment to leave the gang, but gang members begin to question its efficacy. These doubts can be emergent and reside in the back of the mind, but over time they gain ascendancy and lead to the next stage. Anticipatory socialization marks the next step in the

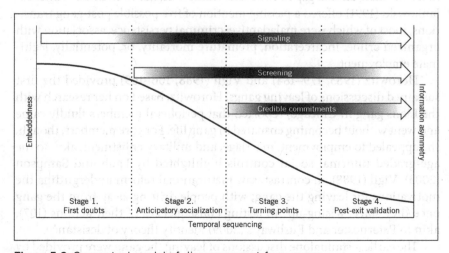

Figure 5.2 Conceptual model of disengagement from gangs
Note: Adapted from Densley and Pyrooz (2019). The shade gradation in the arrows represents the ramping up and tailing off of mechanisms, where darker shades indicate greater activity. Signaling, screening, and credible commitments are interrelated and overlap temporally.

role exit model, where gang members actively look for and weigh alternative roles. This stage is rife with uncertainty, described as a teeter-tottering between the comfortable, known world of the gang and the uncertain world outside of it. But, internally, the action occurs at the turning points stage. This is when gang members experience the "crystallization of discontent" with their current role, when specific events or imperatives prompt the transformation from current to former gang member, some of which may be internal to the gang (i.e., pushes) and others external (i.e., pulls). That transformation is fully realized with postexit validation, which entails internal self-evaluations and external public evaluations offering confirmation of one's former role of "gang member." From the San Francisco Bay Area (Berger et al. 2017) to South Africa (Dziewanski 2020), studies of disengagement from gangs have found support for the role exit model.

Whereas Decker and colleagues' (2014) role exit model focuses primarily on the within, or motivations for leaving, another theoretical perspective—rooted in signaling theory—focuses primarily on the without, or methods for leaving (Densley and Pyrooz 2019). Signaling theory tackles the fundamental problem of information asymmetry: how can someone who is perceived as a gang member convince others that her or his cognitive transformation to former gang status is honest and real? Clearly, the perceived gang member is in a better position to know the truth than any others who may have a stake in this decision, such as the gang, rival gangs, family members, schoolteachers, the neighborhood, and criminal justice agents. The process of closing the information gap involves strategies of action for making public gang status transitions. In some instances, passive exits may be possible, owing to motivations for leaving that are deemed legitimate, or if peripheral status in the gang does not invite scrutiny; while in other instances, active exits are required, such as when leaving is viewed as a betrayal to the gang. When conflicts arise between participating in gang life and something else, efforts to reduce information asymmetry will entail (1) signaling of prosocial tendencies that are costly or hard to fake, (2) credible commitments involving burning bridges to gang life or building bridges to non-gang life, and (3) screening by relying on credible sources to vouch for the legitimacy of transitions or undertaking ceremonies marking exit from the gang. These are strategies of action. Each of these efforts occurs throughout the disengagement process, although their timing, utility, and weight likely differ. Signaling theory represents a new way of thinking about disengagement from gangs as a communicative exchange, and initial support is found in research on religious transformation in Brazilian prisons (A. Johnson and Densley 2018).

We contend that there is merit to both arguments surrounding debates over agency and structure in the disengagement process. Gang members make decisions to transform their identity, yet those decisions can occur in the context of controls exerted by other influential roles. In some ways, this is the gang redux of the "chicken and the egg." When pressed, however, we find ourselves siding with Paternoster and Bushway (2009; Paternoster et al. 2015). While there are instances where gang members indeed stumble haphazardly into marriage, parenthood, jobs, or other "hooks for change" (Giordano et al. 2002) that bring about identity transformation, these external forces are unavailable to the typical gang member in her or his teenage years and thus are less relevant to the lives of gang members. Regardless of developmental periods, we see gang members as active agents in the disengagement process, weighing the costs and benefits of life in the gang versus life after the gang. Yes, choices (costs and benefits) are shaped by outside forces, but to deny that gang members make choices is to ignore the evidence from a large body of research on the motivations and methods for leaving the gang.

Why Do People Leave Gangs?

Now that we have elaborated on the processes of disengagement, what does the leading research on this topic reveal about the motives and methods for leaving the gang? Table 5.3 provides an overview of the key empirical, review, and theoretical works that contribute to the state of knowledge on disengagement from gangs.

Motivations for leaving gangs can be categorized into pushes and pulls. This is the mirror of gang entry discussed in Chapter 4, where pushes now mean factors internal to the gang and pulls are factors external to the gang. While we rely primarily on the narratives provided by gang members, we should be clear that it is not always possible to discern the core motivations for leaving. And while we organize the following discussion by pushes and pulls, we should be clear that they rarely operate in isolation from one another.

Push factors include disillusionment, triggering events, criminal justice involvement, and gang structure. Among all the motivations for leaving, disillusionment is most commonly cited.

Disillusionment refers to a state of discontent brought about by unmet expectations that disrupt the alignment of personal and collective identity. Bubolz and Simi (2015) positioned disillusionment at the core of their cognitive-emotional theory of motivations for leaving gangs. There are several variants of disillusionment. Maturational reform is perhaps the most prevalent. Gang membership is a young man's game. Former gang members, especially those who left at younger ages, often say something along the lines of:

> It was a young thing. I experienced the life and now it is time to experience something else. (Decker and Pyrooz 2011, 13)

Many will say they "just felt like it" or that the gang was "not me." These are not words that suggest a strong impetus to leave. Young people "try on" all

TABLE 5.3 RESEARCH ON THE MOTIVES AND METHODS FOR GANG LEAVING

Author(s) (year of publication)	Location, type of sample	Year of data collection	Sample characteristics	Study design	Study focus
Fong and Vogel (1995)	Texas, prisoners	1993	N = 48, former, adult, male	Quantitative	Motives
Decker and Lauritsen (2002)	St. Louis, street	1990–1993	N = 24, former, youth/adult, male/female	Qualitative	Motives, methods
Varriale (2008)	United States, population	1997–2003	N = 139, current/former, youth/adult, female	Quantitative	Motives
Moloney et al. (2009)	San Francisco, street	2004–2006	N = 91, current/former, youth/adult, male	Qualitative	Motives, methods
Moloney et al. (2011)	San Francisco area, street	N/A	N = 65, current/former, youth/adult, female	Qualitative	Motives, methods
Pyrooz and Decker (2011)	Maricopa County (Arizona), detention	1999–2003	N = 84, former, youth, male/female	Quantitative	Motives, methods
Bolden (2013)	Bexar (Texas) and Orange (Florida) Counties, street	2005	N = 48, current/former, youth/adult, male/female	Qualitative	Motives, methods
Densley (2013)	London, street	2008–2010	N = 69, current/former, youth/adult, male/female	Qualitative	Motives, methods
D. Carson, Peterson, and Esbensen (2013)	Seven U.S. cities, school	2006–2011	N = 473, former, youth, male/female	Quantitative	Motives, methods
Flores (2013)	Los Angeles, religious	2008–2009	N = 34, former, adult, male	Qualitative	Methods
Flores and Hondagneu-Sotelo (2013)	Los Angeles, religious	2008–2009	N = 34, former, adult, male	Qualitative	Methods
MacRae-Krisa (2013)	N/A	N/A	N/A	Theory/review	Motives, methods
Pyrooz and Decker (2014)	N/A	N/A	N/A	Theory/review	Motives, methods
Brenneman (2011)	Central America, religious	2007–2008	N = 63, former, N/A, male/female	Qualitative	Motives, methods

(Continued)

TABLE 5.3 RESEARCH ON THE MOTIVES AND METHODS FOR GANG LEAVING (*Continued*)					
Author(s) (year of publication)	Location, type of sample	Year of data collection	Sample characteristics	Study design	Study focus
Brenneman (2014)	Central America, religious	2007–2008	N = 63, formers, N/A, male/female	Qualitative	Motives, methods
Decker et al. (2014)	Five U.S. cities, high-risk/mixed	2010–2011	N = 260, formers, youth/adult, male/female	Qualitative, quantitative	Motives, methods
Gormally (2014)	Glasgow, street	N/A	N = 15, current/former, youth/adult, male/female	Qualitative	Motives, methods
D. Carson and Vecchio (2015)	N/A	N/A	N/A	Theory/review	Motives, methods
Bubolz and Simi (2015)	N/A	N/A	N/A	Theory/review	Motives
Flores (2016)	Los Angeles, religious	2008–2009	N = 34, former, adult, male	Qualitative	Methods
O'Neal et al. (2016)	Los Angeles and Phoenix, intervention	2010–2011	N = 143, former, youth/adult, male/female	Quantitative	Motives, methods
Deuchar et al. (2016)	Copenhagen, intervention	2014	N = 22, former, youth/adult, male	Qualitative	Motives, methods
J. Sharkey, Stifel, and Mayworm (2015)	California, detention	2011	N = 58, current/former, youth, male	Qualitative	Methods
D. Carson and Esbensen (2016)	Seven U.S. cities, school	2006–2011, 2012	N = 82, former, youth, male/female	Mixed	Motives, methods
Berger et al. (2017)	Los Angeles and San Francisco, intervention	N/A	N = 39, former, adult, male/female	Qualitative	Motives, methods
Chalas and Grekul (2017)	Alberta, prison	2009	N = 175, current/former, adult, male/female	Qualitative	Motives
Maitra, McLean, and Holligan (2017)	England and Scotland, prison	2012–2016	N = 74, current/former, adult, male	Qualitative	Motives

TABLE 5.3 RESEARCH ON THE MOTIVES AND METHODS FOR GANG LEAVING (*Continued*)

Author(s) (year of publication)	Location, type of sample	Year of data collection	Sample characteristics	Study design	Study focus
Pyrooz, McGloin, and Decker (2017)	United States, population	1997–2005	N = 629, current/former, youth/adult, male/female	Quantitative	Motives
Roman, Decker, and Pyrooz (2017)	Four U.S. cities, street	2010–2011	N = 260, former, youth/adult, male/female	Quantitative	Motives
Roman, Decker, and Pyrooz (2017)	Philadelphia, street	2013–2015	N = 51, former, youth/adult, male/female	Quantitative	Motives
D. Carson (2018)	Seven U.S. cities, school	2006–2011, 2012	N = 377, current/former, youth, male/female	Mixed	Motives
A. Johnson and Densley (2018)	Brazil, prisoners	2010–2011, 2012–2013	N = 15, current/former, adult, male	Qualitative	Methods
Roks (2018)	The Hague, street	2011–2013	N = 20, former, youth/adult, male	Qualitative	Motives, methods
Pyrooz and Decker (2019)	Texas, prisoners	2016	N = 301, former, adult, male	Mixed	Motives, methods
Tonks and Stephenson (2019)	N/A	N/A	N/A	Theory/review	Motives
J. Rosen and Cruz (2019)	El Salvador, high-risk/mixed	2017	N = 1,196, current/former, youth/adult, male/female	Mixed	Methods
Cruz and Rosen (2020)	El Salvador, high-risk/mixed	2017	N = 1,196, current/former, youth/adult, male/female	Mixed	Motives
Decker and Pyrooz (2020b)	Texas, prisoners	2016	N = 301, former, adult, male	Mixed	Motives, methods
Bubolz and Lee (2020)	Midwest United States, street	2011–2013	N = 30, former, adult, male/female	Qualitative	Methods
Deuchar (2020)	Denmark, intervention	2016, 2018	N = 17, current/former, adult, male	Qualitative	Methods

(*Continued*)

Author(s) (year of publication)	Location, type of sample	Year of data collection	Sample characteristics	Study design	Study focus
Dziewanski (2020)	Cape Town, street	N/A	N = 24, former, adult, male/female	Qualitative	Motives, methods
Kelly and Ward (2020)	Cape Town, religious	N/A	N = 12, former, adult, male	Qualitative	Motives, methods
Whitney-Snel, Valdez, and Totaan (2020)	N/A	N/A	N = 32, former, adult, male/female	Qualitative	Motives

TABLE 5.3 RESEARCH ON THE MOTIVES AND METHODS FOR GANG LEAVING (*Continued*)

Abbreviations: N refers to the sample size of current/former gang members; N/A indicates that information was not available or deviated from the purpose of the research.

sorts of identities, some longer than others, including gang membership. After all, gang membership typically has its onset during adolescence or late adolescence, periods of experimentation with different lifestyles and beliefs.

The incongruence between personal (individual) and collective identity can also be accelerated by burnout or shifts in gang politics. Former gang members will share that they are tired of the gang lifestyle. Sometimes these sentiments can be expressed unemotionally:

> I use to be affiliated with Crip, I'm not anymore . . . it's just, it's annoying. Too much drama, and too much [pause] pointless violence. (D. Carson 2018)

But other times the exasperation is apparent:

> I am leaving this whole lifestyle behind me. I've had enough. Too old for this shit. Basically, I'm sitting here [in prison] for somebody else's stupidity and activities. (Chalas and Grekul 2017, 376)

Gang membership is high stakes. The prospect of reducing the liabilities and obligations of life in the gang is highly appealing after years of having to "watch one's back." In some cases, former gang members allude to being sold a "bill of goods," where promises of comradery, protection, and economic returns go unfulfilled:

> They paint a pretty picture for you, but that is not what it is. If anything, you really just get yourself in more trouble. (Pyrooz and Decker 2019, 209)

Those unmet expectations can emerge during times of crisis or transition. Shifts in gang politics may be one of those instances. Although most gangs lack political orientations (see Chapter 10 for exceptions), a key factor that distinguishes them from political extremist groups (see Chapter 3), "politics" in gangs refers to a dynamic interplay of alliances, conflicts, and interactions that can breed cynicism—for example,

> For one, the way they were doing things. They were going to start taxing people, take commissary from people, abuse and use people for prostitution. There was a lot of hate and violence. I didn't like that. If anything, I try to help people. It was pretty bad. (Pyrooz and Decker 2019, 235)

Such responses are more likely to be found among gangs that are more organized or composed of older individuals, but they represent yet another form of disillusionment. Roman, Decker, and Pyrooz (2017) found that disillusionment was listed as the motivation for leaving the gang by the majority of former gang members in three different studies, including a high-risk justice-involved sample (85 percent; Decker and Pyrooz 2011), a high-risk street-based sample (89 percent; Eidson, Roman, and Cahill 2017), and a school-based sample (55 percent; D. Carson, Peterson, and Esbensen 2013). As we noted above, disillusionment reflects general social processes, from leaving behind religion to employment to substance use to romantic relationships. The content may be different, but the processes are similar.

Triggering events are another common motivation for leaving. Whereas disillusionment gradually builds up over time, triggering events operate more like a shock to the system. Victimization is commonly cited as a turning point:

> I didn't want to live that type of life. One time, I got seriously stabbed and I was in the hospital for like three months. Right in my back. Close to the kidney. . . . After I got out of the hospital I tried to cope with it a little more, but I just faded away from it. (Decker and Lauritsen 2002, 57)

> Life looks very different you've been shot at or stabbed several times and your insides are on the outside and the doctors are looking at you like "shit, how he not dead." (Densley 2013, 135)

Victimization does not have to be personal, as the fear of violence or vicarious victimization can serve as a triggering event:

> My cousin died, one of the ones that I was close to. He died and everything was screwed up and I started seeing everything and everybody was acting all reckless. (Bolden 2013, 14)

Because we might get shot. Somebody in our hood got shot last night and the day before that. They killing for no reason. (Decker and Lauritsen 2002, 57)

Violence has an upper limit in gangs. The awakening that comes with violent events operates as a moment of clarity to motivate the next stage of identity transformation. Between 31 and 42 percent of the former gang members in the studies summarized by Roman, Decker, and Pyrooz (2017) cited violence as a motivation for leaving the gang.

Criminal justice involvement is a push factor closely related to disillusionment and violence. Harassment or punishment perceived to be associated with gang membership serves as a motivation for anywhere from 24 to 38 percent of former gang members (Roman, Decker, and Pyrooz 2017). Police or correctional policies or practices are cited as the primary driver. There are elements of tiring of police harassment in the narratives of former gang members, but most understand that law enforcement will never view them as reformed—"Once a gang member, always a gang member" (Decker and Pyrooz 2011, 15; Lee and Bubolz 2020). Instead, former gang members note that they grew tired of the long reach of the law, including the enhanced monitoring and penalties applied to gang members:

I am trying to make it home [from prison]. . . . It stayed on my record, parole denies you for being confirmed [as a gang member], you don't qualify for certain TDCJ [Texas Department of Criminal Justice] activities when you are confirmed. (Pyrooz and Decker 2019, 235)

In the last five decades, gangs have been a criminal justice system priority in the United States (see Chapters 11–13). Heavy-handed suppressive responses to gangs by police, courts, and corrections also contribute as a motivating force for leaving.

The final push motive, gang structure, is less commonly observed than the others yet focuses on practical issues of the gang: dissolution and adverse selection. One of the core characteristics of gangs—which is included in the definition—is the ability of the group to survive turnover in membership. Bolden (2013, 15), for example, cited instances when one gang member decided to leave, which created a bandwagon effect:

I think there was a lot of us feeling the same way I did, but just nobody said nothing. I know this from when I got out, because a few other people were like "Yeah, I'm done too." I don't want to feel like I started anything, but I kinda think I did by speaking up that time.

Knowing people who left the gang can serve as an important motivator for leaving, regardless of the gang's continuity and change (Cruz and Rosen 2020). Some groups fall apart as a result of excess incarceration, death, or departures (Ouellet, Bouchard, and Charette 2019), as this former member in Phoenix told us:

> The gang disbanded. Everybody stopped hanging out, and everybody else locked up, got killed, moved away, or started a family. Some [pause] and there's a couple that committed suicide.

These issues take on greater salience in smaller and more tight-knit gangs. In the absence of members, there is no gang. Gangs can also splinter into different directions, such as when the Nevada Trece (a Latino prison gang in Nevada) broke into three distinct groups—Nevada Gangsters, Nevada 89, and Nevada Organization. Members need to decide a path, but the decision to disengage out of frustration would be considered disillusionment, not gang structure. About one-quarter of the gang members in Decker and Pyrooz's (2011) study left for these reasons (Roman, Decker, and Pyrooz 2017).

Adverse selection is also a practical issue of the gang that results in exits. Roman, Decker, and Pyrooz (2017) reported that 11 percent of the former gang members in their study were forced out of the gang. It is not unusual to hear that gang members were kicked out because they violated gang rules by refusing to carry out violence or snitching (Fong and Vogel 1995), or, just as gangs seek to avoid admitting uncontrollable members (Densley 2013), they expel those who present a liability to the gang. A former MS-13 member in El Salvador explained:

> It matters what a gang member has achieved within the gang. For example, let's say you are in charge of a clique and you see that there is an outstanding member. You will keep this member. It is easier for a bad gang member to leave. He is less useful for the gang. (J. Rosen and Cruz 2019, 1501)

Cruz and Rosen (2020) made a compelling point about the power of gangs to regulate social life, particularly in developing countries such as El Salvador. They found that gangs with larger numbers of members per clique had stronger intentions to leave, while affiliation with more powerful gangs (e.g., MS-13) was associated with lower intentions of leaving. Missing from much of the last decade of research on disengagement were the compositional and structural features of the gang itself, a void that Cruz and Rosen addressed.

Pull factors include family, employment, religion, and mobility. Family influence is the most common pull factor. Former gang members pointed primarily to children and romantic partners but also to parents (especially mothers) and mentors as motivations for leaving the gang. There are two dimensions to family that are important to illustrate. One dimension is identity. The arrival of a child is a dramatic life event, ushering in a new identity of father or mother regardless of whether the title is seized or ignored. Parenthood offers a transformation narrative, and gang members realize its significance, such as this young man:

> I was still off the hook, hella violent. And I didn't give a fuck if I lived or died. . . . When she was pregnant I didn't feel shit! When he was born and I see his little face, that when I got a lotta feelins like, "that's my little man right here." (Moloney et al. 2009, 315)

The stakes are undeniably higher for girls and women, however. Indeed, motherhood is often portrayed as reflecting the core of female identity, reflected in this quote from a young woman:

> It kind of made me grow up faster than I should have because now it's like I think about my baby first before I think about myself. . . . Before, I don't care about nothing and, you know, I'm goin to do what I want to do. And then when I had my baby, I thought of him first and I changed my way of thinking. (Moloney et al. 2011, 13)

Parenthood is a clear example of a turning point, redirecting one's identity in unescapable ways. For young female gang members, there is a marked discrepancy between the gang and mother identity.

But parenthood works in other ways, including notable changes in expectations and routines. Accompanying motherhood are the extensive responsibilities with infants, along with the burdens to support a family, leading mothers to "retreat from the street" (Moloney et al. 2011, 1). The transformations of identity and routines are what probably cause a 93 percent reduction in the likelihood of gang membership when young gang-involved females become mothers (Pyrooz, McGloin, and Decker 2017). The results for males, in contrast, are less universal and, in fact, at least partly help to disentangle identity and responsibilities or routines. Fathers who were involved in the child's life, as measured by whether they lived together, reduced their likelihood of gang membership by 72 percent, while fathers who were residentially absent saw no changes in their gang membership, reflecting sentiments such as the following:

> I didn't even wanna be out there. I wanted to get a legal job . . . Instead of being out on the street, I was in the house or the hospital . . . I wasn't smoking weed or doin' drugs . . . Bein' more responsible, more disciplined. And stopped chillin' outside as much . . . I stopped robbin' people, stealin' cars. (Moloney et al. 2009, 312)

It is not simply the role transition to father that matters; it is performing the role of father that brings change.

Romantic partners—such as a girlfriend, baby's mother, or wife—also serve to pull gang members out of the gang. This school-aged former gang member exemplifies this influence clearly:

> You find a girlfriend . . . You stop talkin' to your friends because your girlfriend's telling you "Your friends are all hoodlums." And she starts describing all your friends as bad people. And then one day you realize, like, if she keeps talking about all these friends, that I used to be exactly just like, and she's saying so much bad things, like, "Why would I want to be like that?" (D. Carson 2018, 460)

In this instance, the girlfriend is prompting the first doubts about gang identity, consistent with Sampson and Laub's (2016) contentions about structure inducing transformation. In slight contrast, a former gang member from Southern California stated,

> The crazy stuff wasn't for me no more. I saw other guys go down and I knew it was just a matter of time before I paid the price, you know. I met my girlfriend and she was always on me about getting out of the gang. She gave me a reason, but I was already tired. I was tired of fighting all the time, running around all the time. (Vigil 2002, 63)

In this instance, both the push and the pull work together, consistent with Giordano et al.'s (2002) contention that people must be open to change and perceive the "hook" (i.e., the romantic partner) as important for social controls to truly act as a hook for change. We should further acknowledge that age matters a great deal when balancing questions of identity and structure. For gang members in their midteens, romantic partners may have the influence but rarely the staying power to prompt such cognitive openness to change. Neither male nor female gang members afforded much influence to relationships in the motivation to leave the gangs (O'Neal et al. 2016).

"Nothing stops a bullet like a job" was once the slogan of Homeboy Industries, a celebrated gang intervention project (G. Boyle 2010). Much like family, jobs perform as turning points because they correspond with role transitions to new identity and status, restructure routine activities along the lines of the workday, and impose social controls that promote stakes in conformity. Just under half of the former gang members included in Roman, Decker, and Pyrooz's (2017) summary of studies reported job responsibilities as the reason for leaving. It is important to highlight the precarious economic position of gang members, who rarely have the education or training to secure primary labor market employment and as such have spotty and unlucrative legal work histories (Augustyn, McGloin, and Pyrooz 2019; Chapter 10).

Religious transformation is a motivation for leaving gangs. Religiosity and spirituality can promote identity transformation from a "man of the street" to a "man of God" (Deuchar 2020; Flores 2013). Qualitative studies point to the religious awakening observed in the disengagement process—for example,

> [I left] because I found God. I needed God in my life, so I decided to serve God. (Decker and Pyrooz 2020)

"Gang member" and "follower of God" are viewed as discordant identities. It is not that gang members cannot go to church or be spiritual but that both identities assume outsized roles requiring a fair amount of cognitive dissonance—for example,

> Got closer with God and I was not in agreement with what they were doing. If I was going to be part of something, I want to help others and do good thing. I also want to live for my family and shouldn't have joined a gang in the first place. (Decker and Pyrooz 2020)

For men in transition between the gang and a "normal" life, a religion-infused narrative can transform individual dispositions and understandings of manhood in a way that prevents ex-gang members from feeling emasculated by the process (Flores 2013, 2016; Flores and Hondagneu-Sotelo 2013). Gang members can even use religion strategically to signal their disengagement from gangs and convince a skeptical audience of their professed redemption by essentially using Pascal's wager that it is better to trust in God than not (Densley and Pyrooz 2019; A. Johnson and Densley 2018).

An emerging body of research finds that ex-gang members who convert and commit to religion may understand aspects of faith in ways that their non-gang coreligionists cannot (Deuchar 2018). There is something about hope, transformation, forgiveness, and grace that cannot be learned in a seminary or yoga class or by reading a self-help book; instead, it has to be learned and earned by repenting one's sins. Gang victims and offenders suffer from deep wounds, the kinds that do not heal on their own (Deuchar 2018). Still, upon observing that only 8 percent of the 277 former gang members they interviewed identified religion as a motivation for leaving, Decker and Pyrooz (2020) held that religion was an influential yet narrow pathway for leaving. Religion, they held, did not "produce miracles" but instead functioned more as a method rather than a motive for leaving, results that we return to in the next section and in Chapter 10.

Mobility is the final pull factor identified in research on gang disengagement. Residential and school mobility can both function as pulls that knife off connections to the gang. About 14 percent of the 473 former school-age gang members in D. Carson, Peterson, and Esbensen (2013) reported school transitions or residential transitions as motivations for leaving. Emotional and social ties to the gang may transfer to the new location but likely subside over time as new relationships form and roles are assumed. Other forms of mobility may also knife off gang membership, such as prison:

> When you go to prison, you go to prison alone. I know 'cus I've been there. You've got to remember that in prison you get moved . . . you could get moved overnight. You could get moved to Scotland where it's like, "Who are you?" Your gang is nothing to them up there. (Densley 2013, 136)

Imprisonment in such instances is distinguishable from deterrent forces wrapped up in the criminal justice motivations highlighted above. People leave gangs not because they are tired of the consequences but because there is no gang with which to affiliate. Of course, prison gang dynamics are different in England than in the United States, but street gang affiliations take a backseat to prison politics, especially race and organizations (see also Bolden 2020; Maitra, McLean, and Holligan 2017).

Both pushes and pulls are critical to the disengagement process; they are complementary, not competitive. Rarely do former gang members identify only one reason, much less solely pulls or pushes, for leaving the gang (Roman, Decker, and Pyrooz 2017). Age appears to moderate the motivations for leaving the gang, as disengagement after the teenage years involved twice as many motivations for leaving than during them (Roman, Decker, and Pyrooz 2017). Outside of family reasons (namely, parenthood), gender did not correspond with much if any difference in the motivation for leaving (O'Neal et al. 2016). D. Carson (2018) observed racial/ethnic differences in motivations for leaving—61 percent of White youth, 48 percent of Latino youth, and 40 percent of Black youth reported pull motivations, while 52 percent of White youth, 66 percent of Latino youth, and 48 percent of Black youth reported push motivations. Correctional settings do not appear to heavily moderate the motivations for leaving; Pyrooz and Decker (2019) found similarities in the motivations for leaving on the street and in prison.

Whether the identity transformation that occurs with leaving the gang is spurred by rational future-oriented decision-making or by the structural imposition of social controls, it is important to understand that motivation may undergird action but does not guarantee it. Again, leaving the gang is a process, one that involves unwinding the ties that bind. This is why we need to examine the methods of exit. How does someone transition from peak to trivial levels of gang embeddedness?

How Do People Leave Gangs?

Methods for leaving gangs fall on a continuum of active to passive exits. Active exits entail a communicative exchange between the gang member and the gang, which can range from physical to verbal. Passive exits, in contrast, lack such communication, occurring without ceremony or hostility. Both involve taking steps to leave the gang behind emotionally and socially. These steps can by characterized by intensity and duration. Some exits are intense and abrupt, while others are mild and gradual. We organize our discussion of the methods for leaving by active and passive exits, moving from more to less extreme.

A common refrain is that leaving the gang requires ceremonial violence—Decker and Lauritsen (2002) reported that many gang members believed they would have to "kill their mother" to leave their gang. To be sure, none of the mothers of the twenty-four former gang members they interviewed in St. Louis were harmed. But the notion of "blood in, blood out" does indeed have some merit. A nontrivial minority of former gang members indicated that they were "jumped out" or "smashed out" of the gangs, similar to being "jumped in" to join. This entails subjecting oneself to a beating by members of the gang, as this former prison gang member told us:

> I got jumped out by 20 or 30 people beating me up for a long time.
> That is when my ribs were broken. I was supposed to be dead, but by
> the grace of God I was able to leave. (Pyrooz and Decker 2019, 236)

Fourteen percent of former gang members in Texas prisons stated that they were jumped out of the gang. Other studies with large samples across diverse study sites have similar findings. For example, D. Carson, Peterson, and Esbensen's (2013) study of school-age youth in seven U.S. cities revealed that 24 percent of the former gang members reported having to fight other members to leave. In the signaling perspective, such departures represent "costly extractions" (Densley and Pyrooz 2019). They are costly because they are physically expensive—gang members literally pay a physical price to leave. They represent honest signals of exiting because they are public and hard to fake. As one former member stated,

> I mean I took off my shirt; I was ready to get beat down. And it would've been worth it to me to be out of here. And I told them no matter what, when I leave tonight, that I'm done and it's over with and I don't want to hear anything that I didn't get jumped out because I was letting them know right then, "let's do this right now, I don't care how; it has to happen tonight, I was leaving—I'm out." (Bolden 2013, 12)

Ceremonial violence is indeed intense but of low duration, tantamount to ripping off the Band-Aid—painful, but short-lived. Rather than dragging out identity transformation, these rituals help facilitate the role exit expeditiously, especially as gossip works its way through public channels to validate post-gang status.

Other active exits can involve low intensity and duration, such as seeking permission or giving notice. Both exits involve notification of intentions to leave the gang, but they differ in whether someone is asking or telling the gang. For example, 23 percent of the former gang members in D. Carson, Peterson, and Esbensen's (2013) study indicated that they were allowed out by gang leaders. The gang often vets the motivations for leaving, as evidenced in this quote by a former prison gang member in Texas:

> Spoke with my fellow gang members and the leaders or the ones that were leading on the unit, the top rank. I told them what my plans were, what I wanted to do, that I wanted to get out, but still be in good standing. They asked me why. Said my age and I was just tired of this shit. They took a vote among the rank there, took it to the table which is the main man and let me know their decision. They got a positive response, favorable vote, and they put me in retirement. (Pyrooz and Decker 2019, 238)

Conveying the right signals for leaving is important in this regard. As Pyrooz and Decker (2011) found, none of the gang members who left for pull reasons, such as family or employment, were subject to hostile exits, whereas 30 percent of the gang members who left for push reasons were. In the eyes of the gang, some reasons appear more valid than others (which we guess is true about many decisions in life). "Giving notice" was not exactly seeking permission but giving the gang a heads-up that they were leaving. Pyrooz and Decker (2019) reported that giving notice was quite common in prison, as 34 percent of the 213 former gang members who left their gang in prison endorsed this method.

Interventions designed to facilitate disengagement from gangs are typically of prolonged duration but check off the boxes of signaling (i.e., enrolling/participation is hard to fake), screening (i.e., vouching for true intentions), and credible commitments (i.e., separating the past and present) (Densley and Pyrooz 2019). Some of these interventions are therapeutically grounded (e.g., FFT-G; Thornberry et al. 2018), some are activity-based (e.g., boxing; Deuchar 2020), and still others maintain a religious foundation (e.g., Pentecostalism; A. Johnson and Densley 2018). In Chapter 14, we examine interventions that work in facilitating exit from gangs. Suffice it to say, in all instances interventions are age-graded. Rarely do interventions appear in the narratives of adolescent gang members, but they are found more regularly among adult gang members. About 12 percent of former gang members in Texas indicated that they had leveraged a prison-based intervention to leave the gang, called Gang Renouncement and Disassociation, or GRAD:

> I had to contact someone in the gang and tell them I was going to attend GRAD. Had to write an I-60 to gang intelligence and tell them I wanted to renounce being a member of the Aryan Brotherhood. I had to tell someone at rank of the Aryan Brotherhood. I shot him a kite explaining that I was wanting to get out. Doesn't mean I got his good graces, just means that I can do what I have to do and it doesn't mean I won't be retaliated against. (Pyrooz and Decker 2019, 238)

This, of course, is an extreme example, as giving notice will not absolve the risk of intense reactions from the gang. Moreover, the GRAD program is prison-based, requires two years, and is moored to exiting solitary confinement. There are many street-based interventions that can be leveraged for exit purposes, but we know little about their efficacy (Roman, Decker, and Pyrooz 2017; Chapter 14).

Religion may not sound like an intervention, but it absolutely constitutes a viable pathway out of the gang. We attribute this to two developments. The first is Father Greg Boyle's initiative to establish Homeboy Industries as a leading gang rehabilitation program where spiritual transformation serves as a core mechanism for change. Flores (2013, 2016) found that the religious practices of Homeboy Industries and Victory Outreach facilitate a new "moral universe" oriented around conventional rather than street masculinity. Status comes with being a "man of God" and "family man," not a shot-caller or fighter. Flores expertly highlighted "the podium" provided by the church to validate the role exit, serving as a strong and public signal of disengagement (Decker at al. 2014; Densley and Pyrooz 2019).

Studies in the canon of life-course criminology (e.g., Veysey, Martinez, and Christian 2013; Loomis 2019) contend that religion works as a "hook for change" for gang offenders, as a form of social capital, by teaching and encouraging prosocial behavior, by serving as a resource for emotional coping, and by providing opportunities to build prosocial relationships. This is especially true in Latin America, where religious groups are even inspired by gangs and incorporate aspects of gang organization into their work (Brenneman 2011, 2014; A. Johnson and Densley 2018; J. Rosen and Cruz 2019; Salas-Wright, Olate, and Vaughn 2013). In these settings, gangs constitute a form of governance that highly respects the church and its religious practices, as a Brazilian prisoner explained:

> I started to praise the name of Jesus Christ my savior right there in prison, you know . . . The gang let me leave because they could see the sincerity in my heart. They could see that it wasn't lies leaving my lips, and that the tears rolling down my cheeks were not lies. (A. Johnson and Densley 2018, 12)

Intentions matter, however, as exploiting religion as a false flag could be consequential. Although less common, gangs also respect religious transformations in the United States. Even though religion was not a factor in leaving, a former prison gang member shared,

> I told [Texas Chicano Brotherhood] what I planned to do and if they had a problem with it, to take care of it. They didn't have a problem with it, but they wanted me to make sure to tell people that I was an ex-member because of my religion. So it would put out a better worldly image. (Pyrooz and Decker 2019, 239)

This is why Decker and Pyrooz (2020) viewed religion more as a method than as a motive for leaving the gang, although it appears to be the path less taken in the United States than in Latin America.

Mobility is also a method of leaving the gang. D. Carson, Peterson, and Esbensen (2013) found that "moving away" was reported as the method of leaving the gang for 14 percent of former gang members in their study. It is important to distinguish between purposive and normative mobility. For example, Bolden (2013) highlighted actions taken by gang members to join the military or families moving to new cities to escape the gang. In contrast, the normative transitions, such as moving from middle to high school or residential mobility unrelated to gangs, may indeed knife off connections to gang peers, but they are not purposive—more of a motive than a method. One former gang member said,

I was talking to my friend the other day, he's like "Man, if you woulda kept going to [Previous School]" he's like "Who know where you woulda been right now" and I was like "Yeah that's pretty crazy" I could be, my life could be, you know, totally different direction, but yeah, goin' over to [Current School]' and settling down, focusing on school and college. (D. Carson et al. 2017, 405)

D. Carson and colleagues (2017) examined normative and nonnormative school transitions, finding that both were associated with gang leaving—27 percent of all instances of gang leaving were timed with a school transition. However, once accounting for time trends, only normative transitions mattered, a likely consequence of observing far more normative (2,263 total) than nonnormative (573 total) school transitions in their sample. They further demonstrated that school transitions (of both types) corresponded with reductions in peer group size, more prosocial peers, greater school commitment, lower parental monitoring, and less violence neutralization and anger. In this sense, mobility is a positive for current and former gang members. When asking gang-involved youth what would help facilitate exit from gangs, J. Sharkey, Stifel, and Mayworm (2015) reported a strong need for confidentiality to support sustained identity transformation, which included moving to a new town, name changes, and witness protection.

The final method of leaving the gang is the most common yet involves the least intensity: walking away. Fifteen of the twenty-four former gang members in Decker and Lauritsen's (2002) study in St. Louis simply stopped hanging out with the gang. Nearly 80 percent of the eighty-four youth arrestees in Maricopa County reported that they walked away from their gang (Pyrooz and Decker 2011). D. Carson, Peterson, and Esbensen (2013) found that about half of the former youth gang members in their multicity study "just left" the gang. Among Texas prisoners who left the gang while incarcerated, 12 percent said they stopped associating, while 27 percent offered no explanation for their method of departure. This may reflect the transient nature of most group memberships.

We should clarify that there are several variants of this theme, all of which represent passive exits that lack a shared understanding brought about by a communicative exchange between gang and gang member. Stopping associating with the gang is not easy, however. In the context of prisoner reentry, Taxman (2017) poignantly titled her essay on social networks, "Are You Asking Me to Change My Friends?" This is a big ask, regardless of developmental stage—one that requires exercising a great deal of discretion. One former gang member in Phoenix explained to us the steps she took:

Well, like, first of all, like when they would call me to hang out I wouldn't answer my phone. I wouldn't answer my text messages.

> When they would go to my house, I'd tell everybody to tell them I wasn't home, but just mainly trying to avoid them. It was over in like a couple weeks.

There is no ceremony or ritual in her statement, even though actions were taken to avoid the gang. Other passive exits involve what Brenneman (2011) termed "calmado," or gradually fading away from the gang. Often gang members describe this as "doing nothing" or "just leaving" because this method is devoid of action. People fade away from the gang without much fanfare. This might seem like add odd method of departure, but comparable movements away from church or community organizations are indeed common.

We have taken pains to establish that gang leaving is typically a process, not an event, in the life course. It does not unfold overnight. And with that process of unwinding gang ties, a "residue" is left behind well after deidentification as a gang member (Bubolz and Lee 2020). That residue can be described by Flores's (2013) emphasis on the embodiments of gang life, some soft and malleable, like a shaved head, tattoos, and clothing, others hard and inflexible, like a criminal record, drug addiction, and subconscious reactions. There are also emotional and social ties to the gang, which subside with time, but not necessarily quickly or without effort (Pyrooz, Decker, and Webb 2014). Bubolz and Lee (2020) emphasized several dimensions of the residue, including symbolic forms (e.g., self-presentation, including gang symbols), demeanor (e.g., aggressive posturing), and worldview (e.g., gang codes), which are conveyed in statements like the following:

> White shirts, I like wearing white shirts with black jeans or the opposite . . . maybe to a certain extent I could still feel like I'm still that tough guy, that macho guy, that guy from Fremont Street [gang name] but I don't have to display those colors and represent it in that aspect . . . there's maybe a little bit of power there still. (Bubolz and Lee 2020, 8–9)

The residue of gang life is important to understand, as violence or incarceration can reignite gang ties and potentially affiliations—intermittency in gang members is quite common (Pyrooz 2014b; Thornberry et al. 2003). Those who retain ties to the gang remain at greater risk of victimization (Pyrooz, Decker, and Webb 2014), and the stigma of the gang far exceeds exit, potentially even as gang embeddedness falls to trivial levels (Lee and Bubolz 2020; J. Rosen and Cruz 2018). What former gang members are most concerned about is not negative reactions from their gang or rival gangs but the police (Decker et al. 2014), reflected in this quote:

I could take a walk from here down to the store and I might get, you know, pulled over by an officer and . . . they might just jump out on me and want to pat me down and I'm wondering why, because I'm wearing this. (Lee and Bubolz 2020, 72)

Plenty of ex-gang members remain stuck in police gang databases (Chapter 11). This is why effective signaling is so important. Eliminating information asymmetry avoids role ambiguity, which is important across many different roles, but in the case of gang members it could determine whether they get placed in a gang database, receive a gang sentencing enhancement, or even live or die.

Conclusion

This chapter has demonstrated that gang membership is not a lifelong commitment. Nearly everyone who joins a gang also leaves one. The norm is to leave the gang after one to two years; the exception is prolonged membership across developmental stages. Leaving the gang is a process, not an event. This helps explain why it is not always straightforward to distinguish current and former gang members. Reducing levels of embeddedness is central to the disengagement process, which is undergirded by the motivations and methods for leaving the gang. Although gangs are distinct from other types of pro- and antisocial groups, the exit process is not unlike leaving these groups. A collection of pushes and pulls are the motivating factors for leaving, with disillusionment and family as the most common reasons, which typically act in tandem rather than isolation. Gang members leave the gang through active and passive methods, although most walk away from the group on their own accord. The residue of gang life far outlasts membership, resulting in discrimination and victimization, which is why reducing information asymmetry is so important to establishing public identity as a former gang member and trivial levels of gang embeddedness.

6

Gangs, Crime, and Violence

Turn up or die on Tooka
u Nobody until Somebody kill u dats jst real Shyt
—@Tyquan Assassin, April 10, 2014

Gakirah Barnes, who went by the Twitter handle @TyquanAssassin, was shot dead the day after the above tweet was posted. Gakirah was featured in A&E's *Secret Life of a Gang Girl* (https://www.aetv.com/spe cials/secret-life-of-a-gang-girl-the-untold-story), credited with up to seventeen shootings or killings to her name. She joined a Gangster Disciple set—Tookaville—located on Chicago's South Side, about one mile down the road from the University of Chicago, at age thirteen after a close friend was murdered. Gakirah was very active on social media and was an early adopter of Twitter, using it to express aggression and grief to her large group of followers (Patton, Sanchez, et al. 2017). On April 11, 2014, she tweeted her location to a friend, and not long after she was shot nine times and died in the heart of her gang's Woodlawn territory at age seventeen. The shooter was likely a member of the rival Black Disciples set who lived a few blocks away.

Accounts of gangs in popular imagery—such as news and social media—are often criminal, focusing on drug dealing, school violence, prison riots, stabbings, and drive-by shootings. Dynamics found within gangs have long been thought to give rise to crime and violence. Yet there is not perfect agreement among policymakers, practitioners, and researchers that the gang itself is responsible for these violent actions. Instead, some view gangs as reified and exploited by news media for sensationalized coverage, elected officials for political gain, the criminal justice system to inflate budgets, and academics—like ourselves—to support their careers.

The purpose of this chapter is to understand gang violence and the criminal activities and victimization experiences of gang members. What role did the gang play in influencing the violence Gakirah perpetrated and experienced? More importantly, had Gakirah never affiliated with the Gangster Disciples, would she still be alive today? In this chapter, we take stock of what we know about the following questions:

- Are gang members overrepresented as perpetrators and victims of crime?
- What types of crime are perpetrated and experienced by gang members, from property to drug to violent crimes?
- What explains the relationship between gang membership, offending, and victimization?
- How do the group processes of the gang aid in understanding the nature of gangs and their implications for offending, victimization, and their overlap?

These areas of study have been among the most important in research on gangs. Part of what has drawn such interest is that the implications of these findings are far-reaching. If gangs do not cause crime, as J. Katz and Jackson-Jacobs (2004, 94) noted, the literature on gangs would "be read very differently, to the extent that it would be read at all." The stakes are higher than that. As M. Klein and Maxson (2006) observed, gangs have required sustained political responses at the local, state, and federal levels and special attention from criminal justice and other agencies. Why devote precious resources to gangs if other causes are to blame?

Overrepresentation of Gang Members as Offenders and Victims

The homicide rate in the United States is around 5 per 100,000 people, but for young Black men classified as gang members by St. Louis–area law enforcement, the murder rate was around 950 per 100,000 persons, according to a recent study (Pyrooz, Masters, et al. 2020). Compared to young Black males in the United States and in St. Louis, gang members were around twelve and three times more likely to die of homicide, respectively. What makes these differences starker is that St. Louis suffers from high rates of violence (Hipple et al. 2019). But St. Louis is not unique in this regard. Studies from across the country—Chicago (Levitt and Venkatesh 2001), Milwaukee (Hagedorn 1998a), Philadelphia and Phoenix (Chassin et al. 2013), and Pittsburgh (Loeber and Farrington 2011)—all point to exceptional risk of premature death among gang members. In contrast, El Salvador, which ranks among the most violent countries in the world, logs "only" 61 homicides per one hundred thousand persons. United States military casualties from Operation Iraqi Freedom maintained an annual rate of 335 hostile deaths per 100,000 soldiers between 2003 and 2007 (Goldberg 2010). It is clear that isolating gang membership from other sources of mortality captures acute risk of early death.

Gang members are also involved disproportionately in crime and delinquency. Esbensen and colleagues (2010) compared patterns of violent offending between 522 youth in gangs and 5,226 non-gang youth in the first national evaluation of the school-based G.R.E.A.T. program. In the year prior to being interviewed, 78 percent of gang youth reported hitting someone (vs. 44 percent of non-gang youth), 47 percent attacked someone with a weapon (vs. 9 percent), 26 percent robbed someone (vs. 3 percent), 79 percent participated in a gang fight (vs. 11 percent), and 30 percent shot at someone (vs. 2 percent). Altogether, 84 percent of gang youth reported engaging in serious violence, while just 17 percent of non-gang youth reported the same behaviors. And it is not just a difference of proportions that emerges; it is also a difference in rates. Gang youth reported an average of thirteen violent incidents, compared to five among non-gang youth.

Table 6.1 displays a summary of findings from eleven meta-analyses—quantitative syntheses of an empirical relationship—of fifteen different factors associated with offending, which covers most leading criminological theories. Studies are rank-ordered by the standardized effect size, where larger values indicate a strong association with offending. There have been 179 studies derived from 107 independent datasets that have quantified the relationship between gang membership and criminal offending a total of 1,649 times, revealing a meaningful and robust association ($Mz = 0.23$). Gang membership was not the strongest correlate, but it did rank among the top five, landing between low self-control and differential association theories of criminal offending.

If gang members are involved in so much crime, just what types of crimes do they commit? Determining whether gang members are generalists or specialists and low-level or violent offenders are also important issues to address. Traditionally, gangs were thought to engage in specialized offending, such as drug dealing or robbery. Yet several decades ago, M. Klein (1971, 125) was among the first to push back against that claim, instead contending that gang members are generalists who engage in the "cafeteria-style" offending we highlighted in Chapter 1.

Drug Use

Most ethnographic studies (e.g., Decker and Van Winkle 1996; Fleisher 1998; Hagedorn 1998; Joan Moore 1991; Padilla 1992) document regular marijuana use by gang members. Survey researchers have also documented

TABLE 6.1 SUMMARY OF EFFECT SIZES FROM 11 META-ANALYSES ON FACTORS ASSOCIATED WITH OFFENDING

Authors	Year	Explanatory variable	Effect size (Mz)
Vazsonyi, Mikuška, and Kelley	2017	Low self-control	0.350
Gallupe, McLevey, and Brown	2019	Peer influence	0.321
Ogilvie et al.	2011	Executive functioning	0.292
Pratt and Cullen	2000	Low self-control	0.257
Pyrooz et al.	2016	Gang membership	0.227
Pratt et al.	2010	Differential association	0.225
Pratt et al.	2010	Definitions of law violation	0.218
Ttofi, Farrington, and Lösel	2012	School bullying perpetration	0.193
P. Kelly et al.	2015	Religiosity	|0.190|
P. Kelly et al.	2015	Church attendance	|0.180|
Pratt et al.	2002	ADHD	0.155
Moule and Fox	2020	Code of the street	0.110
Pratt et al.	2010	Modeling/imitation	0.103
Pratt et al.	2010	Differential reinforcement	0.097
Ttofi, Farrington, and Lösel	2012	School bullying victimization	0.096
Pratt, Turanovic, and Cullen	2016	2D:4D (finger) ratio	0.047

Note: Mz refers to the standardized correlation coefficient. Vertical lines indicate an absolute value.

extensive drug use among gang members. As one gang member in St. Louis put it, "everybody and they mama smoke weed" (Decker and Van Winkle 1996, 134). But there is less agreement with regard to harder drugs, such as cocaine, methamphetamine, and heroin. Some gangs take a stance against hard drug use:

> We might smoke every once in a while but no cocaine, no Primos [marijuana mixed with cocaine]. I know what that shit can do to you and if I catch anybody, [for example] like one of my boys, he used to sell dope, he turned into a smoker. I beat the piss out of that man. I said you in violation, you lucky you don't get capped. We don't want you around no more and the homie ain't around no more. (Decker and Van Winkle 1996, 136)

But this isn't necessarily the case for all gangs. Some gangs consider how drug use impacts the gang's drug-dealing activities:

> We'll tell them don't take no losses. You wait until you finish selling and then you can buy whatever you want to buy with your own

money but don't fuck up our profits. You mess our things up . . . we will beat his motherfucking ass cause we took a loss. (Decker and Van Winkle 1996, 139)

And still other gangs take no stance on drug use among members. When asked what the gang would do to hard drug users, one member said,

Nothing, that's they life they wasting. (Decker and Van Winkle 1996, 137)

While we use St. Louis gangs to illustrate these opposing viewpoints, we believe this provides a strong characterization of drug use within gangs.

Over the last two decades, we have gained a better understanding of the patterns of drug use among gang members through urinalysis and self-report research. The Arrestee Drug Abuse Monitoring system was designed to monitor drug patterns among arrestees using urinalysis. Decker (2000) and C. Katz, Webb, and Decker (2005) studied drug use in an eleven-city sample of nearly eight thousand arrestees and an Arizona subset with over nine hundred juvenile arrestees, respectively. The arrestees were questioned about their experiences using drugs, guns, gang membership, and drug sales. In addition, all subjects provided a urine sample to test for the presence of drugs. Decker (2000) found that gang members were more likely to test positive for marijuana use than non-gang subjects, but the opposite was true for cocaine usage. In the Arizona study, however, even after accounting for demographic factors, criminal history, and school attendance, current gang members were more likely to test positive for marijuana, crack cocaine, and powder cocaine usage. Similar findings are observed regardless of using self-report or urinalysis data, meaning that gang members are reliably reporting their usage.

Drug Dealing

The distribution of drugs is closely associated with gangs. We discussed this in Chapter 3 as it relates to the organizational structure of gangs. The weight of the evidence suggests that the coordinated distribution and reinvestment in drug sales by the gang was the exception, while the norm appeared to be that gangs are composed of individual drug-dealing entrepreneurs.

There is considerable variation across gangs in their involvement in drug sales. Nearly all field studies find that gangs are involved in drug dealing to at least some degree. Joan Moore (1991) observed among gangs in East Los Angeles that drug-dealing gang members typically turned to their fellow gang members as dealers and customers. In contrast, as Felix Padilla (1992) documented among the "Diamonds" gang of second-generation Puerto Rican immigrants in Chicago, drug dealing was the primary criminal activity of the gang, and many gang members referred to it as "work" in the very same way they referred to legitimate jobs. A prison gang member we interviewed in Texas indicated that selling was part of the initiation:

> I had to prospect for six months. I had to follow the rules and do what they asked me to do, like selling drugs and cooking drugs. Methamphetamine was my specialty.

But Decker and Van Winkle (1996) made an important observation among St. Louis gangs—only 20 percent of their participants were involved in drug dealing:

> All of the gangs in our sample contain particular cliques and individuals who are more heavily involved in drug trafficking, both as sellers and suppliers. To some extent this is age dependent, as well as dependent on length of membership. (170)

Not all members of gangs participate in drug dealing at the same level. Younger, newer, and less embedded gang members may encounter barriers to drug dealing, as they have not accrued the criminal capital (i.e., experience, "doing dirt") to generate the necessary trust and responsibility. Research in the United Kingdom suggests that some people selling drugs for gangs are not necessarily "gang members" at all but rather exploited youth and vulnerable adults who are coerced into drug dealing through debt bondage (Harding 2020; McLean, Robinson, and Densley 2020). Also, not all gang members want to or are able to participate in the drug-related activities of the gang. Together, this leads to the conclusion that most gangs are involved in the distribution of drugs, but not all gang members sell drugs.

Gangs offer many advantages to those who sell drugs, regardless of whether drugs are distributed among gang members in an instrumental or informal manner. These advantages include opportunity, economic, substance, and protective components. Gang membership offers the convenience of a (generally) reliable point person or contact who provides the access to drugs. As a result of this convenience, gang membership creates the opportunity to sell drugs for profit or for personal use, all while maintaining the backing of the gang, thereby reducing victimization risk (Decker and Van Winkle 1996; Fagan 1989; Waldorf 1993; Valdez and Sifaneck 2004). The opportunity to sell drugs is therefore widespread among gangs, allowing members to sell at some point in their gang careers.

Further evidence suggests that drug dealing might not live up to the hype. Large amounts of capital were rarely accumulated (e.g., Padilla 1992), and the money generated from drug dealing was spent as quickly as it was earned (e.g., Decker and Van Winkle 1996; Hagedorn 1998; Joan Moore 1991). An early study on the returns to drug dealing among gang members in Chicago (Levitt and Venkatesh 2000) revealed that it does not pay the bills; hourly wages for gang leaders ranged from thirty-two to ninety-seven dollars and for foot soldiers or lower-level gang members from two to seven dollars. A larger quantitative study, which tracked individual gang members over time (Augustyn, McGloin, and Pyrooz 2019), revealed that illegal earnings were higher when someone joined a gang and continued their involvement but dropped when they left their gang, compared to periods when they were not in a gang (see Chapter 10).

Gun Ownership and Carrying

In his study of the Fremont Hustlers in Kansas City, Fleisher (1998) reported that the front door of the Hustlers' house was riddled by bullet holes from a drive-by shooting. Fleisher marveled at the firepower in Fremont's arsenal of stolen guns. In their interviews in St. Louis, Decker and Van Winkle (1996) found that nearly 80 percent of gang members owned a gun—four on average. A gun was the weapon of choice among St. Louis gang members, and like the Fremont Hustlers, they would burglarize houses in search of guns. In a study completed by two of the authors of this book (Decker and Pyrooz 2011), when a current gang member in Phoenix was asked about firearm carrying, he patted his waistband and said, "I got it right here." Of course, legislation in Arizona (SB1108, enacted in 2010) made concealed weapon carrying legal, although such nuances are typically lost on gang populations.

It comes as no surprise that gang members seek out weapons. Violence is a regular feature of gang life, and members have to be prepared to respond to assailants at any time. In her study of a Chicano gang in Chicago, Horowitz (1983) noted that gang members armed themselves in the belief that their rivals had guns; they sought to increase the sophistication of their weaponry in the hope that they would not be "left short"—that is, that they would not be caught in a shootout with less firepower than their rivals. Gangs engage in some form of a "weapons race," especially when immersed in conflict. Ninety-six percent, or 135 of 141, of homicides observed among individuals listed in the St. Louis–area police gang database were assault-by-firearm deaths (Tostlebe et al. 2020).

The link between gangs and guns was not always the case (Carlock and Lizotte 2015), as gun violence was the exception in gang research before the 1970s. Joan Moore (1978) reported that gang problems were handled with fists, bats, or even knives in East Los Angeles until the White Fence gang violated universal gang codes, including using guns to battle and carrying out drive-by shootings into households. Guns are more prevalent today than when these early observations took place.

One key question is how gangs obtain their weaponry. Hureau and Braga (2018) conducted what is undoubtedly the most comprehensive study on this topic. They studied the underground gun market among three gangs in Boston. The characteristics of 837 gang guns, or guns recovered from Boston gang members, and 1,359 non-gang guns differed. Gang guns were more likely to be handguns, to be recovered more recently after manufacturing, to be possessed by someone different from the purchaser, and to be sourced from New Hampshire, Maine, or I-95 southern states. Higher-caliber (e.g., .40 or .45) and higher-quality (e.g., Smith & Wesson) guns were rather common. Based on interviews, Hureau and Braga obtained the purchase price for 58 of the 77 handguns in the networks and compared it to the Blue Book of Gun Values, finding that gang members paid inflated prices from gun traffickers, a 200 percent markup on fair market value and 64 percent over full manufacturer suggested retail price; the markup was even greater for less expensive guns, pistols, and high-caliber guns.

Victimization

Focusing only on criminal activity could lead to the erroneous conclusion that gang members are not also victims of crimes. That could not be further from the truth. We should start with the recognition that adverse childhood experiences, or ACEs, are concentrated among gang populations, a point we elaborate on in Chapter 10. A twenty-six-year-old gang member in Fresno tattooed a paw print on his seven-year-old's hip, a symbol used by the Bulldog gang, making national headlines. The father was charged with six felonies involving child abuse and mayhem, facing life imprisonment, but was ultimately convicted of a corporal injury to a child and gang sentencing enhancements, receiving a six-year sentence.

Barrientez (2018) described the rampant emotional, physical, and sexual abuse that gang members from the Denver area experienced in their households as children. This included being forced to fight siblings (47–49), play Russian roulette (50), or physically assault their biological mother (51). One of her respondents reported instances of uncles blowing marijuana smoke in his face or taking LSD at age seven. Boys were expected to be men, protectors of the household, such as this example:

Nathan reported a time when he was six years old and a man broke into his house while his mom was out drinking. He ran into the closet with his five-year-old brother, as his mom had told him to do if this ever happened when she left them home alone. When the man opened the closet door, Nathan shot him in the neck with the shotgun that was hidden in the closet. For the next five hours, while he waited for his mom to come home, he described watching the life go out of the man, as the blood crept closer to his feet. (58–59)

We should be clear that the examples highlighted in Barrientez's research may not be representative, but they concentrate in gang populations to such a degree that they cannot be ignored. Childhood trauma has consequences that reverberate over the life course, including functioning as a pathway into gangs (H. Klein 2020; Wolff et al. 2020).

Yet, it is experiences within the gangs that are perhaps more commonly highlighted as examples of victimization. Ice Cube, in his song "Ghetto Vet," described the transition from being a triggerman to being confined to a wheelchair (https://www.youtube.com/watch?v=izofEX-NQEU). The trials and tribulations of being the veteran gangster that Ice Cube described are perhaps best exemplified in L. Ralph's (2014) *Renegade Dreams*. We started this chapter by illustrating the homicide mortality rate associated with gang members (in St. Louis), but nonfatal injuries like those described by Ice Cube are far more common. As part of his wide-ranging study, Ralph focused on renegade gang members turned paraplegic or quadriplegic in the Crippled Footprint Collective who would speak with young audiences across Chicago, sharing stories such as this:

Y'all know when you gotta use the washroom—you get that feeling, right? Well, when you're in a situation like ours, you no longer get that sensation. . . . So, what happens is that you gotta be on the clock. You know every four to six hours, you have to manually extract the urine. (128)

It would be a mistake to believe that firearm violence is the only, or even primary, source of victimization among gang members. In our interviews with older gang members, those who are original gangsters or veteranos, it is common to hear the refrain that "youngsters" resort too quickly to guns because they are afraid of the status loss from getting beat down in a fist fight. But these fights still occur, often involving weapons other than guns, such as bats, chains, brass knuckles, or knives. McLean and Densley (2020, 101) described a fight between two "teams" of gangs in Glasgow:

Jay drew out a large kitchen devil knife and ran into the crowd. As the Red Team fled, Ali ended up cornered, at which point Jay handed out several weapons to his peers. One Yellow Team youth took a set of knuckledusters, put them on and hooked Ali in the mouth so hard that he not only broke Ali's jaw but also his own hand. That same hand was lacerated from colliding with Ali's teeth, which were knocked out.

The key issue regarding the victimization of gang members is whether the gang is a refuge for people who have been victimized or worsens risk of victimization for people with or without such victimization histories. In other words, is the gang context the cause of this victimization? And, by the same token, is the gang context the cause of the elevated involvement in criminal offending? We now turn to theoretical issues at play.

Theoretical Models of Gang Membership, Crime, and Victimization

The study of street gangs has an important place in the history of criminology. In social disorganization theory, covered in Chapter 2, gangs were the primary transmitters of delinquent traditions across generations of youth (Shaw and McKay 1942; Thrasher 1927). In the "golden era" of criminological theory (Laub 2004), lasting through the 1960s, the explanation of gang behavior *was* the study of juvenile delinquency in several criminological classics (Cloward and Ohlin 1960; A. Cohen 1955; M. Klein 1971; W. Miller 1958; Short and Strodtbeck 1965; see M. Klein 1995, 52–57). But such high levels of interest in gang-related behaviors and processes soon gave way to broader criminological trends in theory and method. The focus of delinquency research shifted away from groups as the primary unit of analysis in criminology, either aggregating up to neighborhoods or disaggregating down to individuals (Bookin-Weiner and Horowitz 1983; Kreager, Rulison, and Moody 2011). While some viewed social processes as the bridge between macro and individual levels of explanation (Short 1974, 1985, 1998), gangs all but vanished from the mainstream criminological landscape in the 1970s. But this sabbatical did not last long. Beginning in the late 1980s, there was an explosion of gang research that has continued to this day.

Fueling this renewed interest was an eroding consensus concerning whether the street gang was indeed the primary source of the criminal behaviors we outlined above. This was not a new criticism (Glueck and Glueck 1950; Hirschi 1969), but gangs and gang membership found themselves wedged within the theoretical crosshairs of thorny debates surrounding control/propensity theories and learning/socialization theories (Akers 1985; M. Gottfredson and Hirschi 1990; Nagin and Paternoster 1991). Thornberry and colleagues (1993, 55–56) seized on the sentiment of the times, stating, "The link between gang membership and delinquency appears indisputable, but there is little information about the causal mechanisms that bring it about"

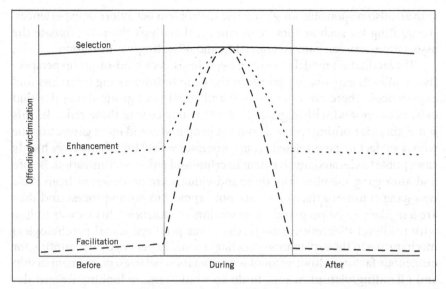

Figure 6.1 Theoretical models of the consequences of gang membership

Note: Between- and within-individual comparisons are made. "Before" refers to prospective gang members, "during" refers to active gang members, and "after" refers to former gang members.

(1993, 55–56). The primary issue was determining the extent to which gangs attracted or created delinquents. As a result, Thornberry and colleagues (1993) introduced a tripartite theoretical model—selection, facilitation, and enhancement—to bring the study of the gang membership–offending link into the broader debates in the criminological community. Figure 6.1 provides a visual representation of the empirical predictions from these models.

Thornberry et al.'s Selection, Facilitation, and Enhancement Models

The selection model is a spuriousness hypothesis. As a kind-of-people perspective, it holds that there is nothing special about the gang in bringing about problem behaviors or experiences. In this sense, gangs are a distraction, as purported gang members are highly prone to crime and violence regardless of their affiliation. Instead, gangs are a collection of young people with shared personal deficits. Some of these deficits could be resistant to change, such as impulsivity, risk-taking, intelligence, or neurological functioning, while others could be mutable yet unrelated to gangs, such as family, school, and negative life events. Whether factors are static or dynamic in the life course, what is important about the selection model is that both gang membership and offending share the same underlying tendencies. In other words, the same factors that are responsible for giving rise to gang membership are also responsible for giving rise to problem behaviors or experiences. Accounting for such factors in an empirical analysis should eliminate the association between gang membership and offending/victimization.

The facilitation model is a causal hypothesis. As a kind-of-group perspective, it affords explanatory power to the gang in influencing behaviors and experiences. There are interactional and situational group dynamics that exist between and within gangs that ultimately elevate these risks. In this sense, there is nothing special about the people who end up in gangs; anyone who is subject to gang-related group processes would find themselves highly susceptible to elevated involvement in crime and risk of victimization. Before and after gang membership, these individuals are no different from their non-gang counterparts, as they are not exposed to group process and thus are less likely to be perpetrators or victims of violence. This view is in line with midlevel theoretical perspectives that privilege social psychological mechanisms in the explanation of behaviors and experiences. Accounting for exogenous factors cannot account for association between gang membership and offending/victimization—to do so would require looking toward dynamics found within the group (issues we detail in the next section).

The enhancement model is a blended hypothesis. It acknowledges both people and groups in the explanation of behaviors and experiences. In contrast to a pure version of the selection perspective, the group maintains causal influence on its members. In contrast to a pure version of the facilitation perspective, the people who select into gangs are at greater risk of offending and victimization for reasons that have little or nothing to do with the group. What matters in the enhancement model is precisely how large a causal effect the group maintains. We now take stock of the research that has examined these models.

State of the Evidence on Theoretical Models

In the predecessor to this book, *Confronting Gangs* (third edition), Curry, Decker, and Pyrooz (2014) included a table summarizing twenty-eight empirical studies testing the selection, facilitation, and enhancement models. Since early 2012, when that table was produced, there have been many developments in the literature. While the volume of research has changed, the conclusions have not, at least not beyond having more confidence in them. There is some evidence in support of the pure facilitation model and little evidence for the pure selection model, while the enhancement model best represents the relationship between gang membership and offending. This conclusion is reached regardless of demographics of study participants, research design used to test the relationship, geographical location of the research, and measurement of gang membership and offending.

A recent meta-analysis isolated 825 effect sizes consistent with the facilitation model, which ignored complementary or rival explanations, and 109 effect sizes consistent with the selection model, which controlled for time-stable and/or exogenous influences (Pyrooz et al. 2016). There were notable differences in the effects of gang membership on offending between the facilitation (Mz = 0.262) and selection (Mz = 0.154) models, the latter of which was clearly weaker yet was nonetheless statistically and substantively significant. The authors stated that these patterns "seem to indicate a lack of adherence to either a pure selection or pure facilitation model" (381). Thus, the prevailing empirical reality is consistent with the enhancement model. Despite the value of meta-analysis to take stock of research findings, disentangling these models will always be in the domain of the single study, and we highlight one that perhaps best illustrates the pattern of enhancement.

Bjerk (2009) used five annual waves of data from nearly three thousand males in the National Longitudinal Survey of Youth 1997 who were between ages twelve and sixteen when they were first interviewed. He compared two groups of youth: those who were in gangs at least once during the five-year period and those who were never in a gang. First, there were differences in offending between these groups: gang members committed more crime than non-gang members, the very correlation confronted by Thornberry et al. (1993) nearly three decades ago. Second, offending was higher when people were active in gangs than when they were not, a within-individual comparison providing evidence of a facilitation effect. Third, when compared to people who never joined gangs, levels of offending were higher for people during periods when they were not active in gangs, a between-individual comparison providing evidence of a selection effect. Bjerk's findings in support of the enhancement model take on added significance since these data were representative of young people in the United States.

We believe that the debate over the causal effect of gang membership on offending is largely settled, but the specter of extraneous influences is likely to always remain because classic experiments to randomize gang membership are obviously unethical and natural experiments are rare to implausible, which means that researcher-controlled quasi-experiments (e.g., propensity score matching, within-family analyses) are about the best we can hope for. The accounting of biological and genetic confounding is one of the few areas that have yet to be granted serious consideration as jointly predisposing to gang membership and offending (e.g., Connolly and Jackson 2019). What remains perhaps the biggest gap in this literature is the inability to fully account for the gang membership–offending link. There is nothing inherently criminal about gang membership (even though some states have criminalized gang membership, see Chapter 13), and as such, the correlation with offending should be explained away. Despite rigorous research on the topic (e.g., Melde and Esbensen 2014), little progress has been made to this end. Isolating the precise mechanisms giving rise to elevated offending among gang members should be a top priority in future research, a point we return to shortly.

Controversy over Findings on Victimization

We have purposefully used language of "behaviors" and "experiences" to acknowledge that the consequences of gang membership are not limited to criminal offending. A small but growing body of research indicates that gang membership is linked to a broader spectrum of personal and social harms, including economic and social outcomes, such as education, joblessness, and family dynamics (Augustyn, Thornberry, and Krohn 2014; Gilman, Hill, and Hawkins 2014; Krohn et al. 2011; Pyrooz 2014a), as well as consequences for mental and physical health, such as anxiety, depression, PTSD, and suicidality (Coid et al. 2013; Connolly and Jackson 2019; Watkins and Melde 2016). This is on top of the gunshot wounds and other physical injuries associated with gang life. Such are the deleterious outcomes of gang membership that in his public talks, Father Greg Boyle describes joining a gang as a socially and culturally acceptable form of suicide among racialized and marginalized youth. Still, one area that has sparked controversy over the last decade is the empirical study of the impact of gang membership on victimization.

Does gang membership decrease, increase, or exert no influence on risk of victimization? Standing in contrast to hypotheses on offending, there are good reasons to anticipate that all three relationships may characterize the gang membership–victimization link. As discussed in Chapter 4, gang members regularly cite protection and safety as motivations for joining gangs; affiliating with a gang could thwart attempts at intimidation, robbery, theft, or violence, especially in dangerous neighborhoods. That must be contrasted against group processes in gangs that elevate risk of violence, as well as the fact that offenders and victims are often one and the same. Criminologists also began to point to the nonrandomness of victimization, emphasizing risky lifestyles, routine activities, and individual propensities (see Turanovic and Pratt 2019). Beginning in the 1990s, qualitative researchers began reporting on the victimization experiences of gang members in places such as Columbus (Jody Miller 1998), Kansas City (Fleisher 1998), St. Louis (Decker and Van Winkle 1996), and Texas (Molidor 1996). Those findings were bolstered by quantitative studies in the 2000s, particularly those by researchers working on the longitudinal evaluation of G.R.E.A.T. (D. Peterson, Taylor, and Esbensen 2004; T. Taylor et al. 2007, 2008). The consensus from this work was that gang membership exacerbated rather than lowered victimization risk.

Gibson and colleagues (2009) put the field on notice. They applied the Thornberry et al. (1993) models to victimization and reanalyzed the G.R.E.A.T.

data using methods that aimed to approximate an experimental research design. They concluded,

> Our results showed support for the selection perspective because the relationship between joining a gang and becoming violently victimized was explained by pre-existing differences that perhaps lead gang members to join a gang in the first place. (639)

The significance of their conclusion is that it locates the sources of gang members' high rates of victimization among the characteristics of the person, not the context of the gang. Not too long after, Ozer and Engel (2012) responded with a "cautionary tale" about the work of Gibson and colleagues, which they held was problematic because it ignored important correlates of gang membership, analyzed data only prospectively and not contemporaneously, inappropriately deflated variation in the measurement of victimization, and was built on a small sample size of twenty-two gang joiners matched to twenty-two non-gang joiners. They reached the following conclusion:

> Our reanalysis of these data call into question Gibson et al.'s (2009) reported support for the selection perspective, and demonstrate new findings that are consistent with the growing body of research examining the relationship between gang membership and victimization. . . . Researchers should be more cautious, and not blindly apply the statistical technique "de jour" without regard for its fit with the data available. (119)

This, of course, prompted a response from Gibson and colleagues (2012), who indeed offered thoughtful methodological commentary, including an excellent table summarizing studies on the topic. Unfortunately, they devoted much of their space to (fair) critiques of Ozer and Engel's work rather than acknowledging the limitations of their own. Controversy is nothing new to gang research, which has long entertained competing viewpoints, yet it is rare to observe such a methodologically heavy controversy unfold, much less in a flagship journal (*Justice Quarterly*).

Our view is that neither the Gibson and colleagues study nor the Ozer and Engel study brings solid (quasi-experimental) evidence to bear on the topic. Several methodological areas must be addressed to make (quantitative) contributions to research on the gang membership–victimization link:

- Use larger sample sizes. Studies seeking to detect between-group differences in victimization must be appropriately powered or run the risk of Type I (false negatives) error.

- Consider the measurement of victimization. Unless there is a theoretical rationale, victimization should be studied using prevalence and counts, since similarities in the former could mask differences in the latter.
- Estimate contemporaneous and prospective effects. Victimization recall periods must overlap with the contours of gang membership, or the effect of gang membership on victimization will be underestimated.
- Keep time in order. Measure confounding and mediating factors before and during gang membership, as joining a gang influences attitudes, behaviors, and experiences.
- Do not select on types of gang members. Allow gang onset to perform as a treatment condition by not selecting on cases with prolonged involvement unless there is theoretical reason to do so.

Our aim is to illustrate lessons learned from this important exchange, not to target the authors, whose works we read and respect. It also illustrates that there are not uniform opinions among the researchers who think about these issues and generate evidence on the topic. More recent evidence has emerged based on rigorous quasi-experimental designs (Barnes, Beaver, and Miller 2010; DeLisi et al. 2009; Ousey, Wilcox, and Fisher 2011; Sweeten, Pyrooz, and Piquero 2013; Turanovic and Pratt 2014; Wu and Pyrooz 2016; Watkins and Melde 2018), which universally reach the following conclusion: gang membership elevates risk of victimization.

Group Process and the Enhancement Effect

Short and Strodtbeck wrote one of the most impactful books in the annals of gang research, *Group Process and Gang Delinquency* (1965). Based on probably the most ambitious data collection effort undertaken in gang research (see Hughes 2015), Short and Strodtbeck reached the conclusion that individual- and community-level characteristics could not account for the elevated levels of delinquency found in gangs; instead, the explanation was centered on midlevel dynamics internal and external to the gang. In a key statement about gang violence, Papachristos captured this stance effectively:

> "Youth" does not pull a trigger nor anomie strangle a victim. *Murder is an action* . . . Gang members do not kill because they are poor, black, or young or live in a socially disadvantaged neighborhood. They kill because they live in a structured set of social relations in which violence works its way through a series of connected individuals. The gang qua group carries with it a set of extra-individual

adversaries and allies that shape individual choices of action, including the selection of murder victims. (2009, 75–76; emphasis added)

This has become known as the group process perspective, which refers to interactional and situational microlevel social processes. We have alluded to group process throughout this book and chapter, and we now elaborate on its core features. To do so, we draw heavily on the work of McGloin and Collins (2015), who wrote a key statement organizing and summarizing the bundle of group process mechanisms. Our take is that group process is what allows gangs to accomplish far more than they would as a sum of their individual members. The reasons are as follows.

Opportunity Structures

Gang ethnographers have long noted that gang members spend their time hanging around in parks and on street corners and cruising the avenues and boulevards (Decker and Van Winkle 1996; Densley 2013; Thrasher 1927; Vigil 1988). There are few social phenomena as street oriented as the gang. Papachristos and Hughes (2015) observed that gangs are defined by the streets, acquire power from the streets, and secure their mystique from the streets. In recalling his observations of gang members in Los Angeles, M. Klein (1995) notably summarized life in the gang as follows:

> For the most part, gang members do very little—sleep, get up late, hang around, brag a lot, eat again, drink, hang around some more. It's a boring life; the only thing that is equally boring is being a researcher watching gang members. (11)

Missing from these accounts is the purpose and structure typically found in rational organizations, such as businesses, professional organizations, or religious institutions. For example, a service organization like Rotary International maintains a membership roster with internal structure and meetings and committees to develop and advance their humanitarian goals.

Osgood and colleagues (1996) viewed unstructured and unsupervised socializing among adolescents as a situational inducement for crime and deviance. While some people may spend more time than others in such settings, this is a situational rather than individual theory. In contrast to structured activities, such as youth athletics or extracurricular groups, unstructured socializing is akin to the phrase that "idle hands are the devil's workshop." When in the company of peers, deviant acts are easier to accomplish (e.g., lookouts and backup) and are more symbolically rewarding (e.g., shared experiences and storytelling). The unsupervised nature of this socializing also means that authority figures, such as parents, teachers, or religious leaders, cannot exercise social control over youth.

Although this perspective was not developed with gangs in mind, it naturally fits the description of gang delinquency and the group process. Hughes and Short (2014) revisited the data that Short and Strodtbeck gathered in Chicago between 1959 and 1962, comparing the unstructured and unsupervised routine collective activities of 490 young people in 31 Black and White gangs and middle- and lower-class groups. Hughes and Short found that greater time spent hanging out together in the street, riding in cars, or at house parties resulted in more situational provocations resulting in fights. Based on panel data from the first national evaluation of G.R.E.A.T., Melde and Esbensen (2011) found that joining a gang increased the amount of time spent socializing in unstructured settings, which in turn increased levels of delinquency. The spontaneity of behavior also accords with opportunity structures in gangs, as Papachristos and colleagues (2015) have highlighted how social network proximity to gang members puts even non-gang members—by virtue of being linked through a police field interrogation report—at risk of gunshot victimization in Newark.

The relevance of opportunity structures extends beyond the situational inducements encountered while socializing with peers. From a criminal capital perspective (McCarthy and Hagan 1995, 2001), involvement in a gang widens the network of people with whom individuals associate. At the most basic level, this avails to gang members opportunities to identify co-offenders who maintain interests or skills to support the engagement in criminal activities. It also makes available information about potential lucrative criminal opportunities. For example, members can collaborate to sell drugs and capitalize on ties to wholesale distributors. But the criminal capital perspective extends beyond that, as the mentors and experiences in the gang allow members to develop competence and skills in ways that could or would not be achieved in the absence of the gang (McLean and Densley 2020; Morselli, Tremblay, and McCarthy 2006; Nguyen and Bouchard 2013). It is one thing to sell drugs but something much different to do it successfully.

Normative Influence

Psychologists and sociologists have long recognized the role of groups—families, schools, neighborhoods, political groups, and peers—in influencing attitudes and behaviors. The gang is one such group that takes on major significance in the lives of young people. In their study of ninety-nine active gang members in St. Louis, Decker and Van Winkle (1996) noted that:

> involvement in legitimate social institutions or with nongang peers
> and relatives drops dramatically following gang initiation. In most

> cases, gang life has an obsessively deadly attraction for our subjects, one which constricts and diminishes their life to the friendship group of the gang. (187)

It is a truism to recognize that all gangs are groups but not all groups are gangs. But gangs appear to maintain normative influences above and beyond typical delinquent peers and peer groups (Battin et al. 1998; D. Carson, Wiley, and Esbensen 2017; Dong and Krohn 2016). For example, Melde and Esbensen (2011) found that joining a gang reduced prosocial peers, school commitment, and guilt and increased violence neutralizations, negative peer commitment, anger and temper, and delinquent peer associations. The consensus from this research is that gangs are not simply extreme delinquent peer groups; socialization into the gang milieu shapes the actions and worldviews of their members. The unfolding of these processes bears a strong resemblance to social learning theory (Akers 2009), but personal and social identity and in-group/out-group boundaries in gangs take on a life of their own.

Social identity theory can explain the universal effects of social categorization on gang membership (Tajfel and Turner 2004) and is one of several major theories of intergroup relations that are relevant to gangs (Densley and Peterson 2018). The others are realistic conflict theory, an economic theory that assumes that people act in self-interest and intergroup conflicts are thus caused by people's drive to maximize their own or their group's rewards to the detriment of other groups' interests (Sherif 1966); equity theory, which argues that perceptions of injustice cause personal distress and intergroup conflict and explain why gang members may view the traits of their own gang, such as a tendency for violent retaliation, as virtuous but perceive those same traits as vices in rival gangs (Densley 2013); and relative deprivation theory, a theory that focuses on perceptions of inequality between groups, such as unequal access to territory or illicit markets, resulting in intergroup conflicts and oppression (Stouffer et al. 1949).

The gang offers definitions in support of law-violating behaviors. Some of this could involve the complete dismissal of the law as a governing authority (e.g., "the sale of drugs should *not* be illegal"), while some of this could entail temporary moral reprieve to neutralize actions (e.g., "they would have attacked us if we did not shoot first"). Normative beliefs are what shape the use of violence in the resolution of disputes and responses to intergroup provocations. This is why gang violence is more contagious than non-gang violence, leading to more offspring events (P. J. Brantingham et al. 2020). While gangs are known for their age-gradedness, more seasoned or respected members serve as models to imitate idealized performances and social roles. It is not uncommon for a younger member to adopt the moniker of a veteran member, sometimes with the prefix "younger" or "tiny" attached (Densley 2013). In some instances, entire gangs are named after a deceased member, such as

Gakirah Barnes's set being renamed after Shondale "Tooka" Gregory's murder. Given its resources and standing, the gang serves to differentially reinforce instrumental and symbolic expressions through the introduction or removal of positive or aversive stimuli. For example, standing up to a rival gang despite being outnumbered could yield status and prestige; backing down might result in guilt and shaming.

Identity is particularly salient in the gang context. Lauger (2020) recently outlined the value of identity for understanding gang performances, such as violence. Collective identity captures the distinction between in-group and out-group, typically expressed through names, symbols, signs, attire, shared experiences, and institutional memory, as well as alliance and rival gangs. Provocations, threats, and violence—which can occur online or offline—contribute to establishing group boundaries (Van Hellemont and Densley 2019). "Gang member" is one of many identities people embrace as a sense of self. This is why researchers typically rely on self-reports of gang status, as it allows the individual to self-identify rather than imposing the gang label on someone. Physical and verbal gang embodiments, such as visible gang tattoos, gang pronouncements on music videos, or public displays of gang violence, also serve as hard-to-fake but imperfect indicators of gang identification (Densley 2012b). The salience of gang identity, however, depends on how people prioritize their multiple social roles and the breadth and depth of gang to non-gang relationships. Stronger identification as a gang member should correspond with greater normative influences, leading to idealized expressions of gang performance. This could explain why gang embeddedness, which taps group identification and relationships, is related to higher involvement in crime and victimization (Sweeten, Pyrooz, and Piquero 2013).

Status Concerns

As we highlighted in Chapter 2, social status has occupied a central place in gang theories (Cloward and Ohlin 1960; A. Cohen 1955; W. Miller 1958). In places characterized by disadvantage, isolation, and marginalization, the gang represents one viable avenue to attain status. Social status refers to social standing and value assigned to people by others. Ascribed status is unearned, afforded by virtue of constitutional (e.g., height, gender, or race) or ancestral (e.g., class or wealth) characteristics. Achieved status is earned, typically based on meritorious actions (e.g., effort or competency). In relation to the delinquency of gang members, we are obviously interested in latter since it privileges social processes found in the group context.

While evaluations of ascribed and achieved status can be made by various social groups, from teachers to church leaders to community organizers,

Gravel and colleagues (2018) outlined the importance of social proximity. Meaningful status evaluations are made by people who share cultural and demographic similarities, such as age, class, gender, geography, offending, and race. For example, a young Latino gang member in Boyle Heights, Los Angeles, will not put much stock in a negative (or positive) evaluation from an elderly White woman in Bel Air, Los Angeles; there is simply too much social distance for that evaluation to hold sway. Instead, that same gang member would be concerned about reputational evaluations from gangs who share social similarity (Lauger 2012). Gravel and colleagues demonstrated with game-theoretical mathematical models that even minimal social distance is enough to bring about a sturdy fact about gangs: their group composition is highly homogenous and their violence almost exclusively intraracial, even in heterogeneous communities.

While these are broad statements about gangs and status, it is within the group context where status concerns can be particularly explosive. Short and Strodtbeck (1963, 1965) viewed status concerns as a core group process responsible for the instigation of acts of aggression. They focused primarily on the appraisal of actions and inactions among gang members. We must acknowledge that the age of gang members—typically teenagers—plays a role in the significance of status concerns. Teenagers are well known for their concerns about the opinions of their peers, and such concerns often motivate both prosocial and antisocial behavior (Ragan 2020; Steinberg and Monahan 2007). The maintenance of status within a group requires some level of adherence to group norms and consistency with the behavior of other members of the group. Groups are powerful socializing influences throughout the life course, but perhaps never more important than during adolescence. Establishing one's status in a group requires participation in what are defined as key activities—or what W. Miller (1958) termed "focal concerns"—by the group. For gangs, those activities include crime and violence.

Based on reports from street outreach workers, Short and Strodtbeck (1965) highlighted eight case studies in which interactions or situations could be construed as influenced by status concerns, and they often involved threats of status loss. A classic example is found in "Duke," a leader of the now-defunct King Rattlers, a Black gang with around fifty teenage members. Duke caught a case for a shooting, which he ultimately beat, spending over two months in jail. Yet Duke's status as a leader was not acknowledged upon his return to the community, which led to out-group provocations with the Junior Lords at a basketball game—publicly declaring, "The Lords ain't shit"—that were atypical for Duke and his leadership style (573). Short and Strodtbeck interpreted this behavior as a response to clarify leadership uncertainty, as Duke returned to his "cool image" once the status ambiguity was resolved.

McGloin and Collins (2015) highlighted the importance of inaction, especially in the company of fellow gang members or even third parties. This comports with Strodtbeck and Short's (1964) introduction of the utility-risk paradigm, which proposes that behavioral options and outcomes for (non) participation in gang violence are better described by aleatory risk calculation than by hedonism or irrational tendencies. Ridicule and social exclusion are important for all youth, but especially in the settings where gangs operate since opportunities for alternative status enhancements are limited (E. Anderson 1999). Based on observations about current and former gang members reentering society from prison, one of G. Scott's (2004) study participants noted,

> There's always that urgency when you get out, you know. You feel like you've lost two to three years. And the little guy you used to see out on the street, when you had a Cadillac and he only had a bicycle. And now you lost your Caddie, and you done your time in jail and come back out. Now he's got a Park Avenue, and you ain't got nothing . . . well, you gotta catch up now. Until you're lookin' for shortcuts, which makes you more vulnerable for getting popped off [arrested] again. (125)

Prisoner reentry is a humbling experience, made difficult due to material and nonmaterial deprivations. Missing out on street developments, especially witnessing children surpass former prisoners on the social ladder, could lead to status-enhancing, risky behavior. Status concerns are exacerbated in the gang context because the staging grounds where (in)actions occur typically include an audience of observers, primarily those who share a similar social standing. This can result in public displays of "costly" behaviors such as crime that are strategically cultivated in order to signal status to others (Densley 2012b).

Collective Behavior

There would be no such thing as a "gang" if it were composed solely of atomized individuals lacking collective identity. Yet it strains credulity to envision groups united only in collective identity without occupying physical space together. There are some instances of gang-like entities existing in the absence of physical connections, such as prison gang members locked away in solitary confinement or cybercriminal groups dispersed across the globe. Such groups, however, are situated at the margins of the distribution of gangs, and definitional accommodations must be made to incorporate them into the mainstream study.

Part of what makes gangs the subject of scientific inquiry as well as policy and practice is their collective behavior. As we noted in Chapter 1, Thrasher (1927) explicitly located collective behavior in the definition of a gang:

> an interstitial group originally formed spontaneously, and then integrated through conflict. (57)

Of course, nearly a century later, it is now possible for conflict to unfold online rather than on the street (Densley 2020; Lane 2018; Pyrooz, Decker, and Moule 2015). But Thrasher's next sentence directly engages the very collective behaviors that are critical to our discussion:

> [The gang] is characterized by the following types of behavior: meeting face to face, movement through space as a unit, conflict, and planning. (57)

Thrasher viewed these collective behaviors as central to the creation of group awareness and boundaries, attachment to place and space, and the development of tradition. He also viewed these collective behaviors as critical to group cohesiveness, a group process that took on an added importance in light of observations from succeeding generations of scholars.

M. Klein (1995, 43) referred to gang cohesiveness as the "quintessential group process." Cohesiveness is conceptualized in a variety of ways (M. Klein and Crawford 1967) but generally refers to the "sense of togetherness, solidarity, morale, or *esprit de corps*" of the gang (Papachristos 2013a, 51). This excerpt from Fleisher's (1998) *Dead End Kids* captures cohesiveness in action:

> Roger ran up and shouted, "Northeast is coming" . . . and the van's pass-through set in motion events that were terrifying: boys going to war. Fremont prepared for battle.
>
> Roger and a few others ran to the abandoned house where they kept their arsenal. One boy stood inside and tossed out the weapons one by one through the window. A boy standing outside took them and handed them to a third and fourth kid, who loaded each one and handed it to its owner. Shawn reached for his 12-gauge, Wayne for his, and so it went.
>
> At the same time boys came running from houses up and down Fremont carrying handguns; some concealed 9-millimeter handguns in their shorts. The excitement, the anticipation of the impending firefight electrified the air. Kids buzzed excitedly and talked about other shootings they'd been in and bragged in anticipation of this one. A few boys climbed onto the roof over Wendy's front porch and stood holding rifles and handguns.

Armed boys darted back and forth along the ridge between Wendy's and Afro's . . . "It's some funny shit, man" said a young warrior. "I'm gonna jump right out in the middle of the street. It's the Fourth of July!" . . . "I'm ready to rock 'n roll, ready to ride," exclaimed another. A boy holding a weapon announced, "I'm rollin on everybody that I fuckin' feel like shootin.'"

We waited—5 minutes, 10, 15. The Cruz brothers didn't show up. Afro, Chucky D, and House of Pain walked into Fremont's armed camp and said, "Da motherfuckers ain't around. Pussies." (54–55)

While cohesiveness is a characteristic of the gang, it is not immutable; cohesiveness fluctuates with dynamics internal and external to the group. In the case of the Fremont Hustlers observed by Fleisher, cohesiveness was amplified as kids were taking cover, guns were gripped tightly, and excitement and tension filled the air. It didn't matter that the threat petered out with little more than a whimper. What mattered was the imprint left in the memories of Fremont youth: they were prepared to fight (and die) on the gang's behalf.

M. Klein (1971, 1995; M. Klein and Maxson 2006) has long contended that these fluctuations are critically important to understanding gang crime and violence. Based on his early observations from the Group Guidance Project in Los Angeles, Klein found that increases in gang cohesiveness—via the assignment of street outreach workers—corresponded with increases in gang crime. His argument was that cohesiveness ensnares individuals in the gang, limiting members from prosocial influences outside of the gang—a group-level effect on gang member embeddedness. Cohesive groups are also more in tune with their normative orientations and can engage in the tit-for-tat violence so common in gangs, a point we return to in the following section. This is what leads to generalized violence, where all members of the gang are held liable for a single act of perpetration; likewise, all members of the aggrieved gang are responsible for responding to the shared victimization, creating a multiplier effect.

Gang researchers were not the only scholars who had something to say about the collective behaviors of gangs. In fact, M. Gottfredson and Hirschi (1990), who are perhaps most closely associated with the selection model discussed above, were attentive to the subtleties of the relationship between gangs and crime, interpreting it within their classical framework:

Groups imply immunity from sanction; they diffuse and confuse responsibility for the act, and they shelter the perpetrator from immediate identification and from long term risk of retribution. In some cases, they prevent sanctions through threats of retaliation. Groups, then, act as a mask and a shield, as a cover for activities that would not otherwise be performed. (209)

Gottfredson and Hirschi speak to what social psychologists call "deindividuation" (see Densley and Peterson 2018), their contention being that the anonymity and conformity within groups alter the utility function of crime, particularly its costs. While it may be true that the group maintains a causal effect on crime, as neither the "mask" nor the "shield" exists without it, the mechanism that brings about such behavior is the altering of preferences for risks and rewards (McGloin and Thomas 2019). This could help explain why Buchanan and Krohn (2020) found that deviant labels associated with arrest were not as stigmatizing—in terms of impacting self-esteem—for gang members and youth in delinquent groups as for youth without these peers. Just as the collective behaviors of gangs ease the commission of crime, they also mitigate the sting of responses to it.

Gangs, Networks, and the Cycle of Violence

In 1992, just a few miles from the Stanford University campus, located on the sunny Bay Area peninsula, there were fifteen separate shootings in twelve hours in East Palo Alto (Armstrong 1994), a small town with around twenty-five thousand residents plagued by crime and poverty. Drugs and gangs were believed to be the drivers of the violence. While homicide rates across the country remained around all-time highs in 1992, East Palo Alto received the dubious distinction of the murder capital of the United States, with 175 homicides per one hundred thousand persons. The cycle of gang violence and institutionalized networks of conflict are believed to give rise to extreme levels of violence observed in East Palo Alto and other cities across the nation. Indeed, the weekend Gakirah Barnes was murdered, another thirty-five people were also shot in Chicago, three fatally. Although last collected in 2012, the National Youth Gang Survey of law enforcement agencies indicated that there were 2,363 victims of gang-related homicide that year (Egley, Howell, and Harris 2014)—across the country there are six homicides each day that bear a resemblance to what occurred in Chicago and East Palo Alto.

Figure 6.2 displays an expanded model of the cycle of gang violence. This model began with Decker's (1996) observations in St. Louis, was visualized by Decker and Pyrooz (2010a), and was elaborated on to incorporate multilevel influences by Moule, Decker, and Pyrooz (2017). The solid straight lines represent direct effects, the dashed lines capture possible effects, and the zigzag lines are effects moderated by gangs and gang member characteristics.

The model begins with threat identification. Gangs bonds are generally loose, revolving around neighborhood arrangements, shared interests, and collective activities. Since the neighborhoods where gangs congregate typically maintain high levels of disadvantage and criminal activity and limited social

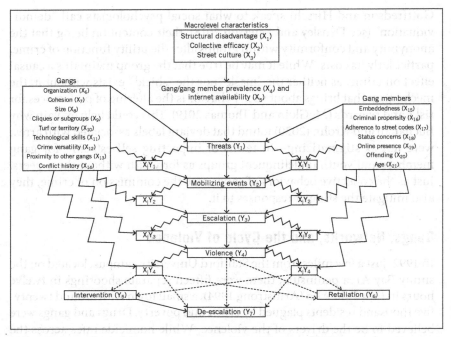

Figure 6.2 An expanded model of the cycle of gang violence with multilevel moderators
Note: This model was originally developed in Moule, Decker, and Pyrooz (2017).

controls, threats remain elevated from within and beyond the community. Lauger (2012) described the inter-gang landscape as a social field of boundaries, interactions, and reputational legitimacy. But gangs also provide a platform from which violence can be launched, where an insult, a wayward stare, or crossed-out graffiti is enough to function as a mobilizing event— that is, something that arouses the acrimony of the group. It is at this point that group processes ramp up, as gang members, from young to old, from clique to set, are made aware of the incident, whether real or perceived. Threat identification and mobilizing events can unfold slowly or quickly, not unlike Fleisher's (1998) observations in Kansas City.

The escalation of activity is where gang violence departs from other types of violence. Gangs have resources—access to weapons and manpower— to support engaging in the type of warfare that Vigil (1988, 132) termed an "endless cycle of revenge." Activities can escalate due to instrumental reasons, such as the economic functioning of the gang, or expressive reasons, such as disrespect, status, or honor. Whatever its sources, the next stage, violence, can set off conflicts that last for days, months, or even years. Violence begets violence, leading to retaliation, which is why Papachristos (2009) held that gangs are situated in institutionalized networks of conflict, where there are norms of reciprocity to violence:

They always comin' at [attacking] us. Everybody knows it, and they watchin' to see what you do. The thing is, what can a nigga' do? If you don't get yourself some payback, you ain't shit. People'll see you [are] weak and your mob's [gang] weak. Then, next thing you know, everyone be stepping at [attacking or insulting] you. You got to hold on to your rep. And, the only thing to do is to go back and fuck some fools [members of opposing group] up. If someone steps to you, you best roll right-the-fuck- back-up on them! Get you some revenge. If we back down from those motherfuckers [Latin Counts], they think they got the best of us. They'd think they got more heart than we do. (117)

In cities, many gang members in many gangs are often unaware of exactly why they are fighting, but they know exactly to whom their antipathy should be directed. In this sense, gang violence can be thought of as a contagious disease, as it passes through individuals in the extended network that constitutes the field of gangs in a city.

At some point, however, the barrage of violence and intensification of group process will eventually lead to intervention and de-escalation. Group processes are not invariant over time. If they were, we would not expect to find the emergence of new gangs, the elimination of old gangs, or the emergence or elimination of gang rivalries. Gang members are not indispensable. As a gang member in Phoenix recalled to one of our interviewers, he saw all of his homeboys either go to prison or die from violence or suicide. As gang members died or went to prison, so went the gang. There is no such thing as a one-man gang. Interventions can occur formally, typically originating from law enforcement, where key players in the violence are arrested; interventions can also occur informally, through external means, such as community stakeholders brokering peace (e.g., priests), or internal means, such as demoralizing violence where the loss of a leader or influential member occurs or the gang loses face. More often than not, it is a combination of formal and informal interventions that leads to the de-escalation of gang violence. We focus on strategies to reduce gang violence in Chapter 14.

Much evidence supports the cycle of gang violence, especially in recent years as criminologists have examined the network properties of gangs. Papachristos has operated at the forefront of this area of study, using law enforcement data—primarily field interrogation cards and gunshot victimizations—to study gang violence. In a study of Chicago gang homicides in 2008–2009 and Boston gang shootings, Papachristos, Hureau, and Braga (2013) found that turf adjacency (i.e., geographic proximity), historical conflict (i.e., preexisting violence), and reciprocity (i.e., retaliation) were all associated with inter-gang violence in both cities. In a different study, Green, Horel, and Papachristos (2017) demonstrated that social contagion, as opposed to demographics, could account for over 60 percent of the 11,123 gunshot victimizations among 140,000 arrestees in Chicago; gang members were the majority of victims (52 percent) despite being under one-quarter of the arrestees. A more recent study, based on gang homicides in Chicago, revealed much more variation in the "rules of the game" (Lewis and Papachristos 2020). Intraracial violence, retaliation, resistance to domination, and generalized exchanges (Gang A attacks B, who attacks C, who attacks A) differed based on gang, race, and time period. This led Lewis and Papachristos to suggest that "it could be that strategies gangs pursue to advance their positions are much more opportunistic than enduring," a conclusion that seems consistent with the precarity of the lives of young males living in dangerous urban environments.

Findings from network research help explain a stronger victim-offender overlap among gang members, which Pyrooz, Moule, and Decker (2014) first uncovered in a study of six hundred people with various levels of system involvement in five U.S. cities. Traditional explanations of the victim-offender overlap (such as the code of the street, low self-control, and routine activities) could not account for this fact, which led the authors to attribute the unexplained variance to group processes best tapped in social network analysis. Reciprocal exchanges of violence between gangs could explain why the triggerman of today is the dead man of tomorrow. They also help put into action the collective liabilities and obligations people assume when they become involved in gangs, as they inherit alliances and rivalries that could result in serious violence despite no stake in or responsibility for past acts.

Conclusion

This chapter has established that gangs produce serious consequences for people and communities. Gang members are overrepresented as offenders and victims of crime, a finding that is invariant with age, crime type, gender, geography, and race. It is the context of the gang rather than the characteristics of gang members that is primarily responsible for this overrepresentation. The victim-offender overlap is especially strong among gang members, which could be explained by the unique properties of gangs. Group processes are believed to be responsible for the elevated involvement in offending and victimization, which includes opportunity structures, normative influences, status concerns, collective behaviors, and institutionalized conflict networks. While crime is included in the legislative and scientific definitions of gangs, crime is also their defining feature in the eyes of the public. And few features draw as much attention to gangs—from news media to documentaries to policymakers to criminal justice authorities—as do their violent actions. Our following chapters examine the nature of gangs under different conditions ranging from gender to race to country.

II

Emerging and Critical Issues

7

Women, Gender, and Gangs

Before the 1980s, there was little attention paid to female gang membership. Gangs were stereotypically depicted as hypermasculine, violent, and the preserve of (minority) men. Women and girls who were gang members were often labeled as "tomboys." They were depicted as subservient to male gang members, or, if they had independence from male gangs, they were described with male attributes. As readers will see, this perception of the role of women is problematic and clearly incorrect. Beginning in the 1980s, the number of females in gangs began to grow, and the picture became increasingly complex. A change in views corresponded to the growing number of female scholars and a general perception that gendered stereotypes rather than solid evidence were used to create such conceptions. In the 1990s, this interest in gang involvement of females continued to grow. Some of this growth was in response to a number of media depictions of girl gangs in highly stylized and exaggerated ways. Gender identity has emerged more recently as a topic of interest in understanding gangs, as has the role of masculinities. Looking at female gangs and gang members over time highlights both divergence from and convergence with their male counterparts. From our perspective, the divergence of female gang membership from male gang membership has grown substantially in the past two decades. Despite that, female gangs and gang members share some structures, activities, and processes in common with male gangs and gang members.

In this chapter, we discuss the role of gender and gang involvement by:

- Examining available information on the level of female gang involvement
- Identifying common misperceptions of female gang involvement that resulted from a male-centric view of gangs
- Outlining the similarities and differences between male and female gangs and gang members, particularly in a life-course framework
- Presenting emerging work on gender identity, masculinities, and gang membership

We frame our discussion around selected examples that we feel have shaped (or are shaping) research and responses to female gang involvement. Early work on female gang involvement is found in the research of male sociologists such as Thrasher in Chicago, Whyte and Miller in Boston, and Spergel in New York. Our thinking about female gang involvement is challenged by the work of Campbell in New York, Moore in East Los Angeles, Fleisher in Kansas City, and Miller in Columbus (Ohio) and St. Louis. Panfil's work with gay and bisexual male gang members in Columbus represents a new view of sexuality in gangs that Thrasher and others had identified. Finally, we integrate masculinities in our discussion of gender and gangs, relying on the recent work of Deuchar (2018), Lauger and Horning (2020), and Mullins and Kavish (2020).

The state of knowledge about female gang involvement has grown in the last decade. It has generally become more quantitative, as researchers utilize larger, nationally representative data sources to address comparative issues between male and female gang members. We see this as a sign of progress. Life-course frameworks have also been used to assess the role of women in gangs. Current research tells us a lot about female gang involvement, especially about how life in the gang for females compares to that for males. While there is overlap between the experiences of females and males in gangs, they have somewhat unique roles as gang members. A broader consideration of gender has led us to include a discussion of sexual behaviors in the gang as well.

The Scope of Female Gang Involvement

In 1975, Walter Miller provided a "general estimate" that 10 percent or fewer of the gang members in the cities that he studied were female. Miller was no stranger to female gang involvement, as his study of Boston's Roxbury neighborhood contained female gangs and gang members, most famously "the Molls" (1973). In the first national gang survey that Miller led, not one city reported an estimate of female gang involvement that exceeded 10 percent. The New York City Police Department reported that half of their city's male gangs had female auxiliary gangs yet estimated females to account for only 6 percent of all gang members. In Chicago, the estimate of female gang involvement was "almost" 10 percent. As a result, many see "the Miller 10 percent" as a rule of thumb in estimating the level of female gang involvement (Spergel 1990).

Does Miller's appraisal still apply today? The short answer: it depends on whom you ask. But it is important to note something Miller sensed about his data—when using police data, only the older and more serious gang members come to their attention. Thus, while there may have been a larger number of gang members in the cities he surveyed, they wouldn't show up in police data because they were younger or less involved in serious crime. Future self-report work conducted in schools would confirm this suspicion.

Miller's pioneering work provided the foundation for the National Gang Center gang surveys of law enforcement that we discussed in Chapters 1 and 2. Still, there was a growing perception among members of the criminal justice system that females were increasingly involved in gang activity above and beyond what the surveys were capturing. Chesney-Lind, Shelden, and Joe (1996) argued that earlier researchers and police had "gendered habits" that had rendered females in gangs "invisible" in much the same way that women were invisible in many other aspects of life. This coupled with the growth of large-scale federally funded studies with greater breadth of coverage (i.e., not just police) challenged the early assumptions about women in gangs. These surveys typically included as many females as males and large numbers of respondents; thus, they provided a good setting for evaluating female gang involvement that wasn't tied to just one source.

In Table 7.1, we provide estimates of the prevalence of female gang involvement from a number of different reports on gender and gang membership. The values in the column labeled "Percentage of female gang members" indicate the percentages of gang members in the data source who were female. We rank the data sources from high to low female involvement in gangs, and we find that estimates range from as low as 2 percent to as high as 40 percent. For every hundred gang members, in other words, only two would be female in one data source, but as many as forty would be female in another.

What explains such large differences across the data sources? And why does it matter? Table 7.1 provides a brief description of the study and the sample type. Our view is that the composition of the samples—particularly in terms of age and criminal justice involvement—are what mainly explain the large differences across these studies. There is evidence of convergence

TABLE 7.1 THE PREVALENCE OF FEMALE GANG MEMBERSHIP IN TEN STUDIES

Study sample	Sample type	Percentage of female gang members	Reference
Gang Resistance Education and Training II (G.R.E.A.T. II)	School youth, ages 11 to 15, seven U.S. cities	40%	Esbensen and Carson (2012)
Gang Resistance Education and Training I (G.R.E.A.T. I)	Middle school youth surveyed in eleven U.S. cities	38%	Esbensen, Deschenes, and Winfree (1999)
Ethnographic study of East Los Angeles gangs	Rosters of two gangs: White Fence and Hoyo Maravilla	33%	Joan Moore (1991)
National Longitudinal Survey of Youth (NLSY), 1997	Nationally representative sample of youth born 1980–1984	29%	Pyrooz (2014b)
Arrestee Drug Abuse Monitoring (ADAM)	Juvenile arrestees surveyed in Maricopa County, Arizona, facilities	17%	Decker et al. (2008)
Fresno County, California, jail	Adult inmates surveyed in Fresno County, California, jail	16%	Kissner and Pyrooz (2009)
Florida County jails	Adult inmates surveyed in Florida jails	15%	K. Fox, Lane, and Akers (2010)
National Gang Center	Nationally representative sample of 3,018 police agencies	6%	https://www.nationalgangcenter.gov/Survey-Analysis/Demographics#anchorregm
California police departments	CalGang database, listed 2017–2018	6%	https://oag.ca.gov/sites/all/files/agweb/pdfs/calgang/ag-annual-report-calgang-2018.pdf
St. Louis–area police departments	Police gang intelligence list, entry 1993–2003	2%	Tostlebe et al. (2020)

in the number of male and female gang members at the "shallow end" surveys, those conducted in schools, compared to those at the "deep end," with criminal justice system involvement. Male/female differences in problem behaviors, aggression, delinquency, crime, and violence are well established in the study of youths and young adults in criminology, psychology, social work, and a host of other disciplines. Consequently, as the involvement in crime of the sample increases, the likelihood of male overrepresentation should increase as well. For example, Jody Miller and Decker (2001) found that male gang members were victims of homicide at roughly ten times the rate of females. Similarly, as the age of the sample increases, female involvement should decrease.

Of key interest is that the prevalence of female gang involvement changes according to the criminal justice involvement of the sample. The first four samples provide estimates from non-law-enforcement sources. These studies allow the respondents to self-report as gang members. Esbensen and colleagues (Deschenes and Esbensen 1999; Esbensen and Carson 2012) provide high estimates of female gang involvement based on samples of middle school and young high school students. These studies, however, impose the criterion of school attendance, and it is possible that absence, tardiness, suspension, expulsion, or confinement, as well as youthfulness, could reduce serious gang delinquents' participation in such studies. After all, males are more likely to be disciplined in school, including suspensions and expulsions, two process that reduce their presence in school-based samples. That said, there is no reason to think that the gender balance in male-female gang membership would be affected to such a large degree by such a consideration. Joan Moore (1991) found a 33 percent female prevalence rate based on the rosters of two East Los Angeles gangs and their subgroups or cliques. Of course, these findings may not be generalizable to other gangs or neighborhoods, but rarely do researchers have access to the rosters of gangs, including information about gender. Pyrooz's (2014b) estimate of 29 percent was based on data that were nationally representative based on household sampling, providing a good sense of female gang involvement. Together, these studies provide a general representation of female gang involvement that is determined by youth themselves and avoids any association with the criminal justice system. These studies also show higher gang membership by females than is found in other studies based on law enforcement samples, exceeding Miller's 10 percent rule.

The next three samples come from criminal justice sources. These studies were conducted with individuals in detention facilities (e.g., booking area or jail). Decker et al. (2008) report findings from interviews with recently arrested juveniles after being booked into a juvenile detention facility in Maricopa County, Arizona. They find that 17 percent of gang members were females, decidedly lower than the self-reported data. Similarly, Kissner and Pyrooz (2009) and K. Fox, Lane, and Akers (2010) identified almost identical female and male rates of gang involvement in Fresno County, California, and counties in Florida, respectively. These estimates derived in criminal justice settings represent a large drop (around fifteen percentage points) from the studies discuss above that were conducted outside of criminal justice settings. In other words, once an arrest criterion is imposed, the likelihood of finding female gang involvement decreases.

The final three samples are derived from law enforcement agencies where gang membership is determined by law enforcement criteria—one national, one state, and one local estimate. First, the National Gang Center estimates are based on surveys of over three thousand law enforcement agencies across the United States asking agencies to report the number of male and female gang members they have on record. Their estimate of 6 percent is close to the Miller 10 percent despite being collected nearly thirty years later. Second, as part of California's Assembly Bill 90, the Fair and Accurate Gang Database Act of 2017, the state attorney general is required to produce an annual report on CalGang, the statewide shared gang database, the largest of its kind in the country. The 2018 report indicated that 5,500 of the 89,000 people listed in the database were female, translating into 6 percent of total gang members, which was spot-on with the National Gang Center's estimate. Finally, and at the local level, we report the proportion of females in a database population maintained by St. Louis–area law enforcement agencies. Females composed only 2 percent of all gang members documented. When contrasting gang intelligence with surveys of arrestees, we find a similar drop, this time slightly over ten percentage points.

These disparate findings matter because different data sources and samples produce different answers, which in turn describe different problems. To government agencies and specialized police gang units, female gang members are a small minority of gang members and gang problems. The question is whether this reflects the reality of the streets or the gender biases of the people collecting the data or both. Regardless, this gender gap has consequences. In a policy environment where resources are distributed according to the magnitude of a problem, those resources would go toward male gangs and gang members. To those who conduct research or make policy among incarcerated youth, institutionalized female gang members are clearly not an inconsequential minority and should not be excluded or minimized. M. Klein (2001, xi) perhaps said it best when referring to his study of four Los Angeles gangs in the 1960s: "How could it be that the originators of the research ignored 26% of the members of these gangs?" Since then, as Curry (1998) and Jody Miller (2001) observed, understanding gangs and gang membership from a female-based perspective has been a major theme of research. We now turn to perspectives on females and gangs.

Perspectives on Females and Gangs: Liberated, Exploited, or Marginalized?

The Molls were a gang in the Boston area comprising White (mostly Irish), Catholic girls. A field worker in W. Miller's (1973) study observed the girls for 2.5 years, when the girls were ages fourteen to sixteen. The Molls were the neighborhood "bad girls"—they ditched school, vandalized property, stole, drank alcohol in public places, and mocked do-gooders with obscene language. "Bad" is relative to the times. Occasionally, the police arrested members of the Molls for their delinquent behaviors. But as Miller pointed out, the Molls also wanted to be recognized as the girls of the "Hoods," a notorious male gang. The Molls "were aware that the wish to gain acceptance by the Hoods was an important reason for committing crimes" (W. Miller 1973, 34). Some of the criminal and deviant behaviors of the Molls could be attributable to their search for respect and identification with the "baddest" male gang. The strong interdependence between a dominant male gang and a female gang that derived its identity through its relationship with that male gang speaks to one model of gang membership where females fit into male gangs. But this clearly is not the only form that the relationship between male and female gangs can take.

Short and Strodtbeck's (1965) work in Chicago offers a contrast to Miller's observation of the Molls. Of particular importance is the reanalysis of those data by Hughes and colleagues (Hughes, Botchkovar, and Short 2019). While the female gangs in the study adopted "feminized" names that corresponded to the male gangs dominant in the area (such as the Vice Ladies and Cobraettes), they engaged in regular inter-gang conflict that played out within friendship networks in their gang. The bonds among female gang members were relatively loose and built largely along the lines of utilitarian gain rather than affective bonds. These female gang members exercised a good deal of autonomy within their gang, particularly in their relationships with other women. Not unlike other research, girls who traded sex for status within the gang were held in the lowest esteem.

The contrast between these girl gangs leads us to our consideration of three different perspectives—marginalization, social injury, and liberation—on the relationship between females, males, and gangs. These perspectives differ on three factors: (1) the recognition of female gang members as equal and the respect afforded to them; (2) the exploitation, typically sexually, of female gang members; and (3) the autonomy of the female gang and gang members. We highlight classic and contemporary research and emphasize the behaviors and motives of the Molls in relation to a lively debate on female gang involvement.

The Marginalization Hypothesis: Frederic Thrasher and Female Invisibility

The marginalization hypothesis takes the position that females are "invisible" in gangs. Their presence, value, and activities in the gang depend on the presence and acceptance of males, who call the shots. In these circumstances, women are afterthoughts, and they reside at the periphery of the gang. Thrasher (1927) espoused these views and promulgated this conclusion. Thrasher identified only six "all-girl gangs" from his 1,313 gangs in Chicago. Of course, this was nearly a century ago, but Thrasher's conclusions about female gang involvement legitimized beliefs that dominated views of female gang involvement for decades and women's involvement in crime more generally. The work of Whyte (1943) in Boston and Spergel (1964) in Chicago are examples of this. Many of Thrasher's observations reflect male bias and privilege, pervasive among the academy and society at large.

Thrasher believed that females did not form or participate in gangs. He gave some consideration to the notion that there was some sort of "ganging instinct" to be found among males but not among females (80). Ultimately, though, Thrasher (161) concluded that females did not participate in gangs because of social reasons rather than biological factors. He specifically focused on the male need to form groups and the observation that females were socialized to anticipate their adult roles as caregivers. Thrasher identified two social factors that he believed prevented females from being involved in gangs in the ways that males were. First, he believed that there were "traditions" and "customs" deeply rooted in society that instilled different values and norms for social behavior in females than in males. In contemporary delinquency theory, this perspective is very similar to one that has been labeled a subculture of gender. It is rooted in studies in anthropology and social psychology that have found that females are imbued with different values than males. For some, these differing values—specifically, a greater tendency to altruism and caring about the needs of others—are linked to women bearing a larger role in the nurture of children.

A second social factor that Thrasher thought to be important to females not participating in gangs was the greater parental supervision of females compared to males. According to Thrasher, in the urbanized, socially disorganized areas where gangs flourished (see Chapter 2), young males were subject to less supervision than young males in more stable communities. Even in such "disorganized" communities, young females were much more closely supervised and guarded than young males, even in the same family. Females were also more likely to be involved in daily activities and responsibilities inside the home, while males were given unsupervised time that made gang involvement possible. The observation that greater parental supervision of females results in greater levels of delinquent behavior in males is a central proposition in the theory of delinquency known as power control theory (Hagan, Simpson, and Gillis 1988).

According to Thrasher (1927, 151), in the uncommon instances when females were involved in gangs, they tended to be younger. He used the term *tomboy* to describe them. Generally, their roles in gangs were the same as those taken by younger males. This kind of gang involvement by females was pictured as short-lived. Puberty drove a wedge between these females and the predominantly male-dominated gangs they had been involved in. As Thrasher (161) put it, "They took the roles of boys until they began to wear their hair up and put on long skirts."

When older females were involved in gangs, Thrasher (1927, 155, 164–166) described their role as exclusively sexual. Females were described by male gang members in terms of their capacity for sexual exploitation rather than any aspect of their personalities or other contributions to gang activities. In support of the allegation of sexual exploitation, Thrasher provided examples of female participation in "orgiastic" or "immoral" gangs. He emphasized that these orgiastic gangs were not true conflict groups and not a central part of ganging behavior. For the true conflict gangs, even sexual exploitation was more occasional than regular. Most common among these occasional conflict gang contacts with females were "stag" parties where female nude dancers would perform. Male gang members often regaled Thrasher with accounts of "gang shags" in which multiple male gang members would have sex with the same female.

For Thrasher, females played their most significant role for the gang from a position outside the gang. Females held a position in the lives of adolescent males that made them the greatest threat to the collectivity and solidarity that was the basis of gang life as described by Thrasher. As he put it, as gang members grew older, "sex got more attention." He did not mean sexual exploitation. He was referring to what he called "the biological function of sex." In this function, sex was associated with love, marriage, and family formation. To the degree that it was associated with love and marriage, sex was for Thrasher "the chief disintegrating force in the gang" (170). Marriage brought the imposition of family structures, responsibilities, and relationships. The male who was lured away from the family by the attractive excitement of the gang peer group was in the end usually lured back into the institution of the family by individual females as wives. In Thrasher's words, "The gang which once supplanted the home, now succumbs to it" (242). Whether as tomboys or as forces that lead to the dissolution of the gang through marriage and parenthood, girls are not ascribed a central role in the gang and find their gang identity through their relationships to gang boys.

The Liberation Hypothesis: Anne Campbell and Female Autonomy

The liberation hypothesis is derived from the feminist perspective. Researchers in this tradition view gang involvement as an act of female independence, female solidarity, and positive movement in the social hierarchy (i.e., equality). Campbell's (1984) *The Girls in the Gang* marked a turning point in how researchers thought about females and gangs. While the prior work of W. Miller (1973) in Boston, W. Brown (1977) in Philadelphia, and Quicker (1983) in Southern California helped transcend the male-centered stereotypes found in Thrasher's work, none of them had an impact like the work of Campbell.

Campbell embraced this role and set out to "write a book about young women by a woman." She stressed that this was important since most research in the social sciences had previously been limited by being "about men and by men," especially research on gangs. Campbell argued that understanding social behavior required vicariously experiencing "its lived reality" through the eyes of its participants. She relied on an NYPD gang unit officer and the leader of a nonprofit group to connect her with gang members. She produced social biographies of three gang members from different gangs that she felt to be most representative of the diversity of gang life in New York. Campbell worked with each of the women from 1979 into the early 1980s. As such, the biographies represent a specific type of female gang member.

Connie was the first of the women profiled by Campbell. She was Puerto Rican, in her early thirties, and a mother of four. Her gang was the Sandman Ladies, a female auxiliary gang of the Sandman. The Sandman was identified by police as a Manhattan drug-selling gang. Campbell devoted a great deal of attention to Connie's efforts to be a good mother and be a part of the gang, which for her was a form of extended family. Connie expressed a desire that her children would have a life similar to her own in the gang. She adorned her children in gang colors and symbols and took photographs of them. While Campbell gave less attention to violence and the gang's marijuana-selling operation, their importance to Connie's day-to-day existence could not be ignored. To be a Sandman Lady, she had to be willing to fight. Threats on Connie's life and the lives of her children led Connie into hiding.

Weeza was the second woman profiled by Campbell. She was also Puerto Rican, in her late twenties, and a mother of two. Weeza was a member of the Sex Girls, the female auxiliary gang of the Sex Boys. In Campbell's opinion, the Sex Boys and Sex Girls corresponded most to "the classic New York street gang." She described the gang as being in the final stages of disintegration at the time of her research. Heavy police suppression and rivalries with neighboring gangs had taken their toll on the group. While the police described an eight-year gang history characterized by violence, robbery, and auto theft, Campbell observed only drug use and petty sales. The central theme in Campbell's account of Weeza was life with her live-in boyfriend Popeye and their children. Weeza's story ended with a poignant description of the execution-style murder of Popeye.

Sun-Africa was the third subject of Campbell's biographies. She was a Black teenager whose parents had immigrated to New York City from Panama. Sun-Africa was a member of the Five Percenters, a self-described religious (Islamic) and cultural movement. The NYPD described them as a gang with a history of criminal activity dating back to the early 1960s. Prior to her involvement with the Five Percenters, Sun-Africa had joined an independent female gang called the Puma Crew at age eleven. Most of the Puma Crew were younger girls, and their delinquency was limited to drug use and fist fighting. Around age fourteen, she and the other members of the Puma Crew began to hang out with male members of the Five Percenters. After she ran away from home, her boyfriend was killed in an attempted robbery, and her brother was sent to prison. Shortly thereafter, Sun-Africa became seriously involved with the Five Percenters. They required her to accept the teachings of Islam, which meant accepting her role as subordinate to males and behaving as a good Muslim woman. Each female who entered the Five Percenter Nation had to be accepted and ruled over by a male group member, referred to as her "god." When Campbell interviewed her, she was leading a life of docility and servitude under the care of her second "god" since joining the group.

From these three profiles, Campbell arrived at two major conclusions about female gang involvement. First, males play a major role in getting females involved in gangs and gang-related crime: "It is still the male gang that paves the way for the female affiliate and opens the door into many illegitimate opportunities and into areas that serve as proving grounds" (32). This was certainly the case for the females who were the subjects of Campbell's three case studies. This conclusion also suggests that female gang auxiliaries, through their association with male gangs, become involved in delinquent and criminal activity. Second, once a female is involved in a gang, "a more visible solidarity or 'sisterhood' within the gang appears. A female's status depends to a larger extent on her female peers." Rank and worth within the gang are not matters dependent on relationships with males or "simple sexual attractiveness." This suggests that for females in the gang, there are opportunities for self-actualization and equality not available to them in other ways.

Liberation, then, was formed in resistance to recurring male gang member efforts to control and exploit women. Some studies require less qualification about what constitutes female resistance than others. For example, Harris (1988) found active resistance to male gang members in her in-depth interviews with Latinas in Southern California. Lauderback, Hansen, and Waldorf (1992) studied a completely independent female Black gang called the Potrero Hill Posse that broke off on their own due to uneven distributions of drug profits. And C. Taylor (1993) reported that women in Detroit and elsewhere have become empowered by the dope business and engage in crime like never before.

The Social Injury Hypothesis: Joan Moore and Female Exploitation

The social injury hypothesis is a blend of the marginalization and liberation hypotheses. Female gang members remain largely dependent on male gangs, and while they play a role in mixed-sex gangs and in the form of their female auxiliary gangs, their net gain in gang involvement is trivial or negative. In other words, the benefits they achieve from freedom are lost after accounting for "social injuries" such as abuse, arrest, and in some cases, imprisonment. Joan Moore's (1991) work in East Los Angeles is most closely linked to this perspective. Moore's work was based on a sample of gang members from several cliques within two of Los Angeles' most long-standing gangs: White Fence and El Hoyo Maravilla. She conducted interviews with 156 gang members from two generations of the gangs, from the late 1940s and early 1950s and from the 1960s and 1970s.

To some extent, Moore's findings were consistent with those of Campbell. Moore, however, took exception to Campbell's version of the liberation proposition, charging that Campbell's assertion of sisterhood and solidarity amounted to an argument that "gang girls have outgrown their sexist image." To speak of liberation in a new sisterhood and solidarity for females in gangs was unacceptable for Moore in the social world of gangs, where she found extreme levels of sexism both in word and in deed. Despite protestations to the contrary from many of the female gang members, Moore discovered that a significant number of male gang members thought of their female compatriots as sexual possessions. Moore (1991, 54) identified three basic conclusions about females prevalent among male gang members:

1. The gang is a male preserve where women don't belong.
2. Male dominance of females is natural and legitimate.
3. For the greater good of the group, male gang members require the sexual use of females.

Sexist attitudes and behavior were not limited to males. In many cases, females supported or engaged in the sexual exploitation of their "sisters." Moore (55–56) offered an account provided by a female gang member in which all female members of one gang showed up in court to support a homeboy accused of rape by one of their homegirls. Their purpose, according to the girl, was to assist the male gang member's defense lawyer to make the rape victim "look like a tramp." Sexist attitudes did not become less common among gang members in the more recent gang generations studied by Moore.

More important to Moore than the pervasive sexism she found in gangs has been her belief that the harms associated with gang involvement for females simply outweigh any benefits. She has contended that gang membership has more long-term harmful effects on females than on male gang members. Female gang members were more likely than male gang members to be responsible for rearing their children (114). The children of female gang members were significantly more likely than the children of male gang members to become gang members themselves. Through this greater impact of gang membership on their children, Moore has suggested that the ultimate harm done to community and society may be greater for females than for males.

A woman in her late thirties who had left her gang described it in stark terms consistent with Moore's view of the social injury hypothesis:

> My life was almost tooken (taken). A female individual should never have to go through what I went through as far as getting robbed for a lot of dope and the things I went through, you know. I was beat, raped and left for dead over a drug deal. I was pronounced dead, I wasn't gonna make it. (Curry, Decker, and Pyrooz 2014, 109)

Where Do the Molls Stand?

Based on the evidence presented above, we draw two main conclusions about females in gangs such as the Molls. First, female gang membership matters. By sheer numbers alone, we should be concerned about the volume and nature of women and girls in gangs. Female gang members are not invisible and should not be viewed as invisible. Researchers and policymakers who treat female gang members as invisible do so at their own peril and that of the females themselves. In this sense, Campbell (1984) and others (e.g., Chesney-Lind, Shelden, and Joe 1996) were correct in pushing for a feminist movement in gang research, a call picked up by Jody Miller (2001) and continued by Peterson and Panfil (2015). Advocating for a female-oriented view of gangs provides a more accurate description of the problem. From this perspective, the Molls play a primary, not secondary, role in their relationship to the Hoods and in their decision-making. While criminal involvement might be viewed vis-à-vis the male gang, this is probably no different from what other age-similar delinquent and nondelinquent cliques of boys and girls do, including the Hoods.

Second, while female gang involvement may be liberating in some sense, the playing field for gangs is not gender neutral. For every female in gangs like the Potrero Hill Posse, there may be as many as ten females in gangs that view women as subservient, like the Five Percenters. Jody Miller (2001) stated in *One of the Guys: Gangs, Girls, and Gender,* based on her research with gang members in Columbus and St. Louis, that female gang members are viewed as weaker than males, their decisions are discounted by male members, they are less willing to put themselves in danger, and the upper tier of the social hierarchy is "males only." Miller referred to this as the "Patriarchal Bargain," where women are forced to balance their gender in a setting dominated by males. Female gang members practice this in various ways. They trade off certain assets to men, such as their sexuality, in return for other things, such as protection or status. Females also exhibit greater degrees of aggression and victim-blaming attitudes toward fellow victimized females. Participation in "masculine" activities draws acceptance from male gang members in terms of gang status but also puts females at greater risk of victimization (Jody Miller 1998). At the same time, these behaviors—especially sexual behaviors—compromise their femininity in the eyes of fellow gang members and in defining their identity (Laidler and Hunt 2001).

Fleisher (1998) observed a similar perception of women and gangs in his research in Kansas City. Males and females would engage in "verbal duels," a form of street theater where they would insult each other publicly regarding genitalia, sexual prowess, and fighting ability (46). Cara, a bright and engaging young woman, and Wendy, recognized as one of the founders, were central to Fleisher's firsthand account of gang life among the Fremont Hustlers. The friendship of these two women developed when they were incarcerated in a juvenile facility. While Cara and Wendy were gregarious and often the center of attention, they experienced violence at the hands of other gangs, violence at the hands of their boyfriends in their own gang, rampant substance use, unsupportive family lives, and miscarriages and abortions. As Fleisher put it, "Cara and Wendy are trapped in poverty or at best on the margin of poverty, and no one seems willing to get close to them, except the police" (224). For females, though, the gang provided an emotional barrier and something they could identify with, which is why Deschenes and Esbensen (1999) found that females were more likely to report that the gang made them feel important and like they belonged and that it was like a family (44).

Are females who have close ties to the gang but are not members subject to similar perceptions? Cepeda and Valdez (2003) introduced a typology to understand the relationships of gang-associated females (not necessarily members) with male gang members, based on the themes of sexuality, partying, substance use, and crime. *Girlfriends* are the steady partners of male gang members. Girls who fit this typology are afforded respect by male gang members, ultimately meaning fewer sexual advances, fewer partying expectations, and less harassment from the community. *Hoodrats* are typically autonomous from male gang partners. They have a reputation for substance use, sexual promiscuity, and heavy partying, which makes them less respected among their peers and community. *Good girls* avoid the party scenes and maintain positive reputations among their neighborhood peers but have ties to gangs because of the neighborhood. *Relatives* are the sisters and cousins of gang members, which results in an elevated status and protection due to bloodline kinship. They are essentially "blessed-in" to gangs (K. Quinn et al. 2016, 156) without gang initiation rites, which results in an elevated status and protection from the gang. In short, it appears that the farther females enter the social domain of males and seek the status and respect of males, the more susceptible females are to the physically and verbally aggressive actions and expectations of male gang members. This differentiation illustrates the role played by gangs in conferring identity to young men and women who grow up in neighborhoods where gangs are visible and active.

We conclude this section by asking: Even if the social hierarchy of the gang were gender neutral, would it make a difference for women? It would not, based on our understanding of gangs and gang membership. There are very few positive aspects of gang life, and females who secure the respect of their male counterparts as part of the patriarchal bargain that Miller identified are unlikely to experience a net positive gain in their lives. The point is that gang life affects males and females. Campbell, Miller, Chesney-Lind, Curry, and others who argue for a feminist perspective on gang involvement contend that by concentrating only on males, the criminal justice system, social workers and other practitioners, and researchers are blind to a nontrivial portion of the problem and a part that affects both female and male gang members. Therefore, the best view of females and gang membership—and, quite frankly, males and gang membership—is the social injury hypothesis. The key, then, is to understand the similarities and differences in gang life across genders.

Girls in the Gang

We now compare several different aspects of gang life among female and male gang members. We do so by using an approach that depends on life-course explanations of gang membership, its pathways in and out of the gang.

Pathways into Gang Membership

Are the pathways into gang membership "gendered"? In Jody Miller's (2001) interviews with female gang members, she identified three central themes that were associated with gang membership. The first related to family. Consistent with Moore, Chesney-Lind, and Joe-Laidler, trouble in the family was very important in pushing a female away from her family and toward the gang. The females Miller interviewed had troubled family lives. When compared to their female non-gang counterparts, female gang members were much more likely to report witnessing and experiencing domestic violence, being the object of sexual abuse (often by family members), and being exposed to substance abuse problems at home.

However, social context mattered as well. The second and third pathways to gang membership were gang activity in the neighborhood and gang members in the family. Exposure to gang members in the neighborhood, at family functions, in the household, or at other gatherings led the females in Miller's sample into gangs. Notably, females in Columbus referenced the influence of male family members, while the females in St. Louis referenced female family member influences (Jody Miller 2001, 52). Altogether, over three-fourths of the females in Miller's study reported one or more of these explanations as their pathway into gangs. This finding has garnered considerable support in the literature, as highlighted by Sutton (2017) in her review of female gang research.

The pathways that Miller identified aren't exclusive to female gang membership. As outlined in Chapter 4, there are numerous risk factors leading youth into gangs. The factors that lead to female gang membership overlap with the factors that lead to male gang membership. This is evidence of a convergence in risk factors for males and females who join gangs. One key difference must be underscored, however. While protection from violence is a common denominator for the decision by both females and males to join a gang, protection has divergent motives across gender. For males, the motivation to join the gang has its origins in street victimization, and for females it lies in victimization at home. In each case, the group provides a refuge of sorts, but the sources of threats for males (street) and females (home) are different.

In their book *Gangs and Delinquency in Developmental Perspective*, Thornberry and his colleagues (2003) examined differences in reasons for gang joining between gang boys and girls in Rochester, New York. Recall from Chapter 4 that we discussed how the researchers organized the reasons for gang joining into five domains: (1) family and friends, including boyfriends, brothers, and close friends in gangs; (2) protection, including avoiding gang harassment; (3) fun and action, including statements that gang involvement was something to do and it was exciting; (4) belonging, excitement, or status, which comes with the routine activities of life in the gang; and (5) other reasons, including statements that they just felt like it and it was what they believed in. When comparing males and females, there were few differences in the reasons for joining. Females were more likely to report family/friend influences and slightly less likely to report protection, fun/action, or other reasons. Notably, the opportunity to sell drugs or make money was rarely mentioned as a motivating factor for gang membership. Esbensen,

Deschenes, and Winfree (1999) found similar results when comparing the reasons for joining among male and female gang members, with the only difference being that males were more likely to report economic motivations for joining.

In summary, there isn't much evidence that the pathways into gang membership differ for females and males. However, pathways do differ within sexes. A recent study comparing and contrasting the experiences of female gang members in Los Angeles and Glasgow, Scotland, found that women entering gangs in "deficit" owing to histories of domestic abuse, drug dependency, and debt had radically different offending and victimization trajectories than more networked women who entered the gang in "credit," bringing social skills, professional expertise, and agency to the group (Deuchar et al. 2020). Gang members in credit exercised far greater agency over their offending and, in most cases, enjoyed greater success in criminal endeavors.

One major difference in gang joining between males and females is the additional option generally offered to females to enter the gang: getting "sexed in." In their interviews with female gang members, Jody Miller (2001) and Portillos (1999) discussed getting sexed into the gang in relation to the other options (jumped in or born in). While girls get jumped into the gang like boys do, girls who get sexed in engage in sexual activities with one, several, or all of the male gang members. Both Miller and Portillos, however, point out two important facts about getting sexed in. First, it is relatively rare. Second, gang girls who follow this path are not respected by their fellow male or female gang members. Fellow gang members think that these girls are weak and that they lack heart because they were unwilling to withstand getting jumped into the gang. These results are consistent with those reported by Lori Hughes and her colleagues (2019), as we noted above. Very few studies can gather information from girls who are sexed in. As Erica, a gang girl in Jody Miller's (2001, 171) study, put it, "If they have [been sexed in], they ain't saying nothing." But recent work by K. Quinn et al. (2019) calls these conclusions into question. Semistructured interviews with fifty-eight gang members identified favorable attitudes toward what the research team deemed "high-risk sexual practices." This came in the form of norms and expectations that provided support for sexual victimization of females by male gang members. Both group processes and cohesion were strengthened through these behaviors. It is clear that the power differences between males and females in gangs as well as the physical and emotional consequences of such victimization require greater attention to these practices and the norms and processes that support them.

The issue of sexual behavior among gang members has received scant attention in the research (with a notable exception or two of late). Thrasher makes passing reference to "weak" male gang members who may be sexually victimized by other male gang members, and Short and Strodtbeck (1965) discuss an incident of apparent homosexuality. The work of Panfil (2020) in this regard is of interest, as she studied gay (male) gang members and the nature of their gang activity. In *City Gangs*, W. Miller (2011) devoted a full chapter each to female and male "sexual and mating behavior." It is ironic that the teenage years seem to be consumed by interest in sex and sexuality, yet so little research on gangs and gang members has been conducted in this important arena of adolescent (gang) life. Miller concluded that sexual behavior as well as braggadocio about sexual behavior occupied a central place in gang life.

Life in the Gang

As we discussed in Chapter 6, there is a well-established relationship between criminal offending, serious victimization, and gang membership. If we were to track an individual's involvement in crime and experiences with victimization, we would observe much higher rates of offending and victimization during active periods of gang membership than before or after his or her involvement. Here, we concentrate on involvement in crime and violence and on victimization and exploitation experiences to determine whether they differ between male and female gang members.

Weerman (2012) compared the offending patterns of teenage male and female gang members in the Netherlands. He made two important observations that we see as central to this line of research. First, gang members, regardless of gender, engage in more criminal activities than non-gang members. After considering several background characteristics, Weerman found that both male and female gang members committed about 50 percent more forms of criminal offenses than non-gang male and female youth with otherwise similar backgrounds. Second, despite this, male gang members were involved in more criminal activities than their female counterparts. This male-to-female gang member difference may have to do with gendered involvement in serious delinquency, especially the fights that boys seem to get involved in (Esbensen, Deschenes, and Winfree 1999; St. Cyr and Decker 2003). The ethnographic work of Fleisher (1998) and Jody Miller (2001) reflects such differences. Females are involved in fewer interpersonal forms of crime than males, such as drug use, drug dealing, and property crimes, particularly serious forms of criminal activity such as violence. Jody Miller (2001) observed, "Most serious affronts to the gang were committed by young men. When girls were involved, young women reported that except for in very unusual circumstances male gang members left retaliation against the rival girls to young women in the gang" (138).

Still, we should not overlook the role of girls in gangs. A male gang member in Fresno indicated that women play a substantial role in the gangs he is familiar with:

> Girls have something to do with at least fifty percent of the crime. Most people wouldn't expect a girl to be a suspect right away.

Harding's (2014) ethnography of gangs in London also reminds us not to overlook the important role that women play in gangs in terms of using their sexuality and social and emotional skills to help facilitate gang crime, negotiate social gains, and navigate the streets. There have even been reports of women posing as "honey traps" to attract male gang members and set them up for victimization (Densley, Davis, and Mason 2013).

Jody Miller (2001) made an important observation about female gang membership, offending, and victimization: females who engaged in criminal activities were also the females who experienced victimization. The victim-offender overlap ranks among the most well-documented findings in criminology (M. Berg 2012). The risk of victimization among females, however, is much lower than among males, who tend to engage in serious forms of crime (such as gun violence). In reviewing police homicide reports in St. Louis, Jody Miller and Decker (2001) found that female gang members were much less likely to be the victims of gang homicide than males and that, unlike males, they were more often unintended targets of such violence. However, the fact that rates of victimization tend to be lower for females than males doesn't mean female gang members aren't concerned about violence—they are constantly looking over their shoulder because of the sporadic nature of neighborhood violence in combination with being a gang member.

One risk faced more often by female gang members than their male counterparts is that females in the gang may be subject to sexual violence. We've described how some women get sexed into the gang, although this is more myth than reality. Jody Miller (2001) described an incident of inter-gang conflict when a female gang associate tipped off a rival gang of impending activities, resulting in the serious assault of a fellow gang member. The gang kidnapped the female gang associate and handed her over to the females to be beaten. After this was carried out, however, the male gang members ripped off her clothes and proceeded to viciously sexually assault her. While events like this tend to be the exception rather than the norm in gangs, it is an example of the additional layer of violence females can experience. As one female gang member put it, "We could have just shot her . . . but they went farther than that" (140). If the gender were switched, the male would have "simply" been shot and killed.

Wesche and Dickson-Gomez's (2019) survey of 281 gang members across 32 gangs found that women and girls perceived by men as gang members faced an increased risk of intimate partner violence (as offenders and victims), forced sex victimization, and gang rape. The risk was elevated in gangs with a higher ratio of male members to female members. However, when women and girls were viewed more as romantic and sexual partners, they experienced less (sexual) violence and coercion. Sexual violence in gangs has in recent years become a central theme of research conducted in the United Kingdom (Beckett et al. 2013; Firmin 2010). Studies have found young girls and women being targeted by men who create the impression of a romantic relationship before subjecting them to coercive control (Densley, Davis, and Mason 2013). In the age of social media (see Chapter 10), gang members use tactics such as sextortion and revenge porn (i.e., threatening to expose or embarrass young women by sharing private sexual photographs or films) to manipulate them into supporting gang activity (Storrod and Densley 2017).

Do characteristics of the gang influence criminal offending and victimization patterns? This is an important question for our discussion of gangs, as it provides insight into the impact of gang characteristics and types on the behavior of members. This highlights the distinction between the role of individual characteristics and group processes in explaining the behavior of gangs and gang members. Gender composition is one such gang measure. D. Peterson, Miller, and Esbensen (2001) examined the impact of gender composition on delinquency in gangs. Using data from the eleven-city G.R.E.A.T. evaluation, they compared the delinquency patterns of male and female gang members in all-female, majority-female, sex-balanced, majority-male, and all-male gangs. Males in all-male gangs had lower rates of delinquency than males in majority-male and sex-balanced gangs *and* females in majority-male gangs. Males in gangs where females were present engaged in the highest rates of delinquency. Furthermore, the findings were general to both property and serious delinquency. The authors attributed these findings to majority-group power, where, unlike in all-male gangs, male gang members assert their masculinity in gangs with nontrivial female minority groups to maintain higher group status. It may be that all-male gangs more closely resemble neighborhood groups that coalesce over common concerns and have weaker bonds. In an update of this work, D. Peterson, Carson, and Fowler (2018) reexamined the impact of sex and sex composition of the gang on offending and victimization. Both respondent sex and the sex composition of their gang have strong relationships to these key outcomes (offending and victimization). Gender dynamics and normative orientations within the gang play an important role in these outcomes. It is rare in criminology that studies can be reassessed over time to validate earlier findings, a strong positive feature of this work.

Laidler and Hunt (1997) compared conflict situations for Black, Hispanic, and Samoan female gang members in San Francisco. While the Black females were a gang independent from males, the Hispanic and Samoan females were part of auxiliary gangs connected to males. This is an important distinction because of the presence or absence of male gang members in day-to-day activities and the impact of males on gang activities. For the independent gang, the sources of conflict and violence included confronting gender stereotypes when selling drugs, rivalries with other female gangs, and domestic situations with boyfriends. For the auxiliary gangs, the sources of conflict and violence included gang initiations, rivalries with other gangs irrespective of gender, rivalries with girls from other gangs, internal conflicts with fellow female gang members that occurred as a result of "talking shit," internal conflicts with male gang members, and domestic situations with boyfriends. In summary, females in auxiliary gangs were exposed to a wider range of conflicts than females in independent gangs, most of which pertained to the natural extension of exposure to being organized in relation to male gang members. Consistent with other research, where women are seen as "tokens" within the context of male-dominated street gangs, they may attempt to adopt "honorary male" status; but when they belong to more gender-balanced gangs, they may have a greater ability to "affect the culture of the group" (Jody Miller and Brunson 2000, 421).

Leaving the Gang

The final area of gang life to compare males and females is leaving the gang. As we discovered in Chapters 4 and 5, almost everyone who joins a gang leaves a gang, and most do so after a relatively short period. In conceptualizing disengagement from gangs, as we detailed in Chapter 5, there are two key aspects in the transition from current to former gang member: (1) the motives for leaving and (2) the methods for leaving. When people leave the gang, they follow either an abrupt, more active disengagement process or a gradual, more passive disengagement process (O'Neal et al. 2016; Quicker 1983; Vigil 1988). This applies to male and female gang members.

One of the key findings from work by Decker, Pyrooz, and Moule (2014) is that the reason an individual left the gang had an impact on the method by which the gang member left. O'Neal et al. (2016) examined this issue among a sample that compared men and women who had left their gang. Few differences across three domains (motivations for leaving, supports for leaving, and perceived negative consequences of leaving) were found between men and women. Those differences included concerns about family among women and reports of continued police harassment among men. Concerns about family among women were often linked to having children.

This is a salient concern, as pregnancy might leave a teenage gang member with her hands tied, where she is forced to retreat from gang events and support her child. Jody Miller (2001) reported that as the female gang members in her study grew older, their ties to the gang weakened and remained only for economic purposes: "Challenging rival gang members and fighting over colors, Yvette said, was 'just getting so old, you know what I'm saying.' She suggested that because 'most of my partners got kids,' they 'don't do all that stuff like we used to do'" (95). Miller pointed out that female gang members have greater aspirations than males and that kids might expedite reducing ties to the gang, but together these aren't guarantees of future life successes (see also Fleisher 1998).

Violence plays an important role as well. A young female in Phoenix who had successfully left her gang told us the following:

Interviewer: When did you first think about leaving the gang?

Interviewee: I first thought of it when I got in, like, my third fight, and the girl pulled out her knife on me. That was when I first thought about it. The time when I was actually like, "I'm quitting for real," was when my friend got shot.

Except for pregnancy (Fleisher and Krienert 2004), the motives for leaving appear similar between males and females. In her review of the research on female gang members, Sutton (2017) underscores that the similarities are many but that in the case of female gang disengagement, it appears that young women leave their gangs at an earlier age than their male counterparts. Pyrooz, Sweeten, and Piquero (2013) studied the patterns of gang membership among male and female gang members arrested in Phoenix and Philadelphia. They tracked gang members over a five-year period from the time of their court appearance to see if females left the gang faster than males. This was indeed the case. Males were far more likely to remain gang-involved throughout the study, whereas females were able to cut their ties to the gang and end their gang involvement. This is an important finding because it confirms one of our female gang membership prevalence hypotheses from Table 6.1 above: females cycle out of gangs faster than males, which is why we observe higher prevalence rates in youth samples (e.g., Esbensen, Winfree, et al.'s study) and lower prevalence rates in older samples of gang members.

To say that pregnancy has different impacts on males and females is to restate the obvious. This holds even among gang members. As Pyrooz, McGloin, and Decker (2017) demonstrated, both parenthood and the residence of a new child have differential impacts on female and male gang members. For men, parenthood shows a small net change in gang behavior, and living in a residence with a newborn child shows reductions in gang-related behavior. For women, childbirth alone is sufficient to promote changes in gang behavior. Moloney et al. (2011) conducted interviews with sixty-five female gang members in San Francisco and found that motherhood entailed a retreat from the street and a renewed emphasis on time spent at home because respect came from being a good mother, not being involved in gangs.

Masculinities, Gender, and Gangs

We conclude this chapter with a discussion of the role of "masculinities" in gangs. To do so first requires us to examine the concept of femininity in gangs. Jody Miller (2002) has argued that "gender crossing" in gangs can occur whereby young women heavily identify with the young men in their gangs and construct themselves as "one of the guys" through acts of violence (443). However, masculinities scholar Messerschmidt (2002) disputed this, arguing instead that violent women in gangs had constructed a form of "bad girl femininity" as a means to earn respect within an otherwise patriarchal power structure (463). For some women, "looking bad" (as opposed to being bad) was merely a protective strategy within the patriarchal environment of the street and a means of demonstrating a sense of power in an environment that afforded them "little status" (Laidler and Hunt 2001, 676). However, the societal reaction to women performing the "bad girl" role can be quite negative because it is seen as an affront to traditional gender roles (Hunt and Joe-Laidler 2001). Peterson and Panfil (2015) identified another group of gang members: those who do not identify as male or female but instead choose another gendered identity. These individuals, in particular, highlight the power of highly masculinized groups such as gangs and the challenges of finding identity in such groups.

Masculinities refers to the set of values, generally held by males, that promote individualism, strength, and often oppositional behavior. Other common or "hegemonic" masculine ideals include social respect, physical strength, and sexual potency (Messerschmidt 2005). Many of these beliefs have become stereotypical or highly stylized, reflecting a broader cultural style of values and behavior. Mullins and Kavish (2020) referred to the role of such beliefs in street life, particularly among individuals and groups that are marginalized. They locate the development of street life in the multiple marginalization faced by minority males in urban areas. Vigil (1988, 2020) has written extensively about the multiple marginalities faced by Mexican Americans who face cultural and institutional marginalization as a consequence of their heritage and experiences with U.S. institutions. Their marginalized state leads them to adopt values, group associations, and institutional adaptations to this exclusion from mainstream institutions and values, a process often exacerbated by experiences with the criminal justice system.

Masculinities have a place in a long tradition of research on gangs and other marginalized groups. In simple terms, for racialized and marginalized young men, gangs represent a route to an idealized masculinity, not least because gangs enable them to "do gender" when conventional means of doing gender, such as getting a job, are out of reach (Messerschmidt 1993). Certainly, W. Miller's (1958) six focal concerns (fate, autonomy, smartness, toughness, excitement, and trouble) provide a set of values that are at once a reaction to institutional and cultural marginalization and a road map for gang behavior. Clearly, the "code of the street" (E. Anderson 1999) emphasized the oppositional nature of behavior with a locus on the street and the importance of maintaining toughness. Mitchell and colleagues (2017) examined the overlap between street codes, prison codes, street gang codes, and prison gang codes. They found considerable overlap among the four value systems, each emphasizing oppositionality, toughness, and rejection of authority. Lauger and Horning (2020) described the internal struggle over which values street-oriented males should embrace. In the end, this struggle is often resolved in favor of accommodations that emphasize respect and masculinity. Such a resolution is often the difference between "victory" and "defeat" on the street as images are projected and assessed in interactions. As Deuchar (2018) noted, the resolution of these challenges to identity, toughness, and viability may lead to what he terms "aggressive masculinity." For women caught in the middle of performances of such masculinities, affiliating with others may appear as a strategy to mitigate the risks of residing in such places. Indeed, as we noted above, concerns about victimization by family members are often motivations for young women to affiliate with a gang.

Conclusion

This chapter examined gender and gangs and found that women have extensive involvement in gangs. Their patterns of membership differ from those of males, with less involvement in crime and shorter stints as gang members. An expanding body of research has documented that female involvement in gangs need not be considered in comparison to males but has a character of its own. That character is conditioned by gender roles as well as demography and neighborhood characteristics. The patterns of leaving and joining a gang share many similarities between males and females, with protection against violence being a common thread in the decision of both genders to join their gang. Maturational processes, including family formation, also are at work for both male and female gang members. However, the locus of violence for joining the gang differs for males and females. Male gang members regard the gang as potential protection against violence on the street, while females regard it as protection against family-based violence. Although underdeveloped, the role of gender identity, particularly masculinities, seems a topic worthy of more attention. Descriptions of masculinities and gang membership are more recent, but descriptions of gang values consistent with depictions of masculinity have a long-standing tradition in criminology.

8

Race, Ethnicity, and Gangs

As discussed in Chapter 1, one of the more contentious issues in addressing gangs is the racial and ethnic status of gang members (for a review, see Freng 2019). There is considerable concern that racial and ethnic minorities are overidentified as gang members, largely as a consequence of the ability and intention of people in positions of power and influence to criminalize the culture and behavior of racial/ethnic minorities (Garland 2002). The perception is that "gang membership" is code or shorthand for Black, Latino, and other racial/ethnic minority males. Some (W. Brown 1977) have gone so far as to claim that gangs represent an extension of the Black family, while others state that identifying young minority males as gang members is part of an effort to label and hold back an entire race (Durán 2013; Durán and Campos 2020). The exclusion of racist skinheads and hate groups from the traditional definition of gangs adds to the concern over the use of gang terms to describe exclusively the behavior of Black, Latino, and other minority ethnic youth (Reid and Valasik 2020).

In this chapter, we examine the following:

- The racialized construction of criminal gangs
- The prevalence of Black, Latino, and other minority ethnic people in gangs
- Racial and ethnic homophily in gangs
- The role of immigration in gang formation
- The (hidden) role of racism in gang formation

In an extension of the discussion in Chapter 2, this chapter also examines how culture, subculture, and global "street culture" contribute to our understanding of gangs.

The Racialized Construction of Criminal Gangs

Marginalized and racialized urban youth are the overwhelming recipients of the "gang member" label (Durán 2013; Rios 2011a; Tapia 2011a, 2011b). While the underclass process outlined in Chapter 2 produces gangs, so too does the labeling process. Critical criminologists argue that the primary function of legal gang definitions is to legitimize the identification, surveillance, and suppression of Black, Latino, and minority racial/ethnic youth and to justify enhanced prison sentences for them (Brotherton 2015). In the tradition of Stan Cohen's (1973) *Folk Devils and Moral Panics*, they contend that "gang talkers'" exaggerated and sensationalized depictions of Black, Latino, and other minority ethnic youth as "gang members" not only defame and demonize but also compound existing social anxieties around race, thus prompting authorities to react disproportionately to perceived moral threats (Fraser 2017; Gunter 2017; Hallsworth and Young 2008; Patrick Williams 2015). A number of scholars have examined racialized depictions of gangs in the media through the lens of "moral panic" (McCorkle and Miethe 2001; Welch, Price, and Yankey 2002; Zatz 1987). Conquergood (1996, 11) summarized this notion as follows:

> The gang member is our urban savage, an all-purpose devil figure onto which we project our deepest fears about social disorder and demographic change. The stereotypical gang member is a young minority male from the impoverished inner city. . . . [and] there is terrible slippage between the terms "gang members," "minority youth," and "Black and Latino teenagers." Labeling someone a gang member licenses the most rabid racism and class bias, and underwrites a formidable legal-juridical apparatus of surveillance and incarceration.

It wasn't always this way. The study of gangs once was the study of delinquency (Pyrooz and Mitchell 2015), but from the 1920s to the 1970s, gangs were not typically subject to harsh criminal justice sanctions. Instead, street gangs were a curiosity, a laboratory, and were perceived publicly as boisterous young peer groups from working-class ethnic communities that displayed some subcultural values (W. Miller 1958; Matza 1990). Amid rising juvenile violent crime in the 1970s and 1980s, however, there was a notable shift in gang research emphasis (W. Miller 1975), what Pitts (2008, 10) described as a "correctional turn" from etiology to control. Solving the gang problem soon became a national priority. Spurred by sensationalist media coverage of a "new breed" (Dilulio 1995, 23) of "fatherless, Godless, and jobless" juvenile "super-predators" (W. Bennett, DiIulio, and Walters 1996, 27) and an impending juvenile "crime wave storm" (J. Fox 1995) that never actually materialized, legislatures across the country adopted a more punitive stance toward juvenile gang offenders (we discuss this in detail in Chapters 11 to 14). The United States went to war against gangs. And the war against gangs was an extension of another war the country was waging—on drugs.

The war on drugs presents narcotics as a macro destructive force, but racism was at the heart of many early drug laws, and to this day, Black and Latino youth are targets for increased drug enforcement and stricter sentencing conditions (Alexander 2010). Early efforts to criminalize illicit drugs framed the issues as applying to "aliens"—Black, Mexican, and Chinese people. Mexican migrants were the focus of early antimarijuana legislation, and the 1914 Harrison Narcotics Tax Act, which regulated opiates and coca products, was born of fear of "Negro cocaine fiends" allegedly assaulting White women in the South (E. Williams 1914) and debauched Chinese Americans running underground opium dens in the coastal states (McLean, Robinson, and Densley 2018). The war on gangs just continues this tradition, some argue, by framing the issue of youth violence not around endemic social and structural problems but around individual action, thus absolving powerful actors of any responsibility for the status quo or the collateral consequences of their attempts to reinforce it.

In his ethnography of gang life in two cities, Denver, Colorado, and Ogden, Utah, Durán (2013) argues that repressive police tactics in theory focus on targeting violent gang members. In practice, however, he finds that gang enforcement targets *all* minority youth living in urban settings because police officers overestimate the percentage of street crime that is gang related (e.g., Kennedy, Braga, and Piehl 1997), and they view urban Blacks and Latinos as a threat for gang membership. Police have waged a long war on drugs and of attrition against gangs on the street level. A recent report on policing gangs in New York City (Trujillo and Vitale 2019, 6) found that "over 20,000 people were added into the NYPD's gang database" over a ten-year period, of whom 99 percent were non-White. People often were included because of superficial characteristics such as an interest in certain music, colors, jewelry, or clothing, confirming existing stereotypes about Black and Latino youth (see Chapter 11 for a discussion of gang policing and databases). Alleged gang members were "subjected to harassment, intimidation, surveillance, and threats" (2), the report claimed, leading Trujillo and Vitale (2019, 29) to conclude, "Gang policing replicates the harms of mass incarceration . . . [it is] racist policing at its worst."

Owing to special sentencing enhancements, (a lack of) prosecutorial discretion, and other anti-gang measures (see Chapter 13), Black and Latino "gang members" have steadily and systematically moved from the streets to the penitentiaries, which have become catalyst sites for the intergenerational transmission of gang membership and the institutionalization of gangs beyond prison walls (Wacquant 2001, 2009; Chapter 12). For example, Tapia's (2019) work on the El Paso (U.S.) and Ciudad Juárez (Mexico) border shows that ties to drug cartels and subsequent federal prosecutions that landed people in prison facilitated the evolution of Mexican American subcultures into binational crime syndicates.

Still, perhaps the best illustration of the uneven application of the gang label is the treatment of White supremacist "gangs," which exist largely in opposition to Black, Latino, and other minority ethnic groups (Reid and Valasik 2020). White gangs are the "Schrödinger's cat" of gangs, Valasik and Reid (2019) argued—simultaneously gang and not gang. The Ku Klux Klan, racist skinheads, neo-Nazis, Boogaloo, and Proud Boys, etc., are relatively durable groups that employ gang-like symbols and rituals of allegiance, but as discussed in Chapter 3, they traditionally have been regarded as social movements, hate groups, or terrorist groups distinct from gangs (Curry, Decker, and Pyrooz 2014; Howell and Griffiths 2015; M. Klein 1995). At the same time, emphasis on their subscription to political ideology, their perceived lack of street orientation, and their sporadic offending patterns have resulted in White gangs being labeled "specialty" gangs (M. Klein and Maxson 2006).

Reid and Valasik (2020) challenged this thinking, demonstrating that right-wing groups easily qualify as street gangs based on the Eurogang and other leading gang definitions. After all, hate crime is still crime, and Black and Latino gangs are no less ideological or rooted in racial/ethnic pride and identity politics than their White power counterparts (Brotherton and Barrios 2004; Cureton 2008; Joan Moore 1978, 1991; Vigil 1996). Reid and Valasik's (2020) invention of the "alt-right gang" is perhaps an overcorrection, however, because if alt-right groups like the Proud Boys are gangs and even self-nominate as such, then surely no further clarification is necessary. As M. Klein (1995) famously observed, you cannot define a gang by descriptors alone.

Durán (2013) spent five years conducting interviews with gang members and control agents. He discovered that gangs had developed from colonial racial oppression, which subjected Latinos in the American Southwest to second-class living standards in marginalized barrios. Urban decay and racism were the perfect conditions for gang development. Nascent gangs provided informal support to marginalized youth, but as the Latino population grew, living conditions in the barrios declined further, and control agents viewed rising youth activism and the organization and mobilization of civil rights activists as threats to the prevailing racial hierarchy. The resulting criminalization of Latino culture forced youth to band together in solidarity to resist racial oppression. Gangs were manifestations of resistance against White supremacy, Durán argued, and violent gang suppression tactics only further entrenched these groups within the barrio. The marginalization felt by racial and ethnic minority youth and their communities was further perpetuated by the "racialization" (Durán 2013) of policies enacted out of fear and misunderstanding of diverse cultures—for example, "zero-tolerance" in schools (Kupchik 2010; Rios 2017; M. Wang and Dishion 2012; see also Chapter 11). By criminalizing activities and behavior that were unremarkable and legal in other contexts (e.g., associating in public), supposedly "race-neutral" policies such as civil gang injunctions functioned the same way, criminalizing certain racial groups and minority spaces (Muniz 2014; see also Chapter 13).

As a former gang member, Durán (2013) is one of a handful of scholars who bring an insider perspective to gang research (see also Bolden 2020; Rios 2011b). Work such as his presents an important challenge to mainstream criminological thinking on gangs and dominant paradigms that either willfully ignore or mistakenly exclude Black, Latino, and other minority ethnic voices from debates about what gangs represent, how best to study them, and how best to intervene with them. By studying gangs in Europe and in other countries around the world, projects such as Eurogang (Chapter 9) have similarly expanded our knowledge of the role of race and ethnicity, as well as immigration and migration, in gangs, by adding diverse experiences and perspectives to the body of work (Van Gemert, Peterson, and Lien 2008).

The Prevalence of Gang Membership by Race and Ethnicity

Clearly, the concept of the gang itself is highly racialized, which could easily explain Black, Latino, and other minority ethnic youth being overtargeted by police and arrested and labeled as gang members more than their White counterparts. Discriminatory policing may also connect to the systematic portrayal of crime by the media and how Blacks and Latinos are overrepresented as perpetrators of crime in news stories (Bjornstrom et al. 2010).

As discussed in Chapter 1, however, relative to their composition in the larger population, racial and ethnic minorities are overrepresented in gangs. Police gang data provide strong evidence that Blacks and Latinos are the primary members of gangs. According to police estimates, 46 percent of gang members are Latino and 35 percent are Black, with the balance being Asian American, White, or other (National Gang Intelligence Center 2015). Prevalence rates of White gang membership are the lowest in larger areas but significantly higher in smaller areas. Critics argue that these percentages merely reflect racial biases in policing (and police records and surveying), not least because self-report studies place rates of White gang membership much higher (Esbensen et al. 2010; Pyrooz 2014b). Table 8.1 presents the prevalence of White, Black, and Latino people in police gang databases from Boston, Chicago, Los Angeles, New York City, and Portland (Oregon) and their relative risk of inclusion compared to their numbers in the general population (for a detailed discussion of police gang databases, see Chapter 11). As can be observed, Whites are dramatically underrepresented, whereas Blacks are anything from two to eleven times overrepresented in police gang data. Latinos are mostly proportional, but in most databases Blacks and Latinos combined account for 76–99 percent of entries.

These data are striking, but less so when placed in the context of other data from a nationally representative survey of youth that required respondents to nominate themselves as gang members. This survey revealed that Blacks and Latinos were twice as likely as Whites to self-report as gang members in adolescence and three to four times more likely in adulthood (Pyrooz 2014b). In fact, Blacks and Latinos were disproportionately involved in gangs by a factor of 60 percent compared to their population base. In other words, the overrepresentation of Blacks and Latinos in gangs is not

		Boston[1]	Chicago[2]	Los Angeles[3]	New York[4]	Portland[5]
Database	Year	2019	2018	2019	2018	2016
	N	5,300	123,242	19,249	18,084	359
White	% of gang	2.3	4.0	2.5	<1.0	18.3
	% of city	44.5	32.7	28.5	32.1	70.5
	Risk ratio	0.05	0.1	0.1	0.03	0.3
Black	% of gang	76.1	69.8	36.5	66.0	64.1
	% of city	25.3	30.5	8.9	24.3	5.8
	Risk ratio	3.7	2.3	4.1	2.7	11.0
Hispanic	% of gang	14.1	25.2	58.2	31.7	12.8
	% of city	19.7	29.0	48.6	29.1	9.7
	Risk ratio	0.7	0.9	1.2	1.1	1.3

TABLE 8.1 PREVALENCE AND RELATIVE RISK OF PLACEMENT IN POLICE GANG DATABASES OF WHITE, BLACK, AND HISPANIC PEOPLE IN FIVE CITIES

Sources:
1. https://www.wbur.org/news/2019/07/26/boston-police-gang-database-immigration.
2. https://igchicago.org/wp-content/uploads/2019/04/OIG-CPD-Gang-Database-Review.pdf.
3. CalGang LAPD data only. https://oag.ca.gov/calgang/reports.
4. https://www.hrw.org/news/2020/09/22/groups-urge-nypd-inspector-general-audit-nypd-gang-database#_ftn12.
5. https://projects.oregonlive.com/police/gang-list/.
U.S. Census Bureau.

solely an artifact of conscious or unconscious bias against people of color, how police collect information, and how the media tell stories. Another factor is the racial composition of gangs themselves.

As discussed in Chapter 4, gangs tend to attract individuals who find themselves at the bottom of the social and economic ladder in society. Gangs also typically reflect the racial and ethnic composition of the multiply deprived neighborhoods they originate from. For a number of reasons (many outlined in Chapter 2 but also later in this chapter), some of the most disadvantaged neighborhoods in the United States are areas with the highest concentrations of Black and Latino residents (Sampson and Wilson 1995; Sampson 2019; Sampson, Wilson, and Katz 2018). Just as the gangs of the 1890s and 1920s were largely composed of Irish and Italian youths (Asbury 1927), representing groups struggling for inclusion in the economic and social mainstream, Blacks and Latinos constitute the modal category of gang membership today.

Pyrooz, Fox, and Decker (2010) examined the argument about gang identification and racial composition in cities. They used police gang data collected by the National Gang Center to study gang membership patterns in the one hundred largest cities in the United States. They argued that while most research on gangs focused on structural disadvantage, race and ethnicity also played an important role in the prevalence of gang membership in communities. They examined racial and ethnic heterogeneity in cities—a key component of social disorganization theory—and its relationship with structural disadvantage and gang membership. As expected, gang membership was more numerous in cities with higher levels of structural disadvantage, but greater racial and ethnic diversity had a much stronger relationship with gang membership. In addition, they found that structural disadvantage mattered much less in cities with low diversity than it did in cities with high diversity.

Differences in involvement in violent or criminal situations between ethnic minority and majority youth also explain away some—but certainly not all—disparities found in police gang data (Densley and Pyrooz 2020). Race and ethnicity have no causal role in the propensity to commit criminal acts (Sampson and Wilson 1995; Sampson, Wilson, and Katz 2018), but crime typically is higher in minority neighborhoods. In 1966, civil rights leader Martin Luther King Jr. (2019) explained this problem as follows: "Criminal responses are environmental and not racial. And the fact is that poverty, social isolation, economic deprivation breed crime whatever the racial group may be." This partly accounts for why law enforcement officers are more heavily deployed in inner-city areas where gang-involved Black and Latino youth are more visible.

Black males in particular are overrepresented in gangs and as both victims and offenders in the sorts of crimes that necessitate police action, such as murders and shootings (Abt 2019; Cooper and Smith 2011). Decker and Curry

(2002a) found that 87 percent of the victims of gang homicide in St. Louis were Black males. The homicide rate for all Blacks in the United States is on average eight times higher than that for Whites, to the extent that over half of all known homicide victims each year are Black. Still, as noted in Chapter 6, when Pyrooz et al. (2020) analyzed Gang Member-Linked Mortality Files from St. Louis, they found that mortality risk for young Black men identified by law enforcement as gang members was three times greater than that of the average young Black male in the city, and the majority of deaths were intentional injuries or homicides. In fact, the age-adjusted homicide rate for gang members in the study was a staggering 950 per 100,000 persons. Compared to all men in the United States, the homicide risk for Black male gang members was forty times greater.

Gangs typically present as racially and ethnically homogeneous groups, to the extent that scholars talk about "Asian gangs," "Black gangs," and "Latino gangs" as distinct groupings (Covey, Menard, and Franzese 1992; Sánchez-Jankowski 1991; Spergel 1995; Tsunokai and Kposowa 2002; Vigil 2002). Some have even dedicated entire textbook chapters to these designations (Huff 1990), using race and ethnicity to differentiate gangs from one another and to explain relative variances in involvement in aspects of gang activity and behavior. However, the research shows that group processes inherent in street gang structures are more important than differences in race/ethnicity. As M. Klein and Maxson (2006, 163) concluded after reviewing the state of the art, "the similarities among various categories of ethnic street gangs are far more common than the differences. . . . Gang structure and group process trump ethnicity." Indeed, most risk factors for gang membership operate similarly across racial and ethnic groups, and there is little variation in the processes of joining and leaving gangs by race/ethnicity (Howell and Griffiths 2015).

Normally, we would provide the results of studies comparing gangs by race/ethnicity in a table, but there is so little reliable work to report on—as M. Klein and Maxson (2006, 221) said, "ethnicity is one of the most widely discussed, and little studied, aspects of gangs"—that we just enumerate it here. Vigil's (2002) study of different gang ethnicities (Blacks, Mexicans, Salvadorians, and Vietnamese) and Sánchez-Jankowski's (1991) comparative study in three cities (Boston, Los Angeles, and New York City) both looked for but failed to find qualitative interethnic differences between gangs. Curry and Spergel's (1992) survey of 300 Black and 139 Latino males found that Black gang members were more influenced by having family members and school classmates in a gang than their Latino counterparts, who were motivated more by educational frustration and low school self-esteem.

Using G.R.E.A.T. survey data (Drake and Melde 2014; Esbensen et al. 2010; Freng and Esbensen 2007), studies have found, for example, that Blacks and Latinos were more likely to join gangs when they were less committed to school, had poor opinions of or interactions with the police, and were socialized on the street, whereas White gang members joined owing to heightened levels of social isolation. D. Carson's (2018) study of gang disengagement, also using G.R.E.A.T. data, found that Black youth were least likely to report pulls out of gang life associated with prosocial attachments and feelings of disillusionment, and Latino youth most commonly reported pulls associated with parental encouragement and experiencing official sanctions and pushes centered on direct and vicarious violent experiences; however, the differences were small. The point here is to emphasize that micro explanations for racial and ethnic tendencies in gangs exist beyond the macro context already discussed.

Racial and Ethnic Homophily in Gangs

Homophily—the tendency for "birds of a feather to flock together" (Glueck and Glueck 1950, 164)—is an established pattern of social life (McPherson, Smith-Lovin, and Cook 2001). Individuals tend to form relationships with others who share demographics (e.g., age, gender, and race) or preferences (e.g., academics, athletics, and culture). The literature on co-offending—that is, who offends with whom—demonstrates strong tendencies toward homophily in general and racial and ethnic homophily in particular (Petterson 2003; Sarnecki 2001).

There are two dominant explanations for ethnic homophily in a criminal context. Three recent, related criminological perspectives capture the first explanation: opportunities. Rational choice theory (Clarke and Cornish 1985), routine activity theory (L. Cohen and Felson 1979), and crime pattern theory (P. L. Brantingham and Brantingham 1993) all are predicated on the notion that crime is not random but rather opportunistic. Crime occurs when the everyday activity space (e.g., schools or neighborhoods) of a victim or target intersects with the activity space of a motivated offender and capable controllers or guardians (e.g., police) are absent. Co-offending networks or gangs likewise emerge within an individual offender's activity or awareness space because offenders are commonly sorted into shared environments (e.g., neighborhoods) that are frequently more homogeneous than the population at large, thus resulting in greater opportunities to associate with similar others (Blau 1977; S. Feld 1982). This is exacerbated in communities with high degrees of racial and residential segregation.

Second, individuals might have a psychological preference to co-offend with similar people. This may reflect processes of social categorization and comparison, which, in turn, validate one's own social status and identity (Tajfel and Turner 2004). After all, gangs (like all groups) are grounded in human relationships. Heterogeneity in terms of race/ethnicity as well as age and gender may act as an "energy barrier" to communication and coordinated action (Mayhew et al. 1995, 19). Similarities become shorthand. The implication is that homophily may assist gangs in negotiating the "problems of trust" inherent in criminal cooperation (Densley 2012b; Gambetta 2009). Dwight C. Smith (1975), author of the influential book *The Mafia Mystique*, maintains that "ethnic ties provide the strongest possibility of ensuring trust among persons who cannot rely on the law to protect their rights and obligations within cooperative but outlawed economic activity" (D. Smith 1980, 375). Gangs are not mafias (see Chapter 3), but this concept clearly still applies.

For example, in prison, where problems of trust are perhaps most acute (Skarbek 2014), gang divisions along racial and ethnic lines are extreme. As discussed in Chapter 12, the oldest and largest gangs in state and federal prisons have clear racial and ethnic boundaries. La Eme (Mexican Mafia), La Nuestra Familia, Mexikanemi, and Texas Syndicate are all composed of primarily Mexican Americans and other Latinos. The Black Guerilla Family is a Black gang, while the Aryan Brotherhood is a White supremacist group comprised of White inmates who oppose the racial threat they perceive from Black and Latino inmates (Orlando-Morningstar 1997). In their study of thirty-eight prison gangs in Texas, Pyrooz and Decker (2019) found that racial and ethnic homogeneity was par for the course. The authors observed that in prison, even street rivals like the Bloods and Crips or People and Folks united around race and ethnicity. They wrote, "Race/ethnicity is *the* defining characteristic of prison gangs" (19; emphasis added). In other words, the neighborhood is the great social sorter on the street, but race serves that discriminative function in prison.

Few street gangs today share one single ethnic identity (Hagedorn 2008; Howell, Egley, and Gleason 2002; Valdez 2007). Modern "hybrid" gangs are increasingly diverse in terms of ethnic composition, not least because continuous immigration has facilitated ethnic mixing and some of the traditional gang alliances have fractured (Aspholm 2020; Starbuck, Howell, and Lindquist 2001). Whether some racial/ethnic groups are more likely than others to associate in multi-racial/ethnic gangs is an open question. In Los Angeles, Weide (2015) wrote about the numbers of Blacks in majority Latino gangs and vice versa. Still, ethnic groups, defined as groups of people who identify with each other through a common heritage and distinctive culture, often consisting of a common language, religion, or country of birth (A. Smith 1991), remain important for understanding gangs. For example, Grund and Densley's (2012, 2015) social network analysis of an ostensibly "Black" gang found evidence of ethnic heterogeneity within the group, with people of African, Caribbean, and British heritage. Ethnicity also predicted co-offending patterns within the broader group, with Jamaicans working with other Jamaicans, Somalis cooperating with Somalis, West Africans offending with West Africans, and so on.

Much as the definition of gangs matters (Chapter 1), the criteria used to describe them and the people within them matter too. Although Asian gangs are more similar to than they are different from non-Asian gangs (Lee 2016), the common "Asian" designation could obfuscate potentially important differences between Chinese, Vietnamese, Hmong, and other ethnic gangs, not to mention the participation of Pacific Islanders in gangs, such as Native Hawaiians, Samoan Americans, Tongan Americans, and Guamanian/Chamorro Americans. Lest we forget, over half of the world's population could qualify as Asian. Likewise, not all Black people are African American, and while the two terms often are used interchangeably, the term *Hispanic* refers to native speakers of Spanish or people who have Spanish-speaking ancestry, while *Latino* is used to refer generally to anyone of Latin American origin or ancestry. We must also recognize that great diversity exists at the intersection of race/ethnicity and gender, sexuality, age, geography, faith, culture, and other structures of power (D. Peterson and Panfil 2017). Youth today have multiple identifications, meaning that an exclusive focus on race/ethnicity can ignore wider factors that may contribute to understanding gangs.

Immigration and Gang Formation

A look back at the history of gang formation in the United States sheds light on how immigration has shaped gang composition along racial and ethnic lines (Howell 2015; Howell and Griffiths 2015). Explosive growth transformed America's cities in the late nineteenth century. New industries concentrated in burgeoning urban settings demanded thousands of new workers. The promise of good wages and plentiful jobs attracted many rural and small-town dwellers to the cities. The promise of a better life also attracted millions of old immigrants from northern and western Europe to American cities between 1840 and 1890 and new immigrants, driven from their homelands in southern and eastern Europe by overpopulation, crop failure, famine, and industrial depression, in the three decades after 1890. Their arrival in the United States left an indelible mark on American society—including the first American gangs.

Immigrants who entered the United States with financial and social capital, including many Germans and Scandinavians, commonly traveled west from their port of entry at Ellis Island in New York to Chicago, Milwaukee, and the prairies beyond. But most of the Irish and Italian immigrants, largely from poor peasant backgrounds, stayed in the northeastern and north-central states and in cities such as Boston, New York, and Philadelphia, where they filled the lowest-paying jobs. In both cases, immigrants tended to cluster together to ease the transition to life in a new society (Riis 1890). Rates of assimilation varied, and whatever their degree of adaptation to the English language or American culture, all immigrant groups faced hostility from the local population, who disliked the foreigners' customs and feared their growing influence. Such influence is perhaps best represented by the "gangs" who were paid and encouraged by politicians such as "Boss" Tweed of Tammany Hall, the Democratic Party political machine, to assist in elections and drive voters to the polls (Asbury 1927; Chapter 10). Older and larger immigrant groups (e.g., the British and Germans) also sometimes made the adjustment to American society more difficult for members of newer and smaller groups (e.g., the Irish and Italians), such as by blocking their access to information and opportunities.

As powerfully depicted in Martin Scorsese's 2002 movie *Gangs of New York* (based on Herbert Asbury's 1927 nonfiction book of the same name), gangs flourished in America's ethnic enclaves, such as New York City's Five Points. Historian Will Cooley (2016) explains that, in general, the immigrant population was transient, not well acculturated, and disconnected from mainstream society. Existing social controls were weak and stressed by large numbers of unattached young men. Black markets serviced young immigrants' collective and individual needs, and they grew to view crime as a necessary alternative to poverty. Thus, while they were not inherently criminal groups, gangs committed crime, and because they were quick to stake out and defend their turf, "territorial conflicts took on a decidedly ethnoreligious cast" (Cooley 2016, 1).

There is no doubt that immigration to the United States led to the growth of gangs in both the early and late parts of the twentieth century (Covey 2010). As Adamson (2000, 276) observed, "Immigrant children, who found themselves caught between old-world communal practices of their parents and the norms of an often hostile host society, frequently got together in corner groups and gangs." However, immigration is not typically thought of as a cause of gang activity, even today when different immigrant groups wind up in gangs. Instead, explanations for the presence of gangs in immigrant communities speak to classic "structural control" and "structural adaptation" perspectives on gangs (Curry, Decker, and Pyrooz 2014). The former hold that gangs are naturally occurring phenomena (Thrasher 1927) in neighborhoods characterized by economic disadvantage, racial/ethnic heterogeneity, and residential mobility—the traditional "social disorganization" cocktail (e.g., Bursik and Grasmick 1993; Kornhauser 1978; Shaw and McKay 1942; Sampson and Groves 1989). Such neighborhoods attract diverse racial and ethnic groups, especially immigrants, but also experience greater population turnover. Subsequent social distance between residents limits social cohesion and complicates the informal social control of problems, what Sampson, Raudenbush, and Earls (1997) called "collective efficacy."

Structural adaptation perspectives argue that gangs form in response to a blocked opportunity structure and to redefine what constitutes success and the legitimate means of achieving it (A. Cohen 1955; Cloward and Ohlin 1960). There is no question that immigrants experience strain (Merton 1938). However, macro theories about structural change can only partially explain why gangs form. Micro context matters (Decker, Van Gemert, and Pyrooz 2009). As Adamson (2000) observed, gang formation was rooted historically in structural factors such as housing segregation, but gang conflict was explained by what he called "defensive localism"—gangs fighting to protect territory (see also Suttles 1972). Ethnic gangs would band together if a common enemy was present, and that common enemy was often other ethnic gangs. As Thrasher (1927) famously argued, gangs were integrated through conflict, and he frequently observed Jewish and Polish youth at odds over "old world antagonisms" (132).

Pinderhughes's (1997) research on racial and ethnic tensions in New York City in the late 1980s and early 1990s advanced a similar view of neighborhood threat and conflict. In Pinderhughes's study, first-generation ethnic Whites (Albanians) felt compelled to fight back against established second- and third-generation ethnic Whites (Italians), African Americans, and Puerto Rican and Dominican youth, who bullied them in schools and on the streets. Gangs such as the Albanian Boys and the Avenue T Boys formed to ensure respect for their minority group and to "defend" their neighborhood from outsiders. They even embarked on self-described "missions" to attack people of the "wrong color" in their neighborhoods.

Pinderhughes's work is a timely reminder that immigration is as much a part of America's present and future as of its storied past. Large waves of immigrants, mostly originating from Latin American and Asian countries, have found themselves in America's metropolitan areas since the 1970s. The country's largest cities have since become a melting pot of ethnicities, although tensions between home cultures, popular culture, and mainstream culture have contributed to a "culture shock" for first-generation children trying to adapt, potentially feeding the formation of ethnic gangs (Sellin 1938; Decker, Van Gemert, and Pyrooz 2009). To some extent, U.S. immigration policy even facilitated the formation and spread of transnational gangs such as Mara Salvatrucha 13, commonly known as MS-13.

In recent years, especially under the presidency of Donald J. Trump, MS-13 has become "America's most notorious gang," the bogeyman of U.S. immigration policy (Dudley 2020). MS-13 is responsible for a small, albeit grisly, proportion of gang violence in the United States, including an estimated 207 murders between 2012 and 2017 (https://cis.org/Report/MS13-Resurgence

-Immigration-Enforcement-Needed-Take-Back-Our-Streets). That translates to less than 0.3 percent of all U.S. murders during that time and about 2 percent of all gang-related homicides (https://www.nationalgangcenter.gov/survey-analysis/measuring-the-extent-of-gang-problems). Still, MS-13 has been explicitly singled out. As discussed in Chapter 9, MS-13 was first formed on the streets of Los Angeles by the children of Salvadoran immigrants fleeing from that country's civil war in the 1980s (Cruz 2010). The gang was a manifestation of Salvadorian pride and identity (Dudley 2020). But when those children and their families were deported or voluntarily returned to their homelands in Guatemala, El Salvador, and Honduras in the early 1990s, they brought back with them new gang styles and sensibilities that were locally adapted and adopted into hybrid subcultures (Cruz 2010). The United States exported more than just gang culture to Latin America—it also exported gang suppression policies and practices (Chapter 11). Gang crackdowns in Latin America are known as *mano dura*, or iron first (Hume 2007), and like in the United States, they have only helped solidify gangs and overpopulate prisons (M. Klein 1995).

Racism and Gang Formation

History is full of racial injustices (Wilkerson 2020). Proponents of critical race theory (Kendi 2019) argue that racial segregation, wide economic and employment disparities, racial differences in fatal police shootings, higher Black incarceration rates, lower educational attainment for Black and Latino youth, and so on are all evidence of structural racism—that is, racism that is all around us, woven into our laws, policies, and practices. So broadly defined, structural racism and the historical traumas associated with it may well contribute to the nonrandom distribution of gangs and gang members across America. The challenge is that the extant gang literature is not especially well positioned to empirically test this proposition, much less establish thresholds for what is and is not considered racism. Perhaps this in and of itself reflects racial bias in gang scholarship. Yet, racial outcome disparities do not alone prove systemic racism; they only imply disparate behavior and treatment. Racism is purposeful, commonly defined as racial prejudice and discrimination. Unequal group outcomes may yet be driven by internal factors (i.e., skills, attitudes, and behaviors) rather than external treatment (i.e., racial discrimination).

Still, the purpose of this section is to highlight what is best deduced about the hidden role of racism in the history of gang formation. For example, even when not explicitly motivated by racial antagonisms, gang fights in the late nineteenth and early twentieth centuries possessed a distinctive racial dimension, at least from the public's perspective, who viewed criminal gangs as part of a broader "alien conspiracy" of ethnic outsiders (Kefauver 1952). Diamond (2009) observed that gangs composed of members of European ethnic groups that had not yet been fully accepted as "White," including Irish, Italian, and Polish youth, used violence to not only resolve issues of racial and national identity but also stake a claim to "Whiteness" (see also Aspholm 2020). This was particularly true of violence undertaken by said groups against Black people (Diamond 2009; Hagedorn 2006), who occupied the lowest rung on America's racial hierarchy and from whom ethnic Europeans most wanted to distance themselves (Wilkerson 2020).

Driven from skilled trades, confined to low-paying menial jobs, trapped in segregated districts, and excluded from other areas by redlining and restrictive real-estate covenants (i.e., the practice of denying services, either directly or through selectively raising prices, to residents of certain areas based on race), the Black community had no way out of the ghetto. Growing competition between immigrants and Black migrants fleeing persecution in the Jim Crow South left Black people segregated in the poorest sections of northern cities, such as Chicago's "Black Belt" on the South Side (Wilkerson 2011). When Blacks first came to Chicago, they competed with the Irish over a scarce labor and housing market. In 1919, racial animosity reached fever pitch when White beachgoers stoned to death a Black youth swimming in an informally designated "White Only" section of Lake Michigan (Tuttle 1996). The Black youth drowned, and the Black community protested, demanding justice; but for their efforts, they were terrorized by covetous White vigilante mobs. Many Blacks were killed in the ensuing race riots, and as Whites set fire to Black neighborhoods, the Chicago Fire Department was prohibited from intervening (Tuttle 1996).

Hagedorn's (2006) essay "Race Not Space: A Revisionist History of Gangs in Chicago" emphasizes how racism shaped the contrasting trajectories of Chicago's European ethnic and Black gangs. Chicago is the birthplace of many of the country's oldest and most notorious street gangs, including the Black P. Stones, Gangster Disciples, Latin Kings, Mickey Cobras, and various incarnations of the Vice Lords, many of which trace their histories as far back as the 1950s and 1960s (Aspholm 2020; Cooley 2011; Cureton 2008; Dawley 1992). For Hagedorn, the origins of Chicago's Black gangs are undeniably rooted in the discrimination that Black people experienced in employment, housing, health care, and every other opportunity for upward social mobility. Black gangs formed out of economic necessity and a need to protect themselves, Hagedorn (2006) argued, whereas White gangs formed in part to terrorize anyone who dared to defy racist segregation laws.

The government's different responses to White (predominately Irish) and Black street gangs also created contrasting fortunes. "Conventionalized" White gangs or "social athletic clubs" were sponsored by politicians to provide boys and young men of the streets with rehabilitative and recreational opportunities (Hagedorn 2006). It is notable that Chicago mayor Richard J. Daley was once a dedicated gang member in his youth. As White gang members aged, they either graduated into organized crime, which flourished during Prohibition, or were "incorporated into the patronage machine controlled by Irish politicians," becoming firefighters and cops (Hagedorn 2006, 198).

By contrast, Black youth faced blocked access even to organized crime opportunities (Cooley 2011, 2017). Scholars commonly employ the theory of ethnic succession, the idea that once immigrant groups become acculturated and securely "American," they no longer need crime, to explain the shifting dominance of immigrant groups over the underworld economy (Cooley 2016). First, it was Irish immigrants who governed the streets. Later, during Prohibition, Jewish organized crime figures such as Arnold Rothstein seized control of bootlegging, loan sharking, gambling, and bookmaking. Then, Italians such as Johnny Torrio and Al Capone in Chicago and Charles "Lucky" Luciano in New York rose to prominence before and during the Depression, laying the foundation for the infamous American mafia (Cooley 2016). However, the position of Blacks was always worse than that of poor White immigrants, so they never truly competed in this space—notable exceptions being Los Angeles drug trafficker "Freeway" Rick Ross and Frank Lucas, king of the 1970s Harlem drug trade and protagonist of the 2002 movie *American Gangster.*

There was also never any serious attempt to formally rehabilitate Black gang members into society. Instead, the government responded through force, and for years, the Black community suffered in silence as their very existence was met with resistance (Hagedorn 2006). They battled with White gangs at the borderlands of Chicago's various Black enclaves and burgeoning White suburbs, while at the same time they were brutalized by White police officers. The postwar period was "an era of hidden violence" and "chronic urban guerrilla warfare," Hirsch (1998, 40–41) argued. But the racial violence of White society served as the galvanizing force in the defensive formation of Black youth gangs (Hagedorn 2008).

Latinos also were victimized by racialized gang violence—a critical revisiting of the beloved 1961 musical *West Side Story,* set in New York City, suggests as much. Puerto Rican youth in particular experienced the type of acute hostility typically reserved for their Black counterparts, owing to their dark skin and often-distinguishable African ancestry (Diamond 2009). However, the 1943 Zoot Suit Riots in Los Angeles stand as the best example of racial tensions boiling over. The riots were a series of violent clashes during which mobs of U.S. servicemen, off-duty police officers, and civilians fought against young Mexican Americans, who called themselves "pachucos." Rooted in generalized fear of "pachuco hoodlums and baby gangsters" (Castillo 2000), the riots took their name from the baggy suits worn by many minority youths at the time, perceived by Whites as the dress code of gang members and juvenile delinquents.

Racism inspired and intensified new forms of racial consciousness among young Black and Latino gang members (Brotherton and Barrios 2004; Diamond 2009; Hagedorn 2006). During the civil rights era, for example, the Black Panther Party attempted to form an alliance with Chicago's Black street gangs to turn them into activist organizations that could rise up against White supremacy. In the 1960s and 1970s, Chicago's largest and most sophisticated Black gang structure, the Vice Lords, became incorporated and even won government grants that paid for community revitalization projects (Dawley 1992). The Conservative Vice Lords Inc., as they were known, opened small businesses, established prominent social and cultural centers, and launched campaigns to beautify Chicago's Lawndale neighborhood under the slogans "Grass, not glass" and "Making the West Side the best side." However, a zero-tolerance crusade against gangs by Chicago mayor Richard M. Daley (son of Richard J.) brought this promising social experiment to an untimely end, and shortly after its funding was cut off, the gang became a negative presence.

Alonso's (2004) and Davis's (2006) research on Black gang formation in Los Angeles highlights how African Americans on the West Coast, who began arriving from the southern regions of the United States in the 1930s, were met with comparable levels of violence and resistance (Cureton 2008). The old car clubs were the foundation for many of the gangs in South Central Los Angeles, which at the time was a White middle-class community of government employees and white-collar workers. Cruising in hot rods and lowriders was a way for minority youth to exert their freedom over racially restrictive covenants in housing and the urban geography of segregation (G. Brown, Vigil, and Taylor 2012). Before long, however, Black and Latino social clubs came to be known as "gangs," singled out by authorities as more deviant and dangerous than the White car clubs known for drag racing along the paved Los Angeles Riverbed. Rivalries developed among groups, and smaller neighborhoods started to band together for protection. Defensive reaction formation (Alonso 2004) was the root of two of the city's most notorious gangs—the Crips and Bloods.

South Central in the 1960s was an area that exemplified the bleakness of poor urban places (Davis 1990). There was some structure and opportunity, largely through Black churches, but the Watts Riots of 1965 had left the city scorched and scarred, and an entire generation of young Black men were searching for identity and respect, hanging out together in nascent "gangs" for protection in the violent streets (G. Brown, Vigil, and Taylor 2012). As Dr. King (2014) poignantly observed in 1966, "There is nothing more dangerous than to build a society with a large segment of people in that society who feel they have no stake in it, who feel like they have nothing to lose." Undermined by government and labeled a threat to national security, the Black Power movement and its various forms of self-advocacy were waning, and it was out of the crisis of Black leadership after Dr. King's assassination in 1968 and the end of the civil rights era that the Crips emerged (Densley 2019).

The documentaries *Crips and Bloods: Made in America* and *Bastards of the Party* tell this Los Angeles story in vivid detail. In 1969, fifteen-year-old Raymond Washington, who had absorbed much of the Black Panther rhetoric of community control of neighborhoods, fashioned his own quasi-political organization in the Panthers' militant image. Washington, who had a reputation for street fighting, assembled his friends to start a gang near his Seventy-Sixth Street home, initially called the Baby Avenues to pay homage to the Avenues, an older local gang. The Baby Avenues later renamed themselves the Avenue Cribs, shortened to just Cribs, a play on the slag term for "home" as well as the group's youthful composition (i.e., a baby's bed).

Two years after Washington had founded the Cribs on the city's east side, a young bodybuilder with an affinity for street fighting named Stanley "Tookie" Williams was establishing himself across town on the west side (S. Williams 2007). In 1971, Washington's East Side Cribs and Williams's West Side Cribs banded together to defend against other South Central gangs that were harassing them; in so doing, they created the Crips, a backronym for Community Revolution in Progress. As the name implied, Washington and Williams intended to create a resistance movement for Black empowerment, but immaturity and inexperience meant that they failed to apply their vision of neighborhood protection into a broader progressive strategy. Instead, the group's membership became preoccupied with protecting themselves from marauding gangs in the community, and, as Thrasher (1927) predicted, they became integrated through conflict.

The Crips grew via friendship and kinship ties (a process common to many social groups) and a series of mergers, acquisitions, and hostile takeovers of existing LA gangs. However, rapid growth created problems for the fledgling gang. Long-standing enemies such as the Piru Street Boys and the Compton Crips were assumed to cooperate, for example, but grievances festered, and individual personalities clashed (Bakeer 1992). At the same time, non-Crip gangs, including the L.A. Brims, the Athens Park Boys, the Bishops, and the Denver Lanes, sought an effective defense against Crip predation. In 1972, the Pirus split from the Crips, and as a counterweight to Crip supremacy they formed a "Blood" alliance with the other gangs, initiating a war between Bloods and Crips that has claimed and changed countless lives.

Many gangs formed initially in response to racial and ethnic conflict and to defend their neighborhood from outsiders (Adamson 2000; Alonso 2004;

Hagedorn 2006; Suttles 1972). Today, however, gang violence tends to be intraracial. Conversations about intraracial violence often fall back on racist assumptions that crime has cultural, even biological, roots (see Abt [2019] for a discussion of the myth of "Black-on-Black crime"). However, using economic game theory, Gravel et al. (2018) simulate that intraracial violence between racially homogenous gangs merely reflects the social distance between racial groups in a community. Neighborhood drives social sorting, and people tend to fall back on who they know and what's around them as reference points for the status rewards of violence. Status also is conferred primarily within racial and ethnic groups.

Intraracial violence is therefore anchored in persistent structural disadvantages (Sampson and Wilson 1995), but "structural characteristics give rise to cultural adaptations that can manifest as interpersonal violence" (Kubrin and Wadsworth 2003, 28). One such characteristic is "a lack of effective criminal justice," which Leovy (2015, 8) argued contributes to the preponderance of Black gangs in particular. The theory goes that Black people turn to criminal gangs to provide order and safety (Sobel and Osoba 2009) and to deliver "street justice" in the absence of formal justice (B. Jacobs and Wright 2006). To put this point in context, an analysis of nearly twenty years of Chicago police data (Ryley 2019) found that police failed to make an arrest in 85 percent of the violent crimes committed with firearms, including nearly 42,000 shootings that resulted in an injury or fatality and 134,000 rapes, robberies, and assaults at gunpoint. In police districts where more residents were Black, arrests were made in a smaller number of shooting cases, and a larger share of all arrests were for petty crimes such as possessing or purchasing marijuana and other illegal drugs (Ryley 2019). Chicago police also were found saturating Black neighborhoods like an "occupying force," baiting residents and using "dangerous" and "reckless" tactics that frequently resulted in "some of the most problematic shootings" of civilians by police (United States Department of Justice Civil Rights Division and United States Attorney's Office Northern District of Illinois 2017, 30–31). For these reasons, Black people turn to gangs for protection (Chapter 4).

Relatedly, racial and ethnic identity is an important part of self-perception that needs to be accounted for when working with gang members. Mainstream delinquency prevention programs do work equally well for minority and White youth (D. Wilson, Gottfredson, and Najaka 2001), but Black, Latino, and other minority ethnic groups have unique experiences and face specific challenges. In a British context, Densley and Stevens (2015) highlighted the constraints imposed by the social structuring of race, noting that it was the "principal modality" (Hall et al. 1978, 347) through which Black gang members sought to comprehend the disadvantage and discrimination they experienced. Their experience of racism was both current and historically reproduced and thus could not be ignored. Durán (2018) similarly found that gang suppression alienates and criminalizes youth living in the barrios, and in the tradition of other critical scholars (e.g., Brotherton and Barrios 2004), he called for "barrio empowerment" to transcend gangs and integrate marginalized gang members and communities into mainstream society. For example, the marginalization of Black and Latino youth has motivated gangs such as the Almighty Latin Kings and Queens Nation to incorporate a political ideology aimed at promoting ethnic pride and cultural consciousness, fighting for political power, and producing social change in their neglected communities (Kontos, Brotherton, and Barrios 2003). In April 1992, for example, just days before the Rodney King riots, Crips and Bloods fatigued from decades of retaliatory violence in the Watts neighborhood of Los Angeles convened in the Imperial Courts Project gym to negotiate a truce modeled on the 1949 Armistice Agreements signed by Israel and Egypt, Lebanon, Jordan, and Syria. The gang cease-fire held for a number of years, and although shootings continued throughout the truce, violence declined.

(Sub)Culture, Migration, Appropriation, and Gangs

As discussed earlier, macro structures do not alone determine social action (Giddens 2013; Densley and Stevens 2015). Akin to our discussion in Chapter 2, culture, "more than just race," intervenes to influence structure and, in turn, the actions of Black, Latino, and other minority ethnic youth (Sampson and Bean 2006; W. Wilson 2009). It would be wrong to ignore the impact that this culture has on the lives of Black, Latino, and other minority ethnic young men. And, as Decker, Van Gemert, and Pyrooz (2009, 401) observed, "Culture is more than ethnicity and can be confounded with street culture, subculture, and global youth culture" (see also Ilan 2015).

Classic subcultural studies of gangs emphasized class over race (A. Cohen 1955; Cloward and Ohlin 1960). In this view, discussed in Chapter 2, the gang was an organizational form of subculture that adapted to structural conditions associated with the hierarchy of the social class system. Based on his extensive work with gangs in the Roxbury neighborhood of Boston, however, W. Miller (1958, 2011) held that gangs were not a product of frustration with middle-class values. Instead, gangs grew out of the lower-class norms or "focal concerns"—trouble, toughness, smartness, autonomy, fate, and excitement—that they share with their community, not opposition to middle-class value systems. The gang then adheres to these focal concerns, which in turn dictate status among gang members. Gang members do not achieve status by getting good grades; rather, they achieve status by being tough and fearless. Such values distinguish the peer groups of the lower class from those of the middle class.

Contemporary structural adaptation explanations of gang emergence emphasize earning respect and achieving economic success in a highly segregated, postindustrial America. Unlike the structural and cultural context of the 1950s, contemporary urban America is replete with the instrumentalities of violence, including drugs and guns, and any "decent" families living in proximity struggle to raise their children in a way that keeps them away from violence (E. Anderson 1990, 1999). E. Anderson's (1999) "code of the street" portrays Black life in the inner city as dictated by a street code that governs interpersonal relationships and dispute resolution. The perception of dirty looks, wayward stares, and seemingly benign insults could result in violent encounters. Such an oppositional street context emerges as a result of a sorting process that creates stable pockets of poverty, residential segregation, labor market inequality, and other disadvantages. While E. Anderson (1999) did not focus explicitly on street gangs, many of the references to street codes and related behaviors are commonly referenced in research on gangs. For example, the expectation of deferential treatment in public, violent responses to trivial insults, retaliatory violence, status attainment through physical means, and the code of honor are themes in many gang-related studies (e.g., Decker and Van Winkle 1996; Horowitz 1983; W. Miller 1958, 2011; Short and Strodtbeck 1965).

The neighborhood context where these street codes emerge is described by W. Wilson's (1987, 1997) deindustrialization thesis. As discussed in Chapter 2, changes in the structure of the labor market disproportionately affected those from socially and economically marginalized groups, especially African Americans. The transition from a manufacturing to a service-oriented economy in the 1970s brought about many social dislocations in urban America, as the demand for low-skill or blue-collar labor waned. These jobs were a natural fit for racialized and marginalized young people (who were often undereducated and undertrained), because they did not require the "soft skills" for face-to-face interactions with consumers. Gang researchers saw face validity in this thesis and extended Wilson's arguments to gangs, holding that marginalized youth turn to gangs for economic purposes (Hagedorn 1998; Joan Moore 1991; Joan Moore and Pinderhughes 1993; Sullivan 1989). As Venkatesh (2002, 2009) illustrated so well in Chicago, diminished legitimate job prospects for young men promoted underground markets and a secondary economy that was governed by gangs and largely fueled by the drug trade.

The final chapter in Hagedorn's (2006) history of gangs documented the era of deindustrialization and mass incarceration and the subsequent transformation of Chicago's Black gangs into corporate-style drug-selling organizations (Levitt and Venkatesh 2000; Padilla 1992; Popkin et al. 2000; Venkatesh 1997; Venkatesh and Levitt 2000). Aspholm's (2020) recent work added a new chapter—horizontal Black gangs, or "cliques," that have strong neighborhood loyalty but are composed of members from many different, and often rival, traditional gangs, such as the Gangster Disciples and Black P. Stones. Such research implies that different racial and ethnic groups adapt differently to the circumstances they are dealt. Vigil (1988, 2002, 2020) proposed the "multiple marginality" thesis to explain the formation of Latino gangs, for example. From this perspective, youth who are marginalized by poverty, work that is insufficient to sustain a family, poor schools, inadequate parenting, and racism will form and join gangs. These "urban outcasts" have been subjected to the triple forces that Wacquant (2007) described: mass unemployment, relegation to neglected neighborhoods, and stigmatization along class and ethnic lines. These forces played a key role in mass incarceration, a point we examine in Chapter 12. Lee's (2016) synthesis of the literature found that multiple marginality was also the dominant theory for explaining the onset and persistence of Asian gangs.

In poor urban areas hollowed out by deindustrialization and cut off from economic opportunity by racial discrimination, drugs such as crack cocaine provided one of the few lucrative incomes for young Black, Latino, and other minority ethnic men. During the 1980s and 1990s, gang members allegedly began migrating from Chicago and Los Angeles to other U.S. cities to establish new drug markets and other criminal enterprises. This gave rise to gang franchising or importation, whereby Los Angeles gangs would either colonize gangs in other locations or recruit local youth to establish a branch of the gang in an area previously untouched by gangs (Maxson 1998). Police crackdowns and tough new criminal justice sanctions on gangs also resulted in the movement of gang members to state and federal correctional facilities throughout the country (Chapter 12). However, perhaps the greatest contributing factor to the spread of gangs outside of "chronic" (Spergel 1995) gang cities such as Chicago and Los Angeles was popular culture and indigenous influences in communities (Maxson 1998).

Imitation is the greatest form of flattery, and thanks to seductive depictions of gangs in the gangster rap music of the N.W.A. and in Hollywood movies such as *Colors* in 1988, *Boyz n the Hood* in 1991, *South Central, Juice*, and *American Me* in 1992, and *Menace II Society* in 1993, youth gangs across the United States began appropriating big-city gang style. Since the 1990s, gangster style has permeated youth culture. Non-gang youth wear the same colored baggy pants or Levi's jeans, baseball caps, basketball jerseys, and bandanas as their gang counterparts, leading some to rightly conclude that a subculture exists beyond the gang (Covey 2015). Critical and cultural criminologists go further, arguing that the gang and its symbolism have been commodified (Hayward and Yar 2006; Ilan 2015) to sell not only clothing and music (Ilan 2020; Pinkney and Robinson-Edwards 2018) but also

sensational tales of Black and Latino criminality to a mostly White suburban youth market (McCann 2017).

However, as Van Hellemont and Densley (2019) observed, fictional accounts of gangs resonated with racialized and marginalized youth too, including those in faraway locales, because they saw themselves for the first
time in the characters and stories presented; such is the emotional power of
fiction when fueled by popular culture. By embracing the persona of the
"gangster," Black and Latino youth, who otherwise possess little power or
capital, can come to accumulate some (Hagedorn 2008). In fact, the gangster has become a powerful global symbol of resistance to hegemonic racial
oppression (Hagedorn 2008). This explains why "supergangs" (Howell and
Griffiths 2015) such as the Bloods and Crips have outposts in most U.S.
states and sets throughout the world (e.g., Van Gemert 2001). While most
ties to the original version are mythical, in the age of global travel and the
internet, what were once distant or even metaphorical ties between Blood
and Crip sets have in some cases become close, literal connections, with
domestic and foreign gangs following and friending each other on social
media and foreign gang members making pilgrimages to Los Angeles (Roks
and Densley 2020), which remains the gangs' stronghold.

Conclusion

A combination of structural factors (e.g., poverty, disadvantage, and immigration), process factors (e.g., cultural conflict and racial and group threats), and
cultural factors (e.g., street codes and global street culture) has resulted in the
formation, growth, and spread of gangs among immigrant, Black, Latino, and
other minority ethnic youth; and one product of such factors has been the
criminalization and increased marginalization of these populations. This
chapter has presented racial and ethnic homophily in gangs as an outcome of
opportunities and preferences. The overrepresentation of Black, Latino, and
other minority ethnic youth in gangs and in crime statistics does not reflect
any special criminal predisposition on their part. Instead, Black, Latino, and
other minority ethnic youth suffer at disproportionate rates the social exclusion and marginalization, concentrated deprivation, and educational failure
that are linked statistically to higher rates of gang membership. The reality and
perception of racism in America also feed the defensive reaction formation of
gangs, encouraging youth to mobilize in an effort to resist racial discrimination, White supremacy, and aggression. Still, the political economy matters,
and so does social class, because (as discussed in Chapter 2) individuals who
engage in activity classified by control agents as "gang related" are overrepresented in the subproletariat that is now surplus to production in the modern
global economy. In other words, gangs live at the intersection of race and class.

9

Gangs around the World

The majority of the theoretical knowledge and empirical work on gangs has come from the United States. Although there are advantages in learning from the American experience, we cannot assume that all gangs are "the American street gang" (M. Klein 1995). As Pyrooz and Mitchell (2015, 43) observed, an "international turn" in gang research occurred around the millennium, "when the study of gangs was no longer the study of gangs in the United States." Outside of the Eurogang body of research (M. Klein et al. 2000; Decker and Weerman 2005), Herbert Covey's (2003) *Street Gangs throughout the World*, which extended a chapter on "Youth Street Gangs in Other Cultures" from his early textbook *Juvenile Gangs* (Covey, Menard, and Franzese 1992), was perhaps the first book to draw attention to the global diversity of gangs. Covey's work included chapters on gangs in Europe, the Western Hemisphere, Russia, Asia, Africa, and Australia. Then followed John Hagedorn's (2008) *A World of Gangs*, which combined primary research conducted in Chicago with secondary material about gangs in Cape Town and Rio de Janeiro. Hagedorn's study made clear that gangs were a global phenomenon, and, despite some difficulties applying definitions cross-nationally, they can be found in most societies around the world (Decker and Pyrooz 2010a). This chapter, therefore, examines the nature and extent of gang activity globally. We pay close attention to similarities and differences across countries, as well as some of the emerging issues pertaining to gangs and gang crime in different parts of the world.

This chapter starts with a discussion of gangs in Europe, including a review of the influential Eurogang program of research and the emerging TRANSGANG and "gangs, gangsters, and ganglands" studies. It then moves on to examine gangs in the United Kingdom, the site of the largest body of research outside the United States as well as some of the greatest debates about the efficacy of gangs and gang research. Next, we look at Canadian gang research and its tradition of social network analysis. Then we consider gangs in Latin America and the Caribbean, where corruption, drugs, and violence are central themes. We finish with gangs in Africa, Asia, and Oceania.

Note that there is not the scope here to discuss every study of gangs outside the United States, and the literature is more mature in some regions than in others. Owing to certain research traditions and practices, it also tends to be more qualitative than quantitative in places. A recent systematic review of factors associated with youth gang membership in low- and middle-income countries concluded, "The lack of available evidence limits the extent to which we can draw any clear conclusions about the factors associated with youth gang membership" (Higginson et al. 2018, 6). However, as can be observed, there is still a tremendous amount of scholarship on gangs across the globe.

Gangs in Europe (and Beyond)

The rise of European gang research is intimately tied to the establishment of the Eurogang Working Group. Eurogang has been described at length in a number of outlets, including six volumes of related research (Decker and Weerman 2005; Esbensen and Maxson 2012; M. Klein et al. 2000; Maxson and Esbensen 2016; Melde and Weerman 2020; Van Gemert, Peterson, and Lien 2008), various chapters and articles by its founding members (M. Klein 2012; Esbensen and Maxson 2018), and the group's own training manual of research instruments (Weerman et al. 2009). For the uninitiated, Eurogang's origins are set in the 1980s and 1990s, when leading US gang researcher Malcolm Klein traveled extensively in Europe, gathering evidence of what he believed to be gangs and gang issues. In 1997, he used the occasion of a conference in Leuven, Belgium, to convene a small group of European colleagues, share his travel observations, and pitch the idea of a subsequent meeting to talk more about the prospect of gangs in Europe. At the time, gangs were not part of the criminological vernacular beyond American borders, but the meeting was arranged, and in 1998 what is now known as "Eurogang I" came to fruition in Schmitten, Germany.

At the first Eurogang workshop, European researchers presented evidence of "troublesome youth groups" tantamount to gangs elsewhere (Weerman et al. 2009). It was here that Klein coined the now-famous "Eurogang Paradox"—the denial that there are American-style gangs in Europe based on a vision of the stereotypical American gang that is not at all typical of gangs in America (M. Klein 2001, 10). Klein contended that street gangs in the United States did not fit the stereotype of vertically structured, efficient, formal organizations that was widely held in Europe and among much of the American public and law enforcement (Chapter 3). Europe's inability to foresee gangs, therefore, was a collective failure of imagination, brought about by a constrained view of what Europe was supposed to be imagining. At the center of all this was a great deal of controversy around use of the term *gang*, which was perceived to be ambiguous, racialized, and highly stigmatizing in the European context.

After much debate, the outcome of the first Eurogang meeting was an agenda for collaborative, comparative, multisite, multimethod gang research, incorporating different levels of analysis (Maxson 2001). Two decades and nineteen workshops later (see Table 9.1), the Eurogang network has grown to more than two hundred researchers and practitioners and has come to resemble its own "invisible college," unburdened by traditional borders such as academic disciplines, universities, or even countries (Pyrooz and Mitchell 2015, 45). Eurogang is a hub for information sharing and disseminates research via edited volumes, an email listserv, a Twitter profile (@Euro_Gang), and a website (https://eurogangproject.com). It has also designed, pretested, and translated five open-access research instruments and protocols (see Weerman et al. 2009). Perhaps most importantly, Eurogang has advanced a consensus, yet still contentious, definition of a street gang to surmount language, cultural, demographic, and regional differences. Recall from Chapter 1, the Eurogang definition of "any durable, street-oriented youth group whose involvement in illegal activity is part of its group identity" (M. Klein and Maxson 2006, 4) emphasizes the following:

- Durability (with respect to the group over time)
- Street-oriented lifestyle (activities are oriented around places open to the public)
- Youthfulness (members tend to be in their teens and early twenties)
- Illegal activity (law-violating—delinquent or criminal—behavior)
- Identity (in that illegal activities help define the group identity)

The Eurogang definition provides a basis for the consistent identification of gangs across jurisdictions, uniting gang research across countries and continents. Variables that are not part of the Eurogang definition—such as the gang's size, structure, organization, ethnicity, symbols, gender, and

TABLE 9.1 TIMELINE OF THE EUROGANG PROJECT

Workshop	Date	Location
I	September 1998	Schmitten, Germany
II	September 1999	Oslo, Norway
III	October 1999	Leuven, Belgium
IV	September 2000	Egmond an Zee, the Netherlands
The Eurogang Paradox (M. Klein et al. 2001)		
V	July 2002	Straubing, Germany
VI	July 2003	Straubing, Germany
VII	July 2004	Albany, New York, United States
VIII	May 2005	Onati, Spain
European Street Gangs and Troublesome Youth Groups (Decker and Weerman 2005)		
VIX	May 2008	Los Angeles, California, United States
Street Gangs, Migration and Ethnicity (Van Gemert, Peterson, and Lien 2008) *Eurogang Program Manual* (Weerman et al. 2009)		
X	June 2010	Neustadt an der Weinstrasse, Germany
XI	September 2011	Hillerod, Denmark
XII	May 2012	Stockholm, Sweden
Youth Gangs in International Perspective (Esbensen and Maxson 2012)		
XIII	June 2013	Canterbury, United Kingdom
XIV	June 2014	Stavern, Norway
XV	June 2015	Blaubeuren, Germany
XVI	June 2016	Gothenburg, Sweden
Gang Transitions and Transformations in an International Context (Maxson and Esbensen 2016)		
XVII	June 2017	East Lansing, Michigan, United States
XVIII	June 2018	Rotterdam and Almen, the Netherlands
XVIX	June 2019	Canterbury, United Kingdom
Gangs in the Era of Internet and Social Media (Melde and Weerman 2020)		

cohesiveness—capture the variation and diversity of gangs, but as descriptors, they are not necessary to defining a group as a gang.

Eurogang definitional indicators were included in the school-based International Self-Report Delinquency studies (ISRD; https://web.northeastern .edu/isrd/; Junger-Tas 2010), which helped yield a baseline for gang prevalence rates in thirty countries in northern, western, eastern, and central European, Anglo-Saxon, Mediterranean, and Latin American regions (Gatti, Haymoz, and Schadee 2011). Lifetime prevalence rates for gang membership in Europe, based on the Eurogang definition, ranged from 4.2 percent in Portugal to 27.2 percent in Ireland, with an average of 11.8 percent (Haymoz, Maxson, and Killias 2014). Despite this wide range, most countries' prevalence rates fall between 8 and 12 percent, not unlike rates in U.S. schools, as we reported in

Chapter 1. You may recall that school-based surveys of teenagers are not necessarily representative of all gang youth. It is likely that in Europe, as in the United States, there is no "single unified gang problem" (Curry 2000, 1254). Survey research tends toward gang members who are younger, delinquent, and marginally embedded in informal-diffuse gangs. Ethnographic research and official data, by contrast, capture gang members who are older, criminal, and deeply embedded in instrumental-rational gangs. Still, these projects are important steps forward in understanding the global diversity of gang activity.

In Europe, comparisons of gang and non-gang youth in terms of risk factors have been conducted in London (Alleyne and Wood 2010), Edinburgh (McAra and McVie 2010), and elsewhere in the United Kingdom (T. Bennett and Holloway 2004; Medina-Ariza et al. 2014; Sharp, Aldridge, and Medina 2006), as well as in Belgium (Pauwels and Svensson 2013; Vettenburg et al. 2013), Denmark (Pedersen and Lindstad 2012; Pedersen 2014), France, Italy, and Switzerland (Blaya and Gatti 2010; Haymoz and Gatti 2010). However, Eurogang's promise of truly comparative gang research has not always borne fruit (M. Klein 2005), in part because of the financial and logistical hurdles to international research projects as well as the compatibility of data.

One solution has been post-hoc research comparisons, such as Weerman, Lovegrove, and Thornberry's (2015) exploration of gang membership transitions drawing on two longitudinal studies—the Rochester Youth Development Study in the United States and the NSCR School Study in the Netherlands. The authors found that in both countries, gang tenure was relatively short-lived, and the modal term in the gang was only one year. Also, in both countries, they found that joining a gang was related to an increasing exposure to negative peer influences, a weakening of conventional bonds, and increasing levels of delinquency and substance use.

A four-year longitudinal study comparing youth in Denver, Colorado, to youth in Bremen, Germany, found that the prevalence of gang membership in each youth sample was comparable—14 percent in Denver and 13 percent in Bremen (Huizinga and Schumann 2001). In both cities, gang members also were overrepresented in violence, with gang youths involved in three to four times more violent acts than non-gang youth in both cities.

A comparison between Dutch and U.S. students came to similar conclusions about the impact of gang membership on involvement in delinquency (Esbensen and Weerman 2005). Both school-based samples were large (nearly six thousand in the United States and two thousand in the Netherlands). Eight percent of the U.S. students reported being in a gang, while 6 percent of the Dutch students reported they were gang members. Similar to the Denver–Bremen findings, gang youth in the Netherlands and the United States were disproportionately involved in violent offenses. Students from both countries were involved in nearly four times more violent delinquency than non-gang youths (Esbensen and Weerman 2005).

A recent ethnographic comparison of reactions to gang-related homicides in the Netherlands and Canada found that gang members in both sites processed death similarly by conducting "pseudo-homicide investigations" and attributing blame to the victim (Urbanik and Roks 2021, 17). However, in Canada, where murder was more frequent and thus more "real," gang members had grown desensitized to the violence and hypervigilance of it, whereas in the Netherlands, where homicide was still rare, fatal violence took on deeper cultural significance, testing or affirming group commitment and becoming a signal of authenticity.

Another comparative study confirms that the levels and severity of gang-related youth violence were generally lower in European countries than in the United States (M. Klein, Weerman, and Thornberry 2006). Gang membership in Europe was correlated with violent offending as in the United States, but it was less lethal in part due to lower levels of firearm use (see also Zimring and Hawkins 1999). A recent study, however, has noted a rise in "explosive violence" in urban Sweden, including shootings and hand grenade attacks attributed to gangs (Sturup, Gerell, and Rostami 2020).

Themes of migration, marginalization, and neighborhood, discussed in detail in Chapters 2 and 8, feature predominately in the etiology of European gangs, as they do in American gangs (Decker, Van Gemert, and Pyrooz 2009; Van Gemert, Peterson, and Lien 2008). Much as there are regional variations among gangs in the United States, gangs in Europe also differ within and between countries. Gangs in Kazan and Russia (Salagaev 2001; Salagaev et al. 2005) and in the Scandinavian countries of Norway (Lien 2005), Denmark (Pedersen and Lindstad 2012), and Sweden (Rostami and Leinfelt 2012; Rostami, Leinfelt, and Holgersson 2012), for example, tend to be more organized, to the extent that while they may fit the Eurogang definition, they better resemble organized crime groups. One exception is Rostami and Leinfelt (2012), both police officials in Stockholm at the time, who described the Swedish gangs they observed in terms much like American gangs as loosely organized, publicly visible, and extensively involved in crime. It is interesting that they conducted extensive field interviews with gang members, something difficult to imagine being done by law enforcement officers in the United States.

Still, a good deal of the early interest in gangs in Scandinavia was focused on outlaw motorcycle gangs, many of which took the names of North American biker gangs such as the Hells Angels (Rostami and Mondani 2019). In her study of Danish gangs, Pedersen (2018) notes that outlaw motorcycle gangs and "adult criminal gangs" are qualitatively different from street gangs because of the age of their members and their level of organization. In Denmark, a growing number of street communities in Copenhagen have militarized significantly in relation to conflicts over local drug markets (Mørck et al. 2013; Deuchar et al. 2016). But, as is common in the American context, crime and violence often are seen as a means for young, marginalized, ethnic minority men to build a sense of "street capital" (Sandberg and Pedersen 2011) in response to experiences of stigmatization and a perceived lack of belonging in mainstream society.

Notwithstanding these contributions, some European scholars take issue with the "quantification of gang research" (Pyrooz and Mitchell 2015, 42) exported from the United States to Europe. The late Jock Young (2004), for example, argues that an "administrative criminology" characterized by "voodoo statistics" dehumanizes and denaturalizes the human experience, reducing gang members to "walking clusters of de-contextualized variables" (Hallsworth and Young 2008, 187). Moreover, by defining gangs as innately criminal and adapting their research assumptions to meet the needs of their justice system sponsors, administrative criminologists inevitably pathologize the gang, thus ignoring more prosocial understandings of them (Brotherton 2015; Mucchielli and Mohammed 2007).

Critical criminologists allege that the Eurogang project, which is open to practitioners and at times utilizes official (police) data, is a major (state-sponsored) contributor to a flourishing gang control industry in Europe (Hallsworth and Brotherton 2011). It is a baseless accusation, rooted in Klein's historical use of law enforcement data and the myth that his early work (M. Klein 1971) played a part in criminalizing gangs and ushering in a new era of repressive anti-gang and youth policies. Writing from experience as active participants in Eurogang, we know that the network is far more diverse than its critics realize, with a host of ethnographers and critical criminologists among its ranks (e.g., Jong 2012; Fraser, Ralphs, and Smithson 2018; Urbanik and Roks 2020; Van Hellemont and Densley 2019).

What is true is that in recent years, Europe has adopted, with varying degrees of success, an array of gang responses (see Chapters 11–14) originally tried and tested in the U.S. context (Densley 2011; Fraser, Ralphs, and Smithson 2018), such as using databases to identify the most violent group members and customize police action (Densley and Pyrooz 2020), "focused deterrence" strategies that target the small number of chronic offenders who are most vulnerable to sanctions with clear incentives for nonviolence (Densley and Jones 2016; Deuchar 2013), and civil gang injunctions that limit gang members' freedoms of association and movement (Carr, Slothower, and Parkinson 2017; Densley 2013). As M. Klein (2001) and Decker (2001) first noted, the myth of the American gang looms large in Europe. If gangs themselves are influenced both by fictional American gangster movies and television shows, such as *New Jack City* and *The Wire*, and by factual (albeit mythologized) American supergangs, such as the Bloods and Crips, it stands to reason that practitioners and policymakers are affected too (Van Hellemont and Densley 2019). Research from the Netherlands finds that the hegemony of the American street gang (M. Klein 1995) is really an expression of the hegemony of American culture, which the rise of the internet and social media have only solidified (Roks and Densley 2020; Van Gemert 2001, 2012; Van Gemert, Roks, and Drogt 2016; Van Gemert and Weerman 2013).

Country-specific case studies, which are juxtaposed rather than properly compared (see Fraser and Hagedorn 2018), make up the majority of Eurogang's output (Irwin-Rogers et al. 2019). One exception is Van Hellemont and Densley's (2019) comparative ethnography of Brussels and London, which merges two datasets in an effort to examine the "glocalization" of gang culture. Outside of the Eurogang framework, moreover, Deuchar (2018) has examined the universal role of religion and spirituality among gangs in Denmark, Scotland, Hong Kong, and the United States. His qualitative research emphasized the role of masculinities in gang engagement and how religious conversion and spiritual practices facilitated disengagement by redefining what it meant to be a man. Deuchar and colleagues (2020) also compared and contrasted female gang membership in Los Angeles and Glasgow, finding local variations on a deficit model of entry into gangs, linked to drug addiction and debt, and a credit model of entry, linked to women's agency and social capital (see Chapter 7).

The TRANSGANG project (Transnational Gangs as Agents of Mediation: Experiences of Conflict Resolution in Street Youth Organizations in Southern Europe, North Africa and the Americas), directed by Carles Feixa Pàmpols at Pompeu Fabra University in Barcelona, Spain, and funded by the European Research Council, seeks to develop a new model for the analysis of transnational youth gangs in the age of globalization (https://www.upf.edu/web /transgang). The project compares and contrasts Hispanic and Arab street youth organizations, both in their countries of origin and in their new immigrant neighborhoods, and highlights examples where gangs have acted as "agents of mediation." For example, in the Spanish community of Catalonia, including its provincial capital, Barcelona, the Almighty Latin King and Queen Nation is accepted as a nonviolent cultural association, whereas in the rest of the country, including the capital, Madrid, the gang is treated as an organized crime group. The TRANSGANG project aims to juxtapose policies of peace and inclusion, such as in Barcelona, Medellín (Colombia), and Casablanca (Morocco), with policies of war and exclusion in Madrid, Marseilles (France), Milan (Italy), Oran (Algeria), Tunis (Tunisia), Cairo (Egypt), Chicago (United States), Santiago de Cuba (Cuba), and San Salvador (El Salvador).

This comparative, multisite ethnography of gangs in southern Europe, North Africa, and the Americas moves gang research away from its typical focus on crime and violence to capture instead the specific cultural practices and creative outputs of gangs, including the perceived benefits of gang membership for marginalized youth. Anchored in the traditions of subcultural research, critical criminology, and postcolonial studies, the project emphasizes the inclusive and positive aspects of gang membership, breaking with the more typical vision of gangs. The research also recognizes that the gang is not a single model but rather a continuum. At one extreme, there are youth subcultures based on leisure and economic activities, and at the other there are gangs in the classic sense, based on illegal activities, with a variety of hybrid groups in between.

The TRANSGANG project complements another ongoing study of gangs funded by the European Research Council titled "Gangs, Gangsters, and Ganglands: Towards a Comparative Global Ethnography." This project, headed by Dennis Rodgers and Stefan Jensen at the Graduate Institute Geneva, aims to systematically compare gang dynamics in France, Nicaragua, and South Africa and follows Rodger's 2014 coedited volume on *Global Gangs* (Hazen and Rodgers 2014), which examined the similarities and differences between gangs in different contexts around the world. This work is still in progress.

Gangs in the United Kingdom

Geographically still in Europe, albeit politically and economically separate post-Brexit, the United Kingdom deserves special attention because nowhere is the debate about gangs and gang violence more intense than in these small islands (Densley, Deuchar, and Harding 2020). For years, Britain avoided any mention of gangs, preferring instead to focus on youth subcultures (Campbell, Munce, and Galea 1982). Patrick's (1973) classic, *A Glasgow Gang Observed*, is notable for being practically the only empirical study of a structured youth gang in Great Britain before 1995. Observers of the British youth scene, notably Downes (1966) and Campbell and Muncer (1989), claimed that the lack of research on gangs in Britain reflected the fact that there simply weren't gangs there. Hallsworth and Young (2008) followed this tradition in the early days of what amounts to a recent explosion in U.K. gang research, arguing that it was not gangs people saw on Britain's streets but "violent street worlds" (Hallsworth 2013) created by young people seeking relief from boredom and structural inequality. Inspired by J. Katz and Jackson-Jacobs's (2004) "criminologists' gang" thesis (i.e., the notion that gangs were the social creation of criminologists whose conceptualization was based not on ethnographic understanding but on official records), Hallsworth and Young (2008) famously advanced the notion that gangs were a social construction and media invention around which both police and academics coalesced in order to keep themselves in paid work. Gangs were exaggerated and—at least partly—imaginary productions of the predilection for "gang talk" by a burgeoning gang industry, Hallsworth and Young (2008) said, thus foreshadowing heavy criticism of subsequent government policy and practice on gangs (e.g., Fraser and Atkinson 2014; Shute and Medina 2014; Smithson and Ralphs 2016). One of the ironies of this criticism is that many of the critics of gang research have received government funding to study gangs.

We know now that the United Kingdom was ground zero for the Euro-gang paradox (M. Klein 2001). It was true that in the early to mid-2000s, the "gang" intervention industry in Britain was disproportionate to the size of its gang problem and was, in many ways, failing to intervene appropriately in the lives of young people (Densley 2011). However, the idea that the media made the whole gang thing up was questionable when several assessments of gangs in the British context, each using different methodologies (e.g., official data, survey data, or ethnographic research), found evidence of gangs in Britain dating back to the 1990s and that gang membership was increasing both the frequency and seriousness of youth offending. This includes the work of Stellfox (1998) with police forces in the United Kingdom; T. Bennett and Holloway (2004) with the NEW-ADAM arrestee survey; Aldridge and Medina (2005) with the 2004 Offending, Crime and Justice Survey for England and Wales; Mares (1998) and Bullock and Tilley (2002), working with offenders in Manchester; and G. Whittaker and colleagues (2017) with London hospital data. Furthermore, amid rising youth violence in London and other urban centers circa 2007, victims' families were actively lobbying the press and government for action on an indigenous gang problem.

John Pitts's (2008) *Reluctant Gangsters: The Changing Face of Youth Crime* was perhaps the first study to challenge head-on the prevailing wisdom that Britain was characterized only by resistant youth subcultures and not by violent street gangs. Drawing on qualitative research in east and south London, Pitts (2008) offered a theoretical explanation centered on the impact of globalization and the concentration of poverty in deprived neighborhoods, which acted as crucibles for gang activity. In an affront to Britain's critical criminologists in general and Hallsworth in particular, Pitts (2012) argued that gangs were a reaction to British society, not the other way around—mass migration, racial discrimination, rising income inequality, and conflict over the control of drug markets had birthed a quintessentially British variety of street gang that had evolved out of traditional youth group structures. Young people were "reluctantly" but pragmatically joining them, Pitts (2008) said, in an effort to negotiate the harsh realities of an increasingly violent, territorial street life.

Pitts's work, a precursor to a "critical realist" perspective that acknowledges the social reality of U.K. gangs in a way that avoids the politics of gang denial and gang blame (Andell 2019), paved the way for a series of studies of gangs in London. Drawing on two years of ethnographic fieldwork in the city and interviews with nearly two hundred people, including sixty-nine gang-involved youth, one of us (Densley 2013) found clear evidence of instrumental-rational gangs with a strong business orientation. For Densley, gang membership was a choice, but one from constrained parameters, and he situates his arguments firmly in young people's lived experiences of social exclusion and poverty (Densley and Stevens 2015). The gang is an "alternate social and economic infrastructure" rather than an "alternative family," Densley (2013, 42) found, as he identified the progression of gangs from formative groupings, which facilitate recreational violence, through criminal activity to criminal enterprise, and ultimately to governance of illegal markets (Densley 2014b). This evolution permits movement from recreational and criminal stages to financial goal orientation. The closer gangs get to resembling organized crime, the more they develop structures for issuing orders, informal rules, and codes of trust (see Chapter 3).

Densley's observation of structural and functional change is quite unique in gang research, but he argued further that trust is central to the gang, which means that testing loyalty becomes an imperative, and this leads to greater selectivity in gang recruitment and membership (Densley 2012b). This process of negotiating trust is inherently linked to the reputation of the gang and its use of symbols. He used signaling theory (see Chapters 4 and 5) to explain how street codes and reputations are reinterpreted by the gang to assess levels of trust and to navigate the uncertainty of the gang disengagement process (see also Densley and Pyrooz 2019).

Densley's (2013) research was also the first to shed light on the "county lines" supply model of illicit drugs in the United Kingdom, whereby gang members in hub cities such as London commute to more profitable and less saturated provincial markets outside of the city to retail crack cocaine and heroin. Subsequent research has examined how county lines feed the goal orientation and articulated structure of U.K. gangs (Harding 2020; McLean, Robinson, and Densley 2020; Robinson, McLean, and Densley 2019). Akin to a "pyramid scheme," gang "elders" at the top exploit their "downline" of drug runners and sellers at the bottom, called "youngers," in order to maximize profits and avoid police attention (Densley 2012a). These findings are reminiscent of Levitt and Venkatesh's (2000) study of a "drug selling gang" in Chicago and the income and risk disparities they found between senior gang members and their foot soldiers.

Research by Hesketh and Robinson (2019) in Merseyside discovered a comparable model of "deviant entrepreneurship" whereby crime gangs effectively employed young people to do the grunt work of drug dealing for them. Hesketh (2019) adds that gang membership gave young people a sense of belonging, identity, and excitement, as well as a way to earn money because some gang members found a substitute for the lack of employment in the local area in "grafting" (drug dealing), similar to some of the U.S. underclass studies described in Chapter 2. A ten-year follow-up study of Pitts's (2008) research, conducted in one of the same London communities as the original, similarly found that local gangs had evolved into more organized and profit-oriented entities with an emphasis on county-lines drug dealing. A. Whittaker and colleagues (2020) found through a series of interviews with practitioners and young people that gang members' expressive and emotional connection to their neighborhood or postcode (zip code) was waning because increasingly, gang turf was regarded as a marketplace to be monetized.

These findings align closely with those of Harding, who conducted his fieldwork in south London around the same time as Densley. Harding (2014) applied Bourdieu's social field theory to create a new theory of gang dynamics called "street capital." (Note that Sandberg and Pedersen [2011] used similar language to describe street life in Oslo, Norway; however, Harding's version is conceptually distinct). Harding argued that young people enter gangs because there is no plausible alternative for them. The gang operates as a unique and highly gendered "social field" with its own rules and logic. The field favors males, but within this social arena of intense competition, youth both survive and thrive by generating, trading, and maintaining personal levels of street capital—a metaphorical points system that determines position in the gang hierarchy and allows others to rank their position, all with the aim of enhancing their status on the streets (Densley [2013, 81] called this "the ratings game"). Harding says this is done by employing the "gang repertoire," a variable collection of criminal activity that allows members to build status and demonstrate social skill. Street capital rises and falls with every action and reaction on the street; thus, to avoid victimization, "players" in the "street casino" must curate their own personal brand and reputation for violence.

Much as gangs in Chicago are different from gangs in Los Angeles, the gang scene in London appears somewhat localized. By interviewing youth in a "research city" two hundred miles north of the capital, for example, Aldridge, Medina-Ariza, and Ralphs were able to identify "gangs" per se, with the caveat that they were more "messy and fluid" than the gangs studied by Pitts and later by Densley, Harding, and others in London (Aldridge and Medina 2008). For young people living in known gang areas, the risks of violent victimization were high (Ralphs, Medina, and Aldridge 2009), but in Manchester, gang violence was less about the drug economy than in London and more about turf, boredom, and personal disputes (Aldridge and Medina 2008). Still, a longitudinal analysis by Medina-Ariza et al. (2014, 3) found

that "gang membership increases the chances of offending, anti-social behavior and drug use amongst young people," which, they argued, "vindicates
the current policy of treating gang membership as a distinct part of crime
prevention and youth policy." At the same time, the Manchester team found
no evidence that gangs were "the changing face of youth crime," as Pitts
(2008) forewarned, or that the numbers of young people joining gangs had
increased over time, thus breathing life back into the waning theory of moral
panic. Back in London, for example, Gunter (2017) advanced the theory that
street violence resulted from a subcultural street code that sat largely outside
of the gang. For Gunter (2017, 7), the very term *gang* was a racist and criminalizing discourse, used by law-and-order politicians to "justify the oppres-
sive policing tactics utilized disproportionately against black and minority
youth" (see also Chapter 8).

In 2011, looting and rioting throughout England was wrongly blamed
on gangs (Densley and Mason 2011; Hallsworth and Brotherton 2011), and,
in terms all too familiar to North American readers, Prime Minister David
Cameron (2011) launched a "concerted, all-out war on gangs and gang culture." A national Ending Gang and Youth Violence (Disley and Liddle 2016)
strategy followed that was later amended to recognize the coercion and
exploitation that lay at the heart of county-lines drug gangs but was still
heavily criticized for failing to establish an evidence-based operational
definition of a "gang" and for funding interventions that were neither clearly described nor comprehensively evaluated (Shute and Medina 2014;
Smithson and Ralphs 2016). Civil gang injunctions and the application of
"joint enterprise" doctrine to gang members were criticized for the collective punishment and criminalization of young people (Cottrell-Boyce 2013;
Patrick Williams and Clark 2016). Scotland Yard's database or "matrix" of
suspected gang members was also discredited on civil liberties grounds and
for unduly labeling and stigmatizing young Black men (Amnesty International U.K. 2018; Patrick Williams 2018). Somewhat lost in all this criticism,
however, is the fact that youth violence, at least in London, is still very much
a gang issue. Based on an analysis of police data, for example, Densley and
Pyrooz (2020) found that nearly half of all youth homicide in the city over
a ten-year period was gang related.

Gangs also are a major driver of violence in another U.K. city that has
seen remarkable success in violence cessation in recent years—Glasgow,
Scotland. Glasgow has long been synonymous with gangs, with a tradition
that dates back over a century (Davies 2013). By the mid-2000s, the city had
six times as many gangs as London and was the per capita murder capital of
Europe (Adam 2018). The city fell on hard times after deindustrialization,
and a number of studies have centered on the unique marginalization of
local housing schemes—the equivalent of housing projects in the United

States—where an attachment to territoriality is a source of identity and masculine distinction (Bannister, Kintrea, and Pickering 2013; Bradshaw 2005; Deuchar 2009; Fraser 2015; Holligan and Deuchar 2009; McLean and Densley 2020; Pickering, Kintrea, and Bannister 2012). Gang membership and public knife carrying in Glasgow are cultural norms handed down from generation to generation via "street socialization" (Johanne Miller 2020), to the extent that Fraser (2015), following Thrasher (1927), saw gangs there as an extension of playgroups, a rite of passage for teens, rooted in local history.

In the Glasgow social housing communities ("schemes") where the drug barons moved in and created new opportunities and preferences for crime and violence, Mclean (2019) found an even sharper end of Glasgow's gang culture. Drawing on Densley's (2014b) gang evolution model, McLean (2018) saw Glasgow's gangs changing from recreational groups into more entrepreneurial outfits. Using McLean's data, recent studies have documented the role of gangs and gang members in street robbery (Harding et al. 2019; McLean and Densley 2022) and in Scotland's drug economy, especially the sale of street drugs such as cocaine and heroin (Densley et al. 2018; McLean, Densley, and Deuchar 2018). There is even evidence of urban Scottish gangs following the county-lines model of drug distribution to travel outside of their territorial borders and deal drugs in outlying areas (Holligan, McLean, and McHugh 2020; McLean, Robinson, and Densley 2020).

However, while drug crime has increased in Glasgow, homicide and street violence have declined (Batchelor, Armstrong, and MacLellan 2019; Skott and McVie 2019), thanks largely to the efforts of the city's Violence Reduction Unit (VRU), which transformed gang-related violence from a policing issue into a public health issue. By working closely with partners in the National Health Service, education, and social work and stressing the importance of positive role models, the VRU has mixed hard deterrence and enforcement with a softer message of empathy and alternatives to gang membership, such as youth clubs, education, employment, and training. Deuchar (2013) conducted a comparative analysis of policing and partnership responses to street violence between Scotland and the United States, where the theory behind this community initiative to reduce violence originated (see Chapters 11 and 14), concluding that the approach has had marked success.

In sum, the United Kingdom has come full circle, from a rejection of the gang premise, in part because of the state crime control implications; to finding more and more examples of gangs that fit the prototypical gang model now largely rejected in the United States; to adopting and adapting gang prevention, intervention, and suppression efforts from the United States that mostly work but at some cost to the individuals and communities targeted. We revisit many of these themes in Chapters 11 through 14, which deal explicitly with policing gangs and gang intervention in policy and practice.

Gangs in Canada

The first recorded work on gangs in Canada was Rogers's (1946) ethnography of Toronto gang life. This study could be compared in many ways to Thrasher's (1927) classic work on gangs in Chicago. Using largely qualitative methods, Rogers documented the nature, characteristics, and social processes of youth gangs and gang members, their forms of social organization, and their involvement in delinquency. Then, in 2003, findings from a national survey on police perceptions of gangs and gang members offered an estimate of the nature and extent of gang activity in Canada (Chettleburgh 2003). Since then, a number of studies have documented the presence of gangs and gang violence in Canada (Chettleburgh 2007; Ezeonu 2010, 2014; Shaffer 2014).

Wortley and Tanner (2004) lament the lack of official data on gangs in Canada (see also Sinclair and Grekul 2012), but they do point to an emerging research literature on these gangs. Using fieldwork techniques, they generated a sample that met the Eurogang definition of gang membership. Their work, conducted in Toronto, revealed that gangs were primarily mixed-race groups. Similar to research conducted in the United States, neighborhood friendship groups often evolved over time into gangs, and these gangs reflected the influence of neighborhoods and often family members who also were involved in gangs (Wortley and Tanner 2006). While protection was a primary motivation for joining the gang, the ability to make money was a factor that kept young people in their gangs, whether that potential was realized or not. Wortley and Tanner (2008) found that many gang members identified a series of social injustices that were linked to their race/ethnicity as well as being young. This led them to conclude that effective gang responses, especially in Toronto, would need to integrate aspects of racial integration.

Immigrant and Aboriginal youth have received perhaps the greatest interest from gang scholars and researchers in Canada in recent years (Bucerius, Jones, and Haggerty 2021). Canada's Aboriginal communities are overrepresented in the criminal justice system and experience high rates of violent offending and victimization (Grekul and LaBoucane-Benson 2008). Aboriginal gangs have existed for decades but are relatively fluid and highly sensitive to law enforcement intervention dictating the form and function of the gang (Sinclair and Grekul 2012; Chalas and Grekul 2017). Members are typically individuals who are on the margins of the legitimate and illegitimate opportunity structures in Canadian society. Some studies indicate that Aboriginal gangs are used by more organized crime groups to carry out "street work" (K. Kelly and Caputo 2005). Aboriginal gang violence is also different from that exhibited by other youth gangs in Canada. Although externalized criminal violence motivated by revenge, retaliation, and reputation is common, internalized violence, such as suicide and drug overdose, is far more common.

Urbanik's ethnographic research with minority ethnic youth in Toronto's disadvantaged Regent Park community highlights the neighborhood context of gang violence. She found that when two rival gangs coexist in the same neighborhood, but their members share a "master status" of being residents of that community versus being part of the gang, local neighborhood identification can suppress inter-gang violence (Urbanik 2018). However, if neighborhood redevelopment displaces the "old heads" in the community, the uneasy peace can be broken by gangs fighting to fill the power vacuum (Urbanik, Thompson, and Bucerius 2017). Urbanik's work also explores how social media creates not only new risks for gang members by blurring their public and private lives but also new tools for managing those risks (Urbanik and Haggerty 2018), which speaks to the ways in which the internet contributes to the spread of a global gang culture (see Chapter 10).

A key theme in Canadian research has been to focus on organizational levels of groups such as gangs. Morselli (2009), known for bringing social network analysis to the masses in criminology, conducted perhaps the most extensive research on Canadian gang networks. He studied the Hells Angels motorcycle gang and two street-level gangs involved with drug distribution in Montreal and the state of Quebec. The conflict that emerged over the control of drug distribution produced 126 murders, 135 attempted murders, and the murder of two prison guards, all over a seven-year period (Morselli 2009, 147–148). Morselli identified the organizational structure of the Hells Angels, as well as two drug distribution groups that we would commonly think of as street gangs, using social network analysis to reproduce the relationships between gang members. The result is an impressive description of the relationships, ties, centrality, and density of the connections between gang members.

There is a strong tradition of social network analysis in Canadian gang research, thanks largely to Morselli as well as Martin Bouchard and colleagues at Simon Fraser University. Bouchard and Hashimi (2017), for example, used police homicide data to differentiate random variation in homicide trends from true waves of gang violence in British Columbia. Using official data on the criminal and social networks of gang associates in Montreal, moreover, Ouellet, Bouchard, and Charette (2019) found that gang duration was a function of their cohesion and local embeddedness, moderated by group size. In short, large gangs with closed structures survived the longest. In this way, gangs are similar to other noncriminal organizations.

Working in Vancouver, Robert Gordon (1998, 2000) identified three types of groups: (1) criminal businesses organizations, (2) street gangs, and (3) wannabe groups. There were important differences between these groups, notably criminal involvement. Bouchard and Spindler (2010) examined gangs in Quebec, while Wortley and Tanner (2004) conducted a study in Toronto. The former surveyed students in school settings, while the Toronto study examined both a school-based and a street-based sample. Consistent with a large body of gang research in Canada, the United States, and Europe, these two pieces of research documented increased levels (frequencies) and seriousness of delinquent involvement among gang members. The Quebec research found a strong correlation between the level of organization in a gang and involvement in delinquency, violence, and drug sales.

Wortley and Tanner (2004) found elevated levels of participation in all forms of property and drug crime as the level of involvement in a gang increased from no involvement through five levels of increasing involvement culminating in current criminal gang membership. Of particular importance to this chapter's focus on gang violence, individuals who self-reported current membership in a criminal gang scored higher on six measures of involvement in violence, with particularly great differences between that group and others for carrying a gun or knife and being involved in a fight.

Gatti et al. (2005) have a long-term cohort study going on in Montreal. Gang questions were first asked of the sample at age fourteen. Consistent with their Canadian colleagues and American research conducted with youth, elevated levels of delinquent involvement for gang members was found for drug use, drug sales, property offending, and violent offending. However, the difference in level of involvement in violence by gang and non-gang members was not as great as is reported in U.S. studies. Perhaps this cleavage in levels of involvement in violence reflects gun availability and differences in societal levels of violence between Canada and the United States. Still, gang-related homicides in Canada have a distinctive character—they occur in public places, and they involve firearms and young victims and offenders far more often than other forms of homicides in Canada. In these ways, Canadian gang homicides resemble gang homicides in the United States (Dauvergne and Li 2006).

Gangs in Latin America and the Caribbean

The literature on gangs in Latin America is both wide and deep and growing rapidly (for reviews, see Rodgers and Baird 2015; Seelke 2016). This section provides an overview of gangs in the region, starting with Mexico and then moving to Colombia, Central America, the Caribbean, and finally, Brazil.

Despite its large shared border with the United States, gang problems in Mexico reflect the presence of a large-scale drug and weapon trade more than the migration or emulation of U.S. gangs. For centuries, drugs have moved north from Mexico to meet demand in the United States, while money and guns have moved south from the United States to Mexico (Decker and Chapman 2008). The problems associated with these commodities (drugs, money, and guns) have grown as Mexican drug cartels have successfully resisted government attempts to curb their activities. Mexico has experienced extremely high levels of violence over the last two decades, with the execution-style killings of journalists, judges, police, and government officials.

It is important to note that the drug cartels in Mexico more closely resemble organized crime groups than gangs (J. Rosen and Zepeda 2016). Because the cartels include many older members, they tend to have more developed organizational structures than street gangs and are more focused on profit. Mexican drug cartels are essentially governance institutions, franchises with branch offices that engage in market-based activities, far different from what we understand most street gangs in the United States to be (J. Rosen and Zepeda 2016). They have pumped money into electoral campaigns and paid off individual politicians and police officers in the border states.

Similar levels of corruption are found in Colombia, which (thanks to the legend of Pablo Escobar) is well known for its cocaine economy. Gangs in Colombia tend to be linked to the drug trade through organized crime groups (Ward 2012) but also are connected to armed actors from the broader historical and political conflict between leftist guerrillas and right-wing paramilitary groups. Ethnographer Adam Baird focuses on urban violence and insecurity in Colombia and in Belize, using masculinities as a lens to understand gang violence and gang members' quest to become the "baddest" there (Baird 2012, 2018a, 2018b, 2019).

There are two types of gangs in Central America: pandillas and maras. They have each now attained an objective and a mythic character. They function as the bogeyman in U.S. immigration policy (Dudley 2020) but are also a serious threat to peace and life for local residents. Pandillas are local indigenous gangs, the origins of which can be traced back to the 1940s and 1950s. They used to be widespread throughout the region but now only really exist in Nicaragua (Rodgers 2006, 2015), Costa Rica, Panama, and Belize (Jütersonke, Muggah, and Rodgers 2009). That is because maras supplanted them in El Salvador, Honduras, and Guatemala. Maras are a product of the mass deportation of criminal and undocumented migrants with Central American origins from the United States, including young people born in or who grew up in Los Angeles, California, who transported North American gang culture and customs with them (Cruz 2010). Although many of these deportees were U.S. gang members, some question the extent to which gangs in Central America are truly connected to gangs in the United States (Zilberg 2011). Still, for this reason, maras often are referred to as "transnational organizations" or gangs that span multiple countries or continents (Cruz 2010; Fontes 2018; Ward 2012). The two largest groups of maras are Mara Salvatrucha (MS-13) and Mara Dieciocho (18th Street).

Maras are overall much more violent than pandillas, in part because they are weakly integrated in the local social fabric but also because they are more embedded in the region's criminal economy—namely, the trafficking of narcotics from south to north and the traffic of weapons from north to south. Maras have essentially evolved from street gangs into protection rackets (Cruz 2010). Pandilla violence was traditionally related to local vigilantism and community protection—at least until the 2000s, when the logic of the gang transformed and they too became organized around drug dealing and protecting drug markets (Rodgers 2017). Across Central America today, local gangs have mixed with transnational gangs, creating hybrid versions.

There are roughly 20,000 gang members in El Salvador, 22,000 in Guatemala, and 12,000 in Honduras, according to government estimates (Seelke 2016). El Salvador has the highest concentration of gang members, with some 323 gang members for every 100,000 citizens, double the level of Guatemala and Honduras. Gang violence in Central America is also highest in El Salvador, followed by Guatemala and Honduras. For comparative purposes, these far outstrip the prevalence of gang members in the United States. While economic conditions play a role in this, these three countries also have the highest number of maras. The northern triangle countries, in turn, have among the highest homicide rates in the world. Like the research from Europe, findings from the research on Latin American gangs are consistent with key findings from the United States. Anywhere between 10 and 60 percent of all criminal violence in the region can be attributed to gangs (Seelke 2016)—although imprecise, even the lower bound estimate is striking. Similar to the United States but different from the situation in Europe, gang youth find that guns are easily accessible. Guns are often seen as symbols of power and respect (Bevan and Florquin 2006), and they are implicated in the vast majority of gang-related homicides.

The relationship between gangs and guns is also a prime factor in Caribbean homicides (Harriott and Katz 2015). The small island nation of Jamaica has one of highest murder rates in the world, and it serves as a strategic transshipment point for cocaine traffickers, including the famed Colombian and Mexican cartels (Pitts 2008). During the Cold War and as a consequence of the war on drugs, guns began flooding the island to service the gangs co-opted by the pro-Cuban PNP (People's National Party) and pro-American JLP (Jamaican Labor Party). Today, gangs still use guns, but the violence is also fueled by kids with personal vendettas or the burgeoning economy of cyber scammers (Edmonds 2016).

In one survey, 15 percent of arrestees on the neighboring Caribbean islands of Trinidad and Tobago told interviewers that they had owned a gun, but 53 percent of gang members reported owning a gun (W. Wells, Katz, and Kim 2010). School youth reported that gang members had greater access to guns than their non-gang peers. As a result, in cross-national comparisons, despite lower levels of organization in gangs (Pyrooz et al. 2012), C. Katz, Maguire, and Choate (2011) observed that gang members in Trinidad and Tobago engaged in higher levels of violence than their U.S. counterparts.

A lack of governmental stability and legitimacy and the failure of the state to provide safety and security for its people have given rise to gangs across Latin America and the Caribbean (Cruz 2016; Kassab and Rosen 2018; Knight 2019). It also makes responding to them difficult. Research with twelve hundred active and former gang members in El Salvador found that when gangs govern communities, regulating the life and peer relationships of their members, disengagement from gangs is especially complicated (Cruz and Rosen 2020; J. Rosen and Cruz 2018, 2019). Worse, when a military dictatorship in Brazil opted to house political prisoners and street criminals together inside the same cellblocks at Ilha Grande, the Brazilian equivalent of Alcatraz prison, the volatile mixture of dissidents and streetwise convicts spawned one of the most violent and tightly organized narco-gangs in the world, the Comando Vermelho (CV; Penglase 2014). The Red Command, as they are known in English, grew into an institutionalized force in the prison system, and the gang's "absolute dominance" within many of the state's prisons has resulted in "de facto segregation" of Rio de Janeiro's prisons by gang affiliation (Lessing 2010, 157; A. Johnson and Densley 2018).

Prison served as an incubator during the CV's early years, but the gang's size and power grew exponentially when it left the cellblocks and entered Rio's socially and geographically isolated favelas (slums) as affiliated inmates were released and returned to their old neighborhoods. The state's chronic absence in these neighborhoods, combined with a collective distrust of the police following the collapse of the military dictatorship in the 1980s, made the favelas ripe for an alternative governing force (Darke 2013). Before long, however, the CV largely abandoned its social welfare emphasis and the leftist political agenda imported by the political prisoners, to focus instead on monetary gain (Arias 2006). This resulted in the escalation of territorial disputes over retail drug sales and a dramatic increase in gang violence and homicides.

Much as we saw in Europe, North America has exported not only gang culture but also the politics and policies of suppression, repression, and incarceration. In Brazil, military police have waged a war of attrition with the CV, leaving scores dead (Arias and Goldstein 2010). The CV, in turn, have militarized the favela and even recruited street children into armed combat (Dowdnwy 2003).

From 2012 to 2014, the government of El Salvador facilitated a historic truce involving the country's largest gangs that contributed to a temporary reduction in homicides (Cruz 2019; Martínez-Reyes and Navarro-Pérez 2020), but the country now is engaged in a war on gangs anchored by military support for anti-gang efforts (Wolf 2017). This has resulted in allegations of extrajudicial killings committed by police engaged in gang suppression (Seelke 2016). The Guatemalan government has generally relied on periodic law-enforcement operations to round up suspected gang members, with some support for community-level prevention programs. Notably, the church plays an important role in gang disengagement efforts throughout Latin America (Brotherton and Gude 2020). Critics point out that gang disengagement through Pentecostal conversion deemphasizes macrosocial and political-economic concerns in Latin America by placing the onus on individual gang members to "save their souls" by adopting a set of dispositions shaped by neoliberal ideas (O'Neill 2015).

However, some Latin American countries have taken a different approach. As discussed in detail in Chapter 10, in 2008, the Ecuadorian government "legalized"—a multipronged approach to integrating the gang into social institutions—one the country's largest street gangs, the Latin Kings, which Brotherton and Gude (2020) argued helped reduce gang-related violence and, in turn, the nation's homicide rate. This stands as an example of social control where the state is committed to polices of social inclusion rather than social exclusion (the latter being the standard practice in both North and South America).

Gangs in Africa, Asia, and Oceania

While gangs have been identified in Africa and the Asia-Pacific region, there is less information about these gangs and their activities than in other parts of the world. This may be due to the general lack of (Western) scholarly attention to these parts of the world, a research focus on other aspects of social behavior, a general lack of measurement of youth behavior (Liu 2008), or the more recent emergence of gang problems in countries in these regions. The knowledge we do have is largely concentrated on a few locations in South Africa, China, and Australia.

In Africa, military actions and civil unrest are more prominent than are gangs. It is true, however, that the line between gangs and armed groups is sometimes hard to find, especially in countries where civil strife seems a regular part of life. A recent study concluded that the inability of law enforcement agencies to control and prevent crime in Nigeria, for example, contributed substantially to the proliferation of gangs (Amali, Moshood, and Iliyasu 2017). Gangs have been documented in a number of African countries including Kenya, Liberia, Nigeria, South Africa, and Uganda (Covey 2010). Despite this, only South Africa has seen much description of the gang problem, although there is emerging research in Nigeria (Amali, Moshood, and Iliyasu 2017; Matusitz and Repass 2009; Salaam 2011a, 2011b).

The history of gangs in South Africa can be traced as far back as the 1920s (Pinnock and Douglas-Hamilton 1998). With the end of apartheid, many of the gangs evolved into larger enterprises (Kynoch 2005). There is evidence that gangs, or "social bandits," are now beginning to grow in South Africa (Petrus and Kinnes 2019), with a strong link between gangs in prisons and gangs on the street (J. Berg and Kinnes 2009). This growth may be due in part to media influences in the cultural transmission of gang images, symbols, and behavior. Pinnock and Douglas-Hamilton (1998) cite figures that estimate as many as 130 gangs and 100,000 gang members in Cape Town, the second-most-populous city in South Africa (after Johannesburg).

Contemporary South African youth gangs engage in a number of acts of violence such as bribery, territorial disputes, robbery, extortion, assaults, and homicides (Burnett 1999; Pinnock 2016). Groups to combat gangs and gang violence such as PAGAD (People against Gangsterism and Drugs) have emerged and ironically have created violence between themselves and other gangs as well as the police in the Western Cape (Dixon and Johns 1999; Kinnes 2014). Schoolteachers in the Western Cape report a rise in "gangsterism" and incidents of gang violence in schools (Maphalala and Mabunda 2014; Reckson and Becker 2005). Gang members are estimated to be responsible for roughly half of all the violent crime in that area (Reckson and Becker 2005; J. Berg and Kinnes 2009). This partly explains why gang exit can be a challenging process in South Africa (Dziewanski 2020; J. Kelly and Ward 2020; Ward and Bakhuis 2010), much like it is in the United States (Pyrooz, Decker, and Webb 2014).

In Asia, organized crime groups such as the Chinese Tongs and Triads and Japanese Yakuza have a long history (P. Hill 2006; P. Wang 2017). A number of Asian countries, including China, Hong Kong, India, Japan, Korean, Pakistan, and Taiwan, also report an emerging gang problem (Covey 2010; Ter Haar 1998). A good deal of what we know in this region is based on journalistic reports. However, there is an emerging body of knowledge about gangs in China.

Because of its population size and increased importance to the global economy, it is especially important to learn more about gangs in China. Some have speculated that recent increases in crime in China are related to a number of cultural and structural changes in the country, although knowledge of this topic is still developing (Liu, Zhang, and Messner 2001; L. Zhang et al. 1997; L. Zhang, Welte, and Wieczorek 1999). Deng and Cordilia (1999) identified rising expectations regarding the standard of living, growing income inequality, and a loosening of formal social control as the primary forces behind the increase in crime in China. A report on crime in China released by the government in 1989 (Dutton 1997) identified an increase in "gang-land crimes" and documented 36,000 gangs and 138,000 gang members. Some have linked changing social and economic conditions, globalization, and the development of the internet to the emergence of gangs in China (Harding 2016; Liang and Lu 2010). A self-reported study conducted in China and the western United States (Jessor et al. 2003) found that almost half of Chinese schoolchildren reported gang-related activity in their neighborhood. This is not a direct measure of gang presence or activity, but it is an indication that a large proportion of Chinese schoolchildren are aware of gangs.

Other work on gangs in China suggests that group context and co-offending are important correlates of juvenile offending in the country. In a study of inmates in prison and reform camps, L. Zhang et al. (1997) identified four key characteristics of gangs in China. First, gang organizational structure was not well developed. Second, gang membership was transitory, and gangs were grouped by age. Third, Chinese gangs identified with turf or geographic territory. Finally, offending patterns were varied, and offenses tended not to be very serious. Other work found that gang members were more likely to recidivate and reoffend at shorter periods (Liu 1999) than non-gang members. With the exception of crime seriousness, these findings are consistent with research in U.S. and European settings that we identified earlier in this chapter.

Webb and colleagues (2011) used the International Self-Report Delinquency (ISRD-2) questionnaire to compare a five-city U.S. sample and a Chinese sample from the city of Hangzhou. They concluded that there was evidence of youth gangs in China, but only about 2 percent of students reported being in a gang. Chinese youth involved in gangs engaged in higher levels of offending and had higher levels of victimization. Pyrooz and Decker (2013) also used a school-based, self-reported delinquency scale in Changzhi. Eleven percent of the sample reported gang membership, and over half of the sample engaged in some form of delinquency. Gang youth were significantly more likely to engage in all forms of delinquency, but especially violence. Interestingly, they found that many of the theoretical variables (delinquent peers, low self-control, household strains, family and school attachment, and parental monitoring) that explained involvement in delinquency and gangs in the United States also explained these activities in the Chinese context.

Harding (2016), best known for his research on gangs in the United Kingdom, argued that street gangs were emerging in China due to an influx of poor rural migrants to the megacities and the influence of the triads in establishing ties between organized crime and juvenile offenders. Likewise, Hong Kong has a long history of organized criminal gangs related to triad society (Harding 2016; Fraser 2017). Triad is a branch of one of the formal secret societies that originated in mainland China (P. Wang 2017), and there is emerging evidence of links between triad society, organized crime, and youth gangs, which has important implications for practice (Lo and Tam 2018). For example, Lo (2012) demonstrated how youth tend to initially join gangs searching for protection and fun, but by working for or on behalf of triad-affiliated gangsters and running criminal errands at the lowest tier of triad society, they are eventually socialized into the triad subculture—a process he calls "triadization."

Research on gangs in Asia has been scarce until recently. The recent work of Ang and colleagues (2012) in Singapore is a welcome addition to our knowledge of gangs in this region. Using the case files of nearly four hundred youthful probationers, they found that gang members and gang-involved youth had higher rates of officially recorded violence than comparable youth who were not gang members or did not have friends involved in gangs. They point to the role of early involvement in aggressive behaviors as a pathway to gang membership. Their work emphasizes the cross-national importance of the role of delinquent peers in gang membership and violent involvement. Ang et al. (2015) later found that aggression and behavioral school engagement were risk factors for self-reported gang membership among a large sample of 1,027 Singapore adolescents, but psychopathy was not.

Finally, there has been a dramatic growth in our understanding of gangs in Australia and New Zealand in recent years (Gilbert 2013, 2016; R. White 2016). In New Zealand, where membership in traditional "patch-wearing" street gangs and outlaw motorcycle clubs has declined, there has been a "reorganization" of gangs in recent years and a rise in "American style" gangs that, like in Europe, borrow the conventional signals of Los Angeles gangs (Gilbert 2016).

R. White's (2013) research on Australian gangs paints a picture that parallels descriptions of European gangs more closely than those of U.S. gangs. For example, White is keen to stress that gang members do not spend all their lives in the gang or all their time doing "gang stuff." He described gang violence in Australia as a rare event with a well-defined set of targets. In Sydney, for example, homicides between gang members are more likely to be generated by petty disputes than over inter-gang issues such as respect or turf. However, youth culture in Australia is characterized by ethnic tension, marginalization, and gang-like groupings of youths in major cities, all conditions that are conducive to gang formation. R. White's (2013) fieldwork with gangs underscored the role of ethnicity and fighting, with little use of guns and more reliance on fists and knives. As in Britain, however, a media panic about "African gangs" speaks to the long-standing racist trope of conflating Blackness with criminality in Australia (Majavu 2020).

Conclusion

Researchers have compared youth gang activity in the United States to that in other regions of the world using several key categories—the prevalence of gang membership, the relationship between gang membership and involvement in crime, trends in gang violence, the nature of gang organization, and the spread of gang membership. Where available, estimates of the presence of gang members in schools seem to produce generally consistent results across countries. Certainly, the European, British, and U.S. research generally shows that 7–12 percent of schoolchildren self-report gang membership. Much lower estimates come from the sparse research that has been done in China, and we lack reliable estimates from Africa and Central and South America.

Another consistent finding across the research has been the relationship between gang membership and criminal behavior. In every location where this has been examined, gang membership increases involvement in crime and delinquency, both in terms of the number of crimes committed (frequency) and their seriousness. This is consistent with our observations in Chapter 6.

On the topic of crime seriousness, levels of gang violence are highest in North and South America (except Canada) and Africa. In contrast, Europe and the Asia-Pacific region have much lower levels of gang violence. Although there are exceptions, by and large it appears that levels of violence are contingent on the propensity of gangs to use firearms during conflict, the ability of states to control this type of behavior, and traditions of violence. While levels of gang violence vary across the geographic regions, motives for gang violence show more similarities than differences. Key contributors to gang violence include racial or ethnic conflict, economic gain, and respect or power. Gang violence can stem from long-standing rivalries or from conflicts that emerge on the spur of the moment. Having read the first eight chapters of this book, you know that these are similar to motives among gangs in the United States. Likewise, research on American gang violence consistently finds that the targets of such violence are typically other gang members. This finding appears to hold in Europe as well as other regions across the world. Overall, this chapter demonstrates that many of the themes discussed thus far in this book transcend borders.

Gang organization varies considerably across countries. It seems lowest in Australia and China, where gangs are newer; it is evolving in Europe, particularly in the United Kingdom; and it is highest in Central America and

Africa, where gang membership is often intertwined with political conflict or operations that involve a lot of money. The most organized groups outside the United States—including Mexican drug cartels, African tribal groups involved in civil wars, and traditional Chinese crime groups such as Tongs and Triads—all have an emphasis on extralegal governance that makes them very different from the majority of gangs in the United States, so different that we might be mistaken to classify them simply as gangs (see Chapter 3).

Finally, as we introduced in Chapter 8, gangs have spread globally through a variety of social processes, including immigration. Gangs have become a part of youth culture and often find their way with their unique styles of dress and behavior through media and social media, especially when the economic and social conditions are right. These are consistent with the ways that gangs spread in the United States and, frankly, are similar to the ways that most trends spread in contemporary society. We find little or no evidence to support a contention that gangs were imported or exported through an organized and planned process. As Densley (2013, 107) memorably said about the Bloods and Crips in England, "nobody from Los Angeles appeared as a recruiting agent." In the case of MS-13, however, it is clear that government actions in combination with native conflict helped spread gangs to a new region.

10

Gangs and Social Institutions

N o gang member is an island. A key to understanding the lives of gang members is to place them in the broader context of social institutions with which they interact. By social institutions, we mean systems critical to the socialization process that provide basic social functions, including the economy, the polity and legal system, education, family, and religion (Rosenfeld and Messner 2011). As with the rest of us, social context in the form of institutions shapes gang members' lives. In this chapter, we place gang members in several key institutional contexts that have important implications for what they do, how they do it, and what their life inside and outside the gang is like. It is important to remember that all but the most core gang members lead a considerable portion of their lives outside the gang. Understanding what life is like in those settings is a key to developing a comprehensive picture of "life in the gang" (Decker and Van Winkle 1996). After all, some commentators argue that gang membership is itself a "performance" limited to certain social contexts (for a review, see Lauger 2020).

In this chapter, we review several social institutions and their impact on the lives of gang members. Our treatment of this topic is derived from a wide range of research and literature on social institutions, especially those pertaining to urban America, where, as we discussed in Chapters 1 and 2, gang activity tends to concentrate. The first few sections review what is known about gangs and gang membership in relation to a number of traditional social institutions, as follows:

- Families
- Schools
- The labor market
- The political system
- Religion

We reserve discussion of the legal system for later chapters.

Here we also examine the role of media and social media in the lives of gang members. This is a burgeoning research area, and with billions of internet users worldwide, we don't have to make much of a case to support the internet as a social institution—people communicate online, they fall in love online, they earn degrees online, they shop online, and, of course, they commit crimes online. Most importantly, all the other social institutions featured in this chapter function and are enhanced by media and technology, including schools, relationships with peers and family, and employment. At the end of the chapter, we discuss whether the gang itself can be classified as an emerging social institution.

Gangs and Traditional Social Institutions

The Family

Appropriately, the first social institution we consider is the family. It is the institution responsible for primary socialization, and it is hard to overestimate the importance of the family in socializing young people, teaching them the rules of behavior in society, and, as agents of informal social control (see Chapter 2), taking the appropriate steps to help them grow within those rules. Recent trends in the status of families in America, especially for the poorest residents of large cities, have caused some researchers to be concerned about the ability of the family to fulfill its traditional function in teaching and supervising youth in contemporary society.

As previewed in Chapters 2 and 8, the Harvard sociologist William Julius Wilson (1987, 1997) has documented the precipitous decline of the family, particularly in poorer Black communities. Wilson linked the emergence of an urban underclass—what he termed "the truly disadvantaged"—and the breakdown of the family to job losses and mass incarceration. First, while the U.S. economy has been growing ever since the 1970s, growth has increasingly been focused at the top. One of the fundamental forces working against less-educated American families is half a century of working poverty and low wages. Real wage decline leads to job decline, and this deterioration in job quality and detachment from the labor force brings misery and loss of earnings, along with a loss of pride. At the same time as their jobs are being outsourced abroad or to robots or gig workers, the working class are experiencing declining marriage rates and attachments to labor unions and employers—the foundations of a meaningful life. Fewer jobs has meant the replacement of the nuclear and pa-triarchal family with extended family units that are matriarchal or female headed (W. Wilson 1987, 1997; E. Anderson 1999).

A second social force that has shaped the structure of families in the underclass is mass incarceration (Pfaff 2017). Despite making up close to 5 percent of the global population, the United States has nearly 25 percent of the world's prison population. Since 1970, the incarcerated population has increased by 700 percent—2.3 million people are in jail and prison today, far outpacing population growth and crime, the latter of which has declined dramatically in the last twenty-five years (Blumstein and Wallman 2005). The burden of mass incarceration falls heaviest on Black, Latino, and other minority ethnic communities (Alexander 2010; Forman 2017), who may be disrupted by the annual return of over six hundred thousand former inmates as young adults to their neighborhoods (Petersilia 2003; Travis and Visher 2005). Combined, the restructuring of the family and the incarceration boom have created two mutually isolated social islands in the underclass commu-nity—one of single mothers and the other of ex-convicts. These two islands are the clay from which stronger underclass communities will have to be built.

A consequence of the deterioration of the family is reduced supervision for young children. Many young children therefore grow up with little or no direction, and the need for socialization and order in their lives is often met on the streets or, perhaps, the internet. Existing research is clear that the structure of the family and the quality of parent-child relationships have an impact on gang involvement. As we showed in Chapters 2 and 4, youth from single-parent households and families living in socioeconom-ic disadvantage are more likely to be involved in gangs. Similar studies have shown a comparable relationship between gang membership and childhood adversity. Adverse childhood experiences (ACEs) are a subset of childhood adversities. The ACEs concept originated from a seminal study by Kaiser Permanente Health Care (Felitti et al. 1998). Between 1995 and 1997, researchers asked 13,500 adults in California about childhood adver-sities in seven categories: physical, sexual, and emotional abuse; having a mother who was treated violently; living with someone who was mentally ill; living with someone who abused alcohol or drugs; and incarceration of a member of the household. They found that the more ACEs adults re-ported from their childhoods, the worse their physical and mental health outcomes.

Thus far, researchers have failed to specify a precise theoretical link between ACEs and gang involvement (H. Klein 2020). A recent longitudinal study of over one hundred thousand juvenile offenders found that ACEs predicted gang involvement by age eighteen, but individual temperament and patterns of substance abuse were more important than ACEs for explaining later gang involvement (Wolff et al. 2020). Still, related factors discussed in Chapter 4, such as low family involvement, inappropriate parental discipline, child abuse and neglect, poor affective relationships, and limited parental education and parental supervision of youth, remain key correlates of gang membership (Esbensen et al. 2010; LeBlanc and Lanctot 1998; Thornberry et al. 2003).

Despite its potential to inform prevention and intervention programming as well as risk factor and life-course approaches to understanding gangs and gang membership, gang scholars have rarely examined the family to the extent they have other correlates of gang involvement. Early gang researchers, most notably Thrasher (1927), spoke about the importance of family life for gang members, and W. Miller's (2011) magnum opus, *City Gangs*, discusses the importance of family ties to gang involvement as well as the role of pseudofamily that the gang plays for its members. Interviews with twenty-four family members also provided important insights into the lives of the gang members in Decker and Van Winkle's (1996) study of gangs in St. Louis. Family members who are already part of the gang play an important role in facilitating gang membership for their siblings or cousins, not least because blood ties in gangs serve as a proxy for trust (Densley 2012b).

It was against the backdrop of family decline that gangs emerged in many cities. Many families were under stress or lacked the resources, financial or emotional, to deal with threats to the welfare of their children. In many instances, gangs filled the void. The work of Joan Moore (1991) and Vigil (1988) in Los Angeles has pointed to the need for order and regulation in the lives of adolescents. Children naturally seek these conditions, and gangs have come to fulfill these needs for a growing number of youths. Just as the status of the family declined, gangs emerged and in many instances provided an alternative form of organization for the lives of young people. As a consequence, the gang has begun to fulfill many of the functions formerly held by the family. For example, gangs attract young men and women because they provide some degree of structure and activities that may otherwise be missing. And given their involvement in illegal activities, gangs also are perceived as a ready source of opportunities to make money. Finally, and perhaps most important, gangs provide social cohesion, emotional support, and status, functions typically fulfilled by a working family. We reserve a more detailed discussion of "the gang as a family" for the section on the gang as a social institution later.

The School

After the family, schools are the most powerful socializing agent in the lives of young people. Children in the United States attend school eight hours a day, 180 days per year, for thirteen consecutive years on average. In school, they interact with students from a variety of backgrounds and influence each other in a variety of ways, both positive and negative. It is no surprise, therefore, that schools have an important impact on the lives of gang and non-gang members, providing the opportunity for non-gang youths to learn about and become involved in gangs. Schools are important staging areas for the performance of gang identities (Garot 2010), and using network data from the Add Health study, Gallupe and Gravel (2018) found that by virtue of their position in the school pecking order, high-status gang members within schools were well placed to influence others to join gangs because they had numerous friendship ties to non-gang members. School transitions can be predictive of gang joining because they thrust youth into the context of the gang and change individual opportunities and preferences for gang membership (D. Carson et al. 2017). In school, for example, a lack of parental guardianship, the potential for bullying and victimization, and the desire to fit in all converge to make gang joining seem like a good option. Perhaps this is why most people who join gangs do so in the school years, around ages twelve to fifteen (see Chapter 4).

As pointed out above, the strength and stability of inner-city families have suffered as a result of national-level changes in the economy over the last four decades. The schools in communities where those families are under stress have also experienced new pressures and problems. Just as strong families produce strong communities, strong communities have historically been associated with effective schools—not least because, in the United States, schools are paid for by local property taxes, which are higher in wealthy neighborhoods. This principle has an obvious converse: weakened communities with struggling households produce schools that have a tenuous place in those communities and a limited capacity to prepare students for participation in mainstream society. Earlier, the work of William Julius Wilson helped us understand how this weakening of families can be associated with an increased risk of gang involvement. Wilson's perceptions of the changing role of schools in these communities make it possible to extend our understanding of the institutional context of gang involvement to include schools as well as families. Wilson (1987, 37) has concluded that "a vicious cycle is perpetuated through the family, through the community, and through the schools." Clearly, the health of these social institutions is linked.

In the "vicious cycle" portrayed by Wilson, schools fail communities, and communities fail schools. Communities fail schools by not providing a safe environment in which teachers can teach and students can learn and by not providing school administrators with the fiscal resources or policy levers needed to overcome a growing host of problems. Schools fail communities by not educating and graduating their students. W. Wilson (1985) noted that in Chicago in the 1980s, more than half of the Black and Latino youths attending public schools dropped out before graduating. Of those graduating, less than half could read at or above the national average level. The social isolation of families from the mainstream economy is paralleled by their isolation from their children's schools. In an extreme example, journalist Alex Kotlowitz (1991, 63), producer of *The Interrupters*, an award-winning documentary about the Cure Violence gang intervention program (see Chapter 14), noted that at one time in Chicago's poor communities, school phone numbers weren't listed in phone books as a way of discouraging poorer Black parents from contacting their children's schools.

The question is, how do gangs fit into this pattern of mutual failure between schools and communities? Data from the two national evaluations of the G.R.E.A.T. program indicate that gang members make up 13 to 17 percent of youth in schools in large cities (Esbensen and Carson 2012; Esbensen et al. 2010). The presence of gangs in schools is a major concern of school officials and policymakers (De La Rue and Forber-Pratt 2018). Gangs are a proxy for school disorder, in part because they are correlated with higher levels of school-based violence and victimization, including cyber bullying (Bouchard, Wang, and Beauregard 2012; D. Carson and Esbensen 2019; G. Gottfredson and Gottfredson 2001; Kupchik and Farina 2016; Wynne and Joo 2011). The relationship between gangs and increased violence and victimization in schools may be more indirect than direct because in schools with a lower capacity to protect and support students, violence is a by-product of other risky behaviors such as truancy, associating with delinquent peers, or drug use (Estrada et al. 2016). Still, studies also find gangs associated with elevated levels of general delinquency and substance use and drug sales in schools (Decker and Van Winkle 1996).

Gang violence in school can be deadly. The term *school shooting* typically recalls the horrors of the 1999 Columbine High School shooting or the 2018 massacre at Marjory Stoneman Douglas High School in Parkland, Florida. However, of the 1,614 times a gun was brandished or fired on school grounds in the United States between January 1970 and October 2020, at least 221 (13.7 percent) incidents were "gang-related." That's according to the K-12 School Shooting Database operated by the Naval Postgraduate School's Center for Homeland Defense and Security (https://www.chds.us/ssdb/), the most comprehensive school shooting database. In one gang assault, at least fifty-six shots were fired during a drive-by shooting in front of the school building. In another, seven people were shot after gang members chased a student into the school cafeteria. Schoolchildren, teachers, parents, bystanders, and even a police officer were all listed as victims of gang-related shootings on school grounds.

Empirical comparisons of gang and non-gang members have shown gang members to have greater levels of school failure, lower educational aspirations, higher frustration with school, and lower school-based self-esteem (Bowker and Klein 1983; Curry and Spergel 1992; LeBlanc and Lanctot 1998; Thornberry et al. 2003; Gilman et al. 2014). Gang members also are more likely to report negative labeling by teachers, poor relationships with teachers, higher educational marginality, and school disciplinary problems (Bjerregaard and Smith 1993; Esbensen and Huizinga 1993; Esbensen, Huizinga, and Weiher 1993; Thornberry et al. 2003). In short, there is a relationship between gangs and schools. This relationship works in both directions, where gangs and gang members are reluctant to conform to the expectations of school administration, while school administration balances a delicate line to meet the needs of all students while sanctioning the disruptive behaviors of gang members.

This relationship is reflected in the lack of educational achievement by gang youth (Gilman, Hill, and Hawkins 2014). Using nationally representative data, Pyrooz (2014a) found that gang members were 30 percent less likely to graduate from high school than their non-gang peers, and while in school, non-gang youth earned half a year more of education than did matched gang members. Pyrooz discovered that at each important stage of educational advancement—graduating high school, attending college, and graduating from college—gang members were less likely to move on to the next stage. Given the strong relationship between educational attainment and success in Western culture, these findings do not bode well for most gang members. As Huerta and colleagues (2020) noted, "college knowledge" is generally lacking among gang-involved youth owing to cultural capital in the family or the sharing of information by school counselors. While college may cross the minds of young gang members, typically the military and continued gang involvement are viewed as more viable pathways (Huerta 2015). Ex-gang members with Ph.D.s are very much the exception, not the rule (Bolden 2020; Durán 2013; Rios 2011b).

In Chapter 2, we introduced A. Cohen's (1955) classic argument that youth form delinquent gangs in an effort to redefine success and status in ways distinct from the "middle class measuring rod" found in schools. Consistent with this idea, research finds that gang members' primary reason for attending school is social (i.e., seeing friends and fighting with enemies) and much of their activity in school is focused on nonschool activities such as cutting classes and breaking rules—often in concert with their gang peers

(K. Boyle 1992; Decker and Van Winkle 1996). Furthermore, the demands of being "down for colors" are too often in clear opposition to school achievement. Decker and Van Winkle (1996) noted that joining gangs reduced participation in extracurricular school activities, and many of the violent incidents that erupted at school (invariably bringing gang members into conflict with school authorities) were rooted in issues and rivalries from outside school.

The greater the level of a youth's commitment to the gang, the lower his or her commitment to the cultural system represented by school participation (Hirschi 1969). Vigil (1988) has portrayed gang involvement as commitment to an alternative culture that is distinctly different from the cultural message of the school. Padilla (1992) also described the difficulties that gang members had with school authority as a form of "oppositional" or "resistance" behavior. Joan Moore (1991) felt that interpreting gang involvement as a resistance that encourages its members to "subvert and defy the norms and ideals of the schools" may be accurate. She cautioned, however, that it is resistance that "dooms" the gang member. It is a form of defiance that she feels assures the gang member of failure in school and in work and that "at worst" can become "an effective socialization for prison." When schools themselves contribute to this trajectory by failing to intervene early in the life of a child, scholars call this the "school to prison pipeline" (Kim, Losen, and Hewitt 2010).

Many gang members who "drop out" of school are actually "kicked out" for fighting (Hagedorn 1998a, 116). Rios (2017) prefers the term *pushed out* because the concept of dropout puts all the blame on the individual, ignoring whatever issues they may have, whereas pushout forces schools and educators to think about who they are failing and what they can do about it. This is especially important because the gang members pushed out of school are disproportionately Black and Latino, and this only exacerbates the myriad struggles they face growing up as people of color in a White world (see Chapter 8). As Decker and Van Winkle (1996, 228) have noted, "Schools do not want students who sell drugs, fight with rivals, show disrespect for teachers and staff, and carry weapons." This is fair, but as M. Klein (1995) has suggested, the school's inability to deal with gang problems in less punitive ways leads to gang suppression by default (Brotherton 1996). In particular, school administrators tend to turn to law enforcement for assistance in dealing with gang problems, and this leads to their "zero-tolerance" for gang members (Kupchik 2010) and thereby gang intervention programs.

Based on National Gang Center data, Clark, Pyrooz, and Randa (2018) report that twenty-seven U.S. states have formal state legislation regarding gangs in schools, although state legislation is the floor, not the ceiling, on gang policies and procedures because local school districts may have their own guidelines. Clark, Pyrooz, and Randa distinguish between programming-based, policy-based, punishment-based, training-based, and discretion-based policies in schools. Programming-based legislation pertains to the funding and implementation of any gang prevention or intervention program in the school such as the G.R.E.A.T. program (see Chapters 11 and 14). Policy-based legislation pertains to any rules around gang symbols, clothing, colors, and so on in schools, such as dress codes. Punishment-based legislation includes laws with special measures for gang-related activities and behaviors, such as sentencing enhancements (see Chapter 13) or the aforementioned zero-tolerance policies, which research finds have led to a marked increase in suspensions and expulsions for alleged gang members (Kupchik 2010; Rios 2017; M. Wang and Dishion 2012). Ironically, research shows that suspensions and expulsions actually drive youth further into gangs, in part by facilitating educational disengagement, dropout, and delinquency (Pyrooz, Decker, and Webb 2014). Training-based legislation pertains to any policies requiring school administrators, faculty, or staff to receive training on gangs and gang responses. Finally, discretion-based legislation speaks to language that leaves culpability and punishment to the discretion of school administrators.

As with many of the ideas that we present in this book, the pull and push propositions of how gang members leave school may both have an element of truth. Future research into gang and school involvement will have to attempt to distinguish between the two types of causal influences as well as identify interactions between them.

The Labor Market

In the life course, there is a natural progression from family to education to the labor market. As we noted above, when there is disruption in this progression—at the micro level for individuals or at the macro level in the economy—this can introduce serious problems to the well-being of individuals, communities, and nations. W. Wilson's (1987) underclass thesis applies to the context of gangs and urban America because the changes in the structure of the labor market disproportionately affected those from socially and economically disadvantaged groups—groups that gang members comprise.

The problem for urban America with the labor market restructuring that took place in the mid-twentieth century was that it introduced spatial and skill mismatches. In urban America, good jobs, often in manufacturing and other blue-collar industries that provided good wages and stability to support a family, were either exported to the suburbs or eliminated entirely. For the jobs that moved to the suburbs, inner-city residents couldn't afford to follow them. This is half of what is referred to as the spatial mismatch. The second half of the spatial mismatch is that urban youth did not meet the qualifications for the jobs remaining in metropolitan centers, which were typically white-collar or skilled positions. This demographic of youth and young adults were either undereducated or undertrained to qualify for jobs. Instead, they were pushed to what Crutchfield (1989) called the "secondary" labor market. Such a market did not necessitate a college education or advanced skills to qualify for employment, but it failed to provide the wages or stability to support individuals or families. As a result, it could not compete with the allure and fast money of an emerging drug market.

As a result, the criminal involvement of gangs made drug dealing a natural fit. Why work conventional jobs when gang members can sell drugs? Decker and Van Winkle (1996) reported that around three-fourths of the gang members they interviewed sold drugs. The estimates of wages earned varied widely among gang members, and Decker and Van Winkle suspected that some of this was simply bragging and exaggeration. Levitt and Venkatesh (2000) found that after they accounted for the average hours worked by drug-selling gang members, wages ranged from $2 to $7 for lower-level gang members and $32 to $97 for gang leaders (or $4–$12 and $55–$168 in 2020 dollars). Of course, these are only estimates based on what the researchers referred to as the financial records of the gang. Padilla (1992) reported that gang members made more than minimum wage. Hagedorn (1998a), however, dismisses drug selling by gang members as just another low-paying job.

Even while gang members sold drugs, Decker and Van Winkle, Levitt and Venkatesh, and others (e.g., Horowitz 1983; Joan Moore 1991) noted that many gang members worked conventional jobs. This might sound counterintuitive to many readers when comparing the benefits of gang membership with the benefits of the conventional job market for those with the skills of gang youth:

> It isn't only earnings that places the legitimate job market at a competitive disadvantage with selling drugs, it is the nature of work, with its requirements of structure and discipline, that conflict with the values of life in the gang. (Decker and Van Winkle 1996, 224)

However, it is important to point out that these jobs were in the secondary job market. Gang members were employed in the service or retail industry, often as janitors, cooks, or cashiers or at amusement parks—low-wage jobs that provided little stability or upward mobility.

As adolescent gang members moved into adulthood, they faced a stark employment reality: they qualified for few jobs in the primary labor market, or at least jobs that could sustain a family. Joan Moore (1991) observed this in East Los Angeles when she compared the employment patterns of earlier and more recent cliques of two gangs. Gang members from the earlier cliques were more likely to be employed and had better work histories than the gang members from the more recent cliques. She attributed this not only to economic restructuring but also to waves of immigration, which oversupplied the labor market and pushed down wages.

Of course, macrolevel changes in the labor market impact all youth and young adults, especially those from inner cities. Joining a gang puts individuals at an additional disadvantage because of the constraining influence of the gang. Not only do gangs work against schools, which puts individuals at a disadvantage when competing for jobs, but also the lifestyle of the gang encourages fast money, instant gratification, and risky behaviors that run counter to conventional workplace culture.

Krohn and colleagues (2011) argued that adolescent gang members will likely do poorly in their adult economic circumstances, even when compared to their similarly situated adolescent peers. Krohn and colleagues found this to be the case, as they held that precocious transitions (e.g., high school dropout, cohabitation, and teenage pregnancy) led to the economic hardships they observed among gang members between the ages of twenty-nine and thirty-one. Using Pathways to Desistance panel data, however, Augustyn, McGloin, and Pyrooz (2019) found that gang membership had little bearing on legal earnings, but illegal earnings increased upon joining a gang and decreased upon leaving it. Former gang members also appeared to pay a penalty in the legal economy for their past affiliations. The implication is that any boost to illegal earnings and total earnings among gang members is short-lived, but to prevent gang entry and reentry, legitimate economic opportunities are needed to counter the pull of gangs.

The Polity

The link between gangs and politics has a notable historical legacy. In his account of early twentieth-century Chicago gangs, Thrasher (1927) devoted an entire chapter to gang involvement in politics. Spergel (1995, 120) has suggested that youth gangs can serve as "a source of stability and potential power" for local politicians. In particular, he described the working relationships between ward bosses and their local gangs. The nature of the involvement between gangs and politics has varied with the structure of local politics. As discussed in Chapter 8, gangs were integrally involved in the operations of the Tweed machine in New York City in the 1800s (Spergel 1995, 120). Furthermore, in Philadelphia during that century, volunteer fire companies were central to local politics, and they frequently recruited their members from local youth gangs. Bursik and Grasmick (1993) also observed how the alliance between the youth gang, the Hamburgs, and politicians in the Bridgeport neighborhood of Chicago in the early decades of the twentieth century laid a political foundation for that community's later control of the city mayor's office. They recalled (177) that the most famous former member of the Hamburgs was the late mayor Richard J. Daley Sr. (see also Hagedorn 2006).

There are a number of ways the relationships between gangs and politicians have proved mutually beneficial. From the politician's perspective, Thrasher (1927, 312) noted, "the political boss finds gangs, whether composed of boys or of men above voting age, very useful in promoting the interests of his machine." Thrasher further suggested that many of the Chicago political bosses knew exactly how to appeal to gang members because they themselves were graduates of the street gangs. He went on to list the ways that street gang members assisted politicians, from distributing campaign literature to posting signs to helping voters get to the polls. Most of those tasks can be assigned to any campaign worker, but gangs have been reported to have gone beyond these kinds of tasks.

Kornblum (1974, 166), for example, reported that Chicago politicians relied on gangs for "the systematic removal of the opposition's street signs and lamp posters." From his study of gangs in three cities, Sánchez-Jankowski (1991, 216) stated, "All thirty-seven gangs observed throughout the ten years of this study established some type of *expedient-exchange* relationship with the politicians in their city." Beyond the list of political services that Thrasher identified, Sánchez-Jankowski (1991, 219–220) observed intimidation through physical presence at the polls on Election Day and occasional harassment of campaign critics and opposition workers. Gangs also were involved in the 1986 primary elections in a predominantly Puerto Rican ward of Chicago (Spergel 1995, 122). Rival gangs supported different candidates, one of whom even named a former gang leader as coordinator of his precinct captains.

As with much gang behavior, reported involvement between gangs and politicians has varied across locales. Spergel (1995, 120) has hypothesized that such relationships are more likely "in times of rapid change and social turmoil." While Sánchez-Jankowski (1991) noted that all the gangs he studied had some relationship with public officials, he reported that only in New York and Boston did gangs have "consistent and direct contact with the offices of elected mayoral and council politicians." None of the gangs that he studied in Los Angeles did. Perhaps another factor is the stability of the gang situation. Most of the examples described above have been taken from chronic gang-problem cities.

The involvement of gangs in politics has the potential for a great deal of social harm. For Thrasher (1927, 320), relationships between gangs and politicians facilitated more extensive alliances between crime and politics and ultimately led to government corruption. Spergel (1995) concluded that gangs are not "ordinarily committed to . . . social and political causes" (121). Spergel found evidence that during the Chicago riots of the 1960s, the police enlisted gang members to assist in quelling the social disorder. Gangs duly obliged, protecting some local merchant property during riots, but only for a fee. Campana and Varese (2018) argued that a criminal group's capacity to generate fear in a community, coerce legal businesses, and influence official figures are all measures of its ability to illegally "govern."

In the contemporary era of Black Lives Matter, scholars see potential for activism among socially conscious gang-involved youth to reduce community violence (Aspholm and Mattaini 2017; Hagedorn 2017). In 2015, rival Bloods and Crips marched side by side in the Baltimore rallies against police brutality, for instance. A positive transformation from "gangs" to "street organizations" has also been documented in the case of the Almighty Latin King and Queen Nation in New York, who reinvented themselves as a community empowerment movement in response to pressure from the state (Brotherton and Barrios 2004). When gangs were "legalized" and the police were reformed in the Republic of Ecuador, the murder rate fell dramatically over the next decade (Brotherton and Gude 2020).

Gangs can become institutionalized as an alternative state (Brotherton 2008) or evolve into social movements and political parties (Fraser and Hagedorn 2018). Particularly noteworthy have been efforts by Chicago street gangs to expand their political influence. As discussed in Chapter 8, during the 1970s, the Vice Lords obtained hundreds of thousands of dollars in external grants from government agencies and private foundations (Dawley 1992). The El Rukns also supported local political candidates and formed voter mobilization groups; that is, until 1986, when their leader, Jeff Forte, was indicted for conspiring to solicit Libyan funding in exchange for engaging in domestic terrorism (Toobin 1994). The 1990s were marked by a foray into political legitimacy by the Black Gangster Disciple Nation (BGDN). The group's letters were argued to stand for Black Growth and Development Network. A community-based group spawned by BGDN leadership, 21st Century Voices of Total Empowerment (VOTE), gained the support of Jesse Jackson's Operation Push, James Compton of the Urban League, a former mayor of Chicago, and at least two members of the city council in its voter registration drives. When federal authorities indicted thirty-nine BGDN leaders in August 1995, leaders of VOTE and candidates for office were included in the indictment along with incarcerated gang leaders.

The Church

Generally speaking, street gang affiliation, with its emphasis on violent retribution, seems to oppose religious affiliation that is predicated on peace and
forgiveness. However, gangs claim to offer many of the things organized religion does—protection, identity, group belonging, and even a sense of solid
militancy (Brenneman 2011). Studies of some larger gangs, such as the Bloods
and Latin Kings, speak to their "street activism" and their use of nonviolent
tactics to end conflicts, anchored in spiritual texts and rituals (Brotherton
and Barrios 2004; Kontos, Brotherton, and Barrios 2003). Indeed, some of the
symbolic rituals of gang matriculation, such as tattoos and blood oaths, also
have religious overtones (Chapter 4). Perhaps it is for this reason that religion
offers a viable alternative form of collective organization to gangs (Deuchar
2018; Flores 2013). Most interesting are examples where religious groups ape
the gang. For example, inside Brazil's prisons (A. Johnson 2017; A. Johnson
and Densley 2018), the Pentecostal church has organized itself in the image
of the gang, borrowing many of its characteristics and customs, in an attempt
to appeal to gang members and give them a credible out.

On its face, a religious life is the anthesis of gang life because religion functions as a source of righteous moral guidance akin to the notion of "belief"
being a central force in promoting conformity in classical control theories of
crime (Hirschi 1969). However, religion and spirituality play an important role
in the lives of gang members. The very prisons where gangs are active are also
religiously vibrant places (Bolden 2020; Decker and Pyrooz 2020; A. Johnson
2017), and from the streets to the penitentiary, gang members attend religious
services, engage in rituals and rites of passage that evoke religious customs,
and bear tattoos with religious motifs. Gang members appear plenty religious,
and in our interviews with them, they routinely express belief in God, although it is unclear how much they fully internalize and prioritize religious
teachings while doing the gang's work.

Gangs, Media, and Technology

Gangs and Film

Film and television are arguably the United States' greatest cultural exports.
It is no surprise, therefore, that how the general public perceives and under-
stands gangs is influenced by media depictions of them (McCorkle and
Miethe 2001). These depictions have changed over time (M. Klein and Maxson 2006), and they often are highly stylized and stereotyped, contributing to
the mythology of gangs (Fraser 2015; Howell 2007; Sánchez-Jankowski 1991).
Research has found that control agents market the gang threat via the news

media (McCorkle and Miethe 2001) but also that they draw inspiration from fiction. As discussed in Chapter 8, so too do gangs and gang members (Decker and Van Winkle 1996; Densley 2012a; Van Hellemont and Densley 2019). The performance of gang membership is informed by stylized narratives of "gangs" and by organized crime groups and mafias. Gang members may fashion themselves in the image of Hollywood gangsters (e.g., their avatars on social media sites) and even borrow mannerisms and lines from gangster movies in order to express themselves in ways generally understood (Gambetta 2009). For these reasons and more, the portrayal of gangs in media is a rich area for study (Hagedorn 2008; Przemieniecki 2012), and we encourage students and scholars of the gang to apprise themselves of these materials, paying close attention to changes in representations over time. As M. Klein and Maxson (2006, 9) note, "gangs have not changed much, but their depiction most certainly has."

Table 10.1 presents a list of some of most iconic and influential media depictions of gangs and gangsters. There is not the scope here for detailed media analysis (see Rafter and Brown 2011); suffice it to say that these films and television shows cover many of the themes discussed in this book. The 1938 movie *Crime School*, starring Humphrey Bogart, offers an interesting take on Thrasher's (1927) playgroups, whereas many of the other 1930s gangster movies (and the 2010 series *Boardwalk Empire*) are stories of immigrants rising in the criminal underworld in Prohibition-era urban America, as described in Chapter 8. There is the historical realism of Martin Scorsese's *Gangs of New York* and the British television series *Peaky Blinders*, and the cinematic realism of coming-of-age dramas such as *Boyz n the Hood* and *Menace II Society*, all of which grapple with issues of neighborhood, race/ethnicity, and class, as discussed in Chapters 2 and 8. These famous "hood" films of the early 1990s also are credited with (and at times blamed for) the migration of gang and street culture, and like *The Wild One* and *The Warriors*, they needle the anxieties of the times.

Films such as *Girl Gang*, *Teenage Gang Debs*, and *Switchblade Sisters* offered a perspective on women in gangs, the subject of Chapter 7, long before gender received sustained treatment in academic research, which perhaps explains the at times (hysterical) stereotypical depictions in these films. *La Haine*, *Cidade de Deus*, *Kidulthood*, *Sin Nombre*, *Bande de Filles*, and others offer an international look at gangs (Chapter 9). *Bad Boys, American Me, Shot Caller* (2017), *American History X*, and others offer insight into prison gangs (Chapter 12). *American History X* also provides a nice illustration of the power of signaling (Chapters 4 and 5), when the main character, a neo-Nazi, removes his shirt in the prison yard to reveal his Swastika tattoo to an unsuspecting Black audience. There is also plenty of signaling going on in episode 70 of the HBO series *The Sopranos* ("Mr. & Mrs. John

TABLE 10.1 POPULAR MEDIA REPRESENTATIONS OF GANGS

Films

1931 *The Public Enemy*
1938 *Angels with Dirty Faces*
1938 *Boys Town*
1938 *Crime School*
1953 *The Wild One*
1954 *Girl Gang*
1955 *Blackboard Jungle*
1958 *Touch of Evil*
1961 *West Side Story*
1966 *Teenage Gang Debs*
1968 *She-Devils on Wheels*
1971 *A Clockwork Orange*
1972 *The Godfather*
1973 *Mean Streets*
1974 *The Godfather Part II*
1975 *Switchblade Sisters*
1976 *Cat Murkil and the Silks*
1978 *Grease*
1979 *Boulevard Nights*
1979 *The Warriors*
1979 *The Wanderers*
1980 *The Long Good Friday*
1983 *Bad Boys*
1983 *Scarface*
1983 *Rumble Fish*
1983 *The Outsiders*
1984 *Once upon a Time in America*
1987 "Bad" (music video)
1987 *The Untouchables*
1988 *Colors*
1990 *The Godfather Part III*
1990 *Goodfellas*
1990 *The Krays*
1990 *The King of New York*
1991 *Boyz n the Hood*
1991 *New Jack City*
1992 *American Me*
1992 *Juice*
1992 *South Central*
1993 *Menace II Society*
1995 *Clockers*
1995 *Heat*
1995 *La Haine*
1996 *Romeo + Juliet*
1996 *Set It Off*
1997 *Donnie Brasco*
1998 *American History X*

1998 *Lock, Stock and Two Smoking Barrels*
2000 *Sexy Beast*
2000 *Snatch*
2001 *Training Day*
2002 *Infernal Affairs*
2002 *Cidade de Deus (City of God)*
2002 *Gangs of New York*
2004 *Layer Cake*
2004 *Bullet Boy*
2005 *Green Street*
2006 *The Departed*
2006 *Kidulthood*
2007 *American Gangster*
2008 *Gran Torino*
2008 *Gomorrah*
2008 *Adulthood*
2009 *Sin Nombre*
2011 *Attack the Block*
2012 *End of Watch*
2013 *The Bling Ring*
2014 *Bande de Filles (Girlhood)*
2015 *Straight Outta Compton*
2017 *Shot Caller*
2019 *The Irishman*
2019 "Gang Shit" (music video)
2020 *Birds of Prey*

Television Series

1999–2007 *The Sopranos*
2002–2008 *The Wire*
2008–2014 *Sons of Anarchy*
2010–2014 *Boardwalk Empire*
2011–2013 *Top Boy*
2013–present *Peaky Blinders*
2015–2020 *Narcos Columbia/Mexico*
2020–present *Gangs of London*

Documentaries

1936 *The March of Time: Crime School*
1979 *80 Blocks from Tiffany's*
1993 *Flyin' Cut Sleeves*
2002 *Gladiator Days*
2005 *Bastards of the Party*
2005 *Slippin': Ten Years with the Bloods*
2005 *Champion*
2008 *Bloods and Crips: Made in America*
2011 *The Interrupters*
2015 *Rubble Kings*

Sacrimoni Request . . . ") when Tony manufactures a confrontation with his younger, fitter bodyguard, simply to prove he's still top dog. And arguably no better line in movie history captures the teeter-tottering in the gang disengagement process (Chapter 5) than "Just when I thought I was out . . . they pull me back in," from *The Godfather: Part III.*

West Side Story is often criticized for its racialized and romanticized vision of gangs (Yablonsky 1997), but the number "Gee, Officer Krupke" satirizes the pushes and pulls of gangs and the jargon of the helping professions (Chapter 4). Sticking with joining the gang, Stanley Kubrick's *A Clockwork Orange* depicts the psychological roots of gang membership, *Scarface* is a master thesis on crime and the American dream, and a scene in the movie *Heat* where the gang debate among themselves whether or not the next heist is worth the risk is a case study in rational choice theory (Chapter 4), especially the "seductions of crime" (J. Katz 1988). Specifically, when one character is advised to sit out the crime because the heat is on and he doesn't need the money, he famously replies, "Well, you know, for me, the action is the juice."

Crime and violence (Chapter 6) are central themes in practically all the movies listed here, which speaks both to the reality of gangs and to the narrow obsessions of gang observers. Policing gangs (Chapter 11) is the subject of *Colors, Training Day, End of Watch*, and the hit HBO series *The Wire*, which is in fact a dissertation on practically every core issue in urban sociology and criminology (see Collins and Brody 2013). The harassment of alleged "gangbangers" in the N.W.A. rap group by LAPD officers outside a recording studio in *Straight Outta Compton* (2015) serves as an interesting example of gang suppression and the rationale for the group's 1988 song "Fuck Tha Police." Marlon Craft's 2019 music video "Gang Shit" takes this further by provocatively portraying the police as a gang (https://www.youtube.com/watch?v=Aqo-hyxjCYE&list=LLoLJsRZ8e6Dklmc4YWPuCnw&index=387). And when law enforcement fails to protect, *Gran Torino* vividly depicts a vigilante response to gangs.

Van Hellemont and Densley (2019) argued that, in the end, the media image of gangs is both related to reality (even if this relation is in many ways distorted) and useful in constructing reality (in the sense that real gang members draw on and take advantage of media myths). Hayward and Young (2004, 259) similarly observed, "The street scripts the screen and the screen scripts the street." And proving just how mainstream gang scripts have become, in the music video for the 2004 Pharrell Williams hit "Drop It Like It's Hot," gangster rapper Snoop Dogg "Crip Walks," a dance step involving quick, intricate footwork, and raps, "I keep a blue flag hanging out my backside, but only on the left side, yeah that's the Crip side"—a direct reference to LA gang symbolism (https://www.youtube.com/watch?v=GtUVQei3nX4&ob=av2e).

Gangs and the Internet

Media and technology have changed our ability to communicate, work, search, and discover. Whereas mainstream media are influenced by corporate and other interests, technology such as the internet is theoretically agnostic and can be used for good and bad purposes. For every prosocial group that harnesses the power of the internet for good, there is an antisocial group equally taking advantage of advances in technology, co-opting them for their personal uses. Terrorists, extremists, and hate groups all maintain an online presence, and so too do gangs and gang members (J. Peterson and Densley 2017). The digital divide has narrowed considerably, especially in urban settings, and for this reason, the internet plays an increasingly important role in everyday life (Lane 2018), including the lives of gang members (Moule, Pyrooz, and Decker 2013).

Back in 2005, Papachristos (2005) observed, "[Few] gang members ever discuss or mention the Internet. Many don't possess the hardware, software, or technical skills (not to mention the necessary telephone lines) to manage the Web" (53). Within two years, however, Apple released the iPhone, putting the full power of the internet in the palm of people's hands, and, as is often the case in the fast-paced world of technology, Papachristos's assessment grew quickly outdated. A brave new world of mobile wireless broadband, unlimited data plans, free Wi-Fi hotspots, apps, social media, streaming, and gig economics emerged. With each passing year, the internet became more deeply entwined in the everyday lives of young people—including gang members—to the point now where their real lives and virtual lives are nearly one and the same (Lane 2018). A digitally mediated world of constant status updates and perfect remembering complicates the already complicated lives of teenagers, forcing them to be "on" all the time for fear of missing out (Boyd 2014). On the "digital street," hanging out online can supplement or even supplant face-to-face communication, potentially amplifying typical adolescent drama (Lane 2018).

There has been an explosion of research looking at gangs' use of the internet in the last decade, including an entire 325-page edited volume titled *Gangs in the Era of Internet and Social Media* (Melde and Weerman 2020). In recent years, the literature has moved from foundational and theoretical to more empirical and applied (for reviews, see J. Peterson and Densley 2017; Pyrooz and Moule 2019). Pyrooz and Moule (2019) categorized this bourgeoning literature according to the methodology employed, thus differentiating between "cyber-ethnographic research," survey research, and "big data" analyses of gang activity online, such as Wijeratne et al.'s (2015, 2016) scraping of Twitter for gang-related key words. Urbanik et al. (2020) elaborated on this typology to distinguish between (a) studies focused on asking gang members about their internet and social media usage; (b) studies that interpret the style and substance of gang-related "artifacts" posted online, such as videos and tweets; and (c) studies that balance the words and deeds of gang members in physical space with analyses of gang content in virtual space.

In the early days of research on gangs' use of the internet, it was necessary to ask gang members if and how they used it, simply to provide some baseline for understanding. Two studies in particular lay this foundation. First, based on a 2006 i-Safe survey, King, Walpole, and Lamon (2007) discovered that 25 percent of gang members used the Internet for at least four hours a week, with many accessing the internet at local community centers. This was helpful in placing gang members in online settings. Second, a study conducted by two of the authors (Decker and Pyrooz 2011) shed light on what gang members actually do while logged on.

The Google Ideas study comprised interviews with current and former gang members, as well as non-gang individuals, in Fresno, Los Angeles, and Phoenix. It found that gang members used the internet and social networking sites at high rates, around 80 and 70 percent, respectively. Facebook and Myspace were the social networks most frequently used (Moule, Pyrooz, and Decker 2013). Gang members reported high rates of offending and victimization in online settings, which included harassment, intimidation, and violent threats. In many respects, technology was shaping the "criminal and routine activities" of gang youth (Pyrooz, Decker, and Moule 2015), to the extent that creating a continuous stream of gang-related content for consumption was fast becoming one of the duties of gang membership. The internet served as a natural extension of the street in part because it met the symbolic needs of gang members as a status enhancer. Gangs used social media to brag about criminal exploits and intimidate rivals. Readers can simply query "gang fights" on YouTube to see what we are referring to. In the Google Ideas study, St. Louis gang members made the following points:

> YouTube is a big deal . . . rapping on videos . . . fights on videos.
>
> Someone's always got a phone recording. Anything you record goes on Facebook or YouTube. (Decker and Pyrooz 2011, 10)

Around the same time, four thousand miles away, another author (Densley 2012a, 2013) was observing similar behavior in London, England. Gang members there would film brief incursions on rival turf and other acts of defiance and disrespect, then post them online, tagging their enemies to rub their noses in it. Gang members would even record their own allies, creating digital *kompromat* to entrap their co-offenders and keep them honest. Still, as Sela-Shayovitz (2012) found through interviews with gang youth in Israel, most gang activity online was social; only in rare cases did gang members venture into the more sophisticated realms of cybercrime. What was true then is true now—much of what gang members do online is the same as what non-gang members do; after all, gang members are human beings. Decker and Pyrooz (2011, 16–17) observe:

> The Internet plays an increasingly important role in gangs, but not to such an extent that it dominates gang activity . . . Gang members use the Internet in ways similar to youth that avoid gangs—they talk to girls (and boys), they listen to music, they watch videos, they post videos of themselves, they look for jobs, and they carry out research for school . . . There is a lot of age-appropriate behavior by gang members in their use of the Internet.

The next phase of research in this area involved scholars reviewing and analyzing social media content, which offered new insights, with the caveat that findings pertained only to publicly available data and, in some cases, the profiles of gangs or gang members with large social media followings (Patton, Lane, et al. 2017). Womer and Bunker (2010) found that Latino gangs maintained a presence on social media, posting references to violence, wealth, drugs, or sex with a deliberate and recognizable message for their audiences. The authors claimed that this was how gangs promoted their criminal activities. Patton, Patel, et al.'s (2017) analysis of millions of tweets posted by individuals identified by Detroit law enforcement as gang members uncovered similar common themes: memorials to deceased gang members, violence, and substance abuse.

Morselli and Décary-Hétu (2013) examined how gang members used three social networking sites, Twitter, Facebook, and MySpace, finding that the internet was used to promote individualized activities of gang members rather than the coordinated behaviors of the gang. Van Hellemont's (2012) analysis of 170 personal "web-blogs" and music videos found Belgian gang members "performing" gang identities in virtual space in a way that conformed to gang stereotypes, thus blurring the boundaries between fantasy and reality. In an ever-global world, gang members were essentially following the common conventions of the gangster genre of music, films, and television shows (Van Hellemont and Densley 2019).

Still, life online remains anchored to the lived reality of the streets, which is why references to physical territory, such as street signs or zip codes, are a fixture of many gangs' social media communication (Irwin-Rogers, Densley, and Pinkney 2018). Leverso and Hsiao (2020) studied digital trace data scraped from a public Facebook about Chicago Latino gangs (resulting in over 140,000 posts, likes, comments, and comment replies) and combined with law enforcement data on the geographic locations of gangs to learn that fighting among gang members in the online environment was conditional on not only the type of post displayed but also the geographic proximity of gang territory. They found gang members using social media to interact with other gangs in faraway locales as well as individuals nearby, but the tone and tenor of that communication often reflected the degree of physical distance. These findings may explain why, in one Philadelphia study, active social media use among gangs appeared to limit the impact of an otherwise effective violence intervention program (Hyatt, Densley, and Roman 2021).

Social media platforms are spaces for gangs to "broadcast badness" (Lauger and Densley 2018) and for gang members to practice the code of the street (Urbanik and Haggerty 2018). When gang members threaten or taunt rivals using social media, this is known as "internet banging" (Patton, Eschmann, and Butler 2013). Content analyses of gang-related rap music videos have found that threatening material posted online is broadly analogous to threats issued on the street (J. Johnson and Schell-Busey 2016; Lauger and Densley 2018; Pinkney and Robinson-Edwards 2018). Both theoretically (Densley 2020; Moule, Decker, and Pyrooz 2017; Lauger, Densley, and Moule 2019) and empirically (Moule, Pyrooz, and Decker 2014), studies have shown how boundaries drawn online can transform virtual spaces into threatening environments (Urbanik and Haggerty 2018) and how certain online behaviors—namely, dissing, calling, and direct threats—can incite violence in physical space (Patton et al. 2019).

At the same time, the social distance that social media creates can help diffuse tensions and deescalate violence. In nature, if you want to protect yourself from predators, you get big and scary (Felson 2006; Howell 2007). Social media affords gangs the same illusion of size, strength, and spread (Densley 2013). And for gang members living in Chicago's most dangerous neighborhoods, Stuart (2020a, 2020b) held that exaggerated virtual identities create barriers to violence. By presenting themselves as scarier and more violent than they are in real life, such as by posting photographs of themselves posing in crowds of dangerous-looking people or holding guns that they borrowed from those people, gang members can deter rival predation. Of course, this is tantamount to a gang member saying out loud that they carry a gun for protection, which only elevates their risk of violent victimization on the streets (Spano and Bolland 2013). In the end, authenticity still matters (Lauger 2012), and if rivals call someone on their bluff or catch them "lacking" (i.e., unwilling to take the bait), especially live on camera, then violent retaliation can follow. These findings hold important implications for law enforcement (see Chapter 11), who have been criticized (e.g., Lane, Ramirez, and Pearce 2018; Patton, Brunton, et al. 2017) for taking online claims at face value and unduly criminalizing actions that *everyone* on social media is guilty of—portraying their lives as more glamorous and exciting than they really are, for the sake of retweets or likes.

Stuart's (2020b) work on the "code of the Tweet" is part of series of recent studies that have combined in-depth interviews or observations with analyses of social media content (Pawelz and Elvers 2018; for a review, see Urbanik and Roks 2020). This work speaks to the "hybridization" of street gang offending—that is, offending that takes place in person and online, often at the same time (Roks, Leukfeldt, and Densley 2020). To counter misinterpretation of any cultural terms or coded language hidden in memes and emojis, scholars have even taken the novel route of incorporating interpretations of social media posts by "domain experts" (i.e., people fluent in gang content), such as ex-gang members, into their studies (Frey et al. 2020). In one study that mixed content analysis with focus groups of young people, gangs were found giving public updates on their drug distribution businesses, such as where they were headed with new supplies of drugs or what they had for sale (Storrod and Densley 2017). At the same time, gangs were using smartphone apps to surveil the activities of drug dealers in their ranks, such as by requiring them to post regular location and status updates. Based in London, England, this study found that the "expressive" work of the gang, done via videos and images online, benefited the gang's "instrumental" criminal activities because it marketed the group as credible suppliers of illicit goods and services (Storrod and Densley 2017). As Marshall McLuhan famously said, "The medium is the message" (McLuhan and Fiore 1967).

When Decker and Pyrooz (2011) first asked about how the gang, not gang members, used the internet, the most common responses involved the following:

> That's a no-no. Only idiots do that. Why would you do that [organize drug deals or other crime online]? That's not the attention you would want.

They also found that very few gang members reported that the gang organizes activities online or recruits new members online, behaviors that the media and law enforcement routinely warn about (e.g., National Gang Intelligence Center 2011). That online gang activity is poorly organized is consistent with what we highlighted about gangs in street settings in earlier chapters. However, new research finds some nuance in this area. A study of gangs in London (A. Whittaker, Densley, and Moser 2020) found that there were "differential adaptations" to social media among gangs, including gangs that occupied the same geographic spaces. The authors attributed this to a "generation gap." They argued that newer gangs and younger gang members, especially those with tenuous "street capital" (Harding 2014), had more to gain and less to lose from signaling their reputations online. In contrast, more durable gangs and more senior gang members had street capital in the bank and could not afford the extra scrutiny that social media attention provided.

In sum, as technologies advance, we expect that they will spread and diffuse to marginalized populations, such as gang members, who often actively attempt to avoid conventional advances. But as technologies become available and knowledge extends to populations at the shadow of the margins, we expect them to adopt it, especially when it proves useful for promoting the very attitudes and behaviors that attract individuals to gangs. The internet qualifies as one such technology, and we expect to find more attention devoted to this topic—from researchers, the criminal justice system, and policymakers—in the upcoming years.

Is the Gang a Social Institution?

In this section, we consider whether the gang itself is a social institution, distinguishable from others, and qualitatively different from a regular peer group. We answer this question by exploring the extent to which gangs provide basic functions for their members, their community, and ordinary citizens, and in some cases overtake the influences of the social institutions we have discussed previously.

Has the Gang Become a Family?

Students, concerned citizens, and policymakers often ask us whether the gang has become a family. Many gang members talk about their gang as if it were a family and use that exact term to describe the gang. Some commentators (Perkins 1987; W. Brown 1977) have argued that the gang is a natural extension of the Black family, sort of the next step in the evolution of the Black experience in cities. In Phoenix, a former female gang member in her late teens described being in her gang as "a sense of belonging. I had a family. They supported me in everything I did, and I didn't find that at home." A young male gang member in Phoenix told us that the gang had an attraction similar to being in a family:

> 'Cause, like, it's hard livin' on the streets. Know what I mean? It's hard. And when you with the gang, you feel like everything is so much better. 'Cause you get . . . get what you need. Like, you get all kind of shit, and you make a living off of livin' in the gang.

These are strong sentiments expressed by young gang members, often reflecting the realities of a breakdown of traditional social institutions.

Still, despite the weakened condition of the American family in many large cities, most gang members continue to be more committed to their natal families than to their gang. This is understandable given the harsh realities of life in the gang. As one of the authors memorably noted, "if the gang is a family . . . it is an abusive one—gang love is very much conditional" (Densley 2013, 36). Densley's study in London is part of a small body of research that has asked gang members directly about the relative importance of the gang and the family. For example, Decker and Van Winkle (1996) learned from their sample of ninety-nine active gang members that only one would choose the gang over his or her family if forced to make such a choice. These same authors and Vigil (2020) also report that few gang members want their children to grow up and become gang members.

One of the emerging issues in the study of gangs and families is the intergenerational character of many gangs. As gangs proliferate and last longer, we have begun to see gang members become parents and raise children who are at risk for gang membership. This condition is most pronounced among the Latino gangs of Southern California (Vigil 1988). But Black gangs in cities like Chicago have been around long enough to see second-, third-, and even fourth-generation gang members within the same family (Aspholm 2020). It is important to note that second- and third-generation gang members enter the gang for many of the same reasons their parents did: they are raised in neighborhoods with few social and economic opportunities, and they are exposed to gang lifestyles on a daily basis. There is not a solid body of evidence that parents are purposely encouraging their offspring to become gang members by socializing them into the gang lifestyle, but kinship ties certainly facilitate entry into gangs (see Chapter 4). Furthermore, the condition of the family, especially in poor neighborhoods, will have important implications for the presence and power of gangs in urban and suburban neighborhoods.

Do Gangs "Run" Public Schools?

Gangs do not make decisions for public schools, but they do influence decision-making. Based on his interviews with school officials, W. Miller (1975, 46) argued that gangs were "operating *within* as well as outside" of schools in several of the nation's largest cities, holding that gangs posed "serious obstacles" to the education of students and "a serious threat to the physical safety of students and teachers." W. Miller (1982, 131–132) suggested that an increase in school-based gangs in the 1970s was related to the weakened ability of schools to control students and a greater emphasis on keeping troublesome adolescents in school.

Miller's conclusions were reflected in a local Chicago study. Troman-hauser, a professor at Chicago State University, and his colleagues conducted a massive survey of more than twelve thousand students in Chicago public schools that was published in 1981 (Tromanhauser, Corcoran, and Lollino 1981). The report concluded that school-based gang activity could be found in all twenty of Chicago's school districts. More than half of the students surveyed reported that gangs were active in their schools. Ten percent re-ported being either intimidated or attacked by gang members or solicited for membership. The minority dropout rate in Chicago schools in the 1980s was one of the largest, if not the largest, in the nation. Hutchison and Kyle (1993) published a study that blamed the high rates of school dropout on gangs. As part of his Ph.D. research at Northwestern University, Kyle, a college admin-istrator and Roman Catholic priest, interviewed random samples of the 1979 entering classes of two predominantly Latino high schools in Chicago. On the basis of these interviews, the researchers concluded that gangs controlled specific classrooms and whole floors at the two schools included in the study. Drugs, including cocaine and heroin, were reported to be routinely sold in-side the schools by gang members. Administrators had failed to control this situation. Non-gang students and students who were members of rival gangs (those not in control in their schools) transitioned from avoiding gang-controlled parts of the schools by cutting classes and ultimately, dropping out.

A little-known fact about Frederic Thrasher is that he was one of the founding fathers not only of gang research but also of the field of educa-tional sociology. His master's thesis was on the Boy Scouts, and in 1927, the year *The Gang* was published, Thrasher was hired as an educational sociolo-gist by New York University (Dimitriadis 2006). Writing in the *Journal of Educational Sociology*, which he edited after World War II, Thrasher (1933) observed that gang problems in schools were less serious than gang problems outside schools. The durability of Thrasher's conclusion was substantiated by a 1980s study of the Chicago Public Schools by Spergel (1985). Spergel ana-lyzed official records data from the Chicago Police Department and Chicago Public Schools. A key finding was that only 9 percent of Chicago's officially recorded gang crime occurred in or near public schools. Spergel concluded, in concurrence with Thrasher, that the school gang problem was distinctly different from the street gang problem. Based on his analysis of official re-cords and his decades of conducting and reviewing research on gangs, Sper-gel (1995) described the gang problem as it is manifested in public schools as representing the activity of younger gang members and involving less serious offenses. In contrast, the gang problem as it is manifested on the streets in-volves older gang members and more serious offenses.

Decker and Van Winkle (1996, 194–195) interviewed active gang mem-bers in St. Louis. Some of what gang members told them could be selectively used to support the belief that gangs control schools. For example, one twenty-year-old gang member recollected that during his school days, he had carried two pistols to school every day. By his account, he had bribed school security guards with crack cocaine. Other gang members recalled bribing teachers and selling drugs to teachers. Yet, Decker and Van Winkle were emphatic in their conclusions that gangs *did not* run schools or even parts of schools. They labeled accounts of gangs controlling schools "alarmist and unfounded" (191). They concluded, "We would not deny that drug sales, gang fights, and gun carrying are serious problems in the schools our subjects attended. But, these schools are not controlled by omnipotent gangs who hold the student and adult populations in terror" (204). Hagedorn (2017) takes this further and finds that gangs in Milwaukee and Chicago have at times played *positive* roles in schools, becoming catalysts for disruptive change. Hagedorn argued that educational policies of exclusion and punishment, often enacted in response to gangs, do more harm to racialized and marginalized youth than the gangs themselves.

More recent work by D. Carson and Esbensen (2019) confirms that gangs do not run schools, although they are certainly present in them (e.g., Garot 2010), and gang members exert influence over schoolchildren (e.g., Gallupe and Gravel 2018). An additional measure of the extent to which gangs have become integrated into the fabric of the institution can be seen in the participation of gang members in high school and college athletics. In a study of athletic directors and coaches at Division I Bowl Championship Series schools, Alpert and colleagues (2011) found that two-thirds of each group thought that there were gang members playing on a Division I athletic team. More than 80 percent of each group believed that gang members had an impact on Division I football and men's basketball programs. The team also conducted interviews with football team members at two prominent Division I football programs. At one of the universities, nearly 90 percent of the players believed that gang members were participating on their own football team or that of another university, and 61 percent of the members of the other team responded that way. Eighteen percent of the players at one of the universities believed that there were active gang members on their own team. One measure of the institutionalization of an activity is if it makes its way into other realms of life. If there are active gang members participating in high school and college athletics, as this study demonstrates, this is further evidence of the institutionalization of gangs into American life (Rojek et al. 2013).

Do Gangs Replace Conventional Employment?

The informal social order of gangs can play a functional role in grey or illicit economies, street justice, and territorial protectionism (Sánchez-Jankowski

1991). And, as we discussed above, being a gang member can be a lucrative job, especially with regard to wages earned from dealing drugs and the perks of being in a gang (Augustyn, McGloin, and Pyrooz 2019). Yet, while we know that the opportunity to make money can motivate gang joining (Levitt and Venkatesh 2001), we remain skeptical about the possibility that gangs replace conventional employment for several reasons. First, many gang members who deal drugs continue to have part-time jobs, even though they tend to be in the secondary labor market. Second, as revealed in several studies, the wages associated with selling drugs are neither high nor stable, reflecting the character of drug dealing and gang membership (Levitt and Venkatesh 2000). Third, as we reviewed in Chapter 5, very few individuals remain in gangs for an extended period. If we observed lifetime involvement or if even five to ten years was the norm, then we might expect that the gang provides for the gang member. Most gang members know that this isn't the case—any increase in illegal earnings is short-lived, which is why "drug dealers still live with their moms" (Levitt and Dubner 2005, 85).

Conclusion

This chapter has explored gang membership in the context of conventional social institutions—families, schools, religion, the labor market, the political system, religion, and the internet. We find that gang membership intersects with these bodies in many and important ways, but in the end, despite its best efforts, the gang can rarely provide (at least consistently) the types of outcomes these other contexts can. Just how closely a gang can be considered as an institution is a subject of disagreement. Based on what we have reviewed above, it is premature to refer to a gang as a social institution. In select areas throughout the country, mostly in neighborhoods in larger cities with high levels of concentrated poverty that lack strong families and employment opportunities, there is the possibility that some gangs can operate in this capacity, providing the basic functions necessary for a community (e.g., Chicago). This situation is clearly the exception. Instead, we believe that it is safe to conclude that gangs are quasi-institutions for individuals operating at the margins of society. They provide a sense of belonging for those who do not get it at home, an opportunity to make money for those without conventional qualifications, and status for those who cannot earn it in the classroom. We could even say that gang membership constitutes an alternative form of education. Much like how formal education enhances cultural, human, and social capital, the gang provides experiences, skills, connections, and opportunities that some might say supersede the need to perform well in school. Combined, we think of these resources that are offered in the context of the gang as forms of "criminal capital," transformed from positive social and human capital in the conventional sense (e.g., education and social relationships) to capital in the criminal sense, where some are more successful in their criminal endeavors (McCarthy and Hagan 1995, 2001). In sum, the gang itself shares many attributes with the social institutions outlined above, but even though it is central to the lives of its members and in many settings has become intergenerational and integrated into mainstream culture, it is not yet an institution in its own right.

III

Responding to Gangs

11

Policing Gangs

The police are the sole domestic agency empowered to enforce the law and apply force on behalf of the state. At time of writing, however, American policing is facing a "legitimacy crisis" (Cook 2015). Police violence and misconduct, primarily against Black people and increasingly captured on video and posted on social media, has sparked civil unrest in many cities (Cobbina 2019) and led some commentators to forecast the "end of policing" as we know it (Vitale 2017). Police abolitionists envision replacing the police with a strong social safety net, creating a society in which the police are largely unnecessary because basic human needs such as a living wage, safe affordable housing, and access to mental health care are universally met (Gimbel and Muhammad 2019). There is no doubt that social services and antipoverty measures could reduce the appeal of gangs and therefore the need to police them. However, opponents to police abolition fear a rise in crime and see the idea as a threat to public safety.

This is important context for thinking about policing gangs. Critical and cultural criminologists argue that by defining gangs as inherently criminal, academics and state actors conspired to narrowly construct the gang as something solely to be policed, and mostly on malum prohibitum behaviors (J. Katz and Jackson-Jacobs 2004). More mainstream criminologists point to the fact that gang members are responsible for a disproportionate amount of malum in se crimes, including about 13 percent of all U.S. homicides despite being a fraction of 1 percent of the population (Egley, Howell, and Harris, 2014), for the reason why the police target gang members. Either way, crime reduction is a mandate that falls to police, but as discussed in Chapter 8, police sometimes approach this task based on stereotypical or inaccurate depictions of gangs, and this can land them in trouble (Esbensen and Tusinski 2007).

Most field studies of gangs report that almost all gang members have been arrested, and school-based surveys of gang members consistently find that gang members—especially Black, Latino, and other minority ethnic youth—are arrested more often than their non-gang peers (Tapia 2011a). One analysis of data from the 1997 National Longitudinal Survey of Youth found that the likelihood of arrest nearly doubles when someone joins a gang and remains rather stable in the succeeding years when someone remains active (Densley and Pyrooz 2020). Gang members therefore see the police regularly, although police interactions with gang members vary (for reviews, see Mora 2020; Novich 2018).

The aim of this chapter is to provide a broad discussion of the nature of police tactics and strategies in dealing with gangs. We begin by examining the police role in gang prevention, including the well-evaluated Gang Resistance Education and Training (G.R.E.A.T.) program deployed in schools, before moving on to explore the more conventional role of police in gang suppression. The section on gang suppression takes a critical view of police intervention but also presents examples of the more promising and proven gang violence reduction strategies, such Group Violence Intervention and Project Safe Neighborhoods. Police gang units and the controversy over police gang databases are other important topics examined in this chapter.

The Police Role in Gang Prevention

Owing to their unique knowledge of gangs and access to the communities where gangs organize and operate (Kennedy, Braga, and Piehl 1997; Sierra-Arévalo and Papachristos 2015a), law enforcement officers have a role to play in outreach to the people and places at risk of gang involvement and activity. Nearly half of police gang units surveyed in 2007 participated in some form of gang prevention programming (Langton 2010). Distributing literature to schools, parents, and community groups was the most common activity, but police also were involved in more hands-on initiatives.

In primary prevention programs, police help develop and deliver information sessions and education programs for the general population, thus attempting to positively engage with as many people as possible, regardless of their risk of involvement in gangs and crime. After-school activities and late-night sports programs in a community center are common examples (Gravel et al. 2013). In secondary prevention efforts, by contrast, police specifically target the people most at risk of gang membership (based on individual, family, school, peer group, and neighborhood factors), at times and in places where that risk is elevated (e.g., in known gang neighborhoods or after high-profile incidents of gang violence), and help refer them to other social service providers (Gravel et al. 2013; Wong et al. 2016).

Perhaps the best example of police involvement in primary prevention is the Gang Resistance Education and Training (G.R.E.A.T.) program (Esbensen 2015). We discuss this program more in Chapter 14. Suffice it to say that few primary prevention programs enjoy G.R.E.A.T.'s longevity or "name recognition" (Papachristos 2013b, 370); it even inspired a similar program, titled Growing against Gangs and Violence, that has been delivered in hundreds of schools to thousands of children in the United Kingdom (Densley et al. 2017). G.R.E.A.T. sees police officers deliver thirteen educational sessions in schools to early adolescents, with three main objectives: (1) to reduce student involvement in violent crime, (2) to teach the consequences of gang affiliation, and (3) to improve relationships with and attitudes toward police (Esbensen et al. 2011).

G.R.E.A.T. has been rigorously evaluated. The first version of G.R.E.A.T. was subject to two multisite evaluations. The first, a cross-sectional study, found some evidence of outcome success (Esbensen and Osgood 1999). The second, a longitudinal evaluation, was less supportive of program efficacy, finding no significant differences between the students in the program and those students who did not receive the program in terms of gang membership, drug use, and delinquency, although there was a "sleeper" effect at years three and four of follow-up (Esbensen et al. 2011). Rather than throw in the towel, the agency responsible for the program sought the advice of the evaluation team to help revise the curriculum, train instructors, and design better training modules. This is relatively unheard of in program evaluation, and G.R.E.A.T. was completely retooled because of it.

G.R.E.A.T. II's expanded curriculum incorporated problem-solving strategies and cooperative learning activities, along with evidence-based risk factors for gang membership (Esbensen et al. 2011, 2012). The rehearsed lecture-style delivery was replaced with a more conversational tone. G.R.E.A.T. II showed "great results" (Howell 2013) in a seven-city randomized controlled trial with four-year follow-up, involving 3,820 students (Esbensen et al. 2012, 2013, 2016). The program reduced the odds of gang membership by 39 percent over one year while also fostering more negative views of gangs and improving youth-police relations. However, there was no concomitant reduction in offending. We discuss this further in Chapter 14.

In terms of secondary prevention, San Francisco police were involved in identifying at-risk youth and referring them to the Youth Development Workers program, where they received job skills training from City Hall employees (Sivilli, Yin, and Nugent 1996). Similarly, police worked in a referral capacity for the Los Angeles Gang Reduction and Youth Development (GRYD) program, which gave direct services to youth at risk of joining gangs and their families (Hennigan et al. 2014). Both programs showed evidence of success.

An evaluation of GRYD, for example, found that program participation reduced clients' engagement in violence and weapons-carrying and in gang-related behaviors (Cahill et al. 2016). However, it is worth noting that the role of the police was minimal—they simply were one avenue of entry into the program. Carlsson and Decker (2005) described a more informal prevention technique whereby police in Norway initiate a "worrying conversation" with young people at risk of gang involvement. They invite youth to visit the police station with their parents to discuss the possible negative consequences of delinquency and find ways to prevent them from progressing further down the path to gang membership. This is a softer, Scandinavian version of the "custom notification" approach to active gang member suppression (Kennedy and Friedrich 2014).

The Police Role in Gang Suppression

Gangs are "street oriented" groups, and gang members spend a lot of time "hanging out," standing on street corners, in parks, and outside their houses (M. Klein and Maxson 2006). This makes gangs and gang members highly visible to the police. It is not surprising, therefore, that officers avail themselves of the opportunity to connect with gang members. Depending on the nature of the assignment and activities of the gang, these interactions can be hostile and aggressive or merely spirited exchanges that are mostly benign. During these interactions, the police may provide curbstone justice—informal adjustments that involve admonishments, advice, alternatives to gang life, and even opportunity provision.

However, many of the tactics and strategies employed by the police in responding to gangs are similar to those employed against other groups that engage in high levels of violence, drug sales, and group activity (C. Katz and Webb 2006). These include activities that are largely oriented around suppression. Such tactics may include saturation patrol, a police policy that floods an area with a heavy concentration of police, whether on foot, in patrol cars, on horseback, or otherwise. "Stop and talks" are a police tactic that engages the police in pulling individuals over, either from their vehicle or more typically on the street, to "chat them up" and ask what they are up to, where they are going, and who their friends are. This practice is very closely aligned with completing field interrogation (FI) cards. These cards are a primary way for the police to collect information from individuals about their activities, their associates, and their neighborhood that provides basic information for the police to better understand neighborhoods, actors, and the relationship between the two (C. Katz and Webb 2006). In recent years, researchers have used FI card data for important research into patterns of gang activity and police surveillance (Papachristos, Hureau, and Braga 2013; Papachristos et al. 2015; Valasik, Reid, and Phillips 2016).

The police act proactively to serve warrants on individuals, especially gang members, who they have reasonable grounds to suspect have recently participated in serious criminal offenses. In many jurisdictions, the police are working with a broad coalition of groups to develop rosters of high-rate offenders whom they will target with enforcement and social service supports. These lists are known by a number of names, most commonly the "Worst of the Worst" list (McDevitt 2006). They comprise individuals who have committed a number of violent crimes and often include gang members. Many of the gang members we interviewed experienced these tactics firsthand:

> Like, I'll be walking down the street, and these boys got pulled over. And I guess the cops thought I was with them, so they pulled me over too. And then they started questioning me about my tattoos and all that. They started taking pictures and the like and put my name in the computer. (Twenty-one-year-old Phoenix ex-gang member)

A former gang member in Los Angeles related a similar story:

> They took me into custody and told me that I couldn't be on the streets of Venice [California]. I told them I had just left my dad's house, you know? And they were like, "Oh well, you're not supposed to be in the streets after ten o'clock at night." They took me in, and I did a five-month violation.

Another former LA gang member in his late forties told us that the "stain" of being a gang member was hard to shed in the eyes of the police:

> Their [the police's] attitude is everybody's a gang member. You know, until they actually pull them over or something and they realize, you know, and, like, a lot of times, I'll ask the police officers, "What is the aggression for; why you stereotyping us?"

A Fresno gang member said that he feared the police worse than a rival gang: "They [the police] kicked the shit out of me." Experiences like these contribute to the perception that the police are in fact "the biggest gang" (Densley 2013, 158).

Many cities have created special gang intelligence units whose function is to gather information for policy formulation, plan strategic interventions, or tip off other police units about upcoming gang activities. Because arrests often are left to other units in the department, gang members can develop rapport with these officers, and some report having positive relationships with such officers. However, most gang members, not surprisingly, see the police as an occupying force in their communities and report antagonistic relationships with police officers and a generalized distrust of the criminal justice system. This a matter of concern since the first agent of government most citizens interact with is typically a law enforcement officer, and those perceptions are generalized to government (Tyler 2006). Black Americans in particular say they do not cooperate because they do not believe the police can protect them from retaliation (Leovy 2015). Because citizens in predominantly poor, Black communities refuse to cooperate with the authorities, the burden of unsolved crimes falls disproportionately on the very people that need and deserve justice the most (Brunson and Wade 2019).

In Novich and Hunt's (2017) study on gang members who deal drugs, interviewees reported being handcuffed too tightly, shoved, pushed, and in many cases choked by police officers. They also reported perceived disrespect from police in the form of abusive and degrading language. However, if gang members were approached for reasons they felt were justified—namely, being caught drug dealing—they awarded legitimacy to the interaction and to the police officer. If they felt they were approached under circumstances where they were not actively criminally involved, then respect for police was lost (Novich and Hunt 2018).

Another study found that drug arrests in Black neighborhoods and of Black people primarily stemmed from officers' greater use of discretionary stops, Terry frisks or searches related to outstanding warrants, suspicion of ambiguous demeanor, or minor infractions (Gaston 2019a). Drug arrests in White neighborhoods or of White citizens, by contrast, resulted simply from reactive policing. Officers also engaged in "out-of-place" racial profiling in drug enforcement, targeting suspects whose race was incongruent with the neighborhood racial context (Gaston 2019b).

As discussed in Chapter 8, there are concerns (real and perceived) that gang members are subject to a differential and discriminatory pattern of policing that serves to stereotype whole sections of Black, Latino, and other minority ethnic communities, especially young men, as involved or potentially involved in crime (Trujillo and Vitale 2019). Such a pattern of policing neutralizes the position of gang members, and by extension Black, Latino, and other minority ethnic people, as victims of crime—especially the types of crime that most adversely affect them, such as gun violence. In fact, some argue that the Black community in particular has suffered from such inadequate policing, highlighted by low homicide and violent crime clearance rates, that gangs exist mostly to help people police themselves (Leovy 2015; Sobel and Osoba 2009; Venkatesh 1997). Cook and Ludwig (2018) observed, "Arresting less than 10% of shooters (as is currently the case in Chicago) may not assuage the instinct of survivors, their families, and their gangs to avenge their victimization."

The rise of suppression as the dominant response to gang crime problems started in the late 1970s and the 1980s as either a function of growing political conservatism or a reaction to increased levels of gang violence (W. Miller 1975). Under the category of suppression, which we further discuss in Chapter 14, Spergel and Curry (1990) included activities such as arrest, special prosecution, incarceration, intensive supervision, gang intelligence, and networking among criminal justice agencies to the exclusion of nonjustice agencies. Suppression is now a pejorative term in policing, but it can capture more innovative and community-oriented strategies. For example, the Los Angeles Police Department used traffic barriers to create cul-de-sacs in some neighborhoods to decrease gang violence in the 1990s, an intervention that led to a 20 percent decrease in violent crime within a year of implementation (Lasley 1999). Under the umbrella of suppression, M. Klein (1998) also includes specialized enforcement efforts, specialized probation, targeting of gang members by the California Youth Authority, summer projects, and the use of gang injunctions.

The Office of Community Oriented Policing Services' (COPS) Anti-Gang Initiative (AGI) is one of the best examples of gang suppression (McGarrell et al. 2013). The COPS office was established under the U.S. Department of Justice through a provision in the 1994 Violent Crime Control and Law Enforcement Act (see Chapter 13). In 1996, COPS launched a fifteen-city AGI. In total, $11 million was made available to the cities in $1 million or $500,000 allocations depending on city size. These jurisdictions included Austin, Texas; Boston, Massachusetts; Chicago, Illinois; Dallas, Texas; Detroit, Michigan; Indianapolis, Indiana; Jersey City, New Jersey; Kansas City, Missouri; Los Angeles, California; Miami, Florida; Oakland, California; Orange County, California; Phoenix, Arizona; Salt Lake City, Utah; and St. Louis, Missouri. Two of the jurisdictions, Los Angeles and Orange County, were area multiagency partnerships.

There were three goals of the AGI: (1) to develop strategies to reduce gang-related problems, (2) to develop strategies to reduce gang-related drug trafficking problems, and (3) to reduce the fear instilled by gang-related activities. Jurisdictions were required to present a characterization of their gang problem as a means of developing a response strategy. Such descriptions of the local gang problem were to include the number of gangs, the number of members, the age ranges of gang members, why individuals joined a gang, the source of recruitment, locations of recruitment, locations of activities, reasons for migration, and incidents of gang-related crime. These analyses of the local gang problem resulted in a variety of response strategies. Eight specific strategies were identified in the materials provided to the COPS office in the requests for funding. These included special curfews, coordination of services, bringing new partners to the table, information sharing, the use of geographic information systems (GIS), tracking gang members with intelligence systems, school involvement, and the use of community organizing.

Three departments (Detroit, Jersey City, and St. Louis) chose to use special curfew enforcement strategies to target juveniles out after curfew hours. Six jurisdictions (Boston, Indianapolis, Miami, Oakland, Phoenix, and St. Louis) emphasized the need to coordinate their funded activities with efforts already in place to combat drugs and gangs. In Boston, this meant that the AGI effort was specifically linked to the Safe Futures funding received from the Office of Juvenile Justice and Delinquency Prevention (OJJDP), and in Phoenix a link was developed between the G.R.E.A.T. prevention program in middle schools and AGI efforts. The integration of these efforts with other programs, including those that are not law enforcement oriented, makes them notable because such efforts are rare.

The most popular strategy among the fifteen departments was an effort to produce organizational change. Spergel and Curry (1990) have identified this as a core response strategy of law enforcement to gang problems. Not surprisingly, eleven of the fifteen departments used some form of this strategy. Typically, this approach attempts to enhance existing interventions by changing an overall organization or strategic response by bringing new partners to the table. This often meant that police departments sought out the assistance of other law enforcement partners, but some also turned to the schools or social service agencies for help. Six cities saw information sharing as a key strategy to be funded by AGI monies. Often, this meant the use of enhanced technology to provide presentations, transfer data, or conduct analyses. For example, many cities took the opportunity to use GIS technology to map gang, drug, and youth crime activities.

Eight of the jurisdictions chose to track gang members through the use of an enhanced or expanded database. In this way, they sought to better understand the size and nature of membership and use that information for developing additional strategies and tactics of suppression. Nine of the jurisdictions specifically included schools as partners in their COPS-funded AGI. Often, this meant enhancing G.R.E.A.T. or PAL (Police Athletic League) activities, but in some cases new partnerships were developed. Finally, eight of the jurisdictions mounted a community organization strategy, seeking to engage citizens and neighborhoods in crime prevention and control. Typically, this meant that presentations and meetings were held.

Policing Gangs beyond Suppression

In most cities, no law enforcement agency relies on suppression strategies alone in responding to gang crime problems. This brings us to one of the most important police responses to gangs, a hybrid approach that combines prevention, intervention, and suppression (see Chapter 14)—the Boston Gun Project, otherwise known (at the time) as Operation Ceasefire (Braga et al. 2001). Operation Ceasefire was a data-driven effort that involved local police, federal law enforcement, state and federal prosecutors, and probation and parole officers (Kennedy, Piehl, and Braga 1996). In addition, the Boston Ceasefire project had a strong community component, with high levels of participation by activist Black clergy and community organizers. Police–Black clergy partnerships helped improve police legitimacy in minority communities and enhanced informal social control elements of the program (Brunson et al. 2015). At each phase of this project, data were used to determine the nature of homicide cases, firearms, victims, offenders, and the legal status of individuals involved in violence (Sierra-Arévalo and Papachristos 2017). As a consequence of the analysis of police data, several strategies were devised.

The first was an emphasis on law enforcement, or as it came to be known, "pulling levers" (Braga 2008, 2014; Kennedy 1997; McGarrell et al. 2006). This involved using notification meetings between law enforcement, prosecution, community groups, and gang members to explain the possible legal consequences of continued involvement in crime and to find any and all legal mechanisms that could produce deterrence. The conviction of a well-known Boston gang member on a federal firearms charge for having a bullet in his pocket was particularly important to the success of this project. At notification meetings, the picture and background of this individual were presented, and prosecutors and police officers described the manner in which such enforcement efforts could be used against other gang members. At these meetings, ministers and social service groups were available to present viable alternatives to a life of crime to individuals interested in them (Kennedy 2012).

Another key component of the Boston Ceasefire strategy was the use of Operation Nightlight. This program combined the efforts of police and probation officers. The examination of data on violent incidents in Boston demonstrated that a large number of perpetrators and victims were on probation. Police officers and probation officers teamed together to visit the homes of juveniles deemed to be at the greatest risk. The goal of these visits was to ensure that juveniles were obeying the orders of their probation with regard to curfew, as well as to send an additional message that they were being watched. The results of the Boston Ceasefire project were very promising. Juvenile homicides, the target of the intervention, declined dramatically, and there was strong evidence that the interventions were responsible for the declines (McDevitt 2006).

What began life as Operation Ceasefire in Boston is now codified by the National Network for Safe Communities (https://nnscommunities.org/strate gies/group-violence-intervention/) and is called Group Violence Intervention (GVI). GVI has been implemented in multiple high-crime cites, including Oakland, Chicago, Detroit, and New Orleans (Braga and Weisburd 2012). Results have shown that focused deterrence strategies not only work in reducing gang violence but can even generate a "spillover" deterrent effect on any rival gangs tied to those directly targeted by the intervention (Braga, Apel, and Welsh 2013).

One of the most notable replications of GVI was in Indianapolis, where youth violence increased dramatically in the 1990s (Lauger 2012). Indianapolis employed similar strategies to those used in Boston. Specifically, research was used to determine the categories of individuals most likely to be at risk for involvement in homicide as victims or offenders. The Indianapolis Violence Reduction Partnership, or VIPER, was initiated (McGarrell and Chermak 2003). Similar to the Ceasefire project in Boston, this project depended on solid data analysis, a key use of police resources, and a focus on gangs. Interviews with individuals held after arrest indicated low levels of awareness of the specific program but generally high levels of awareness of greater federal penalties for firearms use. This strategy parallels the Hollenbeck Problem Solving Project initiated by the Los Angeles Police Department against gangs in one of that city's most notorious gang neighborhoods.

Another replication of the Boston Ceasefire program occurred in Cincinnati. Led by the policing scholar Robin Engel, a collaborative team formed the Cincinnati Initiative to Reduce Violence (CIRV) in 2007 (Engel, Tillyer, and Corsaro 2013). The explicit goal was to reduce gang violence. Team members included researchers, law enforcement, and social service providers. A unique feature of this intervention was its emphasis on sustainability, as successful interventions are all too often short-lived. This was accomplished through a unique partnership with a large corporation that lent their expertise to form an organizational team and structure that could be sustainable beyond the short term. Using the focused deterrence strategy made popular by Boston Ceasefire, CIRV worked to identify the criminal behavior of a small number of high-rate offenders and provide them with direct messages about the immediate consequences of their actions. The two targeted crime types—gang-member-involved homicides and violent crimes with firearms—declined significantly. Perhaps even more importantly, these declines were observed over periods of twenty-four and forty-two months, indicating that these crimes could be deterred for a long period. The enforcement component of CIRV was more effective than the social service component. This is a very important intervention for responding to gang crime because of its specific focus on gang homicide and firearms as well as its sustainability (Tillyer, Engel, and Lovins 2012). We return to this in Chapter 14.

Finally, Project Safe Neighborhoods (PSN), a federal program operated through the U.S. Department of Justice and administered by local U.S. district attorneys' offices, likewise features interagency law enforcement partnerships (i.e., task forces), data-driven processes, deterrence messaging, and focused enforcement and accountability (McGarrell et al. 2018; Papachristos, Meares, and Fagan 2007). One notable aspect of PSN programs is enhanced federal, state, and local prosecution for violent gang offenders. An analysis of PSN across eighty-two cities from 2001 to 2006 revealed an associated 13 percent reduction in violent crimes and a 10 percent reduction in firearm homicides, but only for sites that included all aspects of the program, thus making the precise mechanism for change unclear (McGarrell et al. 2010). Concerns about sustainability also exist. Grunwald and Papachristos (2017) found that the significant effects of PSN in Chicago were evident only during the first few years of the program. We return to these issues when we examine what works in gang intervention in Chapter 14.

Police Gang Units

One trend in the response to gangs by the police has been the formation of specialized gang units (Braga 2015; C. Katz and Webb 2006; Weisel and Shelley 2004). There are about sixteen thousand nonfederal police departments in the United States, and about half of them have fewer than ten officers; but specialized police gang units have been part of large departments with one hundred or more sworn officers (such as the Chicago Police Department) since the late 1960s (Shabazz 2015). According to data collected by the Bureau of Justice Statistics (Langton 2010), 365 of the nation's large police departments and sheriff's offices had specialized gang units in 2007, employing a median of five officers per unit and more than forty-three hundred full-time equivalent officers nationwide. About a third of these units were first established between 2004 and 2007. A full breakdown of the characteristics of gang units can be found in Table 11.1.

TABLE 11.1 CHARACTERISTICS OF GANG UNITS IN NONFEDERAL LAW ENFORCEMENT AGENCIES (N = 365)					
	Valid N	Mean (SD)	Percentage	Min.	Max.
Number of gang unit officers					
Full-time sworn	361	11.40 (29.34)	—	0	346
Part-time sworn	63	6.46 (12.94)	—	1	99
Full-time unsworn	363	0.71 (2.66)	—	0	35
Decade gang unit formed					
1970s	337	—	2.1%	—	—
1980s	337	—	10.7%	—	—
1990s	337	—	38.9%	—	—
2000–2007	337	—	48.4%	—	—
Training of officers					
Specialized	363	—	84.6%	—	—
On-the-job	365	—	96.2%	—	—
Conferences	363	—	95.3%	—	—

(Continued)

TABLE 11.1 CHARACTERISTICS OF GANG UNITS IN NONFEDERAL LAW ENFORCEMENT AGENCIES (*N* = 365) (*Continued*)					
	Valid *N*	Mean (SD)	Percentage	Min.	Max.
Groups addressed by unit					
Street gangs	363	—	98.3%	—	—
Outlaw motorcycle groups	365	—	56.7%	—	—
Prison gangs	365	—	43.2%	—	—
Extremists	365	—	42.5%	—	—
Terrorists	365	—	14.0%	—	—
Organized crime	365	—	14.5%	—	—
Time spent on activities (1 = most, 5 = least)					
Intelligence	362	2.24 (1.17)	—	1	5
Investigation	363	2.38 (1.30)	—	1	5
Support	362	2.68 (1.29)	—	1	5
Suppression	362	3.21 (1.19)	—	1	5
Prevention	362	4.33 (1.08)	—	1	5
Operational activities					
General calls for service	363	—	40.5%	—	—
Foot patrol	363	—	47.9%	—	—
Bicycle patrol	365	—	17.2%	—	—
Directed patrol	365	—	91.0%	—	—
Routine patrol	365	—	75.6%	—	—
Gang infiltration	365	—	23.0%	—	—
Undercover surveillance	365	—	78.1%	—	—
Assistance in civil gang injunctions	363	—	17.9%	—	—
Cross-agency assignments					
Housing authority	363	—	9.1%	—	—
Probation	365	—	48.2%	—	—
Parole	365	—	42.7%	—	—
Prosecutors	365	—	45.2%	—	—
Detention facilities	365	—	36.4%	—	—
Local/regional task force	363	—	62.5%	—	—
Federal task force	365	—	51.5%	—	—

TABLE 11.1 CHARACTERISTICS OF GANG UNITS IN NONFEDERAL LAW ENFORCEMENT AGENCIES (N = 365) (Continued)					
	Valid N	Mean (SD)	Percentage	Min.	Max.
Gang prevention activities					
Primary (non-gang youth)	352	—	56.3%	—	—
Secondary (gang youth)	351	—	48.1%	—	—
G.R.E.A.T.	351	—	32.8%	—	—
Providing literature	351	—	74.1%	—	—
Faith-based organizations	351	—	49.0%	—	—
Gang intelligence data					
Monitoring gang graffiti	363	—	93.7%	—	—
Monitoring internet sites	363	—	92.8%	—	—
Tracking gang members	363	—	92.8%	—	—
Paper tracking	335	—	46.0%	—	—
Computerized tracking	336	—	91.1%	—	—
Auditing for database removal					
Deceased members	336	—	73.2%	—	—
Incarcerated members	336	—	42.6%	—	—
Inactive members	336	—	73.5%	—	—
Sharing gang intelligence with					
Agency command staff	363	—	98.3%	—	—
Other units in agency	365	—	99.5%	—	—
Neighboring agencies	365	—	97.5%	—	—
Other criminal justice agencies	365	—	69.6%	—	—

Note: These data were collected as part of a Bureau of Justice Statistics survey of gang units in nonfederal law enforcement agencies with over one hundred full-time sworn officers (Langton 2010). Seven state-level gang units were removed from the analysis.

McCorkle and Miethe (1998) argued that police gang units were formed owing to a moral panic in a community over gangs, not as the result of a reasoned assessment of the problem. M. Klein (1998) also complained that the creation of specialized units gives greater recognition and identity to gang members, thus making gang problems worse. He argued that all too often, law enforcement settled for "small wins" such as the arrest of a gang member rather than implementing strategies that would disrupt gang activities, solve problems, or lead to long-term solutions. Attempts to disrupt gangs by targeting and arresting gang leaders, moreover, can have the adverse effect of increasing gang crime and violence. Vargas's (2014) research suggested that removing the head of more organized gangs was largely irrelevant because they have groomed successors ready and able to assume leadership positions. Cutting the head off of less organized gangs, by contrast, created a power vacuum that permitted elevated levels of violence among gangs vying for control and supremacy (Vargas 2014).

However, the rise of police gang units parallels another important development in American law enforcement—the shift toward proactive, community policing. Community policing can mean many things, but we understand it as referring to the federal effort to respond to crime in a way that integrates law enforcement into community problem solving. Nationwide surveys showed that police develop gang units in response to the nature of the problem, as suggested by Decker (2007). The fact that the earliest gang units were formed in the 1970s and 1980s in the West and Midwest before spreading to the South and Northeast in the 1990s and 2000s (Braga 2015) lends support to the idea that the units follow the gang problem, not the other way around (Langton 2010). Police gang units spend the bulk of their time gathering intelligence by monitoring gang graffiti, tracking individual gang members, monitoring the internet for gang communications, and conducting both direct patrols and undercover investigations (Langton 2010).

The best study of police gang units comes from Charles Katz and his colleagues (C. Katz 2001; C. Katz, Maguire, and Roncek 2002), who spent nearly a year studying the creation of a police gang unit in a midwestern city. They concluded that the community and political environment shaped this response. There was "no evidence suggesting that police had created the gang units to control marginalized populations who they perceived as threatening"; instead, "minority communities played a major role in shaping the nature of the police organization's response to gangs" (C. Katz and Webb 2004, ix). However, Katz's research pointed to the role of officer culture in shaping the response to gangs in a community, raising questions about the ability of specialized police units to develop knowledge and technical efficiency to address a gang problem (C. Katz and Webb 2004). There was an absence of control and accountability over the gang unit, and gang officers were afforded too much autonomy. Moreover, they rarely practiced community policing but rather used policing tactics that other research has found to be predicated on racial profiling, such as "stop, question, and frisk" (M. White and Fradella 2016).

A recent ride-along study (Rios, Prieto, and Ibarra 2020) found that officers' general adherence to traditional, punitive policing practices such as stop-and-frisk was undermining courtesy policing efforts designed to improve community trust and legitimacy. The paradox of policing Latino gangs, the authors found, was treating suspects with respect (*mano suave*) while continuing to reinforce the racial bias at the heart of stop-and-frisk (*mano dura*). These findings echo those of Durán (2018, 163), who found that "gang units legitimated the social control of people beyond involvement in crime to include perceived criminality." Durán claimed that gang units fabricated intelligence and initiated frequent, unwelcome, and even violent contact with Mexican American gang youth, thus contributing to the "legitimated oppression" of already marginalized communities (Durán 2009).

The story of the Minnesota Gang Strike Force is illustrative in this regard (Bumgarner, Hilal, and Densley 2016). This statewide task force of gang officers was created in 1997, restructured and renamed the Metro Gang Strike Force in 2005 (to reflect its focus on gangs in the Twin Cities metro area), and then disbanded in 2009 owing to a litany of abuses. A state investigation concluded that much of the task force's police work was ineffective and the unit was guilty of widespread impropriety, excessive force, and illegal searches and seizures. A legislative audit found that the unit was unable to account for 202 of its 545 cash seizures, totaling $165,650. Thirteen out of eighty confiscated vehicles were also missing, and one unit commander had illegally sold a seized television to a student employee in his office. They were eventually ordered to pay $3 million to victims of misconduct, including $6,000 to a two-year-old who was kicked in the head by police during an illegal search and $35,500 to two immigrants who were afraid to report their experience of excessive force owing to threats of deportation (Bumgarner, Hilal, and Densley 2016).

The way that the police structure themselves in responding to gangs remains an open question. We don't know whether highly focused units that concentrate on gang issues are the best way to proceed or whether generalized law enforcement is more effective, in part because both have problems. However, a recent study found that the temporary disbandment of the Los Angeles Police Department's gang unit negatively impacted the collection of intelligence on gang members by officers and curtailed gang suppression efforts, including gang member arrests (Valasik, Reid, and Phillips 2016). And there are cascading consequences of cuts to gang units. For example, the National Alliance of Gang Investigators Associations (http://www.nagia.org/), formed in 1998, represents twenty-three state and regional gang investigator associations with over twenty thousand members. Their mission is to provide professional development to law enforcement personnel based on practitioner experience and expertise in policing gangs, which obviously cannot be done in the absence of a specific law enforcement emphasis on gangs, gang members, and gang crime.

Braga (2015, 309) observed, if "properly oriented," police gang units "have great potential to reduce gang violence problems." Of course, "properly oriented" is the important point here. As presented in Table 11.1, not all gang units are created equal. Some units take regular calls for service. Others gather intelligence and enforce the law against gang members. Others still just gather intelligence. While the LAPD's Community Resources against Street Hoodlums (CRASH) program was synonymous with executing no-knock warrants and forcefully taking people into custody (M. Klein 1998), today the department's

Gang Impact Team is far more focused on intelligence gathering and "predictive policing" (Brayne 2020)—that is, using machine learning to mine the LAPD's criminal data and gang territory maps to automate the classification of gang-related crimes and, in theory, prevent crime before it ever occurs.

Of course, an algorithm is only as good as its trainer, and deep learning is only as good as its data, so there are concerns that the errors and biases in police gang data will be baked into the computer models and reinforced (Meijer and Wessels 2019). Critics say that predictive policing algorithms risk reinforcing existing racial biases in the system because they are overreliant on information such as arrest records from overpoliced communities (Noble 2018). At the same time, the expansion of the internet has presented new challenges for law enforcement, and because the world is increasingly global, law enforcement needs to respond appropriately. Civil liberties groups and internet scholars worry that Facebook and YouTube are becoming a mode of surveillance for police, to the extent that "hanging out" on social media can create guilt by association (Lane, Ramirez, and Pearce 2018; Patton, Brunton, et al. 2017). For example, sharing a rap video or other perceived gang content online is now a potential criterion for inclusion in a police gang database (Ilan 2020), our next topic of conversation.

Police Gang Databases

In an attempt to respond to gangs, many law enforcement agencies maintain gang databases (Huff and Barrows 2015). As J. Jacobs (2009, 705) noted, "long before computers were so widespread, individual police offices and the gang intelligence units of big city police departments maintained intelligence files on gangs and gang members." C. Johnson et al. (1995) provided an early overview of the practice of building and using gang databases. Their survey of nearly 150 police departments and over 190 prosecutors found that 70 percent of police departments and 20 percent of prosecutors used an automated database to track gang membership. Into the 2000s, computerized gang databases were commonplace (Barrows and Huff 2009). Nearly every gang unit (93 percent) included in the Bureau of Justice Statistics 2007 survey of 365 policing agencies tracked gang members, using mostly computerized systems (91 percent) but also paper systems (46 percent) (Langton 2010, 5). Twelve U.S. states have even passed laws pertaining to the development and use of gang databases, including how data should be gathered, stored, and shared (see Chapter 13).

As discussed in Chapter 12, many jails and prisons also maintain some sort of database to track the membership of prisoners. The databases maintained in correctional facilities are used primarily to maintain officer safety and prevent housing rival gang members in the same cells or cellblocks. The information found in police gang databases is similar, focused on the characteristics of individuals and groups. For example, the St. Louis city and county gang database includes individual details such as a person's name, contact information (e.g., residence and phone number), physical and demographic information (e.g., age, gender, race, height, and weight), identifying marks (e.g., tattoos), socio-economic information (e.g., employer and marital status), criminal history, gang affiliation, date entered into the database, and information used to validate individuals as gang members. Group details include the evolution of gang symbols, the location of gang turf, and a gang's alliances and rivalries.

Law enforcement argue that these data increase officer safety and help solve gang-related crimes, which is especially important because the burden of unsolved crimes falls disproportionately on the most dangerous and vulnerable communities (Ryley, Singer-Vine, and Campbell 2019; Ryley 2019). The Boston Ceasefire project described earlier, for example, used police data to identify patterns, places, and motivations for gang violence (Braga, Papachristos, and Hureau 2014). Still, because all policing is local and most gang databases are kept by individual police departments, there is considerable variation in what information is stored, the definitions applied to that information, who can access the information, and how the information from the gang database can be used.

There are four main arguments against gang databases, which can be summarized in the broad categories of validity and civil liberties concerns (see Densley and Pyrooz 2020). The first is that gang membership is not measured accurately. Support for this claim is bolstered not only by the lack of a universal definition of a gang (see Chapter 1) but also by subjective and overbroad interpretations of gangs and gang membership. Critical and cultural criminologists argue that police have a vested interest in exaggerating the nature and scale of youth gangs (Fraser, Armstrong, and Hobbs 2021; Hallsworth and Young 2008). Densley (2013; Van Hellemont and Densley 2019) even observed how, in a post-9/11 context, London police overemphasized the threat of the Muslim Boys gang in order to tap into the counterterrorism budget and bring state resources to eliminate them.

Who gets counted as a gang member, and whether those counts include people only marginally embedded in gangs, can vary widely across countries, states, cities, and even neighborhoods. For example, a 2016 audit of California's gang database, CalGang, revealed that babies and ex-gang members were listed, prompting legislation to overhaul the system (California State Auditor 2016). There are concerns that too many individuals are included in gang databases and that police net-widening entraps innocent people (S. Cohen 1979), but also that too few individuals become identified as gang members.

Errors in accurately counting the number of gang members can harm public safety and make law enforcement less efficient in performing their job. Only around 70 percent of police gang units audit their gang databases for deceased, incarcerated, or inactive gang members (Langton 2010), but the data suggest that law enforcement likely undercount gang members anyway. Pyrooz and Sweeten (2015) compared reports of juvenile gang members from the National

Gang Center, based on a representative survey of law enforcement agencies, to the self-reports of gang membership from juveniles in a representative survey of youth, finding that the police may underestimate juvenile gang membership by 70 percent. This should not come as a surprise to readers given that police undercount crime in nearly all forms, known as the "dark figure" of crime (Lynch and Addington 2006).

This problem is exacerbated by the criteria used to document gang members. D. Scott (2020) found variations in methods of gang member identification, as reported by law enforcement, across regions in the United States. The West was more likely to identify gang members through associations or arrests with known gang members, gang symbols, or self-nomination, whereas the South, Northeast, and Midwest regions were more likely to identify gang members through a reliable informant. However, Scott's regional focus was odd because legislation governing gang identification criteria is the purview of individual states rather than regions (see Chapter 13). In Minnesota, for example, someone has to commit a gross misdemeanor or felony to even be entered into a gang database, and if within a three-year period they have not been arrested or convicted of another crime, they must be removed (Bumgarner, Hilal, and Densley 2016). While this makes intuitive sense, it is important to remember that not all gang members are criminals and not all criminals are gang members.

In California (California State Auditor 2016, 15), someone who meets two of the following criteria can be designated as a gang member: admitting to gang membership (used in 58 percent of cases), associating with documented gang members (44 percent), having gang tattoos (43 percent), frequenting gang areas (30 percent), wearing gang dress (25 percent), having an in-custody classification interview (24 percent), being arrested for offences consistent with usual gang activity (11 percent), displaying gang symbols or hand signs (7 percent), being identified by a reliable informant or source (6 percent), or being identified by an untested informant (1 percent). In the best examples, therefore, law enforcement may be more conservative in their measures of gang membership than even gang researchers. But California is the exception, not the rule. In the worst examples, law enforcement may rely almost exclusively on highly questionable criteria, such as wearing gang attire, associations, and informants. Paradoxically, critical and cultural criminologists could get behind the fact that more subjective, ethnographic gang descriptors such as clothing are recognized as important, but not if they are de facto criminalized.

In some jurisdictions, points are assigned to the criteria, and an individual must meet a threshold of points to be included in the gang database; in other jurisdictions, individuals must have a certain number of criteria to be defined as gang members. Still, the fact remains that these criteria can vary substantially, and they may be applied subjectively. Only individuals who come to the attention of the police will be subject to such criteria. In many cases, the police may not have full information or be able to verify that their "reliable source" really was reliable. This can result in strange fluctuations in the number of certified gang members year over year. For example, M. Klein (2009) found that estimates of the number of gang members made by the Los Angeles County Sheriff's department varied by as much as 45 percent in a two-year period. However, other studies have found high, albeit imperfect, correspondence between self-reports of gang membership and the names found in gang databases (Curry 2000). Police data on gang homicides also correspond with newspaper coverage on gang violence (Jensen and Thibodeaux 2013) and are reported consistently (C. Katz, Webb, and Schaefer 2000; C. Katz et al. 2012), especially in agencies with specialized police gang units (Decker and Pyrooz 2010b).

The second main argument against gang databases is similarly tied to problems of validity—that is, they are discriminatory because males and people of color are overrepresented in them. As we learned earlier in Chapter 7, women comprise a large share of gang members, yet they rarely show up in gang databases. Novich and Hunt (2017) found that male gang members were stopped twice as often as their female counterparts. And, as we discovered in Chapter 8, if the police perceive that "any black kid is in a gang" (Manasseh 2017), they overcount minorities as gang members too. The following quote from a gang member in London, England, captures this problem succinctly:

> You're automatically stereotyped. It's like all Black people are criminals. [The police] got this policy where, more than three [people in a group], you're considered a gang so you automatically get stopped. . . . After a time, you feel like, "oh we a gang now? Okay, we'll show you gang." (Densley and Stevens 2015, 133)

The perception that "police don't like Black people" (Brunson 2007) is widespread in the United States too. Racial disparities were the primary driver behind the abolition of Portland, Oregon's twenty-year-old gang database, and as we showed in Chapter 8, in New York, less than 1 percent of the 17,441 people in the gang database were White. In Chicago, under 5 percent of the 128,037 people entered in the gang database between 1999 and 2018 were White. Horror stories from Denver, Colorado (D. Johnson 1993), and Los Angeles, California (Stolberg 1992), revealed that nearly two-thirds and one-half of all young Black men in these respective cities were labeled as gang members, helping fuel suspicion that gang databases are not only invalid but a racist instrument of oppression. Critics say these numbers reflect an entrenched (over)policing philosophy that has always criminalized racialized and marginalized populations (Vitale 2017).

As discussed in Chapter 8, the overrepresentation of Black and Latino young men in gang databases is not solely an artifact of how police collect information. Differences in involvement in violent or criminal situations between White and non-White Americans may explain away some—but certainly not all—disparities. Another factor is the racial composition of gangs themselves or reporting on the validity of measuring gang membership. With regard to gang composition, a representative study of young people in the United States revealed that Blacks and Latinos were twice as likely as Whites to self-report as gang members in adolescence and three to four times more likely in adulthood (Pyrooz 2014b). Age is important here because gang databases are overwhelmingly populated with young adults, not juveniles. In other words, as discussed in Chapter 8, some racial and ethnic disparities in gang data should be expected because the disparities are largely reflective of the realities of gangs.

The third main argument against gang databases is that they are often kept secret (Winston 2016); therefore, there is a lack of due process surrounding placement in databases. In some states, gang members are aware of such lists and how they get on them. A thirty-one-year-old former Phoenix gang member told us:

> They got something out here in Phoenix called the "Gang File," and, I mean, you can make "Gang File" just by having on a red shirt and maybe red shoes or a Chicago Bulls jersey. You could be matching or something, and they pull you over and take all kind of pictures of you and put you in the Gang File. And, say, if you do a crime to where you end up in prison, bein' in the Gang File enhances your sentence.

However, people listed in gang databases are rarely made aware of the designation and have little to no recourse to challenge it. The California State Auditor (2016, 36), for example, found that "agencies have failed to ensure that Cal-Gang records are added, removed, and shared in a way that maintains the accuracy of the system and safeguards individuals' rights." In response to this, California's Fair and Accurate Gang Database Act of 2017 now requires law enforcement to notify individuals in writing when they are entered into a gang database. It also affords purported gang members the opportunity to appeal the designation. Still, adding the "right to know" is controversial because disclosing information about persons on a gang list to those persons may compromise an active criminal investigation and the ability of law enforcement to build a case (J. Jacobs 2009). Intelligence is, after all, considered "intelligence" because it is private information.

Questions of due process extend beyond whether someone is in a database to how long they should remain in it. A total of two to five years of placement in gang databases is the standard in some states, but no sunset periods of gang membership to automatically trigger removal are the rule in others. In fact, it is not uncommon for police and, for that matter, the general public (Howell 2007) to hold the view that "once a gangbanger, always a gangbanger," even if, as discussed in Chapter 5, people disengage from gangs and desist from crime all the time. California's 2017 Fair and Accurate Gang Database Act now requires "retention periods for information about a person in a shared gang database that is consistent with empirical research on the duration of gang membership" (Penal Code 186.36 [L2]), thus ensuring that gang lists better reflect the temporary status of gang membership and the fact that even the "Worst of the Worst" are not beyond redemption (McDevitt 2006).

To this point, the fourth main argument against gang databases is that the (collateral) consequences of being named in one can be serious (J. Jacobs 2009). By having a central registrar of identified gang members, police agencies can more readily determine the gang status of an individual they are questioning or have detained for the purposes of arrest. But this can also escalate a routine stop by police, resulting in unnecessary arrests or use of force. In their analysis of the New York City Police Department's "precision policing" of gangs, Trujillo and Vitale (2019, 13) described a pattern of "harassment and hyper-policing" that influences court proceedings and creates employment issues, housing instability, and even deportation risks for certified gang members.

The stigma and scrutiny of being named in a database can far outlast actual affiliation with a gang (Curry and Decker 1998; Densley and Pyrooz 2020). In an era of data-driven policing (Ferguson 2019), collateral concerns are important, especially because who has access to gang data is not always defined within law. In most cases, officers are uploading license plate numbers, field interview notes, and potential gang affiliations onto a private industry data platform (Brayne 2020). Databases maintained at the state level facilitate information sharing not just across police agencies but also among educational, housing, and immigration authorities. Multiple pieces of legislation place a duty on the police and other public bodies to share information for the purposes of crime reduction, safeguarding, and promoting welfare and well-being. However, as a form of extrajudicial punishment, disproportionately directed at poor people of color, this can be destructive if not properly managed. Databases often are accessed by prosecutors to seek additional sentencing enhancements against gang members, contributing to a "gang penalty" in sentencing (D. Walker and Cesar 2020). In Chapter 13, we examine gang sentencing enhancements in detail; suffice it to say, studies show that gang affiliation can affect pretrial and prosecutorial outcomes (Caudill et al. 2017). One undocumented Chicagoan was entered into a gang database simply for "loitering" in a neighborhood with high gang activity and wound up in deportation proceedings (Felton 2018).

In their examination of London's controversial database of purported gang members, known as the Matrix, Densley and Pyrooz (2020) found that while many of the concerns about gang databases are justified, police gang data can be a force for good if properly managed and maintained. They concluded:

Gang databases must function in a way that upholds the civil rights of those included in them, and without any unlawful discrimination. Police must ensure that the right people are entered into the database in the first place, and that people are added and removed in a standardized way, consistent with empirical research on gangs. Criteria for entry should be consistent and codified, and the databases should be audited regularly so that individuals do not stay in them any longer than necessary and that once removed, the gang label does not follow them indefinitely. People entered into gang databases should also have the right to appeal their designation. Gang databases must also comply with data privacy laws and data protection best practices, ensuring that any sharing of personal information is necessary and proportionate. And the function and operation of gang databases should be as transparent as possible, with appropriate oversight. (Densley and Pyrooz 2020, 15)

These simple steps can improve the efficacy of gang databases as well as build public trust in their use.

Conclusion

This chapter has outlined the myriad ways that law enforcement confronts gangs. While gangs and gang members remain problematic from a law enforcement standpoint, there are a number of ways in which police fail to adequately respond to the challenges that gangs create (Van Hellemont and Densley 2021). The key challenges for the police include the ability to collect and share information, to cooperate and coordinate activities across different agencies and with communities, and to police in a way that is fair and impartial, focused squarely on delivering justice. Until these things happen, it is difficult to see how much progress can be made in dealing with gangs.

As the wider debate about police abolition rages (Vitale 2017), a recent report by the John Jay College Research Advisory Group on Preventing and Reducing Community Violence (2020) identified several evidence-backed strategies for improving public safety without depending on law enforcement. These include place-based interventions that help design out crime; outreach programs like Cure Violence (see Chapter 14) that rely on people respected in the community (e.g., former gang members and local pastors) to intervene among people who are at risk for violent behavior, strengthening antiviolence social norms and peer relationships; engagement and support for the people most responsible for community violence; and comprehensive and uniform policies that limit access to the tools of violence (namely, firearms). However, it is clear that these measures alone, or even in conjunction with greater public spending on social services, cannot and will not replace a police response to gangs entirely.

12

Gangs and Gang Members in Prison

On March 13, 2013, Tom Clements, the head of Colorado's Department of Corrections, was shot and killed on his doorstep by a former prisoner and affiliate of the 211 Crew, a notorious prison gang. The gang member had absconded on parole, killed a pizza delivery driver, and knocked on Clements's door wearing the uniform (Prendergast 2014).

In the summer of 2013, nearly thirty thousand prisoners in California undertook a prolonged hunger strike—to the point where the prison system was preparing to force-feed prisoners—to protest the indeterminate placement of gang affiliates in solitary confinement. The hunger strike was orchestrated by affiliates of the Aryan Brotherhood, Black Guerilla Family, Mexican Mafia, and Nuestra Familia (Reiter 2016).

In April 2018, inter-gang conflicts over the control of contraband cellphone markets resulted in the largest prison riot in the last twenty-five years, leaving seven dead in South Carolina's Lee Correctional Institute. Not even two years later, clashes between the Black Gangster Disciples and the Vice Lords in Mississippi prisons wrought four of the five homicides, which the *New York Times* called a "blood bath."

It is common for the general public to believe that once criminals are locked up, they are no longer free to prey on the community and thus do not warrant the attention that street gangs and street violence receive. But as J. Jacobs (2001, vi) noted and as the aforementioned anecdotes illustrate:

It is hard to understand why the prison gang phenomenon does not attract more attention from the media, scholars, and policy analysts. One would think it would be big news that powerful race and ethnically based gangs are an entrenched feature of many American (and foreign) prisons and that this phenomenon has only gotten bigger. . . . Criminal schemes are hatched in prison and carried out on the street and vice versa. Within the prison, gang members are never out of the sight of their peers and leaders. Thus, the gang becomes a larger force in a low-level member's life. The chance that, upon release from prison, the gang inmate will make a clean break with his gang banging is sharply diminished.

The previous chapters illustrated that there are gaps in our knowledge about many aspects of gangs. This is even more true of the state of knowledge regarding prison gangs and gang members. There are several reasons for this, including difficulty accessing prisons, a lack of consistent institutional data, the reluctance of prisoners generally and prison gang members specifically to talk with prison officials or researchers, and the difficulty in doing such work on the part of researchers (not the least of which is finding funding for such ventures).

But, as the saying goes, absence of evidence is not evidence of absence. As this chapter shows, knowledge about prison gangs is rather haphazard. This chapter explores a range of issues related to prison gangs, piecing together the leading theory and evidence on the following:

- Defining and measuring gangs and gang membership in prison
- Documenting the emergence and proliferation of prison gangs
- Outlining the leading theories on gang emergence in prison
- Reviewing the evidence on the association between gang membership, misconduct, and victimization
- Describing the patterning of gang membership in relation to imprisonment, including joining, avoiding, and leaving gangs
- Detailing the leading responses to gangs in prison, as well as reviewing the leading research on reentry and recidivism

There has been a small resurgence of interest in prison gangs in recent years, partly in the United States (e.g., Bolden 2020; Gundur 2020; Ortiz 2019; Pyrooz, Gartner, and Smith 2017; Roth 2020; Skarbek 2014; Tapia 2019; Weide 2020) but also in Europe (e.g., Maitra 2020; Phillips 2012; Kaminski 2004; Wood et al. 2014) and Latin America (e.g., Butler, Slade, and Dias 2018; Cruz 2016; Lessing 2016). We draw heavily on our recent work on these topics based on the LoneStar Project, a study involving 802 prisoners in Texas, half of whom were gang affiliated, first interviewed in prison and then reinterviewed one and ten months after their release (Pyrooz and Decker 2019).

Defining and Measuring Gangs and Gang Membership in Prison

Definitions matter in understanding and responding to problems. One of the key arguments we make in this book is the need for valid and reliable measurement of concepts. This is the foundation from which data collection and ultimately prevention and intervention efforts must be launched (see Chapter 14). While criminology is replete with examples of bad measurement and exaggerated imagery ("super-predators," "young and the ruthless," and "immigrant threat") perhaps no topic generates as much distortion as gangs. Unfortunately, the definitions around prison gangs and gang members are not as well developed as we may like, especially when compared to definitions of street gangs and gang members. We offer three definitions to highlight the controversy over prison gangs.

The first is Lyman's (1989) definition, which has been used widely owing to its breadth and wide applicability. Based on his observations of groups in prison that were organized in the pursuit of criminal ends, Lyman defined a prison gang as:

> an organization which operates within the prison system as a self-perpetuating criminally oriented entity, consisting of a select group of inmates who have established an organized chain of command and are governed by an established code of conduct. (48)

This definition has several key features that differentiate it from the more general definitions of a gang offered in Chapter 1. Notably, the self-perpetuating nature of the group and its governance characteristics (chain of command, code of conduct, and governance) identify prison gangs as something more serious than street gangs. Similarly, Skarbek (2014, 8–9) argued:

> A prison gang is an inmate organization that operates within a prison system, that has a corporate entity, exists into perpetuity, and whose membership is restrictive, mutually exclusive, and often requires a lifetime commitment.

As readers can easily see, this definition emphasizes the power Skarbek ascribes to the structure of the prison gang, especially perpetuity. These rigid definitions sharply depart from the definitions of street gangs covered in Chapter 1.

Many prison systems have opted for a more generic definition, one that emphasizes the perceived dangerousness of the gang and lumps traditional street gangs, groups that deal largely in protection and criminal goods inside prison, gangs that are based on ideological factors such as race militancy or supremacy, and protection groups organized around race or ethnicity under one banner: "security threat group" (STG). For example, the Texas Department of Criminal Justice (TDCJ 2007) defines an STG as follows:

> Any group of offenders TDCJ reasonably believes poses a threat to the physical safety of other offenders and staff due to the very nature of said Security Threat Group.

This is a definition notable for its brevity but also for the tautology of its "threat" assessment (i.e., an STG is threatening because it is an STG, and it is an STG because it is threatening). Still, beyond Texas, in the Federal Bureau of Prisons, gangs are referred to as STGs, allowing the classification of a broader array of groups than the term *gang* would typically allow. This has proved particularly important in efforts to control groups who organize along racial lines and engage in racially motivated violence.

The STG approach to defining groups as gangs is particularly important for institutional purposes of identification and control of inmates. It extends the view of prison gangs beyond those only found on the street and includes race- and ideology-based groups—and, in theory, it allows for assignments to work and cells that would isolate rivals and not strengthen existing groups. As such, it may be more useful as a tool of prison management, for classification and assignment purposes in prison to keep gang rivals apart, than as an objective assessment of groups. Corrections officials in Texas, for example, have identified seven of the twelve STGs as posing a threat grave enough to warrant indeterminate placement in administrative segregation (Pyrooz and Decker 2019).

This brings us to a third approach, which is to define and measure gang membership in prison. Just as we observe in Chapters 1 and 13, agencies lack definitions of gang membership, instead opting to focus on indicators to validate prisoners as gang affiliated, known as affiliation identifiers or source items. C. Hill (2009) compiled a list of these items based on survey responses received from forty-three of the fifty state prison systems. We organized these responses into five domains:

1. Personal possessions: gang-related clothing, shoes, or other property
2. Physical embodiments: gang-related tattoos or branding
3. Self-admission: self-identification as a gang affiliate

4. Associations: photos, communication, or graffiti indicating affiliation
5. Observations: court records, informants, or staff reports of affiliation

Typically, prison systems will employ a summative "ballot box" approach, where confirmed gang members meet three or more of the criteria, whereas suspected gang members meet fewer than three but more than zero. But the question is, how reliable and valid is this approach in prison? There have been few if any tests of the measurement properties of self-nomination in prison.

Pyrooz, Decker, and Owens (2020) examined the concordance between the prison system's identification of an individual as a member of an STG and their self-reports of gang membership during interviews conducted in 2016. Eighty-two percent of individuals recognized as gang members by the prison system self-reported that they were gang members to the interviewers—a high degree of correspondence, slightly higher than Maxson and colleagues (2012) observed (71 percent) among juveniles incarcerated in California. In addition, of those whom the prison system identified as gang members, 86 percent gave the name of a "concordant" gang—that is, a gang of the same name. This means that not only did gang members self-report whether they were gang members per se, they also provided specific information about the gang they were a member of. Recall our discussion of self-nomination as a means of identifying gang members in Chapter 1. The parallel between that finding (on the street or in a school setting, for example) and the current one (in prison) provides credibility to the conclusion that under the right research circumstances, gang members are truthful in their answers.

The Contested Emergence and Proliferation of Gangs in Prison

As one correctional official contended, "I'm convinced that if you put three people on an island somewhere, two would clique up and become predatory against the other at some point" (Trulson, Marquart, and Kawucha 2006, 26). Given the controversies over gang definitions, it is fitting that there is debate over the origins of prison gangs. It should be clear from our work in Chapters 1, 2, and 8 that gangs have been around for quite some time, at least since the early part of the twentieth century. The impact of Prohibition on the formation of organized crime groups must have resulted in the incarceration of "gangsters" from these groups. The disproportionate involvement of gang members in crime (Chapter 6) makes it likely that they would eventually be identified and processed by the criminal justice system and end up in prison. It also makes sense that once in prison, street gang members would seek out both allies and foes. We know that some of the characteristics of life in prison, such as the inmate social system and the convict code (Sykes and Messinger 1960)—which provide a set of rules to guide conduct while in prison—are consistent with the formation and existence of prison gangs (Mitchell et al. 2017). The formation of gangs in the presence of such group norms and structures is not at all surprising, but the origins of prison gangs remains contested, historically and theoretically.

Lewis Laws, who served as long-term warden of Sing Sing prison in New York state, identified over 130 gangs in his prison in a 1931 article in the *New York Times*. Warden Laws did not identify any of these gangs by name or describe their activities or structure. There were very few studies of prisons or gangs in the 1930s or 1940s, save Clemmer's (1940) groundbreaking work. Despite this lack of attention to prison gangs during these two decades, someone found prison gangs a suitable topic for attention: Hollywood. During the 1930s, at least fifty-five movies were produced in the United States depicting prison gangs, and roughly half that number were made during the 1940s (https://www.prisonmovies.net/movies-by-era). The models for the gangs and gangsters depicted in these films (many of which are now enjoying a resurgence with the popularity of film noir) must have come from somewhere other than just the imagination of a screenwriter or director.

It has conventionally been argued, though without concrete evidence, that the first documented American prison gang was the Gypsy Jokers (Stastny and Tyrnauer 1982). This prison gang was formed in the 1950s in Walla Walla prison in Washington state. The lasting vitality of this claim is likely due to the stature of Camp and Camp (1985) in correctional circles and the retelling of their version of events by such sources as Orlando-Morningstar (1997) and two of the authors of this book, among others. Smith (2016) has cast doubt on this history of prison gangs, arguing that the Gypsy Jokers were in fact a motorcycle gang with roots in the community, not in prison. Roth (2020) argued in his book on the history of prison gangs, *Power on the Inside*, that there was little evidence to support the claim of the Gypsy Jokers being the first prison gang. This underscores the continued importance of original research in prisons.

Gangs are active in nearly every prison system. Pyrooz and Decker (2019) reviewed published documents and survey reports to determine the proliferation of prison gangs. They located information on gang emergence in forty-six of the fifty state prison systems, with the exceptions being Alaska, Kansas, Louisiana, and Maine. The 1980s were not only the buildup to mass incarceration in the United States (Alexander 2010; Pfaff 2017) but also the period that witnessed the widespread emergence of prison gangs. By the end of the 1980s, there were thirty-one prison systems with gang activity, up from sixteen at the conclusion of the 1970s. Another round of prison gang emergence occurred in the 1990s. These patterns closely mirrored the proliferation of gangs in street settings covered in Chapter 1.

Just as it is difficult to measure the number of street gangs and street gang members, it is also difficult to obtain reliable data on the number of prison gangs and gang members. Based on a survey of prison officials, Camp and Camp (1985) determined that there were 114 prison gangs in the United States with a membership of approximately thirteen thousand inmates. Pennsylvania and Illinois reported the most gangs in their prison systems with fifteen and fourteen, respectively. It was further estimated that about one-third of inmates in California belonged to a prison gang (Camp and Camp 1985). The reader will note that the Camp and Camp work is thirty-five years old, hardly a contemporary estimate.

Since Camp and Camp (1985), there have been multiple estimates of the number and proportion of prison gang affiliates. These attempts are represented in Figure 12.1. All of these findings are based on official reports from the prison system; there has never been a national estimate of the prevalence of gang affiliation in prison based on surveys of prisoners. But as we noted

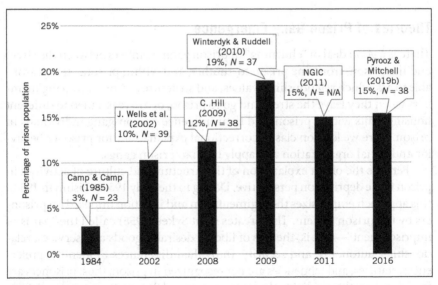

Figure 12.1 Estimates of the proportion of prisoners affiliated with gangs in U.S. prisons

Note: Individual prison system data were analyzed to produce national estimates of the prevalence of gang membership in U.S. prisons for Camp and Camp (1985), J. Wells et al. (2002), C. Hill (2009), and Pyrooz and Mitchell (2019b). The remaining studies only reported state-level average prevalence (Winterdyk and Ruddell 2010) or national count (National Gang Intelligence Center 2011) of gang membership. N/A, not applicable.

above, official reports are a close—but not perfect—proxy for survey reports. A lot of time passed between the first results from 1984 (Camp and Camp 1985) and the second results from 2002 (J. Wells et al. 2002), but the rise in prevalence from 3 percent to 10 percent is notable. The remaining estimates all peg the proportion of prisoners affiliated with gangs above 10 percent (C. Hill 2009; National Gang Intelligence Center 2011; Pyrooz and Mitchell 2019b; J. Wells et al. 2002; Winterdyk and Ruddell 2010), with Winterdyk and Ruddell's 2009 estimate of 19 percent being the highest and Pyrooz and Mitchell's 2016 estimate of 15 percent being the most recent. It is reasonable to conclude that around 1 out of every 7 of the 1.5 million people incarcerated in federal and state prisons are affiliated with a gang. That figure is around seventy-five times greater than the estimate of the number of gang members in noninstitutional settings (Egley, Howell, and Harris 2014; Pyrooz, Gartner, and Smith 2017). Of course, there are more gang members in street than prison settings, but gang members on the street are dispersed across the United States, while in prison they are highly concentrated in the facilities of institutions. This raises the question: Does gang membership originate in prison, or is it imported from the street?

Theories of Prison Gang Emergence

There is a good deal of "churning" of prison gang members between the street and the prison, from one prison to another, and within prisons. It is reasonable to ask which relationships, values, and structures accompany gang members when they leave the street and go to prison, or are reassigned to different housing units within prison, and their influence on non-gang individuals in prison. Here we lean on classic correctional explanations for prisoner behavior and social organization and apply them to prison gangs.

Perhaps the oldest explanation of the structure and culture of activities in prison is the deprivation perspective. Dating to the early 1930s (Fishman 1934), this approach emphasizes the regimentation and isolation imposed on prisoners by the prison system. This creates what Sykes (1958) called the "pains of imprisonment"—that is, the loss of liberty, desirable goods and services, relationships, autonomy, and security. Individual differences in identity, preferences, statuses, and tendencies are not recognized in prison; thus, prisoners are forced to deny their individual or group wants and desires. Prison order dictates what individuals can do, with whom, and when. As inmates become acquainted with the prison routine, they experience "prisonization" and succumb to the social order imposed by the prison. One response to this state of deprivation is the convict code (Sykes and Messinger 1960), a set of rules created by prisoners and accepted as a way to "do your time." This is akin to a tabula rasa, or blank slate, argument. The influence of prisonization is so great that it overcomes any individual differences. Prisons constitute islands unto themselves, and the free-world antipathies on the street are reorganized with admission into prison. Deprivation may play a role in the emergence of prison gangs, as inmates form a collective to gain the esteem of belonging to a group and in so doing gain allies in the search for illicit goods and services in the prison, such as contraband and protection.

A second approach to understanding the emergence of codes and structures in prison is importation. Importation focuses attention on the values, groups, and allegiances that are brought with prisoners from the street or neighborhood into the institution. This may include fealty to the gang that a prisoner belonged to on the street. In some cases, street gang members make a smooth transition to the institution as their gang has a presence within it (Joan Moore 1978). It is not unheard of for one's status in the gang (leader, shot-caller, etc.) to transfer into the prison. Race or ethnicity can also be a master status that transcends other allegiances or relationships. Through our years of interviews, many prison gang members have told us that above all else, race and ethnicity trump other allegiances. But such importation can work the other way, as individuals with a reputation as a "punk" or weak on the street are likely to be preyed on once in the institution.

The churning of inmates through prisons helps facilitate importation. As gang members are arrested and sentenced to prison, they bring their social capital to the prison gang, not just in numbers but also in their experiences. Sentencing a gang member to a prison where other members of their gang are serving time eases the transition for them, providing a ready-made support group. What such a process does not do is make prison management or the lives of rival gang members any easier. The addition of fellow street gang members to the ranks of prison gangs expands their networks and, in many cases, enhances their expertise, or criminal capital.

A close corollary of the importation perspective has been developed in recent years and is known as the exportation perspective. Hummer and Ahlin (2018) combined the deprivation and importation perspectives to contend that violence is also exported out of prison. Prisoners bring elements of the institution back to the street, which include their personal and vicarious experiences with violence and acculturation to the violent scripts of the convict code. Indeed, this can be seen in many aspects of popular culture (e.g., *Orange Is the New Black*, prison tattoo styles being available at tattoo parlors, and Death Row Records) as well as relationships on the street. Prison culture and styles are exported not only through the large numbers of individuals incarcerated but also through the numbers released—nearly six hundred thousand people were released from federal and state prisons in 2019.

A third approach to understanding the origins of prison gangs is the governance perspective. We noted earlier in this book (Chapter 3) that economists and political scientists, such as Lessing and Skarbek, have focused on the structure and control exercised by prison gangs. Their work is consistent with Schelling's (1967) distinction between "organized crime" and "crime that is organized," insomuch that it is the characteristics of that organization that they are most interested in. This approach denies the validity of importation and deprivation perspectives on the origins of prison culture, organization, and activities. Coupled with the challenges to prison governance presented by mass incarceration, Skarbek (2014) argued that there was a void in the management of prison life in the 1980s. Rejecting the power of cultural explanations of control (the inmate or gang code), he makes a case that prison gangs provide an important commodity that the authorities cannot or do not provide: governance. By regulating violence and contraband (drugs, alcohol, sex, and illegal goods), gangs exert control over inmate behavior. Disorder is bad for business (like Wall Street, prison gangs prefer certainty to uncertainty); therefore, gangs have a stake in regulating conduct.

Lessing (2016) too dismisses the influence of cultural explanations of control within prison. He focuses on three factors that accompanied the rise of prison gangs: (1) consolidation of power, (2) propagation of relationships between and within the prison and the street, and (3) projection of power—essentially, the model of gang emergence and governance popularized by the Mexican Mafia that was chronicled in 1992 film *American Me*. He argued that gangs in prison gained control of inmate behavior generally (i.e., not just of gang members) through the consolidation of these factors. Like Skarbek, Lessing identified the unforeseen consequences of crackdowns and the expanded use of segregated housing that played right into the hands of gangs. What better confirmation of the notion that your gang is powerful and in control than to be targeted by authorities?

These are important arguments, particularly because our understanding of prison gangs is poorly developed and with few exceptions lacks much in the way of an empirical foundation. In addition, the perspectives of political scientists can provide an important understanding of the emergence and influence of alternative governance structures in prison. To date, however, empirical evidence in support of these perspectives is wanting. To a great extent, when the governance perspective has been applied to extralegal groups such as prison gangs, drug smugglers, and the like, it is based on case studies that lack representativeness or replicability. Additionally, much of the data used in support of such arguments are institutional data obtained from prison administrators or in some cases interviews with prison administrators. The ability to assess the validity and reliability of such measures remains limited. There is also the issue of simultaneity to deal with, as street gangs and prison gangs emerged at roughly the same points in time within states. This makes it difficult to sort out the nature of the reciprocal influence between street and prison gangs, an important part of the argument in support of prison gangs assuming roles of extralegal governance. As the power of prison gangs eroded in the face of larger numbers of gangs, moreover, it makes sense that younger gang members with less discipline and commitment to gangs would undermine the governance that gangs are purported to provide (Gundur 2020).

The Characteristics of Prison Gangs

Table 12.1 lists the key points of comparison between prison gangs and street gangs and provides a side-by-side contrast with what we have learned about prison gangs. Thus, it demonstrates both the points in common and the differences between the two groups. The primary differences can be seen in the age, organizational structure, and criminal orientation of the groups. Prison gang members are older than street gang members, and this accounts for a good deal of the purpose-oriented nature of prison gangs, including trading in contraband and purposive violence. As a consequence, prison gangs exhibit more sophistication and skills, including organization. The organizational structure of prison gangs is very different from that of street gangs and reflects the ability of older prison gang members to organize and discipline themselves and others. The hierarchical structure of the prison gang facilitates

TABLE 12.1 COMPARISON OF PRISON AND STREET GANGS		
Variable	Prison gang	Street gang
Race	Single race or ethnicity	Mostly single race or ethnicity
Age	Concentrated in the midtwenties, with members into the thirties and forties	Average age in the upper teens
Organizational structure	Hierarchical	Situational/hierarchical
Sources of violence	Symbolic and instrumental	Symbolic
Offending style	Entrepreneurial	Cafeteria style
Visibility of behavior	Covert	Overt
Drug trafficking	Major activity; organized, collective	Varies; mostly individualistic
Loyalty to gang	Strong ties to the gang	Weak bonds
Key to membership	Strong observance of gang rules; willingness to engage in violence	Real or perceived allegiance to the gang; hanging out; commitment to street rules
Key psychological attribute	Opposition, intimidation, control, manipulation	Opposition, intimidation, camaraderie
Adapted from Pyrooz, Decker, and Fleisher (2011).		

the entrepreneurial orientation of these groups, who despite being in prison still manage to control substantial drug and contraband exchanges. The expressive violence of street gangs reflects the age of members for whom revenge alone is a goal worth pursuing. Prison gang offending is more purposive and focused, perhaps owing to the narrower range of targets and opportunities in prison than in the street.

Prison gangs have many organizational similarities with street gangs. These groups usually have a structure that designates one person as a leader who oversees a group of members and makes decisions on behalf of the group. However, there is much more structure and discipline in prison gangs than in street gangs. This provides prison gang leadership with an open slate on which to fulfill their interests in protection and contraband.

Prison gangs require loyalty (e.g., P. Ralph et al. 1996) and secrecy (e.g., Fong 1990). Violent behavior is common both within and between prison gangs, and the use of violence can propel a member upward in the prison hierarchy (Gambetta 2009). Indeed, gang violence or its threat (i.e., projection) is a primary means of accomplishing other goals in prison. A reputation for violence is important, as Lessing (2016) noted, because it allows gangs to project themselves as being able to make good on their promises, control contraband, and protect their members. Prison gangs have a central focus on money-making enterprises, generally through drug trafficking. Gang members are the essential capital in crime-oriented social groups such as the prison gang. Gang members are valued for the protection they can provide and the income they can generate. As such, gang members who express a desire to leave the gang jeopardize group security, and such movement may be met with threats of violence.

Within prison, there is variation in the characteristics of gangs. Buentello, Fong, and Vogel (1991) presented stages of prison gang development, which they developed based on official data and their observations in Texas as an STG manager (Buentello), a special monitor in the *Ruiz v. Estelle* (1980) lawsuit over cruel and unusual punishment (Fong), and a researcher (Vogel). They identify the typical social sorting with entry into prison as the first stage, where prisoners search to find others with similar demographics and preferences. Beyond that, there are "cliques," "protection groups," "predatory groups," and "prison gangs." What differentiated these groups was nine features, including exclusive members, long-term commitment, group-defined goals and benefits, rules regulating conduct, leadership, group-based criminal activity, locus of influence, out-group recognition, and emergent group process. After a collective moves from a clique to a prison gang, the group becomes more exclusive, influential and powerful, criminally and profit oriented, and organized and structured (Gundur 2018; Pyrooz and Decker 2019).

Recall in our discussion of the organizational structure of gangs in Chapter 3 that we emphasized the diversity and dynamic nature of gangs. Street gangs evolve over time, as they face new challenges and attempt to integrate new members (Ayling 2011; Densley 2014b; Ouellet, Bouchard, and Charette 2019). The same can be said of prison gangs, and though the evidence is not great, we believe that prison gangs evolve more slowly than do street gangs. There may be individual movement from group to group, as members of a clique may move to protection groups. But there may also be changes in groups over time, as a predatory group may lose a key member through transfer or release, and the group ceases to exhibit the organization it once had. This diversity can be seen in the strong patterns of racial identification across prison gangs. There are at least seven major prison gangs in state and federal prisons. A major source of their variation is found in race/ethnicity. Many of these gangs function as umbrella groups imitated by inmates in other prison systems, often without direct communication with groups with a similar name in other prisons. These seven gangs include:

1. The Mexican Mafia (also known as La Eme) was started at the Deuel Vocational Center in Tracy, California, in the 1950s. California's first prison gang (Camp and Camp 1985; Hunt et al. 1993), La Eme is primarily composed of Mexican Americans.
2. The Aryan Brotherhood (AB), a White supremacist group, was started in 1967 in California's San Quentin Prison by White inmates who opposed the racial threat they perceived Black and Latino inmates presented to them (Orlando-Morningstar 1997).
3. La Nuestra Familia (Our Family) was established in the 1960s in California's Soledad Prison, though some argue it began in the Deuel Vocational Center (Landre, Miller, and Porter 1997). The original members were Latinos from Northern California's agricultural Central Valley who aligned to protect themselves from the Los Angeles–based Mexican Mafia.
4. The Texas Syndicate (Syndicato Tejano) emerged in the 1970s, originally formed by Tejanos, or Mexican Americans, incarcerated in California, and is thought to be the first Texas prison gang (Aguilar 2019).
5. The Mexikanemi (known also as the Texas Mexican Mafia) was established in 1984. Its name and symbols cause confusion with the California-based Mexican Mafia. The Mexikanemi fights with the Mexican Mafia and the Texas Syndicate, although there is some evidence that the Mexikanemi and the Texas Syndicate are aligning themselves against the Mexican Mafia (Orlando-Morningstar 1997).
6. The Crips and Bloods, traditional Los Angeles street gangs whose names and style have been copied across the country, have gained strength in the prisons. They are the most prominent Black gang

in prisons and emerged in San Quentin prison in 1971, a product of radicalization among Black prisoners (Cummins 1994).

7. People Nation and Folk Nation are traditional African American Street gangs. Folk Nation is aligned with Crip gangs and is active in the Midwest and South. People Nation is aligned with Blood gangs, also active in the Midwest and South. Both had their origins in Chicago. (Knox, Etter, and Smith 2019)

As the names and racial/ethnic compositions of the seven prison gangs identified above show, race and ethnicity are key orienting features of prison gang membership, more so than on the street (Chapter 8). While Black gangs may fight each other on the street (Crips vs. Bloods, People vs. Folk), in prison race trumps most street-based rivalries. In many southwestern states, moreover, Latino gangs form allegiances based on ethnicity as well as immigration status, with place of birth often determining what gangs are available to which individuals for membership.

A Phoenix gang member who had done time in both juvenile and adult prisons told us that race and ethnicity were more important than gang affiliations once you got to prison:

Gangs are not really associated in incarceration. You gonna have to get along with Bloods; you gonna have to get along with Crips. Incarceration is more of a color thing. You with your color. It's about race in jail [and prison]. It's all about Blacks with Blacks, kinfolk with kinfolk, Chicanos with Chicanos. The Woods [Whites] with the Woods, the Chiefs [Native Americans] with Chiefs.

The role of race inside prison was underscored by a White former Fresno gang member who had a mixed-race grandchild:

I was in prison with the skinheads and got a picture of my grandson, who is half Black. My bunkie [cellmate] saw it and got five more guys who came back and beat me up. They said, "We can't have that in the gang."

As Goodman (2008) put it, based on observations of interactions between correctional officers and prisoners at a prison reception center in California, "it's just Black, White, or Hispanic," alluding to the role of the prison system in manufacturing racial distinctions (see also M. Walker 2016).

Maxson (2012) has been cautious in differentiating between street and prison gangs, and rightly so given the limited research available. Based on

her interviews with staff and gang members in California youth correctional facilities, she found that the organizational features of prison gangs were
similar to the organizational features of street gangs. However, the gang
profiles Maxson developed did not include racial homogeneity, structural
hierarchy, and strong bonds and loyalty to the gang. Based on research carried out on gangs in adult prisons (e.g., Hunt et al. 1993; Irwin 1980; J. Jacobs
1977), we would expect different conclusions about the similarities and di-
vergences between street and prison gangs composed of adults. The differences between Maxson's conclusions and ours may hinge on the fact that
her work comes from inside of youth facilities. Pyrooz and Decker (2019)
found limited differences in the characteristics of street and prison gangs
based on self-reports of an adult sample of imprisoned current and former
gang members in Texas. Regardless of the source of the differences, more
work is called for in this important area of gangs, and researchers and policymakers should remain open to the similarities between street and prison
gang members.

Transitions in Prison Gang Membership

Prison plays an increasingly important role in the lives of gang members for two
reasons. First, as gang members become more involved in crime, their likelihood of being arrested, being convicted, and going to prison increases substantially. Thus, prison becomes a natural extension of the gang life (Joan Moore
1978). Gangs can play an important role in prison life, regulating the lives of
members, non-gang members, and in some cases correctional officials. But
there is a second reason why the prison is increasingly important to gang members. Many of the older gang members in prison were leaders in their gangs on
the street. The gangs they leave behind often continue to depend on them for
support and direction. Thus, gang members on the street may find that imprisoned gang members are calling the shots, such as where to sell drugs, who to
target for violence, and which new coalitions to form, for gang members on the
street. The leader of the largest street gang in Chicago, Larry Hoover of the
Gangster Disciples, is reputed to have run his gang for years (and some claim
more effectively) while incarcerated in the Illinois prison system (Aspholm
2020). While this is perhaps an extreme example, it does illustrate the status and
power that can come with imprisonment.

Two authors of this book spent a number of years leading a team that interviewed over eight hundred Texas prisoners with strong gang representation
among those interviewed. We learned a good many things that challenged the
conventional wisdom about the life course of prison gangs and prison gang
membership.

Joining Gangs in Prison

We devoted the entirety of Chapter 4 to discussing the onset of gang membership. There we noted the processes involved in joining a street gang, including the methods and motives. We take up that topic in this section of the prison gang chapter because we believe that understanding parallels between street and prison gang processes, structures, motivations, and consequences is important. Indeed, the primary motivations for joining a street or a prison gang (protection, status, access to contraband, and group processes) are generally consistent. And the proximate methods for joining (violent initiation, just joining, and existing ties to a gang from the street) also closely parallel those for street gangs. There are two pathways to gang membership in prison, which align with the importation and deprivation perspectives described earlier (Pyrooz, Gartner, and Smith 2017).

The first pathway is perhaps the most straightforward: street gang members bring their gang affiliation with them to the institution. Once in prison, prior affiliations may determine in-prison affiliations, as there is continuity between their street and prison affiliations. This continuity may be enhanced by the presence of associates from their old street gang or the neighborhood they lived in. New inmates with recent street gang ties add value to their prison gang not only by providing strength in numbers but also by providing intelligence—updating the status of members of the street gang, detailing new animosities with other gangs, and facilitating business between prison gangs and street gangs. They may also play a role in passing along information that may lead to the discipline of imprisoned individuals who have gotten out of line. This illustrates the power of intelligence for decision-making within the gang.

The second pathway into a prison gang occurs among individuals who were not gang members on the street but decide to affiliate in prison. This process is consistent with the deprivation perspective, whereby recently imprisoned individuals find gang membership necessary, either for their physical survival or to gain access to contraband in prison. The "pains of imprisonment" are not just psychic; physical danger in prison is real, and prisoners include such threats in their calculations about what activities to engage in, whom to affiliate with, and perhaps most importantly, whom to avoid. Lacking the protection that comes with affiliating with a specific group or gang in prison deprives inmates of a key possession in the institution: personal safety.

While the motivations for joining gangs in prison may diverge from those on the street, the methods for gang joining in prison closely parallel those on the street. Being "jumped in" appears to be the primary method for joining, as Pyrooz and Decker (2019) report that just over half of the members in their sample (53 percent) joined in this way. Being "prospected" (sought out for membership and forced to commit crimes to benefit the gang) was the next most prevalent method of joining, reported by 15 percent of the LoneStar sample (201). The Texas gang members interviewed for this study also reported variation across gang types in the method of joining, with race-segregated gangs more likely to use violence as part of the process of entering their gang.

Regardless of the pathway, prison officials are concerned with the prison gang affiliations of their custodial populations. That is why in most prisons, the intake process includes efforts to understand street gang affiliation and prior prison gang affiliation. This process, known as "jacketing," is designed to understand the groups new prisoners have belonged to on the street as well as the groups they are feuding with and those they get along with. Typically, jacketing has led to the use of solitary confinement or being housed in higher levels of security. Gang members are highly overrepresented in solitary confinement—by a factor of three—which Pyrooz and Mitchell (2019b) attributed to three core pathways: disciplinary (i.e., they "earned it"), protection (i.e., they "needed it"), or administrative (i.e., they "pose a threat"). Likewise, most prison systems have STG officers whose job it is to understand and document gang affiliations in the institution, whether they originated on the street or in prison. Knowledge of gang affiliation is an important management tool for such things as housing assignments, including cellmates and pods, as well as programming and work assignments.

Avoiding Gangs in Prison

Two groups are characterized by their decision to avoid involvement with prison gangs regardless of their patterns of affiliation before being imprisoned. The first of these groups is represented by street gang members who decide to maintain an affiliation with their street gang but not affiliate with a prison gang. This decision may reflect the experience of individuals from small towns whose gangs are not well represented or active in prison or individuals who are older and decide to "do their time" and not become involved in activities that may lead to discipline or sentence enhancements (see Bolden's [2020] firsthand account of these issues). This illustrates that the power of a gang in prison has important implications for its ability to control members, hence the struggles for power at the top and the bottom of the prison gang hierarchy.

The second group consists of those individuals who were not affiliated with a gang on the street and decide that they will not affiliate with one in prison. This group represents a majority of incarcerated persons. We believe that those who choose avoidance of prison gangs are older prisoners, perhaps those with families or those with shorter sentences. Such individuals, particularly older prisoners, are more likely to see the entanglements of gang membership as placing constraints on their ability to do their time and be released. These street and prison gang avoiders represent little in the way of challenges to prison gangs and may include individuals not likely to be of interest to gangs, whether because of their inability to bring personal attributes to the gang (such as fighting ability) or because they represent stigmatized groups based on their offenses (i.e., sex offenders).

Leaving Gangs in Prison

We believe that there is a good deal more "conventional wisdom" about prison gangs than empirical evidence, and we have been contributors to said conventional wisdom in several synthetic reviews of the prison gang literature (e.g., Pyrooz, Decker, and Fleisher 2011). As is the case with gang joining in prison, a good deal of the wisdom regarding gang leaving in prison needs to be challenged. This is particularly true of the process of leaving a prison gang. Most of Chapter 5 is devoted to leaving street gangs, a process that until recently had not been acknowledged by researchers, policymakers, or practitioners. As strong as the bonds between gang members and street gangs were believed to be, those of prison gangs and prison gang members were seen as much stronger. After all, it was believed that leaving a prison gang was accompanied by severe, often fatal violence. Whether prison gangs are White supremacists or have members in a large number of institutions, they are viewed as "lifetime memberships" that cannot be renounced. Popular culture, through movies such as *American Me* and *American History X*, underscores the violent nature of such gangs and the view that membership cannot be renounced without the gang imposing the supreme penalty, death. *American Me* made it clear that prison gang membership meant "blood in, blood out." And this has been the bedrock of the conventional wisdom regarding the nature of prison gang membership. Skarbek (2014, 116), for example, cited the Aryan Brotherhood credo that a member "does not leave or terminate his membership except through death. Once in, always in." Such a perception certainly helps the gang project power, as Lessing notes, a key component of control.

But what does the evidence (systematic samples of prisoners with validated data) say about disengaging from prison gangs? The three of us have conducted a good deal of research on disengagement from street gangs. Some of the motivations and processes for leaving street gangs must overlap with those for prison gangs, though it is not clear how much overlap there is. The first issue to address is whether there is evidence that individuals do leave their gang while incarcerated. Until the LoneStar Project, the most recent study of gang leaving (the authors referred to it as "defecting") was published in 1995 by Fong and Vogel and was based on forty-eight former gang members in protective custody and conducted by a prison employee. In their surveys of 802 Texas prisoners, Pyrooz and Decker (2019) used both qualitative and quantitative data to identify the primary motives for leaving a gang in prison and the methods by which they did so. They found evidence of both pushes and pulls at work in the decision to disengage from the gang. The processes of disengagement include taking active steps to leave (through an intervention or being jumped out) as well as some passive steps (moving, just quitting, and doing nothing).

The key finding from the assessment of disengagement from prison gangs was that roughly 70 percent of the respondents had disengaged from a gang in their lifetime. This exposes the myth that prison gang membership is immutable and cannot be renounced and suggests implications for the power of prison gangs to control inmate behavior. The primary motivation prisoners noted for leaving their gang was disillusionment, a consequence of unmet expectations and discontent. Such disillusionment was also a product of gang lifestyles blocking pathways to desired stages of life, being with family, being free from the fear of violence and the pressures of gang membership, and eliminating associations that could affect a release date.

Evidence of violence accompanying gang exits was also found, but it was certainly not present in a majority of cases. Indeed, "giving notice" accompanied a substantial minority of those who disengaged from their prison gang. This method was especially prominent among long-term members. Age and intimate commitments (marriage or family) also were correlates of successful disengagement from gangs. A. Johnson and Densley's (2018) ethnographic work in two Brazilian prisons also identified "religious commitment" as a key in the staged process of exiting from a prison gang. This finding about disengagement from prison is important, as Brazilian prisons are notorious for their high levels of violence, and this method of departure does not involve threats of violence. These findings underscore the need to draw conclusions based on data—a need that continues to exist in most areas of our knowledge of prison gangs.

Offending and Victimization in Prison

Prison gangs share a number of characteristics and experiences with street gangs. This appears to be true of offending in prison as well as victimization. This should not come as a surprise, as the relationship between gang membership, offending, and victimization is quite strong (Esbensen et al. 2010; Pyrooz, Moule, and Decker 2014). And most prison gang members have prior experience (either on the street or in prison) with offending and victimization, consistent with the importation perspective on prison violence (DeLisi et al. 2011).

In terms of misconduct, the evidence is clear: gang affiliates are disproportionately involved in misconduct, including physical violence, assaults on staff, threats, possession and distribution of contraband, and institutional disorder and unrest. These findings are observed in research relying on official data to measure misconduct and gang affiliation in Arizona (Griffin and Hepburn 2006), Nevada (Shelden 1991), Texas (Worrall and Morris 2012), and the Federal Bureau of Prisons (Gaes et al. 2002). They are also supported based on survey data from Huebner's (2003) analysis of the 1991 Survey of Inmates of State Correctional Facilities. Pyrooz and Decker (2019) found support for this relationship using both official and survey measures of gang affiliation and misconduct in the LoneStar Project.

There is an interesting debate about the effect of prison gang membership on victimization. Those who argue for the protective nature of prison gang membership include theorists such as Skarbek, whose work we highlighted earlier in this chapter. From his perspective, gangs perform a protective function by projecting toughness and intervening with violent retaliation against those who threaten or harm gang members in prison. This view reflects Skarbek's view of prison gangs as effective structures for working to the advantage of gangs and gang members in the movement of contraband, including protection against assaults. Empirical support for this view is found in the work of Wooldredge and Steiner (2012, 2014). They found that gang membership was unrelated to assault victimization and was negatively related to theft victimization. These findings are generally taken to identify a protective aspect of prison gang membership, something missing from street gang membership.

In contrast to identifying the protective aspects of gang membership, Pyrooz and Decker (2019) found that current prison gang members had higher rates of misconduct and victimization than did former gang members or those who had never been gang members. The disparities between those who had been gang members (current and former) and those who had never been in a gang were greatest, with the offending and victimization experiences of current and former gang members being greater than those who had never been in a gang. This was most pronounced for the relationship between violent offending and victimization but was tempered for former gang members when the recall period changed to the last six months, since they were no longer susceptible to the group processes of the gang. Regardless of the offending or victimization type, prisoners who had been in a gang were much more likely to engage in misconduct and be victimized.

Prison gangs often dominate the drug business inside and outside the prison walls (Fleisher 1989; Skarbek 2014). Furthermore, many researchers argue that prison gangs are responsible for most prison violence, and there is evidence in support of this contention (e.g., Useem and Reisig 1999). Prison gangs exploit prison operations through their desire to make money and control the institution's inmate power structure. The task of watching thousands of prisoners at all times of day and night (even with cameras) is beyond the capability of staff in most prisons. Where profits are at stake, violence is often an outcome of attempts to cut into sales. Camp and Camp (1985) noted that prison gang members represented only 3 percent of the prison population but caused 50 percent or more of the prison violence. In a small, confined area with a finite number of drug customers and dealers, as well as other gang-related services such as gambling and prostitution (Fleisher 1989), the possibility for competition between gangs is high. Such competition often leads to violence.

Gang members often import violence from the street to the prison. The rivalries that they hold on the street are often translated to the prison setting, though in some cases they are altered. Race and ethnicity become very important elements of gang identification in prison, often trumping rivalries that existed on the street. It is not surprising given the high levels of violence perpetrated by gang members both on the street and in prison that they are among the individuals most likely to be "written up" in prison for violating prison rules. While these violations often include petty drug dealing and providing other contraband services, they can also involve serious assault and murder (Griffin and Hepburn 2006).

Responding to Prison Gangs

Prisons have implemented a number of strategies to respond to gangs. The strategies include using inmate informants and segregation units for prison gang members, isolating prison gang leaders, locking down the entire institution, vigorously prosecuting crimes committed by prison gang members, monitoring prison gang members' internal and external communications, and the case-by-case examination of prison gang offenses. There are, however, no published research evaluations testing the efficacy of these suppression strategies in curbing prison gang violence and other criminal conduct inside correctional institutions.

The state of responses to prison gangs is captured nicely in two surveys of prison management strategies spaced ten years apart. Winterdyk and Ruddell (2010) surveyed all prison systems (and two private systems) in the U.S. regarding their management strategies for STG members. Their response rate was 69.8 percent, which is quite high for this kind of survey of public officials. The two strategies perceived to be most effective were "segregation" and the use of "specialized housing units." "Program participation" was perceived to be very effective by 30 percent of respondents. Generally, there was a lack of consensus or consistency in the choice of responses, despite support for conclusions that STGs were growing in number and their use of violence. Notable by its absence was the evaluation of the effectiveness of such strategies.

A decade later, McGrath (2020) conducted a systematic review of the effectiveness of gang interventions and management strategies in prisons. He found eleven studies that met the criteria for inclusion in the review. Ten of the eleven studies used research designs that permitted an evaluation of a response or strategy's impact, although he concluded, "Many evaluations are too weak to draw reliable conclusions about effectiveness with small, unrepresentative samples and poor reporting quality being particularly problematic." He also stated that "promising" interventions are used least often, while "less promising" interventions are used most often. "Less promising" interventions are characterized by the lack of a rehabilitative focus and dependence on suppression approaches such as jacketing, isolation, and denial of privileges. The promising interventions include reentry and employment, drug treatment, and therapeutic communities. McGrath argued that future work should assess the impact of promising interventions, find researchers to work in concert with prison administrators, and employ strong research designs (see our discussion of this in Chapter 14). It is hoped we do not wait ten years for the next review and evaluation of prison efforts to deal with gang members.

One response to the presence of gangs in prison, introduced earlier, is jacketing. This involves putting an official note in an inmate's file if he or she is suspected of being a gang member. This note allows authorities to transfer the prisoner to a high-security facility or solitary confinement. Many find this process inappropriate because it may involve suspected but unconfirmed gang activity, often reported by a snitch, which may lead to incorrectly labeling an inmate as a prison gang member or associate (Toch 2007). Once labeled, a prisoner may be controlled with threats of segregation and transfer. Like so many other prison gang interventions, there are no published evaluations of the success of this approach.

It is important to revisit Camp and Camp (1985), not least because they were the first to ask questions about how prison systems were responding to the emerging threat of gangs. In their survey of thirty-three prison facilities, they asked officials which strategies they would most likely employ against prison gangs. Transfer was cited by twenty-seven of the thirty-three agencies, the use of informers was cited twenty-one times, gang member segregation was cited twenty times, gang leader segregation was cited twenty times, facility lockdown was cited eighteen times, and vigorous prosecution and interception of prison gang members' communications was cited sixteen times. These interventions reflect the heavy reliance on suppression techniques in responding to prison gangs. Knox and Tromanhauser (1991) surveyed prison wardens regarding prison gang control and found that 70.9 percent advocated "bus therapy," the transfer of prisoners to other institutions. These researchers show that fewer than half of the prisons surveyed provided any type of prison gang training; but more recently, Knox (2000) showed that correctional officer training has improved, with a finding that more than two-thirds of the 133 facilities surveyed provided some gang training in 1999. These findings are at least twenty years old and strongly underscore the need for more research and evaluation in this area. The same is true of the findings from Winterdyk and Ruddell (2010), the most recent work in the area, which was published over a decade ago. But it is clear from the Winterdyk and Ruddell work that approaches that emphasize suppression remain in widespread use, a practice that may result from a limited response repertoire in prison or the attempt to balance the safety of inmates and staff.

A promising intervention found in state prison systems is "gang renunciation" programs. Not many states offer them (Pyrooz and Mitchell 2019a), but such interventions offer gang members an exit ramp out of the gang. Such programs require gang members to follow a path that would lead them to leave their gang. This program in Texas, known as GRAD (Gang Renouncement and Disassociation), began in 2000 (Burman 2012). It requires that participants "renounce" their gang membership to institutional representatives and enter a "step-down" housing assignment in which they move from solitary confinement to special population housing. As mentioned earlier, gang members are housed in restrictive housing prison cells and units at much higher rates than non-gang inmates (Pyrooz and Mitchell 2019b). Some argue that this is for the protection of prisoners and prison employees; however, it may also speak to policies unrelated to gangs, such as staffing ratios and demographic changes to the prison system. Reformers often demand the abolition of solitary confinement, but in many prisons, there are precious few alternatives. As is typical of reentry programs, the tension between maintaining order among inmates and reintegration exists for GRAD too. The program is based on the behavioral economics principle of "nudges," the use of incentives to produce behavioral change that leads to healthy outcomes. To date there has not been a high-quality outcomes assessment of the impact of GRAD (and other step-down programs), but the approach is notable owing to the paucity of evidence, the magnitude of the program, and its skill-based component. A preliminary assessment of GRAD's impact suggested that the program was associated with lower levels of embeddedness in gangs (Pyrooz and Decker 2019).

Gang Members, Reentry, and Recidivism

There are 1.5 million people in prison in the United States (E. Carson 2020). While there is a lot of talk about "locking people up and throwing away the key," the reality is that most prisoners will be released. Indeed, more than 90 percent of all persons currently incarcerated will be back on the street at some point in their life. Roughly six hundred thousand individuals are released from prison each year, a sizable fraction of whom are gang members. But just as we lack good estimates of how many jail or prison inmates are gang members, we have no idea how many of the individuals released into the community each year are gang members. Not surprisingly, we do not have much good policy or research in this area either.

There is a small, emerging body of literature that examines the transitions made by gang members from prison to the community. As documented by

Petersilia (2003) and Western (2018), prisoner reentry is complicated by a variety of factors. Gang affiliation adds another layer of complication. Joan Moore's (1978, 1991) work in East Los Angeles found strong bonds between gang members who entered prison and returned to the community, ties that complicated that return. Based on qualitative results from the interviews of nineteen gang members returning to the community in Chicago, G. Scott (2004) found gangs to be a "self-defeating" correlate of individuals returning to the community. Gang membership had a negative effect on most of the processes (housing, family ties, employment prospects, and prosocial activities) that would lead to a successful reentry. Bender, Cobbina, and McGarrell's (2016) interviews with returning prisoners identified a need for programming with a specific focus on escaping the persistent tentacles of gang membership.

What little work has been done in this area underscores the difficulties gang members have once they are released from prison. Because gang members have a large number of associations with peers involved in crime and negative lifestyles, they bring a number of deficits to prison. Unfortunately, gang members who go to prison do not do much to cut their ties to negative peers while in prison, and in many cases, those ties are magnified. Huebner, Varano, and Bynum (2007) underscored the role of prior peer associations, drug use, concentrated disadvantage, and other factors limiting the success of gang members upon release from prison. They argue that there is something "uniquely important" about gang membership when it comes to successful reintegration following a prison term. The unique characteristics of gang membership provide "difficult barriers" (208) for gang members once they return to the community. Huebner and colleagues argued that the most appropriate response to gang members who leave prison is to provide supervised release in the community, a finding supported by Fleisher and Decker (2001).

Not surprisingly, researchers have found that gang affiliation is associated with recidivism, including rearrest, reconviction, parole violation, and reincarceration (Dooley, Seals, and Skarbek 2014; Huebner, Varano, and Bynum 2007; McShane, Williams, and Dolny 2003; Saunders, Sweeten, and Katz 2009). The precepts from the street gang literature were further applied in recent work by Pyrooz, Clark, et al. (2020), who demonstrated that recidivism rates differed by gang status. Current and former prison gang members were more likely to be arrested, convicted, and incarcerated upon release from prison than individuals who never belonged to a gang. These differences were substantial enough to lead the authors to conclude that identifying current and former gang status of individuals about to be released from prison has important policy implications for their releasee plans. Owing to the stigma attached to the gang and ex-prisoner labels, moreover, it is especially important for gang members returning from prison to the community to signal their commitment to conventional life (Densley and Pyrooz 2019). Bushway and Apel (2012) found that offenders who volunteered to participate in a rigorous and challenging employment program, and especially those who successfully completed such a program, signaled that they were fundamentally different from other offenders who do not choose to participate in programming—an important finding for practitioners and policymakers interested in breaking the cycle of recidivism.

Conclusion

A key conclusion about prison gangs and gang members is that the research foundation for evidence-based decision-making about this critical subpopulation is so small that it often is not sufficient to support solid programming and planning decisions. In addition, the media has had a widespread effect on public perceptions of prison gangs and gang members that is contradicted by much emerging research. It is also important to conclude by noting that there are many parallels between street gangs and prison gangs as well as between street gang members and prison gang members. The processes and motives of joining and leaving appear to overlap considerably. The same may be said of the levels of crime (misconduct in prison) and victimization. Being a gang member poses a great deal of risk to individuals whether they are in prison or on the street.

Perhaps the biggest gap in knowledge exists in the impact of responses to prison gang members by institutions. The few studies that do exist document higher recidivism rates for gang members than for non-gang inmates. And there appear to be residual effects of gang membership, even for those individuals who have disengaged from their gang in prison. We have evidence of very few programming efforts targeting gang members in prison and virtually no solid evaluations. If ever there was a gang topic ripe for more attention, it would be to catalog prison gang member interventions and begin to document their impact.

13

Anti-gang Legislation and Legal Responses

The State of California is in a state of crisis which has been
caused by violent street gangs whose members threaten,
terrorize, and commit a multitude of crimes against the
peaceful citizens of their neighborhoods. . . . It is the intent of
the Legislature in enacting [Chapter 11. Street Terrorism
Enforcement and Prevention, or STEP, Act] to seek the
eradication of criminal activity by street gangs.
—CALIFORNIA PENAL CODE 186.21

The passage of California's STEP act in 1988 marked a turning point in
responding to gangs. It represented the culmination of a popular shift
from the "rehabilitative ideal" to the "get tough" era of responses to the
problems of youth gangs and violence. E. Rosen and Venkatesh (2007) held that
the social work approaches to youth gangs—which emphasized treatment and
nonstate intervention—faded with the retrenchment of the welfare state and
the rise of punitiveness in criminal justice policy and practice. Gangs became
a criminal justice problem, and federal and state governments provided what
M. Klein (1997, 518) called the "legal armament" to respond accordingly. Anti-
gang legislation was enacted across nearly every state, and "Criminal Street
Gangs" was a title in the 1994 Crime Bill. This is why Bjerregaard (2015) categorized legalistic approaches to gangs under the banner of suppression.

The core premise underlying gang legislation is that gangs are qualitatively
different and the problems they pose warrant something distinct from what
the law offers. E. Rosen and Venkatesh (2007, 264) drew on the argument as-
serted by Raffy Astvasadoorian, Los Angeles deputy city attorney, in noting
that "the nature of gang crime—in that it involves a group of people—renders
it in a class of its own meriting special legal treatment." Accordingly, the purpose of this chapter is to examine the special class of laws and legalistic strategies applied to the problem of gangs, which includes the following:

- Understand the theoretical rationale underlying legislation devised to respond to gangs

- Review the origins, proliferation, and variation of targeted gang legislation, including gang definitions, databases, and sentencing enhancements
- Describe legislation that has been repurposed to target gangs, including criminal enterprise and public nuisance laws
- Detail the legacy of federal legislation where gangs were an auxiliary focus—namely, the 1994 Crime Bill
- Identify the consequences of gang affiliation in the courtroom, including the challenges gangs present to prosecutors and the burden of gang affiliation for defendants

Of all the chapters in this book, there is far less to take stock of when it comes to gangs and the law. The many inroads that have been established at the intersection of social science and the law unfortunately exclude issues related to gangs. Academic treatments of the topic involve far more storytelling than science (e.g., Hagedorn 2021; Yablonsky 2005). This is why our aims are primarily descriptive and legalistic, not empirical and explanatory, focusing on documenting the legal scaffolding permitting criminal justice responses to gangs. One last caveat is in order: this chapter focuses exclusively on anti-gang legislation in the United States. As little as we know about the efficacy of this legislation in the United States, our knowledge outside of the United States pales in comparison.

The Purpose of Anti-gang Legislation

Cesare Beccaria's (1764) *Essay on Crimes and Punishments* formed the basis of the classical school, a foundational perspective on crime and justice. The core assumptions of the classical perspective are that humans are rational, exercise free will, pursue self-interest, and seek to maximize pleasure and minimize pain. People weigh the benefits and costs of many behaviors, including crime. Nobel laureate and economist Gary Becker (1968) established a rational choice model of criminal offending, where the expected utility of the behavior was determined by benefits, including personal and social rewards, and costs, including formal and informal sanctions (see also Clarke and Cornish 1985). Altering the expected utility of crime, by either reducing the benefits or increasing the costs, should lower its prevalence and frequency in the population. These assumptions about human behavior serve as the foundation for criminal justice in the United States and elsewhere and have been leveraged to support anti-gang legislation.

Anti-gang legislation focuses almost exclusively on the formal costs of gang activity. This represents a narrow component of G. Becker's (1968) rational choice model, as the informal costs and the benefits of gang activity are typically omitted. Gang databases, sentencing enhancements, juvenile transfers to adult court, and civil gang injunctions do not address the intrinsic rewards and the social acceptability of gang activity. Instead, the overarching purpose of anti-gang legislation is deterrence (Maxson, Matsuda, and Hennigan 2011, 58). Elements of incapacitation (i.e., gang activity is reduced while under surveillance or confinement) or retribution (i.e., "just deserts" for gang crime) may indeed be a goal, but the primary aim of anti-gang legislation is to alter the choice calculus by increasing (1) the certainty of detection and apprehension, (2) the severity of sanctions for gang activity, and (3) the celerity, or swiftness, of detection and sanctions. Legislative definitions of gangs and gang members, along with shared police gang databases, allow for intelligence-led policing and selective enforcement to heighten the certainty of arrest. Sentencing enhancements for gang-motivated crime impose harsher punishments than for crimes without a gang nexus. Those punished should learn from their mistakes, as should their fellow gang members, and should discourage young people from joining gangs and participating in gang activity. That is the basis for general, focused, and specific deterrence.

Whereas anti-gang legislation is typically enacted at the state or federal level, Maxson, Hennigan, and Sloane (2005) and E. Rosen and Venkatesh (2007) highlighted the localized nature of place-based interventions such as gang abatement laws and civil gang injunctions. Both groups of authors identified how legal tactics empower local entities to exercise social control over gang activity. Maxson's team noted that civil gang injunctions could result in strengthening collective efficacy—social cohesion and informal social control—in communities as fear and intimidation subside with the retreat of gang activity from public spaces. Rosen and Venkatesh invoked a similar line of reasoning, although rooted in perspectives on the physical and social forms of disorder in communities—that is, observable signs of disorder function as a signal of the absence of guardianship in the community and thus a magnet for serious crime. Gang abatement laws and civil gang injunctions are not solely about community since elements of deterrence are evident in both, which we will return to shortly.

Courtroom actors are also likely to use gang affiliation as a marker to guide decision-making. Gang affiliation fits Goffman's (1963, 5) concept of a "spoiled identity," especially within conventional and rigid bureaucracies, as the label imputes "the wide range of imperfections on the basis of the original one." Digital surveillance, gang databases, presentencing reports, and self-admission could infuse gang affiliation into conversations and dynamics in the courtroom, which in turn could lead to inequitable outcomes in case processing and sentencing. Miethe and McCorkle (1997) held that gang affiliation was a master status because it generated social and legal condemnation, the differences between gang and non-gang members were dramatized in formal court procedures, and auxiliary traits (e.g., young racial/ethnic minorities, gun and group offenses, and witness intimidation) typified gang cases. D. Walker and

Cesar (2020) emphasized that gang affiliates checked off the boxes of the focal concerns of courtroom actors, especially greater culpability or blameworthiness of the defendant and perceptions of future criminality vis-à-vis the imperative to protect the community. The courtroom workgroup uses gang affiliation in countervailing ways, where prosecutors perceive it as an aggravating factor and defense attorneys a mitigating factor. Given the "get tough" swing of the criminal justice pendulum, beginning in the 1970s, gang affiliation could be exploited to result in an extralegal penalty on charging decisions, pretrial detention, juvenile transfers to adult court, sentences to confinement, and longer sentences.

Targeted Gang Legislation

On September 24, 1988, the governor of California, George Deukmejian, signed into law the first anti-gang legislation in the United States, which was termed the Street Terrorism Enforcement and Prevention, or STEP, Act. Since that time, according to the National Gang Center's overview, all states, along with the District of Columbia and the federal government, have enacted gang legislation (https://www.nationalgangcenter.gov/Legislation/Highlights), resulting in 1,790 gang-related laws. While many of these laws are related to gangs only indirectly, most are designed to enhance or expand the sanctions for gang activity. Figure 13.1 reports the year of the first documented legislation on gangs across jurisdictions in the United States. Note that our review revealed that forty-six governmental jurisdictions maintained anti-gang legislation, in contrast to the National Gang Center's reporting. What is clear is that the rise of anti-gang legislation is a recent shift in the law, occurring over the last three decades and primarily in the 1990s.

In this section, we summarize anti-gang legislation pertaining to four main themes: (1) definitions of gang activity, (2) gang databases, (3) sentencing enhancements, and (4) gang participation and recruitment. Table 13.1 provides a summary of the existence of legislation on each of these themes for all fifty states and the federal government. We use California as an example throughout, partly because anti-gang legislation originated in the state but also because this legislation has been altered as a result of direct democracy (e.g., popular vote on a constitutional amendment: Proposition 21—Juvenile Crime) and legislative action (e.g., a process requiring the governor's signature: Assembly Bill 90—Fair and Accurate Gang Database Act).

Defining Gang Activity

Chapter 1 covered definitions of gangs, gang members, and gang activity. Here, we focus on summarizing the similarities and differences across stat-

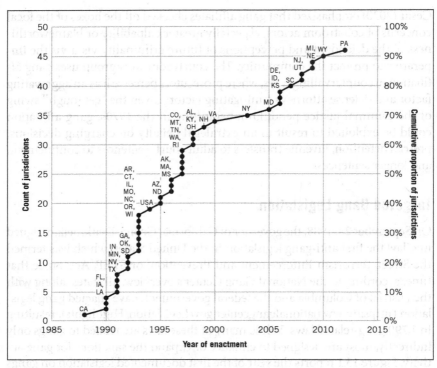

Figure 13.1 Proliferation of anti-gang legislation in the United States

utes. In terms of gangs, we find that nearly all states, forty-five of them, and the federal government maintain a statutory definition of a gang. While our findings update the work of Barrows and Huff, who observed forty-one (Barrows and Huff 2009) and forty-five (Huff and Barrows 2015) statutory definitions, our conclusions are no different from theirs (2015, 63):

1. Most statutes require at least three individuals to be considered a gang, although some do not specify a number (e.g., Arizona), while others require five or more (e.g., Oklahoma).
2. All statutes include criminal activity in the definition of a gang; while most require a pattern of criminal activity, others specify a list of offenses (and some include both).
3. Most statutes, but not all, require that gangs maintain a common name, sign, or symbol.
4. Some statutes, but not many, require a gang to maintain an established hierarchy.
5. Some statutes, but not many, require a gang to maintain an alliance, conspiracy, or shared understanding among members.

TABLE 13.1 SUMMARY OF ANTI-GANG LEGISLATION

| | Year enacted | Definitions | | Shared database | Sentencing enhancement | | Recruiting | Gang |
		Gang	Member		Misdemeanor	Felony		Participation
Federal	1994	X		X		X		
AK	1996	X			X	X	X	
AL	1998	X						X
AR	1993	X			X	X	X	X
AZ	1995	X	X			X	X	X
CA	1988	X		X		X	X	X
CO	1997	X		X			X	
CT	1993	X					X	
DE	2006	X			X	X	X	X
FL	1990	X	X	X	X	X	X	
GA	1992	X		X		X	X	X
HI								
IA	1990	X					X	X
ID	2006	X	X		X	X	X	
IL	1993	X	X	X		X	X	
IN	1991	X				X	X	X
KS	2006	X	X			X	X	
KY	1998	X				X	X	

(Continued)

TABLE 13.1 SUMMARY OF ANTI-GANG LEGISLATION (*Continued*)

	Year enacted	Definitions		Shared database	Sentencing enhancement		Recruiting	Gang Participation
		Gang	Member		Misdemeanor	Felony		
LA	1990	X				X	X	
MA	1996	X					X	
MD	2005	X					X	
ME								
MI	2009	X	X			X	X	X
MN	1991	X		X		X	X	
MO	1993	X				X		X
MS	1996	X	X			X	X	
MT	1997	X				X	X	
NC	1993	X	X			X	X	X
ND	1995	X				X	X	
NE	2009	X	X				X	
NH	1999	X	X			X	X	
NJ	2008	X	X			X	X	X
NM								
NV	1991	X				X	X	
NY	2003	X	X					
OH	1998	X				X		X

State	Year							
OK	1992	X				X	X	
OR	1993	X					X	
PA	2012	X				X		
RI	2014	X				X		
SC	2007	X	X	X		X	X	
SD	1992	X	X			X	X	
TN	1997	X	X	X		X	X	
TX	1991	X					X	
UT	2008	X				X	X	
VA	2000	X	X	X		X	X	X
VT				X				
WA	1997	X	X	X		X	X	
WI	1993	X	X					
WV								
WY	2010	X				X	X	
Total states		46	18	12	5	33	36	14

Overall, there are far more similarities than differences in gang definitions across statutes.

Unlike definitions of gangs, only a minority of statutes define a gang member. Most statutes assume that members are a given or simply define a gang member as a person who is a member of a gang—statutory declarations that are not exactly useful for estimating the size of the gang problem or understanding its dimensions. The first state to introduce gang legislation, California, does not provide such criteria, nor do the federal government, Illinois, or New York, jurisdictions that all maintain a large presence of gang activity. There is considerable variation across the eighteen states that provide gang membership criteria. All include self-admission, but beyond that, there is no universality. Most statutes specify a large list of criteria while requiring that two conditions be met. Virginia requires only one, while Kansas, South Carolina, and Texas also allow for a single criterion of self-admission. Beyond that, all criteria are treated equally—someone who has been convicted of gang crimes and who has gang-related tattoos is equal to someone who wears gang-related clothing and who associates with known gang members.

Defining gang activity is especially important for the purpose of sentencing enhancements, which we cover in more detail below. While some states permit enhancements based on someone's status as a gang member, the vast majority require that criminal activity maintain a gang nexus, not unlike Maxson and Klein's (1996) distinction between gang-related and gang-motivated homicide discussed in Chapter 1. California, for example, defined gang-related criminal activity as:

> committed for the benefit of, at the direction of, or in association with any criminal street gang, with the specific intent to promote, further, or assist in any criminal conduct by gang members. (California Penal Code § 186.22 [b] [1])

These crimes do not have to be committed by gang members, whether current or former, nor do the victims have to be other gang members. Charles Denton's (2014) guidance on STEP, which runs ninety-two pages long, reviewed legal precedent, including establishing a gang nexus, and identified two key issues. First, there is the issue of "benefit of" and "in association with" the gang. Examples of the former include exacting retaliation, gaining respect or intimidation, elevating one's standing in the gang, gaining advantage in a rivalry or ongoing conflict, intimidating witnesses, preventing arrests, or framing rival gang members. Examples of the latter include not only co-offending and cooperation among gang members in the commission of a crime but also solo offending, should a "gang gun" be used in the commission of a crime. Second, there is the issue of "specific intent." Denton noted that "nearly every word in this phrase has been parsed by the courts" (19)—"promote" refers to contributing to progress or growth of the gang, "further" refers to helping the gang's progress, and "assist" refers to giving aid or support to the gang. Legal precedent is broad, as co-offending with known gang members and the location of crimes in gang territory are used to establish the nexus, but not absolute, especially when it comes to solo offending and offending outside of gang territory.

Shared Gang Databases

There is no doubt that gang databases are controversial. In Chapter 11, we covered those issues, from measurement to civil liberties, along with the nature and frequency of the use of gang databases. The federal government and eleven states have enacted legislation regulating gang databases, including California, Colorado, Florida, Georgia, Illinois, Minnesota, South Carolina, Tennessee, Texas, Virginia, and Washington. CalGang is the most well-known example of a shared gang database. Section 186.34 of Title 11 in the California Penal Code includes a definition of a gang database:

> Any database accessed by a law enforcement agency that designates a person as a gang member or associate, or includes or points to information, including, but not limited to, fact-based or uncorroborated information, that reflects a designation of that person as gang member or associate.

This section also includes a definition of a shared gang database:

> A gang database that is accessed by an agency or person outside of the agency that created the records that populate the database.

In 2019, for example, there were 78,096 individuals listed in the CalGang database from 196 law enforcement agencies. That means, for example, that information on the 1,573 people recorded as gang members by the Long Beach Police Department could be accessed by other contributing agencies.

A shared gang database exists at the federal level. The federal government established in 34 U.S.C. § 41507 that the attorney general "shall establish a National Gang Intelligence Center and gang information database to be housed at and administered by the Federal Bureau of Investigation to collect, analyze, and disseminate gang activity information" from the FBI, the Bureau of Alcohol, Tobacco, Firearms, and Explosives, the Drug Enforcement Administration, and the U.S. Marshalls Service, among other federal agencies. This includes appropriations of $10 million annually to carry out these activities, along with an annual report to Congress. State and federal agencies share data with each other. For example, a memorandum of understanding was established in 2006 that permitted the California Department of Justice and the U.S. Immigration and Customs Enforcement read-only access to their respective gang databases, CalGang and ICEGangs. That agreement ended in 2016 with the dissolution of the ICEGangs database.

Some states have statutes in place but do not use a shared gang database. Colorado, for example, permits the state's Bureau of Investigation to "develop and maintain a computerized data base system which tracks the whereabouts of identified gang members," yet despite the 2016 legislative declaration codified in C.R.S. § 24-33.5-415.3, we are unaware of whether such a database exists. In March 2019, a group of assembly members in Nevada proposed the creation of the "Nevada Database of Gangs," yet as enacted, this was revised in scope to instead establish "provisions governing the use of a gang database by a local law enforcement agency." Nevada would have been the thirteenth federal/state government with legislation permitting a shared gang database, but they ultimately scaled back their efforts as Assembly Bill 307 was referred to the judiciary committee.

We return to California owing to Assembly Bill 90 (AB90), or the Fair and Accurate Gang Database Act of 2017, which resulted in sweeping reforms to CalGang. San Diego assemblywoman Shirley Weber, who introduced the legislation, claimed that her own son was threatened with entry into CalGang based on circumstantial evidence (Winston 2016). She pushed for an audit of the database, which made headlines because it revealed babies and dead people in the records. AB90 made several notable changes. First, the California Department of Justice became responsible for overseeing the database, removing authority from the CalGang Executive Board. Second, a Gang Database Technical Advisory Committee was created and staffed with eleven individuals, over half of whom represent law enforcement but the rest of whom are not law enforcement, including someone impacted by gang labeling and an immigration representative. Third, new regulations governing the use, operation, and oversight of the database, which required public input and support of empirical research, were introduced. Fourth, the bill codified that records in the database are not to be disclosed for the purposes of military screening, employment, or federal immigration enforcement. Finally, regular auditing of the database and the production of annual reports were required, including reporting at the agency level the number of people, the number of petitioned and purged removals, and demographics broken down by age, race/ethnicity, and gender.

Reforming shared gang databases will not decrease the need for or use of gang intelligence. After all, the absence of legislation on gang databases does not mean that local law enforcement agencies do not maintain such databases. The New York City Police Department, for example, has a well-developed criminal intelligence apparatus that also includes a gang database, despite the fact that the State of New York lacks legislation (Trujillo and Vitale 2019). But it does appear that legislation like AB90 could hamper the sharing of gang intelligence across agencies. Between 2017 and 2019, the number of agencies contributing to CalGang fell from 214 to 196. The number of individuals listed in CalGang also fell from 104,000 to 78,000, which likely reflects rules around purging. California agencies added 6,575 records to the database in 2019, but 18,548 were automatically purged because they exceeded retention periods of five years. In response to allegations of misuse and falsification by its officers, the Los Angeles Police Department announced that it would no longer enter records into CalGang. The likely consequence is the retrenchment of shared gang databases, with agencies continuing their local documentation of gang members and sharing information with neighboring agencies on an informal basis.

Gang Sentencing Enhancements

Sentencing enhancements prolong incarceration terms for criminal convictions based on the conduct or status of the offender. Hate crime laws are perhaps the most well-known sentencing enhancements. Except Arkansas, South Carolina, and Wyoming, the remaining forty-seven states and the federal government enhance the criminal sentences of offenders convicted of crimes that are motivated by bias, such as race/ethnicity, religion, and sex/gender. For example, the Matthew Shepard and James Byrd Jr. Hate Crimes Prevention Act of 2009, which expanded the class of victims—gender, gender identity, sexual orientation, and disability—protected under hate crime laws, enhances incarceration terms by ten years or life sentences.

Gang sentencing enhancements bear a strong resemblance to hate crime laws. Table 13.1 indicates the existence of gang enhancements in thirty-two states and the federal government. United States Code § 521 establishes that the sentence of a person convicted of a federal felony involving a controlled substance, violence or attempted violence, or a conspiracy may be increased by up ten years if the offender (1) participates in a criminal street gang, (2) intends to promote or further felonious activities of the gang or his or her position in the gang, and (3) has been convicted of various federal or state offenses in the last five years. The federal gang enhancement thus combines the conduct and status of the offender. While all of the thirty-three governmental jurisdictions enhance sentences for felony conviction, five also enhance sentences for misdemeanors. For example, the State of Idaho, as set out in § 18-8503, enhances misdemeanor convictions by "an additional term of imprisonment in the county jail for not more than one (1) year" for criminal gang activity.

California's STEP act, which first established the use of gang sentencing enhancements, has undergone changes resulting in greater punishment for gang members. As Section 186.22 (b) is currently written, felonies committed "for the benefit of, at the direction of, or in association with any criminal street gang" with the "specific intent to promote, further, or assist in any criminal conduct by gang members" could result in the following:

- An additional term of two, three, or four years at the court's discretion
- An additional five years if the felony is serious (as defined in subdivision [c] of Section 1192.7, which outlines forty-two crimes)
- An additional ten years if the felony is violent (as defined in subdivision [c] of Section 667.5, which outlines twenty-three crimes)

Yoshino (2008) highlighted how STEP originally added terms of one, two, or three years, and then in 1994 the lowest term was increased to sixteen months. When California voters approved Proposition 21 in 2000, Yoshino reported, the "gang enhancement terms changed drastically" (119), upping the additional terms to two, three, and four years while also upping terms for serious and violent felonies to five and ten years. Those convicted of gang-related homicide were also made eligible for the death penalty.

The impacts of gang sentencing enhancements are largely unknown. California's Legislative Analyst's Office examined the proposed fiscal effects of Proposition 21 and estimated that it could result in one-time costs of $70 million to construct facilities and ongoing annual costs of about $30 million to pay to incarcerate those convicted of these offenses. These numbers are not insubstantial, especially with the dot-com recession that devastated California's budget in the years following the act's passage. About 6 percent of prisoners in California were subject to a gang sentencing enhancement according to a report by *The Guardian* (Clayton 2019). That said, gang enhancements pale in comparison to the prevalence and frequency of other forms of sentencing enhancements. Dagenais and colleagues (2019) analyzed nearly eight thousand cases from criminal charges resulting in an imprisonment sentence in the San Francisco District Attorney's Office between 2005 and 2017. They found that sentencing enhancements appeared in 13 percent of cases yet accounted for 26 percent of time served. Gang enhancements, in contrast, accounted for only about 4 percent of all sentencing enhancements and enhancement time served. Mandatory minimum sentences, such as three strikes and prior convictions, accounted for the bulk of sentencing enhancements and additional time served.

The biggest question surrounding gang enhancements is whether they reduce crime and violence. The public may be willing to stomach the cost if they are effective. Insiders are skeptical, however. A judge in Arizona interviewed by Zatz and Krecker (2003) shortly after the enactment of anti-gang legislation commented that gang enhancements are supposed to be a deterrent, a deterrent to gang activity. [Interviewer: do you think it works that way?] No, I do not believe it. I don't believe that sentencing enhancements of that kind are a deterrent to gang activity any more than I believe that capital punishment is a deterrent to murder. (186–187)

We are unaware of evidence that supports or refutes the judge's point in Arizona or elsewhere. Although unrelated to gang enhancements, Owens (2009) found that changes to Maryland's sentencing guidelines, which reduced recommended sentences of twenty-three- to twenty-five-year-olds on the basis of excluding juvenile criminal history, thus shortening imprisonment terms by over two hundred days, corresponded with 1.5 additional FBI Part I index crimes per person per year. Sentencing enhancements thus maintained an incapacitation effect, not a deterrent effect, one that likely applies to gang members.

Gang Participation and Recruitment

The most controversial aspect of California's STEP Act was the creation of a substantive offense category for participation in a gang. In other words, STEP criminalized gang membership. Section 186.22 (a) of the California Penal Code states,

> Any person who actively participates in any criminal street gang with knowledge that its members engage in, or have engaged in, a pattern of criminal gang activity, and who willfully promotes, furthers, or assists in any felonious criminal conduct by member of that gang, shall be punished by imprisonment in a county jail for a period not to exceed one year, or by imprisonment in the state prison for 16 months, or two or three years.

It did not take long for civil liberties groups to attack what they viewed as an egregious intrusion into the freedom of association. Molina (1992) referred to the gang participation law as unconstitutional because it could not withstand challenges of strict scrutiny (i.e., the state's interest in fighting crime does not permit violating civil liberties), overbreadth (i.e., punishing constitutionally protected behaviors), and vagueness (i.e., discriminatorily applied to certain groups). Other states were unconcerned with these issues, as another twelve opted to follow California's lead. Yet as Yoshino (2008) observed, this component of STEP is used infrequently by prosecutors. The California Penal Code bars multiple punishments for the same conduct. In other words, the evidence used to activate the "active participation" (i.e., 186.22 [a]) offense cannot be redundant to the evidence used to activate the "conduct enhancement" (i.e., 186.22 [b]), unless it were demonstrated that the objectives for the two offenses differed (Denton 2014, 15).

Anti-gang legislation also criminalizes recruitment into gangs. Targeting the selection process into gangs is critical to undermining their capacity to exist in the face of convictions and shootings that thin their ranks. While gang prevention programs such as G.R.E.A.T. aim to accomplish this through education and skill-building, the anti-gang legislation found in thirty-six states seeks to disrupt pathways into gangs by punishing recruitment. In California, for example, Section 186.26 (a) states,

> Any person who solicits or recruits another to actively participate in a criminal street gang . . . with the intent that the person solicited or recruited participate in a pattern of criminal street gang activity . . . or with the intent that the person solicited or recruited promote, further, or assist in any felonious conduct by members of the criminal street gang, shall be punished by imprisonment in the state prison for 16 months, or two or three years.

California further codifies the use of threats and physical violence in gang recruitment and enhances punishments if the targeted person is a minor. It is unclear how commonly gang recruitment laws are prosecuted. Denton's (2014) exhaustive review of legal precedent made only passing mention of 186.26 (a), suggesting that recruitment has not been prosecuted or has been prosecuted but not challenged constitutionally. We think the former is the likely scenario. This may have been legislation that sounded good on the floor of a political arena but did not translate so well to action in the courtroom.

Repurposed Gang Legislation

There are two broad categories of legislation—criminal enterprise and public nuisance laws—that have been repurposed to combat gangs. That is to say, the original intention of these laws was not to target gangs, but they have been appropriated by prosecutors for this purpose.

Criminal Enterprise Laws

Criminal enterprise laws used to target gangs include the Racketeer Influenced and Corrupt Organizations act (RICO, 18 U.S.C. §§ 1961–1968) and the Continuing Criminal Enterprise statute (CCE, 21 U.S.C. § 848), as well as the Violent Crimes in Aid of Racketeering Act (VICAR, 18 U.S.C. § 1959). Both RICO and CCE were enacted by the federal government in 1970 and target criminal enterprises that engage in a pattern of criminal activity over time. Whereas RICO focused generally on organized crime, CCE was more narrowly tailored to target drug-trafficking organizations. Both laws involve criminal penalties as well as forfeiture of ill-gotten assets. As many as thirty-three states and territories have since followed suit (Floyd 1998), enacting what are termed "little" or "baby" RICO laws that are equally broad as if not broader than the federal legislation.

The criminal penalties for violating criminal enterprise laws are substantial—twenty years of imprisonment for participating in a racketeering conspiracy or continuing criminal enterprise. A RICO conspiracy offense, for example, requires the government to prove five elements beyond a reasonable doubt:

1. A criminal enterprise exists, which may be formal (e.g., multinational corporations and labor unions) or informal (e.g., affinity groups and unincorporated associations); the existence of this enterprise is demonstrated through a shared purpose, relationships among those in the enterprise, and longevity as a continuing unit.
2. The enterprise's collective activities affected, however minimally, interstate or foreign commerce, which refers to the movement of money, goods, services, or persons across state or country lines and can be demonstrated through drug trafficking, extortion, or robbery.
3. A conspirator was employed by or associated with the enterprise during some period of its existence, which is proved through actions that establish joining or connecting with the enterprise.
4. The defendant conducted or participated in the affairs of the enterprise, which involves at least one conspirator (who may be the defendant) involved in the operation or management of the enterprise.
5. The defendant agreed that a conspirator would engage in a pattern of racketeering activity, which includes committing, causing, or aiding and abetting two or more acts with a nexus to the enterprise, at least one of which occurred in the last ten years.

The government need not prove that a defendant maintained complete knowledge of the details of the conspiracy, nor must all conspirators share the same knowledge or role. Agreements among conspirators can be inferred from their collective behavior, such as working together in the commission of a crime or planning such crimes. CCE bears a strong resemblance to RICO, albeit focused on occupying a position in an enterprise of five or more people engaged in continued felonious drug activity. Both RICO and CCE, which casts a broad net with its conspiratorial legal focus, are exceptionally powerful tools the government has at its disposal.

RICO and CCE were not designed with street and prison gangs in mind. As Wheatley (2008, 84) noted, the Mafia was the "archetypal enterprise under RICO," and indeed, various organized crime groups have been subject to RICO prosecutions, including the Bonanno, Gambino, and Lucchese crime families as well as groups as diverse as the Chicago Outfit (a traditional family-based organized crime group) and Hells Angels (a motorcycle gang heavily involved in narcotics trafficking). CCE, in contrast, has been used to incarcerate Felix "the Cat" Mitchell and Joaquin "El Chapo" Guzman, consistent with its aims to target "drug kingpins." Applications of RICO and CCE to gangs did not occur until well over a decade after they were signed into law by President Nixon. Truman (1995) attributed the first application of RICO to *United States v. Louie* (1985), a case involving twenty-five defendants of the Ghost Shadows Chinese street gang in Manhattan, and the first application of CCE to *United States v. Jackson* (1992), a case involving crack cocaine dealing in Charlotte.

The early application of criminal enterprise laws to gangs did not exactly open the floodgates, although the impetus was there. The rise of gang violence was a strong motivation. RICO was deemed to be highly successful in dismantling the Mafia, emboldening the federal government to shift its interests to "a new public enemy" (Blumenstein 2009, 216). Moreover, there was increased availability of federal manpower, as M. Klein (1995, 167) noted:

> Attorney General William Barr (George Bush's last attorney general) [and President Trump's last attorney general] assigned more [than] one hundred FBI agents to street gang control, following the agents' release from cold war duty when the Soviet Union collapsed. These agents knew nothing about street gangs because they had had no experience with them. But they knew about conspiracies and federal interstate statutes such as RICO and other antiracketeering laws.

It is hard to fully enumerate charges or convictions of gangs under RICO and CCE laws—that information simply is not reported (Blumenstein 2009, 217; Woods 2011, 311). The United States Sentencing Commission reports 1,104 people convicted of extortion or racketeering between 2015 and 2019. Of course, that does not guarantee convictions of gang members. C. Johnson and colleagues (1995) surveyed prosecutors' offices about their approaches to gangs, finding that 17 percent of large-county prosecutors and 10 percent of small-county prosecutor have used RICO for gang prosecutions, while 36 percent of the 191 prosecutor's offices reported using drug kingpin statutes against gang members. Simply because a prosecutor's office uses criminal enterprise laws does not tell us how often they are used.

N. Moore and Williams (2011) and Brotherton and Barrios (2004) chronicled RICO charges against the El Rukns in Chicago and Latin Kings in New York City, respectively. Blumenstein (2009) documented thirty instances of federal prosecutors bringing RICO charges against gang members between 2000 and 2007, including gangs in the following states:

1. California: 18th Street, Aryan Brotherhood, Florencia 13, Mexican Mafia (Los Angeles), Mexican Mafia (San Diego), Nuestra Familia, Vineland Boys, and West Myrtle Street Gang
2. Florida: Latin Kings
3. Georgia: Brownside Locos and Sur-13
4. Kansas: Crips
5. Maryland: MS-13
6. Massachusetts: Stonehurst Gang
7. Nevada: Crips and Hells Angels
8. New Jersey: Double II Bloods
9. New York: Boot Camp Gang, Brighton Brigade, Elk Block Gang, and Jungle Junkies
10. Oklahoma: Hoover Crips
11. Tennessee: MS-13
12. Texas: Texas Syndicate (Dallas), Texas Syndicate (Houston), and Texas Syndicate (McAllen)
13. Utah: King Mafia Associates, Solders of the Aryan Culture, and Tiny Oriental Posse
14. Virginia: Dragon Family
15. Washington: Hells Angels

Using broader search criteria, data sources, and time period (2001 to 2010), Woods (2011) identified 160 prosecutions brought against 115 gangs and 2,915 gang members across the states. Among Black gangs, this included nineteen cases against Bloods and eight cases against Crips. Among Latino gangs, this included eight cases against the Latin Kings, twelve against MS-13, and six against the Texas Syndicate. Among White gangs, this included three cases against organized crime groups (e.g., Armenian Power and Chicago Outfit), eleven against outlaw motorcycle groups (e.g., Hells Angels and Pagans), and seven targeting prison gangs (e.g., Aryan Brotherhood and Nazi Low Riders). Overall, it is apparent that criminal enterprise laws are used against gangs, but we lack a clear sense of the frequency with which they are used, much less the motivation for targeting any one gang among the thirty thousand or so that exist in the United States.

Are criminal enterprise laws effective? In summarizing the state of knowledge on various forms of anti-gang legislation, Bjerregaard (2015, 361) noted,

One of the most troubling aspects of these approaches is that although many extol the virtues of these approaches, very little empirical research has been conducted examining either the extent to which they are being utilized and/or their actual effectiveness.

The evidence is sparsest when it comes to RICO and CCE. Indeed, Bjerregaard's (2015, 362–364) table on statutory and judicial approaches to gangs does not contain a single empirical study examining the effectiveness of criminal enterprise laws. Proponents of RICO argue that it acts as a deterrent for gangs and gang members. Punishment for participating in a RICO enterprise is more severe than the penalties for the underlying predicate crimes; thus, criminal sentences can be severe. However, critics argue that the threat of long federal sentences may simply encourage more coerced guilty pleas and false confessions (Blumenstein 2009). They also challenge the practice on constitutional grounds, arguing that RICO "federalizes" criminal activity that traditionally has been prosecuted by the states. The fact that police disproportionately target Black and Latino gangs (Chapter 8) also has some commentators worried about the inequitable impact of RICO prosecutions across races (Blumenstein 2009).

While there are anecdotal reports of crime declining in the aftermath of a federal indictment, the evidence does not rise to social science standards (see Chapter 14's discussion of research designs capable of detecting a program effect). Blumenstein (2009, 217–218) reported that Representative Tom Davis, ranking member of the U.S. House Committee on Oversight and Government Reform in 2007, "requested that the Government Accounting Office undertake a study of the effectiveness of RICO prosecutions against gangs to determine whether there may be ways to alter the law to make it more efficacious." We are unaware of the results of the request, nor can we find a study documenting such an effect.

Public Nuisance Laws

Civil gang injunctions rely on public nuisance laws found in state civil codes. We highlight the State of California, namely Civil Code § 3479 and § 3480, where civil gang injunctions originated and the state where they have been used most often. A public nuisance is "injurious to health" and "interferes with the comfortable enjoyment of life or property" for "an entire community or neighborhood." Local police and prosecutors collaborate to establish the gang as a nuisance by (1) identifying a geographic area the gang claims as territory or set space, (2) gathering written declarations from police officers who patrol the area and residents and business owners in the area about gang activity, and (3) collecting the criminal histories of gang members to be listed in the injunction.

The prosecutor uses this information to file a civil lawsuit against the gang and its named members to obtain a restraining order, which, if granted, prohibits a wide range of criminal and noncriminal activity in the injunction zone; such things as congregating, using social media, and riding together in cars, among others, are prohibited. The manifest goal of such programs is to disrupt the routine activities of gang members and remove gang members, especially concentrations of gang members, from neighborhoods. Such actions, it is believed, provide residents and business owners with a respite from the violence and disorder created by gangs. In addition, it is thought that community development may be more likely once gang member concentrations are reduced. Because the essence of gang life is concentrated social interaction, civil gang injunctions seek to disrupt this process. But like many interventions, the internal logic does not always stand up to external scrutiny.

O'Deane's (2011) book *Gang Injunctions and Abatement* charts the origins and evolution of gang injunctions. The application of gang injunctions began in Los Angeles in 1982, when the city attorney filed suit against three gangs—Dogtown, Primera Flats, and 62nd Street East Coast Crips—as unincorporated associations. That lawsuit focused narrowly on gang graffiti, an activity that already violates the law; many have therefore viewed the civil gang injunction against the Playboy Gangster Crips in 1987 as the original since it sought to prohibit legal activity. The injunction targeted an area then known as "Cadillac-Corning" on the west side of Los Angeles, equidistant from the skyscrapers of downtown and the beaches of Santa Monica. In reconstructing the origins of this injunction, Muniz (2014) argued that the selection of this gang and this area was highly racialized since it was close to affluent and White neighborhoods seeking to protect their cultural and economic interests.

The operative word in civil gang injunctions is *civil*—prosecutors rely on civil rather than criminal codes to target gangs. The significance of this legal strategy is threefold. First, the standard of guilt is lower in civil than in criminal proceedings (i.e., preponderance of the evidence versus beyond a reasonable doubt). Second, there is no right to counsel or speedy trial in civil court (although see Werdegar 1999), which takes on added significance in light of the low socioeconomic standing of most gang members. Third, there is little recourse for individuals when they are named in an injunction, which is typically permanent (Crawford 2009). Violating the prohibited activities listed in the restraining order can result in being held in contempt of court, a misdemeanor resulting in jail time and/or a $1,000 fine—an immediate sanction imposed on enjoined gang members. The original injunction against the Playboy Gangster Crips sought to prohibit legal activities in the injunction zone, including wearing gang-related clothing, publicly associating with enjoined gang members, and violating evening curfews. While a judge ultimately declared the prohibition of these activities as overbroad (O'Deane 2011, 322), supporting the ACLU's legal contestation of the injunction, the groundwork was laid for future attempts by local prosecutors. In 1997, the California Supreme Court, in *People ex rel. Gallo v. Acuna*, overturned an appeals court ruling that only criminal conduct could be prohibited under public nuisance law.

Civil gang injunctions grew in popularity through the 1990s and the 2000s. O'Deane (2011, 316) reported that over 150 injunctions in California have led to targeting 7,394 gang members and 250 square miles as "safety zones." It is important to highlight that the prohibited activities, such as loitering and association, only apply to individuals named in the injunction *and* occurring within the safety zone. This is why the size of the injunction zones is highly contested. For example, an injunction in Oxnard, California, *People v. Colonia Chiques*, included 6.6 square miles, or nearly one-quarter of the city, as a safety zone—an area remarkably greater than the size of territories observed among gangs.

While Southern California typically receives outsized attention, a civil gang injunction in Orange Cove, California, ranks among the most controversial because the Fresno County District Attorney's Office established a safety zone that covered all two square miles of the small agricultural town—about the size of a university campus. Orange Cove, with a population of about ten thousand residents, nearly all of whom are Latino and nearly half of whom live in poverty, is among the smallest municipalities subject to a civil gang injunction. The geographic parameters of the safety zone meant that the twenty-two members of Varrio Orange Cove Rifa Bulldogs and sixteen members of Orange Cove Sur would have to migrate to the fields and orchards surrounding the city to avoid the conditions of the injunction.

The evidence suggests that, on balance, civil gang injunctions reduce crime in the safety zones without displacing crime to the outlying areas. The most definitive results are from the work of Ridgeway and colleagues (2018), who studied the effect of implementing forty-six civil gang injunctions in Los Angeles over two decades (1993–2013), crediting them with long-term reductions in total crime, especially aggravated assaults. What explains these reductions?

Maxson, Hennigan, and Sloane (2005) conducted surveys of residents in San Bernardino eighteen months before and six months after the implementation of a gang injunction. They found a mixed bag of results that partially supported social disorganization, deterrence, and deindividuation (i.e., increasing personal rather than group responsibility) theories. Residents in the injunction zone reported less gang presence, intimidation, and fear of gang members in the short term. However, except fear of crime, there was little evidence to support intermediate and long-term outcome goals, such as reductions in perceptions of disorder, violent and property victimization, social cohesion, information social control, and police relations. Hennigan and Sloan (2013) further advanced this line of inquiry by interviewing 416 young people—27 percent of whom were gang-involved—in two areas subject to a gang injunction and one area as a control group northeast and east of downtown Los Angeles. The twist was that one area contained a gang injunction that was group- and suppression-based, while the other favored individuation coupled with social services, the latter of which was associated with weakening identification with gangs, which in turn was related to lower criminal activity.

Valasik (2014), in contrast, used police gang data in Hollenbeck to find that civil gang injunctions disrupted the patterns of associations among gang members, who were less likely to hang out and associate in public spaces and have encounters with police. This, in turn, corresponded with changes in the nature of gang violence, which moved "indoors" and resulted in more intra-gang homicides. Valasik interpreted these findings in the routine activity perspective, as the opportunity structure for violence—perpetration and victimization—shifted with the retreat from the street. Bichler et al.'s (2019) social network study of Bloods and Crips in California in fact found that gang injunctions *increased* gang violence by disrupting the social order of the neighborhood, fracturing existing gang structures, and creating uncertainty around the established inter-gang hierarchy. They found that the tool unintentionally intensified the need for gangs to fight for control and dominance of the area under injunction.

These mixed findings suggest that civil gang injunctions are not a panacea. They are expensive and time-consuming to put into place; they have a high opportunity cost. Grogger (2005) noted that a civil gang injunction required a full year of a Los Angeles assistant prosecutor's time at $100,000–$150,000. That must be considered in tandem with law enforcement canvassing the community for written declarations of the gang as public nuisance. Then there is the question of enforcement once the injunction is implemented. Grogger juxtaposed the startup and enforcement expenses against the savings from crime reduction, concluding that while it is hard to pin down accurate numbers, the benefits likely exceed the costs.

Of course, economics are not the final word on the matter, nor are gains in social order and reductions in crime, as there are legitimate threats to civil liberties associated with gang injunctions. Werdegar (1999) contended that the California Supreme Court erred in their *Acuna* ruling, in terms of their handling of vagueness (i.e., who is and is not a gang member) and application of guilt by association (i.e., all are punished for the actions of some). Furthermore, while the majority opinion in *Acuna* contended that gang injunctions were not overly broad since they applied only to the thirty-eight gang members of Varrio Sureno Locos/Treces in the Rocksprings neighborhood of San Jose, many remain concerned about the criminalization of legal behavior and its racialized application.

Bloch and Meyer (2019), for example, opened their article by highlighting how Peter Arellano violated a court order for associating with a fellow gang member in the safety zone in the Echo Park neighborhood of Los Angeles. That gang member was Arellano's own father. And in early 2018, all of the 7,300 individuals listed in a civil gang injunction in Los Angeles were released from their conditions owing to due process violations claimed by the ACLU and supported by a district court judge, with Long Beach and Orange County following suit shortly thereafter (Queally 2018). The future of civil gang injunctions is highly uncertain. Owing to the substantial restrictions they place on individual liberty (Caldwell 2009), crime reduction alone is not enough to overcome political opposition.

Auxiliary Gang Legislation: The 1994 Crime Bill

The Violent Crime Control and Law Enforcement Act of 1994, known as the Crime Bill, was signed by President Bill Clinton on September 13, 1994. Then-senator Joe Biden, who helped spearhead the Crime Bill, was seated just behind Clinton in a show of support as the president delivered his speech on the South Lawn at the White House, declaring:

> Today the bickering stops, the era of excuses is over, the law-abiding citizens of our country have made their voices heard. Never again should Washington put politics and party above law and order.

And with the stroke of a pen, President Clinton signed into law what is the largest bill on crime in the history of the United States, which included nearly $11 billion for local and state law enforcement, $10 billion for prison construction, $7 billion for prevention programs, and $3 billion for federal law enforcement. Bipartisan agreement was reached to ban certain types of assault weapons, expand the death penalty, implement sex offender registries, impose three-strikes sentences for serious (federal) offenders, implement juvenile transfer to criminal court, and support victims of crime. Altogether, the Crime Bill codified a wide-ranging approach to crime control, with thirty-three separate titles.

Gangs were not the central feature of the Crime Bill, but they did factor into it prominently. With the homicide rate at nearly 10 per 100,000 in the early 1990s and gangs proliferating across the United States (see Chapter 1), gang violence was fresh in the minds of the public, including President Clinton, who made three statements about gangs in his speech (emphasis added):

First:

> *Gangs* and drugs have taken over our streets and undermined our schools. Every day we read about somebody else who has literally gotten away with murder.

Second:

[The funding] will be used to give our young people something to say yes to, places where they can go after school where they are safe, where they can do constructive things that will help them to build their lives, where teachers replace *gang leaders* as role models.

Third:

Even when we keep our schools open late and give our children an alternative to drugs and *gangs*, your children won't learn the difference between right and wrong unless you teach them and they're in those schools when they're open.

In the 356 pages of the Crime Bill, the word *gang* or *gangs* appeared forty-one times. Gangs were the sole focus of two titles, X and XV. The significance of gangs to federal legislators, the U.S. Department of Justice, state prosecutors, and federal, state, and local law enforcement was codified in the Crime Bill.

"Criminal Street Gangs" were addressed in Title XV. There were seven subsections covering topics that included defining and punishing criminal street gangs, adult prosecution of juvenile offenders, the addition of anti-gang Byrne-grant funding objectives, mentoring programs, juvenile antidrug and anti-gang grants in federally assisted low-income housing, gang investigation coordination and information collection, and multijurisdictional gang task forces. The Crime Bill did little to ameliorate issues related to definitions of gangs and in fact may have helped institutionalize differences between law enforcement (criminal street gangs) and corrections (security threat groups) as well as among academic, school, and community groups. The funding for gang suppression that followed gave suppression-oriented efforts primacy in the response to gangs, despite efforts to integrate intervention and prevention with suppression. There was no method for integrating community members and their perspectives into the formulation and implementation of the comprehensive responses to gangs. The Office of Community Oriented Policing, known as the COPS office, funded law enforcement task forces in fifteen cities through the Anti-Gang Initiative. Each task force was to be in a single jurisdiction, to be led by local law enforcement, and to include a research partner. The addition of a research partner was a somewhat unique requirement, one that would come to be a staple of many other gang and criminal justice interventions.

Title X was devoted to the Gang Resistance Education and Training program, or G.R.E.A.T. Whereas the subsections of Title XV were largely enforcement and prosecution oriented, support for G.R.E.A.T. in Title X was preventive in orientation. Title X included explicit language for the institutionalization and expansion of G.R.E.A.T., giving it a "home" in federal law enforcement (the Bureau of Alcohol, Tobacco, and Firearms), and provided a common structure for implementation in no fewer than fifty sites, as tasked in the Crime Bill, with over $45 million in appropriations through 2000. Perhaps the most distinctive feature of G.R.E.A.T. was its leaders' willingness to leverage other federal agencies (e.g., the National Institute of Justice) to fund multiple comprehensive, multisite evaluations of the program. This is an example of the direct influence of the Crime Bill on responding to gangs and is a unique aspect of the bill because of its focus on prevention before the peak age of gang membership. Today, G.R.E.A.T. still functions, with over thirteen thousand officers having provided curriculum and training to over six million students. This is clearly a legacy of the Crime Bill in responding to gangs.

The Crime Bill certainly helped institutionalize the presence of gangs in the minds of the public and law enforcement. It also provided support for continued attention to the gang problem. There was an explosion of basic and applied research on gangs after the passage of the Crime Bill. We see this as coincidental, with the exception of G.R.E.A.T. A subsection of Title XV called for the FBI to "acquire and collect information on incidents of gang violence for inclusion in its annual uniform crime report." But beyond the inclusion of poorly defined measures of "gang/organized crime-related" and "youth gang activity" in the Supplementary Homicide Reports (SHR), little of the data specified was ever collected. Few scholars use the SHR data to study gang homicide, instead opting for the data collected as part of the National Youth Gang Survey (as we have throughout this book and our past research; Decker and Pyrooz 2010b; Pyrooz 2012b). The National Institute of Justice added targeted solicitations on gang research and filled an important role in fostering basic research as well as evaluations of programmatic and criminal justice responses to gangs. The access that was created for researchers to collect primary data and use archived secondary data seems to be an unintended consequence of the Crime Bill. Following the COPS office, many law enforcement initiatives included a mandate to have a research component or a research partner (e.g., Youth Firearms Violence Initiative, Project Safe Neighborhoods, Safe Futures, and OJJDP Comprehensive Strategy).

There are unintended consequences of the Crime Bill relevant to gangs; two of the most prominent are mass incarceration and disproportionate minority contact. Targeting gangs and gang membership clearly played a role in mass incarceration and increasing contacts with criminal justice for Blacks and Latinos, demographic groups overrepresented in gangs (especially in law enforcement data). Gang members are more likely to be subject to federal prosecution and receive (gang and gun) sentence enhancements and mandatory minimums. *The Guardian* reported that 6 percent of prisoners in California were subject to a gang sentencing enhancement, 92 percent of whom were Blacks or Latinos

(Clayton 2019). Findings such as these are what led Zatz and Krecker (2003) to conclude that anti-gang legislation and initiatives are racialized rather than race-neutral policies.

In sum, the Crime Bill had profound effects on programming and law enforcement approaches to gangs. While some of the Crime Bill's provisions dealing with gangs were not fully implemented, particularly those having to do with prevention and intervention, those that were led to several important changes in the response to gangs and violent crime more generally. This was true in several specific areas: an expansion of gang task forces, increased federal attention to what had been primarily a local problem, institutionalization of gangs as an object of criminal justice response and research, and criminal gang sentencing enhancements. The focus on gangs also likely contributed to the problems of mass incarceration and disproportionate minority confinement. Many other developments in understanding and responding to gangs had little or nothing to do with the Crime Bill, beyond coincidental timing. The legacy of the Crime Bill regarding gangs produced increased identification and focus on the part of the criminal justice system, largely through policing, prosecution, and incarceration. The attempt to balance suppression with intervention and prevention has proved challenging, from its earliest days in the 1960s to the present. The G.R.E.A.T. program remains a very important legacy of the Crime Bill in the area of gangs. Aggressive suppression efforts focusing on gang members by law enforcement and prosecution helped fuel mass incarceration and, in some circumstances, aggravated police-community tensions and led to racialized enforcement practices.

Gangs and the Courtroom

The crimes committed by gang members typically are not complicated or sophisticated (see Chapter 6). Although the FBI has warned that "street gangs have become more involved in white-collar crimes" (National Gang Intelligence Center 2015, 12), it remains the exception to observe gangs or gang members engaging in complex financial crimes, highly technical cybercrimes, or large-scale conspiracies. Despite this, many of the characteristics of gangs make the prosecution of their criminal cases very difficult. There is often a lack of solid information about motives, which is part of the reason why researchers use homicides involving gang members as perpetrators or victims as a close proxy (Maxson and Klein 1996). The group nature of most gang crime provides a "mask" and a "shield" to diffuse and deflect culpability. There is also a lack of cooperation by both victims and witnesses in gang crimes, which can make prosecution especially difficult. A parallel system of rules and regulations means that street justice trumps criminal justice (Leovy 2015; see also Chapter 8). Many victims of gang crimes are intimidated and unwilling to come forward and report their crimes, much less appear in court. A 1992 survey of 191 prosecutors' offices (C. Johnson et al. 1995) indicated that victim and witness cooperation and intimidation were the top two problems they faced in gang-related cases.

John Anderson, at the time assistant district attorney in Orange County (California), shared a textbook example of witness intimidation. A gang-related mass shooting in Garden Grove, California, in the early 1990s resulted in two deaths (a seventeen-year-old boy and four-year-old boy) along with three teenage girls seriously wounded:

> The only witness to come forward was "Ralph," an older, self-proclaimed former member of the victim gang who was living in the perpetrator gang's neighborhood at the time of the crime. He provided critical statements to the police and necessary testimony during the jury trial in the case. Four gang members were charged in the drive-by. . . . Prior to trial, relatives were told that Ralph would be killed if he continued to cooperate with the case or testify. Gang members frequently drove down his street, staring at him or members of his family. He was twice assaulted in the courthouse and a few times outside his house. One time he was stabbed. His wife was also verbally and physically accosted on occasion. His new car was firebombed. Each time he testified, several members of the defendants' gang crowded into the courtroom. For years following his cooperation, pieces of cheese were thrown onto the lawn in front of his house. (J. Anderson 2007, 7)

In most instances, witnesses lack the audacity of people like Ralph, instead succumbing to the intimidation so easily facilitated by the collective behaviors and normative orientations of gangs. Miethe and McCorkle (1997) compared 168 felony gang cases to 202 felony non-gang cases in Clark County, Nevada, and found that the gang cases were six times more likely to result in the dismissal of charges. They attributed these findings to the aforementioned challenges of gang cases, leading prosecutors to overcharge in the hope of securing a plea agreement. What are prosecutors to do in order to combat the influence of gangs in such cases?

One development has been the creation of specialized prosecution units with district or state attorney's offices. Los Angeles was a pioneer in this regard. With support from the federal government, the Los Angeles District Attorney's Office established such a unit devoted to violent gang crimes in 1979, known as Operation Hardcore (M. Klein 1995). Prosecutors in this unit only handled gang-related cases. Their caseloads were reduced in order to respond to the challenges of such cases. Additional investigative support was also provided, such as funds for witness relocation. Each gang case was handled by prosecutors vertically rather than horizontally, which meant that a prosecutor would see the case through all stages of processing, not simply hand off the case as it advanced from the bail hearing to indictment to plea bargaining to trial and sentencing. Prosecutors would begin their work earlier, too. Rather than wait for the police to bring them a case, prosecutors would help draw up search warrants and assist in serving them. This is a more proactive rather than reactive approach, one that should yield dividends in producing positive case outcomes. Drawing on the original report of Dahmann (1982), Pyrooz, Wolfe, and Spohn (2011) examined charging decisions in 614 homicide cases before and after the creation of the specialized unit. They found that charges were dismissed 22 percent of the time if prosecuted by Operation Hardcore, compared to 51 percent of the time if not. These results, combined with Dahmann's findings that the unit generated more convictions and prison commitments, indicate that the specialized prosecutor's units may be effective in combating the challenges posed by gang cases. Of the 118 and 73 prosecutors' offices in large (serving populations over 250,000) and small (50,000 to 250,000) jurisdictions, 32 percent and 5 percent maintained a specialized gang unit, respectively (C. Johnson et al. 1995, 199). We are unaware of more recent data on trends in the structuring of prosecutors' offices to address gang cases.

While it is true that gang cases present great challenges to prosecutors, it would be inaccurate to contend that gang members maintain an advantage in the courtroom. In fact, it is quite the opposite. Anti-gang legislation favors the prosecution, not the defense. In recounting his observations of gangs in court, M. Klein (1997, 518) held:

> With special laws, special prosecution procedures, and special police experts, the prosecution's general theme in gang cases is simple and straightforward: prove the defendant's gang affiliation and thereby increase the likelihood of conviction and of sentence enhancement. Gang membership *per se* is taken as evidence of guilt and of commitment to a career of crime.

Criminal sentencing enhancements targeting gang-related crimes are a powerful bargaining chip for prosecutors. Furthermore, the specialized units have yielded tremendous knowledge about how to best prosecute gang cases, from vertical prosecution to attaining special search warrants to declining plea bargaining to resources for witness protection. Expert witnesses are called on by the state, such as police officers in gang units. As M. Klein (1997, 518) noted, "there are few defense experts whose profession it is to know the local gangs as the gang police do." Criminologists (like ourselves) can speak to patterns and trends but rarely to the particulars of a single gang. A judge ruled that Klein, whom gang researchers fondly refer to as the "Old Silverback" owing to his legacy of contributions to knowledge on gangs (Maxson 2015), was unqualified to serve as an expert on a gang case.

Surprisingly, there is little empirical research on how gang affiliation is used in the courtroom, including its consequences for case outcomes. In late 2007 and early 2008, Yoshino (2008) interviewed three deputy district attorneys, four deputy public defenders, and three law enforcement officers in Los Angeles about the STEP act. Public defenders felt that district attorneys used gang enhancements excessively, persuaded by the expansion of eligible crimes and the incentive of prolonged prison sentences, which a deputy district attorney also attributed to organizational pressure to use enhancements (133). Both defense and prosecuting attorneys agreed that gang enhancements can predispose jurors to negative appraisals of defendants, which, as a result of *People v. Hernandez* (2004), led to bifurcation of trials on the enhancement charge. Gang enhancements also altered the plea-bargaining calculus. One public defender indicated that "any hint of gang activity" would lead to advising his client to accept a prosecutor's offer, "even if no gang enhancement has been filed or if the case otherwise appears beatable" (139). The gang allegation was too prejudicial and the sentencing enhancement too consequential to take the risk (Eisen et al. 2013).

D. Walker and Cesar (2020) expected that gang affiliation should produce more punitive case outcomes since it taps the focal concerns of courtroom actors—namely, blameworthiness and criminal propensity. They studied 1,067 juveniles in Philadelphia and Phoenix who had been adjudicated guilty of a serious offense, comparing incarceration dispositions between self-reported gang (21 percent) and non-gang (79 percent) affiliates. They found that gang affiliates were 2.3 times more likely to be incarcerated than non-gang affiliates. Zatz and Krecker (2003) interviewed courtroom actors in Arizona in 1996 and 1997, including nine juvenile court judges and commissioners, along with eight juvenile probation officers. One judge stated:

> I have to tell you, for me personally, whether they were or were not members of a gang did not necessarily influence my decision as to what should happen. . . . What was important to me was behavior. (184)

Observations such as these take on added importance in light of the fact that Walker and Cesar's research design accounted for factors that might concern the judge, such as crime type, prior referrals, and felony charges (legal factors), along with age, gender, race, and parental criminality (extralegal factors). This is important because unless a juvenile is transferred to adult court, dispositions in juvenile court come from judges, not a jury of a juvenile's peers. Another judge in Zatz and Krecker's study, when commenting on a risk assessment scale that included gang affiliation, noted,

When I see it there it is a red flag, I'll ask questions. I take it into consideration, but you weigh and you balance the situation. (186)

To the extent that gang membership is a master status (Miethe and McCorkle 1997), one that the criminal justice system has mobilized to target, it is difficult to shake the possibility that gang affiliation *does not* creep into the decision-making calculus of courtroom actors, whether consciously or unconsciously (Hagedorn 2021).

Still, much remains unknown about whether and how gang affiliation influences the decisions of courtroom actors. We are unaware of any research on juvenile transfers to adult court. Researchers typically focus on age and race as correlates of transfers rather than other seemingly important factors, such as gang involvement (Mears et al. 2014). It is possible that the vestiges of the "get tough" era of juvenile justice, as well as criminal justice, remain in place by operating through gang membership. Yet, emerging trends with the election of "progressive prosecutors" in urban districts suggest that prosecutors may be moving away from gang affiliation as a focal concern. Chesa Boudin was elected as the district attorney of San Francisco in late 2019, and one of his first declarations was to no longer charge defendants with gang sentencing enhancements (Sernoffsky 2019). George Gascon was the former district attorney of San Francisco. Although he used gang enhancements sparingly, he changed his position and claims that he will no longer use them upon assuming office as the district attorney of Los Angeles in 2020. This is a remarkable statement given Los Angeles's position in enacting STEP and Gascon's former position as a police chief.

Conclusion

This chapter examined legislation and legal processes directed at gangs. We established that the theoretical rationale underlying anti-gang legislation is founded primarily in deterrence but also in incapacitation and community empowerment. Anti-gang legislation, which has been categorized as suppression, is far ranging. Since California first enacted anti-gang legislation in 1988, statutes designed to target gangs have been embraced differentially across governmental jurisdictions in the United States. Other statutes have been repurposed as innovative solutions to target gangs. Perhaps the most significant takeaway from this chapter is just how little we know about the efficacy of anti-gang legislation. We conclude with an observation made by M. Klein (1995, 182) just a few years after STEP was signed into law:

My only wish at this point is that competent research could have been done in conjunction with these STEP acts. This has been our best opportunity to assess the deterrent capacity of a gang suppression program that actually uses at least some elements of deterrence theory. Once again, an opportunity to learn from our responses to gang activity has been lost.

This observation rings as true today as it did a quarter-century ago. Any efforts to unwind the legal scaffolding underpinning the criminal justice system's response to gangs should be guided by evidence on the efficacy of the various types of anti-gang legislation. We recognize the irony of this call given that the buildup was heavy on (deterrence) theory and light on (systematic) evidence.

14

What Works, What Doesn't, and How Do We Know?

Nearly forty years ago, Walter Miller (1982, 47) observed that we have spent "over half a century responding to gang-related crime with programs and policies. It is a shame we haven't spent nearly as much time trying to figure out if they work." Criminologist Ron Huff, editor of the *Gangs in America* series, observed at the annual Office of Justice Programs Research Conference in the late 1990s that he could sum up most of the evaluations of gang interventions in one sentence: "You can't 'find' the program." A leading delinquency and gang researcher, Terence Thornberry, would display a blank piece of paper (or blank PowerPoint slide) at conferences, which he claimed contained the name of every successful gang prevention program.

Were Miller, Huff, and Thornberry right? This chapter tackles that issue by examining the evolution of gang programming from the 1940s on. We also examine what we see as the key impediments to more successful gang interventions. Best and promising practices in responding to gangs are the next topic for consideration. The chapter concludes with a short case study of a very promising gang intervention that went bad.

Much progress has been made since the observations of Miller, Huff, and Thornberry. At the same time, the more things change, the more they stay the same.

What Works and Best Practices in Gang Intervention

There is a good deal of talk about best practices, often without a foundation that identifies what such a practice is. In general, a best practice is an intervention, practice, or program that, through careful assessment and rigorous research, has been shown to be effective. The key to this definition is careful assessment. This implies that there are clear, definable program elements whose implementation can be measured and whose impact can be established through a scientific process that rules out rival hypotheses. As the quotes at the start of the chapter imply, finding such interventions in criminology generally and the area of gangs specifically is difficult. Why? Some of the difficulty lies in implementing programs in a manner consistent with their plans, and some of it lies in the failure to use a rigorous evaluation design.

There are a variety of reasons that programs and practices do not establish their effectiveness. But as Huff noted above, rarely are programs implemented according to their blueprint or plan. Implementation failure is more likely as the number of participating agencies increases. This is particularly important in the area of gangs because the gang problem typically is defined (as we have chosen to do) as a failure of multiple domains (individual, group, and societal; proximate and root causes). In her assessment of over one hundred prevention programs in schools, D. Gottfredson (2000) estimated that only about two-thirds of prevention programs targeting junior high students were ever implemented. In order for an intervention to be effective, it needs to be fully implemented. Without full implementation (or something very close to that standard), programs will not have a chance to work. Implementation failure can happen for a variety of reasons, often because the pressure to do something is greater than the pressure to do something right. When murders increase, when innocent bystanders are shot, when mothers grieve for children lost to violence, the public demands action, and policymakers need something to satisfy their constituents.

This pressure leads to a rather common outcome observed by many program evaluators: "Ready. Fire. Aim." It is understandable why some projects get off the ground without adequate planning. But that does not excuse their lack of effectiveness. That said, we have been involved in projects that get diverted from their design in order to address the concerns of increased violence.

Our definition of a best practice includes a careful evaluation with a research design where alternative explanations for outcomes other than the program can be identified and controlled, either statistically or through random assignment. Random assignment of people, groups, or neighborhoods is the researchers' remedy. Many researchers have heard promises of "random assignment" from agency heads, program directors, or police chiefs, only for them to explain that random assignment means researchers control which cases get treatment and which cases don't. That can be a hard pill to swallow, resulting in promises of random assignment going unfulfilled. Other impediments such as funding cuts, personnel changes, elections, and myriad other challenges can undermine random assignment.

In this context, we acknowledge three approaches to identifying best practices. Sherman and colleagues (Sherman et al. 1998; Farrington et al. 2002) developed the Maryland Scientific Scale (MSS; https://whatworksgrowth.org /resources/the-scientific-maryland-scale/). The scale has five levels that assess the rigor of the research design. By *rigor* we mean the likelihood that the study results draw conclusions about the effect of the program or intervention that are valid and defensible—to the point that the research would support spending millions of dollars and the potential for positively impacting hundreds if not thousands of lives (i.e., scalable). Rigor also refers to the ability of a research design to rule out rival hypotheses to the claim that the program led to the change in the outcome. The Maryland Scientific Scale has five levels, ordered by least to most robust, as follows:

Level 1: Cross-sectional comparison of a treatment and control group or a single treatment group comparison before and after an intervention without control variables.

Level 2: Cross-sectional or pre- and postcomparisons with adequate control variables.

Level 3: Comparison of outcomes for treatment and control groups that were statistically equivalent prior to the intervention.

Level 4: Quasi-randomization of the treatment that is established using exogenous instruments or discontinuity.

Level 5: Random assignment of cases into treatment and control groups with careful attention to differential attrition and contamination effects.

The University of Colorado Blueprints for Healthy Youth Development have a formal process for including an intervention as "promising" or "proven" (Mihalic and Elliott 2015). This is a higher bar to meet than the Maryland Scientific Scale and includes multiple trials of the program before a program is "scalable" or implemented more widely. To date, only one gang intervention—Functional Family Therapy—approaches the Blueprints standard (Thornberry et al. 2018), although there are several model programs for delinquency, including life skills training and multisystemic therapy, that are relevant. Although these programs can be expensive and require precision in implementation, their benefits are estimated to be anywhere from two to seven times their costs. Perhaps the biggest challenge is finding programs with discrete implementation strategies that can be carefully controlled and satisfy standards of program integrity.

Another means of assessing the quality of research designs is presented by the noted police and crime prevention scholar, Jerry Ratcliffe (https://www .jratcliffe.net/post/not-all-evidence-is-created-equally). Ratcliffe classifies evidence regarding the impact of a program, policy, or intervention into four categories: (1) what works, (2) what's promising, (3) what's interesting, and (4) what's suspect. His call for decision-making based on data from high-quality research designs parallels that of the Maryland Scientific Scale. Meta-analytical reviews of high-quality studies and random assignment of treatment and control groups comprise the best designs. Promising evidence of impact can be determined when a study design is truly longitudinal or has data pre- and postintervention across multiple trials or locations. Another design that can be used to produce evidence of a promising intervention is when there is pre-post measurement across a single site that includes a comparison group. Ratcliffe classifies findings as "interesting" when there are cross-site comparisons of treatment and control groups or before-and-after measurements of the treatment group alone. Finally, he classifies as "suspect" findings of effectiveness based on commercial, non-peer-reviewed studies or those based on expert opinion or case studies.

The purpose of this level of detail in a research design is to address the question of "What if?"—that is, what if there was something about the group that received the treatment that made them special or more amenable to the treatment? Or what if they would have improved without the intervention? Or what if doing nothing produced the same results? The stakes are very high because programs are expensive, and the involvement of gang members in crime takes a toll on their lives, those of the community, and society at large. We need the best evidence possible, and that means well-developed research designs. To date, we find such designs all too rarely.

The quest for best practices presents a high bar to surmount. But it also speaks to the lack of attention to solid evaluation work in the examination of gang programming. Often the argument is made that we cannot wait for those results or that denying treatment to some of the "cases" is unethical. At the time of this writing, it is 2021, and we cannot reasonably determine whether the millions and millions of dollars spent on the great majority of gang programming made things better, did not change them at all, or made them worse (Rubenson et al. 2020). We doubt that such conclusions about medical practices would be acceptable, such as cancer treatment drugs or vaccines for infectious diseases; why should the decision-making criteria for gang programming be any different? It is our conclusion that very few gang interventions have been subject to high-level evaluations. The result is that despite decades of research examining the effect of gang interventions, we still have very little solid evidence about the impact of interventions.

Gang Response Strategies

W. Miller (1990) argued that an effective response to America's gang crime problems required reliable information and a link between explanations and programs. We address this question with the response pyramid in Figure 14.1. This pyramid offers a view of the individuals most involved in crime as well as their prevalence in the general population. The diagram makes it clear that a small number of individuals, the serious and chronic offenders and the most influential gang members, commit a large number of offenses, and thus warrant responses concomitant to the nature and extent of the problem.

In this section, we identify the major categories of response strategies to gangs and briefly describe prominent programs under each category, concentrating (where possible) on interventions that have been evaluated. Many of the earliest programs we describe as foundational because they form a basis for knowledge about gangs both in the programs they describe and in the characteristics of gangs that they describe. The focus here is on programs specifically designed to respond to gangs rather than to general or non-gang related problems.

From its inception, the study of gangs has been inextricably tied to gang prevention. Indeed, many of the most important studies of the behavior of gangs and gang members have their origins in assessments of gang programming. And at a minimum, the study of gang programming has produced some of the foundations of our understanding of gangs, delinquency, and criminality.

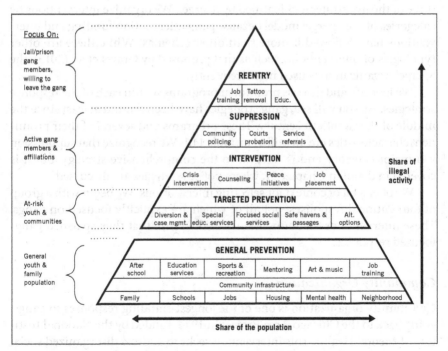

Figure 14.1 Response pyramid of criminal involvement and population prevalence

Perhaps the best example of this is the G.R.E.A.T. evaluations, which, according to the archival records on ICPSR, have yielded over 225 published works and produced important methodological advances in criminology, including the development of sophisticated self-report surveys (Short and Nye 1957; Thornberry and Krohn 2000). Another example is Thrasher's (1927) *The Gang*, which produced the impetus for programming that focused on gang prevention and intervention in schools (Thrasher 1933). While these programs were not well defined, the book did identify that an effective gang intervention would include multiple levels of intervention (individual, group, and societal), presaging Spergel's (1995) celebrated "comprehensive strategy."

In 1988, Spergel and Curry (1990, 1993) surveyed 254 agency representatives from forty-five cities and six institutional sites about their responses to gangs. From their analysis, the researchers identified five categories, which we use to organize the responses included in Table 14.1: community organization, social intervention, opportunities provision, organizational change, and suppression. Spergel (1995, 171) suggested that the strategies identified in the survey "have assumed some dominance in a particular historical period." This observation holds true today. However, as M. Klein and Maxson (2006) and Gravel and colleagues (2013) have noted, a sixth category, comprehensive or hybrid strategies, must also be considered. Such a group includes at least three of the five strategies identified by Spergel. We organize interventions by categories of the Spergel model because gang intervention funding and interventions have followed it more than other schemas. While there are other typologies of interventions, such as that proposed by Gravel et al. (2013), the Spergel organization is used most frequently.

We identify and discuss prominent programs within each of the response strategies. As you will see, gang strategies have been around at least since the middle of the twentieth century. These programs and several of their prominent characteristics are identified in Table 14.1. We recognize that suppression is a major category and is integral to the comprehensive strategy, but it is covered in detail in Chapter 11, where police strategies are discussed.

We offer a bit of context for selecting interventions. We begin with a group of foundational responses, not all of which are explicitly focused on gangs. These interventions are foundational in the sense that they spawned gang-focused responses.

Community Organization

Community organization is one of the longest-standing responses to gangs, going back to the Chicago Area Project in 1944, funded by the National Institute of Mental Health. This intervention seeks to address disorganized social institutions and disorganized neighborhoods. The sources of disorganization

TABLE 14.1 SUMMARY OF MAJOR GANG INTERVENTIONS

Title (funder) —Evaluation(s)	Years active	Unit of intervention	Comm. org.	Social intervention	Opp. provision	Suppression	Org. change	Evaluated? Effective?
Chicago Area Project (NIMH) —Schlossman and Sedlak (1983)	1930s–present	Community	X					Yes. Weak design.
Mobilization for Youth (NIMH) —Cloward and Ohlin (1960)	1961–1967	Community	X					No.
Crisis Intervention Network (City of Philadelphia) —Needle and Stapleton (1983)	1974–1987	Community	X					No.
Mid-City Project (NIMH) —W. Miller (1962)	1954–1957	Community, family, gang	X	X	X			Evaluated.
Chicago Youth Development Project (Ford Foundation) —Gold and Mattick (1974)	1960–1965	Group		X				Evaluated. No effect on delinquency.
Group Guidance Project. (LA City, County) —M. Klein (1971)	1961–1965	Group		X				Yes. Iatrogenic effect.

(Continued)

TABLE 14.1 SUMMARY OF MAJOR GANG INTERVENTIONS (*Continued*)

Title (funder) —Evaluation(s)	Years active	Unit of intervention	Comm. org.	Social intervention	Opp. provision	Suppression	Org. change	Evaluated? Effective?
Ladino Hills Program (LA City, County) —M. Klein (1971)	1966–1967	Group		X				Gang reduced in size; gang crime did not.
G.R.E.A.T. (BATF) —Esbensen and Osgood (1999); Esbensen et al. (2013)	1991–present	Classroom		X				Yes. Beneficial effects.
Comprehensive Strategy (OJJDP) —Spergel (2007); Gebo, Bond, and Campos (2015)	1991–present	Individuals		X	X	X	X	Yes. Outcome results mixed. Implementation difficult.
Boys and Girls Club (nationwide) —Arbreton and McClanahan (2002)	1995–present	Individuals		X	X			No.
Homeboy Industries (private donations) —Leap et al. (2010)	1998–present	Individuals			X			Weak design. Limited effect.
Gang Reduction and Youth Development (City of LA) —Dunworth et al. (2010)	2007–present	Individuals	X		X			Comparative design. Effects detected.

Anti-Gang Initiative (COPS Office) —Fearn, Decker, and Curry (2001)	1996–1998	Individuals			X		No.
Federal gang crackdowns (USDOJ) —Ratcliffe, Perenzin, and Sorg (2017); T. Smith (2020)	2013	Groups, individuals			X		Yes. Strong effects detected.
Civil gang injunctions (local funding) —Maxson, Hennigan, and Sloane (2005); Ridgeway et al. (2018)	1982–present	Community, group, people			X		Yes. Mixed results.
Comprehensive Anti-Gang Initiative (USDOJ) —McGarrell et al. (2013)	2006–2010	City			X		Yes. Small effect at city level on overall violence.
Shannon Grant Program (Massachusetts —Varano and Wolff (2012)	2006–present	Community				X	Yes. Mixed results across sites.
Gang Free Schools and Communities (U.S. Dept. of Education) —Schrer, Dorsey, and Catzva (2009)	2000	Individuals		X		X	Yes. Weak design.

(Continued)

TABLE 14.1 SUMMARY OF MAJOR GANG INTERVENTIONS (*Continued*)

Title (funder) —Evaluation(s)	Years active	Unit of intervention	Comm. org.	Social intervention	Opp. provision	Suppression	Org. change	Evaluated? Effective?
Cure Violence (federal, state foundation) —Skogan et al. (2008); Butts et al. (2015)	2000–present	Groups, individuals		X			X	Yes. Strong program effect in violence reduction.
Group Violence Intervention (federal/local) —Braga, Weisburd, and Turchan (2018)	1996–present	Groups, individuals		X		X	X	Yes. Results vary by site.

Abbreviations: comm, community; org, organization; opp., opportunities; NIMH, National Institute of Mental Health; USDOJ, U.S. Department of Justice; BATF, Bureau of Alcohol, Tobacco, and Firearms; OJJDP, Office of Juvenile Justice and Delinquency Prevention.

can be internal to the neighborhood (the lack of adult supervision of children) or external (dysfunctional labor markets and corrupt political systems) as well as have an institutional source in structural processes (such as the class system) or conflict in conduct norms that regulate the behavior of youth and young adults. In many cases, lower-class youth were isolated from positive socializing influences and exposed to a large number of negative socializing influences such as joblessness, poor schools, and family disruption. In such cases, they often found themselves competing in a world of middle-class norms without the skills and values to succeed.

Spergel (1964, 183) included "organization" as one of three major categories of social control. He subsequently identified *inter-organizing* as "efforts at enhancing, modification, or change in intergroup or interorganizational relationships to cope with a community problem." From this perspective, strategies that seek to create community solidarity, education, and involvement are forms of "community organizations," a point we made in Chapter 2 regarding collective efficacy. "Networking" was considered the most basic community organization strategy as long as it was not restricted to justice system agencies. Multiple-agency prevention efforts and advocacy for victims were also included in this strategic area. Building relationships among groups and individuals was the underlying logic in efforts to increase community organization.

The Chicago Area Project

The Chicago Area Project (CAP) was developed to designate program target sectors that were labeled "delinquency areas" by Shaw and McKay (1942; see also Roberts 1998; Schlossman and Sedlak 1983). These community assessments were used to develop local community organizations, to fill gaps in social control, and to develop indigenous leadership and neighborhood organization (M. Klein 1971, 44). The guiding theory was Shaw and McKay's concept of "social disorganization," an approach to understanding delinquency that examines the social ecology of neighborhoods. This concept was discussed in Chapter 2. The centrality of social disorganization (Bursik and Grasmick 1993) to theories of gang origin and behavior is of such import that we include a discussion of CAP despite its lack of specific focus on gangs.

Six neighborhood committees were formed in selected Chicago delinquency areas. Each committee was empowered to choose its own director and to make decisions about responding to delinquency in its community. In 1944, Clifford Shaw, who served as director and lead researcher of CAP, produced a statistical study that showed reductions in delinquency rates in at least one out of the six CAP target communities. Subsequent criticism of his statistical methods and his interpretations of the social processes of community life led Shaw to emphasize the intervention over analysis. Schlossman and Sedlak (1983, 459) concluded that program implementation was successful. However, as to reducing delinquency, measurement issues make impact evaluation conclusions impossible. The lack of focus on measures of crime and delinquency is a common feature of many contemporary evaluations of gang and delinquency programs.

Mobilization for Youth, New York City

The goals of the Mobilization for Youth (MFY) (1961–1967) were to restructure the social organization of the Lower East Side of Manhattan through community participation and special programs to involve residents in expanded opportunities. Originally funded by the National Institute of Mental Health, in 1962 the MFY was the recipient of an action grant from the President's Committee on Juvenile Delinquency and Youth Crime. This was among the first federally funded gang initiatives (but see W. Miller 1962). Richard Cloward was the theoretical progenitor and, briefly, research director of MFY. Just as Shaw's social disorganization theory defined CAP, Cloward and Ohlin's (1960) opportunity theory shaped MFY. Opportunities provision and community service were primary goals in the context of community organization and the creation of indigenous institutions. The project was central to the War on Poverty and Great Society strategies of the thirty-sixth president of the United States, Lyndon B. Johnson. A youth service corps was established, first hiring unemployed youths and using many of them to teach younger children to read. MFY began as a community organization focused on mobilizing local resources. It grew into a social action movement that challenged New York City's traditional institutions (Bursik and Grasmick 1993, 168). No specific outcome evaluations of MFY programs were produced. As with CAP, there is sufficient evidence (Bibb 1967; Kahn 1967) that MFY was a success in terms of process evaluation outcomes and the development of the desired community organizations. However, the lack of a systematic evaluation of its impact on delinquency or gang involvement remains problematic and a lost opportunity. This is not the only gang initiative to fall in this category.

Crisis Intervention Network, Philadelphia

Philadelphia's Crisis Intervention Network (CIN) (1974–1987) was primarily a community organization approach. However, like CAP and MFY, CIN reflected other strategic approaches and coexisted with a grassroots community organization, the House of Umoja. With street work and a probation/parole unit, CIN represented a coalition of neighborhood-level community organizations. The House of Umoja was an independent shelter for at-risk youths with an emphasis on building self-respect through an awareness of Black culture and traditions. The House of Umoja pioneered the utilization of gang summits and truces to reduce street violence. However, there are no solid evaluations of the impact of such strategies. In fact, there is no systematic process or outcome evaluation of the CIN project, and it was based not on any particular theory of gangs or delinquency but rather on a broader theory of cultural identity.

Summary

The three community organization projects share several things in common. First, they each share a focus on the organization of community agencies, groups, and norms. In this context, these projects recognize the role that institutions such as family, employment, and public services play in the lives of youth. Second, each has a theoretical foundation for the intervention, whether it be social disorganization (Shaw in Chicago), opportunity theory (Cloward in New York City), or cultural identity (House of Umoja in Philadelphia), and these foundations remain important today. In addition, major theoretical perspectives in the understanding of gangs, crime, and delinquency are found in these approaches. While the results are not promising in the two cases where evaluations (outcome and process) were completed, they were at least competently done.

Social Intervention

Social intervention encompasses both social service agency programs and what are generally referred to as "street work" or "detached worker" programs. Social service agency programs include such things as providing services to clients or linking them with agencies that can lead to jobs, family support, or other forms of government assistance. Spergel (1966, 27) defined street work as

> the systematic effort of an agency worker, through social work or treatment techniques within the neighborhood context, to help a group of young people who are described as delinquent or partially delinquent to achieve a conventional adaptation. It involves the redirection or conversion of youth gangs to legitimate social gangs or conventional organizations.

For M. Klein (1971, 44), only the detached worker program "has been identified as a 'pure' gang approach." This is to say that other approaches have their roots in addressing a broader range of problems rather than a more narrowly defined set of gang issues. Whether a general delinquency intervention will work for gang problems or a gang-specific approach is necessary is an ongoing debate in contemporary criminology (Thornberry et al. 2018). An assumption of the detached worker approach was that "the juvenile gang had positive potential; only selected negative structural and process elements required modification. . . . The gang itself was to be a vehicle of its own transformation"

(Spergel 1995, 174). Gang outreach workers would be an important component of such interventions. The goal of including gang outreach workers was to forge ties with gang members in ways that law enforcement or social service agencies could not (Cheng 2018; Decker et al. 2008). Many street outreach workers are former gang members or have some involvement in gang life. The theory in such circumstances is that gang members are more responsive to individuals who understand the entanglements and obligations of gang life. This has prompted at least one observer (Goldstein and Glick 1994) to argue that gang structures could be used to positive ends as a form of "prosocial gang" and be a vehicle through which to deliver aggression replacement therapy. To date, there is no evidence to suggest that this is an effective strategy. Indeed, Klein later found that attention to the gang strengthened the group's appeal without altering its involvement in crime.

Midcity Project, Boston

The Boston Midcity Project (1954–1957) combined street work with community mobilization. Walter Miller, the project director, described the project as "directed at three societal units seen to figure importantly in the genesis and perpetuation of delinquent behavior—the community, the family, and the gang" (1962, 169). Seven detached workers were assigned to "an area, group, or groups (gangs) with a mandate to contact, establish relationships with, and attempt to change resident gangs." Each worker was professionally trained and had access to psychiatric services for their clients. The target gangs included Black and White gangs and male and female groups, the first formal acknowledgment in gang programming that girls joined gangs (see Chapter 7). The program was successfully implemented, and the outcome evaluation was able to measure changes in involvement in crime. Miller concluded that there was no observable program impact. Miller is perhaps best known for his development of the "focal concerns" of gang members (see Chapters 2 and 8), which have been a foundation for cultural explanations of gangs—that is, those that focus on values as the key explanatory variable (Mitchell et al. 2017). These and other details of his work in the Midcity Project are now available in his book *City Gangs* (W. Miller 2011), which is free online.

Chicago Youth Development Project

The Chicago Youth Development Project (CYDP) (1960–1965) was a joint effort between the Chicago Boys Clubs and the Institute for Social Research of the University of Michigan supported by the Ford Foundation (Mattick and Caplan 1967, 107). Though detached street work coordinated by the Boys Clubs was the major focus of the project, a supplementary community organization component was also included. This component included gang and non-gang youths, and the research component involved continued feedback to field-workers throughout the project program (Caplan et al. 1967). The evaluation report (Gold and Mattick 1974) showed no impact on delinquency. In fact, youths who reported being closest to their program workers showed the greatest levels of delinquency, a finding Klein (1971) would replicate in Los Angeles just a few years later. Klein's conclusion in Los Angeles for this "perverse" finding was that the attention from the workers reinforced the gang status—that is to say, the attention was perceived as contingent on gang membership. The impact evaluation results did not suggest that the kind of "aggressive street work" employed had an impact on reducing delinquency.

The Group Guidance Project and the Ladino Hills Program, Los Angeles

The Group Guidance Project (GGP) (1961–1965) was the first major gang intervention effort on the West Coast. It followed the general design of the projects described in Boston and Chicago, while Malcolm Klein (1971) anchored the Ladino Hills Program (LHP) (1966–1967) to the issue of group cohesion. In the GGP, the detached street workers served four gangs and eight hundred gang members through contacts in the Los Angeles County Probation Department. The primary goals of the street workers were to control and prevent gang violence. The results of the evaluation, however, brought Klein to the unsettling conclusion that the GGP itself may have increased delinquency among gang members. Specifically, he found that delinquency increased among gang members who received the most services. Cohesion among gang members increased in direct proportion to the attention paid to the gang by street workers, and delinquency increased in conjunction with cohesiveness. These findings led Klein (1971) to the conclusion that detached street worker programs do not work because they enhance gang solidarity, which promotes violence (see Chapter 6).

The LHP provided an opportunity for Klein to test his conclusions from the GGP. In the LHP, Klein took a detached work program with group programming for a Mexican American gang cluster of about 140 members and incrementally decreased group programming services while increasing the access to individual non-gang alternative services and activities. As a result, he observed decreases in his measures of cohesion and in the size of the gang. While the number of offenses for active gang members did not decline, overall offenses for gang members declined by 35 percent, largely due to a reduction in the size of the gang.

Summary

These four projects in Boston, Chicago, and Los Angeles share several things in common. Again, each was led by an individual researcher. In the case of Miller in Boston and Klein in Los Angeles, the researcher became one of the dominant figures in gang and delinquency research. In today's parlance, we would call these action researchers. A second common feature was their willingness to change the focus of their projects (e.g., the Klein pivot from detached workers assigned to a gang to broader opportunities provision) in the face of negative impact results from evaluations. But in three of the instances, the programs shared an outcome not desired, as the program failed to reduce delinquency.

Opportunities Provision

Two major theoretical perspectives of the 1950s and 1960s were strain and differential opportunity theories. Both of these theories receive extensive treatment in Chapter 2 and are foundational to the study of criminology. Strain and differential opportunity underscore the importance of access to legitimate means and opportunities for preventing gang involvement. When the conventional means to achieve culturally valued goals are not socially available, youth "innovate" and pursue illegitimate means to achieve material success (Merton 1938). Opportunities provision approaches attempt to offer youth at risk for involvement in crime legitimate opportunities as well as means to access those opportunities.

Spergel and Curry (1993) found that opportunities strategies were the least likely primary strategy in gang interventions. They are among the most expensive and most challenging to implement but also carry great appeal. Job preparation, training, and placement programs, as well as enhancing educational opportunities for gang youths that might enhance careers, are included under this heading. For example, in 1967, the U.S. Office of Economic Opportunity funded two job training and job referral centers through Chicago's Woodlawn Organization that were actually staffed and operated by two Chicago gangs: the Gangster Disciples and the Blackstone Rangers. A congressional investigation ultimately led to fraud charges against at least one gang leader. Spergel and Curry (1993) found that gang violence increased over the one-year period of the project. This all-too-common finding receives further discussion later in this chapter.

In 1988, Father Greg Boyle created a program known as Jobs for a Future (JFF) in Boyle Heights, the storied gang neighborhood in Los Angeles discussed in Chapter 2. In 2001, Homeboy Industries (HBI) became independent from JFF. The primary mission of HBI was to find jobs for gang members, a difficult but vital task, because "nothing stops a bullet like a job," Boyle thought. Currently, there is a location just north of downtown Los Angeles that provides counseling services to gang members and at-risk youth, tattoo removal, job placement, and outreach services. HBI provides a variety of jobs within the agency, including the Homegirls Café, an independently run bakery and restaurant that often serves police officers (including former Los

Angeles police chief Charlie Beck) as their clients. Homegirls Café recently opened a restaurant at Los Angeles International Airport (LAX).

There is a faith-based component to HBI, which makes sense given that Father Boyle is a Catholic priest, a component that has received additional attention in gang programming and research. Flores (2013) and Deuchar (2018) both underscore the value of spirituality in exiting from the gang, and Decker and Pyrooz (2020) find evidence that spirituality can be a component of the decision and process to disengage from a gang.

To be placed in a job by HBI, an individual must pass drug tests, receive counseling, participate in job readiness training, and, if they wish, participate in a tattoo removal program. Unlike other programs, Father Greg takes individuals who have few alternatives and are at very high risk for reoffending and victimization. HBI makes a large number of items that are for sale to the public through their website at https://homeboyindustries.org. Unfortunately, the model has been the subject of implementation evaluations but not yet of a rigorous outcome evaluation that would meet level 3 of the Maryland Scientific Scale or level 4 of the Ratcliffe typology (Leap et al. 2010).

Suppression

As discussed in Chapter 11, suppression became the dominant response to gang crime problems in the late 1970s. This may be a function of political conservatism of the "get tough" era on crime (B. Feld 2019), or it may represent a reaction to increased levels of gang violence. It is worth noting that murder rates increased during the "get tough" era in the 1990s. Suppression includes activities such as arrest, specialized or targeted prosecution, incarceration, intensive supervision, gang intelligence, and networking among criminal justice agencies. As we wrote in Chapter 8, this was also the era when commentators such as John DiIulio warned of the coming wave of "super-predators" (W. Bennett, DiIulio, and Walters 1996) that would push rates of violence in a dramatic upward direction. Criminologists such as J. Fox (1992) spoke of such individuals as the "young and the ruthless," which was criticized at length in the bestselling book *Freakonomics* (Levitt and Dubner 2005). Suppression has become the most common response to gang problems, and police department gang crime units are the primary form of suppression (Chapter 11). Many of these are modeled after the LAPD's Community Resources against Street Hoodlums (CRASH) program.

Organizational Development and Change

Organizational development and change are not primary strategies but incorporate a variety of responses to gangs. These may include efforts focused on institutional and policy adaptation and development including gang legislation as well as expanding available resources. From this perspective, establishing a gang unit can be viewed as an organizational development strategy that elaborates a suppression strategy.

Gang legislation constitutes a form of organizational development and change. Many law enforcement agencies engage in efforts to initiate or modify legislation related to gangs or the gang problem or try to influence legislation pertaining to gangs. Discussed thoroughly in Chapter 13, perhaps the best-known gang legislation, which has served as a model for other jurisdictions, was California's 1988 STEP (Street Terrorism Enforcement and Prevention) Act (California Penal Code Section 182.22). The 1994 Crime Bill also contained a separate title that dealt with gangs and proposed the involvement of and support for a number of agencies primarily in the form of suppression (Decker and Pyrooz, forthcoming). The notable exception to the endorsement of gang suppression in the Crime Bill is in the funding and other support for the Gang Resistance Education and Training (G.R.E.A.T.) program, a topic we return to under "Prevention."

Gang Crime Prevention Center, Illinois
In 1996, the Illinois attorney general initiated the Gang Crime Prevention Center (GCPC). This center was designed to focus attention on the problem of gangs across the state. Interventions were funded in six different jurisdictions. These interventions focused on schools, social agencies, after-school programs, and prevention programs. The GCPC enjoyed widespread political support in large part because it placed programs in multiple jurisdictions and worked locally to fund interventions that fit their needs. The GCPC did not produce program models that could be replicated, and while an evaluation was commissioned, in the end, it did not provide outcome measures. This is a very good example of a response to gangs that focuses on organizational development and change. It is important to note that the political power of the office of the attorney general as well as providing funding to local sites made GCPC function.

Shannon Gang Program, Massachusetts
The Shannon Gang intervention in Massachusetts is another example of organizational change and development. Massachusetts provided funding in 2006 to eight sites across the state. Using money from the Edward Byrne Memorial Justice Assistance Grant Program in the Bureau of Justice Assistance, named for a New York City police officer who was killed in the line of duty in 1988 while protecting a witness who agreed to testify against drug dealers, the state provided funding for comprehensive programs that included law enforcement, supervision (probation and parole), and community partners. Each participating site had a mandate to expand their intervention and ser-

vices beyond law enforcement. There was a good deal of independence for the local sites. The evaluation completed by Gebo, Bond, and Campos (2015) demonstrated that cities with experience in coordinating gang programming (primarily larger cities such as Boston) were more successful in producing positive outcomes. That said, a number of the participating jurisdictions implemented models consistent with the mandate. Successful implementation in gang prevention and intervention is still all too rare.

Prevention

People often express frustration with gang problems and wonder what is being done to prevent the issues that result in costs to the taxpayer (in terms of criminal justice expenditures), costs to communities (in terms of fear, disengagement, and reduced quality of life), costs to gang members and their families (in terms of lost potential and broken households), and stressors of inadequate education and unstable employment. We highlight one program that has established itself as a leader in efforts to prevent gang membership. We chose to do this because G.R.E.A.T. is a well-designed program, has used feedback from researchers and other individuals who study and work in prevention, and has national status.

Gang Resistance Education and Training (G.R.E.A.T.)

The G.R.E.A.T. program was developed in 1991 by law enforcement in Phoenix with the goal of a partnership between educators, community leaders, and law enforcement. It is supported with funding from the U.S. Bureau of Alcohol, Tobacco, and Firearms. The program is primarily a gang prevention program that is targeted at and tailored to middle school students. Because of its focus on sixth and seventh graders, the G.R.E.A.T. program can best be considered primary prevention—that is, a program targeted at individuals before they reach the age at risk for involvement in gangs. In its original format, there were eight lessons provided in nine one-hour sessions. The lessons provided both structured activities and classroom instruction that were targeted to help students avoid joining gangs as well as develop into responsible citizens. Topics such as victims' rights and responsibilities, cultural diversity, goal setting, drugs, and personal responsibility were covered in the lessons. This was accomplished by giving students both skills and self-assurance that, in theory, enabled them to resist pressures for involvement in violence and other social problems.

Unlike most gang programs, there have been high-quality evaluations of the G.R.E.A.T. program. Finn-Aage Esbensen of the University of Missouri–St. Louis has been engaged in an evaluation of the implementation, outcome, and impact of the program since 1994 (Esbensen 2015). The G.R.E.A.T. program evaluation can be distinguished from those of other gang programs on other important counts. The first is the receptiveness of program staff to external evaluation. The evaluation was funded for multiple years in multiple sites, and at a level that would allow for meaningful conclusions to be drawn from the study. All too often, program evaluations cannot draw reliable conclusions about the impact of a program because a study is not conducted for a long enough period or is done with too little support. A second distinctive feature of the evaluation is its use of both a quasi-experimental research design and a longitudinal research design. In the 1995–1996 school year, six cities were used for evaluation purposes.

The evaluation examined both short-term and long-term program effects and found that students in the G.R.E.A.T. program were more likely to have prosocial attitudes and fewer problem behaviors than students not in the program (Esbensen and Osgood 1999; Esbensen, Osgood, et al. 2001). However, the major finding from the longitudinal evaluation was that there were not significant differences between the students in the program and those students who did not receive the program in terms of gang membership, drug use, and delinquency. It is important to note that the agency responsible for the program sought the advice of the evaluation team to help restructure the curriculum, train instructors, and design better training modules. This is an all-too-rare occurrence in program evaluation.

Based on the work of a review committee (consisting of the evaluation team, G.R.E.A.T. officers, and school-based prevention experts), the program was revised to promote cooperative learning, proactive classroom management, self-management skills, social skills, and information about drug abuse. The modified core curriculum now consisted of thirteen lessons. Esbensen and colleagues (2012, 2013) recently reported on the program outcomes from the second evaluation of G.R.E.A.T., finding much more positive results in terms of achieving program goals. Importantly, they found that students in the G.R.E.A.T. program had a much lower likelihood of being a gang member— around 40 percent less likely at the conclusion of the program and nearly one year later. This is an important finding indeed, as it is the first to find a program that prevents gang membership and meets the strict demands of experimental criteria. In addition to the supportive gang membership results, the authors find that G.R.E.A.T. helped in other attitudinal categories: reducing anger, self-centeredness, peer pressure, delinquent peer exposure, and hitting neutralizations, and improving attitudes to the police, prosocial peers, refusal skills, prosocial involvement, collective efficacy, and attitudes about gangs. Notable by their omission from these results are the lack of declines in delinquency among program participants compared to control group members. Maxson (2013, 423) called this "surprising," and Pyrooz (2013, 427) called it an "inconvenient truth." Programs that reduce gang membership should also reduce delinquency along with many other adverse outcomes.

Multicomponent Approaches

The Legacy of Irving Spergel and the Comprehensive Gang Strategy

Few programs are as strongly identified with a single individual as is the Comprehensive Gang Model. Spergel, a social work professor at the University of Chicago, worked to develop the principles of the model, saw that it was implemented in the Little Village neighborhood in Chicago, and helped foster its growth across the country. Indeed, many still refer to it as the "Spergel Model." Spergel began the model in 1993 in an attempt to reduce levels of gang membership and violence. The program was operational there for nearly a decade, and outcome evaluation results published in 2007 showed reductions in serious and violent crime and gang involvement, as well as enhanced job and school opportunities for participants. The research design was a level 2 on the Maryland Scientific Scale and the analysis largely correlational, leading some to question its impact (M. Klein 1995; M. Klein and Maxson 2006). The program has been endorsed by the Office of Juvenile Justice and Delinquency Prevention (OJJDP), which funds the National Gang Center to provide training and technical assistance in the implementation of the model nationwide.

There have been several major attempts funded by OJJDP to implement the Comprehensive Gang Model. Five sites (Bloomington, Illinois; Mesa and Tucson, Arizona; Riverside, California; and San Antonio, Texas) were selected to test the model in 1995. There was variation in the level of implementation across the sites, but crime reductions and expanded social opportunities were observed in Riverside. This initial attempt to test the model was followed by (1) the Rural Gang Initiative, which was based in six sites in 1998; (2) four sites in the Gang-Free Schools and Communities Initiative in 2000; and (3) four sites in the Gang Reduction Program in 2003.

The Comprehensive Gang Model is not without its critics. M. Klein (2011) and M. Klein and Maxson (2006) noted that it was difficult to coordinate comprehensive programs and that implementation was at best uneven both within sites and across sites. M. Klein and Maxson (2006) also point to the presence of a path model with a multivariate structure, though a model that fails to take into account the implementation challenges and the length of time between program implementation and results. While the final report (Spergel et al. 2002) does include some multivariate results and a longitudinal design with a matched control area, the sample size (202 gang youth), loose matches between control and target areas, and the frequency of measurement make it difficult to attribute change to program participation. The Comprehensive Gang Model may be most important not for its own impact but for motivating others to develop interventions with multiple program components. And, perhaps most importantly, Spergel's approach constitutes an intervention framework that recognizes single component approaches to gang intervention are unlikely to be successful.

Hybrid Programs

Los Angeles Gang Reduction Youth Development (GRYD)

It should come as no surprise that along with Chicago, Los Angeles has a large number of gang prevention and intervention programs. In 2007, under the leadership of Mayor Antonio Villaraigosa, Los Angeles consolidated its many gang prevention and intervention programs. This decision was difficult because many gang and youth programs in Los Angeles had developed political allies and community support; in short, just like the gangs they served, these groups had their own "turf." But it was unclear what impact, if any, the uncoordinated and unfocused programs had. GRYD identified targeted zones of intervention where services were organized and concentrated. The program emphasized prevention and intervention services and used a Social Embeddedness Tool (SET) to measure the degree of gang embeddedness of youth, as well as risk and protective factors related to gang embeddedness and violent behavior. GRYD further used a Youth Services Eligibility Tool (YSET) composed of nine scales (antisocial tendencies; weak parental supervision; critical life events; impulsive risk taking; guilt neutralization; negative peer influence; peer delinquency; family gang influence; and self-reported delinquency). To be eligible for GRYD services, a youth aged 10–15 had to meet or exceed the risk threshold in four or more of these areas (Hennigan et al. 2015). The GRYD program is housed in the Mayor's Office of Gang Reduction and Youth Development, a location that gives it some clout in the political arena. Its $26 million budget in 2019–2020 makes it the largest in the country, and it adopted a comprehensive approach.

The significance of this intervention is that it created mayoral-level accountability, control, and funding for a citywide gang intervention. This level of control and leadership is often lacking in gang interventions. In some cases, this leaves programs vulnerable to changes in administrations and funding priorities. In addition, an externally funded evaluation monitored the implementation of programs and services as well as the impact of those programs and services.

Group Violence Intervention and Cure Violence

We consider Group Violence Intervention and Cure Violence to be hybrid programs. That is because they combine many of the elements of the Comprehensive Gang Model (prevention, intervention, and suppression) with a unique form of outreach. The key to each of these approaches is their use of outreach workers to "spread the message" either of criminal justice levers (pressure points) that will be activated or of the need to diffuse situations with the potential for violence. What these programs add that was largely lacking in the other approaches was the targeted approach and consistent messages delivered to perpetrators of violence (including gang members) following an incident in which violence was used.

Group Violence Intervention (GVI) started life as the Boston Gun Project in 1995, later Operation Ceasefire, and has been credited with sustained reductions in youth homicide of over 60 percent in Boston (Abt 2019). The intervention is built on "lever pulling," using focused deterrence with groups (or individuals) on the brink of engaging in violence. This approach is consistent with the review by the National Academies of Sciences, Engineering, and Medicine (2018) regarding the impact of focused deterrence on violence, especially the kind of street violence that gang members are at risk for. As discussed in Chapter 11, in Boston, the GVI was paired with a variety of other interventions that included clergy-police cooperation and public health efforts. The public health efforts placed an emphasis on changing community norms toward violence—especially among individuals of prime ages for gang joining and activity. Street outreach workers are the key actors in this aspect of the intervention. The police play a crucial role in selling the message that violence must stop or high-intensity suppression efforts will be brought to bear in a neighborhood. The retailing of the message by street outreach workers and community "moral voices," who share a common cultural understanding of community norms, processes, and treatment, is crucial to the operation of this model. The threat from authorities is clear and unequivocal that even minor offenses will receive substantial attention and that law enforcement will be a highly visible and intrusive presence if violence continues.

From Oakland to Chicago and Detroit to New Orleans, focused deterrence has a strong record of preventing gang and group violence (Braga, Hureau, and Papachristos 2014; Braga and Weisburd 2012), although the studies often are characterized by weak identification strategies (i.e., comparing the program site to a nearby place without the program) and evaluations with more rigorous, matched quasi-experimental designs tend to show weaker program effects (Braga and Weisburd 2014; Braga, Weisburd, and Turchan 2018, 2019). This is a common finding in program evaluations, largely because more rigorous tests set a higher bar for a program to meet; hence, they more frequently fall short. However, sustainability is another concern with GVI (Tillyer, Engel, and Lovins 2012). Several evaluations have noted that GVI's effects appear to be short-lived. A. Fox and Novak (2018), in an evaluation of Kansas City's focused deterrence program, found that there was an immediate reduction in violence during the first twelve months of the intervention, but these rates returned to preintervention levels three years into the program. Even the original "Boston Miracle" did not last, in part because of a breakdown in trust between police and the community (Braga, Hureau, and Winship 2008; Braga, Hureau, and Papachristos 2014; Brunson et al. 2015).

Cure Violence (Butts et al. 2015) is another popular hybrid intervention. It is a public health intervention that depends heavily on the efforts of street outreach workers. It seeks to change norms that regulate the use of guns and violence by gang members. This is the public health component of the intervention, that violence is harmful to the community, families, and the individuals involved. The goal of street outreach workers is to continue to push the message ("violence harms your family"; "violence harms the things you care about"). Street outreach workers bring many assets to communities with high levels of gang-related violence. Perhaps most importantly, the core of the Cure Violence approach is the hiring, supervision, and training of outreach workers who share some of the background characteristics of individual gang members, perhaps having been members (shooters or survivors) themselves at an earlier stage of their life. As such, they can "speak the language" of such individuals, particularly after instances of violence, when retaliation is likely. The retailing of the message is especially intense during periods of violence, and outreach workers attempt to head off nascent violence. The program perhaps enjoyed its greatest success in Chicago, where Skogan et al.'s (2008) evaluation underscored its success in reducing violence.

The most promising feature of Cure Violence, based on independent external evaluations, is the application of public health principles aimed at preventing gang violence (P. J. Brantingham et al. 2018) through the use of "violence interrupters." It is the job of these trained individuals, many of whom are former gang members, to monitor disputes, offer input to individuals at risk for engaging in or becoming victims of gun violence, and attempt to defuse and disrupt potentially violent situations. The "theory of change" in such interventions includes (1) interrupting the transmission of beliefs favoring retaliation and the use of guns, (2) identifying and change the thinking of the most influential "transmitters" such as leaders and other high-status individuals in the group, and (3) changing group norms regarding the use of gun violence to achieve group goals. Evaluations of violence interrupters in two New York City neighborhoods offer promising results (Delgado et al. 2017). Efforts to control gun violence through the use of such techniques have enjoyed success in Oakland (Abt 2019; Webster 2019) based on the results of internal evaluations.

Group Violence Intervention and Cure Violence are often viewed as competing programs, but the reality is that they can be used together in a coordinated approach, provided the roles for street outreach workers and law enforcement are clearly defined and communities are committed to a comprehensive social services model. Evidence suggests that GVI can achieve results quickly largely because it is built primarily on existing police resources and community intelligence on gangs and gang violence, but finding the right balance between enforcement (the stick) and social services (the carrot) can be tricky; so too can keeping momentum going once violence is no longer the problem it once was. Cure Violence takes longer to get off the ground because it needs its own sustainable source of funding, a storefront to serve as a home base or safe haven for victims and offenders in the target area, and support for staff, many of whom still are learning to cope with their own criminal past. However, it can help bring the community together in violence intervention and lay the foundation for peer relationships that facilitate meaningful behavior change.

Assessing the Gang Intervention Findings

We have not reviewed every gang or gang crime response. We have included programs with a definable strategy that have been implemented to some measurable degree of fidelity to their blueprint and have produced outcomes. Table 14.1 includes programs in each of the five major gang intervention categories of the Comprehensive Gang Model as well as what we call "hybrid" programs. Several key observations are in order following this review.

First, there are no clear best practices, at least when it comes to identifying the most effective of the response strategies. The single-purpose strategies seem to fall short of reducing the gang problem in the long term. Because the gang problem is multifaceted, suppression is not likely to solve the need for employment skills, and individual counseling is unlikely to have much effect on long-term gang leaders. This is why we find the hybrid approaches (GVI and Cure Violence) more promising.

Second, while there has been a lot of research examining gang programs, there are few studies with level 5 designs on the Maryland Scientific Scale. That poses a dilemma for practitioners and elected officials who have limited resources to marshal in responding to gangs. This circumstance also places the research community in a difficult spot: What do you tell "authorities" is the best course of action? If pressed, our response would be to collect data on your local gang problem, have clearly defined goals for your interventions, coordinate across intervention types, use the most prominent element of the hybrid interventions (street outreach workers), and evaluate closely.

Third, it is no coincidence that many of the interventions are associated with some of the most important work and researchers in criminology. Though not reviewed here, Thrasher proposed a program for delinquent youth that emphasized the characteristics of their organizational structure. Almost every introductory criminology course reviews theories of delinquency built on the work of Cloward and Ohlin, Miller, Klein, and Spergel and Curry. Esbensen's work on G.R.E.A.T. has resulted in countless books, articles, and dissertations and is a mainstay of our understanding of gangs. Braga, whose work is central to the focused deterrence approach of GVI, is a must-read in policing work. The point here is that gang research has been integral to the field of criminology since its common inception. In addition, the struggle for solid evaluations of gang programming is hardly new; it covers the last half of the twentieth century, and the struggles remain in the current century.

Fourth, while comprehensive interventions appear to have the most promise, that observation has yet to be fully tested. A logic model that engages multiple forms of interventions (suppression, outreach, prevention, etc.) makes sense in addressing gang problems. The problem is that the evaluation literature is replete with work that documents the substantial challenges in coordinating those efforts. Indeed, Decker and Curry (2002b) raised the question of whether it is harder to gain the cooperation of those who respond to gangs (police, prosecutors, outreach workers, job counselors, etc.) than that of gang members themselves. Paul Callanan, who was the director of the Gang Reduction Initiative of Denver for a decade, noted that "turf, ego, and dollars" matter to seemingly rational organizations as much as they do to the gangs themselves (Pyrooz, Weltman, and Sanchez 2019).

Finally, there is light on the horizon. It is not a bright light, but it is a start. Building on the multimillion-dollar Rochester Youth Development Study, Thornberry and colleagues (2018) have taken a larger step forward in their evaluation of Functional Family Therapy (FFT). FFT is one of the Blueprints for Health Youth Development "proven practices" demonstrated to reduce general delinquency (Mihalic and Elliott 2015). After the convening of a panel of subject-matter experts over a period of several years, the decision was made to apply one of the Blueprint programs to gang members, with modifications approved by the creator of FFT and pretested by the research team. It should be noted that this process began in 2009 and resulted in a 2018 publication documenting the process of "translating" FFT to gang members and their families as well as the research results (D. Gottfredson et al. 2018; Thornberry et al. 2018).

FFT typically involves twelve to fifteen face-to-face sessions of approximately one hour during which trained therapists work with the targeted youth and caregivers, usually in a home setting. The entire program lasts about three months. A randomized-controlled trial involving 129 low-income families in Philadelphia found that FFT lowered the recidivism risk among justice-involved boys with a mean age of fifteen (D. Gottfredson et al. 2018; Thornberry et al. 2018). The treatment group ($N = 66$) received FFT, while the control group ($N = 63$) received an alternative family therapy program. Three sets of intent-to-treat estimates were reported: (1) self-reports six months postrandomization, (2) official records (of arrest) six and eighteen months later, and (3) both self-reports and official records conditional on gang "risk" status, a measure that was comparable to level of gang embeddedness. The study found no group differences in self-reports of delinquency and substance use, but differences emerged for more deeply embedded gang members, arguably the population in the greatest need of FFT services. Recidivism was lower for the treatment group at six-month and eighteen-month follow-up periods, and the differences increased in magnitude over time.

The good news, therefore, is that the evaluation provided evidence that gang members and their families completed the program and the treatment group had lower rates of recidivism. The bad news is that science . . . moves . . . slowly. This assessment provides very strong evidence about this program and should encourage replication and extension of this work. But what do we do about gangs in the interim?

There is some evidence in 2020 and 2021 that after years of decline (P. Sharkey 2018), urban violence is on the rise in many cities, and street gangs appear to play a central role in this increase. Just as is the case in the medical and biological sciences, the pressure is on researchers and program development teams to come up with testable programs and to assess their fidelity (i.e., whether they can be implemented according to design) and their effectiveness. This clearly puts pressure on government and foundations to fund such work and have some degree of patience about the time it takes to do implementation and evaluation the right way. But it also puts pressure on the public to provide support for longer-term research that can answer such questions as: Does it work? For whom? Under what circumstances? How big an effect does it have?

At time of writing, the Biden administration has announced significant funding streams to support community violence intervention with the aim of coordinating responses across federal agencies. This is noteworthy because from 2000 to 2020, under Presidents Bush, Obama, and Trump, the National Institute of Justice (NIJ), the research arm of the U.S. Department of Justice (DOJ), awarded just $18.5 million to twenty-four different research, development, and evaluation projects focused on gangs. This represents only 0.6 percent of NIJ's total awards during that period (https://nij. ojp.gov/funding/awards/list). Of course, other offices at the DOJ (e.g., the Office of Community Oriented Policing Services and the Office of Juvenile Justice and Delinquency Prevention), as well as other federal agencies (e.g., Health and Human Services), have appropriated millions of dollars for implementing and evaluating programs and practices designed to respond to gangs and violence in recent decades, but it is clear more needs to be done to stem the tide of violence.

The Thornberry et al. (2018) test of Functional Family Therapy is consistent with what we would call a "best practice." This applies to the formulation of the intervention, its implementation, the research design, and (finally) the results. But are there other ways to fast-track the results of gang program evaluations and develop interventions based on a review of the existing evaluation literature?

Two processes offer direction here. The first is through synthetic reviews, and the second is through meta-analysis. A synthetic review gathers all program evaluations that meet a certain implementation, methodological, and statistical standard and compares the results of the evaluations. These reviews have considerable utility, as they allow an assessment of a large volume of information organized in a way that allows for conclusions. Table 14.1 resembles what some synthetic reviews might look like. The key to the utility of such reviews is the inclusion of studies that meet important criteria such as sample size, program integrity, study dropouts, and the magnitude of the effect of the program. But such "cataloguing" is hardly a substitute for solid evaluation; frankly, even a level 2 score on the Maryland Scientific Scale is better than a cataloguing of interventions and their characteristics.

A Canadian team led by Gravel (Gravel et al. 2013; Wong et al. 2016), a U.S.-based team of Rubenson and her colleagues (2020), and a British-based team of Mallion and Wood (2020) provide four synthetic reviews or meta-analyses. Gravel et al. take important strides in developing appropriate categories of contemporary interventions for future work in their review of forty-five different program evaluations. They point to shortcomings of many gang program evaluations that inhibit further analysis. In their systematic review and meta-analysis of forty-one gang interventions, Rubenson et al. point to an important yet often-overlooked point: some interventions make things worse. Specifically, they find evidence that "adverse effects" such as increased police contacts and arrests among program participants were associated with law enforcement interventions but not any other types of interventions (e.g., street outreach) or characteristics of research design (e.g., random assignment). More recently, Mallion and Wood (2020) used a public health approach in assessing gang intervention programs. They found that many programs fail to address one or more of the key elements of a public health approach: surveillance, risk and protective factors, developing primary and secondary prevention to accompany tertiary intervention, and implementation of evidence-based programs. They find that the Good Lives Model, a strengths-based rehabilitation theory that guides therapeutic work with offenders, produced positive outcomes including motivation to change. They identified Functional Family Therapy (tested by Thornberry et al. 2018) as promising. Multiple sources of support for the same conclusion strengthen that conclusion.

Abt and Winship (2016) conducted a metareview of fourteen hundred studies that were capsulized in forty-three reviews. They identified focused deterrence as having "the strongest and most consistent anti-violence effects" (Abt 2019, 88). There is great utility in such synthetic reviews or metareviews. However, a stronger methodological approach is the use of meta-analyses. A meta-analysis codes and quantifies the characteristics of an intervention and "effect size" (how much it changed behavior per unit of intervention). The work of Wong et al. (2016) on gang prevention and Braga, Weisburd, and Turchan (2018, 2019) on focused deterrence provide the best examples of meta-analyses in the area of gang interventions.

Our review of existing gang interventions has made several points. The prevalence of suppression-only or suppression-first programs demonstrates that programming emphasizes what works the least and underrepresents what works the best. With few exceptions (for an exception, see Ratcliffe, Perenzin, and Sorg 2017), suppression-only strategies have little effect on gang crime, yet interventions prioritize this strategy. And it is equally clear that prevention is the most effective tool against gang membership and gang crime, yet it is often an afterthought or so poorly funded that it has no chance of working. A second conclusion drawn from this review is that there are lots of experiments in programming but little systematic and strategic building on past successes and failures. Gang programming is replete with home-grown programs that fail to build on existing successes and are equally likely to embrace failed models. Such approaches carry the strong likelihood of failure, adding to the perception that nothing works. Finally, nomenclature matters. Distinguishing between "programs" and "strategies" is important. The Colorado Blueprints project identifies programs with specific interventions that demand a high degree of fidelity in their implementation and maintenance. Strategies are flexible approaches to dealing with gang problems and allow a hybrid mixture of multiple interventions. The Comprehensive Gang Model is a good example of such an approach. When researchers fail to find effects of such programs on gang membership or gang crime, supporters argue that because it is a strategy, the same rules of evaluation do not apply, or that the elements of the strategy were not implemented with fidelity. The reality is that a strategy that cannot be implemented with fidelity in most of its versions is not much of a strategy.

Assessing a "Promising Practice": A Case of Implementation Failure

In answering the question, "Why has the United States failed to solve its youth gang problem?" W. Miller (1990, 272–273) asserts, "The virtual abandonment of sound evaluation of gang control efforts is a major reason for our failure to reduce the gang problems." He argues that "as gang problems have increased, the conduct of program evaluation has decreased." It is clear from our review of the multimillion-dollar SafeFutures intervention below that the need for evaluation is greater than ever. Equally great is the need to heed the lessons of prior evaluations and not repeat the same mistakes over and over.

SafeFutures is the program that every city would like to have. This is because it had many of the features that are necessary for success, including a multiyear commitment for funding, time to plan, a geographically targeted intervention, a multidisciplinary intervention team, and a fully funded implementation and outcome analysis. It represents "the program that should have worked"—except in St. Louis, it did not. SafeFutures was based on the Spergel model and funded by OJJDP. It provided substantial funding—$1.4 million a year for six years, including a planning year. It had a substantial roster of training and technical assistance providers that ranged from Boys and Girls Clubs of America to the National Council on Crime and Delinquency and the National Crime Prevention Council to cabinet-level support from the U.S. Department of Housing and Urban Development. Empowerment Zones and Enterprise Communities were present to assist with services and crime alternatives. The approach was to be targeted and include a small part of the city so that program management and fiscal support were integrated. A signed memorandum of understanding was obtained from the mayor, alderpersons (i.e., city council members), police chief, juvenile court, circuit court, prosecutor, public schools, archdiocese, neighborhood groups, and the faith community.

And then there was a municipal election in 1997. The election brought a new mayor, who appointed a new police chief, and the city schools continued to struggle with declining enrollment and a shrinking funding base. The new police chief declined to participate, and political support for SafeFutures vanished. What had once been a comprehensive team with memoranda of understanding, assigned service domains, and cooperative planning became focused only on gang intervention.

In its final review, the local research team arrived at a simple conclusion. When it came to implementation, the local evaluation determined that the program model was not implemented. The most prominent successes also faced challenges. Several of the outreach workers ran afoul of the law; one was arrested with crack cocaine in large enough quantities that he was charged with possession with intent to sell. Another outreach worker was shot. And the shining success, a group of high-risk gang members who met in a church basement weekly, were told that they were no longer welcome at the church because their presence was scaring parishioners away. The evaluation team concluded its outcome evaluation by noting,

> As this evaluation report has made all too clear, the initiative failed on both accounts (implementation and outcome). The model was not implemented as it was designed and failed to produce positive outcomes for the target group (gang members and at-risk youth). (Curry and Decker 2002, 113)

This finding applied to each of the outcome measures: delinquency, arrests, and court appearances.

How could things go so wrong with a solid project model, adequate funding, multiple years to produce, and (at least initially) widespread support? The evaluators concluded with another sobering observation: it may be harder to change the behavior of the adults whose job it is to serve the needs of youth than to change the behavior of the youth themselves.

Continuing Issues in Responding to Gangs

Delinquency Programs or Gang Programs?

An ongoing issue in responding to gangs is whether the response should be focused on gangs specifically or crime and delinquency more broadly. This issue is complicated by the tendency of many researchers, practitioners, and policymakers to not distinguish between gang crime and crime that is not gang related, a topic we discussed in Chapters 1 and 6. Faced with reduced funds for youth programs, policymakers and community representatives often feel that they have to make choices about which youths are to receive program services when program resources are in short supply. Two programs reviewed above, Group Violence Intervention and Cure Violence, are focused on violence, but not explicitly gang violence. In this context it is important to note that Family Functional Therapy, a general delinquency program, was found to be effective with gang members, further reinforcing the overlap between the two. In some ways, the overlap between gang and non-gang crime may broaden the inventory of programs to address gang crime.

There are two challenges here. The first is to decide whether scarce prevention and intervention resources should be focused only on gang members or on delinquents more generally. The second is whether prevention and intervention practices are equally effective in addressing delinquency and gang crime. We believe that this is largely a decision based on the availability of resources and careful analyses of the nature of crime in a community. Where gang crime is the driving force in community disruption and youth development, it should be the target of scarce resources. Alternatively, in communities that do not experience high levels of gang crime, a broader approach that targets delinquency seems more appropriate. At its heart, we argue that this is a decision that should be driven by careful analysis of data. Data are particularly important to define and describe the gang problem. As Decker and Kempf (1991) demonstrated, the differences in views of law enforcement, practitioners, and gang members about the definition of a gang, gang activities, and the problems faced by gang youth could hardly be greater. Common definitions and data are necessary to achieve success—a point made clear by the results of the work by Kennedy and Braga (2002) in Boston.

Denial

It is impossible to develop a response to gang problems in a setting where they are not acknowledged. Alternatively, when a "gang response" is developed in a setting where gangs are not a problem, this produces "moral panic" (Hagedorn 1988; McCorkle and Miethe 2001; Joan Moore 1991). Huff (1989) identified Ohio's three largest cities as being in a state of denial that they had gangs. In Columbus, Ohio, the denial ended quickly when there was a high-visibility gang-related murder and separate gang-related attacks on the governor's daughter and the mayor's son. Huff argued that official denial "appears to facilitate victimization by gangs, especially in the public schools" (530). While city officials are busy denying the existence of gangs in their community, they allow gang membership and popularity to grow. In St. Louis, politicians and police leaders denied the existence of "real gangs" in their city in the 1990s, claiming that because they weren't Los Angeles Bloods or Crips, the gangs in St. Louis didn't merit identification or attention. While they publicly proclaimed such a stance, the gangs of St. Louis were able to grow and gain strength.

From his research on gangs in Milwaukee, Hagedorn (1988, 151–158) described the role that denial can play in shaping the course of a community's response to its gang problem. According to Hagedorn, the motivations for Milwaukee's policy of denial grew out of two kinds of fear. On one hand, political and business leaders of the community feared that recognition of a gang problem would undermine tourism and the potential for attracting prospective employers and economic ventures. On the other hand, some segments of the community feared that law enforcement would use "gang problems" as an excuse to crack down on poor and minority communities and that any recognition of a gang problem constituted a form of racism.

The Role of Gang Members in Responding to Gang Crime Problems

In offering his "practical agenda" for gang reform, Hagedorn (1988, 167) listed as his first principle,

> Gang members must participate in any meaningful programs. By "participate" we mean gang programs need to train and hire former local gang members as staff, utilize older gang members as consultants in developing new programs, and make sure input from the gang "clients" takes place and is genuine.

Echoing Hagedorn, Bursik and Grasmick (1993) proposed the recruitment of gang members as core members of locally based crime prevention programs. They base this recommendation on gang members' knowledge of crime in the community, gang identification with communities as turf, and a number of historical examples where gang involvement in positive actions has led to short-term reductions in criminal violence. Abt (2019) repeats this stance in his thoughtful assessment of gang and violence intervention programs, noting that the presence of gang members in efforts to reduce gang problems increases the legitimacy and credibility of those interventions. This is also a core tenet of Cure Violence.

While several communities have used former gang members to reduce violence (Chicago, Ft. Worth, St. Louis, Boston, and others), the approach remains controversial. M. Klein (2011) was particularly critical of the use of former gang members as "interventionists." He offered several reasons for his skepticism. First, the credibility they earn as program participants glorifies their prior gang activities and even incentivizes ex-gang members embellishing their old street record to appear credible to youth today. Second, they push the assumption that only former gang members can function as interventionists because non-gang workers have not "walked in my shoes." Paraphrasing the old *New York Times* columnist Red Smith, Densley (2013, 164) observed that you do not need to have experienced something in order to do it: "If that were true, then only dead men could write obituaries." Third, former gang members, like the police, are reluctant to share information with others about their clients and can sometimes push away others interested in helping. Finally, former gang members face the burden of reversing a street socialization cycle they have undergone for a long period, which can challenge their identity and self-concept. Indeed, we have seen headlines about former gang members who end up as the victims of serious crimes. Even for experienced and respected "old heads" on the street, life is dangerous (see Chapter 5). When the Shannon Program, funded by the governor's office in Massachusetts, used former gang members for outreach programs (Decker et al. 2008), the approach generated criticism. However, supervision, screening, and training seem the appropriate antidote to many of the concerns listed.

Variation and Change in Gang Crime Problems

Rarely are gang programs the only game in town. That is to say, most cities have multiple interventions and programming going on. Indeed, D. Gottfredson (2000) found that the average middle school student participated in seven prevention programs in a typical school year. With social service, school, law enforcement, and special programs taking place at the same time, and sometimes with the same youth and in the same geographic locations, it is hard to disentangle which program created change in the lives of the people it targeted. For multiyear programs, maturational reform becomes a concern as youth transition from adolescence to teenagers and in some cases adults.

We have alluded to program integrity, another concern in isolating the effect of a gang program. Program integrity refers to the need to implement a program as defined, an especially important issue for interventions in the University of Colorado's Blueprints registry. Strategies and interventions that involve multiple agencies with different cultures and structures often have difficulty working together. This is particularly true of programs that integrate suppression (police-led) with opportunities provision or forms of counseling (social service agencies). The immediacy of gang problems can also affect program integrity, leading otherwise well-intentioned individuals to "do something." And in the rush to do something, often symbolic efforts or unfocused, nonstrategic crackdowns are used that reflect the need for urgency but lack the focus of integration with other initiatives to be successful.

Gang responses must consider variations in the structure and dynamics of gang crime. The distinction between chronic and emerging gang cities is comparable to the one noted by Joan Moore (1988) and Hagedorn (1988) between "new" and "old" gang cities. Chronic gang cities are jurisdictions where a gang problem was reported to have existed prior to 1980. Emerging cities were those where gang crime problems had only been reported more recently. In chronic gang problem cities, gangs appeared to be better organized and more involved in serious crime, including drug trafficking. Not to maintain sensitivity to these community and social differences in gang involvement would undermine the potential for effectively responding to gang crime problems. Maxson, Hennigan, and Sloane (2005) make this point when discussing the efficacy of a civil gang injunction in Southern California, where the application of the strategy would be challenging if presented to gangs with different structural dynamics. Clearly, the widespread availability of the internet and social media has changed the behavior of gangs and continues to do so at a rapid pace (Chapter 10). Understanding and tracking individuals and crime groups is now a sophisticated technological chore.

Connecting Practice to Theory

Our responses to gangs have proceeded without a solid theory of gang behavior and gang programming. Those who have the ultimate responsibility for developing and implementing programs are policymakers and practitioners who do not have extensive training in theory, while researchers, who have extensive training in theory, do not often have a significant role in the practical aspects of responding to gang problems. Researchers need to assume the responsibility of linking practice to theory. This is important because it allows for a deeper understanding of the mechanisms by which programs or program elements work. Three excellent examples are readily available. The G.R.E.A.T. program was developed and implemented by practitioners, but the evaluation team of the G.R.E.A.T. program, Winfree, Esbensen, and Osgood (1996), has carefully and systematically linked the components of the G.R.E.A.T. program to M. Gottfredson and Hirschi's (1990) self-control theory and Akers's (2009) social learning theory. Similarly, Spergel and Grossman (1997) began a preliminary evaluation of the Little Village Gang Violence Reduction Project by linking program components to several theories, specifically anomie, socialization, differential association, and social control, including community and personal disorganization, in explaining gang-related violence among hard-core older gang youths.

Finally, Thornberry has built on his longitudinal work on gang risk and protective factors to conduct a randomized controlled trial of Functional Family Therapy for gang members and their families. This merger of the best research design, theory, and programming is more of what is needed. This calls for partnerships between practitioners, criminal justice system actors, and researchers. Such partnerships may draw the ire of critical scholars, who argue that researchers who engage in such practices lose their independence and exacerbate ethnic and racial disparities while increasing punishment. Such partnerships take work on all sides and critical reflection on the part of researchers. But as the history of gang research has demonstrated, much of the best information comes from program evaluation, such as G.R.E.A.T.

Conclusion

There are multiple and diverse strategies of responding to gangs and gang-related crime. Many of the best-known responses to gangs provided important data in describing the nature of gang membership, gang crime, and gang organization as well as theories of crime. Interventions primarily have focused on the characteristics of neighborhoods, opportunities, and families. Five sometimes-overlapping strategies have dominated the past forty years of responding to gangs: (1) community organization, (2) social intervention, (3) opportunities provision, (4) suppression, and (5) organizational development and change. A recent development has been the growth of hybrid interventions, those with multiple strategies and the addition of either focused deterrence or public health strategies. Evaluation research has found few successes, but such research in this area has been plagued by weak designs, with few comparison groups or neighborhoods.

We did find a growing reliance on more sophisticated evaluations of gang programs. It is clear that the emphasis on best practices has taken root among funding agencies, many of which now insist on randomized controlled trials, synthetic controls, or other sophisticated research designs. It is important in this context to also assess the extent to which programs are implemented with fidelity. Researchers, program staff, and the public all have a stake in the use of better research to assess the important question of what works.

M. Klein and Maxson (2006) pushed the field ahead in their critical analysis of social control efforts directed at street gangs. Fifteen years after their work, the focus on data quality, definitions of concepts (especially gang membership), and clear specification of treatments still rings true. While much progress has been made since their seminal book was published, there is still the need for more. We hope that such work builds on the Klein and Maxson foundation, and fifteen years hence, we will be able to reflect back and find that we are closing the gap between our knowledge of the gang problem and our ability to successfully address that problem.

References

Abt, Thomas. 2019. *Bleeding Out: The Devastating Consequences of Urban Violence—and a Bold New Plan for Peace in the Street*. New York: Basic Books.

Abt, Thomas, and Christopher Winship. 2016. *What Works in Reducing Community Violence: A Meta-review and Field Study for the Northern Triangle*. Washington, DC: U.S. Agency for International Development.

Adam, Karla. 2018. "Glasgow Was Once the 'Murder Capital of Europe.' Now It's a Model for Cutting Crime." *Washington Post*, October 27, 2018. https://www.washingtonpost.com/world/europe/glasgow-was-once-the-murder-capital-of-europe-now-its-a-model-for-cutting-crime/2018/10/27/0b167e68-6e02-4795-92f8-adb1020b7434_story.html.

Adamson, Christopher. 2000. "Defensive Localism in White and Black: A Comparative History of European-American and African-American Youth Gangs." *Ethnic and Racial Studies* 23 (2): 272–298.

Agnew, Robert. 1992. "Foundation for a General Strain Theory of Crime and Delinquency." *Criminology* 30 (1): 47–88.

———. 2017. "Revitalizing Merton: General Strain Theory." In *The Origins of American Criminology*, edited by Francis T. Cullen, Cheryl L. Johnson, Andrew J. Myer, and Freda Adler, 137–158 New York: Routledge.

Aguilar, Alfredo. 2019. "Murder and Prison Gangs: A Mexican American Experience inside a Texas Prison." *NEXO*, Spring 2019. https://jsri.msu.edu/upload/nexo/NEXO%20Excerpt%20S19.pdf.

Akers, Ronald L. 1985. *Deviant Behavior: A Social Learning Approach*. 3rd ed. Belmont, CA: Wadsworth.

———. 2009. *Social Learning and Social Structure: A General Theory of Crime and Deviance*. Piscataway, NJ: Transaction.

Aldridge, Judith, and Juanjo Medina. 2005. *Gangs and Delinquent Behaviour: Findings from the 2004 Offending, Crime and Justice Survey*. London: Home Office.

———. 2008. "Youth Gangs in an English City: Social Exclusion, Drugs and Violence." Full Research Report ESRC End of Award Report, RES-000-23-0615. Swindon: ESRC.

Aldridge, Judith, Juanjo Medina-Ariz, and Robert Ralphs. 2012. "Counting Gangs: Conceptual and Validity Problems with the Eurogang Definition." In *Youth Gangs in International Perspective*, edited by Finn-Aage Esbensen and Cheryl L. Maxson, 35–51. New York: Springer.

Alexander, Michelle. 2010. *The New Jim Crow: Mass Incarceration in the Age of Colorblindness*. New York: New Press.

Alleyne, Emma, and Jane L. Wood. 2010. "Gang Involvement: Psychological and Behavioral Characteristics of Gang Members, Peripheral Youth, and Nongang Youth." *Aggressive Behavior* 36 (6): 423–436.

Alonso, Alejandroa. 2004. "Racialized Identities in the Formation of Black Gangs in Los Angeles." *Urban Geography* 25 (7): 658–674.

Alpert, Geoffrey P., Jeff Rojek, J. Andrew Hansen, Randy L. Shannon, and Scott H. Decker. 2011. "Examining the Prevalence and Impact of Gangs in College Athletic Programs Using Multiple Sources." Washington, DC: Bureau of Justice Assistance.

Amali, Sadiq Ewaoda, Issah Moshood, and Mubarak Bala Iliyasu. 2017. "Impact and Implications of Youth Involvement in Urban Gangs: A Case Study from Nasarawa, Kano State, Nigeria." *Acta Criminologica: African Journal of Criminology and Victimology* 30 (5): 150–169.

Amnesty International U.K. 2018. *Trapped in the Matrix*. London: Amnesty International U.K.

Andell, Paul. 2019. *Thinking Seriously about Gangs: Towards a Critical Realist Approach*. Cham, Switzerland: Palgrave Macmillan.

Anderson, Elijah. 1990. *Streetwise: Race, Class, and Change in an Urban Community*. Chicago: University of Chicago Press.

———. 1999. *Code of the Street: Decency, Violence, and the Moral Life of the Inner City*. New York: W. W. Norton.

Anderson, John. 2007. "Gang-Related Witness Intimidation." National Gang Center Bulletin 1. Tallahassee, FL: National Gang Center.

Anderson, Nells. 1923. *The Hobo*. Chicago: University of Chicago Press.

Ang, Rebecca P., Vivien S. Huan, Wei Teng Chan, Siew Ann Cheong, and Jia Ning Leaw. 2015. "The Role of Delinquency, Proactive Aggression, Psychopathy and Behavioral School Engagement in Reported Youth Gang Membership." *Journal of Adolescence* 41:148–156.

Ang, Rebecca P., Vivien S. Huan, Sok Hoon Chua, and Si Huan Lim. 2012. "Gang Affiliation, Aggression, and Violent Offending in a Sample of Youth Offenders." *Psychology, Crime and Law* 18 (8): 703–711.

Arbreton, Amy J. A., and Wendy S. McClanahan. 2002. *Targeted Outreach: Boys and Girls Clubs of America's Approach to Gang Prevention and Intervention*. Philadelphia: Public/Private Ventures.

Arias, Enrique Desmond. 2006. *Drugs and Democracy in Rio de Janeiro: Trafficking, Social Networks, and Public Security*. New ed. Chapel Hill: University of North Carolina Press.

Arias, Enrique Desmond, and Daniel M. Goldstein, eds. 2010. *Violent Democracies in Latin America*. Durham, NC: Duke University Press Books.

Armstrong, Scott. 1994. "East Palo Alto Takes Back Its Mean Streets." *Christian Science Monitor*, February 14, 1994. https://www.csmonitor.com/1994/0214/14081.html.

Aronowitz, Alexis A. 2001. "Smuggling and Trafficking in Human Beings: The Phenomenon, the Markets That Drive It and the Organisations That Promote It." *European Journal on Criminal Policy and Research* 9 (2): 163–195.

Asbury, Herbert. 1927. *The Gangs of New York: An Informal History of the Underworld*. New York: Vintage.

Asher, Jeff. 2017. "Gang Stats Aren't Remotely Reliable, but Voters Keep Hearing about Them Anyway." *FiveThirtyEight*, November 3, 2017. https://fivethirtyeight.com/features /gang-stats-arent-remotely-reliable-but-voters-keep-hearing-about-them-anyway/.

Askey, Amber Perenzin. 2017. "Quantifying Gang Locations: Systematically Testing Validity Using a Partial Test of Messick's Unified Perspective." Ph.D. diss., Temple University. https://search.proquest.com/docview/2014419746/abstract/1E5523E6820047BAPQ/1.

Aspholm, Roberto. 2020. *Views from the Streets: The Transformation of Gangs and Violence on Chicago*. New York: Columbia University Press.

Aspholm, Roberto R., and Mark A. Mattaini. 2017. "Youth Activism as Violence Prevention." In *The Wiley Handbook of Violence and Aggression*, edited by Peter Sturmey, 1–12. New Brunswick, NJ: John Wiley and Sons.

Augustyn, Megan Bears, Jean M. McGloin, and David C. Pyrooz. 2019. "Does Gang Membership Pay? Illegal and Legal Earnings through Emerging Adulthood." *Criminology* 57 (3): 452–480.

Augustyn, Megan Bears, Terence P. Thornberry, and Marvin D. Krohn. 2014. "Gang Membership and Pathways to Maladaptive Parenting." *Journal of Research on Adolescence* 24 (2): 252–267.

Augustyn, Megan Bears, Jeffrey T. Ward, and Marvin D. Krohn. 2017. "Exploring Intergenerational Continuity in Gang Membership." *Journal of Crime and Justice* 40 (3): 252–274.

Ayling, Julie. 2011. "Gang Change and Evolutionary Theory." *Crime, Law and Social Change* 56 (1): 1–26.

Baird, Adam. 2012. "The Violent Gang and the Construction of Masculinity amongst Socially Excluded Young Men." *Safer Communities* 11 (4): 179–190.

———. 2018a. "Becoming the Baddest: Masculine Trajectories of Gang Violence in Medellín." *Journal of Latin American Studies* 5 (1): 183–210.

———. 2018b. "Dancing with Danger: Ethnographic Safety, Male Bravado and Gang Research in Colombia." *Qualitative Research* 18 (3): 342–360.

———. 2019. "Man a Kill a Man for Nutin': Gang Transnationalism, Masculinities, and Violence in Belize City." *Men and Masculinities*. https://doi.org/10.1177/1097184X19872787.

Bakeer, Donald. 1992. *Crips: The Story of the LA Street Gang from 1971–1985*. Los Angeles: Precocious Pub.

Bannister, Jon, Keith Kintrea, and Jonny Pickering. 2013. "Young People and Violent Territorial Conflict: Exclusion, Culture and the Search for Identity." *Journal of Youth Studies* 16 (4): 474–490.

Barnes, J. C., Kevin M. Beaver, and J. Mitchell Miller. 2010. "Estimating the Effect of Gang Membership on Nonviolent and Violent Delinquency: A Counterfactual Analysis." *Aggressive Behavior* 36 (6): 437–451.

Barrientez, Amanda. 2018. "Toward Rehabilitative Justice: The Journey from De-Habilitated Boys to Re-Habilitated Men." Ph.D. Diss., University of Colorado Boulder.

Barrows, Julie, and C. Ronald Huff. 2009. "Gangs and Public Policy: Constructing and Deconstructing Gang Databases." *Criminology and Public Policy* 8 (4): 675–703.

Barton, Michael S., Matthew A. Valasik, Elizabeth Brault, and George Tita. 2020. "'Gentefication' in the Barrio: Examining the Relationship between Gentrification and Homicide in East Los Angeles." *Crime and Delinquency* 66 (13–14): 1888–1913.

Batchelor, Susan, Sarah Armstrong, and Donna MacLellan. 2019. *Taking Stock of Violence in Scotland*. Glasgow: Scottish Centre for Crime and Justice Research.

Battin, Sara R., Karl G. Hill, Robert D. Abbott, Richard F. Catalano, and J. David Hawkins. 1998. "The Contribution of Gang Membership to Delinquency beyond Delinquent Friends." *Criminology* 36 (1): 93–116.

Beaver, Kevin M., Matt DeLisi, Michael G. Vaughn, and J. C. Barnes. 2010. "Monoamine Oxidase A Genotype Is Associated with Gang Membership and Weapon Use." *Comprehensive Psychiatry* 51 (2): 130–134.

Beccaria, Cesare. 1764. *An Essay on Crimes and Punishments.* Indianapolis: Hackett.

Becker, Gary S. 1968. "Crime and Punishment: An Economic Approach." *Journal of Political Economy* 76 (2): 169–217.

Becker, Michael H., Scott H. Decker, Gary LaFree, David C. Pyrooz, Kyle Ernest, and Patrick A. James. 2020. "A Comparative Study of Initial Involvement in Gangs and Political Extremism." *Terrorism and Political Violence.* https://doi.org/10.1080/09546553.2020.1828079.

Beckett, Helen, Isabelle Brodie, Fiona Factor, Margaret Melrose, Jenny J. Pearce, John Pitts, Lucie Shuker, and Camille Warrington. 2013. *"It's Wrong—but You Get Used to It": A Qualitative Study of Gang-Associated Sexual Violence towards, and Exploitation of, Young People in England.* Luton: University of Bedfordshire.

Bender, Kimberly A., Jennifer E. Cobbina, and Edmund F. McGarrell. 2016. "Reentry Programming for High-Risk Offenders: Insights from Participants." *International Journal of Offender Therapy and Comparative Criminology* 60 (13): 1479–1508.

Bennett, Trevor, and Katy Holloway. 2004. "Gang Membership, Drugs and Crime in the UK." *British Journal of Criminology* 44:305–323.

Bennett, William J., John J. DiIulio Jr., and John P. Walters. 1996. *Body Count: Moral Poverty, and How to Win America's War against Crime and Drugs.* New York: Simon and Schuster.

Benson, Jana S., and Scott H. Decker. 2010. "The Organizational Structure of International Drug Smuggling." *Journal of Criminal Justice* 38 (2): 130–138.

Berg, Julie, and Irvin Kinnes. 2009. "An Overview of Crime in South Africa." *The Criminologist* 34 (3): 22–24.

Berg, Mark T. 2012. "The Overlap of Violent Offending and Violent Victimization: Assessing the Evidence and Explanations." In *Violent Offenders: Theory, Research, Policy, and Practice,* edited by Matt DeLisi and Peter J. Conis, 17–38. Burlington, MA: Jones and Bartlett Learning.

Berger, Rony, Hisham Abu-Raiya, Yotam Heineberg, and Philip Zimbardo. 2017. "The Process of Desistance among Core Ex-Gang Members." *American Journal of Orthopsychiatry* 87 (4): 487.

Best, Joel, and Mary M. Hutchinson. 1996. "The Gang Initiation Rite as a Motif in Contemporary Crime Discourse." *Justice Quarterly* 13 (3): 383–404.

Bevan, James, and Nicolas Florquin. 2006. "Few Options but the Gun: Angry Young Men." In *Small Arms Survey 2006,* 294–321. Geneva: Oxford University Press http://www.smallarmssurvey.org/fileadmin/docs/A-Yearbook/2006/en/Small-Arms-Survey-2006-Chapter-12-EN.pdf.

Bibb, Marylyn. 1967. "Gang-Related Services of Mobilization for Youth." In *Juvenile Gangs in Context: Theory, Research, and Action,* edited by Malcolm W. Klein, 175–182 Englewood Cliffs, NJ: Prentice Hall.

Bichler, Gisela, Alexis Norris, Jared R. Dmello, and Jasmin Randle. 2019. "The Impact of Civil Gang Injunctions on Networked Violence between the Bloods and the Crips." *Crime & Delinquency* 65 (7): 875–915. https://doi.org/10.1177/0011128717739607.

Bjerk, David. 2009. "How Much Can We Trust Causal Interpretations of Fixed-Effects Estimators in the Context of Criminality?" *Journal of Quantitative Criminology* 25 (4): 391–417.

Bjerregaard, Beth. 2002. "Self-Definitions of Gang Membership and Involvement in Delinquent Activities." *Youth and Society* 34 (1): 31–54.

———. 2015. "Legislative Approaches to Addressing Gangs and Gang-Related Crime." In *The Handbook of Gangs*, edited by Scott H. Decker and David C. Pyrooz, 345–368. Chichester, U.K.: Wiley.

Bjerregaard, Beth, and Carolyn Smith. 1993. "Gender Differences in Gang Participation, Delinquency, and Substance Use." *Journal of Quantitative Criminology* 9 (4): 329–355.

Bjornstrom, Eileen E. S., Robert L. Kaufman, Ruth D. Peterson, and Michael D. Slater. 2010. "Race and Ethnic Representations of Lawbreakers and Victims in Crime News: A National Study of Television Coverage." *Social Problems* 57 (2): 269–293.

Blau, Peter Michael. 1977. *Inequality and Heterogeneity: A Primitive Theory of Social Structure*. New York: Free Press.

Blaya, Catherine, and Uberto Gatti. 2010. "Deviant Youth Groups in Italy and France: Prevalence and Characteristics." *European Journal on Criminal Policy and Research* 16 (2): 127–144.

Bloch, Stefano. 2019. "Broken Windows Ideology and the (Mis) Reading of Graffiti." *Critical Criminology* 28:703–720.

Bloch, Stefano, and Dugan Meyer. 2019. "Implicit Revanchism: Gang Injunctions and the Security Politics of White Liberalism." *Environment and Planning D: Society and Space* 37 (6): 1100–1118.

Blumenstein, Matthew H. 2009. "RICO Overreach: How the Federal Government's Escalating Offensive against Gangs Has Run Afoul of the Constitution." *Vanderbilt Law Review* 62 (1): 211–238.

Blumstein, Alfred, and Joel Wallman. 2005. *The Crime Drop in America*. 2nd ed. New York: Cambridge University Press.

Bogardus, Emory S. 1926. *The City Boy and His Problems: A Survey of Boy Life in Los Angeles*. Los Angeles: House of Ralston.

Bolden, Christian. 2013. "Tales from the Hood: An Emic Perspective on Gang Joining and Gang Desistance." *Criminal Justice Review* 38 (4): 473–490.

———. 2020. *Out of the Red: My Life of Gangs, Prison, and Redemption*. New Brunswick, NJ: Rutgers University Press.

Bookin-Weiner, Hedy, and Ruth Horowitz. 1983. "The End of the Youth Gang: Fad or Fact?" *Criminology* 21 (4): 585–602.

Bouchard, Martin, and Sadaf Hashimi. 2017. "When Is a 'War' a 'Wave?' Two Approaches for the Detection of Waves in Gang Homicides." *Canadian Journal of Criminology and Criminal Justice* 59 (2): 198–226.

Bouchard, Martin, and Andrea Spindler. 2010. "Groups, Gangs, and Delinquency: Does Organization Matter?" *Journal of Criminal Justice* 38 (5): 921–933.

Bouchard, Martin, Wei Wang, and Eric Beauregard. 2012. "Social Capital, Opportunity, and School-Based Victimization." *Violence and Victims* 27 (5): 656–673.

Bowker, Lee H., and Malcolm W. Klein. 1983. "The Etiology of Female Juvenile Delinquency and Gang Membership: A Test of Psychological and Social Structural Explanations." *Adolescence* 18:739–751.

Boyd, Danah. 2014. *It's Complicated: The Social Lives of Networked Teens*. New Haven: Yale University Press.

Boyle, Greg. 2010. *Tattoos on the Heart: The Power of Boundless Compassion*. New York: Simon and Schuster.

Boyle, Kathleen 1992. *School's a Rough Place: Youth Gangs, Drug Users, and Family Life in Los Angeles*. Washington, DC: Department of Education, Office of Educational Research and Improvement.

Bradshaw, Paul. 2005. "Terrors and Young Teams: Youth Gangs and Delinquency in Edinburgh." In *European Street Gangs and Troublesome Youth Groups*, edited by Scott H. Decker and Frank Weerman, 193–218. Lanham, MD: AltaMira.

Braga, Anthony A. 2008. "Pulling Levers Focused Deterrence Strategies and the Prevention of Gun Homicide." *Journal of Criminal Justice* 36 (4): 332–343.

———. 2014. "Pulling Levers Policing." In *Encyclopedia of Criminology and Criminal Justice*, edited by Gerben Bruinsma and David Weisburd, 4174–4185. New York: Springer. https://doi.org/10.1007/978-1-4614-5690-2_173.

———. 2015. "Police Gang Units and Effective Gang Violence Reduction." In *The Handbook of Gangs*, edited by Scott H. Decker and David C. Pyrooz, 309–327. Chichester, U.K.: Wiley-Blackwell.

Braga, Anthony A., Robert Apel, and Brandon C. Welsh. 2013. "The Spillover Effects of Focused Deterrence on Gang Violence." *Evaluation Review* 37 (3–4): 314–342.

Braga, Anthony A., David M. Hureau, and Andrew V. Papachristos. 2014. "Deterring Gang-Involved Gun Violence: Measuring the Impact of Boston's Operation Ceasefire on Street Gang Behavior." *Journal of Quantitative Criminology* 30 (1): 113–139.

Braga, Anthony A., David Hureau, and Christopher Winship. 2008. "Losing Faith-Police, Black Churches, and the Resurgence of Youth Violence in Boston." *Ohio State Journal of Criminal Law* 6:141–172.

Braga, Anthony A., David M. Kennedy, Elin J. Waring, and Anne Morrison Piehl. 2001. "Problem-Oriented Policing, Deterrence, and Youth Violence: An Evaluation of Boston's Operation Ceasefire." *Journal of Research in Crime and Delinquency* 38 (3): 195–225.

Braga, Anthony A., Andrew V. Papachristos, and David M. Hureau. 2014. "The Effects of Hot Spots Policing on Crime: An Updated Systematic Review and Meta-analysis." *Justice Quarterly* 31 (4): 633–663.

Braga, Anthony A., and David L. Weisburd. 2012. "The Effects of Focused Deterrence Strategies on Crime: A Systematic Review and Meta-analysis of the Empirical Evidence." *Journal of Research in Crime and Delinquency* 49 (3): 323–358.

———. 2014. "Must We Settle for Less Rigorous Evaluations in Large Area-Based Crime Prevention Programs? Lessons from a Campbell Review of Focused Deterrence." *Journal of Experimental Criminology* 10 (4): 573–597.

Braga, Anthony A., David Weisburd, and Brandon Turchan. 2018. "Focused Deterrence Strategies and Crime Control: An Updated Systematic Review and Meta-analysis of the Empirical Evidence." *Criminology and Public Policy* 17 (1): 205–250.

Brantingham, P. Jeffrey, Baichuan Yuan, and Denise Herz. 2020. "Is Gang Violent Crime More Contagious than Non-Gang Violent Crime?" *Journal of Quantitative Criminology.* Published ahead of print, September 22, 2020. https://doi.org/10.1007/s10940-020-09479-1.

Brantingham, P. Jeffrey, Baichuan Yuan, Nick Sundback, Frederick P. Schoenberg, Andrea L. Bertozzi, Joshua Gordon, Jorja Leap, Kristine Chan, Molly Kraus, and Sean Malinowski. 2018. "Does Violence Interruption Work?" *Proceedings of the National Academy of Science of the United States of America* 8 (7): 1–6.

Brantingham, Patricia L., and Paul J. Brantingham. 1993. "Environment, Routine, and Situation: Toward a Pattern Theory of Crime." In *Routine Activity and Rational Choice*, edited by Ronald Clarke and Marcus Felson, 259–294. New York: Routledge.

Brayne, Sarah. 2020. *Predict and Surveil: Data, Discretion, and the Future of Policing.* New York: Oxford University Press.

Brenneman, Robert. 2011. *Homies and Hermanos: God and Gangs in Central America.* New York: Oxford University Press.

———. 2014. "Wrestling the Devil: Conversion and Exit from Central American Gangs." *Latin American Research Review* 49:112–128.

Brotherton, David C. 1996. "The Contradictions of Suppression: Notes from a Study of Approaches to Gangs in Three Public High Schools." *Urban Review* 28 (2): 95–117.

———. 2008. "Beyond Social Reproduction: Bringing Resistance Back in Gang Theory." *Theoretical Criminology* 12 (1): 55–77.

———. 2015. *Youth Street Gangs: A Critical Appraisal.* New York: Routledge.

Brotherton, David C., and Luis Barrios. 2004. *The Almighty Latin King and Queen Nation: Street Politics and the Transformation of a New York City Gang.* New York: Columbia University Press.

Brotherton, David C., and Rafael Gude. 2020. "Social Control and the Gang: Lessons from the Legalization of Street Gangs in Ecuador." *Critical Criminology*, May 2020. https://doi.org/10.1007/s10612-020-09505-5.

Brown, Gregory Christopher, James Diego Vigil, and Eric Robert Taylor. 2012. "The Ghettoization of Blacks in Los Angeles: The Emergence of Street Gangs." *Journal of African American Studies* 16 (2): 209–225.

Brown, Waln K. 1977. "Black Female Gangs in Philadelphia." *International Journal of Offender Therapy and Comparative Criminology* 21 (3): 221–228.

Brunson, Rod K. 2007. "'Police Don't Like Black People': African-American Young Men's Accumulated Police Experiences." *Criminology and Public Policy* 6 (1): 71–101.

Brunson, Rod K., Anthony A. Braga, David M. Hureau, and Kashea Pegram. 2015. "We Trust You, but Not That Much: Examining Police–Black Clergy Partnerships to Reduce Youth Violence." *Justice Quarterly* 32 (6): 1006–1036.

Brunson, Rod K., and Brian A. Wade. 2019. "'Oh Hell No, We Don't Talk to Police': Insights on the Lack of Cooperation in Police Investigations of Urban Gun Violence." *Criminology and Public Policy* 18 (3): 623–648.

Bubolz, Bryan F., and Sou Lee. 2020. "'I Still Love My Hood': Passive and Strategic Aspects of Role Residual among Former Gang Members." *Criminal Justice and Behavior*, 48 (6): 846–63. https://doi.org/10.1177/0093854820959115.

Bubolz, Bryan F., and Pete Simi. 2015. "Disillusionment and Change: A Cognitive-Emotional Theory of Gang Exit." *Deviant Behavior* 36 (4): 330–345.

Bucerius, Sandra M., Daniel J. Jones, and Kevin D. Haggerty. 2021. "Indigenous Gangs in Western Canada." In *International Handbook of Critical Gang Studies*, edited by David C. Brotherton and Rafael Gude, 451–472. New York: Routledge.

Buchanan, Molly, and Marvin D. Krohn. 2020. "Does It Matter if Those Who Matter Don't Mind? Effects of Gang versus Delinquent Peer Group Membership on Labeling Processes." *Criminology* 58 (2): 280–306. https://doi.org/10.1111/1745-9125.12237.

Buentello, Salvador, Robert S. Fong, and Ronald E. Vogel. 1991. "Prison Gang Development: A Theoretical Model." *Prison Journal* 71 (2): 3–14.

Bullock, Karen, and Nick Tilley. 2002. *Shootings, Gangs and Violent Incidents in Manchester: Developing a Crime Reduction Strategy.* Crime Reduction Research Series Paper 13. London: Home Office.

Bumgarner, Jeff, Susan Hilal, and James Densley. 2016. *Minnesota's Criminal Justice System.* Durham: Carolina Academic Press.

Burman, Michelle Lynn. 2012. "Resocializing and Repairing Homies within the Texas Prison System: A Case Study on Security Threat Group Management, Administrative Segregation, Prison Gang Renunciation and Safety for All." Austin: University of Texas at Austin.

Burnett, Cora. 1999. "Gang Violence as Survival Strategy in the Context of Poverty in Davidsonville." *Society in Transition* 30 (1): 1–12.

Bursik, Robert J. 2015. "Social Sources of Delinquency and the Second Coming of Shaw and McKay." In *Challenging Criminological Theory: The Legacy of Ruth Rosner Kornhauser,* edited by Francis T. Cullen, Pamela Wilcox, Robert J. Sampson, and Brendan D. Dooley, 105–116. New Brunswick, NJ: Transaction.

Bursik, Robert J., and Harold G. Grasmick. 1993. *Neighborhoods and Crime: The Dimensions of Effective Community Control*. New York: Lexington Books.

Bushway, Shawn D., and Robert Apel. 2012. "A Signaling Perspective on Employment-Based Reentry Programming." *Criminology and Public Policy* 11 (1): 21–50.

Butler, Michelle, Gavin Slade, and Camila Nunes Dias. 2018. "Self-Governing Prisons: Prison Gangs in an International Perspective." *Trends in Organized Crime*. https://doi.org/10.1007/s12117-018-9338-7.

Butts, Jeffrey A., Caterina Gouvis Roman, Lindsay Bostwick, and Jeremy R. Porter. 2015. "Cure Violence: A Public Health Model to Reduce Gun Violence." *Annual Review of Public Health* 36:39–53.

Cahill, Meagan, Jesse Jannetta, Emily Tiry, Samantha S. Lowry, Miriam Becker-Cohen, Ellen Paddock, Maria Serakos, Loraine Parker, and Karen Hennigan. 2016. *Evaluation of the Los Angeles Gang Reduction and Youth Development Program: Year 4 Evaluation Report*. Washington, DC: Urban Institute. https://www.urban.org/research/publication/evaluation-los-angeles-gang-reduction-and-youth-development-program-year-4-evaluation-report.

Caldwell, Beth. 2009. "Criminalizing Day-to-Day Life: A Socio-Legal Critique of Gang Injunctions." *American Journal of Criminal Law* 37 (3): 241–290.

California State Auditor. 2016. *The CalGang Criminal Intelligence System: As the Result of Its Weak Oversight Structure, It Contains Questionable Information That May Violate Individuals' Privacy Rights*. Sacramento: California State Auditor.

Cameron, David. 2011. "Speech on the Fight-Back after the Riots." *New Statesman*, August 15, 2011. http://www.newstatesman.com/politics/2011/08/society-fight-work-rights.

Camp, George M., and Camille Graham Camp. 1985. *Prison Gangs: Their Extent, Nature, and Impact on Prisons*. Washington, DC: U.S. Department of Justice, Government Printing Office.

Campana, Paolo, and Federico Varese. 2013. "Cooperation in Criminal Organizations: Kinship and Violence as Credible Commitments." *Rationality and Society* 25 (3): 263–289.

———. 2018. "Organized Crime in the United Kingdom: Illegal Governance of Markets and Communities." *British Journal of Criminology* 58 (6): 1381–1400.

Campbell, Anne. 1984. *The Girls in the Gang*. New York: Basil Blackwell.

Campbell, Anne, Steven Munce, and John Galea. 1982. "American Gangs and British Subcultures: A Comparison." *International Journal of Offender Therapy and Comparative Criminology* 26 (1): 76–89.

Campbell, Anne, and Steven Muncer. 1989. "Them and Us: A Comparison of the Cultural Context of American Gangs and British Subcultures." *Deviant Behavior* 10 (3): 271–288.

Caplan, Nathan S., Dennis J. Deshaies, Gerald D. Suttles, and Hans W. Mattick. 1967. "The Nature, Variety, and Patterning of Street Club Work in an Urban Setting." In *Juvenile Gangs in Context: Theory, Research, and Action*, edited by Malcolm W. Klein, 194–202. Englewood Cliffs, NJ: Prentice Hall.

Carlock, Arna L., and Alan J. Lizotte. 2015. "Gangs, Guns, and Violence: Synergistic Effects." In *The Handbook of Gangs*, edited by Scott H. Decker and David C. Pyrooz, 178–192. Chichester, U.K.: Wiley-Blackwell.

Carlsson, Yngve, and Scott H. Decker. 2005. "Gang and Youth Violence Prevention and Intervention: Contrasting the Experience of the Scandinavian Welfare State with the United States." In *European Street Gangs and Troublesome Youth Groups*, edited by S. H. Decker and F. Weerman. Walnut Creek, CA: AltaMira.

Carr, Richard, Molly Slothower, and John Parkinson. 2017. "Do Gang Injunctions Reduce Violent Crime? Four Tests in Merseyside, UK." *Cambridge Journal of Evidence-Based Policing* 1 (4): 195–210.

Carson, Dena C. 2018. "Examining Racial and Ethnic Variations in Reasons for Leaving a Youth Gang." *Journal of Developmental and Life-Course Criminology* 4 (4): 449–472.

Carson, Dena C., and Finn-Aage Esbensen. 2016. "Motivations for Leaving Gangs in the USA: A Qualitative Comparison of Leaving Processes across Gang Definitions." In *Gang Transitions and Transformations in an International Context*, edited by Cheryl L. Maxson and Finn-Aage Esbensen, 139–155. Switzerland: Springer.

———. 2019. "Gangs in School: Exploring the Experiences of Gang-Involved Youth." *Youth Violence and Juvenile Justice* 17 (1): 3–23.

Carson, Dena C., Chris Melde, Stephanie A. Wiley, and Finn-Aage Esbensen. 2017. "School Transitions as a Turning Point for Gang Status." *Journal of Crime and Justice* 40 (4): 396–416.

Carson, Dena C., Dana Peterson, and Finn-Aage Esbensen. 2013. "Youth Gang Desistance: An Examination of the Effect of Different Operational Definitions of Desistance on the Motivations, Methods, and Consequences Associated with Leaving the Gang." *Criminal Justice Review* 38 (4): 510–534.

Carson, Dena C., and J. Michael Vecchio. 2015. "Leaving the Gang: A Review and Thoughts on Future Research." In *The Handbook of Gangs*, edited by Scott H. Decker and David C. Pyrooz, 257–275. Chichester, U.K.: Wiley-Blackwell.

Carson, Dena C., Stephanie A. Wiley, and Finn-Aage Esbensen. 2017. "Differentiating between Delinquent Groups and Gangs: Moving beyond Offending Consequences." *Journal of Crime and Justice* 40 (3): 297–315.

Carson, E. Ann. 2020. *Prisoners in 2018*. NCJ 253516. Washington, DC: U.S. Department of Justice, Bureau of Statistics. https://www.bjs.gov/content/pub/pdf/p18.pdf.

Castillo, Richard Griswold del. 2000. "The Los Angeles 'Zoot Suit Riots' Revisited: Mexican and Latin American Perspectives." *Mexican Studies / Estudios Mexicanos* 16 (2): 367–391.

Catino, Maurizio. 2014. "How Do Mafias Organize? Conflict and Violence in Three Mafia Organizations." *European Journal of Sociology / Archives Européennes de Sociologie* 55 (2): 177–220.

Caudill, Jonathan W., Chad R. Trulson, James W. Marquart, and Matt DeLisi. 2017. "On Gang Affiliation, Gang Databases, and Prosecutorial Outcomes." *Crime and Delinquency* 63:210–229.

Cepeda, Alice, and Avelardo Valdez. 2003. "Risk Behaviors among Young Mexican American Gang-Associated Females: Sexual Relations, Partying, Substance Use, and Crime." *Journal of Adolescent Research* 18 (1): 90–106.

Chalas, Dawn Marie, and Jana Grekul. 2017. "I've Had Enough: Exploring Gang Life from the Perspective of (Ex) Members in Alberta." *Prison Journal* 97 (3): 364–386. https://doi.org/10.1177/0032885517705312.

Chassin, Laurie, Alex R. Piquero, Sandra H. Losoya, Andre D. Mansion, and Carol A. Schuber. 2013. "Joint Consideration of Distal and Proximal Predictors of Premature Mortality among Serious Juvenile Offenders." *Journal of Adolescent Health* 52 (6): 689–696.

Cheng, Tony. 2018. "Recruitment through Rule Breaking: Establishing Social Ties with Gang Members." *City and Community* 17(1): 150–169.

Chesney-Lind, Meda, Randall G. Shelden, and Karen A. Joe. 1996. "Girls, Delinquency, and Gang Membership." In *Gangs in America*, vol. 2, edited by C. Ronald Huff, 185–204. Thousand Oaks, CA: Sage.

Chettleburgh, Michael C. 2003. *Results of the 2002 Canadian Police Survey on Youth Gangs*. Toronto: Astwood Strategy Corporation.

———. 2007. *Young Thugs: Inside the Dangerous World of Canadian Street Gangs*. Toronto: HarperCollins.

Chu, Yiu-kong. 2000. *The Triads as Business*. New York: Routledge.

Chwe, Michael Suk-Young. 2001. *Rational Ritual: Culture, Coordination, and Common Knowledge*. Princeton, NJ: Princeton University Press.

Clark, Kendra J., David C. Pyrooz, and Ryan Randa. 2018. "School of Hard Knocks: Gangs, Schools, and Education in the United States." In *The Wiley Handbook on Violence in Education*, edited by Harvey Shapiro, 203–225. Hoboken, NJ: John Wiley and Sons.

Clarke, Ronald V., and Derek B. Cornish. 1985. "Modeling Offenders' Decisions: A Framework for Research and Policy." *Crime and Justice* 6 (January): 147–185.

Clayton, Abené. 2019. "92% Black or Latino: The California Laws That Keep Minorities in Prison." *The Guardian*, November 26, 2019. https://www.theguardian.com/us-news/2019/nov/26/california-gang-enhancements-laws-black-latinos.

Clemmer, Donald. 1940. *The Prison Community*. New York: Rhinehart.

Cloward, Richard A., and Lloyd E. Ohlin. 1960. *Delinquency and Opportunity: A Theory of Delinquent Gangs*. New York: Free Press.

Cobbina, Jennifer E. 2019. *Hands Up, Don't Shoot: Why the Protests in Ferguson and Baltimore Matter, and How They Changed America*. New York: New York University Press.

Cohen, Albert K. 1955. *Delinquent Boys: The Culture of the Gang*. New York: Free Press.

Cohen, Lawrence E., and Marcus Felson. 1979. "Social Change and Crime Rate Trends: A Routine Activity Approach." *American Sociological Review* 44 (4): 588–608.

Cohen, Stanley. 1973. *Folk Devils and Moral Panics: Creation of Mods and Rockers*. St. Albans, U.K.: Paladin.

———. 1979. "The Punitive City: Notes on the Dispersal of Social Control." *Contemporary Crises* 3 (4): 339–363.

Coid, Jeremy W., Simone Ullrich, Robert Keers, Paul Bebbington, Bianca L. DeStavola, Constantinos Kallis, Min Yang, David Reiss, Rachel Jenkins, and Peter Donnelly. 2013. "Gang Membership, Violence, and Psychiatric Morbidity." *American Journal of Psychiatry* 170 (9): 985–993.

Coleman, James S. 1988. "Social Capital and the Creation of Human Capital." *American Journal of Sociology* 94:95–120.

———. 1990. *Foundations of Social Theory*. Cambridge, MA: Harvard University Press.

Collins, Peter, and David Brody. 2013. *Crime and Justice in the City: As Seen through the Wire*. Durham: Carolina Academic Press.

Connolly, Eric J., and Dylan B. Jackson. 2019. "Adolescent Gang Membership and Adverse Behavioral, Mental Health, and Physical Health Outcomes in Young Adulthood: A within-Family Analysis." *Criminal Justice and Behavior* 46 (11): 1566–1586.

Conquergood, Dwight. 1996. "The Power of Symbols." In *One City*, edited by Chicago Council on Urban Affairs, 11–17. Chicago: Chicago Council on Urban Affairs. https://gangresearch.net/GangResearch/Media/Power.htm.

Cook, Phillip. 2015. "Will the Current Crisis in Police Legitimacy Increase Crime? Research Offers a Way Forward." *Psychological Science in the Public Interest* 16 (3): 71–74.

Cook, Phillip, and Jens Ludwig. 2018. "Policing Guns: Why Gun Violence Is Not (Just) a Public Health Problem." *Items: Insights from the Social Science Research Council* (blog), November 6, 2018. https://items.ssrc.org/understanding-gun-violence/policing-guns-why-gun-violence-is-not-just-a-public-health-problem/.

Cooley, Will. 2011. "'Stones Run It': Taking Back Control of Organized Crime in Chicago, 1940–1975." *Journal of Urban History* 37 (October): 911–932.

———. 2016. "Immigration, Ethnicity, Race, and Organized Crime." In *The Oxford Handbook of American Immigration and Ethnicity*, edited by Ronald H. Bayor, 319–337. New York: Oxford University Press.

———. 2017. "Jim Crow Organized Crime: Black Chicago's Underground Economy in the Twentieth Century." In *Building the Black Metropolis: African American Entrepreneurship in Chicago*, edited by Robert Weems and Jason Chambers, 147–170. Chicago: University of Illinois Press.

Cooper, Alexia, and Erica L. Smith. 2011. "Homicide Trends in the United States, 1980–2008." U.S. Department of Justice, Office of Justice Programs, Bureau of Justice Statistics (NCJ 236018). https://bjs.ojp.gov/content/pub/pdf/htus8008.pdf.

Corb, Abbee, and Renee Grozelle. 2014. "A New Kind of Terror: Radicalizing Youth In Canada." *Journal Exit-Deutschland: Zeitschrift Für Deradikalisierung Und Demokratische Kultur* 1 (0): 32–58.

Costanza, S. E., and Ronald Helms. 2012. "Street Gangs and Aggregate Homicides: An Analysis of Effects during the 1990s Violent Crime Peak." *Homicide Studies* 16 (3): 280–307.

Cottrell-Boyce, Joe. 2013. "Ending Gang and Youth Violence: A Critique." *Youth Justice* 13 (3): 193–206.

Covey, Herbert C. 2010. *Street Gangs throughout the World*. Springfield, IL: Charles C. Thomas.

———. 2015. *Crips and Bloods: A Guide to an American Subculture*. Santa Barbara, CA: Greenwood.

Covey, Herbert C., Scott Menard, and Robert J. Franzese. 1992. *Juvenile Gangs*. Springfield, IL: Charles C. Thomas.

Crawford, Lindsay. 2009. "No Way Out: An Analysis of Exit Processes for Gang Injunctions." *California Law Review* 97 (1): 161–193.

Crutchfield, Richard D. 1989. "Labor Stratification and Violent Crime." *Social Forces* 68:489–512.

Cruz, José Miguel. 2010. "Central American Maras: From Youth Street Gangs to Transnational Protection Rackets." *Global Crime* 11 (4): 379–398.

———. 2016. "State and Criminal Violence in Latin America." *Crime, Law and Social Change* 66 (4): 375–396.

———. 2019. "The Politics of Negotiating with Gangs: The Case of El Salvador." *Bulletin of Latin American Research* 38 (5): 547–562. https://doi.org/10.1111/blar.12847.

Cruz, José Miguel, and Jonathan D. Rosen. 2020. "Mara Forever? Factors Associated with Gang Disengagement in El Salvador." *Journal of Criminal Justice* 69 (July): 101705.

Cullen, Francis T., and Pamela Wilcox. 2015. "The Legacy of Ruth Rosner Kornhauser." In *Challenging Criminological Theory: The Legacy of Ruth Rosner Kornhauser*, edited by Francis T. Cullen, Pamela Wilcox, Robert J. Sampson, and Brendan D. Dooley, 1–22. New Brunswick, NJ: Transaction.

Cullen, Francis T., Pamela Wilcox, Robert J. Sampson, and Brendan D. Dooley, eds. 2015. *Challenging Criminological Theory: The Legacy of Ruth Rosner Kornhauser*. Vol. 19 of Advances in Criminological Theory. New Brunswick, NJ: Transaction.

Cummins, Eric. 1994. *The Rise and Fall of California's Radical Prison Movement*. Stanford, CA: Stanford University Press.

Cureton, Steven R. 2008. "Something Wicked This Way Comes: A Historical Account of Black Gangsterism Offers Wisdom and Warning for African American Leadership." *Journal of Black Studies* 40 (2): 347–361.

Curry, G. David. 1998. "Female Gang Involvement." *Journal of Research in Crime and Delinquency* 35 (1): 100–118.

———. 2000. "Self-Reported Gang Involvement and Officially Recorded Delinquency." *Criminology* 38 (4): 1253–1274. https://doi.org/10.1111/j.1745-9125.2000.tb01422.x.

———. 2011. "Gangs, Crime, and Terrorism." In *Criminologists on Terrorism and Homeland Security*, edited by Brian Forst, Jack Greene, and James Lynch, 97–112. Cambridge: Cambridge University Press.

———. 2015. "The Logic of Defining Gangs Revisited." In *The Handbook of Gangs*, edited by Scott H. Decker and David C. Pyrooz, 7–27. Chichester, U.K.: John Wiley and Sons.

Curry, G. David, Richard A. Ball, and Scott H. Decker. 1996. *Estimating the National Scope of Gang Crime from Law Enforcement Data*. Research in Brief. Washington, DC: U.S. Department of Justice, Office of Justice Programs, National Institute of Justice.

Curry, G. David, Richard A. Ball, and Robert Joseph Fox. 1994. *Gang Crime and Law Enforcement Recordkeeping*. Research in Brief. Washington, DC: U.S. Department of Justice, Office of Justice Programs, National Institute of Justice.

Curry, G. David, Richard A. Ball, Robert J. Fox, and Darryl Stone. 1992. *National Assessment of Law Enforcement Anti-gang Information Resources*. Final Report. Washington, DC: National Institute of Justice.

Curry, G. David, and Scott H. Decker. 1998. *Confronting Gangs: Crime and Community*. Los Angeles: Roxbury.

———. 2002. *Safe Futures in St. Louis*. St. Louis: University of Missouri–St. Louis, Department of Criminology and Criminal Justice.

Curry, G. David, Scott H. Decker, and David C. Pyrooz. 2014. *Confronting Gangs: Crime and Community*. Third ed. New York: Oxford University Press.

Curry, G. David, and Irving A. Spergel. 1988. "Gang Homicide, Delinquency, and Community." *Criminology* 26 (3): 381–406.

———. 1992. "Gang Involvement and Delinquency among Hispanic and African-American Adolescent Males." *Journal of Research in Crime and Delinquency* 29 (3): 273–291.

Dagenais, Elan, Raphael Ginsburg, Sharad Goel, Joseph Nudell, and Robert Weisberg. 2019. *Sentencing Enhancements and Incarceration: San Francisco, 2005–2017.* Stanford, CA: Stanford Computational Policy Lab. https://policylab.stanford.edu/media/enhancements _2019-10-17.pdf.

Dahmann, Judith. 1982. *An Evaluation of Operation Hardcore: A Prosecutorial Response to Violent Gang Criminality*. NIJ 19160. McLean, VA: Mitre Corporation.

Darke, Sacha. 2013. "Inmate Governance in Brazilian Prisons." *Howard Journal of Criminal Justice* 52 (3): 272–284.

Dauvergne, Mia, and Geoffrey Li. 2006. "Homicide in Canada, 2005." *Juristat: Statistics Canada Catalogue* 26 (6): 1–26.

Davies, Andrew. 2013. *City of Gangs: Glasgow and the Rise of the British Gangster*. London: Hodder and Stoughton.

Davis, Mike. 2006. *City of Quartz: Excavating the Future in Los Angeles*. New York: Verso.

Dawley, David. 1992. *A Nation of Lords: The Autobiography of the Vice Lords*. 2nd ed. Prospect Heights, IL: Waveland.

Decker, Scott H. 1996. "Collective and Normative Features of Gang Violence." *Justice Quarterly* 13 (2): 243–264.

———. 2000. "Legitimate Drug Use: A Note on the Impact of Gang Membership and Drug Sales on the Use of Illicit Drugs." *Justice Quarterly* 17 (2): 393–410.

———. 2001. "The Impact of Organizational Features on Gang Activities and Relationships." In *The Eurogang Paradox: Street Gangs and Youth Groups in the U.S. and Europe*, edited by Malcolm W. Klein, Hans-Jürgen Kerner, Cheryl L. Maxson, and Elmar G. M. Weitekamp, 21–39. Dordrecht: Springer Netherlands.

———. 2007. "Expand the Use of Police Gang Units." *Criminology and Public Policy* 6 (4): 729–733.

———. 2011. "Revisiting City Gangs." In *City Gangs*. Phoenix: Arizona State University, School of Criminology and Criminal Justice.

Decker, Scott H., Tim Bynum, Jack McDevitt, Amy Farrell, and Sean P. Varano. 2008. "Street Outreach Workers: Best Practices and Lessons Learned." *School of Justice Studies Faculty Papers*, Paper 15, 1–20.

Decker, Scott H., Tim Bynum, and Deborah Weisel. 1998. "A Tale of Two Cities: Gangs as Organized Crime Groups." *Justice Quarterly* 15 (3): 395–425.

Decker, Scott H., and Margaret Townsend Chapman. 2008. *Drug Smugglers on Drug Smuggling*. Philadelphia: Temple University Press.

Decker, Scott H., and G. David Curry. 2000. "Addressing Key Features of Gang Membership: Measuring the Involvement of Young Members." *Journal of Criminal Justice* 28 (6): 473–482.

———. 2002a. "Gangs, Gang Homicides, and Gang Loyalty: Organized Crimes or Disorganized Criminals." *Journal of Criminal Justice* 30 (4): 343–352.

———. 2002b. "I'm Down for My Organization: The Rationality of Responses to Delinquency, Youth Crime, and Gangs." In *Rational Choice and Criminal Behavior: Recent Research and Future Challenges*, edited by Alex R. Piquero and Stephen G Tibbets, 197–218. New York: Routledge.

Decker, Scott H., Charles M. Katz, and Vincent J. Webb. 2008. "Understanding the Black Box of Gang Organization: Implications for Involvement in Violent Crime, Drug Sales, and Violent Victimization." *Crime and Delinquency* 54 (1): 153–172.

Decker, Scott H., and Kimberly Kempf. 1991. "Constructing Gangs: The Social Definition of Youth Activities." *Criminal Justice Policy Review* 5 (4): 271–291.

Decker, Scott H., and Janet L. Lauritsen. 2002. "Leaving the Gang." In *Gangs in America*, edited by C. Ronald Huff, 3:51–70. Newbury Park, CA: Sage.

Decker, Scott H., Chris Melde, and David C. Pyrooz. 2013. "What Do We Know about Gangs and Gang Members and Where Do We Go from Here?" *Justice Quarterly* 30 (3): 369–402.

Decker, Scott H., and David C. Pyrooz. 2010a. "Gang Violence Worldwide: Context, Culture, and Country." In *Small Arms Survey 2010: Gangs, Groups, and Guns*, 128–155. Cambridge: Cambridge University Press.

———. 2010b. "On the Validity and Reliability of Gang Homicide: A Comparison of Disparate Sources." *Homicide Studies* 14 (4): 359–376.

———. 2011. *Leaving the Gang: Logging Off and Moving On*. New York: Council on Foreign Relations. https://www.cfr.org/sites/default/files/pdf/2011/11/SAVE_paper_Decker_Pyrooz.pdf.

———. 2013. "Gangs: Another Form of Organized Crime?" In *Handbook of Organized Crime*, edited by Letizia Paoli, 1–5. New York: Oxford University Press.

———. 2015. "'I'm Down for a Jihad': How 100 Years of Gang Research Can Inform the Study of Terrorism, Radicalization and Extremism." *Perspectives on Terrorism* 9 (1): 104–112.

———. 2020. "The Role of Religion and Spirituality in Disengagement from Gangs." In *Gangs in the Era of Internet and Social Media*, edited by Chris Melde and Frank M. Weerman, 225–249. Cham, Switzerland: Springer.

———. Forthcoming. "Gangs and the 1994 Crime Bill." In *The 1994 Crime Bill: Legacy and Lessons*. Washington, DC: Council on Criminal Justice.

Decker, Scott H., David C. Pyrooz, and Richard K. Moule Jr. 2014. "Disengagement from Gangs as Role Transitions." *Journal of Research on Adolescence* 24 (2): 268–283.

Decker, Scott H., David C. Pyrooz, Gary Sweeten, and Richard K. Moule Jr. 2014. "Validating Self-Nomination in Gang Research: Assessing Differences in Gang Embeddedness across Non-, Current, and Former Gang Members." *Journal of Quantitative Criminology* 30 (4): 577–598.

Decker, Scott H., Frank Van Gemert, and David C. Pyrooz. 2009. "Gangs, Migration, and Crime: The Changing Landscape in Europe and the USA." *Journal of International Migration and Integration* 10 (4): 393–408.

Decker, Scott H., and Barrik Van Winkle. 1994. "'Slinging Dope': The Role of Gangs and Gang Members in Drug Sales." *Justice Quarterly* 11 (4): 583–604.

———. 1996. *Life in the Gang: Family, Friends, and Violence*. Cambridge: Cambridge University Press.

Decker, Scott H., and Frank Weerman, eds. 2005. *European Street Gangs and Troublesome Youth Groups*. San Francisco: AltaMira.

De La Rue, Lisa, and Anjali J. Forber-Pratt. 2018. "When Gangs Are in Schools." In *The Wiley Handbook on Violence in Education*, edited by Harvey Shapiro, 287–302. Hoboken, NJ: John Wiley and Sons. https://doi.org/10.1002/9781118966709.ch14.

Delgado, Sheyla A., Laila Alsabahi, Kevin T. Wolff, Nicole Alexander, Patricia Cobar, and Jeffrey A. Butts. 2017. "The Effects of Cure Violence in the South Bronx and East New York, Brooklyn." In *Denormalizing Violence: A Series of Reports from the John Jay College Evaluation of Cure Violence Programs in New York City*, edited by Jeffrey A. Butts, 1–11. New York: Research and Evaluation Center, John Jay College of Criminal Justice, City University of New York.

DeLisi, Matt, J. C. Barnes, Kevin M. Beaver, and Chris L. Gibson. 2009. "Delinquent Gangs and Adolescent Victimization Revisited: A Propensity Score Matching Approach." *Criminal Justice and Behavior* 36 (8): 808–823.

DeLisi, Matt, Chad R. Trulson, James W. Marquart, Alan J. Drury, and Anna E. Kosloski. 2011. "Inside the Prison Black Box: Toward a Life Course Importation Model of Inmate Behavior." *International Journal of Offender Therapy and Comparative Criminology* 55 (8): 1186–1207.

Deng, Xiaogang, and Ann Cordilia. 1999. "To Get Rich Is Glorious: Rising Expectations, Declining Control and Escalating Crime in Contemporary China." *International Journal of Offender Therapy and Comparative Criminology* 43:211–229.

Densley, James A. 2011. "Ganging Up on Gangs: Why the Gang Intervention Industry Needs an Intervention." *British Journal of Forensic Practice* 13 (1): 12–23.

———. 2012a. "The Organisation of London's Street Gangs." *Global Crime* 13 (1): 42–64.

———. 2012b. "Street Gang Recruitment: Signaling, Screening, and Selection." *Social Problems* 59 (3): 301–321.

———. 2013. *How Gangs Work: An Ethnography of Youth Violence*. New York: Palgrave Macmillan.

———. 2014a. "ISIS: The Street Gang on Steroids." CNN. October 7, 2014. http://www.cnn.com/2014/10/07/opinion/densley-isis-gangs/index.html.

———. 2014b. "It's Gang Life, but Not as We Know It: The Evolution of Gang Business." *Crime and Delinquency* 60 (4): 517–546.

———. 2015. "Joining the Gang: A Process of Supply and Demand." In *The Handbook of Gangs*, edited by Scott H. Decker and David C. Pyrooz, 235–256. Chichester, U.K.: Wiley-Blackwell.

———. 2019. "Crips." In *The SAGE Encyclopedia of Criminal Psychology*, edited by Ron Morgan, 331–335. Thousand Oaks, CA: Sage.

——. 2020. "Collective Violence Online: When Street Gangs Use Social Media." In *The Handbook of Collective Violence: Current Developments and Understanding*, edited by Carol A. Ireland, Michael Lewis, Anthony Lopez, and Jane L. Ireland, 305–316. London: Routledge.

Densley, James A., Joanna R. Adler, Lijun Zhu, and Mackenzie Lambine. 2017. "Growing against Gangs and Violence: Findings from a Process and Outcome Evaluation." *Psychology of Violence* 7 (2): 242–252.

Densley, James A., Tianji Cai, and Susan Hilal. 2014. "Social Dominance Orientation and Trust Propensity in Street Gangs." *Group Processes and Intergroup Relations* 17 (6): 763–779.

Densley, James A., Allen Davis, and Nick Mason. 2013. "Girls and Gangs: Preventing Multiple Perpetrator Rape." In *Handbook on the Study of Multiple Perpetrator Rape*, edited by Miranda Horvath and Jessica Woodhams, 275–301. New York: Routledge.

Densley, James A., Ross Deuchar, and Simon Harding. 2020. "An Introduction to Gangs and Serious Youth Violence in the United Kingdom." *Youth Justice* 20 (1–2): 3–10.

Densley, James A., and David S. Jones. 2016. "Pulling Levers on Gang Violence in London and St. Paul." In *Gang Transitions and Transformations in an International Context*, edited by Cheryl Maxson and Finn-Aage Esbensen, 291–305. Cham, Switzerland: Springer.

Densley, James A., and Nick Mason. 2011. "The London Riots: A Gang Problem?" *Policing Today* 17:14–15.

Densley, James A., Robert McLean, Ross Deuchar, and Simon Harding. 2018. "An Altered State? Emergent Changes to Illicit Drug Markets and Distribution Networks in Scotland." *International Journal of Drug Policy* 58:113–120.

Densley, James A., and Jillian Peterson. 2018. "Group Aggression." *Current Opinion in Psychology, Aggression and Violence* 19 (February): 43–48.

Densley, James A., and David C. Pyrooz. 2019. "A Signaling Perspective on Disengagement from Gangs." *Justice Quarterly* 36 (1): 31–58.

——. 2020. "The Matrix in Context: Taking Stock of Police Gang Databases in London and Beyond." *Youth Justice* 20 (1–2): 11–30.

Densley, James A., and Alex Stevens. 2015. "'We'll Show You Gang': The Subterranean Structuration of Gang Life in London." *Criminology and Criminal Justice* 15 (1): 102–120.

Denton, Charles M. 2014. "Penal Code 186.22: The California Street Terrorism Enforcement and Prevention [S.T.E.P.] Act." http://www.claraweb.us/wp-content/uploads/2015/01/2014-Defending-Gang-Cases-Manual-California-STEP-Act-Denton.pdf.

Department of Homeland Security. 2016. "Targeted Violence and Terrorism Prevention." March 22, 2016. https://www.dhs.gov/tvtpgrants.

Department of Justice, Office of Public Affairs. 2020. "The Department of Justice Announces Takedown of Key MS-13 Criminal Leadership: Joint Task Force Vulcan is a Coordinated Effort to Dismantle and Destroy MS-13." [Press release.] July 15, 2020. https://www.justice.gov/opa/pr/department-justice-announces-takedown-key-ms-13-criminal-leadership.

Deschenes, Elizabeth Piper, and Finn-Aage Esbensen. 1999. "Violence and Gangs: Gender Differences in Perceptions and Behavior." *Journal of Quantitative Criminology* 15 (1): 63–96.

Descormiers, Karine, and Raymond R. Corrado. 2016. "The Right to Belong: Individual Motives and Youth Gang Initiation Rites." *Deviant Behavior* 37 (11): 1341–1359.

Descormiers, Karine, and Carlo Morselli. 2011. "Alliances, Conflicts, and Contradictions in Montreal's Street Gang Landscape." *International Criminal Justice Review* 21 (3): 297–314.

Deuchar, Ross. 2009. *Gangs, Marginalised Youth and Social Capital*. Stoke on Trent, U.K.: Trentham Books.

———. 2013. *Policing Youth Violence: Transatlantic Connections*. London: Institute of Education Press.

———. 2018. *Gangs and Spirituality: Global Perspectives*. New York: Springer.

———. 2020. "'I Get More in Contact with My Soul': Gang Disengagement, Desistance and the Role of Spirituality." *Youth Justice* 20 (1–2): 113–127.

Deuchar, Ross, Simon Harding, Robert McLean, and James A. Densley. 2020. "Deficit or Credit? A Comparative, Qualitative Study of Gender Agency and Female Gang Membership in Los Angeles and Glasgow." *Crime and Delinquency* 66 (8): 1087–1114.

Deuchar, Ross, Thomas Friis Søgaard, Torsten Kolind, Birgitte Thylstrup, and Liam Wells. 2016. "'When You're Boxing You Don't Think So Much': Pugilism, Transitional Masculinities and Criminal Desistance among Young Danish Gang Members." *Journal of Youth Studies* 19 (6): 725–742.

Diamond, Andrew J. 2009. *Mean Streets: Chicago Youths and the Everyday Struggle for Empowerment in the Multiracial City, 1908–1969*. Berkeley: University of California Press.

Dilulio, John J. 1995. "The Coming of the Super-predators." *National Review*, November 27, 1995, 23–28.

Dimitriadis, Greg. 2006. "The Situation Complex: Revisiting Frederic Thrasher's *The Gang: A Study of 1,313 Gangs in Chicago*." *Cultural Studies—Critical Methodologies* 6 (3): 335–353.

Dishman, Chris. 2001. "Terrorism, Crime, and Transformation." *Studies in Conflict and Terrorism* 24 (1): 43–58.

———. 2005. "The Leaderless Nexus: When Crime and Terror Converge." *Studies in Conflict and Terrorism* 28 (3): 237–252.

Disley, Emma, and Mark Liddle. 2016. *Local Perspectives in Ending Gang and Youth Violence Areas: Perceptions of the Nature of Urban Street Gangs*. London: Home Office.

Dixon, Bill, and Lisa-Marie Johns. 1999. *Gangs, Pagad and the State: Vigilantism and Revenge Violence in the Western Cape*. Cape Town: Center for the Study of Violence and Reconciliation.

Dong, Beidi, and Marvin D. Krohn. 2016. "Dual Trajectories of Gang Affiliation and Delinquent Peer Association during Adolescence: An Examination of Long-Term Offending Outcomes." *Journal of Youth and Adolescence* 45 (4): 746–762.

Dooley, Brendan D., Alan Seals, and David Skarbek. 2014. "The Effect of Prison Gang Membership on Recidivism." *Journal of Criminal Justice* 42 (3): 267–275.

Dowdnwy, Luke. 2003. *Children of the Drug Trade: A Case Study of Children*. First thus used ed. Rio de Janeiro: Viveiros De Castro Editoria.

Downes, David. 1966. "The Gang Myth." *The Listener* 75:534–537.

Drake, Gregory, and Chris Melde. 2014. "The Problem of Prediction: The Efficacy of Multiple Marginality in Cross-Sectional versus Prospective Models." *Journal of Crime and Justice* 37 (1): 61–78.

Dudley, Steven. 2020. *MS-13: The Making of America's Most Notorious Gang*. New York: Hanover Square.

Dunworth, Terence, Dave Hayeslip, Morgan Lyons, and Megan Denver. 2010. *Evaluation of the Los Angeles Gang Reduction and Youth Development Program: Final Y1 Report*. Research Report. Washington, DC: Urban Institute.

Durán, Robert J. 2009. "Legitimated Oppression: Inner-City Mexican American Experiences with Police Gang Enforcement." *Journal of Contemporary Ethnography* 38 (2): 143–168.

——. 2013. *Gang Life in Two Cities: An Insiders Journey*. New York: Columbia University Press.

——. 2018. *The Gang Paradox: Inequalities and Miracles on the US-Mexico Border*. New York: Columbia University Press.

Durán, Robert J., and Jason A. Campos. 2020. "Gangs, Gangsters, and the Impact of Settler Colonialism on the Latina/o Experience." *Sociology Compass* 14 (3): e12765.

Dutton, Michael. 1997. "The Basic Character of Crime in Contemporary China." *China Quarterly* 149:160–177.

Dziewanski, Dariusz. 2020. "Leaving Gangs in Cape Town: Disengagement as Role Exit." *Journal of Contemporary Ethnography* 49 (4): 507–535. https://doi.org/10.1177/08912 41620915942.

Ebaugh, Helen Rose Fuchs. 1988. *Becoming an Ex: The Process of Role Exit*. Chicago: University of Chicago Press.

Edmonds, Kevin. 2016. "Guns, Gangs and Garrison Communities in the Politics of Jamaica." *Race and Class* 57 (4): 54–74.

Egley, Arlen, Jr., James C. Howell, and Meena Harris. 2014. *Highlights of the 2012 National Youth Gang Survey*. Washington, DC: U.S. Department of Justice, Office of Juvenile Justice and Delinquency Prevention.

Eidson, Jillian L., Caterina G. Roman, and Meagan Cahill. 2017. "Successes and Challenges in Recruiting and Retaining Gang Members in Longitudinal Research: Lessons Learned from a Multisite Social Network Study." *Youth Violence and Juvenile Justice* 15 (4): 396–418.

Eisen, Mitchell L., Dayna M. Gomes, Lindsey Wandry, David Drachman, Amanda Clemente, and Cheryl Groskopf. 2013. "Examining the Prejudicial Effects of Gang Evidence on Jurors." *Journal of Forensic Psychology Practice* 13 (1): 1–13.

Eitle, David, Steven Gunkel, and Karen Van Gundy. 2004. "Cumulative Exposure to Stressful Life Events and Male Gang Membership." *Journal of Criminal Justice* 32 (2): 95–111.

Elder, Glen H. 1994. "Time, Human Agency, and Social Change: Perspectives on the Life Course." *Social Psychology Quarterly* 57 (1): 4–15.

Engel, Robin S., Marie Skubak Tillyer, and Nicholas Corsaro. 2013. "Reducing Gang Violence Using Focused Deterrence: Evaluating the Cincinnati Initiative to Reduce Violence (CIRV)." *Justice Quarterly* 30 (3): 403–439.

Esbensen, Finn-Aage. 2015. "The Gang Resistance Education and Training (G.R.E.A.T.) Program: An Evaluator's Perspective." In *The Handbook of Gangs*, edited by Scott H. Decker and David C. Pyrooz, 369–391. Chichester, U.K.: Wiley-Blackwell.

Esbensen, Finn-Aage, and Dena C. Carson. 2012. "Who Are the Gangsters? An Examination of the Age, Race/Ethnicity, Sex, and Immigration Status of Self-Reported Gang Members in a Seven-City Study of American Youth." *Journal of Contemporary Criminal Justice* 28 (4): 465–481.

Esbensen, Finn-Aage, Elizabeth Piper Deschenes, and L. Thomas Winfree Jr. 1999. "Differences between Gang Girls and Gang Boys: Results from a Multisite Survey." *Youth and Society* 31 (1): 27–53. https://doi.org/10.1177/0044118X99031001002.

Esbensen, Finn-Aage, and David Huizinga. 1993. "Gangs, Drugs, and Delinquency in a Survey of Urban Youth." *Criminology* 31 (4): 565–589.

Esbensen, Finn-Aage, David Huizinga, and Anne W. Weiher. 1993. "Gang and Non-gang Youth: Differences in Explanatory Factors." *Journal of Contemporary Criminal Justice* 9 (2): 94–116.

Esbensen, Finn-Aage, and Cheryl L. Maxson. 2012. *Youth Gangs in International Perspective: Results from the Eurogang Program of Research*. New York: Springer.

———. 2018. "The Eurogang Program of Research." In *Oxford Research Encyclopedia of Criminology and Criminal Justice.* Article published March 28, 2018. https://doi .org/10.1093/acrefore/9780190264079.013.421.

Esbensen, Finn-Aage, and D. Wayne Osgood. 1999. "Gang Resistance Education and Training (GREAT): Results from the National Evaluation." *Journal of Research in Crime and Delinquency* 36 (2): 194–225.

Esbensen, Finn-Aage, D. Wayne Osgood, Dana Peterson, and Terrance J. Taylor. 2016. *Process and Outcome Evaluation of the Gang Resistance Education and Training (G.R.E.A.T.) Program, 2006–2011.* Ann Arbor, MI: Inter-University Consortium for Political and Social Research. https://doi.org/10.3886/ICPSR34899.v1.

Esbensen, Finn-Aage, D. Wayne Osgood, Dana Peterson, Terrance J. Taylor, and Dena C. Carson. 2013. "Short- and Long-Term Outcome Results from a Multisite Evaluation of the G.R.E.A.T. Program." *Criminology and Public Policy* 12 (3): 375–411.

Esbensen, Finn-Aage, D. Wayne Osgood, Terrance J. Taylor, Dana Peterson, and Adrienne Freng. 2001. "How Great Is G.R.E.A.T.? Results from a Longitudinal Quasi-experimental Design." *Criminology and Public Policy* 1 (1): 87–118.

Esbensen, Finn-Aage, Dana Peterson, Terrance J. Taylor, and Adrienne Freng. 2010. *Youth Violence: Sex and Race Differences in Offending, Victimization, and Gang Membership.* Philadelphia: Temple University Press.

Esbensen, Finn-Aage, Dana Peterson, Terrance J. Taylor, Adrienne Freng, D. Wayne Osgood, Dena Carson, and Kristy Matsuda. 2011. "Evaluation and Evolution of the Gang Resistance Education and Training (G.R.E.A.T.) Program." *Journal of School Violence* 10:53–70.

Esbensen, Finn-Aage, Dana Peterson, Terrance J. Taylor, and D. Wayne Osgood. 2012. "Results from a Multi-site Evaluation of the G.R.E.A.T. Program." *Justice Quarterly* 29 (1): 125–151.

Esbensen, Finn-Aage, and Katin Tusinski. 2007. "Youth Gangs in the Print Media." *Criminal Justice and Popular Culture* 14:21–38.

Esbensen, Finn-Aage, and Frank M. Weerman. 2005. "A Cross-National Comparison of Youth Gangs and Troublesome Youth Groups in the United States and the Netherlands." *European Journal of Criminology* 2:5–37.

Esbensen, Finn-Aage, L. Thomas Winfree, Ni He, and Terrance J. Taylor. 2001. "Youth Gangs and Definitional Issues: When Is a Gang a Gang, and Why Does It Matter?" *Crime and Delinquency* 47 (1): 105–130.

Estrada, Joey Nuñez, Jr., Tamika D. Gilreath, Cathia Y. Sanchez, and Ron Avi Astor. 2016. "Associations between School Violence, Military Connection, and Gang Membership in California Secondary Schools." *American Journal of Orthopsychiatry* 87 (4): 443–451. http://www.ncbi.nlm.nih.gov/pubmed/27414056.

Ezeonu, Ifeanyi. 2010. "Gun Violence in Toronto: Perspectives from the Police." *Howard Journal of Criminal Justice* 49:147–165.

———. 2014. "Doing Gang Research in Canada: Navigating a Different Kaleidoscope." *Contemporary Justice Review* 17 (1): 4–22.

Fagan, Jeffrey. 1989. "The Social Organization of Drug Use and Drug Dealing among Urban Gangs." *Criminology* 27 (4): 633–670.

Farrington, David P., Denise C. Gottfredson, Lawrence W. Sherman, and Brandon C. Welsh. 2002. "The Maryland Scientific Methods Scale." In *Evidence-Based Crime Prevention,* edited by David P. Farrington, Doris Layton MacKenzie, Lawrence W. Sherman, Brandon C. Welsh, 13–21. New York: Routledge.

Feld, Barry C. 2019. *The Evolution of the Juvenile Court: Race, Politics, and the Criminalizing of Juvenile Justice*. New York: New York University Press.

Feld, Scott L. 1982. "Social Structural Determinants of Similarity among Associates." *American Sociological Review* 47 (6): 797–801.

Felitti, Vincent J., Robert F. Anda, Dale Nordenberg, David F. Williamson, Alison M. Spitz, Valerie Edwards, and James S. Marks. 1998. "Relationship of Childhood Abuse and Household Dysfunction to Many of the Leading Causes of Death in Adults: The Adverse Childhood Experiences (ACE) Study." *American Journal of Preventive Medicine* 14 (4): 245–258.

Felson, Marcus. 2006. "The Street Gang Strategy." In *Crime and Nature*, edited by Marcus Felson, 305–324. Thousand Oaks, CA: Sage.

Felton, Emmanuel. 2018. "Gang Databases Are a Life Sentence for Black and Latino Communities." *Pacific Standard*, March 15, 2018. https://psmag.com/social-justice/gang-databases-life-sentence-for-black-and-latino-communities.

Ferguson, Andrew Guthrie. 2019. *The Rise of Big Data Policing: Surveillance, Race, and the Future of Law Enforcement*. New York: New York University Press.

Firmin, Carlene. 2010. *Female Voice in Violence Project: A Study into the Impact of Serious Youth and Gang Violence on Women and Girls*. London: Race on the Agenda. https://www.rota.org.uk/content/female-voice-violence-project-home.

Fishman, Joseph Fulling. 1934. *Sex in Prison: Revealing Sex Conditions in American Prisons*. New York: National Library Press.

Fleisher, Mark S. 1989. *Warehousing Violence*. Newbury Park, CA: Sage.

———. 1995. *Beggars and Thieves: Lives of Urban Street Criminals*. Madison: University of Wisconsin Press.

———. 1998. *Dead End Kids: Gang Girls and the Boys They Know*. Madison: University of Wisconsin Press.

Fleisher, Mark S., and Scott H. Decker. 2001. "Going Home, Staying Home: Integrating Prison Gang Members into the Community." *Corrections Management Quarterly* 5:65–77.

Fleisher, Mark S., and Jessie L. Krienert. 2004. "Life-Course Events, Social Networks, and the Emergence of Violence among Female Gang Members." *Journal of Community Psychology* 32 (5): 607–622.

Flores, Edward Orozco. 2013. *God's Gangs: Barrio Ministry, Masculinity, and Gang Recovery*. New York: New York University Press.

———. 2016. "'Grow Your Hair Out': Chicano Gang Masculinity and Embodiment in Recovery." *Social Problems* 63 (4): 590–604.

Flores, Edward Orozco, and Pierrette Hondagneu-Sotelo. 2013. "Chicano Gang Members in Recovery: The Public Talk of Negotiating Chicano Masculinities." *Social Problems* 60 (4): 476–490.

Floyd, John E. 1998. *RICO State by State: A Guide to Litigation under the State Racketeering Statutes*. Chicago: American Bar Association.

Fong, Robert S. 1990. "The Organizational Structure of Prison Gangs: A Texas Case Study." *Federal Probation* 54:36–43.

Fong, Robert S., and Ronald E. Vogel. 1995. "Blood-in, Blood-out: The Rationale behind Defecting from Prison Gangs." *Journal of Gang Research* 2 (4): 45–51.

Fontes, Anthony W. 2018. *Mortal Doubt: Transnational Gangs and Social Order in Guatemala City*. Berkeley: University of California Press.

Forman, James, Jr. 2017. *Locking Up Our Own: Crime and Punishment in Black America*. New York: Farrar, Straus and Giroux.

Fox, Andrew M., and Kenneth J. Novak. 2018. "Collaborating to Reduce Violence: The Impact of Focused Deterrence in Kansas City." *Police Quarterly* 21 (3): 283–308.

Fox, James Alan. 1992. "Crime: The Young and the Ruthless." *Chicago Tribune*, January 10, 1992. https://www-proquest-com.colorado.idm.oclc.org/docview/283174988/fulltext /7FC6DC5E20554F2EPQ/1?accountid=14503.

———. 1995. "The Calm before the Crime Wave Storm." *Los Angeles Times*, October 30, 1995. http://articles.latimes.com/1995-10-30/local/me-62753_1_crime-wave.

Fox, Kathleen A., Jodi Lane, and Ronald L. Akers. 2010. "Do Perceptions of Neighborhood Disorganization Predict Crime or Victimization? An Examination of Gang Member versus Non–Gang Member Jail Inmates." *Journal of Criminal Justice* 38 (4): 720–729.

Fraser, Alistair. 2015. *Urban Legends: Gang Identity in the Post-industrial City*. Oxford: Oxford University Press.

———. 2017. *Gangs and Crime: Critical Alternatives*. Thousand Oaks, CA: Sage.

Fraser, Alistair, Gary Armstrong, and Dick Hobbs. 2021. "Policing the Olympic Gang: The Rise and Fall of the Portuguese Mafia." *Policing and Society* 31 (2): 195–208.

Fraser, Alistair, and Colin Atkinson. 2014. "Making Up Gangs: Looping, Labelling and the New Politics of Intelligence-Led Policing." *Youth Justice* 14 (2): 154–170.

Fraser, Alistair, and John M. Hagedorn. 2018. "Gangs and a Global Sociological Imagination." *Theoretical Criminology* 22 (1): 42–62.

Fraser, Alistair, Robert Ralphs, and Hannah Smithson. 2018. "European Youth Gang Policy in Comparative Context." *Children and Society* 32 (2): 156–165.

Freng, Adrienne. 2019. "Race, Ethnicity, and Street Gang Involvement in an American Context." In *Oxford Research Encyclopedia of Criminology and Criminal Justice*. Article published February 25, 2019. https://oxfordre.com/criminology/view/10.1093 /acrefore/9780190264079.001.0001/acrefore-9780190264079-e-432.

Freng, Adrienne, and Finn-Aage Esbensen. 2007. "Race and Gang Affiliation: An Examination of Multiple Marginality." *Justice Quarterly* 24 (4): 600–628.

Frey, William R., Desmond U. Patton, Michael B. Gaskell, and Kyle A. McGregor. 2020. "Artificial Intelligence and Inclusion: Formerly Gang-Involved Youth as Domain Experts for Analyzing Unstructured Twitter Data." *Social Science Computer Review* 38 (1): 42–56.

Gaes, Gerald G., Susan Wallace, Evan Gilman, Jody Klein-Saffran, and Sharon Suppa. 2002. "The Influence of Prison Gang Affiliation on Violence and Other Prison Misconduct." *Prison Journal* 82:359–385.

Gallupe, Owen, and Jason Gravel. 2018. "Social Network Position of Gang Members in Schools: Implications for Recruitment and Gang Prevention." *Justice Quarterly* 35 (3): 505–525.

Gallupe, Owen, John McLevey, and Sarah Brown. 2019. "Selection and Influence: A Meta-analysis of the Association between Peer and Personal Offending." *Journal of Quantitative Criminology* 35 (2): 313–335.

Gambetta, Diego. 1996. *The Sicilian Mafia: The Business of Private Protection*. Cambridge, MA: Harvard University Press.

———. 2009. *Codes of the Underworld: How Criminals Communicate*. Princeton, NJ: Princeton University Press.

Garland, David. 2002. *The Culture of Control: Crime and Social Order in Contemporary Society*. Chicago: University of Chicago Press.

Garot, Robert. 2010. *Who You Claim: Performing Gang Identity in School and on the Streets*. New York: New York University Press.

Gaston, Shytierra. 2019a. "Enforcing Race: A Neighborhood-Level Explanation of Black–White Differences in Drug Arrests." *Crime and Delinquency* 65 (4): 499–526.

———. 2019b. "Producing Race Disparities: A Study of Drug Arrests across Place and Race." *Criminology* 57 (3): 424–451.

Gatti, Uberto, Sandrine Haymoz, and Hans M. A. Schadee. 2011. "Deviant Youth Groups in 30 Countries: Results from the Second International Self-Report Delinquency Study." *International Criminal Justice Review* 21 (3): 208–224.

Gatti, Uberto, Richard E. Tremblay, Frank Vitaro, and Pierre McDuff. 2005. "Youth Gangs, Delinquency and Drug Use: A Test of the Selection, Facilitation, and Enhancement Hypotheses." *Journal of Child Psychology and Psychiatry* 46 (11): 1178–1190.

Gebo, Erika, Brenda J. Bond, and Krystal S. Campos. 2015. "The OJJDP Comprehensive Gang Strategy." In *The Handbook of Gangs*, edited by Scott H. Decker and David C. Pyrooz, 392–405. Chichester, U.K.: Wiley-Blackwell.

Gibson, Chris L., J. Mitchell Miller, Wesley G. Jennings, Marc Swatt, and Angela Gover. 2009. "Using Propensity Score Matching to Understand the Relationship between Gang Membership and Violent Victimization: A Research Note." *Justice Quarterly* 26 (4): 625–643.

Gibson, Chris L., Marc L. Swatt, J. Mitchell Miller, Wesley G. Jennings, and Angela R. Gover. 2012. "The Causal Relationship between Gang Joining and Violent Victimization: A Critical Review and Directions for Future Research." *Journal of Criminal Justice* 40 (6): 490–501.

Giddens, Anthony. 2013. *The Constitution of Society: Outline of the Theory of Structuration*. Bristol, U.K.: Polity.

Gilbert, Jarrod. 2013. *Patched: The History of Gangs in New Zealand*. Auckland, New Zealand: Auckland University Press.

———. 2016. "The Reorganisation of Gangs in New Zealand." In *Global Perspectives on Youth Gang Behavior, Violence, and Weapons Use*, edited by Simon Harding and Marek Palasinski, 346–365. Hershey, PA: IGI Global.

Gilman, Amanda B., Karl G. Hill, and J. David Hawkins. 2014. "Long-Term Consequences of Adolescent Gang Membership for Adult Functioning." *American Journal of Public Health* 104 (5): 938–945.

Gilman, Amanda B., Karl G. Hill, J. David Hawkins, James C. Howell, and Rick Kosterman. 2014. "The Developmental Dynamics of Joining a Gang in Adolescence: Patterns and Predictors of Gang Membership." *Journal of Research on Adolescence* 24:204–219.

Gimbel, V. Noah, and Craig Muhammad. 2019. "Are Police Obsolete? Breaking Cycles of Violence through Abolition Democracy." *Cardozo Law Review* 40:1543.

Giordano, Peggy C., Stephen A. Cernkovich, and Jennifer L. Rudolph. 2002. "Gender, Crime, and Desistance: Toward a Theory of Cognitive Transformation." *American Journal of Sociology* 107 (4): 990–1064.

Glueck, Sheldon, and Eleanor Glueck. 1950. *Unraveling Juvenile Delinquency*. New York: Commonwealth Fund.

Goffman, Erving. 1963. *Stigma: Notes on the Management of Spoiled Identity*. New York: Simon and Schuster.

Gold, Martin G., and Hans W. Mattick. 1974. "Experiment in the Streets: The Chicago Youth Development Project." Ann Arbor: University of Michigan, Institute for Social Research.

Goldberg, Matthew S. 2010. "Death and Injury Rates of US Military Personnel in Iraq." *Military Medicine* 175 (4): 220–226.

Goldstein, Arnold P., and Barry Glick. 1994. *The Prosocial Gang: Implementing Aggression Replacement Training*. Thousand Oaks, CA: Sage.

Goodman, Philip. 2008. "It's Just Black, White or Hispanic: An Observational Study of Racializing Moves in California's Segregated Prison Reception Centers." *Law and Society Review* 42 (4): 735–770.

Gordon, Rachel A., Benjamin B. Lahey, Eriko Kawai, Rolf Loeber, Magda Stouthamer-Loeber, and David P. Farrington. 2004. "Antisocial Behavior and Youth Gang Membership: Selection and Socialization." *Criminology* 42 (1): 55–87.

Gordon, Robert M. 1998. "Street Gangs and Criminal Business Organizations: A Canadian Perspective." In *Gangs and Youth Subcultures: International Explorations*, edited by Kayleen Hazlehurst and Cameron Hazlehurst, 165–187. New Brunswick, NJ: Transaction.

———. 2000. "Criminal Business Organizations, Street Gangs and 'Wanna-Be' Groups: A Vancouver Perspective." *Canadian Journal of Criminology* 42 (1): 39–60.

Gormally, Sinéad. 2014. "'I've Been There, Done That . . .': A Study of Youth Gang Desistance." *Youth Justice* 15 (2): 148–165.

Gottfredson, Denise C. 2000. *Schools and Delinquency*. Cambridge: Cambridge University Press.

Gottfredson, Denise C., Brook Kearley, Terence P. Thornberry, Molly Slothower, Deanna Devlin, and Jamie J. Fader. 2018. "Scaling-Up Evidence-Based Programs Using a Public Funding Stream: A Randomized Trial of Functional Family Therapy for Court-Involved Youth." *Prevention Science* 19 (7): 939–953.

Gottfredson, Gary D., and Denise C. Gottfredson. 2001. *Gang Problems and Gang Programs in a National Sample of Schools*. Ellicott City, MD: Gottfredson Associates. https://eric.ed.gov/?id=ED459408.

Gottfredson, Michael R., and Travis Hirschi. 1990. *A General Theory of Crime*. Stanford, CA: Stanford University Press.

Gottschalk, Petter. 2017. "Maturity Levels for Outlaw Groups: The Case of Criminal Street Gangs." *Deviant Behavior* 38 (11): 1267–1278. https://doi.org/10.1080/01639625.2016.1248713.

Gravel, Jason, Blake Allison, Jenny West-Fagan, Michael McBride, and George E. Tita. 2018. "Birds of a Feather Fight Together: Status-Enhancing Violence, Social Distance and the Emergence of Homogenous Gangs." *Journal of Quantitative Criminology* 34 (1): 189–219.

Gravel, Jason, Martin Bouchard, Karine Descormiers, Jennifer S. Wong, and Carlo Morselli. 2013. "Keeping Promises: A Systematic Review and a New Classification of Gang Control Strategies." *Journal of Criminal Justice* 41 (4): 228–242.

Green, Ben, Thibaut Horel, and Andrew V. Papachristos. 2017. "Modeling Contagion through Social Networks to Explain and Predict Gunshot Violence in Chicago, 2006 to 2014." *JAMA Internal Medicine* 177 (3): 326–333.

Grekul, Jana, and Patti LaBoucane-Benson. 2008. "Aboriginal Gangs and Their (Dis) Placement: Contextualizing Recruitment, Membership, and Status." *Canadian Journal of Criminology and Criminal Justice* 50 (1): 59–82.

Griffin, Marie L., and John R. Hepburn. 2006. "The Effect of Gang Affiliation on Violent Misconduct among Inmates during the Early Years of Confinement." *Criminal Justice and Behavior* 33 (4): 419–466.

Grogger, Jeffrey. 2005. "What We Know about Gang Injunctions." *Criminology and Public Policy* 4:637.

Grund, Thomas U., and James A. Densley. 2012. "Ethnic Heterogeneity in the Activity and Structure of a Black Street Gang." *European Journal of Criminology* 9 (4): 388–406. https://doi.org/10.1177/1477370812447738.

————. 2015. "Ethnic Homophily and Triad Closure: Mapping Internal Gang Structure Using Exponential Random Graph Models." *Journal of Contemporary Criminal Justice* 31 (3): 354–370. https://doi.org/10.1177/1043986214553377.

Grunwald, Ben, and Andrew Papachristos. 2017. "Project Safe Neighborhoods in Chicago: Looking Back a Decade Later." *Journal of Criminal Law and Criminology* 107 (1). https://scholarlycommons.law.northwestern.edu/jclc/vol107/iss1/3.

Gundur, R. V. 2018. "The Changing Social Organization of Prison Protection Markets: When Prisoners Choose to Organize Horizontally Rather Than Vertically." *Trends in Organized Crime* (February). https://doi.org/10.1007/s12117-018-9332-0.

————. 2019. "Settings Matter: Examining Protection's Influence on the Illicit Drug Trade in Convergence Settings in the Paso Del Norte Metropolitan Area." *Crime, Law and Social Change* 72 (3): 339–360. https://doi.org/10.1007/s10611-019-09810-3.

————. 2020. "Prison Gangs." In *Oxford Research Encyclopedia of Criminology and Criminal Justice*. Article published November 19, 2020. https://doi.org/10.1093/acrefore/9780190264079.013.397.

Gunter, Anthony. 2017. *Race, Gangs and Youth Violence: Policy, Prevention and Policing*. Bristol, U.K.: Policy Press.

Hagan, John, John Simpson, and A. Ronald Gillis. 1988. "Feminist Scholarship, Relational and Instrumental Control, and a Power-Control Theory of Gender and Delinquency." *British Journal of Sociology* 39 (3): 301–336.

Hagedorn, John M. 1988. *People and Folks: Gangs, Crime and the Underclass in a Rustbelt City*. Chicago: Lake View.

————. 1994. "Homeboys, Dope Fiends, Legits, and New Jacks." *Criminology* 32 (2): 197–219.

————. 1998a. *People and Folks: Gangs, Crime and the Underclass in a Rustbelt City*. 2nd ed. Chicago: Lake View.

————. 1998b. "Gang Violence in the Postindustrial Era." *Crime and Justice* 24 (January): 365–419.

————. 2006. "Race Not Space: A Revisionist History of Gangs in Chicago." *Journal of African American History* 91 (2): 194–208. https://doi.org/10.1086/JAAHv91n2p194.

————. 2008. *A World of Gangs: Armed Young Men and Gangsta Culture*. Minneapolis: University of Minnesota Press.

————. 2017. "Gangs, Schools, and Social Change: An Institutional Analysis." *ANNALS of the American Academy of Political and Social Science* 673 (1): 190–208. https://doi.org/10.1177/0002716217726965.

————. 2021. *Gangs on Trial: Challenging Stereotypes and Demonization in the Courts*. Philadelphia: Temple University Press.

Hall, Stuart, Chas Critcher, Tony Jefferson, John Clarke, and Brian Roberts. 1978. *Policing the Crisis: Mugging, the State, and Law and Order*. 1978 ed. London: Palgrave.

Hallsworth, Simon. 2013. *The Gang and Beyond: Interpreting Violent Street Worlds*. Basingstoke: Palgrave Macmillan.

Hallsworth, Simon, and David C. Brotherton. 2011. *Urban Disorder and Gangs: A Critique and a Warning*. London: Runnymede.

Hallsworth, Simon, and Tara Young. 2008. "Gang Talk and Gang Talkers: A Critique." *Crime, Media, Culture* 4 (2): 175–195.

Harding, Simon. 2014. *The Street Casino: Survival in Violent Street Gangs*. Bristol, U.K.: Policy Press.

————. 2016. "From 'Little Flowers of the Motherland' into 'Carnivorous Plants': The Changing Face of Youth Gang Crime in Contemporary China." In *Global Perspectives on Youth Gang Behavior, Violence, and Weapons Use*, edited by Simon Harding and Marek Palasinski, 295–325. Hershey, PA: IGI Global.

———. 2020. *County Lines: Exploitation and Drug Dealing amongst Urban Street Gangs.* Bristol, U.K.: Bristol University Press.

Harding, Simon, Ross Deuchar, James Densley, and Robert McLean. 2019. "A Typology of Street Robbery and Gang Organization: Insights from Qualitative Research in Scotland." *British Journal of Criminology* 59 (4): 879–897.

Harriott, Anthony, and Charles M. Katz, eds. 2015. *Gangs in the Caribbean: Responses of State and Society.* Kingston, Jamaica: University Press of the West Indies.

Harris, Mary G. 1988. *Cholas: Latino Girls and Gangs.* New York: AMS.

Hashimi, Sadif, Robert Apel, and Sara Wakefield. 2021. "Sibling Transmission of Gang Involvement." *Journal of Research in Crime and Delinquency* 58 (5): 507–544.

Haymoz, Sandrine, and Uberto Gatti. 2010. "Girl Members of Deviant Youth Groups, Offending Behaviour and Victimisation: Results from the ISRD2 in Italy and Switzerland." *European Journal on Criminal Policy and Research* 16 (3): 167–182.

Haymoz, Sandrine, Cheryl Maxson, and Martin Killias. 2014. "Street Gang Participation in Europe: A Comparison of Correlates." *European Journal of Criminology* 11 (6): 659–681.

Hayward, Keith, and Majid Yar. 2006. "The 'Chav' Phenomenon: Consumption, Media and the Construction of a New Underclass." *Crime, Media, Culture* 2 (1): 9–28.

Hayward, Keith J., and Jock Young. 2004. "Cultural Criminology: Some Notes on the Script." *Theoretical Criminology* 8 (3): 259–273.

Hazen, Jennifer M., and Dennis Rodgers. 2014. *Global Gangs: Street Violence across the World.* Minneapolis: University of Minnesota Press.

Hennigan, Karen M., Kathy A. Kolnick, Flor Vindel, and Cheryl L. Maxson. 2015. "Targeting Youth at Risk for Gang Involvement: Validation of a Gang Risk Assessment to Support Individualized Secondary Prevention." *Children and Youth Services Review* 56 (September): 86–96.

Hennigan, Karen M., Cheryl L. Maxson, David C. Sloane, Kathy A. Kolnick, and Flor Vindel. 2014. "Identifying High-Risk Youth for Secondary Gang Prevention." *Journal of Crime and Justice* 37 (1): 104–128.

Hennigan, Karen M., and David Sloane. 2013. "Improving Civil Gang Injunctions: How Implementation Can Affect Gang Dynamics, Crime, and Violence." *Criminology and Public Policy* 12 (1): 7–41.

Hesketh, Robert Francis. 2019. "Joining Gangs: Living on the Edge?" *Journal of Criminological Research, Policy and Practice* 5 (4): 280–294.

Hesketh, Robert Francis, and Grace Robinson. 2019. "Grafting: 'The Boyz' Just Doing Business? Deviant Entrepreneurship in Street Gangs." *Safer Communities* 18 (2): 54–63.

Higginson, Angela, Kathryn Ham Benier, Yulia Shenderovich, Laura Bedford, Lorraine Mazerolle, and Joseph Murray. 2018. *Factors Associated with Youth Gang Membership in Low- and Middle-Income Countries: A Systematic Review.* Oslo: Campbell Collaboration. https://doi.org/10.4073/csr.2018.11.

Hill, Cece. 2009. "Gangs/Security Threat Groups." *Corrections Compendium* 34 (1): 23–37.

Hill, Karl G., James C. Howell, J. David Hawkins, and Sara R. Battin-Pearson. 1999. "Childhood Risk Factors for Adolescent Gang Membership: Results from the Seattle Social Development Project." *Journal of Research in Crime and Delinquency* 36 (3): 300–322.

Hill, Karl G., Christina Lui, and J. David Hawkins. 2001. *Early Precursors of Gang Membership: A Study of Seattle Youth.* Washington, DC: U.S. Department of Justice, Office of Juvenile Justice and Delinquency Prevention.

Hill, Peter B. E. 2006. *The Japanese Mafia: Yakuza, Law, and the State*. Oxford: Oxford University Press.

Hipple, Natalie Kroovand, Beth M. Huebner, Theodore S. Lentz, Edmund F. McGarrell, and Mallory O'Brien. 2019. "The Case for Studying Criminal Nonfatal Shootings: Evidence from Four Midwest Cities." *Justice Evaluation Journal* 3 (1): 1–20.

Hirsch, Arnold R. 1998. *Making the Second Ghetto: Race and Housing in Chicago, 1940–1960*. 1998 ed. Chicago: University of Chicago Press.

Hirschi, Travis. 1969. *Causes of Delinquency*. Berkeley: University of California Press.

Holligan, Chris, Robert McLean, and Richard McHugh. 2020. "Exploring County Lines: Criminal Drug Distribution Practices in Scotland." *Youth Justice* 20 (1–2): 50–63.

Holligan, Chris, and Ross Deuchar. 2009. "Territorialities in Scotland: Perceptions of Young People in Glasgow." *Journal of Youth Studies* 12 (6): 731–746.

Horowitz, Ruth. 1983. *Honor and the American Dream: Culture and Identity in a Chicano Community*. New Brunswick, NJ: Rutgers University Press.

Howell, James C. 1999. "Youth Gang Homicides: A Literature Review." *Crime and Delinquency* 45 (2): 208–241.

———. 2007. "Menacing or Mimicking? Realities of Youth Gangs." *Juvenile and Family Court Journal* 58 (2): 39–50.

———. 2013. "GREAT Results." *Criminology and Public Policy* 12 (3): 413–420.

———. 2015. *The History of Street Gangs in the United States: Their Origins and Transformations*. Lanham, MD: Lexington Books.

Howell, James C., and Arlen Egley Jr. 2005. "Moving Risk Factors into Developmental Theories of Gang Membership." *Youth Violence and Juvenile Justice* 3 (4): 334–354.

Howell, James C., Arlen Egley Jr., and Debra K. Gleason. 2002. "Modern Day Youth Gangs." National Gang Center Bulletin. Washington, DC: Office of Juvenile Justice and Delinquency Prevention.

Howell, James C., and Elizabeth Griffiths. 2015. *Gangs in America's Communities*. 2nd ed. Thousand Oaks, CA: Sage.

Howell, James C., Mark W. Lipsey, and John J. Wilson. 2014. *A Handbook for Evidence-Based Juvenile Justice Systems*. Lanham, MD: Lexington Books.

Huebner, Beth M. 2003. "Administrative Determinants of Inmate Violence." *Journal of Criminal Justice* 31 (2): 107–117.

Huebner, Beth M., Sean P. Varano, and Timothy S. Bynum. 2007. "Gangs, Guns, and Drugs: Recidivism among Serious, Young Offenders." *Criminology and Public Policy* 6 (2): 187–221.

Huerta, Adrian H. 2015. "'I Didn't Want My Life to Be Like That': Gangs, College, or the Military for Latino Male High School Students." *Journal of Latino/Latin American Studies* 7 (2): 119–132.

Huerta, Adrian H., Patricia M. McDonough, Kristan M. Venegas, and Walter R. Allen. 2020. "College Is . . .: Focusing on the College Knowledge of Gang-Associated Latino Young Men." *Urban Education* (July). https://doi.org/10.1177/0042085920934854.

Huff, C. Ronald. 1989. "Youth Gangs and Public Policy." *Crime and Delinquency* 35 (4): 524–537.

———, ed. 1990. *Gangs in America*. Newbury Park, CA: Sage.

———. 1996a. "The Criminal Behavior of Gang Members and Nongang At-Risk Youth." In *Gangs in America*, edited by C. Ronald Huff, 2nd ed., 75–102. Thousand Oaks, CA: Sage.

———, ed. 1996b. *Gangs in America*. 2nd ed. Newbury Park, CA: Sage.

Huff, C. Ronald, and Julie Barrows. 2015. "Documenting Gang Activity: Intelligence Databases." In *The Handbook of Gangs*, edited by Scott H. Decker and David C. Pyrooz, 59–77. Chichester, U.K.: John Wiley and Sons.

Hughes, Lorine A. 2015. "The Legacy of James F. Short, Jr." In *The Handbook of Gangs*, edited by Scott H. Decker and David C. Pyrooz, 440–457. Chichester, U.K.: Wiley-Blackwell.

Hughes, Lorine A., Ekaterina V. Botchkovar, and James F. Short Jr. 2019. "'Bargaining with Patriarchy' and 'Bad Girl Femininity': Relationship and Behaviors among Chicago Girl Gangs, 1959–62." *Social Forces* 98 (2): 493–517.

Hughes, Lorine A., and Lisa M. Broidy. 2020. *Social Bridges and Contexts in Criminology and Sociology: Reflections on the Intellectual Legacy of James F. Short, Jr.* New York: Taylor and Francis.

Hughes, Lorine A., and James F. Short. 2014. "Partying, Cruising, and Hanging in the Streets: Gangs, Routine Activities, and Delinquency and Violence in Chicago, 1959–1962." *Journal of Quantitative Criminology* 30 (3): 415–451.

Huizinga, David, and Karl F. Schumann. 2001. "Gang Membership in Bremen and Denver: Comparative Longitudinal Data." In *The Eurogang Paradox: Street Gangs and Youth Groups in the U.S. and Europe*, edited by Malcolm Klein, Hans-Jurgen Kerner, Cheryl Maxson, and Elmar Weitekamp, 231–246. Dordrecht, Netherlands: Kluwer Academic Publisher.

Hume, Mo. 2007. "Mano Dura: El Salvador Responds to Gangs." *Development in Practice* 17 (6): 739–751.

Hummer, Don, and Eileen M. Ahlin. 2018. "Exportation Hypothesis: Bringing Prison Violence Home to the Community." In *Handbook on the Consequences of Sentencing and Punishment Decisions*, vol. 3, edited by Natasha A. Frost and Beth M. Huebner, 379–399. New York: Routledge.

Hunt, Geoffrey, and Karen Joe-Laidler. 2001. "Situations of Violence in the Lives of Girl Gang Members." *Health Care for Women International* 22 (4): 363–384.

Hunt, Geoffrey, Stephanie Riegel, Tomas Morales, and Dan Waldorf. 1993. "Changes in Prison Culture: Prison Gangs and the Case of the 'Pepsi Generation.'" *Social Problems* 40 (3): 398–409.

Hureau, David M., and Anthony A. Braga. 2018. "The Trade in Tools: The Market for Illicit Guns in High-Risk Networks." *Criminology* 56 (3): 510–545.

Hutchison, Ray, and Charles Kyle. 1993. "Hispanic Street Gangs in Chicago's Public Schools." In *Gangs: The Origins and Impact of Contemporary Youth Gangs in the United States*, edited by Scott Cummings and Daniel J. Monti, 113–136. Albany: State University of New York Press.

Hyatt, Jordan M., James A. Densley, and Caterina G. Roman. 2021. "Social Media and the Variable Impact of Violence Reduction Interventions: Re-examining Focus Deterrence in Philadelphia." *Social Science* 10 (2): 1–17.

Ilan, Jonathan. 2015. *Understanding Street Culture: Poverty, Crime, Youth and Cool.* 2015 ed. Houndmills: Red Globe.

———. 2020. "Digital Street Culture Decoded: Why Criminalizing Drill Music Is Street Illiterate and Counterproductive." *British Journal of Criminology* 60 (4): 994–1013.

Irwin, John. 1980. *Prisons in Turmoil.* Boston: Little, Brown.

Irwin-Rogers, Keir, Scott H. Decker, Amir Rostami, Svetlana Stephenson, and Elke Van Hellemont. 2019. "European Street Gangs and Urban Violence." In *Handbook of Global Urban Health*, edited by Igor Vojnovic, Amber Pearson, Gershim Asiki, Geoff DeVerteuil, and Adriana Allen, 484–508. New York: Routledge.

Irwin-Rogers, Keir, James A. Densley, and Craig Pinkney. 2018. "Gang Violence and Social Media." In *The Routledge International Handbook of Human Aggression*, edited by Jane L. Ireland, Phillip Birch, and Carol A. Ireland, 400–410. New York: Routledge.

Jackson, Pamela Irving. 1991. "Crime, Youth Gangs, and Urban Transition: The Social Dislocations of Postindustrial Economic Development." *Justice Quarterly* 8 (3): 379–397.

Jacobs, Bruce A., and Richard Wright. 2006. *Street Justice: Retaliation in the Criminal Underworld*. New York: Cambridge University Press.

Jacobs, James B. 1977. *Stateville: The Penitentiary in Mass Society*. Chicago: University of Chicago Press.

——. 2001. "Focusing on Prison Gangs." *Corrections Management Quarterly* 5:vi–vii.

——. 2009. "Gang Databases: Context and Questions." *Criminology and Public Policy* 8:705.

Jensen, Gary F., and Jarrett Thibodeaux. 2013. "The Gang Problem: Fabricated Panics or Real Temporal Patterns?" *Homicide Studies* 17 (3): 275–290.

Jessor, Richard, Mark S. Turbin, Frances M. Costa, Qi Dong, Hongchuan Zhang, and Changhai Wang. 2003. "Adolescent Problem Behavior in China and the United States: A Cross-National Study of Psychosocial Protective Factors." *Journal of Research on Adolescence* 13 (3): 329–360.

John Jay College Research Advisory Group on Preventing and Reducing Community Violence. 2020. *College Research Advisory Group on Preventing and Reducing Community Violence*. New York: Research and Evaluation Center, John Jay College of Criminal Justice, City University of New York.

Johnson, Andrew. 2017. *If I Give My Soul: Faith behind Bars in Rio de Janeiro*. New York: Oxford University Press.

Johnson, Andrew, and James Densley. 2018. "Rio's New Social Order: How Religion Signals Disengagement from Prison Gangs." *Qualitative Sociology* 41 (2): 243–262.

Johnson, Claire M., Barbara A. Webster, Edward F. Connors, and Diana J. Saenz. 1995. "Gang Enforcement Problems and Strategies: National Survey Findings." *Journal of Gang Research* 31 (1): 1–18.

Johnson, Dirk. 1993. "2 of 3 Young Black Men in Denver Listed by Police as Suspected Gangsters." *New York Times*, December 11, 1993. https://www.nytimes.com/1993/1 2/11/us/2-of-3-young-black-men-in-denver-listed-by-police-as-suspected-gangsters .html.

Johnson, Joseph, and Natalie Schell-Busey. 2016. "Old Message in a New Bottle: Taking Gang Rivalries Online through Rap Battle Music Videos on YouTube." *Journal of Qualitative Criminal Justice and Criminology* 4 (1): 42–81.

Jong, Jan Dirk de. 2012. "Typically Moroccan? A Group Dynamic Explanation of Nuisance and Criminal Behavior." In *Youth Gangs in International Perspective: Results from the Eurogang Program of Research*, edited by Finn-Aage Esbensen and Cheryl L. Maxson, 225–236. New York: Springer.

Junger-Tas, Josine. 2010. "The Significance of the International Self-Report Delinquency Study (ISRD)." *European Journal on Criminal Policy and Research* 16 (2): 71–87.

Jütersonke, Oliver, Robert Muggah, and Dennis Rodgers. 2009. "Gangs, Urban Violence, and Security Interventions in Central America." *Security Dialogue* 40:373–397.

Kahn, Alfred J. 1967. "From Delinquency Treatment to Community Development." In *The Uses of Sociology*, edited by Harold L. Wilensky, Paul Felix Lazarsfeld, and William H. Sewell, 477–505. New York: Basic Books.

Kaminski, Marek. 2004. *Games Prisoners Play: The Tragicomic Worlds of Polish Prison*. Princeton, NJ: Princeton University Press.

Kassab, Hanna Samir, and Jonathan D. Rosen. 2018. *Corruption, Institutions, and Fragile States*. 1st ed. New York: Palgrave Macmillan.

Katz, Charles M. 2001. "The Establishment of a Police Gang Unit: An Examination of Organizational and Environmental Factors." *Criminology* 39 (1): 37–74.

Katz, Charles M., Andrew Fox, Chester Britt, and Phillip Stevenson. 2012. "Understanding Police Gang Data at the Aggregate Level: An Examination of the Reliability of National Youth Gang Survey Data." *Justice Research and Policy* 14 (2): 103–128.

Katz, Charles M., Edward R. Maguire, and David Choate. 2011. "A Cross-National Comparison of Gangs in the United States and Trinidad and Tobago." *International Criminal Justice Review* 21 (3): 243–262.

Katz, Charles M., Edward R. Maguire, and Dennis W. Roncek. 2002. "The Creation of Specialized Police Gang Units: A Macro-level Analysis of Contingency, Social Threat, and Resource Dependency Explanations." *Policing: An International Journal of Police Strategies and Management* 25:472–506.

Katz, Charles M., and Stephen M. Schnebly. 2011. "Neighborhood Variation in Gang Member Concentrations." *Crime and Delinquency* 57 (3): 377–407.

Katz, Charles M., and Vincent J. Webb. 2004. *Police Response to Gangs: A Multi-site Study*. Washington, DC: National Institute of Justice.

———. 2006. *Policing Gangs in America*. New York: Cambridge University Press.

Katz, Charles M., Vincent J. Webb, and Scott H. Decker. 2005. "Using the Arrestee Drug Abuse Monitoring (ADAM) Program to Further Understand the Relationship between Drug Use and Gang Membership." *Justice Quarterly* 22 (1): 58–88.

Katz, Charles M., Vincent J. Webb, and David R. Schaefer. 2000. "The Validity of Police Gang Intelligence Lists: Examining Differences in Delinquency between Documented Gang Members and Nondocumented Delinquent Youth." *Police Quarterly* 3 (4): 413–437.

Katz, Jack. 1988. *Seductions of Crime*. New York: Basic Books.

Katz, Jack, and Curtis Jackson-Jacobs. 2004. "The Criminologists' Gang." In *The Blackwell Companion to Criminology*, edited by Colin Sumner, 91–124. Malden, MA: Blackwell.

Kazemian, Lila. 2016. "Desistance from Crime: Theoretical, Empirical, Methodological, and Policy Considerations." *Journal of Contemporary Criminal Justice* 23 (1): 5–27. https://doi.org/10.1177/1043986206298940.

Kefauver, C. Estes. 1952. *Special Committee on Organized Crime in Interstate Commerce*. Washington, DC: U.S. Senate. https://www.senate.gov/about/powers-procedures/investigations/kefauver.htm.

Kelly, Jane F., and Catherine L. Ward. 2020. "Narratives of Gang Disengagement among Former Gang Members in South Africa." *Criminal Justice and Behavior* 47 (11): 1509–1528. https://doi.org/10.1177/0093854820949603.

Kelly, Katharine, and Tullio Caputo. 2005. "The Linkages between Street Gangs and Organized Crime: The Canadian Experience." *Journal of Gang Research* 13:17–31.

Kelly, P. Elizabeth, Joshua R. Polanin, Sung Joon Jang, and Byron R. Johnson. 2015. "Religion, Delinquency, and Drug Use: A Meta-analysis." *Criminal Justice Review* 40 (4): 505–523.

Kendi, Ibram X. 2019. *How to Be an Antiracist*. New York: One World.

Kennedy, David. 1997. "Pulling Levers: Chronic Offenders, High-Crime Settings, and a Theory of Prevention." *Valparaiso University Law Review* 31 (2): 449–484.

———. 2012. *Don't Shoot: One Man, A Street Fellowship, and the End of Violence in Inner-City America*. New York: Bloomsbury.

Kennedy, David M. and Anthony A. Braga. 2002. "Reducing Gang Violence in Boston." In *Responding to Gangs: Evaluation and Research*, edited by Winifred Reed and Scott H. Decker, 265–288. Washington, DC: National Institute of Justice.

Kennedy, David M., Anthony A. Braga, and Anne M. Piehl. 1997. "The (Un)Known Universe: Mapping Gangs and Gang Violence in Boston." In *Crime Mapping and Crime Prevention*, edited by David L. Weisburd and J. Thomas McEwen, 219–262. New York: Criminal Justice Press.

Kennedy, David M., and Michael Friedrich. 2014. *Custom Notifications: Individualized Communication in the Group Violence Intervention*. Washington, DC: Office of Community Oriented Policing Services.

Kennedy, David M., Anna Piehl, and Anthony Braga. 1996. "Youth Violence in Boston: Gun Markets, Serious Youth Violence, and a Use-Reduction Strategy." *Law and Contemporary Problems* 59:147–196.

Kim, Catherine Y., Daniel J. Losen, and Damon T. Hewitt. 2010. *The School-to-Prison Pipeline: Structuring Legal Reform*. New York: New York University Press.

King, Jonathan E., Carolyn E. Walpole, and Kristi Lamon. 2007. "Surf and Turf Wars Online—Growing Implications of Internet Gang Violence." *Journal of Adolescent Health* 41 (6): S66–S68.

King, Martin Luther, Jr. 2014. Transcript of Dr. Martin Luther King's speech at SMU on March 17, 1966. https://www.smu.edu/News/2014/mlk-at-smu-transcript-17march1966.

———. 2019. Transcript of Dr. Martin Luther King's speech at Monmouth College on October 6, 1966. https://www.monmouth.edu/about/wp-content/uploads/sites/128/2019/01/MLKJrSpeechatMonmouth.pdf.

Kinnes, Irvin. 2014. "Gangs, Drugs and Policing the Cape Flats." *Acta Criminologica: African Journal of Criminology and Victimology* 2014 (2): 14–26.

Kirk, David S., and Andrew V. Papachristos. 2011. "Cultural Mechanisms and the Persistence of Neighborhood Violence." *American Journal of Sociology* 116 (4): 1190–1233.

Kissner, Jason, and David C. Pyrooz. 2009. "Self-Control, Differential Association, and Gang Membership: A Theoretical and Empirical Extension of the Literature." *Journal of Criminal Justice* 37 (5): 478–487.

Klein, Hannah J. 2020. *Adverse Childhood Experiences and Adolescent Gang Membership: Utilizing Latent Class Analysis to Understand the Relationship*. Philadelphia: Temple University.

Klein, Malcolm W. 1971. *Street Gangs and Street Workers*. Englewood Cliffs, NJ: Prentice-Hall.

———. 1995. *The American Street Gang: Its Nature, Prevalence and Control*. New York: Oxford University Press.

———. 1997. "What Are Street Gangs When They Get to Court?" *Valparaiso University Law Review* 31 (2): 515–522.

———. 1998. "The Problem of Street Gangs and Problem-Oriented Policing." In *Problem Oriented Policing*, edited by Tara O'Connor Shelley and Anne C. Grant, 57–86. Washington, DC: Police Executive Research Forum.

———. 2001. "Resolving the Eurogang Paradox." In *The Eurogang Paradox: Street Gangs and Youth Groups in the U.S. and Europe*, edited by Malcolm W. Klein, Hans-Juergen Kerner, Cheryl L. Maxson, and Elmar G. M. Weitekamp, 7–20. Dordrecht, Netherlands: Kluwer Academic.

———. 2005. "The Value of Comparisons in Street Gang Research." *Journal of Contemporary Criminal Justice* 21 (2): 135–152. https://doi.org/10.1177/1043986204272911.

———. 2009. "Street Gang Databases: A View from the Gang Capitol of the United States." *Criminology and Public Policy* 8 (4): 717–721.

———. 2011. "Comprehensive Gang and Violence Reduction Programs: Reinventing the Square Wheel." *Criminology and Public Policy* 10 (4): 1037–1044.

———. 2012. "The Next Decade of Eurogang Program Research." In *Youth Gangs in International Perspective: Results from the Eurogang Program of Research*, edited by Finn-Aage Esbensen and Cheryl L. Maxson, 291–302. New York: Springer.

Klein, Malcolm W., and Lois Y. Crawford. 1967. "Groups, Gangs, and Cohesiveness." *Journal of Research in Crime and Delinquency* 4 (1): 63–75.

Klein, Malcolm W., Hans-Jürgen Kerner, Cheryl Maxson, and E. Weitekamp. 2000. *The Eurogang Paradox: Street Gangs and Youth Groups in the U.S. and Europe*. Dordrecht, Netherlands: Kluwer Academic.

Klein, Malcolm W., and Cheryl L. Maxson. 2006. *Street Gang Patterns and Policies*. New York: Oxford University Press.

Klein, Malcolm W., Frank M. Weerman, and Terence P. Thornberry. 2006. "Street Gang Violence in Europe." *European Journal of Criminology* 3 (4): 413–437.

Knight, W. Andy. 2019. "The Nexus between Vulnerabilities and Violence in the Caribbean." *Third World Quarterly* 40 (2): 405–424.

Knox, George W., Gregg Etter, and Carter F. Smith. 2019. *Gangs and Organized Crime*. New York: Routledge.

Knox, George, and Edward Tromanhauser. 1991. "Gangs and Their Control in Adult Correctional Institutions." *Prison Journal* 71 (2): 15–22.

Kontos, Louis, David C. Brotherton, and Luis Barrios, eds. 2003. *Gangs and Society: Alternative Perspectives*. New York: Columbia University Press.

Kornblum, William S. 1974. *The Blue Collar Community*. Chicago: University of Chicago Press.

Kornhauser, Ruth Rosner. 1978. *Social Sources of Delinquency: An Appraisal of Analytic Models*. Chicago: University of Chicago Press.

Kotlowitz, Alex. 1991. *There Are No Children Here: The Story of Two Boys Growing Up in the Other America*. New York: Doubleday.

Kreager, Derek A., Kelly Rulison, and James Moody. 2011. "Delinquency and the Structure of Adolescent Peer Groups." *Criminology* 49 (1): 95–127.

Krohn, Marvin D., and Terence P. Thornberry. 2008. "Longitudinal Perspectives on Adolescent Street Gangs." In *The Long View of Crime: A Synthesis of Longitudinal Research*, edited by Akiva M. Liberman, 128–160. New York: Springer.

Krohn, Marvin D., Jeffrey T. Ward, Terence P. Thornberry, Alan J. Lizotte, and Rebekah Chu. 2011. "The Cascading Effects of Adolescent Gang Involvement across the Life Course." *Criminology* 49 (4): 991–1028.

Kubrin, Charis E., and Tim Wadsworth. 2003. "Identifying the Structural Correlates of African American Killings: What Can We Learn from Data Disaggregation?" *Homicide Studies* 7 (1): 3–35.

Kupchik, Aaron. 2010. *Homeroom Security: School Discipline in an Age of Fear*. New York: New York University Press.

Kupchik, Aaron, and Katie A. Farina. 2016. "Imitating Authority: Students' Perceptions of School Punishment and Security, and Bullying Victimization." *Youth Violence and Juvenile Justice* 14 (2): 147–163.

Kynoch, Gary. 2005. *We Are Fighting the World: A History of the Marashea Gangs in South Africa*. Athens: Ohio University Press.

Laidler, Karen Joe, and Geoffrey Hunt. 1997. "Violence and Social Organization in Female Gangs." *Social Justice* 24 (70): 148–169.

———. 2001. "Accomplishing Femininity among the Girls in the Gang." *British Journal of Criminology* 41 (4): 656–678.

Lampe, Klaus von. 2015. *Organized Crime: Analyzing Illegal Activities, Criminal Structures, and Extra-Legal Governance*. Thousand Oaks, CA: Sage.

Lampe, Klaus von, and Arjan Blokland. 2020. "Outlaw Motorcycle Clubs and Organized Crime." *Crime and Justice* 49 (June): 521–578.

Landre, Rick, Mike Miller, and Dee Porter. 1997. *Gangs: A Handbook for Community Awareness*. New York: Facts on File.

Lane, Jeffrey. 2018. *The Digital Street*. New York: Oxford University Press.

Lane, Jeffrey, Fanny A. Ramirez, and Katy E. Pearce. 2018. "Guilty by Visible Association: Socially Mediated Visibility in Gang Prosecutions." *Journal of Computer-Mediated Communication* 23 (6): 354–369.

Langton, Lynn. 2010. *Gang Units in Large Local Law Enforcement Agencies, 2007*. Washington, DC: U.S. Department of Justice, Bureau of Justice Statistics.

Lasley, James. 1999. *"Designing Out" Gang Homicides and Street Assaults, Research in Brief*. Washington, DC: National Institute of Justice. https://nij.ojp.gov/library/publications /designing-out-gang-homicides-and-street-assaults-research-brief.

Laub, John H. 2004. "The Life Course of Criminology in the United States: The American Society of Criminology 2003 Presidential Address." *Criminology* 42 (1): 1–26.

Laub, John H., and Robert J. Sampson. 2003. *Shared Beginnings, Divergent Lives: Delinquent Boys to Age 70*. Cambridge, MA: Harvard University Press. http://psycnet.apa.org /psycinfo/2003-88395-000.

Laub, John H., Robert J. Sampson, and Gary A. Sweeten. 2006. "Assessing Sampson and Laub's Life-Course Theory of Crime." In *Taking Stock: The Status of Criminological Theory*, 313–333. Advances in Criminological Theory. Piscataway, NJ: Transaction.

Lauderback, David, Joy Hansen, and Dan Waldorf. 1992. "Sisters Are Doin' It for Themselves: A Black Female Gang in San Francisco." *Gang Journal* 1 (1): 57–72.

Lauger, Timothy R. 2012. *Real Gangstas: Legitimacy, Reputation, and Violence in the Intergang Environment*. New Brunswick, NJ: Rutgers University Press.

———. 2020. "Gangs, Identity, and Cultural Performance." *Sociology Compass* 14 (4): e12772.

Lauger, Timothy R., and James A. Densley. 2018. "Broadcasting Badness: Violence, Identity, and Performance in the Online Gang Rap Scene." *Justice Quarterly* 35 (5): 816–841.

Lauger, Timothy R., James A. Densley, and Richard K. Moule Jr. 2019. "Social Media, Strain, and Technologically Facilitated Gang Violence." In *The Palgrave Handbook of International Cybercrime and Cyberdeviance*, edited by Thomas J. Holt and Adam M. Bossler, 1375–1395. Cham, Switzerland: Palgrave Macmillan.

Lauger, Timothy R., and Brooke Horning. 2020. "Street Culture and Street Gangs." In *Street Culture*, edited by Jeffrey Ian Ross, 238–248. New York: Routledge.

Leap, Jorja, T. Franke, C. Christie, and Susana Bonis. 2010. "Nothing Stops a Bullet like a Job: Homeboy Industries Gang Prevention and Intervention in Los Angeles." In *Beyond Suppression: Global Perspectives on Youth Justice*, edited by Joan Serra Hoffman, Lyndee Knox, and Robert Cohen, 127–138. Santa Barbara, CA: ABC-CLIO.

Leary, Mark R. 1990. "Responses to Social Exclusion: Social Anxiety, Jealousy, Loneliness, Depression, and Low Self-Esteem." *Journal of Social and Clinical Psychology* 9 (2): 221–229.

LeBlanc, Marc, and Nadine Lanctot. 1998. "Social and Psychological Characteristics of Gang Members According to the Gang Structure and Its Subcultural and Ethnic Makeup." *Journal of Gang Research* 5:15–28.

Lee, Sou. 2016. *Asian Gangs in the United States: A Meta-synthesis*. Carbondale: Southern Illinois University Carbondale.

Lee, Sou, and Bryan F. Bubolz. 2020. "The Gang Member Stands Out: Stigma as a Residual Consequence of Gang Involvement." *Criminal Justice Review* 45 (1): 64–83.

Leovy, Jill. 2015. *Ghettoside: A True Story of Murder in America*. New York: Spiegel and Grau.

Lessing, Benjamin. 2010. "The Danger of Dungeons: Prison Gangs and Incarcerated Militant Groups." *Small Arms Survey* 6:157–183.

———. 2016. *Inside Out: The Challenge of Prison-Based Criminal Organizations*. Washington, DC: Brookings Institution.

———. 2017. "Counterproductive Punishment: How Prison Gangs Undermine State Authority." *Rationality and Society* 29 (3): 257–297.

Lessing, Benjamin, and Graham Denyer Willis. 2019. "Legitimacy in Criminal Governance: Managing a Drug Empire from Behind Bars." *American Political Science Review* 113 (2): 584–606.

Leverso, John, and Yuan Hsiao. 2020. "Gangbangin on the [Face]Book: Understanding Online Interactions of Chicago Latina/o Gangs." *Journal of Research in Crime and Delinquency* 58 (3): 239–268. https://doi.org/10.1177/0022427820952124.

Leverso, John, and Ross L. Matsueda. 2019. "Gang Organization and Gang Identity: An Investigation of Enduring Gang Membership." *Journal of Quantitative Criminology* 35:797–829. https://doi.org/10.1007/s10940-019-09408-x.

Levitt, Steven D., and Stephen J. Dubner. 2005. *Freakonomics: A Rogue Economist Explores the Hidden Side of Everything*. New York: HarperCollins.

Levitt, Steven D., and Sudhir Alladi Venkatesh. 2000. "An Economic Analysis of a Drug-Selling Gang's Finances." *Quarterly Journal of Economics* 115:755–789.

———. 2001. "Growing Up in the Projects: The Economic Lives of a Cohort of Men Who Came of Age in Chicago Public Housing." *American Economic Review* 91 (2): 79–84.

Lewis, Kevin, and Andrew V. Papachristos. 2020. "Rules of the Game: Exponential Random Graph Models of a Gang Homicide Network." *Social Forces* 98 (4): 1829–1858.

Liang, Bin, and Hong Lu. 2010. "Internet Development, Censorship and Cyber-Crimes in China." *Journal of Contemporary Criminal Justice* 26 (1): 103–120.

Lien, Inger-Liese. 2005. "Criminal Gangs and Their Connections: Metaphors, Definitions, and Structures." In *European Street Gangs and Troublesome Youth Groups*, edited by Scott H. Decker and Frank Weerman, 31–50. Lanham, MD: AltaMira.

Liu, Jianhong. 1999. "Social Capital and Covariates of Reoffending Risk in the Chinese Context." *International Criminal Justice Review* 9 (1): 39–55.

———. 2008. "Data Sources in Chinese Crime and Criminal Justice Research." *Crime, Law and Social Change* 50:131–147.

Liu, Jianhong, Lening Zhang, and Steven F. Messner, eds. 2001. *Crime and Social Control in a Changing China*. Westport, CT: Praeger.

Lo, T. Wing. 2012. "Triadization of Youth Gangs in Hong Kong." *British Journal of Criminology* 52 (3): 556–576.

Lo, T. Wing, and H. L. Tam. 2018. "Working with Chinese Triad Youth Gangs: Correct Diagnosis and Strategic Intervention." *International Journal of Offender Therapy and Comparative Criminology* 62 (12): 3708–3726.

Loeber, Rolf, and David P. Farrington. 2011. *Young Male Homicide Offenders and Victims: Risk Factors, Prediction, and Prevention from Childhood*. New York: Springer.

Loomis, Katelyn. 2019. *Spirituality, Religion, and Gang Membership: An Exploratory Analysis*. Tempe: Arizona State University.

Lyman, Michael D. 1989. *Gangland*. Springfield, IL: Charles C. Thomas.

Lynch, James P., and Lynn A. Addington. 2006. *Understanding Crime Statistics: Revisiting the Divergence of the NCVS and the UCR*. Cambridge: Cambridge University Press.

MacRae-Krisa, Leslie. 2013. "Exiting Gangs: Examining Processes and Best Practice within an Alberta Context." *International Journal of Child, Youth and Family Studies* 4 (1): 5–23.

Maitra, Dev, Robert McLean, and Chris Holligan. 2017. "Voices of Quiet Desistance in UK Prisons: Exploring Emergence of New Identities under Desistance Constraint." *Howard Journal of Crime and Justice* 56 (4): 437–453.

Maitra, Dev Rup. 2020. "'If You're Down with a Gang Inside, You Can Lead a Nice Life': Prison Gangs in the Age of Austerity." *Youth Justice* 20 (1–2): 128–145.

Majavu, Mandisi. 2020. "The 'African Gangs' Narrative: Associating Blackness with Criminality and Other Anti-Black Racist Tropes in Australia." *African and Black Diaspora: An International Journal* 13 (1): 27–39.

Mallion, Jaimee S., and Jane L. Wood. 2020. "Good Lives Model and Street Gang Membership: A Review and Application." *Aggression and Violent Behavior* 52:101393.

Manasseh, Tamar. 2017. "To the Chicago Police, Any Black Kid Is in a Gang." *New York Times*, December 25, 2017. https://www.nytimes.com/2017/12/25/opinion/chicago-police-black-kids-gangs.html.

Maphalala, Mncedisi C., and P. L. Mabunda. 2014. "Gangsterism: Internal and External Factors Associated with School Violence in Selected Western Cape High Schools." *Journal of Sociology and Social Anthropology* 5 (1): 61–70.

Mares, Dennis. 1998. "Gangchester: Youth Gang-Cultures in Manchester." MA thesis, Utrecht University.

Martínez-Reyes, Alberto, and José-Javier Navarro-Pérez. 2020. "The Effects of the Gang Truce on Salvadoran Communities and Development Agents." *International Social Work* (April). https://doi.org/10.1177/0020872820901765.

Matsuda, Kristy N., Finn-Aage Esbensen, and Dena C. Carson. 2012. "Putting the 'Gang' in 'Eurogang': Characteristics of Delinquent Youth Groups by Different Definitional Approaches." In *Youth Gangs in International Perspective*, edited by Finn-Aage Esbensen and Cheryl L. Maxson, 17–33. New York: Springer.

Mattick, Hans W., and Nathan S. Caplan. 1967. "Stake Animals, Loud-Talking, and Leading in Do-Nothing and Do-Something Situations." In *Juvenile Gangs in Context: Theory, Research, and Action*, edited by Malcolm W. Klein, 106–119. Englewood Cliffs, NJ: Prentice Hall.

Matusitz, Jonathan, and Michael Repass. 2009. "Gangs in Nigeria: An Updated Examination." *Crime, Law and Social Change* 52:495–511.

Matza, David. 1990. *Delinquency and Drift*. Reprint ed. New Brunswick, NJ: Routledge.

Maxson, Cheryl L. 1998. *Gang Members on the Move*. Washington, DC: U.S. Department of Justice, Office of Juvenile Justice and Delinquency Prevention.

———. 1999. "Gang Homicide: A Review and Extension of the Literature." In *Homicide: A Sourcebook of Social Research*, edited by M. Dwayne Smith and Margaret A. Zahn, 239–254. Thousand Oaks, CA: Sage.

———. 2001. "A Proposal for Multi-site Study of European Gangs and Youth Groups." In *The Eurogang Paradox: Street Gangs and Youth Groups in the U.S. and Europe*, edited by Malcolm W. Klein, Hans-Juergen Kerner, Cheryl L. Maxson, and Elmar G. M. Weitekamp, 299–308. Dordrecht, Netherlands: Kluwer Academic.

———. 2011. "Street Gangs: How Research Can Inform Policy." In *Crime and Public Policy*, 158–182. New York: Oxford University Press.

———. 2012. "Betwixt and between Street and Prison Gangs: Defining Gangs and Structures in Youth Correctional Facilities." In *Youth Gangs in International Perspective*, edited by Finn-Aage Esbensen and Cheryl L. Maxson, 107–124. New York: Springer.

———. 2013. "Do Not Shoot the Messenger: The Utility of Gang Risk Research in Program Targeting and Content." *Criminology and Public Policy* 12 (3): 421–426.

———. 2015. "The Legacy of Malcolm W. Klein." In *The Handbook of Gangs*, edited by Scott H. Decker and David C. Pyrooz, 406. Chichester, U.K.: Wiley-Blackwell.

Maxson, Cheryl L., Charlotte E. Bradstreet, Danny Gascón, Julie Gerlinger, Jessica Grebenkemper, Darin Haerle, Jacob Kang-Brown, et al. 2012. *Gangs and Violence in California's Youth Correctional Facilities: A Research Foundation for Developing Effective Gang Policies*. Irvine: Department of Criminology, Law and Society, University of California, Irvine.

Maxson, Cheryl L., and Finn-Aage Esbensen, eds. 2016. *Gang Transitions and Transformations in an International Context*. 1st ed. New York: Springer.

Maxson, Cheryl L., Karen M. Hennigan, and David C. Sloane. 2005. "'It's Getting Crazy out There': Can a Civil Gang Injunction Change a Community?" *Criminology and Public Policy* 4 (3): 577–605.

Maxson, Cheryl L., and Malcolm W. Klein. 1995. "Investigating Gang Structures." *Journal of Gang Research* 3 (1): 33–40.

———. 1996. "Defining Gang Homicide: An Updated Look at Member and Motive Approaches." In *Gangs in America*, edited by C. Ronald Huff, 2nd ed., 3–20. Thousand Oaks, CA: Sage.

Maxson, Cheryl L., Kristy N. Matsuda, and Karen Hennigan. 2011. "'Deterrability' among Gang and Nongang Juvenile Offenders: Are Gang Members More (or Less) Deterrable Than Other Juvenile Offenders?" *Crime and Delinquency* 57 (4): 516–543.

Maxwell, Joseph A. 2012. *Qualitative Research Design: An Interactive Approach*. 3rd ed. Thousand Oaks, CA: Sage.

Mayhew, Bruce H., J. Miller McPherson, Thomas Rotolo, and Lynn Smith-Lovin. 1995. "Sex and Race Homogeneity in Naturally Occurring Groups." *Social Forces* 74 (1): 15–52. https://doi.org/10.2307/2580623.

McAra, Lesley, and Susan McVie. 2010. "Youth Crime and Justice: Key Messages from the Edinburgh Study of Youth Transitions and Crime." *Criminology and Criminal Justice* 10 (2): 179–209.

McCann, Bryan J. 2017. *The Mark of Criminality: Rhetoric, Race, and Gangsta Rap in the War-on-Crime Era*. 1st ed. Tuscaloosa: University of Alabama Press.

McCarthy, Bill, and John Hagan. 1995. "Getting into Street Crime: The Structure and Process of Criminal Embeddedness." *Social Science Research* 24 (1): 63–95.

———. 2001. "When Crime Pays: Capital, Competence, and Criminal Success." *Social Forces* 79 (3): 1035–1060.

McCorkle, Richard C., and Terance D. Miethe. 1998. "The Political and Organizational Response to Gangs: An Examination of a 'Moral Panic' in Nevada." *Justice Quarterly* 15:41–64.

———. 2001. *Panic: The Social Construction of the Street Gang Problem*. Upper Saddle River, NJ: Prentice Hall.

McDevitt, Jack. 2006. *Project Safe Neighborhoods: Strategic Intervention, Offender Notification Meetings*. Washington, DC: U.S. Department of Justice.

McGarrell, Edmund F., and Steven Chermak. 2003. *Strategic Approaches to Reducing Firearms Violence: Final Report on the Indianapolis Violence Reduction Partnership*. Washington, DC: National Institute of Justice, U.S. Department of Justice.

McGarrell, Edmund F., Steven Chermak, Jeremy M. Wilson, and Nicholas Corsaro. 2006. "Reducing Homicide through a 'Lever-Pulling' Strategy." *Justice Quarterly* 23 (2): 214–231.

McGarrell, Edmund F., Nicholas Corsaro, Natalie Kroovand Hipple, and Timothy S. Bynum. 2010. "Project Safe Neighborhoods and Violent Crime Trends in US Cities: Assessing Violent Crime Impact." *Journal of Quantitative Criminology* 26 (2): 165–190.

McGarrell, Edmund F., Nicholas Corsaro, Chris Melde, Natalie Hipple, Jennifer Cobbina, Timothy Bynum, and Heather Perez. 2013. *An Assessment of the Comprehensive Anti-gang Initiative: Final Project Report.* Washington, DC: U.S. Department of Justice, National Institute of Justice.

McGarrell, Edmund F., Heather Perez, Robyn Carter, and Haley Daffron. 2018. *Project Safe Neighborhoods (PSN): Research Foundation.* East Lansing: Michigan State University.

McGloin, Jean M. 2005. "Policy and Intervention Considerations of a Network Analysis of Street Gangs." *Criminology and Public Policy* 4 (3): 607–635.

McGloin, Jean M., and Megan E. Collins. 2015. "Micro-level Processes of the Gang." In *The Handbook of Gangs,* edited by Scott H. Decker and David C. Pyrooz, 276–293. Chichester, U.K.: Wiley-Blackwell.

McGloin, Jean M., and Kyle J. Thomas. 2019. "Peer Influence and Delinquency." *Annual Review of Criminology* 2:241–264.

McGrath, Karl. 2020. "A Systematic Review of the Effectiveness of Gang Interventions and Management Strategies (GIMS) in Penal Institutions." Technological University Dublin.

McLean, Robert. 2018. "An Evolving Gang Model in Contemporary Scotland." *Deviant Behavior* 39 (3): 309–321.

———. 2019. *Gangs, Drugs and (Dis)Organised Crime.* Bristol, U.K.: Bristol University Press.

McLean, Robert, and James A. Densley. 2020. *Scotland's Gang Members: Life and Crime in Glasgow.* Cham, Switzerland: Palgrave Macmillan.

———. 2022. *Robbery in the Illegal Drugs Trade: Violence and Vengeance.* Bristol, UK: Bristol University Press.

McLean, Robert, James A. Densley, and Ross Deuchar. 2018. "Situating Gangs within Scotland's Illegal Drugs Market(s)." *Trends in Organized Crime* 21 (2): 147–171.

McLean, Robert, Ross Deuchar, Simon Harding, and James A. Densley. 2019. "Putting the 'Street' in Gang: Place and Space in the Organization of Scotland's Drug-Selling Gangs." *British Journal of Criminology* 59 (2): 396–415.

McLean, Robert, Grace Robinson, and James A. Densley. 2018. "The Rise of Drug Dealing in the Life of the North American Street Gang." *Societies* 8 (3): 90.

———. 2020. *County Lines: Criminal Networks and Evolving Drug Markets in Britain.* SpringerBriefs in Criminology. Cham, Switzerland: Springer.

McLuhan, Marshall, and Quentin Fiore. 1967. *The Medium Is the Massage.* New York: Bantum.

McPherson, Miller, Lynn Smith-Lovin, and James M. Cook. 2001. "Birds of a Feather: Homophily in Social Networks." *Annual Review of Sociology* 27 (1): 415–444.

McShane, Marilyn D., Frank P. Williams, and H. Michael Dolny. 2003. "The Effect of Gang Membership on Parole Outcome." *Journal of Gang Research* 10 (4): 25–38.

Mears, Daniel P., Joshua C. Cochran, Brian J. Stults, Sarah J. Greenman, Avinash S. Bhati, and Mark A. Greenwald. 2014. "The 'True' Juvenile Offender: Age Effects and Juvenile Court Sanctioning." *Criminology* 52 (2): 169–194.

Medina-Ariza, Juan Jose, Andreas Cebulla, Judith Aldridge, Jon Shute, and Andy Ross. 2014. "Proximal Adolescent Outcomes of Gang Membership in England and Wales." *Journal of Research in Crime and Delinquency* 51:168–199.

Meijer, Albert, and Martijn Wessels. 2019. "Predictive Policing: Review of Benefits and Drawbacks." *International Journal of Public Administration* 42 (12): 1031–1039.

Melde, Chris. 2016. "Gangs and Gang Crime." In *The Handbook of Measurement Issues in Criminology and Criminal Justice*, edited by Beth M. Huebner and Timothy S. Bynum, 157–180. U.K.: Wiley Blackwell.

Melde, Chris, Chelsea Diem, and Gregory Drake. 2012. "Identifying Correlates of Stable Gang Membership." *Journal of Contemporary Criminal Justice* 28 (4): 482–498.

Melde, Chris, and Finn-Aage Esbensen. 2011. "Gang Membership as a Turning Point in the Life Course." *Criminology* 49 (2): 513–552.

———. 2014. "The Relative Impact of Gang Status Transitions: Identifying the Mechanisms of Change in Delinquency." *Journal of Research in Crime and Delinquency* 51 (3): 349–376.

Melde, Chris, and Frank Weerman, eds. 2020. *Gangs in the Era of Internet and Social Media*. Cham, Switzerland: Springer.

Merton, Robert K. 1938. "Social Structure and Anomie." *American Sociological Review* 3 (5): 672–682.

Messerschmidt, James W. 1993. *Masculinities and Crime: Critique and Reconceptualization of Theory*. Lanham: Rowman and Littlefield.

———. 2002. "On Gang Girls, Gender and a Structured Action Theory: A Reply to Miller." *Theoretical Criminology* 6 (4): 461–475.

———. 2005. "Men, Masculinities, and Crime." In *Handbook of Studies on Men and Masculinities*, edited by Michael S. Kimmel, Jeff Hearn, and Raewyn W. Connell, 196–212. Thousand Oaks, CA: Sage.

Mieczkowski, Thomas. 1986. "Geeking Up and Throwing Down: Heroin Street Life in Detroit." *Criminology* 24 (4): 645–666. https://doi.org/10.1111/j.1745-9125.1986.tb01506.x.

Miethe, Terance D., and Richard C. McCorkle. 1997. "Gang Membership and Criminal Processing: A Test of the 'Master Status' Concept." *Justice Quarterly* 14 (3): 407–427.

Mihalic, Sharon F., and Delbert S. Elliott. 2015. "Evidence-Based Programs Registry: Blueprints for Healthy Youth Development." *Evaluation and Program Planning* 48 (February): 124–131. https://doi.org/10.1016/j.evalprogplan.2014.08.004.

Miller, Jody. 1998. "Gender and Victimization Risk among Young Women in Gangs." *Journal of Research in Crime and Delinquency* 35 (4): 429–453.

———. 2001. *One of the Guys: Girls, Gangs, and Gender*. New York: Oxford University Press.

———. 2002. "The Strengths and Limits of 'Doing Gender' for Understanding Street Crime." *Theoretical Criminology* 6 (4): 433–460.

Miller, Jody, and Rod K. Brunson. 2000. "Gender Dynamics in Youth Gangs: A Comparison of Males' and Females' Accounts." *Justice Quarterly* 17 (3): 419–448.

Miller, Jody, and Scott H. Decker. 2001. "Young Women and Gang Violence: Gender, Street Offending, and Violent Victimization in Gangs." *Justice Quarterly* 18 (1): 115–140.

Miller, Johanne. 2020. "Passing on Gang Culture in the Theatre of the Streets: 'They'll Grow out of It, Then Our Age Will Grow into It and Then We'll Grow out of It.'" *Journal of Youth Studies* 23 (8): 1086–1101.

Miller, Walter B. 1958. "Lower Class Culture as a Generating Milieu of Gang Delinquency." *Journal of Social Issues* 14 (3): 5–19.

———. 1962. "The Impact of a 'Total-Community' Delinquency Control Project." *Social Problems* 10 (2): 168–191.

———. 1973. "The Molls." *Society* 11 (1): 32–35.

———. 1975. *Violence by Youth Gangs and Youth Groups as a Crime Problem in Major American Cities*. Washington, DC: Office of Juvenile Justice and Delinquency Prevention.

———. 1982. *Crime by Youth Gangs and Groups in the United States*. Washington, DC: U.S. Department of Justice, Office of Justice Programs, Office of Juvenile Justice and Delinquency Prevention.

———. 1990. "Why the United States Has Failed to Solve Its Youth Gang Problem." In *Gangs in America*, edited by C. Ronald Huff, 263–287. Newbury Park, CA: Sage.

———. 2011. *City Gangs*. Phoenix: Arizona State University, School of Criminology and Criminal Justice. http://gangresearch.asu.edu/walter_miller_library/walter-b.-miller -book.

Minkenberg, Michael. 1998. "Context and Consequence: The Impact of the New Radical Right on the Political Process in France and Germany." *German Politics and Society* 16, no. 3 (48): 1–23.

Mitchell, Meghan M., Chantal Fahmy, David C. Pyrooz, and Scott H. Decker. 2017. "Criminal Crews, Codes, and Contexts: Differences and Similarities across the Code of the Street, Convict Code, Street Gangs, and Prison Gangs." *Deviant Behavior* 38 (10): 1197–1222.

Mitchell, Meghan M., Kallee McCullough, Jun Wu, David C. Pyrooz, and Scott H. Decker. 2018. "Survey Research with Gang and Non-gang Members in Prison: Opera- tional Lessons from the LoneStar Project." *Trends in Organized Crime* (March). https:// doi.org/10.1007/s12117-018-9331-1.

Molidor, Christian E. 1996. "Female Gang Members: A Profile of Aggression and Victim- ization." *Social Work* 41 (3): 251–257.

Molina, Alexander A. 1992. "California's Anti-gang Street Terrorism Enforcement and Prevention Act: One Step Forward, Two Steps Back." *Southwestern University Law Re- view* 22:457–482.

Moloney, Molly, Geoffrey P. Hunt, Karen Joe-Laidler, and Kathleen MacKenzie. 2011. "Young Mother (in the) Hood: Gang Girls' Negotiation of New Identities." *Journal of Youth Studies* 14 (1): 1–19.

Moloney, Molly, Kathleen MacKenzie, Geoffrey Hunt, and Karen Joe-Laidler. 2009. "The Path and Promise of Fatherhood for Gang Members." *British Journal of Criminology* 49 (3): 305–325.

Moore, Joan W. 1978. *Homeboys: Gangs, Drugs, and Prison in the Barrios of Los Angeles*. Philadelphia: Temple University Press.

———. 1985. "Isolation and Stigmatization in the Development of an Underclass: The Case of Chicano Gangs in East Los Angeles." *Social Problems* 33 (1): 1–12.

———. 1988. "Gangs and the Underclass: A Comparative Perspective." In *People and Folks: Gangs, Crime and the Underclass in a Rustbelt City*, 3–16. Chicago: Lake View Press.

———. 1991. *Going down to the Barrio: Homeboys and Homegirls in Change*. Philadelphia: Temple University Press.

Moore, Joan W., and Raquel Pinderhughes. 1993. *In the Barrios: Latinos and the Underclass Debate*. New York: Russell Sage Foundation.

Moore, John P. 1997. *Highlights of the 1995 National Youth Gang Survey*. Fact Sheet No. 63. Washington, DC: U.S. Department of Justice, Office of Justice Programs, Office of Ju- venile Justice and Delinquency Prevention. https://www.ncjrs.gov/App/Publications /abstract.aspx?ID=186268.

Moore, Natalie Y., and Lance Williams. 2011. *The Almighty Black P Stone Nation: The Rise, Fall, and Resurgence of an American Gang*. Chicago: Lawrence Hill Books.

Mora, Victor. 2020. "Police Response to Juvenile Gangs and Gang Violence." In *Oxford Research Encyclopedia of Criminology and Criminal Justice*. Article published March 31, 2020. https://doi.org/10.1093/acrefore/9780190264079.013.79.

Mørck, Line Lerche, Khaled Hussain, Camilla Møller-Andersen, Tülay Özüpek, Anne-Mette Palm, and Ida Hedegaard Vorbeck. 2013. "Praxis Development in Relation to Gang Conflicts in Copenhagen, Denmark." *Outlines: Critical Practice Studies* 14 (2): 79–105.

Morselli, Carlo. 2001. "Structuring Mr. Nice: Entrepreneurial Opportunities and Brokerage Positioning in the Cannabis Trade." *Crime, Law and Social Change* 35 (3): 203–244.

———. 2009. *Inside Criminal Networks.* New York: Springer.

Morselli, Carlo, and David Décary-Hétu. 2013. "Crime Facilitation Purposes of Social Networking Sites: A Review and Analysis of the 'Cyberbanging' Phenomenon." *Small Wars and Insurgencies* 24 (1): 152–170.

Morselli, Carlo, Pierre Tremblay, and Bill McCarthy. 2006. "Mentors and Criminal Achievement." *Criminology* 44 (1): 17–43.

Moule, Richard K., Jr. 2015. "The Legacy of Walter B. Miller." In *The Handbook of Gangs*, edited by Scott H. Decker and David C. Pyrooz, 458–477. Chichester, U.K.: Wiley-Blackwell.

Moule, Richard K., Jr., Scott H. Decker, and David C. Pyrooz. 2017. "Technology and Conflict: Group Processes and Collective Violence in the Internet Era." *Crime, Law and Social Change*, no. 1–2: 47–73.

Moule, Richard K., Jr., and Bryanna Fox. 2020. "Belief in the Code of the Street and Individual Involvement in Offending: A Meta-analysis." *Youth Violence and Juvenile Justice* 19 (2): 227–247. https://journals.sagepub.com/doi/full/10.1177/1541204020927737.

Moule, Richard K., Jr., David C. Pyrooz, and Scott H. Decker. 2013. "From 'What the F#@% Is a Facebook?' to 'Who Doesn't Use Facebook?': The Role of Criminal Lifestyles in the Adoption and Use of the Internet." *Social Science Research* 42 (6): 1411–1421.

———. 2014. "Internet Adoption and Online Behaviour among American Street Gangs: Integrating Gangs and Organizational Theory." *British Journal of Criminology* 54 (6): 1186–1206.

Mucchielli, Laurent, and Marwan Mohammed. 2007. *Les bandes de jeunes des "blousons noirs" à nos jours.* Paris: La Decouverte.

Mullins, Christopher W., and Daniel R. Kavish. 2020. "Street Life and Masculinities." In *Routledge Handbook of Street Culture*, edited by Jeffrey I. Ross, 183–193. New York: Routledge.

Muniz, Ana. 2014. "Maintaining Racial Boundaries: Criminalization, Neighborhood Context, and the Origins of Gang Injunctions." *Social Problems* 61 (2): 216–236.

Nagin, Daniel S., and Raymond Paternoster. 1991. "On the Relationship of Past to Future Participation in Delinquency." *Criminology* 29 (2): 163–189.

———. 2000. "Population Heterogeneity and State Dependence: State of the Evidence and Directions for Future Research." *Journal of Quantitative Criminology* 16 (2): 117–144.

National Academies of Sciences, Engineering, and Medicine. 2018. *Proactive Policing: Effects on Crime and Communities.* Washington, DC: National Academies Press.

National Gang Intelligence Center. 2011. *2011 National Gang Threat Assessment—Emerging Trends.* Washington, DC: Federal Bureau of Investigation, National Gang Intelligence Center. https://www.fbi.gov/file-repository/stats-services-publications-2011-national -gang-threat-assessment-2011%20national%20gang%20threat%20assessment%20%20 emerging%20trends.pdf/view.

———. 2015. *2015 National Gang Threat Assessment.* Washington, DC: Federal Bureau of Investigation, National Gang Intelligence Center. https://www.fbi.gov/file-repository /stats-services-publications-national-gang-report-2015.pdf/view.

Needle, Jerome, and William Vaughan Stapleton. 1983. *Police Handling of Youth Gangs.* Washington, DC: U.S. Department of Justice, Office of Juvenile Justice and Delinquency Prevention.

Nguyen, Holly, and Martin Bouchard. 2013. "Need, Connections, or Competence? Criminal Achievement among Adolescent Offenders." *Justice Quarterly* 30 (1): 44–83.

Noble, Safiya Umoja. 2018. *Algorithms of Oppression: How Search Engines Reinforce Racism*. New York: New York University Press.

Novich, Madeleine. 2018. "Policing American Gangs and Gang Members." In *Oxford Research Encyclopedia of Criminology and Criminal Justice*. Article published March 28, 2018. https://doi.org/10.1093/acrefore/9780190264079.013.445.

Novich, Madeleine, and Geoffrey Hunt. 2017. "'Get off Me': Perceptions of Disrespectful Police Behaviour among Ethnic Minority Youth Gang Members." *Drugs: Education, Prevention and Policy* 24 (3): 248–255.

———. 2018. "Trust in Police Motivations during Involuntary Encounters: An Examination of Young Gang Members of Colour." *Race and Justice* 8 (1): 51–70.

O'Deane, Matthew D. 2011. *Gang Injunctions and Abatement: Using Civil Remedies to Curb Gang-Related Crimes*. Boca Raton, FL: CRC.

Ogilvie, James M., Anna L. Stewart, Raymond C. K. Chan, and David H. K. Shum. 2011. "Neuropsychological Measures of Executive Function and Antisocial Behavior: A Meta-analysis." *Criminology* 49 (4): 1063–1107.

O'Neal, Eryn Nicole, Scott H. Decker, Richard K. Moule, and David C. Pyrooz. 2016. "Girls, Gangs, and Getting Out: Gender Differences and Similarities in Leaving the Gang." *Youth Violence and Juvenile Justice* 14 (1): 43–60.

O'Neill, Kevin Lewis. 2015. *Secure the Soul: Christian Piety and Gang Prevention in Guatemala*. Berkeley: University of California Press.

Orlando-Morningstar, Dennise. 1997. "Prison Gangs." *Special Needs Offender Bulletin* 2 (August): 1–13.

Ortiz, Jennifer M. 2019. "Gangs and Environment: A Comparative Analysis of Prison and Street Gangs." *American Journal of Qualitative Research* 2 (1): 97–117.

Osgood, D. Wayne, Janet K. Wilson, Patrick M. O'Malley, Jerald G. Bachman, and Lloyd D. Johnston. 1996. "Routine Activities and Individual Deviant Behavior." *American Sociological Review* 61 (4): 635–655.

Ouellet, Marie, Martin Bouchard, and Yanick Charette. 2019. "One Gang Dies, Another Gains? The Network Dynamics of Criminal Group Persistence." *Criminology* 57 (1): 5–33.

Ousey, Graham C., Pamela Wilcox, and Bonnie S. Fisher. 2011. "Something Old, Something New: Revisiting Competing Hypotheses of the Victimization-Offending Relationship among Adolescents." *Journal of Quantitative Criminology* 27 (1): 53–84.

Owens, Emily G. 2009. "More Time, Less Crime? Estimating the Incapacitative Effect of Sentence Enhancements." *Journal of Law and Economics* 52 (3): 551–579.

Ozer, M. Murat, and Robin S. Engel. 2012. "Revisiting the Use of Propensity Score Matching to Understand the Relationship between Gang Membership and Violent Victimization: A Cautionary Note." *Justice Quarterly* 29 (1): 105–124.

Padilla, Felix M. 1992. *The Gang as an American Enterprise*. New Brunswick, NJ: Rutgers University Press.

Panfil, Vanessa R. 2020. "'I Was a Homo Thug, Now I'm Just Homo': Gay Gang Members' Desistance and Persistence." *Criminology* 58 (2): 255–279. https://doi.org/10.1111/1745-9125.12240.

Papachristos, Andrew V. 2005. "Gang World." *Foreign Policy* 147:48–55.

———. 2009. "Murder by Structure: Dominance Relations and the Social Structure of Gang Homicide." *American Journal of Sociology* 115 (1): 74–128.

———. 2013a. "The Importance of Cohesion for Gang Research, Policy, and Practice." *Criminology and Public Policy* 12 (1): 49–58.

———. 2013b. "Two Decades of G.R.E.A.T." *Criminology and Public Policy* 12 (3): 367–371.

Papachristos, Andrew V., Anthony A. Braga, Eric Piza, and Leigh S. Grossman. 2015. "The Company You Keep? The Spillover Effects of Gang Membership on Individual Gunshot Victimization in a Co-offending Network." *Criminology* 53 (4): 624–649.

Papachristos, Andrew V., and Lorine A. Hughes. 2015. "Neighborhoods and Street Gangs." In *The Handbook of Gangs*, edited by Scott H. Decker and David C. Pyrooz, 98–117. Chichester, West Sussex: Wiley-Blackwell.

Papachristos, Andrew V., David M. Hureau, and Anthony A. Braga. 2013. "The Corner and the Crew: The Influence of Geography and Social Networks on Gang Violence." *American Sociological Review* 78 (3): 417–447. https://doi.org/10.1177/0003122413486800.

Papachristos, Andrew V., and David S. Kirk. 2006. "Neighborhood Effects on Street Gang Behavior." In *Studying Youth Gangs*, edited by James F. Short and Lorine A. Hughes, 12:63–83. Lanham, MD: Rowman AltaMira.

Papachristos, Andrew V., Tracey L. Meares, and Jeffrey Fagan. 2007. "Attention Felons: Evaluating Project Safe Neighborhoods in Chicago." *Journal of Empirical Legal Studies* 4 (2): 223–272.

Paternoster, Ray, Ronet Bachman, Shawn Bushway, Erin Kerrison, and Daniel O'Connell. 2015. "Human Agency and Explanations of Criminal Desistance: Arguments for a Rational Choice Theory." *Journal of Developmental and Life-Course Criminology* 1 (3): 209–235.

Paternoster, Ray, and Shawn Bushway. 2009. "Desistance and the 'Feared Self': Toward an Identity Theory of Criminal Desistance." *Journal of Criminal Law and Criminology* 99 (4): 1103–1156.

Patrick, James. 1973. *A Glasgow Gang Observed*. London: Eyre Methuen.

Pattillo, Mary E. 1998. "Sweet Mothers and Gangbangers: Managing Crime in a Black Middle-Class Neighborhood." *Social Forces* 76 (3): 747–774.

———. 1999. *Black Picket Fences: Privilege and Peril among the Black Middle Class*. Chicago: University of Chicago Press.

Patton, Desmond U., Douglas-Wade Brunton, Andrea Dixon, Reuben Jonathan Miller, Patrick Leonard, and Rose Hackman. 2017. "Stop and Frisk Online: Theorizing Everyday Racism in Digital Policing in the Use of Social Media for Identification of Criminal Conduct and Associations." *Social Media + Society* 3 (3): 2056305117733344.

Patton, Desmond U., Robert D. Eschmann, and Dirk A. Butler. 2013. "Internet Banging: New Trends in Social Media, Gang Violence, Masculinity and Hip Hop." *Computers in Human Behavior* 29 (5): A54–A59.

Patton, Desmond U., Jeffrey Lane, Patrick Leonard, Jamie Macbeth, and Jocelyn R. Smith Lee. 2017. "Gang Violence on the Digital Street: Case Study of a South Side Chicago Gang Member's Twitter Communication." *New Media and Society* 19 (7): 1000–1018.

Patton, Desmond U., Sadiq Patel, Jun Sung Hong, Megan Ranney, Marie Crandal, and Lyle Dungy. 2017. "Tweets, Gangs and Guns: A Snapshot of Gang Communications in Detroit." *Violence and Victims* 32 (5): 919–934.

Patton, Desmond U., David Pyrooz, Scott Decker, William R. Frey, and Patrick Leonard. 2019. "When Twitter Fingers Turn to Trigger Fingers: A Qualitative Study of Social Media-Related Gang Violence." *International Journal of Bullying Prevention* 1 (3): 205–217.

Patton, Desmond U., Ninive Sanchez, Dale Fitch, Jamie Macbeth, and Patrick Leonard. 2017. "I Know God's Got a Day 4 Me: Violence, Trauma, and Coping among Gang-Involved Twitter Users." *Social Science Computer Review* 25 (2): 226–243.

Pauwels, Lieven J. R., and Robert Svensson. 2013. "Violent Youth Group Involvement, Self-Reported Offending and Victimisation: An Empirical Assessment of an Integrated Informal Control/Lifestyle Model." *European Journal on Criminal Policy and Research* 19 (4): 369–386.

Pawelz, Janina, and Paul Elvers. 2018. "The Digital Hood of Urban Violence: Exploring Functionalities of Social Media and Music among Gangs." *Journal of Contemporary Criminal Justice* 34:442–459.

Pedersen, Maria Libak. 2014. "Gang Joining in Denmark: Prevalence and Correlates of Street Gang Membership." *Journal of Scandinavian Studies in Criminology and Crime Prevention* 15 (1): 55–72.

———. 2018. *Joining and Leaving Gangs in Denmark: Four Empirical Papers*. Aalborg: Aalborg University. https://search.proquest.com/openview/0802f662406c6dc329b348 876c1bdfbc/1?pq-origsite=gscholar&cbl=1836341.

Pedersen, Maria Libak, and Jonas Markus Lindstad. 2012. "The Danish Gang-Joining Project: Methodological Issues and Preliminary Results." In *Youth Gangs in International Perspective: Results from the Eurogang Program of Research*, edited by Finn-Aage Esbensen and Cheryl L. Maxson, 239–250. New York: Springer.

Penglase, R. Ben. 2014. *Living with Insecurity in a Brazilian Favela: Urban Violence and Daily Life*. New Brunswick, NJ: Rutgers University Press.

Perkins, Useni Eugene. 1987. *Explosion of Chicago's Black Street Gangs*. Chicago: Third World.

Perrow, Charles. 2000. "An Organizational Analysis of Organizational Theory." *Contemporary Sociology* 29 (3): 469.

Petersilia, Joan. 2003. *When Prisoners Come Home: Parole and Prisoner Reentry*. New York: Oxford University Press.

Peterson, Dana, Dena C. Carson, and Eric Fowler. 2018. "What's Sex (Composition) Got to Do with It? The Importance of Sex Composition of Gangs for Female and Male Members' Offending and Victimization." *Justice Quarterly* 35 (6): 941–976.

Peterson, Dana, Jody Miller, and Finn-Aage Esbensen. 2001. "The Impact of Sex Composition on Gangs and Gang Member Delinquency." *Criminology* 39 (2): 411–440.

Peterson, Dana, and Vanessa R. Panfil. 2015. "Gender, Sexuality, and Gangs: Re-envisioning Diversity." In *The Handbook of Gangs*, edited by Scott H. Decker and David C. Pyrooz, 208–234. Chichester, U.K.: Wiley-Blackwell.

———. 2017. "Toward a Multiracial Feminist Framework for Understanding Females' Gang Involvement." *Journal of Crime and Justice* 40 (3): 337–357.

Peterson, Dana, Terrance J. Taylor, and Finn-Aage Esbensen. 2004. "Gang Membership and Violent Victimization." *Justice Quarterly* 21 (4): 793–815.

Peterson, Jillian, and James Densley. 2017. "Cyber Violence: What Do We Know and Where Do We Go from Here?" *Aggression and Violent Behavior* 34: 193–200.

Petrus, Theodore, and Irvin Kinnes. 2019. "New Social Bandits? A Comparative Analysis of Gangsterism in the Western and Eastern Cape Provinces of South Africa." *Criminology and Criminal Justice* 19 (2): 179–196.

Petterson, Tove. 2003. "Ethnicity and Violent Crime: The Ethnic Structure of Networks of Youths Suspected of Violent Offences in Stockholm." *Journal of Scandinavian Studies in Criminology and Crime Prevention* 4 (2): 143–161.

Pfaff, John. 2017. *Locked In: The True Causes of Mass Incarceration—and How to Achieve Real Reform*. New York: Basic Books.

Phillips, Coretta. 2012. "'It Ain't Nothing like America with the Bloods and the Crips': Gang Narratives inside Two English Prisons." *Punishment and Society* 14 (1): 51–68.

Piano, Ennio E. 2017. "Free Riders: The Economics and Organization of Outlaw Motorcycle Gangs." *Public Choice* 171 (3): 283–301.

Pickering, Jonny, Keith Kintrea, and Jon Bannister. 2012. "Invisible Walls and Visible Youth: Territoriality among Young People in British Cities." *Urban Studies* 49 (5): 945–960.

Pinderhughes, Howard. 1997. *Race in the Hood: Conflict and Violence among Urban Youth.* 1st ed. Minneapolis: University of Minnesota Press.

Pinkney, Craig, and Shona Robinson-Edwards. 2018. "Gangs, Music and the Mediatisation of Crime: Expressions, Violations and Validations." *Safer Communities* 17 (2): 103–118.

Pinnock, Don. 2016. *Gang Town.* Cape Town: Tafelberg.

Pinnock, Don, and Mara Douglas-Hamilton. 1998. "Rituals, Rites and Tradition: Rethinking Youth Programs in South Africa." In *Gangs and Youth Subcultures: International Explorations,* edited by Kayleen Hazlehurst and Cameron Hazlehurst, 307–341. New Brunswick, NJ: Transaction.

Piquero, Alex R., David P. Farrington, and Alfred Blumstein. 2003. "The Criminal Career Paradigm." *Crime and Justice* 30 (January): 359–506.

Pitts, John. 2008. *Reluctant Gangsters: The Changing Face of Youth Crime.* Cullompton, U.K.: Willan.

———. 2012. "Reluctant Criminologists: Criminology, Ideology and the Violent Youth Gang." *Youth and Policy* 109:27–45.

Popkin, Susan J., Victoria E. Gwiasda, Lynn M. Olson, Dennis P. Rosenbaum, and Larry Buron. 2000. *The Hidden War: Crime and the Tragedy of Public Housing in Chicago.* New Brunswick, NJ: Rutgers University Press.

Portillos, Edwardo L. 1999. "Women, Men, and Gangs: The Social Construction of Gender in the Barrio." In *Female Gangs in America: Essays on Girls, Gangs and Gender,* edited by Meda Chesney-Lind and John M. Hagedorn, 232–244. Chicago: Lake View.

Possley, Maurice, and William Crawford. 1986. "El Rukns Indicted in Libya Scheme." *Chicago Tribune,* October 31, 1986. https://www.chicagotribune.com/news/ct-xpm-1986-10-31-8603210871-story.html.

Pratt, Travis C., and Francis T. Cullen. 2000. "The Empirical Status of Gottfredson and Hirschi's General Theory of Crime: A Meta-analysis." *Criminology* 38 (3): 931–964.

Pratt, Travis C., Francis T. Cullen, Kristie R. Blevins, Leah Daigle, and James D. Unnever. 2002. "The Relationship of Attention Deficit Hyperactivity Disorder to Crime and Delinquency: A Meta-analysis." *International Journal of Police Science and Management* 4 (4): 344–360.

Pratt, Travis C., Francis T. Cullen, Christine S. Sellers, L. Thomas Winfree, Tamara D. Madensen, Leah E. Daigle, Noelle E. Fearn, and Jacinta M. Gau. 2010. "The Empirical Status of Social Learning Theory: A Meta-analysis." *Justice Quarterly* 27 (6): 765–802.

Pratt, Travis C., Jillian J. Turanovic, and Francis T. Cullen. 2016. "Revisiting the Criminological Consequences of Exposure to Fetal Testosterone: A Meta-analysis of the 2D:4D Digit Ratio." *Criminology* 54 (4): 587–620.

Prendergast, Alan. 2014. "After the Murder of Tom Clements, Can Colorado's Prison System Rehabilitate Itself?" *Westword,* August 21, 2014. http://www.westword.com/news/after-the-murder-of-tom-clements-can-colorados-prison-system-rehabilitate-itself-5125050.

Przemieniecki, Christopher. 2012. "'Reel' Gangs or 'Real' Gangs: A Qualitative Media Analysis of Street Gangs Portrayed in Hollywood Films, 1960–2009." Ph.D. diss., University of North Dakota. https://commons.und.edu/theses/1312.

Puffer, Joseph Adams. 1912. *The Boy and His Gang.* Boston: Houghton.

Pyrooz, David C. 2012. "Structural Covariates of Gang Homicide in Large US Cities." *Journal of Research in Crime and Delinquency* 49 (4): 489–518.

———. 2013. "Gangs, Criminal Offending, and an Inconvenient Truth: Considerations for Gang Prevention and Intervention in the Lives of Youth." *Criminology and Public Policy* 12 (3): 427–436.

———. 2014a. "From Colors and Guns to Caps and Gowns? The Effects of Gang Membership on Educational Attainment." *Journal of Research in Crime and Delinquency* 51 (1): 56–87.

———. 2014b. "'From Your First Cigarette to Your Last Dyin' Day': The Patterning of Gang Membership in the Life-Course." *Journal of Quantitative Criminology* 30 (2): 349–372.

Pyrooz, David C., Kendra J. Clark, Jennifer J. Tostlebe, Scott H. Decker, and Erin Orrick. 2020. "Gang Affiliation and Prisoner Reentry: Discrete-Time Variation in Recidivism by Current, Former, and Non-gang Status." *Journal of Research in Crime and Delinquency* 58 (2): 192–234. https://doi.org/10.1177/0022427820949895.

Pyrooz, David C., and Scott H. Decker. 2011. "Motives and Methods for Leaving the Gang: Understanding the Process of Gang Desistance." *Journal of Criminal Justice* 39 (5): 417–425.

———. 2013. "Delinquent Behavior, Violence, and Gang Involvement in China." *Journal of Quantitative Criminology* 29 (2): 251–272.

———. 2014. "Recent Research on Disengaging from Gangs: Implications for Practice." In *Effective Interventions in the Lives of Criminal Offenders*, edited by John A. Humphrey and Peter Cordella, 81–98. New York: Springer.

———. 2019. *Competing for Control: Gangs and the Social Order of Prisons*. Cambridge: Cambridge University Press.

Pyrooz, David C., Scott H. Decker, and Mark S. Fleisher. 2011. "From the Street to the Prison, from the Prison to the Street: Understanding and Responding to Prison Gangs." *Journal of Aggression, Conflict and Peace Research* 3 (1): 12–24. https://doi.org/10.5042/jacpr.2011.0018.

Pyrooz, David C., Scott H. Decker, and Richard K. Moule Jr. 2015. "Criminal and Routine Activities in Online Settings: Gangs, Offenders, and the Internet." *Justice Quarterly* 32 (3): 471–499.

Pyrooz, David C., Scott H. Decker, and Emily Owens. 2020. "Do Prison Administrative and Survey Data Sources Tell the Same Story? A Multi-trait, Multi-method Examination with Application to Gangs." *Crime and Delinquency* 66 (5): 627–662.

Pyrooz, David C., Scott H. Decker, and Vincent J. Webb. 2014. "The Ties That Bind: Desistance from Gangs." *Crime and Delinquency* 60 (4): 491–516.

Pyrooz, David C., and James A. Densley. 2016. "Selection into Street Gangs: Signaling Theory, Gang Membership, and Criminal Offending." *Journal of Research in Crime and Delinquency* 53 (4): 447–481.

———. 2018. "On Public Protest, Violence, and Street Gangs." *Society* 55 (3): 229–236.

Pyrooz, David C., Andrew M. Fox, and Scott H. Decker. 2010. "Racial and Ethnic Heterogeneity, Economic Disadvantage, and Gangs: A Macro-level Study of Gang Membership in Urban America." *Justice Quarterly* 27 (6): 867–892.

Pyrooz, David C., Andrew M. Fox, Charles M. Katz, and Scott H. Decker. 2012. "Gang Organization, Offending, and Victimization: A Cross-National Analysis." In *Youth Gangs in International Perspective*, edited by Finn-Aage Esbensen and Cheryl L. Maxson, 85–105. New York: Springer.

Pyrooz, David C., Nancy Gartner, and Molly Smith. 2017. "Consequences of Incarceration for Gang Membership: A Longitudinal Study of Serious Offenders in Philadelphia and Phoenix." *Criminology* 55 (2): 273–306.

Pyrooz, David C., Gary LaFree, Scott H. Decker, and Patrick A. James. 2018. "Cut from the Same Cloth? A Comparative Study of Domestic Extremists and Gang Members in the United States." *Justice Quarterly* 35 (1): 1–32.

Pyrooz, David C., Ryan K. Masters, Jennifer J. Tostlebe, and Richard G. Rogers. 2020. "Exceptional Mortality Risk among Police-Identified Young Black Male Gang Members." *Preventive Medicine* 141 (December): 106269.

Pyrooz, David C., Jean M. McGloin, and Scott H. Decker. 2017. "Parenthood as a Turning Point in the Life Course for Male and Female Gang Members: A Study of within-Individual Changes in Gang Membership and Criminal Behavior." *Criminology* 55 (4): 869–899. https://doi.org/10.1111/1745-9125.12162.

Pyrooz, David C., Chris Melde, Donna Coffman, and Ryan Meldrum. 2021. Selection, Stability, and Spuriousness: Testing Gottfredson and Hirschi's Propositions to Reinterpret Street Gangs in Self-Control Perspective." *Criminology*. Published ahead of print, January 15, 2021. https://doi.org/10.1111/1745-9125.12268.

Pyrooz, David C., and Meghan M. Mitchell. 2015. "Little Gang Research, Big Gang Research." In *The Handbook of Gangs*, edited by Scott H. Decker and David C. Pyrooz, 28–58. Chichester, U.K.: Wiley-Blackwell.

———. 2019a. "The Hardest Time: Gang Members in Total Institutions." In *Handbook on the Consequences of Sentencing and Punishment Decisions*, edited by Beth M. Huebner and Natasha A. Frost, 3:361–378. ASC Division on Corrections and Sentences Handbook Series. New York: Routledge.

———. 2019b. "The Use of Restrictive Housing on Gang and Non-gang Affiliated Inmates in U.S. Prisons: Findings from a National Survey of Correctional Agencies." *Justice Quarterly* 37 (4): 590–615.

Pyrooz, David C., and Richard K. Moule Jr. 2019. "Gangs and Social Media." In *Oxford Research Encyclopedia of Criminology and Criminal Justice*. Article published April 26, 2019. https://doi.org/10.1093/acrefore/9780190264079.013.439.

Pyrooz, David C., Richard K. Moule Jr., and Scott H. Decker. 2014. "The Contribution of Gang Membership to the Victim–Offender Overlap." *Journal of Research in Crime and Delinquency* 51 (3): 315–348.

Pyrooz, David C., and Gary Sweeten. 2015. "Gang Membership between Ages 5 and 17 Years in the United States." *Journal of Adolescent Health* 56 (4): 414–419.

Pyrooz, David C., Gary Sweeten, and Alex R. Piquero. 2013. "Continuity and Change in Gang Membership and Gang Embeddedness." *Journal of Research in Crime and Delinquency* 50 (2): 239–271.

Pyrooz, David C., Jillian J. Turanovic, Scott H. Decker, and Jun Wu. 2016. "Taking Stock of the Relationship between Gang Membership and Offending: A Meta-analysis." *Criminal Justice and Behavior* 43 (3): 365–397.

Pyrooz, David C., Elizabeth Weltman, and Jose Sanchez. 2019. "Intervening in the Lives of Gang Members in Denver: A Pilot Evaluation of the Gang Reduction Initiative of Denver." *Justice Evaluation Journal* 2 (2): 139–163.

Pyrooz, David C., Scott E. Wolfe, and Cassia Spohn. 2011. "Gang-Related Homicide Charging Decisions: The Implementation of a Specialized Prosecution Unit in Los Angeles." *Criminal Justice Policy Review* 22 (1): 3–26.

Queally, James. 2018. "California Moving Away from Gang Injunctions amid Criticism, Falling Crime Rates." *Los Angeles Times*, July 8, 2018. https://www.latimes.com/local/lanow/la-me-gang-injunctions-california-20180708-story.html.

Quicker, John Charles. 1983. *Homegirls: Characterizing Chicana Gangs*. San Pedro: International Universities Press.

Quinn, James F. 2001. "Angels, Bandidos, Outlaws, and Pagans: The Evolution of Organized Crime among the Big Four 1% Motorcycle Clubs." *Deviant Behavior* 22 (4): 379–399.

Quinn, James, and D. Shane Koch. 2003. "The Nature of Criminality within One-Percent Motorcycle Clubs." *Deviant Behavior* 24 (3): 281–305.

Quinn, Katherine, Julia Dickson-Gomez, Michelle Broaddus, and Maria Pacella. 2019. "'Running Trains' and 'Sexing-In': The Functions of Sex within Adolescent Gangs." *Youth and Society* 51 (2): 151–169.

Raby, Carlotta, and Fergal Jones. 2016. "Identifying Risks for Male Street Gang Affiliation: A Systematic Review and Narrative Synthesis." *Journal of Forensic Psychiatry and Psychology* 27 (5): 601–644.

Rafter, Nicole, and Michelle Brown. 2011. *Criminology Goes to the Movies: Crime Theory and Popular Culture*. New York: New York University Press.

Ragan, Daniel T. 2020. "Similarity between Deviant Peers: Developmental Trends in Influence and Selection." *Criminology* 58 (2): 336–369. https://doi.org/10.1111/1745-9125.12 238.

Ralph, Laurence. 2014. *Renegade Dreams: Living through Injury in Gangland Chicago*. Chicago: University of Chicago Press.

Ralph, Paige H., Robert J. Hunter, James W. Marquart, Steven J. Cuvelier, and Dorothy Merianos. 1996. "Exploring the Differences between Gang and Non-gang Prisoners." In *Gangs in America*, edited by C. Ronald Huff, 2nd ed., 123–136. Thousand Oaks, CA: Sage.

Ralphs, Robert, Juanjo Medina, and Judith Aldridge. 2009. "Who Needs Enemies with Friends like These? The Importance of Place for Young People Living in Known Gang Areas." *Journal of Youth Studies* 12 (5): 483–500.

Ralphs, Robert, and Hannah Smithson. 2015. "European Responses to Gangs." In *The Handbook of Gangs*, edited by Scott H. Decker and David C. Pyrooz, 520–537. Hoboken, NJ: Wiley.

Ratcliffe, Jerry H., Amber Perenzin, and Evan T. Sorg. 2017. "Operation Thumbs Down: A Quasi-Experimental Evaluation of an FBI Gang Takedown in South Central Los Angeles." *Policing: An International Journal* 40 (2): 442–458.

Reckson, Batya, and Lily Becker. 2005. "Exploration of the Narrative Accounts of South African Teachers Working in a Gang-Violent Community in the Western Cape." *International Journal of Social Welfare* 14:107–115.

Reid, Shannon E., and Matthew Valasik. 2020. *Alt-Right Gangs: A Hazy Shade of White*. Oakland: University of California Press.

Reiss, Albert J., Jr. 1986. "Why Are Communities Important in Understanding Crime?" *Crime and Justice* 8:1–33.

Reiter, Keramet. 2016. *23/7: Pelican Bay Prison and the Rise of Long-Term Solitary Confinement*. New Haven, CT: Yale University Press.

Ridgeway, Greg, Jeffrey Grogger, Ruth A. Moyer, and John M. MacDonald. 2018. "Effect of Gang Injunctions on Crime: A Study of Los Angeles from 1988–2014." *Journal of Quantitative Criminology* 35:517–541. https://doi.org/10.1007/s10940-018-9396-7.

Riis, Jacob A. 1890. *How the Other Half Lives: Studies among the Tenements of New York*. New York: Penguin.

Rios, Victor. 2011a. *Punished: Policing the Lives of Black and Latino Boys*. New York: New York University Press.

———. 2011b. *Street Life: Poverty, Gangs, and a Ph.D.* California: Five Rivers.

———. 2017. *Human Targets: Schools, Police, and the Criminalization of Latino Youth*. Chicago: University of Chicago Press.

Rios, Victor M., Greg Prieto, and Jonathan M. Ibarra. 2020. "Mano Suave–Mano Dura: Legitimacy Policing and Latino Stop-and-Frisk." *American Sociological Review* 85 (January): 58–75.

Roberts, Albert R. 1998. *Juvenile Justice: Policies, Programs, and Services.* 2nd ed. Chicago: Nelson-Hall.

Robinson, Grace, Robert McLean, and James Densley. 2019. "Working County Lines: Child Criminal Exploitation and Illicit Drug Dealing in Glasgow and Merseyside." *International Journal of Offender Therapy and Comparative Criminology* 63 (5): 694–711.

Rodgers, Dennis. 2006. "Living in the Shadow of Death: Gangs, Violence and Social Order in Urban Nicaragua, 1996–2002." *Journal of Latin American Studies* 38:267–292.

———. 2015. "The Moral Economy of Murder: Violence, Death, and Social Order in Gangland Nicaragua." In *Violence at the Urban Margins,* edited by Javier Auyero, Philippe Bourgois, and Nancy Scheper-Hughes. New York: Oxford University Press.

———. 2017. "Of Pandillas, Pirucas, and Pablo Escobar in the Barrio." In *Politics and History of Violence and Crime in Central America,* edited by Sebastian Huhn and Hannes Warnecke-Berger, 65–84. New York: Palgrave Macmillan.

Rodgers, Dennis, and Adam Baird. 2015. "Understanding Gangs in Contemporary Latin America." In *The Handbook of Gangs,* edited by Scott H. Decker and David C. Pyrooz, 478–502. U.K.: John Wiley and Sons. https://doi.org/10.1002/9781118726822.ch26.

Rodríguez, Juan Antonio, Neelie Pérez Santiago, Christopher H. Birkbeck, Freddy Crespo, and Solbey Morillo. 2017. "Internationalizing the Study of Gang Membership: Validation Issues from Latin America." *British Journal of Criminology* 57 (5): 1165–1184.

Rogers, Kenneth H. 1946. *Street Gangs in Toronto: A Study of the Forgotten Boy.* Toronto: Ryerson.

Rojek, Jeff, Scott H. Decker, Geoffrey P. Alpert, and J. Andrew Hansen. 2013. "'Is the Quarterback a "Crip"?': The Presence of Gangs in Collegiate Athletics Programs." *Criminal Justice Review* 38 (4): 452–472.

Roks, Robby, Rutger Leukfeldt, and James Densley. 2020. "The Hybridization of Street Offending in the Netherlands." *British Journal of Criminology.* Published ahead of print, December 29, 2020. https://doi.org/10.1093/bjc/azaa091.

Roks, Robert A. 2018. "Crip or Die? Gang Disengagement in the Netherlands." *Journal of Contemporary Ethnography* 47 (5): 695–716.

Roks, Robert A., and James A. Densley. 2020. "From Breakers to Bikers: The Evolution of the Dutch Crips 'Gang.'" *Deviant Behavior* 41 (4): 525–542.

Roman, Caterina G., Scott H. Decker, and David C. Pyrooz. 2017. "Leveraging the Pushes and Pulls of Gang Disengagement to Improve Gang Intervention: Findings from Three Multi-site Studies and a Review of Relevant Gang Programs." *Journal of Crime and Justice* 40 (3): 316–336.

Rosen, Eva, and Sudhir Venkatesh. 2007. "Legal Innovation and the Control of Gang Behavior." *Annual Review of Law and Social Science* 3 (1): 255–270.

Rosen, Jonathan D., and José Miguel Cruz. 2018. "Overcoming Stigma and Discrimination: Challenges for Reinsertion of Gang Members in Developing Countries." *International Journal of Offender Therapy and Comparative Criminology* 62 (15): 4758–4775.

———. 2019. "Rethinking the Mechanisms of Gang Desistance in a Developing Country." *Deviant Behavior* 40 (12): 1493–1507.

Rosen, Jonathan D., and Roberto Zepeda. 2016. *Organized Crime, Drug Trafficking, and Violence in Mexico: The Transition from Felipe Calderón to Enrique Peña Nieto.* Lanham, MD: Lexington Books.

Rosenfeld, Richard, Timothy M. Bray, and Arlen Egley. 1999. "Facilitating Violence: A Comparison of Gang-Motivated, Gang-Affiliated, and Nongang Youth Homicides." *Journal of Quantitative Criminology* 15 (4): 495–516.

Rosenfeld, Richard, and Steven F. Messner. 2011. "The Intellectual Origins of Institutional-Anomie Theory." In *The Origins of American Criminology: Advances in Criminological Theory*, edited by Francis T. Cullen, Cheryl L. Jonson, Andrew J. Myer, and Freda Adler, vol. 16, 121–135. New Brunswick, NJ: Transaction.

Rostami, Amir, and Fredrik Leinfelt. 2012. "The Stockholm Gang Intervention and Prevention Project (SGIP): Introducing an Holistic Approach to Gang Enforcement." In *Youth Gangs in International Perspective: Results from the Eurogang Program of Research*, edited by Finn-Aage Esbensen and Cheryl Maxson, 251–270. New York: Springer.

Rostami, Amir, Fredrik Leinfelt, and Stefan Holgersson. 2012. "An Exploratory Analysis of Swedish Street Gangs: Applying the Maxson and Klein Typology to a Swedish Gang Dataset." *Journal of Contemporary Criminal Justice* 28 (4): 426–445.

Rostami, Amir, and Hernan Mondani. 2019. "Organizing on Two Wheels: Uncovering the Organizational Patterns of Hells Angels MC in Sweden." *Trends in Organized Crime* 22 (1): 34–50.

Roth, Mitchell. 2020. *Power on the Inside: A Global History of Prison Gangs.* London: Reaktion Books.

Rubenson, Miriam P., Katharine Galbraith, Olivia Shin, Christopher R. Beam, and Stanley J. Huey. 2020. "When Helping Hurts? Toward a Nuanced Interpretation of Adverse Effects in Gang-Focused Interventions." *Clinical Psychology: Science and Practice* 28 (1): 29–39. https://doi.org/10.1111/cpsp.12321.

Ryley, Sarah. 2019. "Most Shooters Go Free in Chicago's Most Violent Neighborhoods—While Police Make Non-stop Drug Arrests." *The Trace*, November 11, 2019. https://www.thetrace.org/2019/11/most-shooters-go-free-in-chicagos-most-violent-neighborhoods-while-police-make-non-stop-drug-arrests/.

Ryley, Sarah, Jeremy Singer-Vine, and Sean Campbell. 2019. "Shoot Someone in a Major US City, and Odds Are You'll Get Away with It." *BuzzFeed*, January 24, 2019. https://www.buzzfeednews.com/article/sarahryley/police-unsolved-shootings.

Sageman, Marc. 2008. *Leaderless Jihad: Terror Networks in the Twenty-First Century.* Philadelphia: University of Pennsylvania Press.

Salaam, Abeeb O. 2011a. "Motivations for Gang Membership in Lagos, Nigeria." *Journal of Adolescent Research* 26:701–726.

———. 2011b. "Street Life Involvement and Substance Use among 'Yandaba' in Kano, Nigeria." *African Journal of Drug and Alcohol Studies* 10 (2): 119–129.

Salagaev, Alexander. 2001. "Podrostkovo-Molodejnoe Territorialnoe Soobshchestvo Delinkventnoy Napravlennosti Kak Ob'ekt Teoreticheskogo Issledovaniya." Doctor of sociology diss., Saint-Petersburg State University.

Salagaev, Alexander, Alexander Shashkin, Irina Sherbakova, and Elias Touriyanskiy. 2005. "Contemporary Russian Gangs: History, Membership and Crime Involvement." In *European Street Gangs and Troublesome Youth Groups*, edited by Scott Decker and Frank Weerman, 169–192. Lanham, MD: AltaMira.

Salas-Wright, Christopher P., René Olate, and Michael G. Vaughn. 2013. "The Protective Effects of Religious Coping and Spirituality on Delinquency: Results among High-Risk and Gang-Involved Salvadoran Youth." *Criminal Justice and Behavior* 40 (9): 988–1008.

Sampson, Robert J. 2002. "Organized for What? Recasting Theories of Social (Dis) Organization." In *Crime and Social Organization*, edited by Elin J. Waring and David Weisburd, 10:95–110. Advances in Criminological Theory. New Brunswick: Transaction Publishers.

Sampson, Robert J. 2019. "Neighbourhood Effects and Beyond: Explaining The Paradoxes of Inequality In The Changing American Metropolis." *Urban Studies* 56 (1): 3–32.

Sampson, Robert J., and Lydia Bean. 2006. "Cultural Mechanisms and Killing Fields: A Revised Theory of Community-Level Racial Inequality." In *The Many Colors of Crime: Inequalities of Race, Ethnicity and Crime in America*, edited by Ruth Peterson, Lauren Krivo, and John Hagan, 8–36. New York: New York University Press.

Sampson, Robert J., and W. Byron Groves. 1989. "Community Structure and Crime: Testing Social-Disorganization Theory." *American Journal of Sociology* 94 (4): 774–802.

Sampson, Robert J., and John H. Laub. 1993. *Crime in the Making: Pathways and Turning Points through Life*. Cambridge, MA: Harvard University Press.

———. 2016. "Turning Points and the Future of Life-Course Criminology: Reflections on the 1986 Criminal Careers Report." *Journal of Research in Crime and Delinquency* 53, (3): 321–335. https://doi.org/10.1177/0022427815616992.

Sampson, Robert J., Stephen W. Raudenbush, and Felton Earls. 1997. "Neighborhoods and Violent Crime: A Multilevel Study of Collective Efficacy." *Science* 277 (5328): 918–924.

Sampson, Robert J., and William Julius Wilson. 1995. "Toward a Theory of Race, Crime, and Urban Inequality." In *Crime and Inequality*, edited by John Hagan and Ruth Peterson, 37–56. Stanford, CA: Stanford University Press.

Sampson, Robert J., William Julius Wilson, and Hanna Katz. 2018. "Reassessing 'Toward a Theory of Race, Crime, and Urban Inequality': Enduring and New Challenges in 21st Century America." *Du Bois Review: Social Science Research on Race* 15 (1): 13–34.

Sánchez-Jankowski, Martin. 1991. *Islands in the Street: Gangs and American Urban Society*. Berkeley: University of California Press.

———. 2003. "Gangs and Social Change." *Theoretical Criminology* 7 (2): 191–216.

Sandberg, Sveinung, and Willy Pedersen. 2011. *Street Capital: Black Cannabis Dealers in a White Welfare State*. Bristol, U.K.: Policy Press. http://books.google.com/books?hl=en&lr=&id=vZerfm0B0bAC&oi=fnd&pg=PR3&dq=Street+capital:+Black+cannabis+dealers+in+a+white+welfare+state.&ots=NajnkHb9eF&sig=8fslZ3BlJLplNa_49BQT8vPwxGM.

Sarnecki, Jerzy. 2001. *Delinquent Networks: Youth Co-offending in Stockholm*. Cambridge: Cambridge University Press.

Saunders, Jessica, Gary Sweeten, and Charles M. Katz. 2009. *Post-release Recidivism among Gang and Non-gang Prisoners in Arizona from 1985 through 2004*. Phoenix: Center for Violence Prevention and Community Service, Arizona State University. https://cvpcs.asu.edu/projects/examination-recidivism-rates-among-arizona-gang-members-and-drug-offenders.

Schelling, Thomas C. 1967. "Economics and Criminal Enterprise." *Public Interest* 7:61.

———. 1985. *Choice and Consequence*. Cambridge, MA: Harvard University Press.

Scherer, Jennifer, Dana Thompson Dorsey, and Daniel Catzva. 2009. "Lessons Learned from the National Evaluation of the Gang-Free Schools and Community Program." *Journal of Gang Research* 17 (1): 29–44.

Schlossman, Steven, and Michael Sedlak. 1983. "The Chicago Area Project Revisited." *Crime and Delinquency* 29 (3): 398–462.

Scott, Daniel. 2020. "Regional Differences in Gang Member Identification Methods among Law Enforcement Jurisdictions in the United States." *Policing: An International Journal* 43 (5): 723–740.

Scott, Daniel, and Cheryl Maxson. 2016. "Gang Organization and Violence in Youth Correctional Facilities." *Journal of Criminological Research, Policy and Practice* 2 (2): 81–94. https://doi.org/10.1108/JCRPP-03-2015-0004.

Scott, Greg. 2004. "'It's a Sucker's Outfit': How Urban Gangs Enable and Impede the Reintegration of Ex-Convicts." *Ethnography* 5 (1): 107–140.

Seelke, Clare R. 2016. *Gangs in Central America*. Washington, DC: Congressional Research Service.

Sela-Shayovitz, Revital. 2012. "Gangs and the Web: Gang Members' Online Behavior." *Journal of Contemporary Criminal Justice* 28 (4): 389–405.

Sellin, Thorsten. 1938. *Culture, Conflict and Crime*. 1st U.S. ed. 1st printing. New York: Social Science Research Council.

Sernoffsky, Evan. 2019. "SF DA-Elect Chesa Boudin Sets New Course in Gang Cases, Citing Charges 'Infused with Racism.'" *San Francisco Chronicle*, December 15, 2019. https://www.sfchronicle.com/crime/article/SF-DA-elect-Chesa-Boudin-sets-new-course-in-gang-14906018.php.

Shabazz, Rashad. 2015. *Spatializing Blackness*. Champaign: University of Illinois Press.

Shaffer, Catherine S. 2014. *Risk and Protective Factors for Youth Gang Involvement in Canada: An Ecological Systems Analysis*. Burnaby, BC: Simon Fraser University.

Sharkey, Jill D., Skye W. F. Stifel, and Ashley Mayworm. 2015. "How to Help Me Get Out of a Gang: Youth Recommendations to Family, School, Community, and Law Enforcement Systems." *Journal of Juvenile Justice* 4 (1): 64–83.

Sharkey, Patrick. 2018. *Uneasy Peace: The Great Crime Decline, the Renewal of City Life, and the Next War on Violence*. New York: W. W. Norton.

Sharp, Clare, Judith Aldridge, and Juanjo Medina. 2006. *Delinquent Youth Groups and Offending Behaviour: Findings from the 2004 Offending, Crime and Justice Survey*. London: Home Office.

Shaw, Clifford R. 1930. *The Jack-Roller*. Chicago: University of Chicago Press.

Shaw, Clifford R., and Henry D. McKay. 1942. *Juvenile Delinquency and Urban Areas*. Chicago: University of Chicago Press.

Sheldon, Henry D. 1898. "The Institutional Activities of American Children." *American Journal of Psychology* 9 (4): 425–448.

Shelden, Randall G. 1991. "A Comparison of Gang Members and Non-gang Members in a Prison Setting." *Prison Journal* 71 (2): 50–60.

Sheley, Joseph F., Joshua Zhang, Charles J. Brody, and James D. Wright. 1995. "Gang Organization, Gang Criminal Activity, and Individual Gang Members' Criminal Behavior." *Social Science Quarterly* 76 (1): 53–68.

Sherif, Muzafer. 1966. *In Common Predicament: Social Psychology of Intergroup Conflict and Cooperation*. Boston: Houghton Mifflin.

Sherman, Lawrence W., Denise C. Gottfredson, Doris Layton MacKenzie, John E. Eck, Peter Reuter, and Shawn D. Bushway. 1998. *Preventing Crime: What Works, What Doesn't, What's Promising*. Research in Brief. Washington, DC: U.S. Department of Justice, National Institute of Justice.

Short, James F., Jr. 1974. "Youth, Gangs, and Society: Micro- and Macro-sociological Processes." *Sociological Quarterly* 15:3–19.

———. 1985. "The Level of Explanation Problem in Criminology." In *Theoretical Methods in Criminology*, edited by Robert F. Meier, 51–72. Beverly Hills, CA: Sage.

———. 1996. *Gangs and Adolescent Violence*. Boulder, CO: Center for the Study and Prevention of Violence. https://citeseerx.ist.psu.edu/viewdoc/download?doi=10.1.1.183.245&rep=rep1&type=pdf.

———. 1998. "The Level of Explanation Problem Revisited—the American Society of Criminology 1997 Presidential Address." *Criminology* 36 (1): 3–36.

Short, James F., Jr., and Lorine A. Hughes. 2006. "Moving Gang Research Forward." In *Studying Youth Gangs*, edited by James F. Short Jr. and Lorine A. Hughes, 225–238. Lanham, MD: Rowman AltaMira.

———. 2015. "Bringing the Study of Street Gangs Back into the Mainstream." In *Emerging Trends in the Social and Behavioral Sciences*, edited by Robert A. Scott and Marlis C. Buchmann. New York: Wiley. http://onlinelibrary.wiley.com/doi/10.1002/9781118900772.etrds0028/abstract.

Short, James F., Jr., and F. Ivan Nye. 1957. "Reported Behavior as a Criterion of Deviant Behavior." *Social Problems* 5 (3): 207–213.

Short, James F., Jr., and Fred L. Strodtbeck. 1963. "The Response of Gang Leaders to Status Threats: An Observation on Group Process and Delinquent Behavior." *American Journal of Sociology* 68 (5): 571–579.

———. 1965. *Group Process and Gang Delinquency*. Chicago: University of Chicago Press.

Shute, Jon, and Juanjo Medina. 2014. "Hunting Gruffalo: 'Gangs', Unreason and the Big Bad Coalition." *Criminal Justice Matters* 96 (1): 26–27.

Sierra-Arévalo, Michael, and Andrew Papachristos. 2015a. "Applying Group Audits to Problem-Oriented Policing." In *Disrupting Criminal Networks: Network Analysis in Crime Prevention*, edited by Gisela Giselle Bichler and Ali Malm, 27–46. Boulder, CO: Lynne Rienner.

———. 2015b. "Social Network Analysis and Gangs." In *The Handbook of Gangs*, edited by Scott H. Decker and David C. Pyrooz, 157–177. Chichester, U.K.: Wiley-Blackwell.

———. 2017. "Social Networks and Gang Violence Reduction." *Annual Review of Law and Social Science* 13 (1): 373–393.

Sinclair, Raven, and Jana Grekul. 2012. "Aboriginal Youth Gangs in Canada: (De)Constructing an Epidemic." *First Peoples Child and Family Review* 7 (1): 2–28.

Sivilli, June, Robert Yin, and M. Elaine Nugent. 1996. *Evaluation of Gang Interventions: Final Report*. Washington, DC: U.S. Department of Justice. https://www.ncjrs.gov/App/abstractdb/AbstractDBDetails.aspx?id=172244.

Skarbek, David. 2011. "Governance and Prison Gangs." *American Political Science Review* 105 (4): 702–716.

———. 2014. *The Social Order of the Underworld: How Prison Gangs Govern the American Penal System*. New York: Oxford University Press.

———. 2020. *The Puzzle of Prison Order: Why Life behind Bars Varies around the World*. New York: Oxford University Press.

Skogan, Wesley G., Susan M. Hartnett, Natalie Bump, and Jill Dubois. 2008. *Evaluation of CeaseFire-Chicago*. Washington, DC: U.S. Department of Justice, National Institute of Justice.

Skolnick, Jerome. 1990. "Gang Organization and Migration / Drugs, Gangs, and Law Enforcement." *California Agencies*, no. 501. https://digitalcommons.law.ggu.edu/caldocs_agencies/501.

Skott, Sarah, and Susan McVie. 2019. "Reduction in Homicide and Violence in Scotland Is Largely Explained by Fewer Gangs and Less Knife Crime." *Applied Quantitative Methods Network Research Briefing* 13:1–5.

Smith, Anthony D. 1991. *The Ethnic Origins of Nations*. Reprint ed. Malden, MA: Wiley-Blackwell.

Smith, Carter F. 2016. "When Is a Prison Gang Not a Prison Gang: A Focused Review of Prison Gang Literature." *Journal of Gang Research* 23 (2): 41–52.

Smith, Chris M. 2014. "The Influence of Gentrification on Gang Homicides in Chicago Neighborhoods, 1994 to 2005." *Crime and Delinquency* 60 (4): 569–591.

Smith, Dwight C. 1975. *The Mafia Mystique*. New York: Basic Books.

———. 1980. "Paragons, Pariahs, and Pirates: A Spectrum-Based Theory of Enterprise." *Crime and Delinquency* 26 (3): 358–386.

Smith, Thomas Bryan. 2020. "Gang Crackdowns and Offender Centrality in a Countywide Co-offending Network: A Networked Evaluation of Operation Triple Beam." *Journal of Criminal Justice* 73: 101755. https://doi.org/10.1016/j.jcrimjus.2020.101755.

Smithson, Hannah, Leanne Monchuk, and Rachel Armitage. 2012. "Gang Member: Who Says? Definitional and Structural Issues." In *Youth Gangs in International Perspective: Results from the Eurogang Program of Research*, edited by Finn-Aage Esbensen and Cheryl L. Maxson, 53–68. New York: Springer.

Smithson, Hannah, and Rob Ralphs. 2016. "Youth in the UK: 99 Problems but the Gang Ain't One?" *Safer Communities* 15 (1): 11–23.

Smithson, Hannah, Rob Ralphs, and Patrick Williams. 2013. "Used and Abused the Problematic: Usage of Gang Terminology in the United Kingdom and Its Implications for Ethnic Minority Youth." *British Journal of Criminology* 53 (1): 113–128.

Sobel, Russell S., and Brian J. Osoba. 2009. "Youth Gangs as Pseudo-governments: Implications for Violent Crime." *Southern Economic Journal* 75 (4): 996–1018.

Spano, Richard, and John Bolland. 2013. "Disentangling the Effects of Violent Victimization, Violent Behavior, and Gun Carrying for Minority Inner-City Youth Living in Extreme Poverty." *Crime and Delinquency* 59 (2): 191–213.

Spence, A. Michael. 1974. *Market Signaling: Informational Transfer in Hiring and Related Screening Processes*. Cambridge, MA: Harvard University Press.

Spergel, Irving A. 1964. *Racketville, Slumtown, Haulburg*. Chicago: University of Chicago Press.

———. 1966. *Street Gang Work: Theory and Practice*. Reading, MA: Addison-Wesley.

———. 1984. "Violent Gangs in Chicago: In Search of Social Policy." *Social Service Review* 58 (2): 199–226.

———. 1985. *Youth Gang Activity and the Chicago Public Schools*. Chicago: University of Chicago, School of Social Service Administration.

———. 1990. "Youth Gangs: Continuity and Change." *Crime and Justice* 12:171–275.

———. 1995. *The Youth Gang Problem: A Community Approach*. New York: Oxford University Press.

———. 2007. *Reducing Youth Gang Violence: The Little Village Project in Chicago*. Lanham, MD: AltaMira.

Spergel, Irving A., and G. David Curry. 1990. "Strategies and Perceived Agency Effectiveness in Dealing with the Youth Gang Problem." In *Gangs in America*, edited by C. Ronald Huff, 288–309. Newbury Park, CA: Sage.

———. 1993. "The National Youth Gang Survey: A Research and Development Process." In *The Gang Intervention Handbook*, edited by Arnold P. Goldstein and C. Ronald Huff, 359–400. Champaign, IL: Research Press.

Spergel, Irving A., and Susan F. Grossman. 1997. "The Little Village Project: A Community Approach to the Gang Problem." *Social Work* 42 (5): 456–470.

Spergel, Irving A., Kwai Ming Wa, S. Choi, S. F. Grossman, Ayad Jacob, Annot Spergel, and Elisa M. Barrios. 2002. *Evaluation of the Gang Violence Reduction Project in Little Village: Final Report Summary*. Chicago: University of Chicago, School of Social Service Administration.

Stack, Carol B. 1975. *All Our Kin: Strategies for Survival in a Black Community*. New York: Basic Books.

Starbuck, David, James C. Howell, and Donna Lindquist. 2001. *Hybrid and Other Modern Gangs*. OJJDP Juvenile Justice Bulletin. Washington, DC: Office of Juvenile Justice and Delinquency Prevention.

Stastny, Charles, and Gabrielle Tyrnauer. 1982. *Who Rules the Joint? The Changing Political Culture of Maximum-Security Prisons in America*. Lexington, MA: Lexington Books.

St. Cyr, Jenna L., and Scott H. Decker. 2003. "Girls, Guys, and Gangs: Convergence or Divergence in the Gendered Construction of Gangs and Groups." *Journal of Criminal Justice* 31 (5): 423–433.

Steinberg, Laurence, and Kathryn C. Monahan. 2007. "Age Differences in Resistance to Peer Influence." *Developmental Psychology* 43 (6): 1531–1543.

Stellfox, Peter. 1998. *Gang Violence: Strategic and Tactical Options*. London: Home Office Research Group.

Stolberg, Sheryl. 1992. "150,000 Are in Gangs, Report by D.A. Claims: Crime: Reiner's Study Says Half of Young Blacks Are Members. But Even Gates Says Numbers May Be Too High." *Los Angeles Times*, May 22, 1992. https://www.latimes.com/archives/la-xpm-1992-05-22-mn-282-story.html.

Storrod, Michelle L., and James A. Densley. 2017. "'Going Viral' and 'Going Country': The Expressive and Instrumental Activities of Street Gangs on Social Media." *Journal of Youth Studies* 20 (6): 677–696.

Stouffer, Samuel A. 1949. "An Analysis of Conflicting Social Norms." *American Sociological Review* 14 (6): 707–717.

Strodtbeck, Fred L., and James F. Short. 1964. "Aleatory Risks versus Short-Run Hedonism in Explanation of Gang Action." *Social Problems* 12 (2): 127–140.

Stuart, Forrest. 2020a. *Ballad of the Bullet: Gangs, Drill Music, and the Power of Online Infamy*. Princeton, NJ: Princeton University Press.

———. 2020b. "Code of the Tweet: Urban Gang Violence in the Social Media Age." *Social Problems* 67:191–207.

Sturup, Joakim, Manne Gerell, and Amir Rostami. 2020. "Explosive Violence: A Near-Repeat Study of Hand Grenade Detonations and Shootings in Urban Sweden." *European Journal of Criminology* 17 (5): 661–677.

Sullivan, Mercer L. 1989. *"Getting Paid": Youth Crime and Work in the Inner City*. New York: Cornell University Press.

Sutherland, Edwin H. 1947. *Principles of Criminology*. 4th ed. Philadelphia: J. B. Lippincott.

Suttles, Gerald D. 1968. *The Social Order of the Slum: Ethnicity and Territory in the Inner City*. Chicago: University of Chicago Press.

———. 1972. *The Social Construction of Communities*. Chicago: University of Chicago Press.

Sutton, Tara E. 2017. "The Lives of Female Gang Members: A Review of the Literature." *Aggression and Violent Behavior* 37:142–152.

Sweeten, Gary, David C. Pyrooz, and Alex R. Piquero. 2013. "Disengaging from Gangs and Desistance from Crime." *Justice Quarterly* 30 (3): 469–500.

Swidler, Ann. 1986. "Culture in Action: Symbols and Strategies." *American Sociological Review* 51 (2): 273–286.

Sykes, Gresham M. 1958. *The Society of Captives*. Princeton, NJ: Princeton University Press.

Sykes, Gresham M., and Sheldon L. Messinger. 1960. "The Inmate Social System." In *Theoretical Studies in Social Organization of the Prison*, edited by Richard A. Cloward, Donald R. Cressey, George H. Grosser, Richard McCleery, Lloyd E. Ohlin, and Gresham M. Sykes, 5–19. New York: Social Science Research Council.

Tajfel, Henri, and John C. Turner. 2004. *The Social Identity Theory of Intergroup Behavior*. Political Psychology: Key Readings. New York: Psychology Press.

Tapia, Mike. 2011a. "Gang Membership and Race as Risk Factors for Juvenile Arrest." *Journal of Research in Crime and Delinquency* 48 (3): 364–395.

———. 2011b. "U.S. Juvenile Arrests: Gang Membership, Social Class, and Labeling Effects." *Youth and Society* 43 (4): 1407–1432. https://doi.org/10.1177/0044118X10386083.

———. 2019. *Gangs of the El Paso-Juárez Borderland: A History*. Albuquerque: University of New Mexico Press.

Taxman, Faye S. 2017. "Are You Asking Me to Change My Friends?" *Criminology and Public Policy* 16 (3): 775–782. https://doi.org/10.1111/1745-9133.12328.

Taylor, Carl S. 1993. *Girls, Gangs, Women and Drugs*. East Lansing: Michigan State University Press.

Taylor, Terrance J., Adrienne Freng, Finn-Aage Esbensen, and Dana Peterson. 2008. "Youth Gang Membership and Serious Violent Victimization: The Importance of Lifestyles and Routine Activities." *Journal of Interpersonal Violence* 23 (10): 1441–1464. https://doi.org/10.1177/0886260508314306.

Taylor, Terrance J., Dana Peterson, Finn-Aage Esbensen, and Adrienne Freng. 2007. "Gang Membership as a Risk Factor for Adolescent Violent Victimization." *Journal of Research in Crime and Delinquency* 44 (4): 351–380.

Ter Haar, Barend. 1998. *The Ritual and Mythology of the Chinese Triads: Creating an Identity*. Leiden: Brill.

Texas Department of Criminal Justice. 2007. *Security Threat Groups "on the Inside."* August 2007. http://www.tdcj.state.tx.us/documents/cid/CID_STGMO_FAQ.pdf.

Thompson, Hunter S. 1996. *Hell's Angels: A Strange and Terrible Saga*. New York: Ballantine Books.

Thornberry, Terence P. 1987. "Toward an Interactional Theory of Delinquency." *Criminology* 25 (4): 863–892.

Thornberry, Terence P., Brook Kearley, Denise C. Gottfredson, Molly P. Slothower, Deanna N. Devlin, and Jamie J. Fader. 2018. "Reducing Crime among Youth at Risk for Gang Involvement." *Criminology and Public Policy* 17 (4): 953–989.

Thornberry, Terence P., and Marvin D. Krohn. 2000. "The Self-Report Method for Measuring Delinquency and Crime." *Criminal Justice* 4 (1): 33–83.

Thornberry, Terence P., Marvin D. Krohn, Alan J. Lizotte, and Deborah Chard-Wierschem. 1993. "The Role of Juvenile Gangs in Facilitating Delinquent Behavior." *Journal of Research in Crime and Delinquency* 30 (1): 55–87.

Thornberry, Terence P., Marvin D. Krohn, Alan J. Lizotte, Carolyn A. Smith, and Kimberly Tobin. 2003. *Gangs and Delinquency in Developmental Perspective*. New York: Cambridge University Press.

Thrasher, Frederic M. 1927. *The Gang: A Study of 1,313 Gangs in Chicago*. Chicago: University of Chicago Press.

———. 1933. "Juvenile Delinquency and Crime Prevention." *Journal of Educational Sociology* 6 (8): 500–509.

Tillyer, Marie Skubak, Robin S. Engel, and Brian Lovins. 2012. "Beyond Boston: Applying Theory to Understand and Address Sustainability Issues in Focused Deterrence Initiatives for Violence Reduction." *Crime and Delinquency* 58 (6): 973–997.

Tita, George E., Jacqueline Cohen, and John Engberg. 2005. "An Ecological Study of the Location of Gang 'Set Space.'" *Social Problems* 52 (2): 272–299.

Tita, George E., and Steven M. Radil. 2011. "Spatializing the Social Networks of Gangs to Explore Patterns of Violence." *Journal of Quantitative Criminology* 27 (4): 521–545.

Tita, George, K. Jack Riley, and Peter Greenwood. 2003. "From Boston to Boyle Heights: The Process and Prospects of a 'Pulling Levers' Strategy in a Los Angeles Barrio." In *Policing Gangs and Youth Violence*, edited by Scott H. Decker, 102–130. Belmont, CA: Wadsworth.

Toch, Hans. 2007. "Sequestering Gang Members, Burning Witches, and Subverting Due Process." *Criminal Justice and Behavior* 34:274–288.

Tonks, Sarah, and Zoe Stephenson. 2019. "Disengagement from Street Gangs: A Systematic Review of the Literature." *Psychiatry, Psychology and Law* 26 (1): 21–49.

Toobin, Jeffrey. 1994. "Capone's Revenge." *New Yorker*, May 23, 1994, 46–59.

Tostlebe, Jennifer J., David C. Pyrooz, Richard G. Rogers, and Ryan K. Masters. 2020. "The National Death Index as a Source of Homicide Data: A Methodological Exposition of Promises and Pitfalls for Criminologists." *Homicide Studies* 25 (1): 5–36. https://doi .org/10.1177/1088767920924450.

Travis, Jeremy, and Christy Visher. 2005. *Prisoner Reentry and Crime in America*. New York: Cambridge University Press.

Tromanhauser, Edward F., Tom Corcoran, and Allen Lollino. 1981. *The Chicago Safe School Study*. Chicago: City of Chicago, Chicago Board of Education.

Trujillo, Josmar, and Alex S. Vitale. 2019. *Gang Takedowns in the De Blasio Era: The Dangers of "Precision Policing."* New York City Gang Policing Report. New York. https:// static1.squarespace.com/static/5de981188ae1bf14a94410f5/t/5df14904887d561d6 cc9455e/1576093963895/2019+New+York+City+Gang+Policing+Report+-+FINAL%29 .pdf.

Trulson, Chad R., James W. Marquart, and Soraya K. Kawucha. 2006. "Gang Suppression and Institutional Control." *Corrections Today* 68 (May): 26–31.

Truman, David R. 1995. "The Jets and Sharks Are Dead: State Statutory Responses to Criminal Street Gangs." *Washington University Law Quarterly* 73:55.

Tsunokai, Glenn T., and Augustine J. Kposowa. 2002. "Asian Gangs in the United States: The Current State of the Research Literature." *Crime, Law and Social Change* 37 (1): 37–50.

Ttofi, Maria M., David P. Farrington, and Friedrich Lösel. 2012. "School Bullying as a Predictor of Violence Later in Life: A Systematic Review and Meta-analysis of Prospective Longitudinal Studies." *Aggression and Violent Behavior* 17 (5): 405–418.

Turanovic, Jillian J., and Travis C. Pratt. 2014. "'Can't Stop, Won't Stop': Self-Control, Risky Lifestyles, and Repeat Victimization." *Journal of Quantitative Criminology* 30 (1): 29–56.

———. 2019. *Thinking about Victimization: Context and Consequences*. London: Routledge.

Turner, Jackie, and Liz Kelly. 2009. "Trade Secrets: Intersections between Diasporas and Crime Groups in the Constitution of the Human Trafficking Chain." *British Journal of Criminology* 49 (2): 184–201. https://doi.org/10.1093/bjc/azn079.

Tuttle, William M. 1996. *Race Riot: Chicago in the Red Summer of 1919*. Urbana: University of Illinois Press.

Tyler, Tom R. 2006. *Why People Obey the Law*. Princeton, NJ: Princeton University Press.

Uggen, Christopher, and Irving Piliavin. 1998. "Asymmetrical Causation and Criminal Desistance." *Journal of Criminal Law and Criminology* 88 (4): 1399–1422.

United States Department of Justice Civil Rights Division and United States Attorney's Office Northern District of Illinois. 2017. *Investigation of the Chicago Police Depart-*

ment. Washington, DC: U.S. Department of Justice. https://www.justice.gov/opa/file /925846/download.

Urbanik, Marta-Marika. 2018. "Drawing Boundaries or Drawing Weapons? Neighborhood Master Status as Suppressor of Gang Violence." *Qualitative Sociology* 41 (4): 497–519.

Urbanik, Marta-Marika, and Kevin D. Haggerty. 2018. "'#It's Dangerous': The Online World of Drug Dealers, Rappers and the Street Code." *British Journal of Criminology* 58 (6): 1343–1360.

Urbanik, Marta-Marika, Robby Roks, Michelle Lyttle Storrod, and James Densley. 2020. "Ethical and Methodological Issues in Gang Ethnography in the Digital Age: Lessons from Four Studies in an Emerging Field." In *Gangs in the Era of Internet and Social Media*, edited by Chris Melde and Frank Weerman, 21–41. Cham, Switzerland: Springer.

Urbanik, Marta-Marika, and Robert A. Roks. 2020. "GangstaLife: Fusing Urban Ethnography with Netnography in Gang Studies." *Qualitative Sociology* 43 (2): 213–233.

———. 2021. "Making Sense of Murder: The Reality versus the Realness of Gang Homicides in Two Contexts." *Social Science* 10 (1): 17.

Urbanik, Marta-Marika, Sara K. Thompson, and Sandra M. Bucerius. 2017. "'Before There Was Danger but There Was Rules. And Safety in Those Rules': Effects of Neighbourhood Redevelopment on Criminal Structures." *British Journal of Criminology* 57 (2): 422–440.

Useem, Bert, and Michael D. Reisig. 1999. "Collective Action in Prisons: Protests, Disturbances, and Riots." *Criminology* 37 (4): 735–760.

Valasik, Matthew. 2014. *Saving the World, One Neighborhood at a Time: The Role of Civil Gang Injunctions at Influencing Gang Behavior.* Irvine: University of California, Irvine.

———. 2018. "Gang Violence Predictability: Using Risk Terrain Modeling to Study Gang Homicides and Gang Assaults in East Los Angeles." *Journal of Criminal Justice* 58 (September): 10–21. https://doi.org/10.1016/j.jcrimjus.2018.06.001.

Valasik, Matthew, Michael S. Barton, Shannon E. Reid, and George E. Tita. 2017. "Barriocide: Investigating the Temporal and Spatial Influence of Neighborhood Structural Characteristics on Gang and Non-gang Homicides in East Los Angeles." *Homicide Studies* 21 (4): 287–311. https://doi.org/10.1177/1088767917726807.

Valasik, Matthew, and Shannon E. Reid. 2019. "The Schrödinger's Cat of Gang Groups: Can Street Gangs Inform Our Comprehension of Skinheads and Alt-Right Groups?" *Deviant Behavior* 40 (10): 1245–1259.

———. 2021. "East Side Story: Disaggregating Gang Homicides in East Los Angeles." *Social Sciences* 10 (2): 48.

Valasik, Matthew, Shannon E. Reid, and Matthew D. Phillips. 2016. "CRASH and Burn: Abatement of a Specialised Gang Unit." Edited by Jane L. Wood. *Journal of Criminological Research, Policy and Practice* 2 (2): 95–106.

Valdez, Avelardo. 2007. *Mexican American Girls and Gang Violence: Beyond Risk.* New York: Palgrave Macmillan. https://doi.org/10.1057/9780230601833.

Valdez, Avelardo, and Stephen J. Sifaneck. 2004. "'Getting High and Getting By': Dimensions of Drug Selling Behaviors among American Mexican Gang Members in South Texas." *Journal of Research in Crime and Delinquency* 41 (1): 82–105.

Van Gemert, Frank. 2001. "Crips in Orange: Gangs and Groups in the Netherlands." In *The Eurogang Paradox: Street Gangs and Youth Groups in the U.S. and Europe*, edited by Malcolm W. Klein, Hans-Jürgen Kerner, Cheryl L. Maxson, and Elmar G. M. Weitekamp, 145–152. Dordrecht: Springer Netherlands.

———. 2012. "Five Decades of Defining Gangs in the Netherlands: The Eurogang Paradox in Practice." In *Youth Gangs in International Perspective: Results from the Eurogang*

Program of Research, edited by Finn-Aage Esbensen and Cheryl L. Maxson, 69–83. New York: Springer.

Van Gemert, Frank, Dana Peterson, and Inger-Lise Lien. 2008. *Street Gangs, Migration and Ethnicity*. Devon, U.K.: Willian.

Van Gemert, Frank, Robby Roks, and Marijke Drogt. 2016. "Dutch Crips Run Dry in Liquid Society." In *Gang Transitions and Transformations in an International Context*, edited by Cheryl Maxson and Finn-Aage Esbensen, 157–172. Cham, Switzerland: Springer.

Van Gemert, Frank, and Frank Weerman. 2013. "Youth Groups and Street Gangs in the Netherlands." In *EU Street Violence: Youth Groups and Violence in Public Spaces*, edited by European Forum for Urban Security. Paris: European Forum for Urban Security. https://research.vu.nl/en/publications/youth-groups-and-street-gangs-in-the-netherlands.

Van Hellemont, Elke. 2012. "Gangland Online: Performing the Real Imaginary World of Gangstas and Ghettos in Brussels." *European Journal of Crime, Criminal Law and Criminal Justice* 20:165–180.

Van Hellemont, Elke, and James A. Densley. 2019. "Gang Glocalization: How the Global Mediascape Creates and Shapes Local Gang Realities." *Crime, Media, Culture* 15 (1): 169–189.

———. 2021. "If Crime is Not the Problem, Crime Fighting is no Solution: Policing Gang Violence in the Age of Abolition". *Journal of Aggression, Conflict and Peace Research* 13 (2–3): 136–147.

Varano, Sean, and Russell Wolff. 2012. "Street Outreach as an Intervention Modality for At-Risk and Gang-Involved Youth." In *Looking beyond Suppression: Community Strategies to Reduce Gang Violence*, edited by Erika Gebo and Brenda J. Bond, 83–104. Lanham, MD: Lexington Books.

Varese, Federico. 2001. *The Russian Mafia: Private Protection in a New Market Economy*. Oxford: Oxford University Press.

———, ed. 2010. *Organized Crime*. London: Routledge.

———. 2011. *Mafias on the Move: How Organized Crime Conquers New Territories*. Princeton, NJ: Princeton University Press.

———. 2018. *Mafia Life: Love, Death, and Money at the Heart of Organized Crime*. New York: Oxford University Press.

Vargas, Robert. 2014. "Criminal Group Embeddedness and the Adverse Effects of Arresting a Gang's Leader: A Comparative Case Study." *Criminology* 52 (2): 143–168.

Varriale, Jennifer A. 2008. "Female Gang Members and Desistance: Pregnancy as a Possible Exit Strategy." *Journal of Gang Research* 15 (4): 35–64.

Vazsonyi, Alexander T., Jakub Mikuška, and Erin L. Kelley. 2017. "It's Time: A Meta-analysis on the Self-Control-Deviance Link." *Journal of Criminal Justice* 48:48–63.

Venkatesh, Sudhir Alladi. 1997. "The Social Organization of Street Gang Activity in an Urban Ghetto." *American Journal of Sociology* 103 (1): 82–111.

———. 2002. *American Project: The Rise and Fall of a Modern Ghetto*. Cambridge, MA: Harvard University Press.

———. 2009. *Off the Books: The Underground Economy of the Urban Poor*. Cambridge, MA: Harvard University Press.

Venkatesh, Sudhir Alledi, and Steven D. Levitt. 2000. "'Are We a Family or a Business?' History and Disjuncture in the Urban American Street Gang." *Theory and Society* 29 (4): 427–462.

Vettenburg, Nicole, Ruben Brondeel, Claire Gavray, and Lieven J. R. Pauwels. 2013. "Societal Vulnerability and Adolescent Offending: The Role of Violent Values, Self-Control and Troublesome Youth Group Involvement." *European Journal of Criminology* 10 (4): 444–461. https://doi.org/10.1177/1477370812470777.

Veysey, Bonita M., Damian J. Martinez, and Johnna Christian. 2013. "'Getting Out': A Summary of Qualitative Research on Desistance across the Life Course." In *Handbook of Life-Course Criminology: Emerging Trends and Directions for Future Research*, edited by Chris L. Gibson and Marvin D. Krohn, 233–260. New York: Springer. https://doi.org/10.1007/978-1-4614-5113-6_14.

Vigil, James Diego. 1988. *Barrio Gangs: Street Life and Identity in Southern California.* Austin: University of Texas Press.

———. 1996. "Street Baptism: Chicano Gang Initiation." *Human Organization* 55 (2): 149–153.

———. 2002. *A Rainbow of Gangs: Street Cultures in the Mega-city.* Austin: University of Texas Press.

———. 2020. *Multiple Marginality and Gangs: Through a Prism Darkly.* Lanham, MD: Lexington Books.

Vigil, James Diego, and John M. Long. 1990. "Emic and Etic Perspectives on Gang Culture: The Chicano Case." In *Gangs in America*, edited by C. Ronald Huff, 55–68. Newbury Park, CA: Sage.

Vitale, Alex S. 2017. *The End of Policing.* New York: Verso.

Wacquant, Loïc. 2001. "Deadly Symbiosis: When Ghetto and Prison Meet and Mesh." *Punishment and Society* 3 (1): 95–133.

———. 2007. *Urban Outcasts: A Comparative Sociology of Advanced Marginality.* Cambridge: Polity.

———. 2009. *Punishing the Poor: The Neoliberal Government of Social Insecurity.* Durham, NC: Duke University Press Books.

Waldorf, Dan. 1993. "Don't Be Your Own Best Customer—Drug Use of San Francisco Gang Drug Sellers." *Crime, Law and Social Change* 19 (1): 1–15.

Walker, D'Andre, and Gabriel T. Cesar. 2020. "Examining the 'Gang Penalty' in the Juvenile Justice System: A Focal Concerns Perspective." *Youth Violence and Juvenile Justice* 18 (4): 315–336. https://doi.org/10.1177/1541204020916238.

Walker, Michael L. 2016. "Race Making in a Penal Institution." *American Journal of Sociology* 121 (4): 1051–1078.

Wang, Ming-Te, and Thomas J. Dishion. 2012. "The Trajectories of Adolescents' Perceptions of School Climate, Deviant Peer Affiliation, and Behavioral Problems during the Middle School Years." *Journal of Research on Adolescence* 22 (1): 40–53.

Wang, Peng. 2017. *The Chinese Mafia: Organized Crime, Corruption, and Extra-legal Protection.* New York: Oxford University Press.

Ward, Catherine, and Karlijn Bakhuis. 2010. "Intervening in Children's Involvement in Gangs: Views of Cape Town's Young People." *Children and Society* 24:50–62.

Ward, Thomas W. 2012. *Gangsters without Borders: An Ethnography of a Salvadoran Street Gang.* New York: Oxford University Press.

Warr, Mark. 2002. *Companions in Crime: The Social Aspects of Criminal Conduct.* Cambridge: Cambridge University Press.

Watkins, Adam M. 2017. "The Labor Market and Gang Membership in Adulthood: Is the Availability, Quality, and Nature of Legal Work Associated with Adult Gang Involvement?" *Journal of Crime and Justice* 40 (3): 376–394. https://doi.org/10.1080/0735648X.2017.1296781.

Watkins, Adam M., and Chris Melde. 2016. "Bad Medicine: The Relationship between Gang Membership, Depression, Self-Esteem, and Suicidal Behavior." *Criminal Justice and Behavior* 43 (8): 1107–1126. https://doi.org/10.1177/0093854816631797.

———. 2018. "Gangs, Gender, and Involvement in Crime, Victimization, and Exposure to Violence." *Journal of Criminal Justice* 57 (July): 11–25.

Webb, Vincent J., Ling Ren, Jihong "Solomon" Zhao, Ni "Phil" He, and Ineke Haen Marshall. 2011. "A Comparative Study of Youth Gangs in China and the United States: Definition, Offending, and Victimization." *International Criminal Justice Review* 21 (3): 225–242.

Webster, Daniel W. 2019. *Public Health Approaches to Reducing Community Gun Violence.* Roundtable on the Future of Justice Policy. New York: Columbia University. https://squareonejustice.org/wp-content/uploads/2019/10/roundtable-oct-2019-Webster-PublicHealthApproachestoReducingCommunityGunViolenceFINAL.pdf.

Weerman, Frank M. 2012. "Are the Correlates and Effects of Gang Membership Sex-Specific? Troublesome Youth Groups and Delinquency among Dutch Girls." In *Youth Gangs in International Perspective*, edited by Finn-Aage Esbensen and Cheryl L. Maxson, 271–287. New York: Springer.

Weerman, Frank M., Peter J. Lovegrove, and Terence Thornberry. 2015. "Gang Membership Transitions and Its Consequences: Exploring Changes Related to Joining and Leaving Gangs in Two Countries." *European Journal of Criminology* 12 (1): 70–91.

Weerman, Frank M., Cheryl L. Maxson, F. Esbensen, Judith Aldridge, Juanjo Medina, and Frank van Gemert. 2009. *Eurogang Program Manual: Background, Development, and Use of the Eurogang Instruments in Multi-site, Multi-method Comparative Research.* Retrieved from the Eurogang Network website: http://www.umsl.edu/~ccj/eurogang/Eurogang_20Manual.pdf.

Weide, Robert D. 2015. *Race War? Inter-racial Conflict between Black and Latino Gang Members in Los Angeles County.* New York: New York University.

———. 2020. "The Invisible Hand of the State: A Critical Historical Analysis of Prison Gangs in California." *Prison Journal* 100 (3): 312–331. https://doi.org/10.1177/0032885520916817.

Weisel, Deborah Lamm, and Tara O'Connor Shelley. 2004. *Specialized Gang Units: Form and Function in Community Policing.* Washington, DC: National Institute of Justice.

Welch, Michael, Erica Price, and Nana Yankey. 2002. "Moral Panic over Youth Violence: Wilding and the Manufacture of Menace in the Media." *Youth and Society* 34 (1): 3–30.

Wells, James B., Kevin I. Minor, Earl Angel, and Lisa Carter. 2002. *A Study of Gangs and Security Threat Groups in America's Adult Prisons and Jails.* Indianapolis: National Major Gang Task Force.

Wells, William Katz, Charles M. Katz, and Jeonglim Kim. 2010. "Firearm Possession among Arrestees in Trinidad and Tobago." Huntsville, TX: Sam Houston University.

Werdegar, Matthew Mickle. 1999. "Enjoining the Constitution: The Use of Public Nuisance Abatement Injunctions against Urban Street Gangs." *Stanford Law Review* 51 (2): 409–445. https://doi.org/10.2307/1229274.

Wesche, Rose, and Julia Dickson-Gomez. 2019. "Gender Attitudes, Sexual Risk, Intimate Partner Violence, and Coercive Sex among Adolescent Gang Members." *Journal of Adolescent Health* 64 (5): 648–656.

Western, Bruce. 2018. *Homeward: Life in the Year after Prison.* New York: Russell Sage Foundation.

Wheatley, Joseph. 2008. "The Flexibility of RICO and Its Use on Street Gangs Engaging in Organized Crime in the United States." *Policing: A Journal of Policy and Practice* 2 (1): 82–91. https://doi.org/10.1093/police/pan003.

White, Michael D., and Henry F. Fradella. 2016. *Stop and Frisk: The Use and Abuse of a Controversial Policing Tactic.* New York: New York University Press.

White, Rob. 2013. *Youth Gangs, Violence and Social Respect: Exploring the Nature of Provocations and Punch-Ups.* 1st ed. Basingstoke: Palgrave Macmillan.

———. 2016. "Youth Gangs and Youth Violence in Australia." In *Global Perspectives on Youth Gang Behavior, Violence, and Weapons Use*, edited by Simon Harding and Marek Palasinski, 327–345. Hershey, PA: IGI Global.

Whitney-Snel, Kendall, Christine E. Valdez, and Jessica Totaan. 2020. "'We Break the Cycle . . . ': Motivations for Prosocial Advocacy among Former Gang Members to End Gang Involvement." *Journal of Community Psychology* 48 (6): 1929–1941.

Whittaker, Andrew, James Densley, Len Cheston, Tajae Tyrell, Martyn Higgins, Claire Felix-Baptiste, and Tirion Havard. 2020. "Reluctant Gangsters Revisited: The Evolution of Gangs from Postcodes to Profits." *European Journal on Criminal Policy and Research* 26 (1): 1–22.

Whittaker, Andrew, James Densley, and Karin S. Moser. 2020. "No Two Gangs Are Alike: The Digital Divide in Street Gangs' Differential Adaptations to Social Media." *Computers in Human Behavior* 110 (September): 106403.

Whittaker, George, Joel Norton, James Densley, and Duncan Bew. 2017. "Epidemiology of Penetrating Injuries in the United Kingdom: A Systematic Review." *International Journal of Surgery* 41:65–69.

Whyte, William F. 1943. *Street Corner Society*. Chicago: University of Chicago Press.

Wijeratne, Sanjaya, Lakshika Balasuriya, Derek Doran, and Amit Sheth. 2016. "Word Embeddings to Enhance Twitter Gang Member Profile Identification." Preprint, submitted October 27, 2016. http://arxiv.org/abs/1610.08597.

Wijeratne, Sanjaya, Derek Doran, Amit Sheth, and Jack L. Dustin. 2015. "Analyzing the Social Media Footprint of Street Gangs." In *2015 IEEE International Conference on Intelligence and Security Informatics (ISI)*, 91–96. http://ieeexplore.ieee.org/abstract/document/7165945/.

Wilkerson, Isabel. 2011. *The Warmth of Other Suns: The Epic Story of America's Great Migration*. New York: Vintage.

———. 2020. *Caste: The Origins of Our Discontents*. New York: Random House.

Williams, Edward. H. 1914. "Negro Cocaine 'Fiends' Are a New Southern Menace." *New York Times*, February 8, 1914. https://www.nytimes.com/1914/02/08/archives/negro-cocaine-fiends-are-a-new-southern-menace-murder-and-insanity.html.

Williams, Patrick. 2015. "Criminalising the Other: Challenging the Race-Gang Nexus." *Race and Class* 56 (3): 18–35.

———. 2018. *Being Matrixed*. London: StopWatch.

Williams, Patrick, and Becky Clark. 2016. *Dangerous Associations: Joint Enterprise, Gangs and Racism*. London: Centre for Crime and Justice Studies.

Williams, Phil. 1998. "The Nature of Drug-Trafficking Networks." *Current History* 97 (618): 154.

Williams, Stanley Tookie. 2007. *Blue Rage, Black Redemption: A Memoir*. New York: Touchstone.

Wilson, David B., Denise C. Gottfredson, and Stacy S. Najaka. 2001. "School-Based Prevention of Problem Behaviors: A Meta-analysis." *Journal of Quantitative Criminology* 17 (3): 247–272.

Wilson, William Julius 1985. "Cycles of Deprivation and the Underclass Debate." *Social Service Review* 59:541–559.

———. 1987. *The Truly Disadvantaged: The Inner City, the Underclass, and Public Policy*. Chicago: University of Chicago Press.

———. 1997. *When Work Disappears: The World of the New Urban Poor*. New York: Vintage.

———. 2009. *More Than Just Race: Being Black and Poor in the Inner City*. New York: W. W. Norton.

Winfree, L. Thomas, Jr., Finn-Aage Esbensen, and D. Wayne Osgood. 1996. "Evaluating a School-Based Gang-Prevention Program: A Theoretical Perspective." *Evaluation Review* 20 (2): 181–203.

Winston, Ali. 2016. "You May Be in California's Gang Database and Not Even Know It." *Reveal*, March 23, 2016. https://www.revealnews.org/article/you-may-be-in-californias-gang-database-and-not-even-know-it/.

Winterdyk, John, and Rick Ruddell. 2010. "Managing Prison Gangs: Results from a Survey of U.S. Prison Systems." *Journal of Criminal Justice* 38 (4): 730–736.

Wise, Robert, and Jerome Robbins, dirs. 1961. *West Side Story*. Mirisch Pictures.

Wolf, Sonja. 2017. *Mano Dura: The Politics of Gang Control in El Salvador*. Austin: University of Texas Press.

Wolff, Kevin T., Michael T. Baglivio, Hannah J. Klein, Alex R. Piquero, Matt DeLisi, and James C. Howell. 2020. "Adverse Childhood Experiences (ACEs) and Gang Involvement among Juvenile Offenders: Assessing the Mediation Effects of Substance Use and Temperament Deficits." *Youth Violence and Juvenile Justice* 18 (1): 24–53.

Womer, Sarah, and Robert J. Bunker. 2010. "Sureños Gangs and Mexican Cartel Use of Social Networking Sites." *Small Wars and Insurgencies* 21 (1): 81–94.

Wong, Jennifer S., Jason Gravel, Martin Bouchard, Karine Descormiers, and Carlo Morselli. 2016. "Promises Kept? A Meta-analysis of Gang Membership Prevention Programs." *Journal of Criminological Research, Policy and Practice* 2 (2): 134–147.

Wood, Jane, and Emma Alleyne. 2010. "Street Gang Theory and Research: Where Are We Now and Where Do We Go from Here?" *Aggression and Violent Behavior* 15 (2): 100–111.

Wood, Jane, Emma Alleyne, Katarina Mozova, and Mark James. 2014. "Predicting Involvement in Prison Gang Activity: Street Gang Membership, Social and Psychological Factors." *Law and Human Behavior* 38 (3): 203.

Woods, Jordan Blair. 2011. "Systemic Racial Bias and RICO's Application to Criminal Street and Prison Gangs." *Michigan Journal of Race and Law* 17 (2): 303–358.

Woodward, Bob, and Carl Bernstein. 2014. *All the President's Men*. Reissue ed. New York: Simon and Schuster.

Wooldredge, John, and Benjamin Steiner. 2012. "Race Group Differences in Prison Victimization Experiences." *Journal of Criminal Justice* 40 (5): 358–369.

———. 2014. "A Bi-level Framework for Understanding Prisoner Victimization." *Journal of Quantitative Criminology* 30 (1): 141–162. https://doi.org/10.1007/s10940-013-9197-y.

Worrall, John L., and Robert G. Morris. 2012. "Prison Gang Integration and Inmate Violence." *Journal of Criminal Justice* 40 (5): 425–432.

Wortley, Scot, and Julian Tanner. 2004. "Social Groups or Criminal Organizations: The Extent and Nature of Youth Gangs in Toronto." In *From Enforcement and Prevention to Civic Engagement: Research on Community Safety*, edited by Jim Phillips and Bruce Kidd, 59–80. Toronto: Centre of Criminology.

———. 2006. "Immigration, Social Disadvantage and Urban Youth Gangs: Results of a Toronto-Area Study." *Canadian Journal of Urban Research* 15 (2): 18–37.

———. 2008. "Respect, Friendship, and Racial Injustice: Justifying Gang Membership in a Canadian City." In *Street Gangs, Migration and Ethnicity*, edited by Frank van Gemert, Dana B. Peterson, and Inger-Lise Lien, 192–208. Uffculme, U.K.: Willan.

Wu, Jun, and David C. Pyrooz. 2016. "Uncovering the Pathways between Gang Membership and Violent Victimization." *Journal of Quantitative Criminology* 32:531–559.

Wynne, Susan L., and Hee-Jong Joo. 2011. "Predictors of School Victimization: Individual, Familial, and School Factors." *Crime and Delinquency* 57 (3): 458–488.

Yablonsky, Lewis. 1962. *The Violent Gang*. New York: Lexington Books. https://www.ncjrs
.gov/App/abstractdb/AbstractDBDetails.aspx?id=149139.
———. 1997. *Gangsters: 50 Years of Madness, Drugs, and Death on the Streets of America*.
New York: New York University Press.
———. 2005. *Gangs in Court*. Tucson: Lawyers and Judges.
Yoshino, Erin R. 2008. "California's Criminal Gang Enhancements: Lessons from Interviews with Practitioners Note." *Southern California Review of Law and Social Justice*
18 (1): 117–152.
Young, Jock. 2004. "Voodoo Criminology and the Numbers Game." In *Cultural Criminol-
ogy Unleashed*, edited by Jeff Ferrell, Keith Hayward, Wayne Morrison, and Mike
Presdee, 27–42. London: Routledge-Cavendish.
Zaitch, Damián. 2002. *Trafficking Cocaine: Colombian Drug Entrepreneurs in the Nether-
lands*. 1st ed. The Hague: Springer.
Zatz, Marjorie S. 1987. "Chicano Youth Gangs and Crime: The Creation of a Moral Panic."
Contemporary Crises 11 (2): 129–158. https://doi.org/10.1007/BF00728588.
Zatz, Marjorie S., and Richard P. Krecker Jr. 2003. "Anti-gang Initiatives as Racialized
Policy." In *Crime Control and Social Justice: The Delicate Balance*, edited by Darnell
Felix Hawkins, Samuel L. Myers, and Randolph N. Stone, 173–196. Santa Barbara, CA:
Greenwood.
Zhang, Lening, Steven F. Messner, Zhou Lu, and Xiaogang Deng. 1997. "Gang Crime and
Its Punishment in China." *Journal of Criminal Justice* 4:289–302.
Zhang, Lening, John W. Welte, and William F. Wieczorek. 1999. "Youth Gangs, Drug Use,
and Delinquency." *Journal of Criminal Justice* 27 (2): 101–109.
Zhang, Sheldon X. 1997. "Task Force Orientation and Dyadic Relations in Organized
Chinese Alien Smuggling." *Journal of Contemporary Criminal Justice* 13 (4): 320–330.
———. 2007. *Smuggling and Trafficking in Human Beings: All Roads Lead to America*.
Westport, CT: Praeger.
———. 2008. *Chinese Human Smuggling Organizations: Families, Social Networks, and
Cultural Imperatives*. Stanford, CA: Stanford University Press.
Zilberg, Elana. 2011. *Space of Detention: The Making of a Transnational Gang Crisis between Los Angeles and San Salvador*. Durham, NC: Duke University Press.
Zimring, Franklin E., and Gordon Hawkins. 1999. *Crime Is Not the Problem: Lethal Violence in America*. 1st ed. New York: Oxford University Press.
Zimring, Franklin E., and Hannah Laqueur. 2015. "Kids, Groups, and Crime: In Defense
of Conventional Wisdom." *Journal of Research in Crime and Delinquency* 52 (3):
403–413.

Index of Names

Index of Subjects

The letter *t* following a page number denotes a table.

Scott H. Decker is Foundation Professor Emeritus in the School of Criminology and Criminal Justice at Arizona State University. His books include *Drug Smugglers on Drug Smuggling* and *Criminology and Public Policy* (Temple), as well as *Life in the Gang: Family, Friends, and Violence* and *Competing for Control: Gangs and the Social Order of Prisons*.

David C. Pyrooz is Associate Professor of Sociology at the University of Colorado Boulder. He is the author of *Confronting Gangs: Crime and Community* and *Competing for Control: Gangs and the Social Order of Prisons*.

James A. Densley is Professor and Department Chair of the School of Law Enforcement and Criminal Justice at Metropolitan State University. He is the author of *How Gangs Work: An Ethnography of Youth Violence* and *Scotland's Gang Members: Life and Crime in Glasgow*.